The BEATS

The BEATS

A Literary Reference

EDITED BY
MATT THEADO

A Bruccoli Clark Layman Book

CARROLL & GRAF PUBLISHERS
NEW YORK

THE BEATS
A Literary Reference

Carroll & Graf Publishers
An Imprint of Avalon Publishing Group Inc.
161 William Street, 16th Floor
New York, NY 10038

First Carroll & Graf paperback edition 2003

Library of Congress Cataloging-in-Publication Data is available.

ISBN: 0-7867-1099-3

Printed in the United States of America
Distributed by Publishers Group West

For my daughter, Bailey

Contents

Acknowledgments

This book was produced by Bruccoli Clark Layman, Inc. Karen L. Rood is senior editor. George Parker Anderson was the in-house editor.

Production manager is Philip B. Dematteis.

Administrative support was provided by Ann M. Cheschi, Dawnca T. Williams, and Mary A. Womble.

Accounting supervisor is Ann-Marie Holland. Accounting assistant is Amber L. Coker.

Copyediting supervisor is Phyllis A. Avant. The copyediting staff includes Brenda Carol Blanton, Allen E. Friend Jr., Melissa D. Hinton, William Tobias Mathes, Nancy E. Smith, and Elizabeth Jo Ann Sumner. Freelance copyeditors are Brenda Cabra and Rebecca Mayo.

Editorial associates are Andrew Choate and Michael S. Martin.

Layout and graphics supervisor is Janet E. Hill. The graphics staff includes Karla Corley Brown and Zoe R. Cook.

Office manager is Kathy Lawler Merlette.

Photography supervisor is Paul Talbot. Photography editors are Charles Mims and Scott Nemzek.

Permissions editor is Jeff Miller.

Digital photographic copy work was performed by Joseph M. Bruccoli.

SGML supervisor is Cory McNair. The SGML staff includes Frank Graham, Linda Dalton Mullinax, Jason Paddock, and Alex Snead.

Systems manager is Marie L. Parker.

Typesetting supervisor is Kathleen M. Flanagan. The typesetting staff includes Patricia Marie Flanagan, Mark J. McEwan, Pamela D. Norton, and Alison Smith. Freelance typesetters are Wanda Adams and Vicki Grivetti.

Walter W. Ross did library research. He was assisted by Steven Gross and the following librarians at the Thomas Cooper Library of the University of South Carolina: circulation department head Tucker Taylor; reference department head Virginia W. Weathers; Brette Barclay, Marilee Birchfield, Paul Cammarata, Gary Geer, Michael Macan, Tom Marcil, Rose Marshall, and Sharon Verba; interlibrary loan department head John Brunswick; and interlibrary loan staff Robert Arndt, Hayden Battle, Barry Bull, Jo Cottingham, Marna Hostetler, Marieum McClary, Erika Peake, and Nelson Rivera.

The editor wishes to thank Carolyn Cassady; Jerome Poynton; Peter Hale; Robert Cowley; John Bennett of the Ohio State University Rare Books Library; Jeff Ritchie; Carol Moore of the Arizona State University Library; John Skarstad of the Special Collections Library at the University of California at Davis; Bernard Crystal of Rare Books and Manuscripts Library, Butler Library, Columbia University; Rodney Phillips of the Berg Collection, New York Public Library; and Mike Simpson.

Special thanks to my hard-working student assistant, Kelly King, and my colleagues in the English Department at Gardner-Webb University, especially Gayle Price.

Permissions

Allen Ginsberg Trust
PHOTOS: Group shot of the Beats, 1944; Ginsberg in 1932; Ginsberg on ship; Burroughs and Kerouac on couch; Huncke (photo booth); Kerouac late in life; Ginsberg with mother, New York World's Fair; Ginsberg yearbook photo; Ginsberg on rooftop; 1010 Montgomery interior; Ginsberg typing; Corso in attic; Corso and Ginsberg head shots; Snyder in diner booth; Cassady with cigarette; Cassady in jacket; Cassady and woman under movie marquee; Cassady on bus with Leary. FACSIMILES: First page of the *Howl* typescript; typescript page for *Howl;* manuscript page for *Howl;* letter to Lucien Carr, 16 January 1956; manuscript page for "Kaddish"; typescript page of "Presidential Skeletons"; manuscript pages for "Popular Tunes"; typescript page for "Popular Tunes"; manuscript pages for "Death and Fame." TEXT: Letter from Ginsberg to Lucien Carr, 4 April 1997; letter from Ginsberg to Lucien Carr, 30 May 1958.

The American Scholar
Frank A. Butler, "On the Beat Nature of Beat," 30, no. 1 (Winter 1960–1961); reproduced from *The American Scholar,* 30, no. 1 (Winter 1960–1961). © 1960 by the Phi Beta Kappa Society.

Archive Photos
Brando on motorcycle; Ginsberg leading prayer meeting; Beatniks in Hollywood coffeehouse; Times Square, NYC, 1949; Columbia University campus, circa 1940s; ad for John Begg Scotch, 1961; stars of *Dobie Gillis;* Ginsberg swinging Buddhist prayer bell; Ginsberg with Peter Orlovsky, Miami, 1972.

The Henry W. and Albert A. Berg Collection of English and American Literature, The New York Public Library, Astor, Lenox, and Tilden Foundations
Junkie (Burroughs) Ace edition; cover for *Pictures of the Gone World* (Ferlinghetti); cover for *The Beat Boys* (Holmes), first British edition; cover for "The Hippos Were Boiled in Their Tanks"; letter from Kerouac to Giroux, 14 February 1963; *Book of Sketches* (Kerouac) typescript; *Book of Sketches* inside page; *Satori in Paris* notebooks; *Mexico City Blues* notebooks; *Mexico City Blues* typescript page; letter from Kerouac to Solomon, 5 August 1952; manuscript page for *Buddha Tells Us; Passing Through* notebooks; letter from Kerouac to Ginsberg, 1 January 1962; *Book of Dreams* typescript, first page; *Maggie Cassady* notebooks; cover for *Uncollected Writings of Jack Kerouac.*

Carolyn Cassady
PHOTOS: Young Neal Cassady on steps; Cassady mug shot; group shot, Hinkles, Thompson, and Carolyn; Cassady and Kerouac in bomber jackets; Cassady in jacket; Kerouac, Cathy, and Cassady; seated Kerouac in boots; Kerouac in sweatshirt; Cassady with kids, 1953; Cassady and kids, Easter, 1957; Carolyn, picture sent to San Quentin, 1959; Carolyn and Cassady, arm in arm. FACSIMILES: Cassady's letter from San Quentin; *Town and the City* inscribed by Kerouac to Carolyn; Cassady's recommendation letter for Kerouac, 1952; calendar page with "goodbye" note to Carolyn; receipt for Ekotape recorder; brakeman instructions manual; brakeman pay stub; April Fools' Day poem on small card; insurance settlement statement; receipt from attorney; hospital bill; hospital receipt; racetrack brochure; racetrack newspaper; Cassady's GED certificate; Buddhism class certificate; aid to needy children statement of revocation of payment; Cassady's death certificate; calendar page written by Cassady to "Dear Ma"; postcard from Cassady to his family, 24 July 1963; postcard from Cassady to his family, 26 July 1963. TEXT: Letter from Cassady to Ginsberg, 14 March 1947; letter from Cassady to Ginsberg, 20 March 1947; letter from Cassady to Kerouac, 27 March 1947; letter from Cassady to Kerouac, 7 January 1948; letter from Cassady to Kerouac, 15 October 1950; letter from Cassady to Kerouac, February 1951.

Ann Charters
PHOTOS: Ginsberg and his father; Kerouac and his mother; Holmes, seated; Anne Waldman; Kerouac funeral; Joyce Johnson.

Chicago Tribune
Stuart Mitchner, "Those Phony Beatniks," *Sunday Tribune Magazine,* 8 November 1959, pp. 47–49.

Permissions

Choice
Review of *Rip Rap,* by Gary Snyder (October 1966): 651.

The Christian Science Monitor
"Polarity Finder," anonymous (24 October 1969). Victor Howes, "Poet's Love Lyrics to Planet Earth" (30 December 1974): 10, © 1969, 1974 by The Christian Science Publishing Society, reproduced with permission. All rights reserved.

Columbia University Rare Books and Manuscript Library
FACSIMILES: Letter from Burroughs to Ginsberg, 7 February 1949; letter from Burroughs to Kerouac, 30 November 1948; letter from Burroughs to Kerouac, 26 September 1949; letter from Burroughs to Kerouac, 10 March 1950; letter from Ginsberg to Carr, 16 January 1956; City Lights Books statement of facts concerning Ginsberg's *Howl.* TEXT: Letter from Ginsberg to Carr, 4 April 1957; letter from Ginsberg to Carr, 30 May 1958.

Commonweal
Daniel Aaron, review of *Nothing to Declare* (5 May 1967). © 1967 by the Commonweal Foundation, reprinted with permission.

Rob Cowley
Letters and memos of Malcolm Cowley about Kerouac's *On the Road.*

Gregory Daurer
PHOTOS: Ginsberg looking at photo of Kerouac; Ginsberg reading, early 1990s; Burroughs reading, 1988; Ginsberg waving, 1988. TEXT: Interview with Ginsberg.

Encounter
Mary McCarthy, "Burroughs's *Naked Lunch*" (April 1963): 92–98.

Esquire
John Clellon Holmes, "The Philosophy of the Beat Generation" (February 1958): 35–38, reprinted by permission of Sterling Lord Literistic, Inc. © 1958.

James Grauerholz
PHOTOS: Burroughs as a child; Burroughs in Harvard yearbook. FACSIMILES: Letter from Burroughs to Ginsberg, 7 February 1949; letter from Burroughs to Ginsberg, 20 October 1955; letter from Burroughs to Kerouac, 30 November 1948; letter from Burroughs to Kerouac, 26 September 1949; letter from Burroughs to Kerouac, 10 March 1950; typescript pages for *Naked Lunch* and *Soft Machine;* typescript page for *The Ticket That Exploded;* typescript pages for *Exterminator!* typescript pages for *Twilight's Last Gleamings.* TEXT: "Statement on Huncke," from *The Huncke Reader;* letter from Burroughs to Ginsberg (excerpt), 15 January 1953; letter from Burroughs to Ginsberg (excerpt), 15 April 1953; letter from Burroughs to Ginsberg (excerpt), 28 October 1957; journal entries (excerpt), as published in *The New Yorker,* 18 August 1997; prologue to *Junky,* Viking Penguin, 1977.

Harper's
Mildred Edie Brody, "The New Cult of Sex and Anarchy" (April 1947): 312–322; Louis Simpson, "New Books of Poems," review concerning Gary Snyder (August 1968): 73–77.

Harry Ransom Humanities Research Center, The University of Texas at Austin
Knopf rejection memo for Kerouac's *On the Road;* excerpt from Kerouac's unpublished *On the Road* journal.

High Times
Gregory Daurer, interview with Allen Ginsberg (February 1992): 13–16. Permission granted by Gregory Daurer.

The Hollywood Reporter
Review of *The Subterraneans* (21 June 1960). Permission granted by Linda Miller.

The Huncke Reader
"Guilty of Everything" excerpt. Permission granted by Jerome Poynton.

Jim Jones
Photograph of *On the Road* scroll.

Robert King
Interview with Gregory Corso, "I'm Poor Simple Human Bones," in *The Beat Vision* (1987).

Library Journal
Excerpt from review of Burroughs's *Naked Lunch* (1 December 1962): 44–54; excerpt from review of Burroughs's *The Ticket That Exploded* (1 June 1967): 21–77; excerpt from review of Kerouac's *Visions of Cody* (15 September 1972); excerpt from review of Snyder's *Turtle Island* (15 November 1974).

Fred W. McDarrah
Photos of Cedar Street Tavern with Beck and Ginsberg and Columbia poetry reading with Dr. Frederick W. Dupee introducing poets. © by Fred W. McDarrah.

James McKenzie
Interview with Gary Snyder, "Moving the World a Millionth of an Inch," in *The Beat Vision* (1987).

The Nation
Gene Bare, "Beatniks Then and Now" (5 September 1959): 115–117; Stephen Koch, "Images of Loathing" (4 July 1966): 25–26.

New Directions Press
Gary Snyder, "Anasazi," in *Turtle Island* (1974).

The New Republic
John Wain, "The Great Burroughs Affair" (1 December 1962); Ted Solotaroff, "The Algebra of Need" (5 August 1967); reprinted by permission of *The New Republic.* © 1962, 1967 The New Republic, Inc.

New Statesman
Ralph Gleason, "Begone, Dull Beats" (2 June 1961); John Gross, "Disorganization Men" (8 February 1963); Alan Brownjohn, "Fblup!" (10 January 1969). © *New Statesman* 1961, 1963, 1969.

New York Daily News
"Heir's Pistol Kills His Wife; He Denies Playing Wm. Tell," 8 September 1951, p. 3; reprinted with permission of AP.

New York Herald Tribune
"Books and Authors," 22 September 1957, p. 2; Clyde Kilby, "Love and Loss," 23 February 1958; Richard Kluger, "Panorama of Perversity," 25 November 1962, p. 8.

New York Post
David Boroff, "Beatsville, USA," February 1958; Boroff, "The Roughnecks," 8 September 1957; "Mike Wallace Asks Jack Kerouac, 'What Is the Beat Generation?'" 21 January 1958, p. 16.

The New York Review of Books
John Wain, "Making It New" (28 April 1966); reprinted with permission from *The New York Review of Books.* © 1966 by NYREV, Inc.

The New York Times
"Columbia Student Kills Friend and Sinks Body in Hudson River," 17 August 1944, p. 1; John Deck, review of *Kerouac,* 15 April 1973, p. 23; Gilbert Milstein, "The Kick that Failed," 9 November 1952, p. 50; Milstein, review of Kerouac's *On the Road,* "Books of the Times" column, 5 September 1957, p. 27; obituary of Ginsberg, online, 7 April 1997; Nancy Wilson Ross, "Beat–and Buddhist," 5 October 1958, pp. 5, 14; "Student is Indicted in 2D-Degree Murder," 25 August 1944, p. 15.

The New York Times Book Review
Herbert Gold, "At Play in the Circles of Hell," 20 March 1966, p. 4, reprinted by permission of Herbert Gold; Gold, "Instead of Love, the Fix," 25 November 1962, pp. 4, 69, reprinted by permission of Herbert Gold; Kenneth Rexroth, review of Kramer's *Allen Ginsberg in America,* 11 May 1969, pp. 8, 41; Richard Rhodes, "Cutting Up," review of Burroughs's *The Ticket That Exploded,* 18 June 1967, p. 4; "West Coast Rhythms," 9 February 1956, p. 7.

The New Yorker
William Burroughs's journal excerpts (18 August 1997): 36–37; excerpt from review of Kerouac's *Dharma Bums* (1 November 1958): 175; review of Kerouac's *Town and the City* (25 March 1950): 115; Donald Malcolm, "The Heroin of Our Times," review of Burroughs's *Naked Lunch* (2 February 1963): 114–115, 118, 120–121.

Newsweek
"The Alluring Cupful" (8 October 1956): 86–88; "Heat on the Beatniks" (17 August 1959): 36; "Bye, Bye, Beatnik" (1 July 1963): 65. © 1956, 1959, 1963 by Newsweek, Inc.; reprinted by permission. All rights reserved.

North Point Press
Gary Snyder, "Axe Handles," in *Axe Handles* (1983).

The Paris Review
Ted Berrigan, interview with Jack Kerouac; reprinted by the permission of Russell & Volkening as agents for the author. © *The Paris Review.*

Partisan Review
Anatole Broyard, "A Portrait of a Hipster," first appeared in *Partisan Review,* 25, no. 2 (1958): 721–728; LeRoi Jones, "Letter to the Editor," first appeared in *Partisan Review,* 25, no. 3 (1958): 472–473; Norman Podhoretz, "The Know-Nothing Bohemians," first appeared in *Partisan Review,* 25, no. 2 (1958): 305–318; Diana Trilling, "The Other Night at Columbia," first appeared in *Partisan Review,* 26, no. 2 (1959): 214–230.

Poetry
Bill Berkson, review of *Planet News* by Allen Ginsberg (July 1969), first appeared in *Poetry,* © 1969 The Modern Poetry Association; reprinted by permission of the Editor of *Poetry.*

Quarterly Review
Tim Hunt, interview with John Clellon Holmes (Winter 1978): 50–58.

The Reporter
Eugene Burdick, "Innocent Nihilists Adrift in Squaresville" (3 April 1958): 30–33.

San Francisco Examiner
"Ginsberg Talks of Kerouac," 23 October 1969, reprinted by permission of AP; Michael Grieg, "That Old Beat Gang Is Breaking Up," 28 September 1958, p. 18.

The Saturday Review
Carlos Baker, "Itching Feet" (7 September 1957): 19; G. Baker, "Avant Garde at the Golden Gate" (August 1957); John Ciardi, "Book Burners and Sweet 16" (27 July 1959): 22–23; Barnaby Conrad, "Barefoot Boy with Dreams of Zen" (22 May 1959): 23; Malcolm Cowley, "Innovation to Innovators" (21 August 1954); EJF, "BeBop and Blues" (11 October 1952): 36; Ralph Gleason, review of Kerouac's *On the Road* (11 January 1958); Herbert Gold, "Squaring Off the Corners" (22 September 1962): 29; H. M. Jones, "Back to the Merrimack" (11 March 1950): 18.

Science Digest
"Beats Just Sick, Sick, Sick" (April 1959): 25–26.

Gary Snyder
"Anasazi" typescript page; "Axe Handles" handwritten manuscript page; "Axe Handles" typescript pages.

St. Martin's Press
Excerpts from *Jack's Book: An Oral Biography*. © 1978 by Barry Gifford and Lawrence Lee. Excerpts reprinted by permission of St. Martin's Press, LLC.

Sterling Lord Literistic
Selected letters of Jack Kerouac. Reprinted by permission of Sterling Lord Literistic, Inc. © 1995 by John Sampas, Literary Representative.

Time-Life Syndication
"Disorganization Men" and "King of the YADS," *Time* (30 November 1962): 96–97.

John Tytell
Interview with John Clellon Holmes (as appeared in *The Beat Book,* the unspeakable visions of the individual 4); interview with William Burroughs (as appeared in *The Beat Diary,* the unspeakable visions of the individual 5); interview with Carl Solomon (as appeared in *The Beat Book,* the unspeakable visions of the individual 4).

University of California, Davis
From Gary Snyder Collection: "Anasazi" typescript page; "Axe Handles" monograph, two pages; "Axe Handles" typescript page (handwritten title); "Axe Handles" typescript page (typed title). Department of Special Collections, University of California Library, Davis, California.

Variety
Review of *The Subterraneans,* 22 June 1960; reprinted with permission of Variety, Inc.

Anne Waldman
"A. Waldman Interviews Diane di Prima," in *The Beat Vision* (1987).

Wired
Steve Silberman, "Burroughs Spun a Legacy of Naked Sense," (5 August 1997): <http://www.wired.com/news/news/culture/story/5771.html> © 1994–1999 Wired Digital, Inc. All Rights Reserved.

The
BEATS

Dictionary of Literary Biography: A Documentary Volume

Chronology of the Beat Generation

1914 William Seward Burroughs is born 5 February in St. Louis, Missouri. He is named for his paternal grandfather, the inventor of the first reliable adding machine and founder of the Burroughs Adding Machine Corporation.

1915 Herbert Edwin Huncke is born 9 January in Greenfield, Massachusetts.

1922 Jean-Louis (Jack) Kerouac is born 12 March in Lowell, Massachusetts.

1926 Neal Cassady is born 18 February in Salt Lake City while his parents are en route from Iowa to California.

Irwin Allen Ginsberg is born 3 June in Paterson, New Jersey.

Kerouac's brother, Gerard, dies at age nine.

1930 Gregory Corso is born 26 March in Greenwich Village in New York City.

1932 Burroughs attends Harvard University as an English major.

1939 Huncke arrives in New York City.

Kerouac enrolls in Horace Mann Preparatory School before matriculating at Columbia University on a football scholarship.

1942 Kerouac serves as a merchant seaman on the S.S. *Dorchester*.

Burroughs works in Chicago as an exterminator.

1943 Burroughs moves to New York City.

Kerouac works on an unpublished novel, "The Sea Is My Brother."

Ginsberg meets Lucien Carr at Columbia University. Carr will introduce Ginsberg to Kerouac and Burroughs.

1944 Carr, Ginsberg, and Kerouac discuss "The New Vision," which presents early tenets of the Beat Generation.

Carr kills David Kammerer on 14 August. He is arrested, and Kerouac is detained as a material witness. On 22 August, Kerouac marries Edie Parker of Grosse Pointe, Michigan, as a means of raising bond money. The marriage lasts only a few months. Carr is convicted and serves two years in prison.
Burroughs meets Herbert Huncke.

1945 Ginsberg is suspended from Columbia University for writing obscenities on his dorm-room window and allowing Kerouac, who was unwelcome on campus because of his involvement in the Kammerer murder, to spend the night in his room. Ginsberg lives for a time in a communal apartment; frequent inhabitants include Kerouac, Parker, and Joan Vollmer, who becomes Burroughs's common-law wife.

1946 Kerouac's father dies; he begins writing his first published novel, *The Town and the City*.
Huncke introduces Burroughs to heroin.
Cassady marries Luanne Henderson, and they arrive in New York City in December. Friendships begin with Kerouac and Ginsberg.
Corso begins a three-year prison sentence for grand theft.

1947 In January, Burroughs moves with Vollmer, his common-law wife, to Texas.
In March, Cassady returns to Denver, with Ginsberg and Kerouac arriving separately that summer.
Cassady meets Carolyn Robinson, who becomes his second wife.
Kerouac travels to Denver, the first of his trips to be recounted in *On the Road*. He goes on to San Francisco.
Cassady, Huncke, and Burroughs harvest marijuana and attempt to sell it in New York.

1948 Burroughs and family move to Algiers, Louisiana.
Kerouac finishes *The Town and the City*.
Ginsberg has a vision of William Blake speaking to him in his East Harlem apartment.
John Clellon Holmes meets Kerouac. The two will be close friends and rival writers for years.
Kerouac coins the phrase "beat generation."
In the winter Kerouac and Cassady embark on further travels that will be included in *On the Road*.

1949 Ginsberg is arrested for helping Huncke and others store stolen goods in his apartment.
Harcourt, Brace accepts *The Town and the City*. Kerouac receives a $1,000 advance.
Kerouac first uses the phrase "beat generation" in a conversation with Holmes.
Burroughs is arrested for illegal possession of drugs and firearms. He moves with his family to Mexico.

1950 Kerouac's *The Town and the City* is published (Harcourt, Brace).
Burroughs begins writing *Junkie*.
Cassady marries Diana Hansen while still married to Carolyn. He soon returns to Carolyn.
Kerouac marries Joan Haverty.
Ginsberg meets Corso in Greenwich Village.

1951 Holmes finishes *Go,* the first novel to tell the story of the Beat Generation.
Burroughs begins writing *Queer*.

Kerouc writes the "scroll version" of *On the Road.*
Burroughs travels to Ecuador in search of a drug called yage.
In Mexico, Burroughs kills Vollmer while attempting to shoot a glass off her head. He later says that he would never have become a writer but for her death.
Kerouac begins "sketching" with words, leading to a technique he calls "spontaneous prose."

1952 Kerouac stays with the Cassadys in San Francisco. While there, he does some of his best writing, including much of *Visions of Cody;* he also has an affair with Carolyn.
Ginsberg sends some of his poems to William Carlos Williams.
Kerouac visits Burroughs in Mexico and writes *Doctor Sax.*
Holmes's *Go* is published by Scribners, and he is asked to write "This Is the Beat Generation" for *The New York Times Magazine.*

1953 Ace Books publishes Burroughs's *Junkie: Confessions of an Unredeemed Drug Addict* under the pseudonym William Lee (later published by Penguin, 1977, as *Junky,* by William S. Burroughs).
Lawrence Ferlinghetti and Peter Martin open City Lights, the first paperback bookstore in the United States.
Gary Snyder works as a forest-service lookout in the Northwest, then enters the University of California, Berkeley, as a graduate student.
Burroughs and Ginsberg have a brief affair. When Ginsberg ends it, Burroughs travels to Europe and Africa, winding up in Tangier, where he will live for five years; he begins *Naked Lunch.*
Kerouac writes *Maggie Cassidy* and *The Subterraneans.*

1954 Kerouac begins his study of Buddhism, writes *San Francisco Blues,* and begins *Some of the Dharma.*
Ginsberg meets Peter Orlovsky in San Francisco.

1955 Corso's first book of poems, *The Vestal Lady on Brattle and Other Poems,* is published by Richard Brukenfield.
In San Francisco, Ginsberg writes most of *Howl.* He enrolls as a graduate student at the University of California, Berkeley, and meets Gary Snyder.
Ferlinghetti publishes the first City Lights book, his own *Pictures of the Gone World.*
Kerouac writes *Mexico City Blues* and begins *Tristessa.* He then meets Snyder and Philip Whalen in Berkeley.
An excerpt from *On the Road,* "Jazz of the Beat Generation," is published in *New World Writing,* and later "The Mexican Girl," another excerpt, is published in *Paris Review.*
7 October: The famous poetry reading hosted by Kenneth Rexroth at the Six Gallery in San Francisco includes Ginsberg, Whalen, Snyder, and McClure. Ferlinghetti, Kerouac, and Cassady are in attendance.

1956 Kerouac finishes *Tristessa* and writes *Visions of Gerard.* He also serves as a forest lookout and writes the first part of *Desolation Angels.*
Ginsberg reads the complete *Howl* in Berkeley. City Lights publishes *Howl and Other Poems,* with an introduction by William Carlos Williams.
Snyder goes to Japan to study Zen and Japanese.

1957 Grove Press's *Evergreen Review* features "The San Francisco Scene."

	Kerouac travels to Tangier, where he meets with Ginsberg and Orlovsky at Burroughs's home. They assist Burroughs in putting together *Naked Lunch.*
	In March, U.S. customs officials confiscate 520 copies of *Howl* as they arrive from the British printer. Officials release the books, but Ferlinghetti and his store manager are arrested by San Francisco police for selling the book. In October, following a celebrated obscenity trial, *Howl* is declared "not obscene."
	Rexroth and Ferlinghetti read poetry to jazz accompaniment in a San Francisco bar.
	On the Road is published by Viking and receives a rave review in *The New York Times.* The book becomes a best-seller and makes Kerouac a celebrity. At the height of his fame, Kerouac writes *The Dharma Bums* and agrees to give live readings from his work at a Greenwich Village nightclub.
	Ginsberg begins *Kaddish* for his mother, who died in 1956.
1958	Ginsberg, Orlovsky, Corso, and Burroughs live in Paris at 9 rue Git-le-Coeur, which becomes known as the "Beat Hotel."
	Corso's *Gasoline* is published (City Lights).
	Kerouac's *The Subterraneans* is published by Grove Press, and *The Dharma Bums* is published by Viking. Kerouac appears on *The Steve Allen Show.*
	An excerpt from *Naked Lunch* is published in the *Chicago Review* fall issue. Its controversial appearance there brings acts of censorship to subsequent issues, and editors Paul Carroll and Irving Rosenthal go on to found *Big Table,* the first issue of which is impounded by the U.S. Postal Service. Carroll and Rosenthal ship the remaining copies by truck to San Francisco and New York, where they sell out.
	Cassady is sentenced to San Quentin for marijuana possession and serves two years.
	Diane di Prima's *This Kind of Bird Flies Backward* is published (Totem Press).
	Ferlinghetti's *A Coney Island of the Mind* is published (New Directions).
	Holmes's *The Horn* is published (Random House).
	Snyder's "Cold Mountain Poems" is published in *Evergreen Review.*
1959	*The Naked Lunch* is published by the Olympia Press in Paris. Grove publishes the book in America in 1962 as *Naked Lunch.*
	Kerouac's *Doctor Sax* (Grove), *Maggie Cassidy* (Avon), *Mexico City Blues* (Grove), and *Excerpts from Visions of Cody* (New Directions) are published.
	Snyder's *Rip Rap* is published by Origin Press in Japan.
	The movie *Pull My Daisy* is produced by Robert Frank and Alfred Leslie. Ginsberg, Corso, and Orlovsky appear in it, and Kerouac extemporizes the narrator's voice.
1960	Burroughs begins to experiment with his "cut-up" technique.
	Kerouac stays in Ferlinghetti's cabin near Big Sur. His *Tristessa* (Avon), *The Scripture of the Golden Eternity* (Totem Press/Corinth), and *Lonesome Traveler* (McGraw-Hill) are published.
	Corso's *The Happy Birthday of Death* is published (New Directions).
	Snyder's *Myths and Texts* is published (Totem/Corinth).
	Grove Press editor Donald Allen publishes *The New American Poetry,* a volume that includes Beat poets.
	Kerouac's *The Subterraneans* is made into a movie by M-G-M.
1961	Burroughs's *The Soft Machine* is published (Olympia)
	Kerouac's *Book of Dreams* (City Lights) and *Pull My Daisy* (Grove) are published. He writes *Big Sur* and the second half of *Desolation Angels.*
	Ginsberg's *Kaddish and Other Poems: 1958–1960* (City Lights) and *Empty Mirror* (Totem/Corinth) are published. Ginsberg travels to the Near and Far East.

1962	Burroughs's *Naked Lunch* is published in the United States (Grove). His *The Ticket That Exploded* is published in France (Olympia). Mary McCarthy and Norman Mailer bring Burroughs worldwide notice with their praise at the International Writer's Conference in Edinburgh, Scotland. Kerouac's *Big Sur* is published (Grove).
1963	Kerouac's *Visions of Gerard* is published (Farrar, Straus). Burroughs and Ginsberg's *Yage Letters* is published (City Lights). Ginsberg's *Reality Sandwiches* is published (City Lights). Ginsberg is awarded a Guggenheim Fellowship for 1963–1964.
1964	Kerouac moves to Tampa, Florida, with his mother. He and Cassady see each other for the last time. Snyder returns to the United States and teaches English at the University of California, Berkeley.
1965	Kerouac travels to France and, after his return, writes *Satori in Paris. Desolation Angels* is published (Coward-McCann). Snyder's *Riprap & Cold Mountain Poems* and *Six Sections from Mountains and Rivers without End* are published (Four Seasons). He returns to Japan.
1966	The Massachusetts Supreme Court rules that *Naked Lunch* is "grossly offensive" but not obscene. Testimony was contributed by Mailer, Ginsberg, and John Ciardi. Burroughs begins living in London. *The Soft Machine* is published in the United States (Grove). Kerouac and his mother move to Hyannis on Cape Cod, Massachusetts, where she suffers a stroke. Kerouac marries his third wife, Stella Sampas, and the three of them move to Lowell, Kerouac's hometown.
1967	Kerouac writes *Vanity of Duluoz* in Lowell. Burroughs's *The Ticket That Exploded* is published in the United States (Grove). Holmes's *Nothing More to Declare* is published (Dutton).
1968	Neal Cassady dies in Mexico. Kerouac's *Vanity of Duluoz* is published (Coward-McCann).
1969	Kerouac completes his final book, *Pic;* dies in Florida; and is buried in Lowell. Snyder's *Earth House Hold* is published (New Directions). Ginsberg is awarded a National Institute of Arts and Letters grant for poetry. Bruce Cook's *The Beat Generation* is published (Scribners).
1970	Burroughs's *The Last Words of Dutch Schultz* is published in London by Cape Goliard (it will be published in a revised and enlarged edition by Viking in 1975).
1973	Burroughs's *Exterminator!* is published (Viking).
1974	Burroughs returns to the United States and teaches briefly at the City College of New York.

Ginsberg is inducted into the American Academy of Arts and Letters. He also wins the National Book Award for *Fall of America.*

With Anne Waldman, Ginsberg founds the Jack Kerouac School of Disembodied Poetics, Naropa Institute, Boulder, Colorado.

1978

Ginsberg's *Mindbreaths: Poems 1972–1977* is published (City Lights).

As Ever: The Collected Correspondence of Allen Ginsberg & Neal Cassady is published (Creative Arts).

1981

Burroughs moves to Lawrence, Kansas.

1982

The Twenty-fifth Anniversary National Celebration of *On the Road* is held at Naropa Institute in Boulder. Attendees include Ginsberg, Burroughs, Corso, Orlovsky, Robert Creeley, Ferlinghetti, Michael McClure, Diane di Prima, Ken Kesey, Carl Solomon, Ray Bremser, Huncke, Anne Waldman, Abbie Hoffman, Timothy Leary, and Jan Kerouac.

1985

Burroughs's *Queer* is published (Viking).

1989

Burroughs appears in the movie *Drugstore Cowboy* as Tom, a junky priest.

1991

The movie *Naked Lunch* is released, starring Peter Weller and directed by David Cronenberg.

Burroughs has triple bypass surgery.

1994

Burroughs appears in advertisements for Nike athletic shoes.

New York University sponsors the Beat Legacy and Celebration, 18–21 May. Honorary chairpersons are Ginsberg and Ann Charters, and speakers include David Amram, Carolyn Cassady, Corso, Ferlinghetti, Joyce Johnson, Hettie Jones, Jan Kerouac, Joanne Kyger, Ray Manzarek, Michael McClure, Ed Sanders, Cecil Taylor, Hunter S. Thompson, and Anne Waldman.

1995

New York University sponsors The Writings of Jack Kerouac Conference, 4–6 June.

1997

Ginsberg dies in April in New York City.

Burroughs dies in August in Lawrence, Kansas.

Primary Bibliography

William S. Burroughs

BOOKS: *Junkie: Confessions of an Unredeemed Drug Addict,* as William Lee, bound with *Narcotic Agent,* by Maurice Helbrant (New York: Ace, 1953; London: Digit, 1957); as William Burroughs (New York: Ace, 1964; London: Olympia/New English Library, 1966); unexpurgated edition published as *Junky,* as William S. Burroughs (New York: Penguin, 1977);

The Naked Lunch (Paris: Olympia, 1959); republished as *Naked Lunch* (New York: Grove, 1962; London: Calder/Olympia, 1964);

The Exterminator, by Burroughs and Brion Gysin (San Francisco: Auerhahn Press, 1960);

Minutes to Go, by Burroughs, Sinclair Beiles, Gregory Corso, and Gysin (Paris: Two Cities, 1960; San Francisco: Beach Books, 1968);

The Soft Machine (Paris: Olympia, 1961; revised and enlarged edition, New York: Grove, 1966; revised and enlarged again, London: Calder & Boyars, 1968);

The Ticket That Exploded (Paris: Olympia, 1962; revised and enlarged edition, New York: Grove, 1967; London: Calder & Boyars, 1968);

Dead Fingers Talk (London: Calder/Olympia, 1963);

The Yage Letters, by Burroughs and Allen Ginsberg (San Francisco: City Lights Books, 1963; enlarged, 1975);

Nova Express (New York: Grove, 1964; London: Cape, 1966);

Roosevelt after Inauguration, as "Willy Lee" alias WSB (New York: Fuck You Press, 1964); enlarged as *Roosevelt after Inauguration and Other Atrocities* (San Francisco: City Lights Books, 1979);

Health Bulletin: APO-33, a Metabolic Regulator (New York: Fuck You Press, 1965); republished as *APO-33 Bulletin: A Metabolic Regulator* (San Francisco: Beach Books, 1966);

Time (New York: "C" Press, 1965);

Valentine's Day Reading (New York: American Theatre for Poets, 1965);

So Who Owns Death TV? by Burroughs, Claude Pélieu, and Carl Weissner (San Francisco: Beach Books, 1967);

The Last Words of Dutch Schultz (London: Cape Goliard, 1970; revised and enlarged edition, New York: Viking/Seaver, 1975);

Ali's Smile (Brighton, U.K.: Unicorn, 1971); enlarged as *Ali's Smile/Naked Scientology* (Göttingen: Expanded Media Editions, 1973);

Electronic Revolution 1970–71 (Cambridge: Blackmoor Head, 1971; enlarged edition, Göttingen: Expanded Media Editions, 1972);

The Wild Boys: A Book of the Dead (New York: Grove, 1971; London: Calder & Boyars, 1972);

Brion Gysin Let the Mice In, by Burroughs, Gysin, and Ian Sommerville, edited by Jan Herman (West Glover, Vt.: Something Else, 1973);

Exterminator! (New York: Seaver/Viking, 1973; London: Calder & Boyars, 1975);

Mayfair Academy Series More or Less (Brighton, U.K.: Urgency Rip-Off, 1973);

Port of Saints (London: Covent Garden Press, 1973; revised edition, Berkeley, Cal.: Blue Wind Press, 1980);

White Subway (London: Aloes, 1973);

The Book of Breeething (Ingatestone, Essex, U.K.: OU, 1974; Berkeley, Cal.: Blue Wind Press, 1975);

Sidetripping, by Burroughs and Charles Gatewood (New York: Strawberry Hill, 1975);

Snack . . . , by Burroughs and Eric Mottram (London: Aloes, 1975);

Cobble Stone Gardens (Cherry Valley, N.Y.: Cherry Valley Editions, 1976);

The Retreat Diaries, bound with *The Dream of Tibet,* by Ginsberg (New York: City Moon, 1976);

The Third Mind, by Burroughs and Gysin (New York: Seaver/Viking, 1978; London: Calder, 1979);

Doctor Benway: A Passage from The Naked Lunch (Santa Barbara, Cal.: Morrow, 1979);

Ah Pook Is Here and Other Texts (London: Calder, 1979; New York: Riverrun, 1982);

Blade Runner (A Movie) (Berkeley, Cal.: Blue Wind Press, 1979);

Cities of the Red Night (New York: Holt, Rinehart & Winston, 1981; London: Calder, 1981);

Early Routines (Santa Barbara: Cadmus, 1981);

The Streets of Chance (New York: Red Ozier, 1981);

A William Burroughs Reader, edited by John Calder (London: Pan/Picador, 1982);
The Place of Dead Roads (New York: Holt, Rinehart & Winston, 1983; London: Calder, 1984);
The Burroughs File (San Francisco: City Lights Books, 1984);
The Adding Machine: Collected Essays (London: Calder, 1985); republished as *The Adding Machine: Selected Essays* (New York: Seaver, 1986);
Queer (New York: Viking, 1985; London: Pan, 1985);
The Cat Inside (New York: Grenfell, 1986);
Routine (London: Plashet, 1987);
The Western Lands (New York: Viking Penguin, 1987; London: Pan, 1987);
Interzone (New York: Viking, 1989; London: Pan, 1989);
Ghost of Chance (New York: High Risk Books, 1995);
My Education: A Book of Dreams (New York: Viking, 1995; London: Pan, 1995).
Collections: *The Soft Machine, Nova Express, The Wild Boys: Three Novels* (New York: Grove/Outrider, 1980);
Word Virus: The Selected Writings of William S. Burroughs, edited by James Grauerholz and Ira Silverberg (New York: Grove/Atlantic, 1998).

PLAY PRODUCTION: *The Black Rider: The Casting of the Magic Bullets,* with songs by Tom Waits, Hamburg, Germany, Thalia Theater, 31 March 1990; New York, Brooklyn Academy of Music, December 1993.

OTHER: John Giorno, *You Got to Burn to Shine: New and Collected Writings,* introduction by Burroughs (New York: Serpent's Tail, 1994).

SELECTED PERIODICAL PUBLICATION–UNCOLLECTED: "My Purpose Is To Write for the Space Age," *New York Times Book Review,* 19 February 1984, p. 910.

INTERVIEWS: *Entretiens avec William Burroughs,* by Burroughs and Daniel Odier (Paris: Belfond, 1969); translated, revised, and enlarged as *The Job: Interviews with William S. Burroughs* (New York: Grove, 1970; London: Cape, 1970; revised and enlarged again, New York: Grove, 1974).

Neal Cassady

BOOK: *The First Third & Other Writings* (San Francisco: City Lights Books, 1971; revised and enlarged, 1981).

LETTERS: *As Ever: The Collected Correspondence of Allen Ginsberg & Neal Cassady,* edited by Barry Gifford (Berkeley, Cal.: Creative Arts, 1977).

OTHER: "Drive Five" (transcription of one of Cassady's "raps" at La Honda), in *The Beat Book,* edited by Arthur and Glee Knight, the unspeakable visions of the individual, volume 4 (California, Pa.: Knight, 1974), pp. 82–87.

Gregory Corso

BOOKS: *The Vestal Lady on Brattle and Other Poems* (Cambridge, Mass.: Richard Brukenfeld, 1955);
Gasoline (San Francisco: City Lights Books, 1958);
A Pulp Magazine for the Dead Generation: Poems, by Corso and Henk Marsman (Paris: Dead Language, 1959);
The Happy Birthday of Death (New York: New Directions, 1960);
Minutes to Go, by Corso, Sinclair Beiles, William Burroughs, and Brion Gysin (Paris: Two Cities, 1960; San Francisco: Beach Books, 1968);
The American Express (Paris: Olympia, 1961);
The Minicab War: The Gotla War-Interview with Minicab Driver and Cabbie (London: Matrix, 1961);
Long Live Man (New York: New Directions, 1962);
Selected Poems (London: Eyre & Spottiswoode, 1962);
The Mutation of the Spirit (New York: Death, 1964);
The Geometric Poem (Milano: Cosmopresse, 1966);
10 Times a Poem (New York: Poets Press, 1967);
Elegiac Feelings American (New York: New Directions, 1970);
Ankh (New York: Phoenix Book Shop, 1971);
Gregory Corso (New York: Phoenix Book Shop, 1971);
The Night Last Night Was at Its Nightest (New York: Phoenix Book Shop, 1972);
Earth Egg (New York: Unmuzzled Ox, 1974);
Way Out: A Poem in Discord (Kathmandu, Nepal: Bardo Matrix, 1974);
Gregory Corso: Writings from Unmuzzled Ox Magazine (New York: Unmuzzled Ox, 1981);
Herald of the Autochthonic Spirit (New York: New Directions, 1981);
Mindfield: New and Selected Poems (New York: Thunder's Mouth Press, 1989).

OTHER: "Biographical Notes," in *The New American Poetry: 1945–1960,* edited by Donald M. Allen (New York: Grove, 1960), pp. 429–430;
Junge Amerikanische Lyrik, edited by Corso and Walter Hollerer, introduction by Corso (Munich: Hanser, 1961);
"Variations on a Generation," in *A Casebook on the Beat,* edited by Thomas Parkinson (New York: Crowell, 1961), pp. 88–97;
Poems, in *Penguin Modern Poets 5* (Harmondsworth, U.K.: Penguin, 1963);

"In This Hung-Up Age: A One-Act Farce Written 1954," in *New Directions in Prose and Poetry,* volume 18, edited by John Laughlin (New York: New Directions, 1964), pp. 149–161;

"Some of My Beginning . . . and What I Feel Right Now," in *Poets on Poetry,* edited by Howard Nemerov (New York: Basic Books, 1966), pp. 172–181;

"That Little Black Door on the Left," in *Pardon Me, Sir, But Is My Eye Hurting Your Elbow?* edited by Bob Booker and George Foster (New York: Geis, 1968), pp. 159–163.

SELECTED PERIODICAL PUBLICATIONS–UNCOLLECTED: "Reply From," *Wagner Literary Magazine* (Spring 1959): 31;

"Detective Frump's Spontaneous & Reflective Testament," *Transatlantic Review,* no. 5 (December 1960): 69–76;

Standing on a Streetcorner: A Little Play, Evergreen Review, 6 (March/April 1962): 63–78;

"Clumping in Soho," *Nugget,* 7 (June 1962): 16–23;

"Moschops! You Are a Loser!," *Nugget,* 7 (October 1962): 52–53, 66;

"Poetry and Religion: An Open Letter from Gregory Corso," *Aylesford Review,* 5 (Summer 1963): 119–126;

"Notes from the Other Side of April: With Negro Eyes, with White," *Esquire,* 62 (July 1964): 86–87, 110;

"Life, Death and Dancing: A Buffalo Shindig," *Esquire,* 64 (July 1965): 34–35;

"Gregory Corso: Sources," transcribed and edited by Douglas Calhoun, *Athanor,* 5 (Winter 1975): 1–6.

Lawrence Ferlinghetti

BOOKS: *Pictures of the Gone World* (San Francisco: City Lights Books, 1955);

A Coney Island of the Mind (Norfolk, Conn.: New Directions, 1958; enlarged edition, London: Hutchinson, 1959; enlarged again, New York: New Directions, 1968);

Tentative Description of a Dinner Given to Promote the Impeachment of President Eisenhower (San Francisco: Golden Mountain, 1958);

Her (Norfolk, Conn.: New Directions, 1960; London: MacGibbon & Kee, 1966);

Starting from San Francisco (Norfolk, Conn.: New Directions, 1961; enlarged edition, New York: New Directions, 1967);

Berlin (San Francisco: Golden Mountain, 1961);

One Thousand Fearful Words for Fidel Castro (San Francisco: City Lights Books, 1961);

Howl of the Censor (San Carlos, Cal.: Nourse, 1961);

Unfair Arguments with Existence (New York: New Directions, 1963);

Routines (New York: New Directions, 1964);

An Eye on the World: Selected Poems (London: MacGibbon & Kee, 1967);

After the Cries of Birds (San Francisco: Dave Haselwood, 1967);

Fuclock (London: Fire, 1968);

The Secret Meaning of Things (New York: New Directions, 1969);

Tyrannus Nix? (New York: New Directions, 1969; revised, 1973);

The Mexican Night: Travel Journal (New York: New Directions, 1970);

Back Roads to Far Places (New York: New Directions, 1971);

Love Is No Stone on the Moon: Automatic Poem (Berkeley, Cal.: ARIF, 1971);

Open Eye, bound with *Open Head,* by Allen Ginsberg (Melbourne: Sun Books, 1972);

Open Eye, Open Heart (New York: New Directions, 1973);

Who Are We Now? (New York: New Directions, 1976);

Director of Alienation: A Poem (Northampton, Mass.: Main Street, 1976);

A Political Pamphlet (San Francisco: Anarchist Resistance, 1976);

Northwest Ecolog (San Francisco: City Lights Books, 1978);

Landscapes of Living and Dying (New York: New Directions, 1979);

The Sea and Ourselves at Cape Ann (Madison, Wis.: Red Ozier, 1979);

Mule Mountain Dreams (Bisbee, Ariz.: Bisbee, 1980);

Literary San Francisco: A Pictorial History from Its Beginnings to the Present Day, by Ferlinghetti and Nancy Joyce Peters (San Francisco: City Lights Books/Harper & Row, 1980);

A Trip to Italy and France (New York: New Directions, 1980);

Endless Life: Selected Poems (New York: New Directions, 1981);

The Populist Manifestos: Plus an Interview with Jean-Jacques Lebel (San Francisco: Grey Fox, 1981);

Leaves of Life (First Series): Fifty Drawings from the Model (San Francisco: City Lights Books, 1983);

Over All the Obscene Boundaries: European Poems & Transitions (New York: New Directions, 1984); republished as *European Poems & Transitions: Over All the Obscene Boundaries* (New York: New Directions, 1988);

Seven Days in Nicaragua Libre (San Francisco: City Lights Books, 1984);

Love in the Days of Rage (New York: Dutton, 1988);

Inside the Trojan Horse (San Francisco: Don't Call It Frisco, 1988);

Amant des Gares (Quebec: Ecrits des Forges, 1990);
When I Look at Pictures (Salt Lake City: Peregrine Smith, 1990);
Spirit of the Crusades (London: Turret, 1991);
These Are My Rivers: New & Selected Poems, 1955–1993 (New York: New Directions, 1993);
The Canticle of Jack Kerouac (Boise: Limberlost, 1993);
Triumph of the Postmodern (Hull, U.K.: Carnivorous Arpeggio, 1993);
Poem, Interview, Photographs (Louisville, Ky.: White Fields, 1994);
A Far Rockaway of the Heart (New York: New Directions, 1997);
The Hopper House at Truro (New York: Lospecchio, 1997).
Collection: *Wild Dreams of a New Beginning* (New York: New Directions, 1988)–comprises *Who Are We Now?* and *Landscapes of Living and Dying.*

RECORDINGS: *Tentative Description of a Dinner Given to Promote the Impeachment of President Eisenhower & Other Poems,* Fantasy Records 7004, 1958;
Poetry Readings in The Cellar, read by Ferlinghetti and Kenneth Rexroth, Fantasy Records 7002, 1959;
Starting from San Francisco, read by Ferlinghetti, Norfolk, Conn.: New Directions, 1961;
The World's Great Poets, volume 1, read by Ferlinghetti, Allen Ginsberg, and Gregory Corso at the 1965 Spoleto Festival, CMS, 1971;
Contemporary American Poets Read Their Works: Lawrence Ferlinghetti, Everett/Edwards, 1972;
Tyrannus Nix? & Assassination Raga, Fantasy Records, 1971;
Lawrence Ferlinghetti: An Interview, Washington, D.C.: Tapes for Readers, 1979;
Into the Deeper Pools, read by Ferlinghetti, Washington, D.C.: Watershed Tapes, 1984.

OTHER: Jacques Prévert, *Selection from Paroles,* translated by Ferlinghetti (San Francisco: City Lights Books, 1958);
Diane Di Prima, *This Kind of Bird Flies Backward,* introduction by Ferlinghetti (New York: Totem, 1958);
Poems, in *Penguin Modern Poets 5* (Harmondsworth, U.K.: Penguin, 1963);
Yevgeny Yevtushenko, "Freedom to Kill," translation adapted by Ferlinghetti, in *Flowers and Bullets, and Freedom to Kill,* by Yevtushenko (San Francisco: City Lights Books, 1970), pp. 1–14;
"Genesis of After the Cries of the Birds," in *The Poetics of the New American Poetry,* edited by Donald Allen and Warren Tallman (New York: Grove, 1973);
City Lights Anthology, edited by Ferlinghetti (San Francisco: City Lights Books, 1974);
Ezra Pound, *Antologia,* epilogue by Ferlinghetti (Madrid: Visor, 1979);
Nicanor Parra, *Antipoems: New and Selected Poems,* edited by David Unger, translated by Ferlinghetti (New York: New Directions, 1985);
Pier Paolo Pasolini, *Roman Poems,* translated by Ferlinghetti (San Francisco: City Lights Books, 1986).

SELECTED PERIODICAL PUBLICATIONS–UNCOLLECTED: "Lawrence Ferlinghetti: Horn on 'HOWL,'" *Evergreen Review,* 1, no. 4 (1957): 145–158;
"Notes on Poetry in San Francisco," *Chicago Review,* 12 (Spring 1958): 3–5.

INTERVIEWS: Gavin Selerie, *An Interview with Lawrence Ferlinghetti Conducted at Riverside Studios 3.7.80* (London: Binnacle, 1980);
The Cool Eye: Lawrence Ferlinghetti Talks to Alexis Lykiard (Exeter, U.K.: Stride, 1993).

Allen Ginsberg
BOOKS: *Howl and Other Poems* (San Francisco: City Lights Books, 1956);
Empty Mirror: Early Poems (New York: Totem Press/Corinth Books, 1961);
Kaddish and Other Poems: 1958–1960 (San Francisco: City Lights Books, 1961);
Reality Sandwiches: 1953–60 (San Francisco: City Lights Books, 1963);
The Yage Letters, by Ginsberg and William Burroughs (San Francisco: City Lights Books, 1963);
T.V. Baby Poems (London: Cape Goliard, 1967; New York: Grossman, 1968);
Airplane Dreams: Compositions from Journals (Toronto: House of Anansi Press, 1968; San Francisco: City Lights Books, 1969);
Ankor Wat (London: Fulcrum, 1968);
Planet News: 1961–1967 (San Francisco: City Lights Books, 1968; London: Villiers, 1968);
Notes after an Evening with William Carlos Williams (New York: Samuel Charters, 1970);
Indian Journals: March 1962–May 1963 (San Francisco: David Haselwood/City Lights Books, 1970);
Ginsberg's Improvised Poetics, edited by Mark Robinson (Buffalo, N.Y.: Anonym, 1971);
The Fall of America: Poems of These States 1965–1971 (San Francisco: City Lights Books, 1972);
The Gates of Wrath: Rhymed Poems, 1948–1952 (Bolinas, Cal.: Grey Fox, 1972);
Iron Horse (Toronto: Coach House, 1972; San Francisco: City Lights Books, 1974);

Allen Verbatim: Lectures on Poetry, Politics, Consciousness, edited by Gordon Ball (New York: McGraw-Hill, 1974);

The Visions of the Great Rememberer (Amherst, Mass.: Mulch, 1974);

Chicago Trial Testimony (San Francisco: City Lights Books, 1975);

First Blues: Rags, Ballads & Harmonium Songs 1971–74 (New York: Full Court Press, 1975);

Journals: Early Fifties Early Sixties, edited by Ball (New York: Grove, 1977);

Mind Breaths: Poems 1972–1977 (San Francisco: City Lights Books, 1978);

Poems All over the Place: Mostly 'Seventies (Cherry Valley, N.Y.: Cherry Valley Editions, 1978);

Composed on the Tongue, edited by Donald Allen (Bolinas, Cal.: Grey Fox, 1980);

Straight Hearts' Delight: Love Poems and Selected Letters, by Ginsberg and Peter Orlovsky, edited by Winston Leyland (San Francisco: Gay Sunshine, 1980);

Plutonian Ode: Poems 1977–1980 (San Francisco: City Lights Books, 1982);

Collected Poems 1947–1980 (New York: Harper & Row, 1984; Harmondsworth, U.K.: Viking, 1985);

Howl: Original Draft Facsimile, Transcript & Variant Versions, Fully Annotated by Author, edited by Barry Miles (New York: Harper & Row, 1986);

White Shroud: Poems 1980–1985 (New York: Harper & Row, 1986);

Your Reason and Blake's System (New York: Hanuman, 1988);

Allen Ginsberg: Photographs (Altadena, Cal.: Twelvetrees, 1990);

Kaddish for Naomi Ginsberg, 1894–1956 (San Francisco: Arion, 1992);

Honorable Courtship: From the Author's Journals, January 1–15, 1955, edited by Ball (San Francisco: Coffee House, 1993);

Snapshot Poetics: A Photographic Memoir of the Beat Era (San Francisco: Chronicle, 1993);

Cosmopolitan Greetings: Poems 1986–1992 (New York: HarperCollins, 1994);

Journals Mid-Fifties, 1954–1958, edited by Ball (New York: HarperCollins, 1995);

Illuminated Poems (New York: Four Walls Eight Windows, 1996).

RECORDINGS: *Allen Ginsberg Reads Howl and Other Poems,* Fantasy-Galaxy Records, 1959;

Allen Ginsberg Reads Kaddish, A Twentieth Century Ecstatic Narrative Poem, Atlantic Verbum Series, 1966;

Allen Ginsberg/William Blake: Songs of Innocence and Experience, M-G-M Records, 1969;

Birdbrain!, by Ginsberg and the Gluons, Alekos Records/Wax Trax Records, 1981;

First Blues: Rags, Ballads and Harmonium Songs, Folkways Records, 1981;

The Lion for Real, Great Jones/Island Records, 1990;

Cosmopolitan Greetings, words by Ginsberg, music by George Gruntz, Migros-Genossenschafts-Bund Musikszene, Scheitz, 1993;

Howls, Raps & Roars: Recordings from the San Francisco Poetry Renaissance, Fantasy Records, 1993;

Hydrogen Jukebox, libretto by Ginsberg, music by Philip Glass, Electra Nonesuch, 1993;

Allen Ginsberg: Holy Soul Jelly Roll–Songs and Poems (1949–1993), Rhino Records, 1994.

LETTERS: Ginsberg and Richard Eberhart, *To Eberhart from Ginsberg: A Letter about Howl 1956* (Lincoln, Mass.: Penmaen Press, 1976);

As Ever: The Collected Correspondence of Allen Ginsberg & Neal Cassady, edited by Barry Gifford (Berkeley, Cal.: Creative Arts, 1977).

John Clellon Holmes

BOOKS: *Go* (New York: Scribners, 1952; abridged edition, New York: Ace, 1958); republished as *The Beat Boys* (London: Ace/Harborough, 1959);

The Horn (New York: Random House, 1958; London: Deutsch, 1959);

Get Home Free (New York: Dutton, 1964; London: Corgi, 1966);

Nothing More to Declare (New York: Dutton, 1967; London: Deutsch, 1968);

The Bowling Green Poems (California, Pa.: the unspeakable visions of the individual, 1977);

Death Drag: Selected Poems 1948–1979 (Pocatello, Idaho: Limberlost Press, 1979);

Visitor: Jack Kerouac in Old Saybrook, the unspeakable visions of the individual, volume 11 (California, Pa.: Knight, 1981);

Displaced Person: The Travel Essays (Fayetteville: University of Arkansas Press, 1987);

Passionate Opinions: The Cultural Essays (Fayetteville: University of Arkansas Press, 1988);

Representative Men: The Biographical Essays (Fayetteville: University of Arkansas Press, 1988);

Night Music: Selected Poems (Fayetteville: University of Arkansas Press, 1989).

OTHER: Carolyn Cassady, *Heartbeat,* introduction by Holmes (Berkeley, Cal.: Creative Arts, 1978).

SELECTED PERIODICAL PUBLICATIONS–UNCOLLECTED:

FICTION

"Tea for Two," *Neurotica,* no. 2 (1948): 36–43;

"A Length of Chain," *Nugget,* 5 (August 1960): 13–14, 21, 43;
"The Next to the Last Time," *Escapade,* 14 (September 1967): 28–31, 36;
"The Manifest Destiny of Mrs. Polk's Sudie," *Penthouse,* 8 (February 1977): 109ff;
"Night Blooming Cereus," *Black Warrior Review,* 4 (Spring 1978): 8–20;
"At Pompeii," *Black Warrior Review,* 7 (Spring 1981): 19–29.

NONFICTION
"20th Century Troubador," *Holiday,* 19 (February 1956): 14, 16, 19–22;
"The Philosophy of the Beat Generation," *Esquire,* 49 (February 1958): 35–38;
"The Golden Age of Jazz/Time Present," *Esquire,* 51 (January 1959): 100–102;
"Existentialism and the Novel," *Chicago Review,* 13 (Summer 1959): 144–151;
"A Few Loves, A Few Deaths: 1945-1951," *Contact,* 13 (July–August 1962): 69–73;
"The Booze and I," *Nugget,* 7 (August 1962): 62–63;
"The New Girl," *Playboy,* 15 (January 1968): 179–182;
"An American Requiem in Paris," *Venture,* 7 (April 1970): 10, 12, 15-16, 19–20, 23–24;
"See Naples and Live," *Playboy,* 17 (June 1970): 124–126, 136, 214, 216-217;
"The New Taste in Humor," by Holmes and Jay Landesman as Alfred Towne, *American Mercury,* 73 (September 1971): 22-27;
"Thanksgiving in Florence," *Playboy,* 18 (November 1971): 130–132, 214, 216–218;
"Encounter in Munich," *Playboy,* 19 (March 1972): 138–140, 207-211;
"In Search of Los Angeles," *Playboy,* 19 (May 1972): 123ff;
"This Is the Beat Generation," *New York Times Magazine,* 16 November 1972, p. 347;
"Gone in October," *Playboy,* 20 (February 1973): 96–99, 140, 158-160, 162, 166;
"Unscrewing the Locks: The Beat Poets," *Poets of the Cities New York and San Francisco 1950–1965* (1975): 64–71;
"Awake in Rome," *Quarterly West,* 5 (Winter 1978): 59–70;
"Exile's London, 1967," *New Letters,* 44 (Spring 1978): 7-31;
"And Here Comes Neal (New York, 1948–51)," *Spit in the Ocean,* 6 (Fall 1981): 7–14.

Herbert Huncke
BOOKS: *Huncke's Journal* (New York: Poets Press, 1965);
Elsie John and Joey Martinez (New York: Pequod Press, 1979);
The Evening Sun Turned Crimson (Cherry Valley, N.Y.: Cherry Valley Editions, 1980);
Guilty of Everything: The Autobiography of Herbert Huncke (New York: Paragon House, 1990).

SELECTED PERIODICAL PUBLICATION–UNCOLLECTED: "Alvarez," *Playboy,* 15 (October 1968): 141, 179.

Jack Kerouac
BOOKS: *The Town & the City* (New York: Harcourt, Brace, 1950; London: Eyre & Spottiswoode, 1951);
On the Road (New York: Viking, 1957; London: Deutsch, 1958);
The Dharma Bums (New York: Viking, 1958; London: Deutsch, 1959);
The Subterraneans (New York: Grove, 1958; London: Deutsch, 1960);
Doctor Sax: Faust Part Three (New York: Grove, 1959; London: Evergreen, 1961);
Excerpts from Visions of Cody (New York: New Directions, 1959);
Maggie Cassidy (New York: Avon, 1959; London: Panther, 1960);
Mexico City Blues (New York: Grove, 1959);
Lonesome Traveler (New York: McGraw-Hill, 1960; London: Deutsch, 1962);
Rimbaud (San Francisco: City Lights Books, 1960);
The Scripture of the Golden Eternity (New York: Totem Press in association with Corinth Books, 1960; London: Centaur, 1960);
Tristessa (New York: Avon, 1960; London: World, 1963);
Book of Dreams (San Francisco: City Lights Books, 1961);
Pull My Daisy (New York: Grove, 1961; London: Evergreen, 1961);
Big Sur (New York: Farrar, Straus & Cudahy, 1962; London: Deutsch, 1963);
Visions of Gerard (New York: Farrar, Straus, 1963);
Visions of Gerard & Tristessa (London: Deutsch, 1964);
Desolation Angels (New York: Coward-McCann, 1965; London: Deutsch, 1966);
Satori in Paris (New York: Grove, 1966; London: Deutsch, 1967);
Vanity of Duluoz: An Adventurous Education 1935–46 (New York: Coward-McCann, 1968; London: Deutsch, 1969);
Pic (New York: Grove, 1971);
Scattered Poems (San Francisco: City Lights Books, 1971);

Visions of Cody (New York: McGraw-Hill, 1972; London: Deutsch, 1973);

Trip Trap Haiku along the Road from San Francisco to New York 1959, by Kerouac, Albert Saijo, and Lew Welch (Bolinas, Cal.: Grey Fox, 1973);

Heaven & Other Poems (Bolinas, Cal.: Grey Fox, 1977);

San Francisco Blues (N.p.: Beat Books, 1983);

Good Blonde & Others, edited by Donald Allen (San Francisco: Grey Fox, 1993);

Atop an Underwood: Early Stories and Other Writings, edited by Paul Marion (New York: Viking, 1999).

Collection: *The Portable Jack Kerouac,* edited by Ann Charters (New York: Viking, 1995).

LETTERS: *Dear Carolyn: Letters to Carolyn Cassady,* edited by Arthur and Kit Knight, the unspeakable visions of the individual, volume 13 (California, Pa.: Estate of Jack Kerouac, 1983);

Jack Kerouac: Selected Letters, 1940–1956, edited by Ann Charters (New York: Viking, 1995);

Jack Kerouac: Selected Letters, 1956–1969, edited by Charters (New York: Viking, 1999).

SELECTED PERIODICAL PUBLICATION–UNCOLLECTED: "The Art of Fiction XLI," *Paris Review,* 43 (Summer 1968).

Gary Snyder

BOOKS: *Riprap* (Kyoto, Japan: Origin Press, 1959); enlarged as *Riprap & Cold Mountain Poems* (San Francisco: Four Seasons Foundation, 1965);

Myths & Texts (New York: Totem Press/Corinth Books, 1960; London: Centaur, 1960; republished with new preface, New York: New Directions, 1978);

Six Sections from Mountains and Rivers without End (San Francisco: Four Seasons Foundation, 1965; London: Fulcrum, 1967); enlarged as *Six Sections from Mountains and Rivers without End Plus One* (San Francisco: Four Seasons Foundation, 1970);

A Range of Poems (London: Fulcrum, 1966);

Three Worlds, Three Realms, Six Roads (Marlboro, Vt.: Griffin, 1966);

The Back Country (London: Fulcrum, 1967; New York: New Directions, 1968);

The Blue Sky (New York: Phoenix Book Shop, 1969);

Earth House Hold: Technical Notes & Queries for Fellow Dharma Revolutionaries (New York: New Directions, 1969; London: Cape, 1970);

Regarding Wave (Iowa City: Windhover, 1969; enlarged edition, New York: New Directions, 1970; London: Fulcrum, 1972);

Manzanita (Bolinas, Cal.: Four Seasons Foundation, 1972);

The Fudo Trilogy (Berkeley, Cal.: Shaman Drum, 1973);

Turtle Island (New York: New Directions, 1974);

The Old Ways: Six Essays (San Francisco: City Lights Books, 1977);

He Who Hunted Birds in His Father's Village: The Dimensions of a Haida Myth (Bolinas, Cal.: Grey Fox, 1979);

The Real Work: Interviews & Talks 1964–1979, edited by William Scott McLean (New York: New Directions, 1980);

True Night (North San Juan, Cal.: Bob Giorgio, 1980);

Axe Handles (San Francisco: North Point, 1983);

Passage through India (San Francisco: Grey Fox, 1983);

Good Wild Sacred (Madley, U.K.: Five Seasons, 1984);

The Fates of Rocks & Trees (San Francisco: James Linden, 1986);

Left Out in the Rain: New Poems 1947–1985 (San Francisco: North Point, 1986);

The Practice of the Wild (San Francisco: North Point, 1990);

No Nature: New and Selected Poems (New York: Pantheon, 1992);

North Pacific Lands & Waters: A Further Six Sections (Waldron Island, Wash.: Brooding Heron, 1993);

A Place in Space: Ethics, Aesthetics, and Watersheds. New and Selected Prose (Washington, D.C.: Counterpoint, 1995);

Mountains and Rivers without End (Washington, D.C.: Counterpoint, 1996);

The Gary Snyder Reader (Washington, D.C.: Counterpoint, 1999).

OTHER: "Statement on Poetics," in *The New American Poetry,* edited by Donald M. Allen (New York: Grove, 1960), pp. 420–421;

Naked Poetry, edited by Stephen Berg and Robert Mezey (New York: Bobbs-Merrill, 1969);

On Bread & Poetry: A Panel Discussion with Gary Snyder, Lew Welch & Philip Whalen, edited by Allen (Bolinas, Cal.: Grey Fox, 1977);

Barry Gifford and Lawrence Lee, *Jack's Book: An Oral Biography of Jack Kerouac,* contribution by Snyder (New York: St. Martin's Press, 1978), p. 202;

Beneath a Single Moon: Buddhism in Contemporary American Poetry, edited by Kent Johnson and Craig Paulenich, introductory essay by Snyder (Boston: Shambhala, 1991).

SELECTED PERIODICAL PUBLICATION–UNCOLLECTED: "A Young Mazama's Idea of a Mount Hood Climb," *Mazama,* 18 (1946): 56.

Carl Solomon

BOOKS: *Mishaps, Perhaps,* edited by Mary Beach (San Francisco: Beach Books Texts & Documents/City Lights Books, 1966);

More Mishaps, edited by Beach (San Francisco: Beach Books Texts & Documents/City Lights Books, 1968);

Emergency Messages: An Autobiographical Miscellany, edited by John Tytell (New York: Paragon House, 1989).

OTHER: *The Beat Book,* edited by Arthur and Glee Knight, contributions by Solomon, the unspeakable visions of the individual, volume 4 (California, Pa.: Knight, 1974);

"Partizani," in *A Decade and Then Some, Intrepid Anthology,* edited by Allen De Loach (Buffalo: Intrepid Press, 1976), p. 332;

The Beat Diary, edited by Arthur and Kit Knight, the unspeakable visions of the individual, volume 5 (California, Pa.: Knight, 1977)–includes contributions by Solomon;

"1977 Reflections," in *New Directions,* no. 37 (New York: New Directions, 1977).

SELECTED PERIODICAL PUBLICATIONS–UNCOLLECTED: "The Conscientious Objectors Speak," as Karl Solomon, *New Leader,* 33 (10 June 1950): 24;

"For the Man Who Knows," *New Leader,* 33 (19 August 1950): 26;

"Danish Gambit," as Carl Gentile, *Neurotica,* no. 7 (Autumn 1950): 19;

"Crime Novel without a Detective," *New Leader,* 33 (16 September 1950): 23;

"Rather Reich than Resident," *New Leader,* 33 (4 December 1950): 25;

"Further Afterthoughts of a Shock Patient," as Carl Goy, *Neurotica,* no. 8 (Spring 1951): 74;

"The Madman in the Looking Glass," *Outsider,* no. 3 (Spring 1963): 56;

Poetry and prose pieces, *Intrepid,* no. 5 (March 1965);

"Age: 36," *El Corno Emplumado,* no. 15 (July 1965): 21;

"From the Files of Carl Solomon–1962," *Intrepid,* no. 6 (September 1966);

"Badinage for Claude Pelieu," *Coldspring Journal,* no. 10 (April 1976): 33;

"Work Day Ended–1976," *Palantir,* no. 4 (November 1976): 41;

"All About Joe Stripp–A Heartwarming Memoir," *Red M(irage),* no. 1 (Summer 1977);

"More Memories and Random Thoughts," *Saturday Morning,* 2 (Summer 1978);

"A Generation Ago," *United Artists,* no. 10 (April 1980);

"*Sens Plastique,* by Malcolm de Chazal," *Poetry Project Newsletter,* no. 76 (September 1980);

"*Aberration of Starlight,* by Gilbert Sorrentino," *American Book Review,* volume 3 (January–February 1981): 5;

"*The Jaime De Angulo Reader,* edited by Bob Callahan," *Poetry Project Newsletter,* no. 82 (April 1981);

"Short Prose Piece for Curtis Sliwa," *Poetry Project Newsletter,* no. 83 (May 1981);

"*Fame and Love in New York,* by Ed Sanders," *American Book Review,* 3 (May–June 1981): 14;

"Paul Celan: Poems," *American Book Review,* 3 (September–October 1981): 13.

Chapter 1
The Beats in New York City

The Beat Phenomenon

The writers who spawned the multifaceted Beat Generation phenomenon spoke for the disaffiliated youth who were coming of age in the late 1940s and 1950s, an era marked by global warfare, the atomic bomb, mass industrialization, suburban sprawl, decaying spiritual values, and a loss of individual identity. These writers both identified the malaise and pointed the way out–through heightened perception and spiritual epiphany. That message was lost on much of the public, though, as the Beats were ensnared instead in the trappings of their lifestyle. Rather than seeing the goal, the public mainly saw the means–the frantic jazz scenes, fast cars, sex, and drugs. Initially, the Beats evoked both fear and disgust, along with a general dismissal of their literary efforts. In fact, their works probably were known best because some of them had been banned as obscene. Allen Ginsberg's Howl and Other Poems *(1955) was seized by customs officials as its English printers sent it into the United States, and later bookstore owner and publisher Lawrence Ferlinghetti was arrested for selling the book. William Burroughs's* Naked Lunch *(1959) maintains the distinction of being, in 1965, the last literary work banned for alleged obscenity in the United States.*

Even though the Beat literature was largely dismissed, the Beat lifestyle, as it came to be seen, threatened America's once-solid Protestant middle-class values. To conservative observers, the Beats embodied immorality and represented the result of frustration and decadence, a social force that jeopardized society with lawlessness. Terms such as revolt, insurrection, *and* mutiny *became associated with* Beat. *Yet, just as Joel Chandler Harris, a writer for the* Atlanta Constitution *in the 1880s, had created the harmless and lovable character of Uncle Remus to allay public fears of the recently freed slaves, the media once again created a harmless representation, this time of the insurrectionist Beats. In April 1958* San Francisco Chronicle *columnist Herb Caen referred to a smattering of young bohemians as "beatniks."*

The term beatnik *softened the image of the Beats, and soon, instead of fearing the Beat insurrection, the public began to ridicule–and sometimes enjoy–the beatniks, young men in beards and sandals who tapped bongo drums and recited poetry while hip chicks in leotards gazed on with a lilting pout. Perhaps not surprisingly, many young people left home to seek adventure and a new life in neighborhoods such as Greenwich Village in New York City or North Beach in San Francisco, and adopted the dress, lingo, and posture of what had been a media bastardization, believing that they were hooking into the real thing.* Squares, *that is, the mainstream, the nonbeat, even had theme parties to which they invited beatniks and dressed as beatniks themselves. Beatniks infested the public domain as objects of derision and easy targets: the unwashed, the deliberately unemployed, the poetasters, and coffeehouse inhabitants who uttered "like" and "wow" and "man" as they discussed Poetry and Life in watered-down discourse.*

This conversion left the original Beat writers in an unusual predicament. They had originally identified an attitude which they shared; now they were seen as inspiring a pattern of ironically conformist behavior that was more a fad than a significantly vital alternative lifestyle. Immediately and frequently, Jack Kerouac sought to distance himself, telling any interviewer who would listen that he was a serious artist and working-class product who had no connection with the hangers-on who toted his books in the back pockets of their blue jeans. Inevitably, Kerouac, Ginsberg, and Burroughs were affiliated with the fad that followed them, captives, in a sense, of the movement they started. In the mid 1960s the Beatniks yielded the cultural center stage, and those who remained transformed themselves and joined the rising generation of young bohemians, the hippies. The hippies were generally more politically charged, set with a clearer agenda of preserving the environment and pursuing global peace, all while exploring sexual love. Ginsberg made the transition seamlessly and became a leading figure in antiwar protest and marches for gay rights.

Despite often being derided, the Beat writers opened up new material and new styles of expression for writing. They also wielded a significant influence as a social force, for people who may have never heard of Kerouac, Ginsberg, or Burroughs benefit from the Beat urges toward freedom of expression in personal terms. Clear lines of influence stretch from artistic pursuits in the twenty-first century back to 1944, when the Beat writers met in New York City and changed their culture.

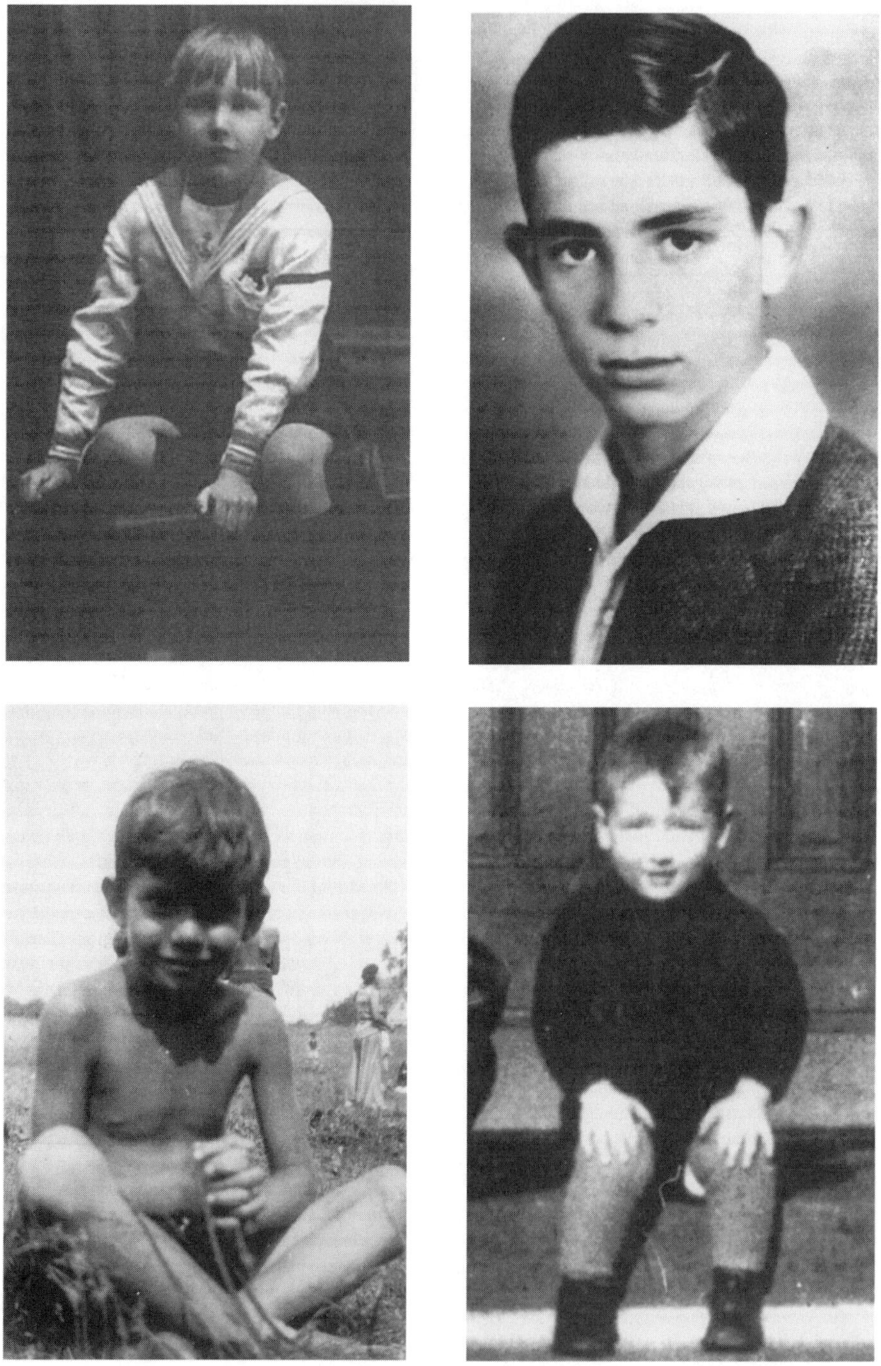

Four key members of the Beat Generation as children: top, William Burroughs and Jack Kerouac; bottom, Allen Ginsberg and Neal Cassady

The Gathering of the Beats

In a 1978 interview Ginsberg discussed the gathering of the founding members of the Beat Movement at Columbia University. Kerouac entered the school in 1940, after a year at Horace Mann Preparatory School in New York City. Ginsberg entered in the fall of 1943, at age seventeen. Burroughs, who had graduated from Harvard in the 1930s, did not have a Columbia connection.

New York in the forties. Well, the main scene, I think, where everybody met–that is to say, Burroughs, Kerouac, myself, Herbert Huncke, Neal Cassady, Joan Vollmer Adams Burroughs, Ed White, Hal Chase, Clellon Holmes, Ed Stringham of *The New Yorker* magazine, Alan Harrington, started around Christmas '43 . . .

Lucien Carr moved into the seventh floor of the Union Theological Seminary on 120th Street, which during wartime was used as a dormitory for Columbia, which was filled with V-8 Navy students. I moved in across the hall in my second term at Columbia, on the seventh floor, and Lucien was at the end of the long, old wooden corridor. And I met him 'cause there was some music coming out of his door. It was very beautiful–Brahms Trio No. 1, which I'd never heard. So I knocked, and he opened the door, and we immediately were struck with each other and started talking.

And he took me down, for the first time, to Greenwich Village, and that Christmas I met Burroughs, who was a friend of Lucien's from St. Louis. Then, around the same time, Lucien met Edie Parker, who was Kerouac's girlfriend, Kerouac was still at sea. Edie, when Kerouac came back from shipping, I think, to Greenland, introduced Lucien to Kerouac at the West End cafeteria, or else at the apartment they had on 118th Street near Amsterdam Avenue. Then Lucien took me over to see Edie, maybe at the West End, or took me over to see Jack, or else gave me the address to go see him.

He described Kerouac in very romantic terms as a seaman who was a novelist or a poet, or writer, Jack Londonesque in style. I don't know what our reference point was then, actually. Soulful.

So I went up to visit Jack one morning when he was eating breakfast, eleven or twelve, and we got into some kind of funny conversation, I don't know what it was about any more. I remember being awed by him and amazed by him, because I'd never met a big jock who was sensitive and intelligent about poetry. Not that I knew anything about poetry, because my idea was A.E. Housman and Shakespeare, or something, I hadn't read any Eliot or Pound or any modern poetry, I didn't have any idea what I was doing, I was writing little rhymed lyrics. And he had just finished a book called *The Sea Is My Brother,* which was written, I guess, aboard the ocean liner. I don't know what we talked about, except prose versus poetry, or something–

That memory is mixed up with another memory, maybe of the same time. I was moving out of the room at the theological seminary. I think I'd moved my stuff out and was going back to pick up the dishes, and Jack walked me down through the Columbia campus, down along 120th Street, I guess, to Union Seminary. And we were talking about the phantomlike, ghostly nature of moving from place to place and saying farewell to old apartments and rooms. And so we walked up the seven flights, and I picked up whatever gear I hadda get, and then turned and bowed and saluted the door as I left, and then saluted the hallway and said, "Goodbye, beautiful steps. Goodbye, second step. Goodbye, third step," and so on, as we went down the seven flights. And so we got into a rapport over the sense of mortal transience, because he said, "Ah, I do that, too, when I say goodbye to a place."

. . . He was aware when he was saying goodbye to a place or when he was passing through the world, that it was a melancholy mortal tearful moment, constantly. Saying goodbye was like arriving or something. I don't know. It was a little poem idea that we had. The

World War II had a profound effect on the generation that was then coming of age. In this 15 July 1942 excerpt from a letter that Kerouac wrote to his girlfriend, Norma Bickfelt, at the height of the war, he reveals his romantic nature and his appreciation of literature. At the same time, he clearly has an affinity for literary groups that grapple with issues.

For one thing, I wish to take part in the war, not because I want to kill anyone, but for a reason directly opposed to killing–the Brotherhood. To be with my American brothers, for that matter, my Russian brothers; for their danger to be my danger; to speak to them quietly, perhaps at dawn, in Arctic mists; to know them, and for them to know myself. . . . an elusive thing, I speak of now, but I know it is there.

. . . .

Have you been reading Thomas Wolfe and William Saroyan? . . . and if so, what do you think of them? I took your advice and read Thomas Mann–he certainly is a great and true Humanist. Speaking of Humanists, I am a member of a young Humanist movement in Boston. We are obscure, and may never dent progress–but we have heated discussions and plenty of intellectual stimulation.

–*Jack Kerouac: Selected Letters, 1940–1956,* pp. 22–23, 25

Columbia University campus. The school was the vortex that drew together Kerouac, Ginsberg, and Burroughs in the mid 1940s. Ginsberg's interest was in studying literature and writing poetry for the campus literary magazine, while Kerouac came to play football.

conversation was a discovery that we both felt the same sensitive, personal self-farewell toward the world, and the occasion was moving out of this college dormitory where I'd fallen in love. So I think that from that conversation we became friends . . .

Jack was introduced to Burroughs by Lucien, I think. We didn't know Burroughs. We just met him once, and I think that was Christmas, '43. David Kammerer, Burroughs' friend, was living at forty-four Morton. So Lucien took me down to visit David's flat, and Burroughs was there that Christmas. I remember Burroughs describing a fight that he'd seen on the floor of some dyke bar, in which this guy had bit somebody's ear. And I think Bill had said, "Tis too starved an argument for my sword." It was the first time I ever heard Shakespeare quoted with intelligence. "In the words of the immortal bard, 'Tis too starved an argument for my sword.'" So I wondered who this intelligent aristocrat was. He hasn't changed at all. I mean, his demeanor is the same now as it was then.

Jack must have met him with Lucien at some point or another, or at the same time, but neither of us knew him. It wasn't until about a half year later, after Lucien left town, that Jack and I decided we ought to go look up Burroughs together and pay him a formal visit and examine his soul and find out who he was and what he was, because he was so interesting and intelligent and worldly wise that he seemed like some sort of international spiritual man of distinction to us. But we couldn't figure out what his secret mystery was, so we decided we'd go find out in his apartment on Riverside Drive.

So Jack and I made a formal visit to Bill, and I remember that he had copies of Yeats' *A Vision,* which Lucien had been carrying around. Shakespeare, Kafka: *The Castle* or *The Trial, The Castle,* I think; Korzybski's *Science and Sanity,* Spengler's *Decline of the West,* Blake, a copy of Hart Crane, which he gave me and I still have, Rimbaud, Cocteau's *Opium.* So those were the books he was reading, and I hadn't read any of those. And he loaned books to us . . .

So we had a long conversation with Burroughs, probably about Spengler and Korzybski. He was pointing out that words were not things that they represented, were not identical . . . Of course, Burroughs was interested from the viewpoint of general semantics, since he studied with Korzybski in Chicago. From his own point of view, also being involved in psychoanalysis, he was interested in . . . "original mind . . . preconceptual primordial mind."

Kerouac in uniform and Ginsberg aboard ship. Both men served in the Merchant Marine during World War II. In February 1943 Kerouac joined the Coast Guard, which was part of the U.S. Navy during the war (estate of Edie Parker Kerouac–Tim Moran, executor).

. . . .

Kerouac and I decided that Burroughs was a big seeker of souls and searcher through cities. I think Kerouac said "the last of the Faustian men." He was taking the terminology from Spengler, and it was from Spengler that Kerouac got his idea of *fellaheen*–the word *fellaheen.*

We all got our whole conception, certainly different from my original, liberal, *New York Post* background, of some kind of spiritual crisis in the west and the possibility of Decline instead of infinite American Century Progress–The idea of an apocalyptic historical change.

Bill moved downtown to an apartment on, I think, Sixtieth Street and Ninth Avenue, above a bar called Riordan's, where he sat around in a vest, as he sat around for the last thirty years since, having tea or coffee and smoking and conversing in his room . . .

So Jack would come in from Long Island and visit him, and I would come down from Columbia and visit him, and I think around that time, he met Huncke and Bill Garver. And so we–living around Eighth Avenue, we all started exploring Eighth Avenue from Fifty-ninth down to Forty-second and the Times Square area, hanging around Bickford's under the Apollo Theater marquee on Forty-second, when it was still there–an all-night population of hustlers and junkies, and just sort of wandering. . . . Street wanderers–intelligent, Melvillean street wanderers of the night.

. . . .

Then a friend of ours from Denver, Hal Chase, told us about Neal Cassady, a bright young poolhall cocksman who was sort of orphaned at thirteen and had gone through the Denver Public Library and read all through Kant and a lot of philosophy. And Chase, on a summer vacation, had told Neal that there were a bunch of poets in New York and that poetry was superior to philosophy, which immediately clicked in Neal's mind. It suddenly delivered him from bondage to rationalistic thinking and to a realization of creative humor, romance. That conversation apparently–according to Neal years later–was crucial. So he told Neal about the poets he met around Columbia, and he told us about the car-thief "Adonis of Denver" with his head full of philosophy. I think there's a line in Yeats about somebody who read all of Immanuel Kant while tilling the field–some Irish peasant or Premier.

So this was all between '44 and '46, these engagements and alliances. And then, around '45, Kerouac's girlfriend Edie Parker's roommate, Joan, who had a baby–newborn–had an apartment on 115th Street between Morningside Drive and Amsterdam Avenue and was broke and needed people to share the apartment with her. So Hal Chase and myself moved in, and Jack would hang around, and so would Ed White and various other people'd visit occasionally.

Then Jack and I decided that Joan, who was very intelligent, should meet Burroughs, it was a match we decided we'd arrange. They were older than us, slightly, and we thought they were kind of intellectual, sardonic equals, because they both had a laconic sense of humor and both were completely untyrannized by normative American stereotypes. They hadn't internalized any of that, as I had, certainly. They both seemed more sophisticated to us, so we thought we should bring these two sophistications together.

So we went to see Bill and he had to move out of his . . . apartment on Riverside Drive. There was an extra room at Joan's, and we were all living there, and so we invited him to come over, and apparently he and Joan hit it off and were very witty together and enjoyed each other's company. . . . Soon Bill had moved in there.

The apartment was a nice, big, old-fashioned apartment with big rooms–six big rooms. Living room facing south, so we got nice light in the daytime. It was me in the first room by the door, staying with Hal Chase, or Hal Chase in another room sometimes. . . Burroughs staying with Joan; a room of his own, but staying with Joan, relating to her, sleeping with her occasionally but very much sort of friends and lovers, actually. Huncke visiting and Kerouac visiting.

I was still taking classes at Columbia, which was right across the street, so I'd go from class to Burroughs' and Kerouac's conversation and back to class. So it was kind of funny, because the conversation in the house was a lot more elegant than the classroom conversation, a lot more curious and investigative and psychically moving.

Jack had nothing to do with Columbia, he was just living there because he had a girl friend on 118th Street, and he had gone there. He wasn't living at home, he was living with his girl. His home base was Ozone Park, and then he'd come for the weekend or two or three days, or just take the subway in and hang around with us and write. Or he'd use the Columbia library occasionally. He had friends at Columbia: myself, Hal Chase, Ed White. . . . And then Burroughs moved up there, so it just became our social center, between there and Times Square.

–*Jack's Book,* pp. 34–36, 38–39, 40–41

Despite their many differences–Kerouac was a tough, working-class Catholic football player while Ginsberg was an unathletic Jewish intellectual–the two young men felt a deep kinship almost immediately.

This excerpt from an October 1944 letter Kerouac wrote to Ginsberg is from early in their correspondence, which continued for more than twenty years.

I find in you a kindred absorption with identity, dramatic meaning, classic unity, and immortality: you pace a stage, yet sit in the boxes and watch. You seek identity in the midst of indistinguishable chaos, in sprawling nameless reality.

–*Jack Kerouac: Selected Letters, 1940–1956,* p. 81

Allen Temko, a Columbia student and a contemporary of Ginsberg, became friends with the East Coast gang and also with the Denver crowd, headed by anthropology student Haldon Chase. In an interview in the latter half of the 1970s, Temko recalls his impressions of the people he knew in the 1940s.

Hal Chase got out of the Army during the war, and I saw him on leave when he was already a civilian. He had been in the ski troops and had come back. And he got into this Dostoevskian scene. It was just like *The Possessed.* Terribly destructive people. And they were the first people I knew who were seriously involved in drugs.

I didn't know about Kerouac, but Burroughs at that time was into drugs seriously, and Kerouac introduced me to Burroughs one night in the West End. It must have been '44. I was on leave.

It was very funny, because Burroughs hated Roosevelt, and he wanted to hire an airplane at some New Jersey airport and fill it with horse shit and pitchfork it out over the White House. He wanted to fly down to Washington, and I was in the Navy. It was very funny, and Burroughs had very good clothes then. But of course, Kerouac was conspicuous for his not dressing the way Ivy League boys dressed. Not that Columbia was ever fashionable the way Yale and Princeton were. Burroughs wore these wonderful Chesterfield coats and bowlers, and he still belonged to the Racquet Club. He had Ginsy there one night. Burroughs was still very much the disreputable member of the Burroughs family of Adding Machine fame–very snobbish, very brilliant, terribly cold.

I knew then he was capable of killing someone. They were all very unattractive in that way. The level of violence was high, and Kerouac liked that, and Ginsberg liked it, but it horrified me. It was very Dostoevski.

Lucien Carr and Burroughs belonged to the real ruling class of this country. I found Burroughs fascinating. Very reptilian, but brilliant. Carr, whom I didn't meet until after the war, I found loathsome. I had no common ground with this spoiled and destructive boy.

. . . .

I felt that these people were very nineteenth century and *Lower Depths*. Very much like St. Petersburg in the under-thing of New York. They were the first people who were talking of Céline, partly because Kerouac read French. I read French, too. In fact, Kerouac spoke a kind of French-Canadian that's really like the English hillbillies in Virginia speak, an English of the seventeenth century. Sometimes Jack and I spoke French, walking on the beach at Far Rockaway and looking out to the Atlantic toward France.

. . . .

It was fun to walk with Kerouac along the railroad line. There was a railroad yard near his house. I think it's all electrified now, but at that time there were locomotives, and they would let off steam. That's when he was at his most winning, because he would yell and holler and whoop when the locomotives chugged. He liked the noise. He liked to write and hear those locomotives chugging and the cars shunting in the yards. He had a good ear–a good, natural ear.

He was very high on Wolfe, and there was then a lot of interest in Scott Fitzgerald and Hemingway as fine writers, versus Wolfe as New York telephone directory writer, putting everything in. We used to talk about that. I didn't think Hemingway was so good then, but one didn't talk to Jack of literature in the same way one talked to Hal Chase, who had a different kind of sensibility. Hal was very precocious, terribly brilliant. He wrote, when we were very young–seventeen years old–an imaginary dialogue between Dostoevski and Nietzsche. Kerouac wasn't capable of that kind of thing. Well–he wouldn't be interested.

Neal Cassady came to Columbia and showed up. The Denver boys [specifically Hal Chase and Ed White] had him around a lot, and he had these idiot girls around. He had one from Denver.

I could never understand the fascination these people held for Kerouac, except that he thought they were America, and they are. He always thought that Neal was Huck Finn and Bob Burford was smart-aleck Tom Sawyer. But Neal isn't Huck Finn. Huck Finn's impulses are always good and constructive. Neal was a terribly treacherous and untrustworthy and destructive person.

There was a born hatred between me and someone like Neal Cassady, because I felt he was just a sponger and useless. I didn't see his charm. He didn't say anything. He just sat around and was just, well, an encumbrance. I didn't ever want to have much to do with him. I thought he was good-looking. I thought he was criminal, in the worst sense. That is, I felt he would perform a criminal ripoff on anyone. I think he had no loyalty to anyone. Kerouac used him for literary material, but I wasn't interested in that.

–*Jack's Book,* pp. 62–64

In this early article, novelist and critic Anatole Broyard identified the character of the hipster, pointing out the hipster's predicament and his reliance upon the language of jive.

A Portrait of the Hipster
Anatole Broyard
Partisan Review, June 1948, pp. 721–728

As he was the illegitimate son of the Lost Generation, the hipster was really *nowhere.* And, just as amputees often seem to localize their strongest sensations in the *missing* limb, so the hipster longed, from the very beginning, to be *somewhere.* He was like a beetle on its back; his life was a struggle to get *straight.* But the law of human gravity kept him overthrown, because he was always of the minority–opposed in race or feeling to those who owned the machinery of recognition.

The hipster began his inevitable quest for self-definition by sulking in a kind of inchoate delinquency. But this delinquency was merely a negative expression of his needs, and, since it led only into the waiting arms of the ubiquitous law, he was finally forced to *formalize* his resentment and express it *symbolically.* This was the birth of a philosophy–a philosophy of *somewhereness* called *jive,* from *jibe:* to agree, or harmonize. By discharging his would-be aggressions *symbolically,* the hipster harmonized or reconciled himself with his society.

At the natural stage in its growth, jive began to talk. It had been content at first with merely making sounds–physiognomic talk–but then it developed language. And, appropriately enough, this language described the world as seen through the hipster's eyes. In fact, that was its function: to re-edit the world with new definitions . . . jive definitions.

Since articulateness is a condition for, if not actually a cause of, anxiety, the hipster relieved his anxiety by disarticulating himself. He cut the world down to size–reduced it to a small stage with a few props and a curtain of jive. In a vocabulary of a dozen verbs, adjectives, and nouns he could describe everything that happened in it. It was poker with no joker, nothing wild.

There were no neutral words in this vocabulary; it was put up or shut up, a purely polemical language in which every word had a job of *evaluation* as well as designation. These evaluations were absolute; the hipster banished all comparatives, qualifiers, and other syntactical uncertainties. Everything was dichotomously *solid, gone, out of this world,* or *nowhere, sad, beat,* a *drag.*

In there was, of course, somewhereness. *Nowhere,* the hipster's favorite pejorative, was an *abracadabra* to make things disappear. *Solid* connoted the stuff, the reality, of existence; it meant concreteness in a bewilderingly abstract world. A *drag* was something which "dragged" implications along with it, something which was embedded in an inseparable, complex, ambiguous–and thus, possible threatening–context.

Because of its polemical character, the language of jive was rich in aggressiveness, much of it couched in sexual metaphors. Since the hipster never did anything as an end in itself, and since he only gave of himself in aggression of one kind or another, sex was subsumed under aggression, and it supplied a vocabulary for the mechanics of aggression. The use of the sexual metaphor was also a form of irony, like certain primitive peoples' habit of parodying civilized modes of intercourse. The person on the tail end of a sexual metaphor was conceived of as lugubriously victimized; i.e., expecting but not receiving.

One of the basic ingredients of the jive language was a priorism. The a priori assumption was a short cut to somewhereness. It arose out of a desperate, unquenchable need to know the score; it was a great projection, a primary, self-preserving postulate. It meant "it is given to us to understand." The indefinable authority it provided was like a powerful primordial or instinctual orientation in a threatening chaos of complex interrelations. The hipster's frequent use of metonymy and metonymous gestures (e.g., brushing palms for handshaking, extending an index finger, without raising the arm, as a form of greeting, etc.) also connoted prior understanding, there is no need to elaborate, I dig you, man, etc.

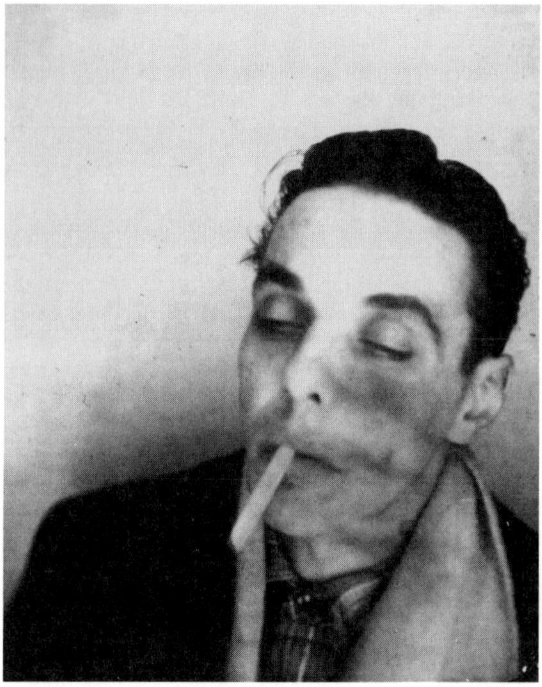

Herbert Edwin Huncke in a Times Square photo booth, circa 1945

Like Broyard, young Kerouac understood the hipster's precarious place in modern urban culture, but he also saw a sympathetic side to the hipster with which he identified. Kerouac's nurturance of the hipster spirit is the beginning of the Beat Generation, and here he describes his first meeting with Herbert Huncke, who embodied the term beat.

The Origins of the Beat Generation
Jack Kerouac
Playboy, June 1959, pp. 31–32, 42, 79

When I first saw the hipsters creeping around Times Square in 1944 I didn't like them either. One of them, Huncke of Chicago, came up to me and said "Man, I'm beat." I knew right away what he meant somehow.

Anyway, the hipsters, whose music was bop, they looked like criminals but they kept talking about the same things I liked, long outlines of personal experience and vision, night-long confessions full of hope that had become illicit and repressed by War, stirrings, rumblings of a new soul (that same old human soul). And so Huncke appeared to us and said "I'm beat" with radiant light shining out of his despairing eyes . . . a word perhaps brought from some midwest carnival or junk cafeteria. It was a new language, actually spade (Negro) jargon but you soon learned it, like "hung up" couldn't be a more economical term to mean so many things. Some of these hipsters were raving mad and talked continually. It was jazzy. Symphony Sid's all-night modern jazz and bop show was always on. By 1948 it began to take shape. That was a wild vibrating year when a group of us would walk down the street and yell hello and even stop and talk to anybody that gave us a friendly look. The hipsters had eyes.

Herbert Huncke

Herbert Huncke was the ultimate Beat character. According to Raymond Foye, Huncke "was Ur-Beat: Kerouac's lonesome traveler, Burroughs's junky, Ginsberg's angelheaded hipster." A significant Beat Generation figure, Huncke is known more for his talking than for his writing, although he had several works published, including Huncke's Journal *(1965) and* Guilty of Everything: The Autobiography of Herbert Huncke *(1990). Born in Greenfield, Massachusetts, on 9 January 1915, Herbert Edwin Huncke (whose name rhymes with "junkie") moved with his parents, Herbert Spencer and Marguerite Bell Huncke, to Chicago where he grew up in the midst of the Roaring Twenties. Early in his life Huncke had contact with Chicago's underworld through his uncle, Oswald Huncke, who was the Illinois State Boxing Commissioner. At twelve years of age Huncke, who was already smoking marijuana, ran away to New York City, but was returned home by the police. He later began to take heroin, which he bought in Chicago's Chinatown. His habit as a youth was to take long late-night walks in downtown Chicago, where he met the "people of the night" in speakeasies: drug addicts, homosexuals, transvestites, and hermaphrodites. He later recalled these experiences in his short piece, "In the Park," which originally appeared in* Huncke's Journal *and was published in revised form in* The Herbert Huncke Reader *(1997):*

> I have always enjoyed walking and much of my life has been spent roving city streets through the hours of darkness. Some of my more welcome memories and recollections have to do with my youth in Chicago and many-many-nights spent wandering through the city streets and parks and along the lakefront, finally resting atop a stone piling perhaps or on a bench watching the sunrise. I had adventures and strange experiences–frequently meeting and becoming involved with other night people. I learned much about sex and about the vast number of people who make up the so-called less desirable element in our American way of life. Haunted people–lonely people–misfits–outcasts–wanderers–those on the skids–drunkards–deviates of all kinds–hustlers of every description–male and female–old people and young people–and they come from every section of the country.

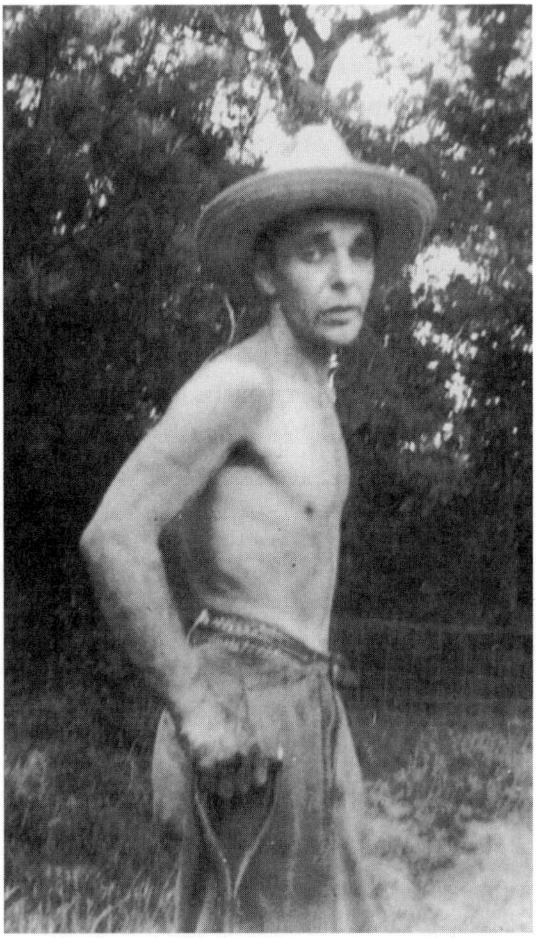

Huncke on Burroughs's farm in New Waverly, Texas, where Burroughs grew marijuana in 1947 (© by Allen Ginsberg Trust)

Huncke traveled about the country for ten years, collecting a vast stock of stories, before arriving in New York City in 1939 at the age of twenty-four. The center of his life then became Times Square, where he lived the hand-to-mouth existence of a small-time hustler. He attracted the attention of and was repeatedly interviewed by Alfred Kinsey, author of Sexual Behavior in the Human Male *(1948), and eventually met William Burroughs, whom he introduced to heroin, as well as Allen Ginsberg and Jack Kerouac. Huncke represented the underground contemporary America that fascinated Kerouac and Ginsberg. His use of the word* beat *to describe his downtrodden circumstances was picked up by Kerouac in his descriptive phrase "Beat Generation." Huncke spent most of the 1950s in prison–Sing Sing, Dannemora, and Rikers Island. He spent his final years in room 828 of the Chelsea Hotel; Jerry Garcia of the rock group Grateful Dead contributed to his rent.*

In the journal he began keeping in 1948, Huncke discussed his sense of himself as a person and recalled a sunny summer morning in Chicago when he was fourteen.

My name; although I'm known generally as Huncke and by a few as Herbert and in the past as Herbie. It is seldom I'm referred to as Mr. Huncke, and when formal introduction is required it is usually–Herbert Huncke.

I mention all this concerning my name simply because recently I've grown to dislike my name–not because my name is Herbert Huncke but rather because I've reached a point where my name (any name I might have had) by its mere utterance creates an almost weary and loathsome feeling in me. When I say it to myself–and frequently I say it to myself–I am immediately aware of a sense of disgust as though the sounds I make are significant of not only me but of a new and strange disease and I am sure, for at least the instant, I am at last slipping into an insanity from which there is no escape.

For several years I've been confident I will become insane, in fact I've felt thusly almost as far back as I am able to recall.

Once, when I thought I would become a writer (I was quite young–fourteen at the time), I made periodic attempts to write poetry, and on this particular occasion I became aware fully of the sense of pending insanity. It was shortly after dawn and a huge glistening sun was ascending a delicate blue sky. It was early summer and people were beginning to enjoy the bright colors of summer attire. I was living on Superior Street just east of North State Street in Chicago in an old wood-frame house that had been converted into what is called studio apartments. The house was well constructed and the rooms were large with high ceilings and windows reaching the full height of each room.

I had spent the few hours just preceding daybreak bathed in moonlight, watching the sky thru one of my windows (there were two in this room–huge windows which could be flung up quite high, letting in all the outside sound and scent and air, on either side of a fireplace with a white mantel with two large brass candlesticks with tall green candles), allowing my thoughts to dwell as they would and pondering over my problems and the magnificence of a daybreak.

I had sent my minute energy quota into the central urge aiding each rent in the block of darkness, tugging at each fold of light to make way for the one great power: the sun.

And now, as I descended the front steps to the street level–the sun was hurling and spiraling across a huge space of blue.

To one side of the steps was a flower bed sparsely filled with yellow jonquils, and I glanced at them and then toward the sidewalk to observe several young women who were rapidly walking past and talking of their work and of something amusing, and when they had almost reached the corner they began laughing. Their costumes were charming and one wore something with large figures of poppy red which I liked.

I was rather frightened and deeply impressed. I stood a long time thinking about it, becoming more convinced each instant, I was doomed.

Several hours later when I had finished my breakfast and returned to my apartment, I tried putting into a poem all which I had felt and I was rather pleased with what I had written, although I can't remember any of it and the actual writing is long misplaced–along with everything of myself at that time.

It wasn't long after I began traveling and ceased considering Chicago as my home.

–*The Herbert Huncke Reader,* pp. 5–6

In *The Thief's Journal,* Genet says there are very few people who have earned the right to think. Huncke had adventures and misadventures that were not available to middle-class, comparatively wealthy college people like Kerouac and me: "Some write home to the old folks for coin. That's their ace in the hole." Huncke had extraordinary experiences that were quite genuine. He isn't a type you find anymore.

–William S. Burroughs, foreword
The Herbert Huncke Reader

In the following two excerpts originally published in Guilty of Everything, *an autobiography that evolved out of a series of interviews, Huncke gives a vivid portrait of his life in Times Square that so intrigued the Beat writers. In the first excerpt he recounts his meeting with sex researcher Alfred Kinsey.*

One afternoon when I was sitting in Chase's cafeteria I was approached by a young girl who asked if she could join me. She was carrying several books in her arms and was obviously a student. "There's someone who wants to meet you," she told me.

I said, "Yes, who?"

"A Professor Kinsey."

I had never heard of him and she went on to say, "Well, he's a professor at Indiana University and he's doing research on sex. He is requesting people to talk about their sex lives, and to be as honest about it as possible."

My immediate reaction was that there was some very strange character in the offing who was too shy to approach people himself, someone who probably had some very weird sex kick and was using this girl to pander for him. But I sounded her down.

She must have known what the score was insofar as sex, but I didn't know that. I didn't want to shock her, but at the same time I wanted to find out exactly what the story was, so I questioned her rather closely about this man. I asked her why he hadn't approached me himself, and she said, "He felt it would be better if someone else spoke with you. He has seen you around, and he thought you might be very interesting to talk to. I'll tell you what I'll do. I'll give you his name and number." At that time he was staying in a very nice East Side hotel. "You can call him and discuss the situation with him."

I had nothing else to do, and I said, "Well, I might as well find out what this is all about."

I called Kinsey and he said, "Oh, yes, I'd like to speak with you very much."

"What exactly is it you're interested in?" I asked him.

"All I want you to do," he said to me, "is tell me about your sex life, what experiences you've had, what your interests are, whether you've masturbated and how often, whether you've had any homosexual experiences."

"That all you want?" I said.

"That's all I want."

"Well, I think it's only fair to tell you," I went on, "and I don't want to be crude–but I do need money."

He said, "I'd certainly be willing to give you some money. Would ten dollars be all right?"

"It certainly would."

We went through a funny exchange. Kinsey wanted me to come up to his place, and I said, "No, I'd rather not do that. I'd rather meet you somewhere first." I did not trust him yet. There was just something about the whole thing that sounded very offbeat to me. I arranged to have him meet me at a bar. "I'll meet you at the bar, but I don't drink," he said. "But I'll buy a drink."

"All right, fair enough."

"I'll know you when I see you," he told me, " so you sit down and order yourself a drink and I'll be there in a while." We were to meet at a popular bar on the square, though not the Angler.

I didn't have enough money to buy myself a drink, and I sort of kicked around in front of the place until I saw a cab pull up and a man get out. Kinsey had a very interesting appearance, strictly professorial. His hair was cut very short, slightly gray. He had a round face that was pleasant appearing, and he was dressed in a suit–obviously a conservative man, I thought.

He walked up to me and said, "I'm Kinsey, you're Herbert Huncke. Let's go in. You'd like to have a drink."

I said, "Yes, I'd like to talk to you a few moments before we go to your hotel." He again gave me much the same story the girl had, and he assured me that the only thing he was interested in was the discussion, though he did say he wanted to measure the size of the penis. He showed me a card which had a phallus drawn on it. He said he'd like to know the length of it when erect and when soft. Naturally, I was wondering when he was going to get to the point. It was all so strange, and I still did not quite believe him, but I thought, Well, hell, I might just as well go along with him and see what it's all about.

As it turned out, it was a very delightful experience. As I started rapping to Kinsey about my sex life, I sort of unburdened myself of many things that I'd long been keeping to myself. For example, I'd always masturbated, all the way up until I kind of lost interest in sex altogether around the age of fifty. When I told others of my confessions to Kinsey they all said I was off my rocker, but I must say I was thankful by that time to get it out of my system. Sex had always played a prominent role in my life. I earned my living from sex at one time and have met all kinds of people, and heard of and had experiences with some very strange fetishes.

I told Kinsey most of these things. In *Huncke's Journal* I describe an interesting experience I had as a young boy, and I spoke to him about this. It tells of a young fellow, about twenty years old, who, after telling me dirty stories and arousing me with pornographic pictures, suggested we go up into a building together. We did, and he suddenly startled me by dropping his pants. There he was with an erection. This thing looked gigantic to me, being eight or nine years old, because it just happened that it was dead in front of my face. I drew back but at the same time I say in all honesty that I was somehow interested. I felt no fear.

He said he wanted to feel me. I was embarrassed. Here was my tiny hunk of flesh and then this gigantic thing standing in front of me. It didn't seem right somehow. Anyway, he did try and convince me that it would be a good idea if I'd allow him to put it up my rectum. I certainly drew the line at that, because I knew it'd be very painful. I assured him I wasn't about to cooperate, and he didn't press the issue. He proceeded to masturbate furiously and then he ejaculated. That was my first experience with anyone other than children my own age. This was

Huncke in New York City, 1953 (Photographs by Allen Ginsberg)

the first thing I thought of when I began to masturbate. It would excite me. Instead of following the normal course and being pleased by visions of a little girl, I was attracted to this big phallus—a cock. It was quite an experience. I had never told anyone about it until I told Kinsey. It was this sort of thing that I unburdened myself of to this man.

As I continued to speak to him, he became so adept at his questioning and his approach that there was no embarrassment on my part, and I found myself relaxing. The one thing I could not supply him with was a size to my penis. He finally gave me a card and asked me to fill it out and send it to him later on, which, incidentally, I never did.

Kinsey turned out to be a very intriguing man, a man that I learned to respect and whom I began to see quite a bit of. We met for interviews several times, but I also began to see him outside of his office. He only remained in New York on that first visit. I believe there was some difficulty about the grants that would enable him to continue his research. He had to return to the university; but he did come back, this time with a companion. He was a nice young man, someone who had studied with Kinsey and that Kinsey had taken on as an assistant in his *Kinsey Reports*.

I believe I was one of the first in New York to be interviewed by Kinsey, and certainly one of the first from Times Square. Kinsey had apparently seen me around the square and was fairly sure I'd have information to give, if he could get it from me. He had walked up and down Forty-second Street, and he realized there was action of some sort going on there. Of course, he didn't know too much about the underworld aspect of it, but it was still pretty obvious. One walked by doorways and saw young men in tight pants with their whole profile on display. And there were the many flagrant queens that used to fly up and down the street, not to mention the more sinister types that could be noticed if one paid attention, and they can still be seen to this day.

Kinsey gave me money for the interviews. I wouldn't have accepted anything from him if I hadn't needed it very badly at the time. He told me, "Now, if there's anyone else you know that you think might be interested in being interviewed, by all means send them up. I'll tell you what. For every person you send up from Forty-second Street, I'll give you two dollars. I know you can use the money."

"Yes, I can."

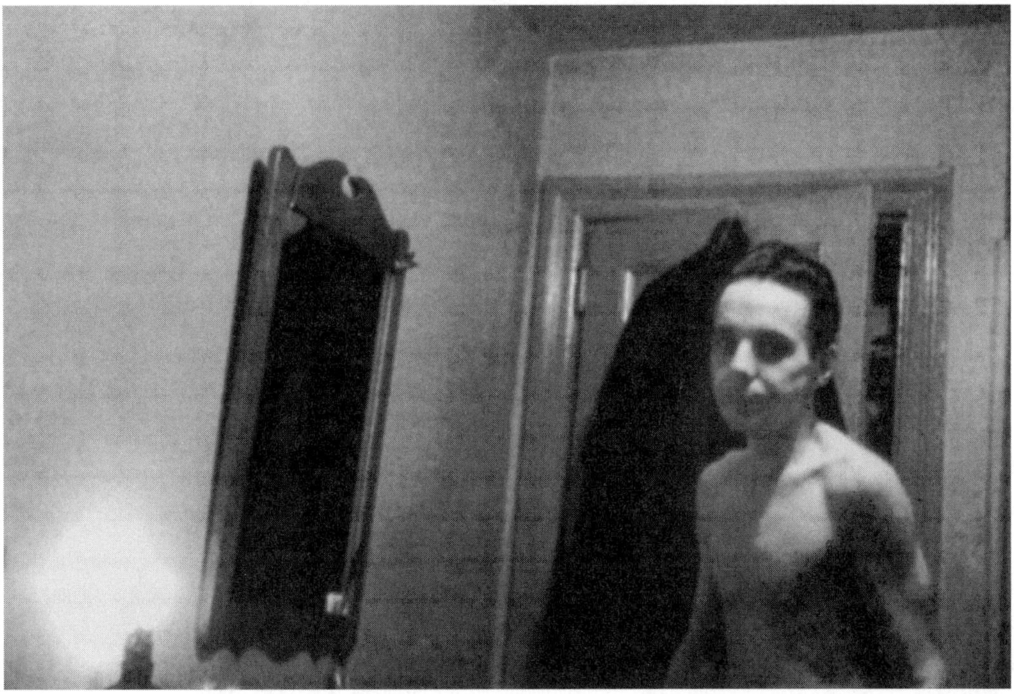

It was nice to know that when I was uptight I could get two dollars. All I'd have to do is waylay somebody I knew and say, "Hey, man, want to make a couple bucks?"

"What do I have to do?"

"Well, all you have to do is sit down and tell this man all there is to tell about your sex life. There's no hanky-panky involved. The man is doing research on sex." Of course, there was no problem. I sent a number of people I knew up to meet with Kinsey. I think I pretty much made his Times Square study. There were others, of course, whom he'd met through me that kind of took over for me. It got to be quite competitive for a while there, what with all the running about for interviewees.

In fact, I introduced Burroughs to Kinsey over at the Angler Bar. Bill, of course, is a very knowledgeable individual. He's been all over the world, and as a young man he had studied medicine in Vienna. The two of them talked the same language. When Kinsey came back to the city the second time, he spent more time out and we'd all meet at the Angler. Joan would come around, and Ginsberg, and though I'm not sure, each of them interviewed with Kinsey as well. It was at these long discussions when we all sat around talking with Kinsey that I came to see that Bill is an extraordinary person.

–*The Herbert Huncke Reader,* pp. 251–255

During his periods out of prison in the 1950s, Huncke became aware of the coincidental rise of the drug culture and bebop jazz.

I ended up doing a bit. Somebody had to do it. When the parole board began their investigation they got in touch with my father. I had begged them not to. "Please, whatever you do, don't bother my people," I asked them, 'because they have nothing to do with me. I have nothing to do with them. They won't want to hear anything about it, and they won't be of any assistance one way or another. So please do me a favor and don't get in touch with them." "Oh, we wouldn't think of it." Immediately they did get in touch. My father sent a letter back, on his own stationery–H. S. Huncke & Co.–and I was so ashamed I hung my head.

It started out by saying he had done everything a father could do. The parole board told me that from what they could judge, my father was a fine man, obviously respected, and a hard worker who had established himself in show business in Chicago. They were just like him. A five-man parole board based their case on the letter. "We can't help but feel that we have to agree with your father's summation of your character. He states that you have always been a weak sister, and apparently this is what you are." I didn't say anything. I simply stood there and let them say what they wanted to. I knew I wasn't going to get out, had known it from the jump. I knew I was a bad parole risk–no real roots, and couldn't depend on the family for a thing. I had to depend on myself always; nobody else was going to help me.

What can I say about prison? This was my first extended bit, my first time at Sing Sing. I knew I'd be going there and I was very curious about this place. I knew, though, I was getting into something entirely different from what I'd ever been in before.

When I got to Sing Sing I tried to take things in stride. I was still very shy about the whole thing. What else can one do? It was difficult for me to adjust. I had no money and the first thing that you do to establish any prestige at all is to go to commissary. If you can't go to commissary, automatically you're uptight, because there are certain things you are going to need. I knew I either had to depend on people I might know or do some kind of scuffle.

I was fortunate. I met a couple of cats that I'd known from Rikers Island. They were glad to see me. Needless to say the feeling was mutual. While I was waiting to be oriented we got together some. Sing Sing is generally a kind of relay prison. They have these tables in the recreation halls instead of courts, and they have long strips of gas plates where you can cook. That's a big item in Sing Sing–you cook meals. There's always a pot of coffee on, and this is your recreation.

I was waiting for my case to be filed in Albany. I was to be established with a number and a file. In my case, where there were no relatives or such, there was no problem of my being sent to one of the upstate prisons. This time I was sent to Greenhaven State. It's not a very good prison; I preferred Dannemora much better. I was sent there on my next bit.

I did my time in Greenhaven, over three years, and I came out in '53 owing a year. In order to get out early I had to get a job. I was grateful to Jackie's brother-in-law for offering me a job in a dye factory.

I started out working, and I was in touch with people who had money. Now the drug scene by this time was flourishing. The pushers had come back out onto the scene again after nearly disappearing at the end of the forties. There was a new attitude among the drug addicts now; it all seemed to be much more wide open.

This coincided with the bebop scene, which followed swing. Bebop jazz clubs were getting to be the big thing, and when it was discovered that a lot of the jazz musicians were using, gradually the drug scene began to erupt all over again.

A couple of hot places began to operate. This one I recall most vividly was the Royal Roost, up on Fifty-second Street. All of the jazz greats at the time played there. The doorman at the Roost was a big connection. You had to go down to the john to shoot, where the guy that ran the men's room would then duke you whatever the doorman had written on a note. You'd pay upstairs and then go downstairs to get the shit.

The funny thing was that the drug scene was no longer confined to just any one neighborhood. It started to happen in all neighborhoods, much more so than previously when you'd cop, say, in Harlem. More and more people, different types, began to use–not only heroin and morphine but amphetamine too. When I came back to the scene after my second bit, in '59, it was even more obvious. It was the younger generation becoming more involved, a batch of new junkies were making their move, and the old-timers–guys that dated back to the days of Welfare Island–were leaving.

–*The Herbert Huncke Reader*, pp. 264–268

Herbert Huncke, the Hipster Who Defined 'Beat,' Dies at 81

Robert McG. Thomas Jr.
The New York Times, 9 August 1996

Herbert Huncke, the charismatic street hustler, petty thief and perennial drug addict who enthralled and inspired a galaxy of acclaimed writers and gave the Beat Generation its name, died yesterday at Beth Israel Hospital. He was 81.

The cause was congestive heart failure, said Jerry Poynton, his friend and literary executor.

Mr. Huncke had lived long enough to become a hero to a new generation of adoring artists and writers, not to mention a reproach to a right-thinking, clean-living establishment that had long predicted his imminent demise.

In an age when it was hip to be hip Mr. Huncke (whose name rhymes with junkie) was the prototypical hipster, the man who gave William S. Burroughs his first fix, who introduced Jack Kerouac to the term beat and who guided them, as well as Allen Ginsberg and John Clellon Holmes, through the netherworld of Times Square in the 1940's.

They honored him in turn by making him an icon of his times. He became the title character (Herbert) in Mr. Burroughs's first book, "Junkie" (1962). He was Ancke in Mr. Holmes's 1952 novel, "Go." He appears under his own name in innumerable Ginsberg poems, including "Howl" (1956) with its haunting reference to "Huncke's bloody feet."

And if it was the fast-talking, fast-driving Neal Cassady who became Mr. Kerouac's chief literary obsession, as the irrepressible Dean Moriarty in Mr. Kerouac's 1957 breakthrough classic, "On the Road," Mr. Huncke (who was Elmo Hassel in "On the Road") was there first.

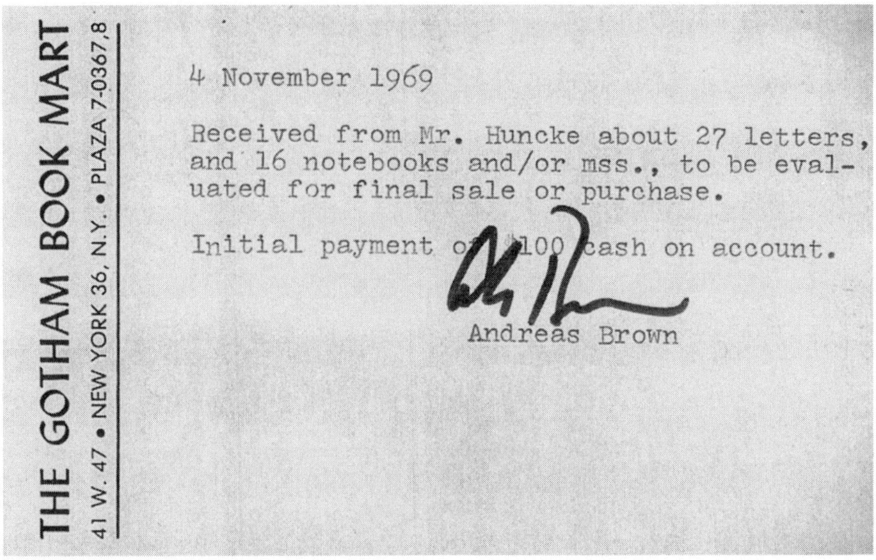

THE GOTHAM BOOK MART
41 W. 47 • NEW YORK 36, N.Y. • PLAZA 7-0367,8

4 November 1969

Received from Mr. Huncke about 27 letters, and 16 notebooks and/or mss., to be evaluated for final sale or purchase.

Initial payment of $100 cash on account.

Andreas Brown

Receipt for Huncke's writings (Collection of Jerry Poynton)

As Junkey, he was the dominant character in the urban half of Mr. Kerouac's first book, "The Town and the City," and made later appearances as Huck in "Visions of Cody" and "Books of Dreams."

All this for a teen-age runaway who said he was using drugs as early as 12, selling sex by the time he was 16, stealing virtually anything he could get his hands throughout his life and never once apologizing for a moment of it.

"I always followed the road of least resistance," he said in a 1992 interview. "I just continued to do what I wanted. I didn't weigh or balance things. I started out this way and I never really changed."

Actually, he didn't quite start out that way. Born into a middle-class family in Greenfield, Mass., on Dec. 9, 1915, he moved with his family to Detroit when he was 4 and two years later to Chicago, where his father ran his own machine-parts distributing company.

By his own accounts he seems to have had an uneventful early childhood, but his parents divorced, and by the time he was in his early teens he was on the street, acquiring a lifelong passion for drugs and discovering the joys–and lucrative possibilities–of sex with men. He was also beginning a life of crime, first as a runner for the Capone gang and later as a burglar and thief.

Hitting the road early, he served for a time with the Depression-era Civilian Conservation Corps. He traveled around the country until 1939, when he arrived in New York and found a psychic home in Times Square.

Making his base of operations the Angler bar at 42d Street and Eighth Avenue, he sold drugs at times and himself at others, not always with notable success. Mr. Huncke once confided to a friend that he had not been a successful hustler: "I was always falling in love," he said.

It was in 1945 that an elegantly dressed man in a Chesterfield coat knocked on the door of an apartment where Mr. Huncke was living. The visitor, who was in search of Mr. Huncke's roommate in the hope of selling him a sawed-off shot gun, was William S. Burroughs. Mr. Huncke would recount that he took one look and told his roommate to get rid of him. "He's the F.B.I.," he said.

Mr. Burroughs proved anything but, and within days Mr. Huncke had introduced him to heroin and sealed a lifelong friendship that included a 1947 visit to a marijuana farm Mr. Burroughs had started in Texas.

It was through Mr. Burroughs that Mr. Huncke soon met Mr. Ginsberg, then a Columbia undergraduate, and Mr. Kerouac, a recent Columbia dropout who became so enchanted with Mr. Huncke's repeated use of the carny term "beat," meaning tired and beaten down, that he later used it as his famous label for the Beat Generation. (Mr. Kerouac later clouded things by suggesting it was derived from "beatific.")

An aspiring, Columbia-centered literary crowd was soon learning at Mr. Huncke's feet. Among other things, he introduced them to Alfred Kinsey,

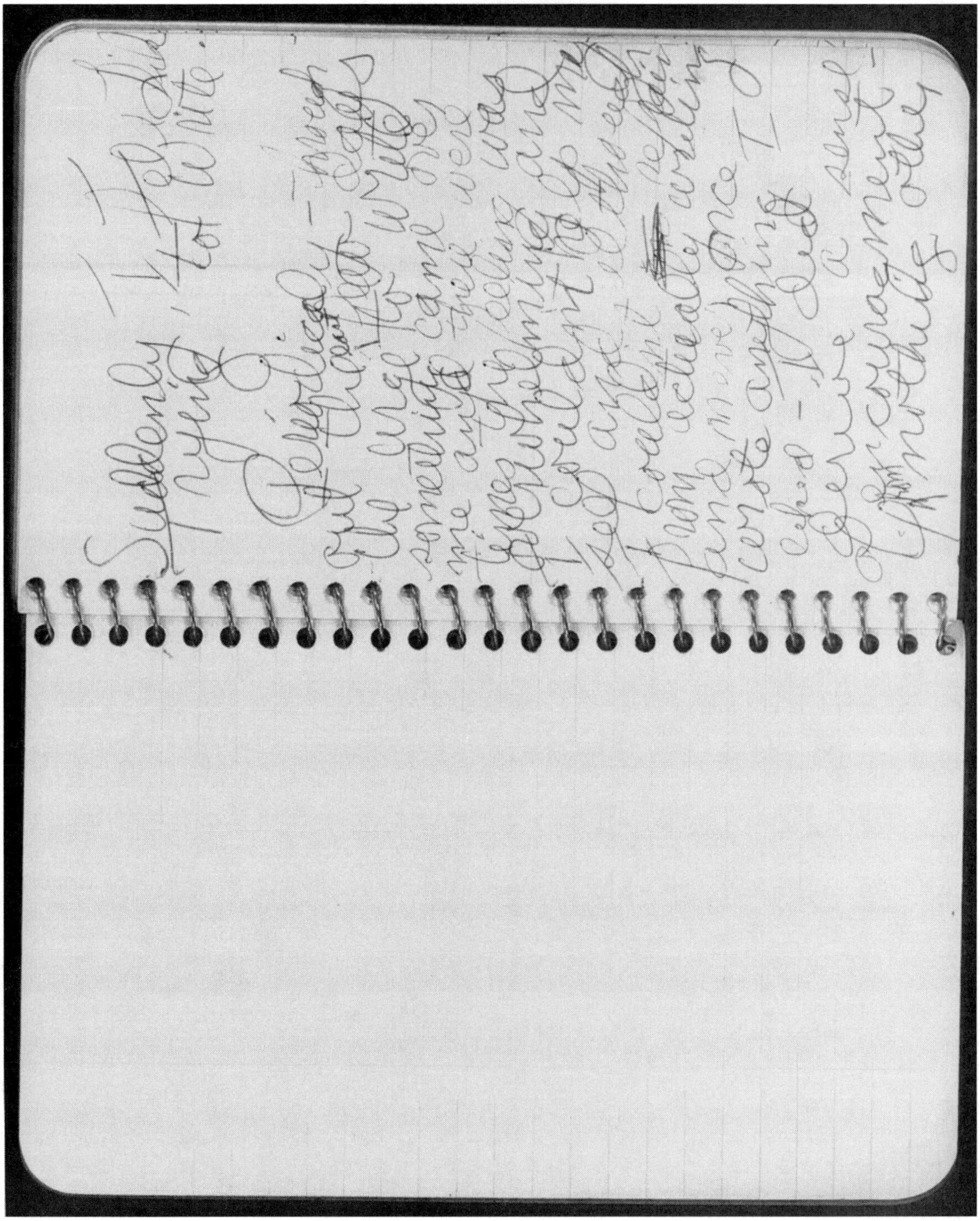

Notebook pages from 1970 in which Huncke observes that "writing is a source of relief for me" (Collection of Jerry Poynton)

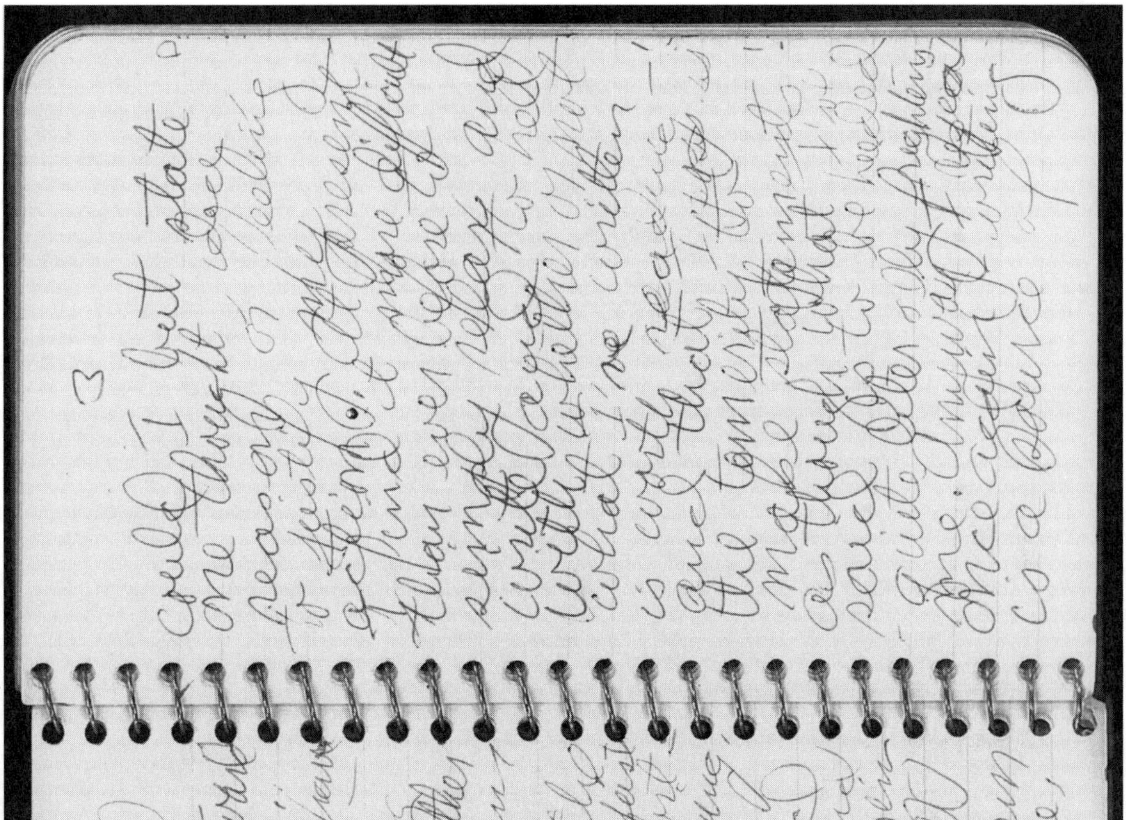

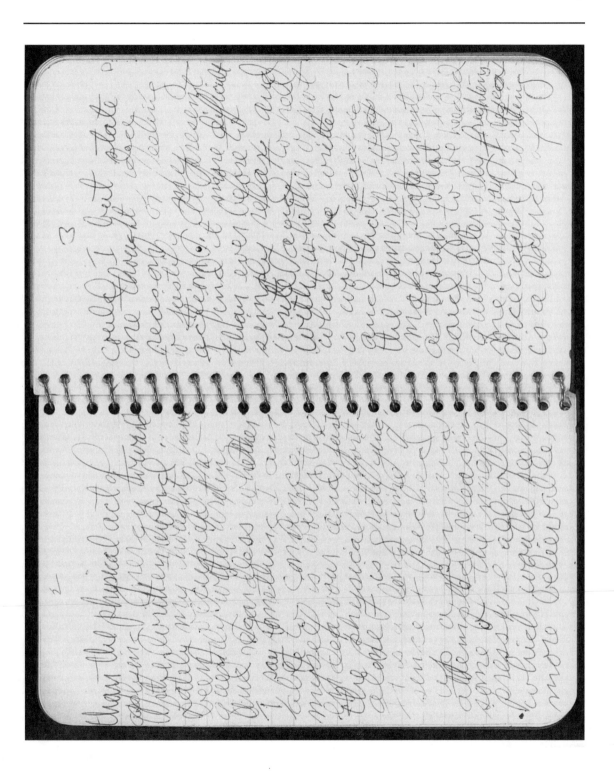

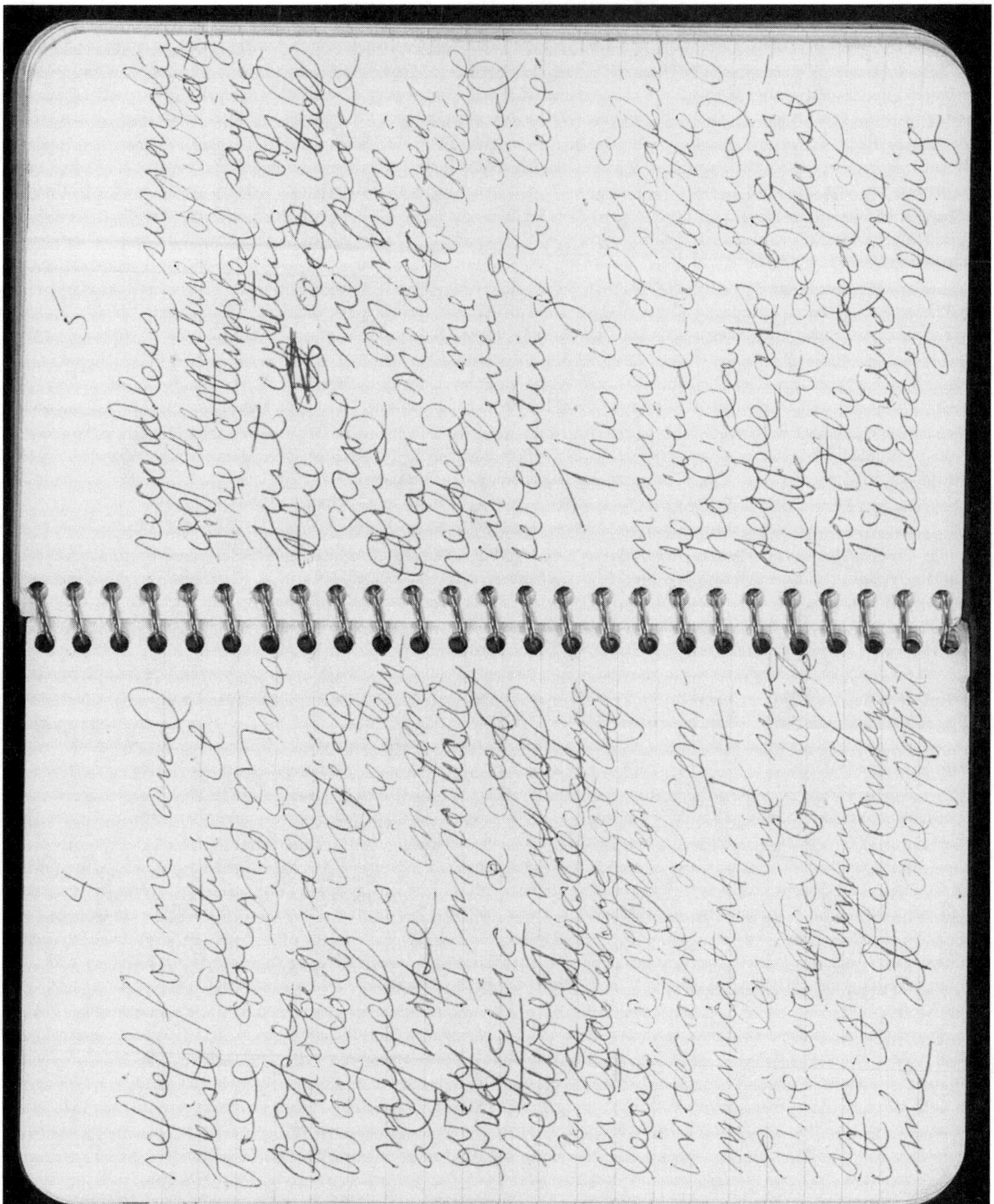

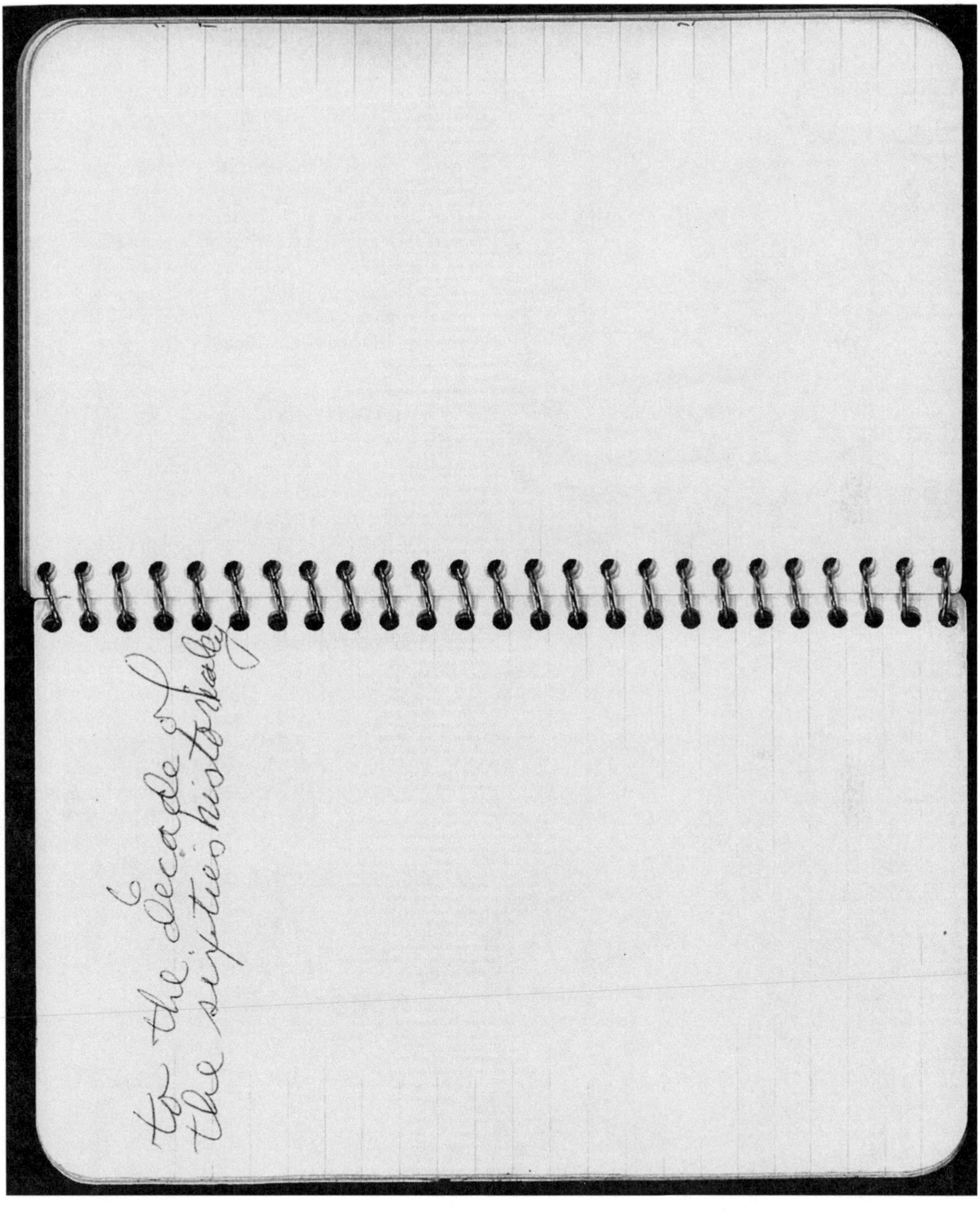
to the decade of
the sixties historically

Huncke with his longtime companion Louis Cartwright (photograph by David Sands)

who after meeting Mr. Huncke at the Angler had interviewed him about his colorful sex life and hired him to recruit other subjects.

Though it seemed strange to some people that such a wide array of literary figures found Mr. Huncke so enchanting, he was always more than he seemed. For all his disreputable pursuits, he had elegant, refined manners and a searing honesty. He was also uncommonly well read for someone who had never been to high school, and such a natural and affecting storyteller that he could keep a table of admirers enthralled until the wee hours.

He also had a code of honor. Yes, he might steal from his friends if he needed a fix, but did not inform on them, something he proved on a number of occasions when the police sought his help in developing charges against his celebrity friends.

Mr. Huncke, who spent a total of 11 years in prison, including almost all of the 1950's, was unrepentant, a man whose acceptance of crime as his fate bolstered his friends' views that he was a victim of a rigid, unfeeling society.

If his friends saw him as fodder for their literary work, Mr. Huncke as he later claimed, saw them as marks. There is, perhaps, a certain paradox in Mr. Huncke's use of his literary friends as literary fodder. Mr. Huncke himself began writing in the 1940's, locking himself in a stall in the men's room in the subway. He described it as the only

Huncke cutting cocaine in his room in the Chelsea Hotel, 1996 (Collection of Jerry Poynton)

place he could work in peace, scribbling away in his notebooks.

Taking the Kerouac idea of writing nearly automatic prose even further than Mr. Kerouac did, Mr. Huncke turned out a series of memoirs that have been praised for their unaffected style. Those who heard him regale listeners say his books read as if he were telling a spontaneous anecdote around a table at the Angler.

"Huncke's Journal," (1965) was followed by "Elsie John and Joey Martinez" (1979), and "The Evening Sun Turned Crimson," (1980) and "Guilty of Everything," published by Hanuman Books in 1990.

The books and Mr. Huncke's role in a brash new literary movement made him famous to a younger generation, and he had several successful lecture tours in recent years.

His books did not make much money, but they didn't need to. Friends contributed willingly to the upkeep of Mr. Huncke, who seemed proud that he had no talent for regular work.

It was a reflection of his continued standing among self-styled counterculturists that one of his most generous benefactors was a man who had never met him: Jerry Garcia of the Grateful Dead, who is said to have helped with his rent at the Chelsea Hotel.

Mr. Huncke, whose longtime companion, Louis Cartwright, was killed in 1994, is survived by his half-brother, Dr. Brian Huncke of Chicago.

A Shocking Murder

By 1944 Kerouac, Ginsberg, and Burroughs had become increasingly involved with the underground New York world of thieves and drug users. Essentially, though, they saw this world in romanticized terms, as if they were characters in a story by Russian novelist Fyodor Dostoyevsky, author of Notes From Underground. *Suddenly, real violence rocked their world when Lucien Carr, one of their intimate circle, killed a homosexual admirer with his Boy Scout knife and sank the dead man's body in the Hudson River. The killing shocked his friends and briefly scattered the group.*

Columbia Student Kills Friend
And Sinks Body in Hudson River
Frank S. Adams
The New York Times, 17 August 1944, p. 1

A fantastic story of a homicide, first revealed to the authorities by the voluntary confession of a

Lucien Carr

19-year-old Columbia sophomore, was converted yesterday from a nightmarish fantasy into a horrible reality by the discovery of the bound and stabbed body of the victim in the murky waters of the Hudson River.

For twenty-four hours previously the police and the district attorney's office, balked by the absence of a body or a particle of evidence corroborating the commission of any crime, had detained the self-proclaimed slayer without a charge. He stayed in the district attorney's office, peacefully reading poetry most of the night.

But with the discovery of the body yesterday afternoon, which the slender, studious youth unshakingly identified as it was lifted from the water, and after he had led detectives to the spot where he had buried his victim's eyeglasses in Morningside Park, the investigators knew that they were dealing with a real homicide and not the imaginings of an overstrained mind.

Lucien Carr, 19 years old, son of a family formerly prominent in St. Louis, but now living in this city, was the youth who admitted the killing. The authorities said that he was the son of Russell Carr of 419 East Fifty-seventh Street, and of Mrs. Carr, who is separated from her husband and lived with her son at 421 West 118th Street.

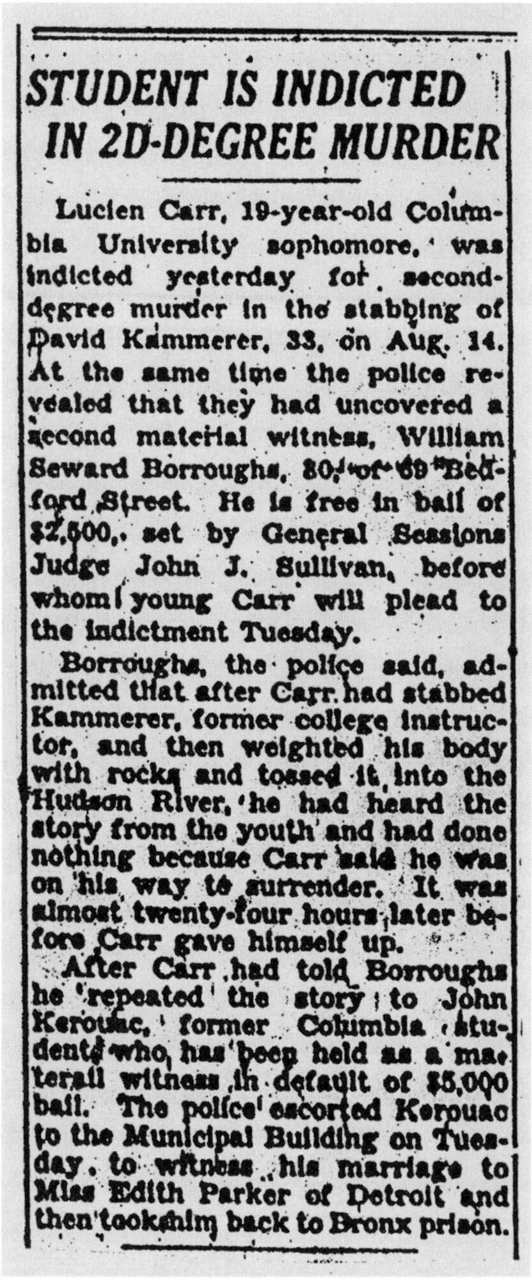

STUDENT IS INDICTED IN 2D-DEGREE MURDER

Lucien Carr, 19-year-old Columbia University sophomore, was indicted yesterday for second-degree murder in the stabbing of David Kammerer, 33, on Aug. 14. At the same time the police revealed that they had uncovered a second material witness, William Seward Borroughs, 30, of 69 Bedford Street. He is free in bail of $2,500, set by General Sessions Judge John J. Sullivan, before whom young Carr will plead to the indictment Tuesday.

Borroughs, the police said, admitted that after Carr had stabbed Kammerer, former college instructor, and then weighted his body with rocks and tossed it into the Hudson River, he had heard the story from the youth and had done nothing because Carr said he was on his way to surrender. It was almost twenty-four hours later before Carr gave himself up.

After Carr had told Borroughs he repeated the story to John Kerouac, former Columbia student who has been held as a material witness in default of $5,000 bail. The police escorted Kerouac to the Municipal Building on Tuesday to witness his marriage to Miss Edith Parker of Detroit and then took him back to Bronx prison.

The New York Times, *25 August 1944, p. 15. Carr eventually served two years in the Elmira State Reformatory for second-degree homicide.*

Young Carr, who had just completed his freshman year and embarked upon his sophomore year in Columbia College, where he was taking a liberal arts course, was described as "definitely a superior student," by Prof. Nicholas McKnight, associate dean of the college, who knew him personally. He was a quiet, well-behaved, intellectual type who had been classified 4F by the Selective Service on medical grounds.

His victim was David Kammerer, 33 years old, formerly a teacher of English and a physical education instructor at Washington University in St. Louis, where he first made the acquaintance of young Carr. The authorities said that Kammerer was a homosexual who had recently earned his living by helping the janitor at 48 Morton Street.

Carr appeared at the office of District Attorney Frank S. Horan on Monday afternoon, accompanied by a lawyer whose name was withheld by the authorities. There he freely told Jacob Grumet, assistant district attorney in charge of the Homicide Bureau, of the killing and of the events leading up to it. At first he was nervous, but as he completed his amazing recital he became astonishingly calm and self-possessed.

Knew Victim Several Years

His story was that he had known Kammerer for several years in St. Louis. During that time, Carr told Mr. Grumet he had been a student at Phillips-Andover Academy at Andover, Mass., at Bowdoin College in Maine, and at the University of Chicago, but he had seen Kammerer during his vacations in St. Louis.

Carr said that several times during their acquaintance Kammerer had made improper advances to him, but that he had always rebuffed the older man. He said that when he entered Columbia last year Kammerer followed him to the city, ostensibly intending to take graduate work at that institution. Columbia University officials said that Kammerer never actually matriculated, however.

Kammerer's personality steadily deteriorated during his year in this city, until he was little more than a derelict, barely keeping himself alive by his janitorial work, according to Carr's story, which was corroborated in this respect yesterday by evidence uncovered by the detectives who checked up on the activities of the older man.

Nevertheless, Carr continued his acquaintance with Kammerer. On Monday morning between 3 and 4 A.M. the two were sitting on the grassy bank below Riverside Drive, at the foot of 115th Street, enjoying a breath of the cool, morning air, according to Carr, when Kammerer once more made an offensive proposal.

Used Knife on Older Man

Carr said that he rejected it indignantly and that a fight ensued. Carr, a slight youth, 5 feet 9 inches tall and weighing 140 pounds, was no match for the burly former physical education instructor who was 6 feet tall and weighed about 185 pounds. He was rapidly getting the worst of it, he said.

In desperation, Carr pulled out of his pocket his Boy Scout knife, a relic of his boyhood, and plunged the blade twice in rapid succession into Kammerer's chest, according to the story he told at the District Attorney's office. The bigger man fell heavily to the ground.

Not knowing whether he was alive or dead, young Carr rolled the fallen man down the grassy embankment to the water's edge. There he took the laces from Kammerer's shoes and used them to tie his hands and feet. He took off Kammerer's shirt and tore it into strips and tied them about the body also, and then fastened Kammerer's belt about his arms.

Working with frantic haste in the darkness, unaware of whether anyone had seen him, the college student gathered together as many small rocks and stones as he could quickly find and shoved them into Kammerer's pockets and inside his clothing. Then he pushed the body into the swift-flowing water.

After he had left the area he toyed with the notion of running away and joining the Merchant Marine, Carr said, but further reflection convinced him that this was not the wisest choice. Unable to make up his mind what to do, he eventually confided in his mother, according to Mr. Grumet. She immediately communicated with a lawyer, who, after hearing young Carr's story took him to the District Attorney's office.

Detectives who went last night to the five-story apartment house at 421 West 118th Street, where Carr and his mother were said by the authorities to have lived, took into custody John Kerouac, a 23-year-old seaman, who lived at that address. He was booked at the West 100th Street station as a material witness in the case, although the detectives refused to discuss his connection with it.

Kerouac and Burroughs were detained by police as material witnesses since they had spent time with Carr before he turned himself in. Kerouac's father refused to pay the $100 set as his son's bail. Instead, Edie Parker's family agreed to provide the bail if Jack and Edie were married. On August 22, with a plainclothes detective acting as witness, they were married.

Kerouac spent the late summer of 1944 in Grosse Pointe, Michigan, with his bride, Edie Parker Kerouac. In October Kerouac returned to New York, leaving Edie in Michigan. She later rejoined him in New York, but for a time Kerouac lived with his parents in Ozone Park, Queens, while Ginsberg attended Columbia University.

In the year following Carr's murder of David Kammerer, Kerouac's output as a writer greatly increased. The following excerpt of Kerouac's 23 August 1945 letter to Ginsberg reveals his realization of the seriousness of his life's pursuit and his teasingly jealous rivalry with Ginsberg.

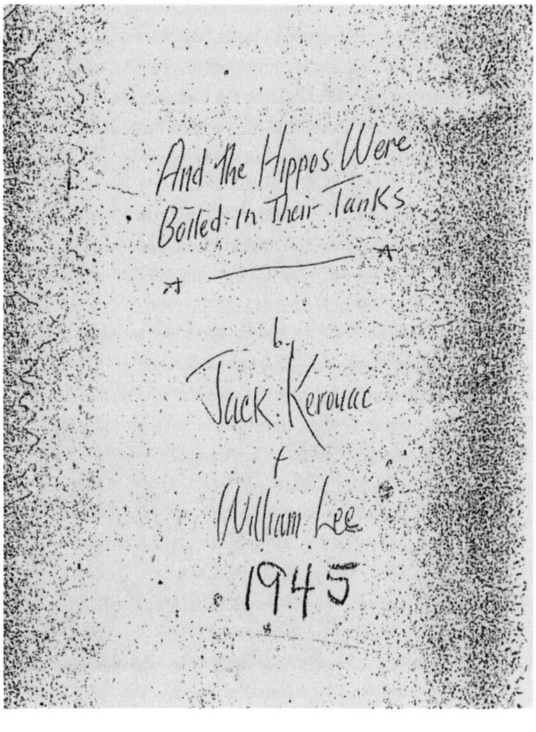

Title page from the manuscript for an unpublished hard-boiled murder mystery modeled on the Lucien Carr case in which Kerouac and Burroughs wrote alternating chapters. The title came from a radio news broadcast Burroughs once heard about a fire at the St. Louis Zoo (New York Public Library).

It may surprise you to know that I have been writing in prodigious amounts. I am writing three novels at this very minute, and keeping a large diary to boot. And reading! . . . I have been reading like a madman. There's nothing else to do. It's one of those things you can do at the moment when all else isn't any more interesting, I mean, when everything else can't exactly prove to be much more worthwhile. I intend to do this sort of thing all my life. As for artistry, that is now a personal problem, something that concerns only me, so that probably I won't bother you about that ever again. All well and good. A line from my diary: "We are all sealed in our own little melancholy atmospheres, like planets, and revolving around the sun, our common but distant desire." Not so good, perhaps, but if you steal that line of mine, I'll actually kill you, for a change.

Bye bye petit,
Jean

–*Jack Kerouac: Selected Letters, 1940–1956,* p. 92

Burroughs and Kerouac in Ginsberg's apartment in New York City, 1953. In addition to their lengthy letters and discussions, Kerouac, Ginsberg, and Burroughs also collaborated on their writing. Kerouac and Ginsberg often read and wrote in each other's journals, sometimes creating back-and-forth dialogues.

Defining a Generation

In this 1947 feature article Brady describes the bohemians she observed in California that Kerouac later labeled the "Beat Generation."

The New Cult of Sex and Anarchy
Mildred Edie Brady
Harper's Magazine, April 1947, pp. 312–322

[T]hese newcomers are a different crowd. They don't have money and most of them are young, with no clamoring public to hide from nor any agent to drum up a demand for their stuff. When you first come upon them in their countryside shacks they are a surprise. You recognize them instantly, for even here in this forest by the ocean the stamp of young bohemia is as unmistakable as a trade mark. But it is their apparent isolation that bothers you. Their beards and sandaled feet, their corduroys and dark shirts; the barren clutter in the one or two uncarpeted rooms: abstract paintings against rude board walls, canned milk and pumpernickel on a rough table, ceramic ash trays and opened books on a packing box–all this is familiar. Except for the bright daylight and the absence of city soot and noise, you'd think you were in a Greenwich Village apartment of twenty years ago. But it is decidedly unlike young bohemia to turn hermit or to take upon itself the disciplined demands of rural self-sufficiency. It doesn't fit.

. . . .

The parties are not plush affairs, as a rule. Neither food nor drink is lavishly plentiful. And the poetry-reading sessions are serious and solemn occasions. They are held weekly in both San Francisco and Berkeley, where thirty or forty at a time can be found crowded together listening gravely to language patterns that are all but incomprehensible to the uninitiated. Poetry is far and away the most popular medium of these young writers, and their poems make no compromise with old standards of communication. Poetry, they hold, "transcending logic, invades the realm where unreason reigns and where the relations between ideas are sympathetic and mysterious–affective–rather than casual."

You could describe it, in brief, as a combination of anarchism and certain concepts related to psychoanalysis which together yield a philosophy–holding on the one hand that you must abandon the church, the state, and the family (even if you do it, as James Joyce preached, "by treachery, cunning, and exile"); and on the other offering sex as the source of individual salvation in a collective world that's going to hell.

. . . .

Your first reaction to all this is almost sure to be: "Anarchism! I suppose we'll all be playing mah jongg next," or, "Sexual salvation, heaven help us, this is where I came in a quarter of a century ago." But to dismiss it simply as nothing more than a stale replica of the twenties, a kind of intellectual measles that every generation has to go through, is to overlook some differences. If it is indeed true, as some are inclined to believe, that what we are witnessing out here on the coast is the characteristic pattern of the postwar bohemia of World War II then it is also true that bohemia has changed its party line to produce a somewhat different spirit from that which sent cultural pioneers after World War I to the grimy walkups in New York's Greenwich Village.

. . . .

So they write poetry. They paint. They write philosophy. They go to galleries and concerts. Only in art, today, can the fettered, mechanically burdened soul of man speak out his revolt against the dead hand of rationalism. Only through art is it any longer possible to reach that all but buried spark of natural life dying under the intolerable weight of modern man's sadistic super-ego. And only through art will man find a path back to his spontaneous, natural creativeness. Here again you are apt to hear Herbert Read quoted, though sometimes not credited, for he has put this part of their view most clearly. "Poetry," he writes, "in its intensest and most creative moments penetrates to the same level as mysticism."

John Clellon Holmes wrote the first major book published on the Beat Generation, Go *(1952). He was a close friend of Kerouac for twenty years. In an interview for* Jack's Book *he describes his initial meeting with and impressions of Kerouac in 1948.*

Up in Spanish Harlem on July 4, 1948 Allen was giving a party. It was terribly hot, and my then-wife was out of town. I went up there with Alan Harrington, who had met them–or met Jack, anyway–a week or two before at somebody else's party.

So up we went, and there they were. I cottoned to them immediately, and we became friends terribly quickly, particularly with Jack. There was something about Jack. I mean, I love Allen and loved him then, or he fascinated me, but there was something about Jack that I sensed immediately. He must have felt something similar, because we became friends very, very rapidly.

I wrote a novel before *Go.* I was working on it then, and I finished it within about eight months after I met Jack. It was never published; it was a terrible novel.

John Clellon Holmes

Since I was four years younger than Jack, he had read more than I had. Also, he had a formal education. I didn't. I was twenty-two and he was twenty-six. Think about that for a minute. And Burroughs was thirty. That seemed like an absolute grayed image.

Jack and I shared certain things. We discovered certain things together. We read Melville together. We read Blake together because of Allen's influence. I turned Jack on to Lawrence. Lawrence always had been a big thing with me. He'd read Lawrence, I think, a little bit, but he hadn't read him seriously.

He turned me on to Céline, whom I had not read. I had read Wolfe. I didn't want to go back and read him, although Jack was still very enthusiastic about Wolfe. Dostoevski was where we intersected again. I had read Dostoevski before and was already very influenced by him. Jack had a tremendously free and easy feeling about Dostoevski. He treated it like reality. So we would talk about characters as if they were real. We'd spend whole nights saying, "Kirilov wouldn't say that, he'd say *this,"* and we'd invent whole conversations and scenes. Novelistically, I think Dostoevski was where we really intersected. We used to laugh and giggle about Dostoevski.

Jack was living with his mother out in Ozone Park. He'd spend most of his time out there, and then he'd come roaring into New York to party, to get laid, drink, and everything. At that particular period he would most often stay at my place because he had to stay somewhere, and he'd be around for two or three days, maybe three or four, and then he'd disappear again.

I went out there to Ozone Park. It was a very, very formalized situation. Mémerê was the other side of Jack wrought to its uttermost. She was very precise and very fastidious and hated disorder, but was herself very irrational.

Every time Jack limped back after three or four days in New York, she would give him a hard time. She was worried about him. He was her baby boy. I used to go out there in the afternoon sometimes. It was pin-neat. Everything was in its place.

Jack had his little room, and he liked it that way. Among his friends of that period, I think she thought I was okay, because I was blond, I was a WASP, and I was polite. I was straight, anyway. I mean, she didn't demand a tie or anything like that, but I've always been respectful of my elders.

When I visited Jack, we talked, we didn't drink. I wasn't constantly trying to draw him out to the bars or back into the city, so she figured I wasn't a pernicious influence. I acted toward Mémerê the way Jack acted toward my mother.

Jack with older women, with parents, was incredibly proper and straight and deferential. My mother, to this day, will break into tears when she thinks about Jack, because Jack was simply so nice to her. He wasn't putting her on. That's what you did with mothers.

Everybody was attracted to Jack. You couldn't not be in those days.

My first wife, Marian, loved Jack. She also recognized him as a potential danger to the tranquility of the house, because he would blow in and everything was going to be in an uproar for who knows how long. Jack never was like Neal. He didn't take things over, didn't con, but it meant–*ooh-la-la,* it meant the phone would ring, and people would come over, and beer would be gotten out. She went along with it, but she saw that his effect on me was a danger to her. It was mainly her war with me, not him, however.

It was my feeling that you had to have as much experience as you could get. But I hadn't decided on what the novel was going to be like–what any novel was going to be like. What the fate of the novel was going to be. I was attracted to this experience because there was no way to understand it except by going through it. Of course, it attracted me because it was open, it was free, anything might happen, and there were fabulous people, interesting people, talking about real things, it seemed to me. That's the way I thought about it. It never occurred to me to write a book about it until I was up to my eyeballs in it.

–*Jack's Book,* pp. 73–76

In these journal excerpts Holmes comments on his generation.

Crazy Days and Numinous Nights, 1948–1950
John Clellon Holmes
The Beat Vision, pp. 73–88

September 8, 1948
The whole world is going berserk and I'm going too, just for laughs . . . I think myself into straitjackets. I wake up yowling out of my dreams. I stay up until two every night and scrape myself out of bed at seven in the morning. It's the binge of the New Age, our Brave New World . . . I don't listen to quite so many news broadcasts anymore, and I've cut myself down to two papers. It was the least I could do to save my stomach . . . I've been listening to bebop. It's the new insane music of this world. It's like the configurations of a wild mind. It pounds on and on, mechanical, disharmonic, the abstraction of an abstraction . . . Look at the young men go off to war! Singing their songs, making their obscene jokes, laughing and uneasy in their hearts. . . Now they go off, without memories, without regrets, the boys who always turned to the sports sections of the daily papers, who went to the shows, who fucked their girls in back alleys or under the stairs in the tenements. They learned to smoke at seven, had their first woman at the whorehouse on 161st street when they were fifteen. They wandered around this city, beating up old men for a lark, writing dirty words in the subway, posting no bills. Now they are finished. Where in hell's name does it lead? . . .There are those of us who don't give a good goddamn anymore. We're sick and tired of caring about the whole rotten swill of life. The boiling cities of the earth swallow us all and masticate us with their cement jaws and spit us out when they can't digest or destroy us. . . . Why shouldn't we take what we can get, possess it absolutely?

December 10, 1948
Kerouac speaks to Harrington (in a letter written and mailed from here) about "the beat generation," the "generation of furtives". . . They are breaking the laws of this country, almost every one of them. They are drug addicts, or they are drug peddlers. Many of them are thieves, some are murderers . . . But it is interesting to note that Huncke, a street-arab as a child, a junkie, a thief, a second-story man, a miserable derelict, listens to Ginsberg, with interest, and comprehends him in a way. Their experience is the same, they recognize the same mental reality, they have been thru it. They comprehend subtleties that are Dostoyevskian, but only because they are "underground" and know what "the man" is talking about . . . I am called out into the street to try to understand the above-mentioned things, to fit them into my patterns, to change my patterns where that is necessary.

Dust jacket for Holmes's first novel, published in 1952. As he was working on the book, he wrote the following journal entry of 28 April 1950: "I rush from place to place eagerly, meeting new hordes of people, engaging each in feverish conversation, only to discover beneath the shiny, fetching surface, the same fears, the same insecurities, the same resolve never to show themselves or what they feel. That is why I have given my heart to our generation . . . ."

In Go, *Holmes based the character Hobbes on himself, Pasternak on Kerouac, and Stofsky on Ginsberg.*

He [Hobbes] came to know their world, at first only indirectly. It was a world of dingy backstairs "pads," Times Square cafeterias, bebop joints, night-long wanderings, meetings on street corners, hitchhiking, a myriad of "hip" bars all over the city, and the streets themselves. It was inhabited by people "hungup" with drugs and other habits, searching out a new degree of craziness; and connected by the invisible threads of need, petty crimes of long ago, or a strange recognition of affinity. They kept going all the time, living by night, rushing around to "make contact," suddenly disappearing into jail or on the road only to turn up again and search one another out. They had a view of life that was underground, mysterious, and they seemed unaware of anything outside the realities of deals, a pad to stay in, "digging the frantic jazz," and keeping everything going. Hobbes ventured into the outskirts of this world suspiciously, even fearfully, but unable to quell his immediate fascination for he had been among older, less active, and more mental people for too long, and needed something new and exciting.

Once Pasternak said to him with peculiar clarity: "You know, everyone I know is kind of furtive, kind of beat. They all go along the street like they were guilty of something, but didn't believe in guilt. I can spot them immediately! And it's happening all over the country, to everyone; a sort of revolution of the soul, I guess *you'd* call it!"

And the more Hobbes saw of Pasternak and Stofsky and heard of their friends, and the more he found himself responding unwillingly to a disorder that he had once condemned, the more he was forced to conclude that Pasternak was right, and that something had happened to all of them.

–*Go,* p. 36

When Holmes's Go *created an interest in New York City's bohemian underground, Gilbert Millstein, book reviewer for* The New York Times, *asked him to write an essay that explained his generation. In this lucid, straightforward account of the postwar attitude of a certain set of young people in America, Holmes gives the little-known Kerouac credit for coming up with the defining phrase he used for his title. Holmes portrayed the Beat Generation as literary and considerate of both ideas and actions and insisted that for his contemporaries "there is no single philosophy, no single party, no single attitude," and that the "problem of modern life is essentially a spiritual problem."*

This Is the Beat Generation

John Clellon Holmes

The New York Times Magazine, 16 November 1952, pp. 10–22

Several months ago, a national magazine ran a story under the heading "Youth" and the subhead "Mother Is Bugged at Me." It concerned an 18-year-old California girl who had been picked up for smoking marijuana and wanted to talk about it. While a reporter took down her ideas in the uptempo language of "tea," someone snapped a picture. In view of her contention that she was part of a whole new culture where one out of every five people you meet is a user, it was an arresting photograph. In the pale, attentive face, with its soft eyes and intelligent mouth, there was no hint of corruption. It was a face which could only be deemed criminal through an enormous effort of righteousness. Its only complaint seemed to be "Why don't people leave us alone?" It was the face of a Beat Generation.

That clean young face has been making the newspapers steadily since the war. Standing before a judge in a Bronx court house, being arraigned for stealing a car, it looked up into the camera with curious laughter and no guilt. The same face, with a more serious bent, stared from the pages of *Life* magazine, representing a graduating class of ex-G.I.'s, and said that as it believed small business to be dead, it intended to become comfortable cog in the largest corporation it could find. A little younger, a little more bewildered, it was this same face that the photographers caught in Illinois when the first non-virgin club was uncovered. The young copywriter, leaning down the bar on Third Avenue, quietly drinking himself into relaxation, and the energetic hot-rod driver of Los Angeles, who plays Russian roulette with a jalopy, are separated only by a continent and a few years. They are the extremes. In between them fall the secretaries wondering whether to sleep with their boyfriends now or wait; the mechanics, beering up with the guys and driving off to Detroit on a whim; the models studiously name-dropping at a cocktail party. But the face is the same. Bright, level, realistic, challenging.

Any attempt to label an entire generation is unrewarding, and yet the generation which went through the last war, or at least could get a drink easily once it was over, seems to possess a uniform, general quality which demands an adjective. It was John Kerouac, the author of a fine, neglected novel *The Town and the City,* who finally came up with it. It was several years ago, when the face was harder to recognize, but he has a sharp, sympathetic eye, and one day he said, "You know, this is really a *beat* generation." The origins of the word "beat" are obscure, but the meaning is only too clear to most Americans. More than mere weariness, it implies the feeling of having been used, of being raw. It involves a sort of nakedness of mind, and, ultimately, of soul; a feeling of being reduced to the bedrock of consciousness. In short, it means being undramatically pushed up against the wall of oneself. A man is beat whenever he goes for broke and wagers the sum of his resources on a single number; and the young generation has done that continually from early youth.

Its members have an instinctive individuality, needing no bohemianism or imposed eccentricity to express it. Brought up during the collective bad circumstances of a dreary depression, weaned during the collective uprooting of a global war, they distrust collectivity. But they have never been able to keep the world out of their dreams. The fancies of their childhood inhabited the half-light of Munich, the Nazi-Soviet pact and the eventual blackout. Their adolescence was spent in a topsy-turvy world of war bonds, swing shifts and troop movements. They grew to independent mind on beachheads, in ginmills and U. S. O.'s, in past-midnight arrivals and pre-dawn departures. Their brothers, husbands, fathers or boy friends turned up dead one day at the other end of a telegram. At the four trembling corners of the world, or in the home town invaded by factories and lonely servicemen, they had intimate experience with the nadir and the zenith of human conduct, and little time for much that came between. The peace they inherited was only as secure as the next headline. It was a cold peace. Their own lust for freedom, and their ability to live at a pace that kills, to which war had adjusted them, led to black markets, bebop, narcotics, sexual promiscuity, hucksterism and Jean-Paul Sartre. The beatness set in later.

It is a postwar generation, and, in a world which seems to mark its cycles by its wars, it is already being compared to that other postwar generation, which dubbed itself "lost." The Roaring Twenties, and the generation that made them roar, are going through a sentimental revival, and the comparison is valuable. The Lost Generation was discovered in a roadster, laughing hysterically because nothing meant anything anymore. It migrated to Europe, unsure whether it was looking for the "orgiastic future" or escaping from the "puritanical past." Its symbols were the flapper, the flask of bootleg whisky, and an attitude of desperate frivolity best expressed by Noel Coward's line: "Tennis, anyone?" It was caught up in the romance of disillusionment, until even that became an illusion. Every act in its drama of lostness was a tragic or an ironic third act, and T. S. Eliot's *The Wasteland* was more than the dead-end statement of a perceptive poet. The pervading atmosphere was an almost objectless sense of loss, through which the reader felt immediately that the cohesion of things had disappeared. It was, for an entire generation, an image which expressed, with dreadful accuracy, its own spiritual condition.

But the wild boys of today are not lost. Their flushed, often scoffing, always intent faces elude the word, and it would sound phony to them. For this generation conspicuously lacks that eloquent air of bereavement which made so many of the exploits of the Lost Generation symbolic actions. Furthermore, the repeated inventory of shattered ideals, and the laments about the mud in moral currents, which so obsessed the Lost Generation, does not concern young people today. They take it frighteningly for granted. They were brought up in these ruins and no longer notice them. They drink to "come down" or to "get high," not to illustrate anything. Their excursions into drugs or promiscuity come out of curiosity, not disillusionment.

Only the most bitter among them would call their reality a nightmare and protest that they have indeed lost something, the future. But ever since they were old enough to imagine one, that has been in jeopardy anyway. The absence of personal and social values is to them, not a revelation shaking the ground beneath them, but a problem demanding a day-to-day solution. *How* to live seems to them much more crucial than *why*. And it is precisely at this point that the copywriter and the hot-rod driver meet, and their identical beatness becomes significant, for, unlike the Lost Generation, which was occupied with the loss of faith, the Beat Generation is becoming more and more occupied with the need for it. As such, it is a disturbing illustration of Voltaire's reliable old joke: "If there were no God, it would be necessary to invent Him." Not content to bemoan His absence, they are busily and haphazardly inventing totems for Him on all sides.

For the giggling nihilist, eating up the highway at ninety miles an hour, and steering with his feet, is no Harry Crosby, the poet of the Lost Generation who flew his plane into the sun one day because he could no longer accept the modern world. On the contrary, the hot-rod driver invites death only to outwit it. He is affirming the life within him in the only way he knows how, at the extreme. The eager-faced girl, picked up on a dope charge, is not one of those "women and girls carried screaming with drink or drugs from public places," of whom Fitzgerald wrote. Instead, with persuasive seriousness, she describes the sense of community she has found in marijuana, which society never gave her. The copywriter, just as drunk by midnight as his Lost Generation counterpart, probably reads *God and Man at Yale* during his Sunday afternoon hangover. The difference is this almost exaggerated will to believe in something, if only in themselves. It is a *will* to believe, even in the face of an inability to do so in conventional terms. And that is bound to lead to excesses in one direction or another.

The shock that older people feel at the sight of this Beat Generation is, at its deepest level, not so much repugnance at the facts, as it is distress at the attitudes which move it. Though worried by this distress, they most often argue or legislate in terms of the facts rather than the attitudes. The newspaper reader, studying the eyes of young dope addicts, can only find an outlet for his horror and bewilderment in demands that passers be given the electric chair. Sociologists, with a more academic concern, are just as troubled by the legions of young men whose topmost ambition seems to be to find a secure berth in a monolithic corporation. Contemporary historians express mild surprise at the lack of organized movements, political, religious or otherwise, among the young. The articles they write remind us that being one's own boss and being a natural joiner are two of our most cherished national traits. Everywhere, people with tidy moralities shake their heads and wonder what is happening to the younger generation.

Perhaps they have not noticed that, behind the excess on the one hand, and the conformity on the other, lies that wait-and-see detachment that results from having to fall back for support more on one's human endurance than on one's philosophy of life. Not that the Beat Generation is immune to ideas: they fascinate it. Its wars, both past and future, were and will be wars of ideas. It knows, however, that in the final, private moment of conflict a man is really fighting another man, and not an idea. And that the same goes for love. So it is a generation with a greater facility for entertaining ideas than for believing in them. But it is also the first generation in several centuries for which the act of faith has been an obsessive problem, quite aside from the reasons for having a particular faith or not having it. It exhibits on every side, and in a bewildering number of facets, a perfect craving to believe. Though it is certainly a generation of extremes, including both the hipster and the "radical" young Republican in its ranks, it renders unto Caesar (i.e., society) what is Caesar's, and unto God what is God's. For in the wildest hipster, making a mystique of bop, drugs and the night life, there is no desire to shatter the "square" society in which he lives, only to elude it. To get on a soapbox or write a manifesto would seem to him absurd. Looking out at the normal world, where most everything is a "drag" for him, he nevertheless says: "Well, that's the Forest of Arden after all. And even it jumps if you look at it right." Equally, the young Republican, though often seeming to hold up Babbitt as the culture hero, is neither vulgar nor materialistic, as Babbitt was. He conforms because he believes it is socially practical, not necessarily virtuous. Both positions, however, are the result of more or less the same conviction–namely that the valueless abyss of modern life is unbearable.

A generation can sometimes be better understood by the books it reads, than by those it writes. The literary hero of the Lost Generation should have been Bazarov, the nihilist in Turgenev's *Fathers and Sons*. Bazarov sat around, usually in the homes of the people he professed to loathe, smashing every icon within his reach. He was a man stunned into irony and rage by the collapse of the moral and intellectual structure of his world.

But he did nothing. The literary hero of the Beat Generation, on the other hand, might be Stavrogin, that most enigmatic character in *The Possessed* by Dostoevski. He is also a nihilist, or at least intimately associated with them.

But there is a difference, for Stavrogin, behind a facade very much like Bazarov's, is possessed by a passion for faith, almost any faith. His very atheism, at its extreme, is metaphysical. But he knows that disbelief is fatal, and when he has failed in every way to overcome it, he commits suicide because he does not have what he calls "greatness of soul." The ground yawned beneath Bazarov, revealing a pit into which he fell: while Stavrogin struggled at the bottom of that pit, trying feverishly to get out. In so far as it resembled Stavrogin, there have been few generations with as natural and profound a craving for convictions as this one, nor have there been many generations as ill-equipped to find them.

For beneath the excess and the conformity, there is something other than detachment. There are the stirrings of a quest. What the hipster is looking for in his "coolness" (withdrawal) or "flipness" (ecstasy) is, after all, a feeling of somewhereness, not just another diversion. The young Republican feels that there is a point beyond which change becomes chaos, and what he wants is not simply privilege or wealth, but a stable position from which to operate. Both have had enough of homelessness, valuelessness, faithlessness.

The variety and the extremity of their solutions is only a final indication that for today's young people there is not as yet a single external pivot around which they can, as a generation, group their observations and their aspirations. There is no single philosophy, no single party, no single attitude. The failure of most orthodox moral and social concepts to reflect fully the life they have known is probably the reason, but because of it each person becomes a walking, self-contained unit, compelled to meet the problem of being young in a seemingly helpless world in his own way, or at least to endure.

More than anything else, this is what is responsible for the generation's reluctance to name itself, its reluctance to discuss itself as a group, sometimes its reluctance to be itself. For invented gods invariably disappoint those who worship them. Only the need for them goes on, and it is this need, exhausting one object after another, which projects the Beat Generation forward into the future and will one day deprive it of its beatness.

Dostoevski wrote in the early 1880s, "Young Russia is talking of nothing but the eternal questions now." With appropriate changes, something very like this is beginning to happen in America, in an American way; a reevaluation of which the exploits and attitudes of this generation are only symptoms. No simple comparison of one generation against another can accurately measure effects, but it seems obvious that a Lost Generation, occupied with disillusionment and trying to keep busy among the broken stones, is poetically moving, not very dangerous. But a Beat Generation, driven by a desperate craving for belief and as yet unable to accept the moderations which are offered it, is quite another matter. Thirty years later, after all, the generation of which Dostoevski wrote, was meeting in cellars and making bombs.

This generation may make no bombs; it will probably be asked to drop some, and have some dropped on it, however, and this fact is never far from its mind. It is one of the pressures which created it and will play a large part in what will happen to it. There are those who believe that in generations such as this there is always the constant possibility of a great new moral idea, conceived in desperation, coming to life. Others note the self-indulgence, the waste, the apparent social irresponsibility, and disagree.

But its ability to keep its eyes open, and yet avoid cynicism; its ever-increasing conviction that the problem of modern life is essentially a spiritual problem; and that capacity for sudden wisdom which people who live hard and go far, possess, are assets and bear watching. And, anyway, the clear, challenging faces are worth it.

Writing several decades after the genesis of the Beat Generation, journalist Bruce Cook summarized the movement's effects on readers.

Yes, according to John Clellon Holmes, it was Kerouac who christened them all, though no one would ever claim that he originated the term. Beat, in the sense of beaten, frustrated, played out, has been around for many, many years. Its fustian, ungrammatical quality suggests it may have originated in the nineteenth-century West or rural South. In the 1940s it had a vogue among jazz musician who used to embellish it with little variations, such as "I'm beat right down to my socks." A friend of Kerouac's, Herbert Huncke, who was then living an underground life as a Times Square hustler, petty thief, and drug addict, had picked it up from the jazzmen and used it often with frequent variations. So there was nothing really remarkable in Jack Kerouac using the word in that way when he attempted to characterize the new attitude he saw in his contemporaries. "It's a sort of furtiveness," Clellon Holmes quotes him as saying, "like we were a generation of furtives. You know, with an inner knowledge there's no use flaunting on that level, the level of the 'public,' a kind of beatness–I mean being right down to it, to ourselves, because we all *really* know where we are–and a weariness with all the forms, all the conventions of the world . . . . It's something like that. So I guess you might say we're a *beat* generation."

A version of this speech found its way into John Clellon Holmes' novel *Go,* a book particularly important for the picture it provides of the early Beat scene in New York in the 1940s. Published in 1952, it has the distinction of being the first Beat Generation novel. But apart from good reviews, it received no real notice and certainly started no movements. It took Jack Kerouac's *On the Road,* published five years later, to do that.

It is difficult, separated as we are by time and temper from that period, to convey the liberating effect that *On the Road* had on young people all over America. There was a sort of instantaneous flash of recognition that seemed to send thousands of them out into the streets, proclaiming that Kerouac had written their story, that *On the Road* was their book. There was such community of feeling in this response that critics began to speak with some certainty, though without much respect, of Kerouac's as the new literary generation.

Their lack of respect was probably due less to the work produced by Kerouac and his friends than to their public performances. Whether at readings, on panels, or in front of television cameras, they could always be depended upon to shock some and dismay many more. There was a sort of programmatic ruthlessness to their impudence. It was as though they had put aside any notion of revolting against the establishment and had decided merely to thumb their noses at it.

The Beat Generation, p. 6

David Halberstam argues that the decade in which the Beats flourished was far more complicated than it is often remembered.

The fifties were captured in black and white, most often by still photographers; by contrast, the decade that followed was, more often than not, caught in living color on tape or film. Not surprisingly, in retrospect the pace of the fifties seemed slower, almost languid. Social ferment, however, was beginning just beneath this placid surface. It was during the fifties, for example, that the basic research in the development of the birth-control pill took place; but it was not until a decade later that this technological advance had a profound effect upon society. Then, apparently overnight, rather conservative–indeed cautious–sexual practices were giving way to what commentators would speak of as the sexual revolution. It was in the fifties that the nation became wired for television, a new medium experimented with by various politicians and social groups. Ten years later television had begun to alter the political and social fabric of the country, with stunning consequences.

Three decades later, the fifties appear to be an orderly era, one with a minimum of social dissent. Photographs from the period tend to show people who dressed carefully: men in suits, ties, and–when outdoors–hats; the women with their hair in modified page-boys, pert and upbeat. Young people seemed, more than anything else, "square" and largely accepting of the given social covenants. At the beginning of the decade their music was still slow and saccharine, mirroring the generally bland popular taste. In the years following the traumatic experiences of the Depression and World War II, the American Dream was to exercise personal freedom not in social and political terms, but rather in economic ones. Eager to be part of the burgeoning middle class, young men and women opted for material well-being, particularly if it came with some form of guaranteed employment. For the young, eager veteran just out of college (which he had attended courtesy of the G.I. Bill), security meant finding a good white-collar job with a large, benevolent company, getting married, having children, and buying a house in the suburbs.

–*The Fifties,* pp. ix-x

In his "The Philosophy of the Beat Generation," originally published in the February 1958 issue of Esquire, *Holmes discusses the importance of James Dean as an emblem.*

A large proportion of this generation lived vicariously in the short, tumultuous career of actor James Dean. He was their idol in much the same way that Valentino was the screen idol of the twenties and Clark Gable was the screen idol of the thirties. But there was a difference, and it was *all* the difference. In Dean, they saw not a daydream Lothario who was more attractive, mysterious and wealthy than they were, or a virile man of action with whom they could fancifully identify to make up for their own feelings of powerlessness, but a wistful, reticent youth, looking over the abyss separating him from older people with a level, saddened eye; living intensely in alternate explosions of tenderness and violence; eager for love and a sense of purpose, but able to accept them only on terms which acknowledged the facts of life as he knew them: in short, themselves.

To many people, Dean's mumbling speech, attenuated silences, and rash gestures seemed the ultimate in empty mannerisms, but the young generation knew that it was not so much that he was inarticulate or affected as it was that he was unable to believe in some of the things his scripts required him to say. He spoke to them right through all the expensive make-believe of million-dollar productions, saying with his sighs, and the prolonged shifting of his weight from foot to foot: "Well, I suppose there's no way out of this, but we know how it really is. . . ." They knew he was lonely, they knew he was flawed, they knew he was confused. But they also knew that he "dug," and so they delighted in his sloppy clothes and untrimmed hair and indifference to the proprieties of fame. He was not what they wanted to be; he was what they were. He lived hard and without complaint; and he died as he lived, going fast.

–*Nothing More to Declare*

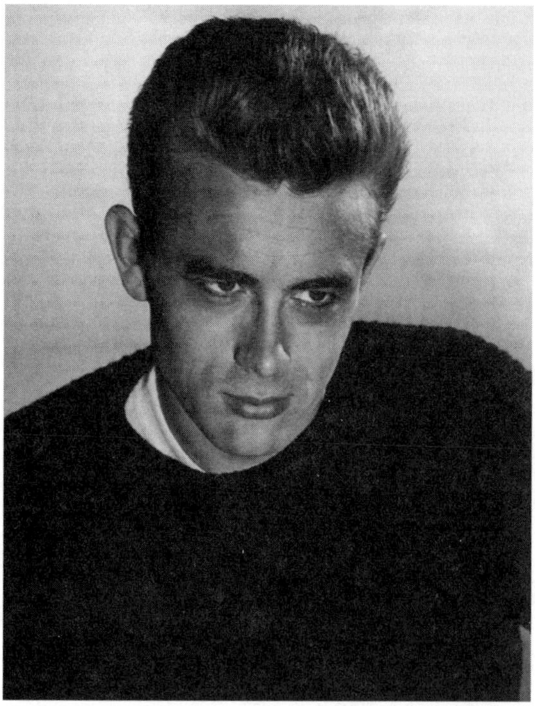

In movies such as Rebel Without a Cause *and* The Wild One *James Dean and Marlon Brando epitomized youthful rebellion against the status quo. Historian and journalist David Halberstam linked James Dean, Marlon Brando, and Kerouac as inaugurators of a "new tradition of American rebels." Millions of moviegoers saw Dean and Brando, paving the way for Kerouac's breakthrough as another in the line of attractive, misunderstood, and possibly dangerous models for teens.*

Malcolm Cowley was well known for his book Exile's Return: A Narrative of Ideas *(1931; revised, 1951) in which he chronicled the Lost Generation writers in Paris. In this feature article Cowley describes the post–World War II generation of writers and singles out Kerouac's unpublished book,* On the Road, *as "the best record" of the Beat Generation. Cowley figured prominently in Kerouac's professional life, for, as an adviser to Viking Press, he was responsible for getting* On the Road *published.*

Invitation to Innovators
Malcolm Cowley
The Saturday Review, 21 August 1954, pp. 7–8, 38–40

The young writers of this age–I am thinking of those born after 1920–belonged to the first generation that really grew up with the automobile, the first for which driving three or four thousand pounds of steel at sixty miles an hour became as instinctive as walking and more habitual; nobody liked to walk any more. They were also the first to grow up with radio, the jukebox, and talking pictures–that is, with omnipresent voices and music–just as still younger persons, born after 1940, would be the first to grow up with television. The effect on both groups was to make them more ear-minded and picture-minded and to occupy much of the time they might have spent in reading. On the average they had probably read fewer books than their elders at the same age–or it might be more accurate to say that the reading, even for future writers, began later in life, when they were in college rather than when they were in high school. They were the first generation to attend new high schools at a time when secondary education had become almost universal and teen-age boys and girls composed an independent society, resentful of interference by older people. The education they received was different, with more stress laid on adjustment to the group and less on competitive achievement in their studies; in high school there were also fewer themes to write, less homework, less study of foreign languages, and a less thorough grounding in English. They were being prepared to get along with people rather than to manipulate words or ideas.

The new writers were children during the depression, which most of them later seemed to have forgotten, although there were signs that the fear of poverty was still embedded in their minds. They served in the Second World War if they were old enough; many of

The Saturday Review
AUGUST 21, 1954

INVITATION TO INNOVATORS

By MALCOLM COWLEY

In this discussion Mr. Cowley, a cosmopolitan critic born in Pennsylvania and polished in the University of Montpellier in France who has long been the friend and editor of many American writers, investigates the natures and conditions of young America, in order to prophesy the type of serious writing the new generation will produce when it finally gets down to work.

Opening page of essay in which Cowley first discusses the work of Kerouac. Cowley later championed the publication of On the Road.

them spent five or six years in uniform. They learned much about warfare, somewhat less about foreign countries, and more about Americans of all types, while they also acquired the habit of looking to the government for food, clothing, and answers to the question, "What shall I do next?" The habit continued for many after their discharge from the armed forces, since the government sent them checks to pay for their education, with a few dollars extra for wives and children; most of them had married young. Meanwhile still younger writers were also having their share of military life–some with assignments in Korea–and were being taught to hold a similar attitude toward an impersonal, all-powerful, and all-nourishing state. In civilian life both groups would benefit from the longest period of prosperity this country has known–the state was also responsible for that, through its military spending–and both would learn to fear a sudden disaster in which their world might go down to ruin.

. . . .

There was one fairly large group that refused to conform and waged a dogged sort of rebellion–against what it is hard to say, because the group had no program, but possibly against the whole body of laws, customs, fears, habits of thought, and literary standards that had been accepted by other members of the generation. The rebellion was individual and nihilistic; each of the rebels simply refused to accept any model, in literature or life, that older people asked him to emulate. Some made a cult out of heavy drinking, promiscuity, smoking marijuana, or almost any other forbidden pleasure, but their real delights were driving fast–if they could get hold of automobiles–and listening to cool jazz. They liked to be "cool," that is, withdrawn. Often they talked about being "underground" and called themselves "the beat generation"; it was John Kerouac who invented the second phrase and his unpublished long narrative, *On the*

Cedar Tavern in Greenwich Village (copyright © by Fred W. McDarrah)

Writer Seymour Krim, who provided an intelligent critical assessment of Kerouac's work in his introduction to Desolation Angels *(1965), describes the milieu of the Cedar Tavern in Greenwich Village and the attraction he felt for the fledgling Beat Generation.*

When I got out of the nuthouse, I didn't return to my old haunts, where the crowd from the *Partisan Review* and *Commentary* hung out, but instead I began to go to the old Cedar Bar, which was then a hangout for abstract expressionist painters, for Beats, and Beat types. It was as simple as that. Just a change of scene made all the difference. Who was there? Well, everybody you might expect–Holmes, Ginsberg, Corso, and occasionally Kerouac and then others that might be thought of more as the Black Mountain crowd–Selby, Gilbert Sorrentino, and for a while Robert Creeley. People like that. But I'm making distinctions and groupings after the fact. It was just a bunch of people back then who came together evening after evening. And a change of bar meant a change of atmosphere for me. That was what was important for me–the change of atmosphere.

–*The Beat Generation,* p. 51

Road, is the best record of their lives. In two respects they were like the more conventional majority of young people: they had no interest in politics, even as a spectator sport, and they were looking for something to believe, an essentially religious faith that would permit them to live at peace with their world.

Carl Solomon

Born in the Bronx, New York, on 30 March 1928, Carl Wolfe Solomon joined the United States Maritime Service and traveled to Europe as a young man. In France he was affected by the Surrealist works of André Breton, Jean Genet, and Antonin Artaud. Back in New York in 1949, he voluntarily entered the Columbia Psychiatric Institute, requesting shock treatment. While he was there he met Allen Ginsberg, who was undergoing psychiatric evaluation after his implication in a sale-of-stolen-goods scheme. Ginsberg later wrote "Howl for Carl Solomon" and repeatedly referred to him in the poem.

After his release, Solomon worked for his uncle, A. A. Wyn of Ace Books, where he oversaw the publication of William Burroughs's Junkie *and tried unsuccessfully to get Kerouac to revise his work, including* On the Road, *into a "marketable product." Ace eventually did publish Kerouac's* Tristessa. *Solomon lived and worked in New York City and published two collections of essays,* Mishaps, Perhaps *(1966) and* More Mishaps *(1968). His memoirs, including his recollections of his Beat associations, were published as* Emergency Messages: An Autobiographical Miscellany *(1989). Solomon's biographer Tom Collins writes that "in many ways Solomon is the secret heart of the Beat movement, far more influential than his own modest output would suggest. Yet despite a life story that is in many ways astounding, he is also a mystery man who has preferred to live the greater part of his life in privacy, deliberately shunning the legend that surrounds him."*

An Interview with Carl Solomon
John Tytell
The Beat Book (1974), pp. 163–171

INTERVIEWER: When did you first travel to Europe?

CS: I joined the Merchant Marine in 1945, just before the war with Japan ended. I went to various places, France among them, and I jumped ship in 1947 in France . . . I stayed there, went to Paris, and learned about Artaud, and Michaux, and Isou.

INT: Isn't it curious that so many writers like Kerouac and Ginsberg were joining the Merchant Marine?

CS: Well, there were movies in those days romanticizing it–"Action in the North Atlantic" with Humphrey Bogart–so that sort of thing was in the air then.

INT: Before going to sea you attended City College?

CS: I started there in 1943, when I was fifteen.

INT: When did you leave City College?

CS: Well, I kept on shipping out intermittently, going to school one term and to sea the next.

INT: So you were an early dropout?

CS: Yes, although I hadn't dropped out completely. I had neglected my studies really, and I got sort of low grades.

INT: Were there any teachers there that you still remember?

CS: Leffert, he was a specialist in Modern Literature–a very sharp, very classy sort of guy who seemed to love Gide.

INT: Was there anyone else?

CS: Then I had Abraham Edel in Philosophy who was very bright.

INT: Was CCNY a very active place politically?

CS: Yes. While I was there I joined the AYD (American Youth for Democracy). This was the Communist front organization of that period when they were anti-axis and for the war. The AYD group was known as the Tom Paine Club. The Communist Party went out of existence then, and they called it the CPA–Communist Political Association during the Browder period which is now regarded as a revisionist period. Browder felt there would be collaboration between capitalism and communism, and that the Party should go out of existence. So I joined the CPA which was part of the progressive movement and it was considered the left.

INT: Is this the origin of what is now known as Progressive Labor?

CS: No, no, no. That's Maoist and from the second wave of leftism in the late fifties or early sixties.

INT: Do you remember whether many students were similarly involved?

CS: Yeah. They had a very large membership. As a matter of fact, during those years the Communists dominated the CIO (Congress of Industrial Organization), and they even elected two members to the New York City Council in those years, Ben Davis and Cacchione in Brooklyn.

INT: Didn't you also attend Brooklyn College at one time?

CS: Well, I broke with my CP friends that I had made at CCNY, and I moved down to the Village and became interested in avant-garde art and existentialism with a circle of people disillusioned with the left, ex-liberals and progressives I should say. I began to read The Partisan Review, and a flock of other little magazines like Horizon. I went to Brooklyn College because I had a friend going there who said that it would be better for my literary interests than CCNY which was geared for engineers and science.

INT: In Mishaps Perhaps, you write that you witnessed an Artaud reading in Paris, 1947.

CS: First of all I was looking for existentialists. So I went wandering around San Germain de Pres and came to a gallery with a crowd standing outside. I can't recall the name of the street, but I read an account about it when I returned in Partisan Review, how Artaud had been screaming his "Damnation of the Flesh"–I've forgotten the Rue (Was it Rue Jacob?), but to me it's the Rue Impasse or Satan. So I stood outside, and first a young man with black hair descended from upstairs, and he was trembling, and he read what I later found out was Artaud's "Ci-Git" preceded by the "Indian Culture": then I remember another man in a

Cover for Solomon's 1966 book that includes "Report from the Asylum: Afterthoughts of a Shock Patient"

turban screaming. He had been there before the young man. Originally, I had thought the young man was Artaud, but later I learned Artaud was an older man then–he was 51. I remember one line the young man read: "Papa, Maman et pederastinne" and that tickled Kerouac in later years. The story I gave to him was that the reader was pointing at me but he was really pointing at the crowd.

INT: Did you have any further interest in Artaud?

CS: Oh yes. In 1948 I worked on a ship again since they hadn't ousted me for deserting and I went back to France. This time I got a couple of days off from my job as a dishwasher, and I made the long trip to Paris just for one day where I bought, in the same neighborhood, Artaud's book on Van Gogh, The Man Suicided by Society.

INT: I wanted to ask you about that. In Mishaps Perhaps you summarize Artaud's condemnation of all psychiatry, and his argument that those who are in turn condemned by psychiatrists are gifted with a superior lucidity and insight. It occurs to me that such notions are extremely prevalent in radical psychiatry in England and America today with people like R. D. Laing, David Cooper and Thomas Szasz.

CS: Yes, today. Artaud began to be absorbed in certain areas later on. When I first read Artaud it was still something very esoteric. Later, when the theater of the absurd became prominent, his theatrical ideas at least came through. Anyway, I got The Man Suicided by Society, and then moved to West Fourth Street and attended Brooklyn College. At that time I was spending a lot of time in the 42nd Street Library where I found the lettrist magazine, La Dictature Lettrice, and I read through that. I was twenty years old at the time, and reading Artaud's letters. Then I cooked up a thing with Leni Grubes and Ronnie Gold–who is now one of the heads of the Gay Activists–and we staged a dadaist demonstration, and threw potato salad at Markfield.

INT: Wallace Markfield?

CS: Yes, he was lecturing on Mallarme.

INT: Isn't there a line in "Howl" about that experience?

CS: Yes. At that time Ronnie and I were discussing the validity of suicide, and I read Lafcadio's Adventures, you know, the idea of the gratuitous crime, but I backed out of all this. I did steal a sandwich at Brooklyn College and showed it to the policeman, got sent to the psychologist, and then they sent me up to the Columbia Psychiatric Institute. I was in a very negative, nihilistic mood, things seemed so sick to me, and I wanted a lobotomy, or to be suicided. I thought I was a madman.

INT: Was this in any way a reaction to a dullness in the culture you felt at the time?

CS: Yeah it was a reaction. Just before that my mother and I had moved to Parkchester, which I used to refer to as a Cubist colony because of the way it was arranged, cold, abstract, futuristic, regular houses which are now very common, but that was the first of the large projects. My old neighborhood, Prospect Avenue in the South Bronx, had been an ordinary sort of Jewish neighborhood with brownstones.

INT: Was this the Amalgamated project?

CS: No, Metropolitan Life Insurance Company, and in the beginning they didn't let Negroes in, you know, it was a place where everybody seemed to be a stereotype. And my rebellion against that led to the avant-garde involvement which led to the insulin shock treatment up at Columbia Psychiatric.

INT: Isn't that where you met Allen Ginsberg in a Dostoevskian encounter with you introducing yourself as Kirilov, and Allen as Myshkin?

CS: Yes, I met Allen after coming down from the insulin ward, just emerging from a coma; comas, no less, to come out of reading and ideas! The story is in

Carl Solomon (right) with interviewer John Tytell

my "Afterthoughts of a Shock Patient." When I came out of the hospital, supposedly cured, Allen introduced me to Neal Cassady and that bunch, and Landesman.

INT: Had you appeared in Neurotica before?

CS: No. Before that I wasn't really interested in Neurotica, although I had seen it around.

INT: What was Landesman like?

CS: He had an art gallery in St. Louis, a patron of the arts, and as Jack Kerouac characterized him he was a playboy.

INT: John Clellon Holmes has an interesting description of him in Nothing More to Declare.

CS: They were close friends.

INT: You met Allen in '49? He had been placed there because of the ride and Little Jack Melody. How many months were you together at that time?

CS: Oh, a couple of months, and I got out before he did.

INT: Did you have freedom to meet?

CS: We used to meet on the ward, and write, and read things to one another. I introduced him to works of Artaud and Genet; he read Yeats to me, Melville, and spoke of his friends, Kerouac and Burroughs. But he was highly critical of me. He thought my ideas at that time would lead me to a worse insanity, and perhaps under his suggestion that's what ultimately happened when I went to Pilgrim State.

INT: Well, that is a kind of negative influence.

CS: I suppose it was.

INT: In More Mishaps, you write that Allen was taking notes on your adventures while at Columbia Psychiatric, and some of those notes appeared in a different form in "Howl."

CS: He sat there, and I used to come out with very surrealistic aphorisms which he would transcribe.

INT: Can you remember some instances in your life that are reflected, however prismatically, in "Howl"?

CS: The remark about the pubic beards was mine, and the harlequin talk of suicide.

INT: In your books, I thought I detected a sign of hostility as well as admiration towards Ginsberg and his literary friends.

CS: I was angry because of my second sickness. I thought that they had all rejected me because I was madder than they were. I thought that they were neurotics and I was a psychotic, an outsider.

INT: In your books you always tease your readers with differences you had with Ginsberg, such as the way you saw Whitman.

CS: We were continually fighting. I saw Whitman as a political revolutionary, and Allen saw him as a sexual revolutionary. When I first met Allen I called him a "dopey daffodil" because he symbolized to me what poetry was then, referring to Wordsworth, I guess, the idea of poets as sensitive souls rather than Artaud's conception of the poet as brute. But Allen turned out not to be a dopey daffodil at all, but that's the way he looked then, a neat haircut and horn rim glasses. He seemed to me to be like the conventional English major who couldn't stand up to me at all. I thought I was much greater than these types, much more unconventional. I identified with the Beat Generation in much the same way as Artaud himself identified with the Surrealists: he felt that they were his ultimate enemy.

INT: You mean as a possible close source of betrayal because they couldn't really live up to his ideals?

CS: Yeah. Like when I escaped from Pilgrim State Hospital once I went over to Allen's brother's house, and while he talked to me, his wife called the hospital.

INT: How did you escape?

CS: I just walked off.

INT: What kind of treatment did you receive at Psychiatric Institute? Was it group therapy or individual analysis?

CS: Individual; they had group therapy at Pilgrim State.

INT: What kind of analyst did you have at Columbia Psychiatric–what school was he from?

CS: She–Washington School–Harry Stack Sullivan.

INT: What about Allen's analyst?

CS: I think he was Freudian. We had many fights about our analysts and their virtues. That happens in all hospitals, by the way. There was a situation out at Pilgrim State where the gentile patients wanted Jungian analysts, and the Jewish patients wanted Freudians.

INT: In Mishaps Perhaps you state that you had been conditioned in illness by classical surrealism.

CS: I meant Artaud's void. Also ideas like the derangement of the senses, and things that Ronnie Gold and I used to do. We used to hang out in gay bars then, Mary's and Main Street which were both on Eighth Street in the Village, hubs of activity then. They were crowded outside and inside, a real super-decadent atmosphere. Ned Rorem used to go there, he was always at the bar. Ronnie Gold and I used to eat benzedrine. To me decadence meant absinthe, or green drinks like pernod, or creme de menthe. My idea of decadence was something that made Jack Kerouac write to me when I was at Pilgrim State: "Lautreamont, cafe noir, sans sucre." I never actually became a junkie or anything like that, and I was probably really afraid of more serious drugs, so I sort of dabbled in safe affectations. Stanley Gould says that I talked my way into all these hospitals, that I gave them the impression of being sick without really being sick.

INT: Do you think you were helped by being in those hospitals?

CS: It was bad as far as my record goes.

INT: I don't mean that, but your general attitudes to life and yourself?

CS: Oh sure. At Pilgrim State, for instance, by urging wholesome things on me, a tame life, the attendant used to treat me like a solider and say to me "front and center." The psychologists tried to steer me away from the Beat Generation.

INT: Did you learn the lesson of psychiatry as being an adjustment, in front an acceptance of exactly what you were rebelling against? I would equate that with aging, with abandoning or forgetting youth.

CS: Well, I find myself in that position now.

INT: In Mishaps Perhaps, you claimed that your friends in 1949 made you assume the role of a "lunatic saint." Who did you mean specifically?

CS: Oh, Leni and that bunch, like Bob Reisner who was in my class at Brooklyn College, he wrote a book on graffiti. They thought that kind of thing was great. Reisner and I used to do many funny things, like I once pretended to be W. H. Auden at some exhibition, and there I was signing Auden's name.

INT: Somewhere in Mishaps Perhaps you mention that you were betrayed by Wilhelm Reich. I couldn't understand what you meant by that?

CS: I have this anger at anybody who has done anything against me or criticized me in any way. So now up in the Bronx I'm just the poor innocent who has returned completely healthy after being driven mad by the captious criticism of all the intellectuals in the Village with their Reich and all the rest of it. And also I go back to the days when I was in high school at James Monroe, where I was into Whitman who seemed to me to be the greatest poet, and all these others were into more sophisticated things like Eliot–but that wasn't so bad–the worst was that some of them were into more Reich. These same people were criticizing me as being overly naive about sexual matters, but to me they were trying to shock me, while generally mocking me.

INT: How did Junkie, Burroughs' first novel, get to you?

CS: My uncle, A. A. Wyn, was the publisher of Ace Books. He gave me a job, and I was trying to make a big impression, and Allen thought it was a great idea to bring out these writers, and if we could make Genet and these others well known to the American public we would be accomplishing something. I don't see what we've accomplished, but we were trying to do that anyway, to change the consciousness. It was largely an educational mission.

INT: And Wyn was interested in this project?

CS: Yes. I don't think he was primarily interested in the commercial end, I think he saw their possibilities as writers.

INT: Did Allen give you the manuscript of Junkie?

CS: We got it chapter by chapter from Burroughs in Mexico City. He would send them to Allen who brought them to me at Ace.

INT: That's about Burroughs' earliest writing, although I've read in correspondence up at Columbia University that he and Kerouac collaborated on a detective book right after World War II.

CS: He sent me another book, Queer.

INT: Why didn't that get published?

CS: My uncle and I didn't feel it was up to Junkie. That's never been published, but it probably should have been, especially for anybody interested in Burroughs' work. I once made him very angry because when he sent up Queer, I suggested that we should change the title to Fag, and Burroughs wrote back to Allen saying that he would cut my balls off because he made a distinction between the words, a fag being someone effeminate and a queer is a masculine type of homosexual.

INT: I have the hunch that parts of Queer may have found a way into Naked Lunch. Did you have any correspondence with Burroughs in later years?

CS: Yes, in Pilgrim State. He once sent me a cryptic note saying I should become a waiter. I didn't know whether he meant that I should wait until I was cured, or whether I should work in restaurants.

INT: He was opposed to psychoanalysis. He profoundly distrusts it.

CS: He probably did.

INT: In your preface to Junkie you call Burroughs a "curious adventurer."

CS: Because of things like his trip to the Amazon.

INT: As well as mental trips inside the mind. By the way, have you read his more recent work, The Wild Boys, for instance?

CS: I glanced at The Exterminator; I've been selling it. I'm a little wary of Burroughs now because he's into a kind of general espousal of youth revolt, and it's necessary for me in my present state to keep a very straight, pro-social, even patriotic outlook. During the Vietnam thing I participated in no protests; I voted for Procaccino, and I was on the verge of voting for Nixon, but I ended up voting for McGovern. But at the same time I'm doing crazy things like reading Marx.

INT: In Mishaps Perhaps you discuss–not in connection with Burroughs but with Surrealism–the impulse to make the ugly beautiful which is just the approach I am taking in my own attempts to describe Burroughs' fiction. You also deal with diabolism.

CS: All this is secondary, later than "The Report from the Asylum" which I still consider the clearest statement of my ideas–after that I was just trying to relate to my legend. That's where the diabolist stuff occurs.

INT: Then you have no chronology in your book because the "Report" is near the end?

CS: Yeah there aren't any dates. At the time I wrote "Report from the Asylum" I was very careful, and I used to edit closely, but I reached a phase where the whole thing got out of my control, sometimes agreeing to things I disliked out of weariness or confusion. Of course legally, I lost my rights in 1956 when I was committed to Pilgrim State.

INT: Getting back to your work as an editor at Ace, I understand that you were also at one time considering publishing Kerouac?

CS: We had paid him an advance of $500, and I had visions of myself as being his Maxwell Perkins and him being my Wolfe because his first novel resembled Wolfe.

INT: I read a letter you wrote to Kerouac at Columbia University Special Collections in which you said that the Wolfean aspect of The Town and the City was a charade that bespoke a repressed surrealism and a repressed homosexuality.

CS: I must have been very erudite in those days.

INT: What happened with the contract because Kerouac never published with Ace Books?

CS: Well, we rejected On the Road–he sent us this long scroll. My uncle said it looked like he took it from his trunk.

INT: The teletype roll. Did he get that from Lucien Carr at United Press?

CS: I don't know where he got it, but we were used to these neat manuscripts, and I thought, "Gee, I can't read this."

INT: You didn't accept it as a surrealist antic, then?

CS: Because at the same time I probably wasn't into that. I went through many phases while I was an editor: a Buddhist phase, then I read this book, Philosophy of a Lunatic, ultimately.

INT: Who wrote that?

CS: John Custance. Nobody has ever heard of the book but me. I bought it in the Gotham Book Mart while working for Ace Books. To me it seemed the ultimate mind-blowing thing, going beyond Zen which was a great step toward the elimination of myself. It was an existentialist version of Armageddon, the forces of God against the forces of the devil.

INT: What was Kerouac's attitude to publishers in general?

CS: Bad! He thought of them as skinflints, and he used the term "Broadway Sams"–he meant Jewish liberal intellectuals. He was snide about anybody who worked in offices.

INT: Was there any problem with getting Kerouac to make revisions?

CS: Yes. He got very angry when I wrote him suggestions.

INT: Did Kerouac send you anything after On the Road?

CS: Then I flipped and was sent to Pilgrim State. But the house continued to deal with him, and they accepted things, and then later reversed themselves.

INT: Did Kerouac try to interest you in publishing Cassady?

CS: He mentioned that Neal Cassady wrote, but he wasn't trying to get us to accept anything. That later became The First Third.

INT: Did you ever meet Neal Cassady?

CS: Oh yeah. When I came out of Columbia Psychiatric Allen wanted me to throw a New Year's Party. So I got a cold water flat on 17th Street and threw a party at which Neal Cassady was one of the star performers. He played one of those sweet potato things that make music, you know, and we were wearing those funny noses with the bebop eyeglasses.

INT: I've heard that Cassady had magnetic sexual appeal?

CS: Not to me.

INT: What was his appeal, then?

CS: He was always bouncing around–sort of kinetic energy more than anything else.

INT: What about his speech? His rambling monologues?

CS: He did one funny routine at the New Year's party, an Amos and Andy routine.

INT: He was influenced by radio?

CS: He knew a lot about popular culture. He was very American where a lot of us were rather frenchified.

INT: What kind of jobs have you worked in your life? In Mishaps Perhaps you have this anecdote about selling ice cream in front of the United Nations.

CS: That was after Howl had just come out, and I was considered to have gone mad again. I was working for Eskimo Ace. I've worked on ships as a messman, in the steward's department, as an editor, with books in bookstores, when I was sixteen on a farm in Smyrna, New York, where I shoveled manure and worked a horse drawn plow trying to make even furrows, and earlier, when I was fourteen I bundled the Sunday Times. I also worked for Nugent National Stores in the garment district, and delivered womens wear. When I met Allen we all worked in market research. I was married then, and my wife and I coded for N.O.R.C. John Holmes also worked there.

INT: Let's talk about your own writing. One of the qualities I love in it is your humor which is so often a function of epigram, puns and word play, like calling Poe's "The Raven", "the ravin". Or saying that if you lose contact with the zeitgeist, never fear, you may reach the poltergeist.

CS: The use of puns is not entirely natural to me. That was the Michaux influence.

INT: Can you find ways to sustain that humor in your own life?

CS: I've tried, but it's dropped off. Now my jokes are very bad. I've exhausted my humor, and can't work my brain to that extent because I have to be responsible for my own functioning.

INT: Do you feel that you were part of a movement?

CS: As matter of fact, I hadn't felt that. I had just been through with a movement, and I had an aversion to movements–after all I had just finished with Communists. I was living on 113th Street, and I knew this guy Don Cook, and he first mentioned the idea of a movement in reference to the Beats, and I was shocked–here I was trapped by something I had been trying to get away from!

Women and the Beat Generation

Ginsberg once had a dream in which he realized that the "social organization which is most true of itself to the artist is the boy gang," and in many ways the Beat writers were just that. The core Beat writers in the late 1940s were all young men–Kerouac, Ginsberg, Burroughs, and Holmes–and their biggest influences at the time were also men–Cassady, Huncke, Solomon, writers such as Dostoevsky and Proust, and musicians such as Charlie Parker and Dexter Gordon. Women for these writers were at best a peripheral interest. The narrator in Kerouac's On the Road *tends to categorize women as virgins (to be worshipped) or whores (to be lusted after). Real women, of course, were not excluded from the real-life scene: Kerouac was always close to his mother, and he told biographer Ann Charters that he wrote* On the Road *for his second wife. He wrote* Vanity of Duluoz *for his third and last wife. In addition, Carolyn Cassady was close enough to the center of activity to be able to write her memoirs, subtitled "My Years with Cassady, Kerouac, and Ginsberg."*

Anne Waldman in 1969. In 1975 she and Allen Ginsberg founded the Jack Kerouac School of Disembodied Poetics at the Naropa Institute in Boulder, Colorado (photograph by Ann Charters).

In her interview with Anne Waldman, Diane de Prima discusses the circumstances of her own life and the plight of a women writer in the 1950s.

Interview with Diane di Prima
Anne Waldman
Boulder, Colorado, July 1978

A: Maybe you can say something about raising 5 children basically on your own, without a strong father figure. It's rather unusual. Also, your children are quite extraordinary and you've come through with tremendous energy and work.

D: Well, I think I probably arranged, I mean I know I did with the first child, but I'm realizing now as I think about it, I probably arranged to not have too strong of a father around altogether, because I didn't want the interference in my own life and in my own process. In some sense, children never were that interference because they come into the world without any particular expectation. They expect to be fed and held, but they don't have any expectation about role. So you don't have to play up to someone's notion of what time dinner goes on the table. Whatever time dinner goes on the table, they'll eat it, and if they're hungry before that they learn very early to open the refrigerator. So, what happens is that given any man I've ever tried to live with there was always some particular notion of how we were going to do it, that I had to work with, or against. And I never got that kind of flack from the kids so I realize now I've probably from the beginning had a sense to avoid strong father figures, to avoid the patriarch. In the first case I simply knew I was ready to have a baby. My body was ready, and emotionally I was ready. I was 23 and I really wanted a child, and didn't especially want to live with a man. I was in a state from 13 to 23 of relative sexual freedom. I had the lovers I wanted, male and female, and there was a kind of coming and going. No one tried to own anyone else. This was, '53-'57, or thereabouts, and at that point I knew the last thing I wanted was to try to do a one-to-one relationship, so I got pregnant and I had a baby and let the dad know when the baby was about 4 months old. Being alone with one child was no trouble. She just went with me everywhere. When she was 2, I was

Diane di Prima, whose books include Dinners and Nightmares *(1961),* Memoirs of a Beatnik *(1969),* Revolutionary Letters *(1971), and* Loba *(1978).*

doing the stage-managing of the Living Theater for Jimmy Waring. She came to all the openings and all the parties and all the readings, that was no problem. The second time I had a child it was because I truly loved the man, and wanted that man's child. And so, against his will I brought a child into the world, a child that I very, very much wanted and have never for a second been sorry. But it was overwhelming to be alone with two children, in the sense I was also ill right then. In the sense that the relationship itself was overwhelming, in the sense there's a lot of repercussions in the world we both shared, the writing in New York. So after that I married. I lived with a married man who was gay and had two children with him. The relationship was more or less matter of fact, almost a contractual relationship, and a warm friendship. He's a very erratic man, but a basically warm person. And we'd made a whole lot of things happen that we really wanted to do. We did a theater together for 4 or 5 years in New York, bought presses and began the Poet's Press, moved a lot of work forward in the world, and that was one of the only times I did indeed have space to make writing rituals. I wrote a book of prose called The Calculus of Variation and then another one called Spring and Autumn Annuals. I also began some religious practices at that time, meditation and so on. If I had had at that point no children I probably would have gone off to a Zen monastery or something and a viable solution was this marriage with a gay man, where the sexuality was very seldom, and was intense when it happened, but in between I led a celibate writing life, which was exactly what I wanted and got a lot done in the arts I really cared about. And I think, moved some things forward in New York at the time, especially in theater. So that's two more of the kids, and the last of the kids I had with a man I loved–a young poet–and we had a very tender relationship. It wasn't a very viable one as time went on and so it came easily to an end at some point for me, and so that's five kids. One of the most amazing things for me was being at the birth of my grandchild, assisting my daughter while she was in labor and beginning to understand the kind of link that that is. The kind of link between mother and daughter, and what that is that you pass on and what that is that binds you together in way of common experience and support. At one point when the baby was crowning, he was just about to be out, Jeanne suddenly had a moment of panic and said, "I can't do this!" And, of course, various folks were rushing about and doing one thing and another, but, well, it became so clear, I simply said, "Your body already knows how to do it. Just let it." And this is the information I have, finally, you know. And this is what I pass on to a daughter, and this began for me to be a whole different understanding of what is between us–not that I didn't always know that we had childbirth in common and all that, but somehow the mother-daughter link is very interesting to me now.

. . . .

AW: Has male energy and consciousness been dominating the poetry scene or do you find you can work with that energy? Have you had trouble getting your own work published in N.Y. for example, in a big publishing house which are on the whole dominated by male editors?

DD: Over the years, let's say for the first 10 or 15 years I never really realized one way or the other or cared that much about what was going on in that way. It wasn't an issue for me. It's only more recently I've come to spend any time realizing or thinking about the fact that indeed if the body of work that I had done, have done, or say had done by the time in '63 when The New Hand Book of Heaven was out and The Calculus of Variation was finished had been done by any of the male writers on that scene at that point, we won't name names, who were my close friends, I think that the acknowledgment that a body of work indeed was in progress would have been much greater. But, in those days, I was just expecting trouble all around, so it never occurred to me. I just kind of grew up with a tough back to the wall, ready-to-fight-anybody attitude. I can't really say why. It seems that the particular kind of head I had and the particular kind of demand I made on the world having never been fulfilled as a child and so on, made one grow up fighting, So that I didn't distinguish which of these things is happening because I'm a woman, which of these things is happening because that's just the way the world is, and there was a lot of that's just how the world is, don't forget, in the air in the '50's, too. We all expected the worst. All of us . . . it's the Jean-Paul Sartre era. We all expected something terrible. But, indeed, yes, I'm sure that a lot of stuff, a lot of like not getting published, is traceable to that. There's another thing there, which is not only am I a woman, but I'm a particular kind of woman–I'm not apologetic. I'm not sad, you know, if . . . Maybe if I was drinking a lot and writing miserable poems about some man and trying to kill myself every three years, maybe that would be okay, because, that makes guys feel okay, too, you know. But, I think it is that I've actually had the balls to enjoy myself. I'm a woman, I've enjoyed myself. My politics is ridiculous, it's not establishment politics. And, although my parents were sort of on the lower edge of the middle class, I'm definitely a street person. All my first writing was completely predicated on getting the slang of N.Y. in the period in the early '50's, down on paper somehow or another. And to this day, Loba may go through several worlds, but my sympathies lie with the street. I can't really untangle what's class prejudice and what's sex prejudice and what's the natural desire of the ruling class to maintain its position. All those things are in there. I didn't even go to college. I left after a year, you know. But, so then, the question is, it's a male dominated scene, the literary scene? Yes, and women are just beginning to get a place in it and I think your generation is the first generation of women that has had access to the information that makes you a proficient writer. Don't forget, however great your visioning and your inspiration, you need the techniques of the craft, and there's no where, really, to get them because these are not passed on in schools. They are passed on person to person, and back then the male naturally passed them on to the male, I think maybe I was one of the first people to break through that in having deep conversations with Charles Olson and so on. And Frank O'Hara. Robert Duncan and I are now conversing on those levels. I'm learning a lot from him these days.

What I learned from Allen Ginsberg was to have confidence in my own spontaneity, more than technical information. I'm talking about things like what's happened with the syntax, what's happened with the line, and also stuff like how do we get to the source material that will shape the new vision for the time. Have you read Nilsson's book on the primitive orders of the time? That kind of stuff was passed on mainly man to man. So, this is the first time there is a really skilled generation of women writers, I think. Not only with a lot to say, but with really the tools to say it. But in my day it was still a question of women just not writing as well. And the fact was, just like with the black children in my neighborhood in school, they were never given the tools to write well with. So, it's a mixed question. I can't say a lot of really great women writers were ignored in my time, but I can say a lot of potentially great women writers wound up dead or crazy. I think of the women on the Beat scene with me in the early '50's, where are they right now? I know Barbara Moraff is a potter and does some writing in Vermont, and that's about all I know. I know some of them OD'ed and some of them got nuts, and one woman that I was running around the Village with in '53 was killed by her parents putting her in a shock treatment place in Pennsylvania, that promised your loved one back to you in three weeks cured. What the parents really wanted was the illegitimate child she had had so they could raise it without making the same mistakes they'd made with her. This was the kind of general atmosphere we were up against. I don't want to rant on about individual cases, but the threat of incarceration or early death in one form or another was very real. A friend and a writer in my crowd were threatened with jail because the parent of one of them discovered that a homosexual affair between the two women was in progress. We were all under threat of being dragged into court for that. This was daily life. I remember sitting on the steps of a house on the lower East Side about a year after I left school and hearing the news of the death of the Rosenbergs. There was a way in which we didn't even dare reach out for too many tools. We wrote the way Virginia Woolf describes Jane Austin hiding her papers under the tablecloth. We really wanted to stay inconspicuous. Most of us. I was a brash little brat. Probably why I'm still alive!

Joyce Johnson, who wrote about her love affair with Jack Kerouac and involvement in the circle of Beat writers in the 1950s in her 1984 memoir, Minor Characters *(photograph by Ann Charters)*

A: I was just going to ask you how you survived.

D: I bluffed a lot. I was very angry. I had enough anger to carry me through almost anything, and I learned how to use it. I was real determined to survive. I never assumed a barrier because I was a woman with anybody that I wanted to know, or any group of people I wanted to associate with. And I didn't necessarily have to associate with them sexually. They were mostly men. I merely assumed I could go where I wanted and do what I wanted.

A: Were you nervous or self-conscious about sending poems to Ezra Pound?

D: A little bit, sure. And they weren't very good poems. He was very sweet about them. This was in '52. I'm sure they weren't very good poems.

A: How did he respond?

D: He wrote me back, right away, and wrote they seem (underlined) to be well written, but no one was ever much use as a critic of the younger generation. And that was the basis on which we went on with our correspondence. Finally I went to visit him. I find now one of the most deadening, killing, and stultifying things that is offered is homage and admiration from the young as opposed to just love and peership and friendship. Duncan once said that if you want to kill an artist, flatter him, but I think if there's no homage, there's also no hostility. Most of the poets and dancers and painters were older than I in those days, and were a lot of my survival because they were a huge protective network. I think a lot of Franz Kilne as a hovering presence protecting all of us, young writers. I think a lot of what helped me to get to the place where I could receive protection and receive the information they had to offer was the love I had for them overrode any awe I had. So it was never just a question of admiration involved. It was a real hug and a shared dinner.

A: But do you think the poetic community now parallels that community you had in the '50's and '60's? Doesn't it seem less intimate now? Everybody's informed even in incredibly out of the way places through the network that's been built up in the last two decades of reading circuits and little magazines, and so on. Don't you think it might be a little discouraging for a younger writer, the overkill?

D: Folks really have to know themselves what to do. Who else can know for them, right? No one else knew for us, but I know that many writers are discouraged because although it's easy to get published, it's not easy to get read. Nobody reads all these magazines that everybody publishes. I'm sure you have students you feel are very fine; I do. And my sense of it is they shouldn't publish. They should hang back 6 or 8 years anyway, of good writing's worth before they burst into that and then have something really solid–get a good book together and not worry so much about the magazines. But there isn't just a small elite creating art now and that's great! It should be that everyone makes art. It should be part of daily life in every village in America as it was in every tribe everywhere. That means that at some point some fine artist in one place emerges and goes to another village and exchanges songs with fine singers there. I urge people to form workshops and situations within their own community. Start working at home.

And I think each piece of this country has its own forms for all the arts. Certainly in poetry, the middle west the poetry is different than the poetry of either coast, and the two coasts don't have that much in common really anymore. That should be a local art, and I think there should be a universal attention on the part of the artists. I mean, they should read stuff from everywhere, but the art still remains a local art. How you filter that stuff back through is yours, you know.

A: The tribal situation was interesting. There was a place for the poet, it was completely natural. And somebody else wove cloth or made pottery and somebody else gathered food and so on. There was a functioning mandala. And somewhere along the way that broke down. Ezra Pound would blame it all on "usury." But in the last ten years there's been more of a demand for the poet. Do you think poetry is essential to life? Or is it just some kind of refinement or distillation of life that can parallel whatever else is happening?

D: I think the poet is the last person who is still speaking the truth when no one else dares to. I think the poet is the first person to begin the shaping and visioning of the new forms and the new consciousness when no one else has begun to sense it, so that there's both of those happening all the time. I think these are two of the most essential human functions. Pound once said, "Artists are the antennae of the race." Whether or not we have an audience, this strong visioning and shaping of a master poem informs the conscience of generations to come. And we see very dramatically in our time how without even reaching that high plane, like Dante or Shakespeare, the work of Allen and Kerouac in the '50's and so on has informed the '70's.

Chapter 2
The Beats in the West

Neal Cassady invited Ginsberg and Kerouac to visit him after he moved to San Francisco with his second wife, Carolyn. Both men visited at different times and stayed for extended periods. At one point Carolyn threw Ginsberg, who was interested in pursuing a love relationship with Neal, out of the house. However, Kerouac, who had an affair with Carolyn, apparently with Neal's blessing, did some of his best writing in the attic of the Cassadys' house. In any case, Kerouac and Ginsberg got to know other writers and poets in the San Francisco area, including Gary Snyder, Michael McClure, Phillip Whalen, Philip Lamantia and the leading literary figure, Kenneth Rexroth. In October 1955 the Six Gallery reading, at which Ginsberg read his breakthrough poem "Howl," launched the San Francisco poetry renaissance.

The Beat Generation writers rose to a level of prominence in San Francisco far beyond that which they had been able to achieve in New York City. San Francisco's North Beach neighborhood was suitably bohemian and ethnic, harboring Chinatown and Little Italy, and the mixing of east coast and west coast writers created a dynamic literary community. Lawrence Ferlinghetti's City Lights bookstore became a mecca for both writers and readers, and his City Lights Books published Ginsberg's Beat manifesto Howl and Other Poems. *San Francisco gained further notoriety as a Beat Generation city when the subsequent obscenity trial for Ginsberg's book was held there. The city was also the setting for Kerouac's novel* The Subterraneans *(1958).*

The Reading at Six Gallery

Allen Ginsberg and Gary Snyder promoted the "6 Poets at 6 Gallery" reading in part by sending postcard invitations. The "small collection for wine" they requested was given to Kerouac, who rushed out for gallon jugs of red wine shortly before the reading began. Kerouac, who encouraged the poets by cheering them on as if he were at a jazz club, and Neal Cassady, dressed in his railroad brakeman's uniform, were part of an audience that numbered well more than one hundred.

Rexroth, who produced a weekly radio show in San Francisco that promoted local writers, participated as one the readers and served as master of ceremonies at the reading. Kerouac biographer Gerald Nicosia described Rexroth as "a middle-aged Chicago poet transplanted to San Francisco, where he held a salon for anarchists and maverick writers" and was "beloved as a 'hip square' and general sponsor of talent."

In an interview for Jack's Book, *Ginsberg recalls the occasion when he, Gary Snyder, Philip Whalen, Philip Lamantia, Michael McClure, and Kenneth Rexroth read in painter Wally Hedrick's gallery at Union and Fillmore Streets in San Francisco on 7 October 1955.*

The Six Gallery reading had come about when Wally Hedrick, who was a painter and one of the major people there, asked Rexroth if he knew any poets that would put on a reading. Maybe Rexroth asked McClure to organize it and McClure didn't know how or didn't have time. Rexroth asked me, so I met McClure and Rexroth suggested I go visit another poet who was living in Berkeley, which was Gary. So I went right over to Gary's house and immediately had a meeting of minds with him over William Carlos Williams, 'cause I had written *Empty Mirror* at that time and he had begun *Myths and Texts,* or *The Berry Feast,* or something, and he told me about his friend Philip Whalen who was due in town the next day. And I told him about my friend Kerouac who was in town that day, and within three or four days we all met. . . .

Jack and I were coming from Berkeley, and had just arrived in San Francisco at the Key System Terminal, the bus terminal there, and we met right out on First and Mission, by accident. Gary was with Phil and I was with Jack, and we all went off immediately and started talking. And then Philip Lamantia was in town, whom I'd known from '48 in New York, and then there was Michael McClure. So there was a whole complement of poets. Then Gary and I decided we ought to invite Rexroth to be the sixth–sixth poet–to introduce at the Six Gallery, be the elder, since he had linked us up.

–*Jack's Book,* pp. 198–199

Kenneth Rexroth reading his work. He is faced by Ruth Witt-Diamant, the director of the Poetry Center at San Francisco State College.

Kerouac evoked the Six Gallery reading in his novel The Dharma Bums *(1958). He fictionalized the names of the participants: Gary Snyder becomes Japhy Ryder; Allen Ginsberg, Alvah Goldbook; Kenneth Rexroth, Rheinhold Cacoethes; Philip Whalen, Warren Coughlin; Philip Lamantia, Francis DaPavia; and Michael McClure, Ike O'Shea. Lamantia read the work of the late John Hoffman, who Kerouac here identifies as Altman.*

. . . It was a great night, a historic night in more ways than one. Japhy Ryder and some other poets (he also wrote poetry and translated Chinese and Japanese poetry into English) were scheduled to give a poetry reading at the Gallery Six in town. They were all meeting in the bar and getting high. But as they stood and sat around I saw that he was the only one who didn't look like a poet, though poet he was indeed. The other poets were either hornrimmed intellectual hepcats with wild black hair like Alvah Goldbook, or delicate pale handsome poets like Ike O'Shay (in a suit), or out-of-this-world genteel-looking Renaissance Italians like Francis DaPavia (who looks like a young priest), or a bow-tied wild-haired old anarchist fuds like Rheinhold Cacoethes, or big fat bespectacled quiet booboos like Warren Coughlin. And all the other hopeful poets were standing around, in various costumes, worn-at-the-sleeves corduroy jackets, scuffly shoes, books sticking out of their pockets. . . .

Anyway, I followed the whole gang of howling poets to the reading at Gallery Six that night, which was, among other important things, the night of the birth of the San Francisco Poetry Renaissance. Everyone was there. It was a mad night. And I was the one who got things jumping by going around collecting dimes and quarters from the rather stiff audience standing around in the gallery and coming back with three huge gallon jugs of California Burgundy and getting them all piffed so that by eleven o'clock when Alvah Goldbook was reading his, wailing his poem "Wail" drunk with arms outspread everybody was yelling "Go! Go! Go!" (like a jam session) and old Rheinhold Cacoethes the father of the Frisco poetry scene was wiping his tears in gladness. Japhy himself read his fine poems about Coyote the God of the North American Plateau Indians (I think), at least the God of the Northwest Indians, Kwakiutl and whatall. "Fuck you! sang Coyote, and ran away!" read Japhy to the distinguished audience, making them all howl with joy, it was so pure, fuck being a dirty word that comes out clean. And he had his tender lyrical lines, like the ones about bears eating berries, showing his love of animals, and great mystery lines about oxen on the Mongolian road showing his knowledge of Oriental literature even on to Hsuan Tsung the great Chinese monk who walked from China to Tibet, Lanchow to Kashgar and Mongolia carrying a stick of incense in his hand. Then Japhy showed his sudden barroom humor with lines about Coyote bringing goodies. And his anarchistic ideas about how Americans

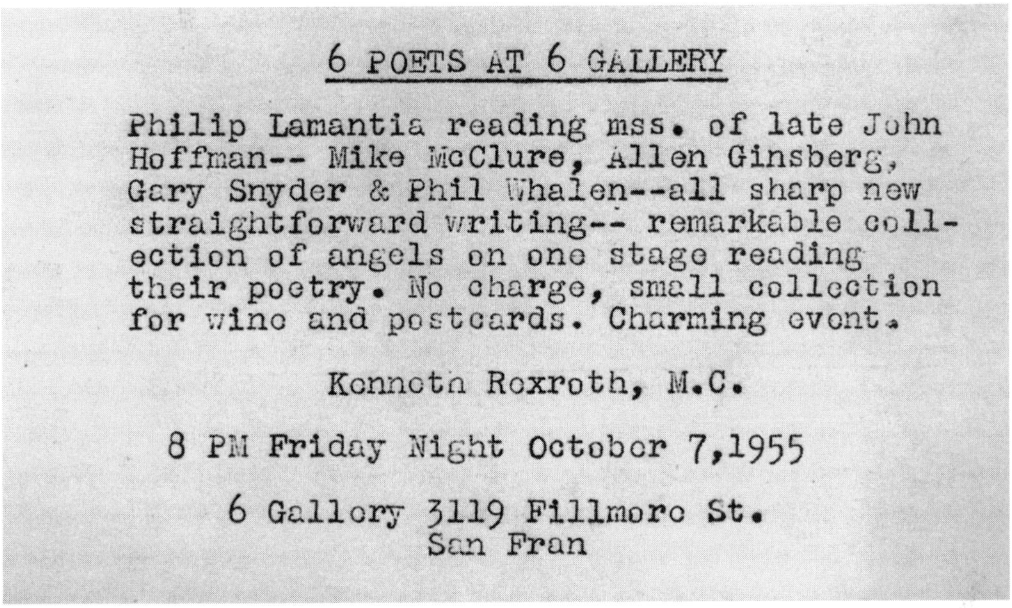

6 POETS AT 6 GALLERY

Philip Lamantia reading mss. of late John Hoffman-- Mike McClure, Allen Ginsberg, Gary Snyder & Phil Whalen--all sharp new straightforward writing-- remarkable collection of angels on one stage reading their poetry. No charge, small collection for wine and postcards. Charming event.

Kenneth Rexroth, M.C.

8 PM Friday Night October 7,1955

6 Gallery 3119 Fillmore St.
San Fran

Invitation for a reading that energized the San Francisco literary scene

Michael McClure, one of the six poets at the Six Gallery, described the setting in his recollection of the reading.

The Six Gallery was a huge room that had been converted from an automobile repair shop into an art gallery. Someone had knocked together a little dais and was exhibiting sculptures by Fred Martin at the back of it–pieces of orange crates that had been swathed in muslin and dipped in plaster of paris to make splintered, sweeping shapes like pieces of surrealist furniture. A hundred and fifty enthusiastic people had come to hear us. Money was collected and jugs of wine were brought back for the audience. I hadn't seen Allen in a few weeks and I had not heard *Howl*–it was new to me. Allen began in a small and intensely lucid voice. At some point Jack Kerouac began shouting "GO" in cadence as Allen read it. In all of our memories no one had been so outspoken in poetry before–we had gone beyond a point of no return–and we were ready for it, for a point of no return. None of us wanted to go back to the gray, chill, militaristic silence, to the intellective void–to the land without poetry–to the spiritual drabness. We wanted to make it new and we wanted to invent it and the process of it as we went into it. We wanted voice and we wanted vision.

– *Scratching the Beat Surface,* p. 13

don't know how to live, with lines about commuters being trapped in living rooms that come from poor trees felled by chainsaws (showing here, also, his background as a logger up north). This voice was deep and resonant and somehow brave, like the voice of oldtime American heroes and orators. Something earnest and strong and humanly hopeful I liked about him, while the other poets were either too dainty in their aestheticism, or too hysterically cynical to hope for anything, or too abstract and indoorsy, or too political, or like Coughlin too incomprehensible to understand (big Coughlin saying things about "unclarified processes" though where Coughlin did say that revelation was a personal thing I noticed the strong Buddhist and idealistic feeling of Japhy, which he'd shared with goodhearted Coughlin in their buddy days at college, as I had shared mine with Alvah in the Eastern scene and with others less apocalyptical and straighter but in no sense more sympathetic and tearful).

Meanwhile scores of people stood around in the darkened gallery straining to hear every word of the amazing poetry reading as I wandered from group to group, facing them and facing away from the stage, urging them to glug a slug from the jug, or wandered back and sat on the right side of the stage giving out little wows and yesses of approval and even whole sentences of comment with nobody's invitation but in the general gaiety nobody's disapproval either. It was a great night. Delicate Francis DaPavia read, from delicate onionskin yellow pages, or pink, which he kept flipping carefully with long white fingers, the poems of his dead chum Altman who'd eaten too much peyote in Chihuahua (or died of polio, one) but read none of his own poems—a charming elegy in itself to the memory of the dead young poet, enough to draw tears from the Cervantes of Chapter Seven, and read them in a delicate Englishy voice that had me crying with inside laughter though I later got to know Francis and liked him. . . .

Between poets, Rheinhold Cacoethes, in his bow tie and shabby old coat, would get up and make a little funny speech in his snide funny voice and introduce the next reader; but as I say come eleven-thirty when all the poems were read and everybody was milling around wondering what had happened and what would come next in American poetry, he was wiping his eyes with his handkerchief.

—*The Dharma Bums*, pp. 10–16

Lawrence Ferlinghetti

Lawrence Ferlinghetti

Born on 24 March 1919 in Yonkers, New York, and educated at the Sorbonne in Paris, Lawrence Ferlinghetti moved in 1951 to San Francisco, where he contributed significantly to the publishing of poetry in America. In June 1953 he and a partner opened the City Lights Pocket Book Shop. Ever since its doors opened, City Lights Books, at 261 North Beach Avenue, has been a mecca for writers and readers of the American avant-garde. Within a year, Ferlinghetti was the sole owner of the business, which he expanded by starting an alternative press, modeled partially on New Directions in New York and partially on the small presses he had seen in Paris. City Lights Books featured inexpensive, pocket-size volumes of poetry. The first book published by the press was Ferlinghetti's own Pictures of the Gone World *(1955). The most successful City Lights book, though, is Allen Ginsberg's* Howl and Other Poems *(1956). Ferlinghetti attended the famous reading held at the Six Gallery on 7 October 1955, at which Ginsberg first read early portions of* Howl *to a wildly receptive audience.* Howl and Other Poems *enjoyed popularity in San Francisco, but it achieved a nationwide reputation when it was seized by United States customs officials en route from England, where the first edition was printed. After Ferlinghetti published another edition printed in the United States, he and his bookstore clerk were arrested and charged with selling obscene material. The American Civil Liberties Union defended City Lights, and after a celebrated court battle that further boosted the book's renown,* Howl *was declared not obscene.* Howl and Other Poems *went on to become one of the best-selling books of poetry in America, and the success of City Lights Books was assured.*

Ferlinghetti's City Lights published the work of other Beat writers, including Jack Kerouac, Gregory Corso, William Burroughs, Diane di Prima, and Bob Kaufman. Years later, Ginsberg described his relationship with Ferlinghetti: "We had a very good arrangement. If he needed more money one year I would give him a larger percentage. We didn't even have a contract for Howl *until the very end. It turned out nobody could find a contract. We had a friendship agreement, and it worked for practically thirty years." Ferlinghetti is more than a successful publisher; one of his own volumes of poetry,* A Coney Island of the Mind *(1958), has sold well and has never gone out of print. He has written a dozen books of poetry, as well as plays and two novels. As for his role as publisher, Ferlinghetti once said, "The function of the small press is discovery."*

Ferlinghetti's City Lights Book Shop in San Francisco has been popular with readers and writers since it was founded in 1953.

Ferlinghetti and poet Gregory Corso in San Francisco, 1969

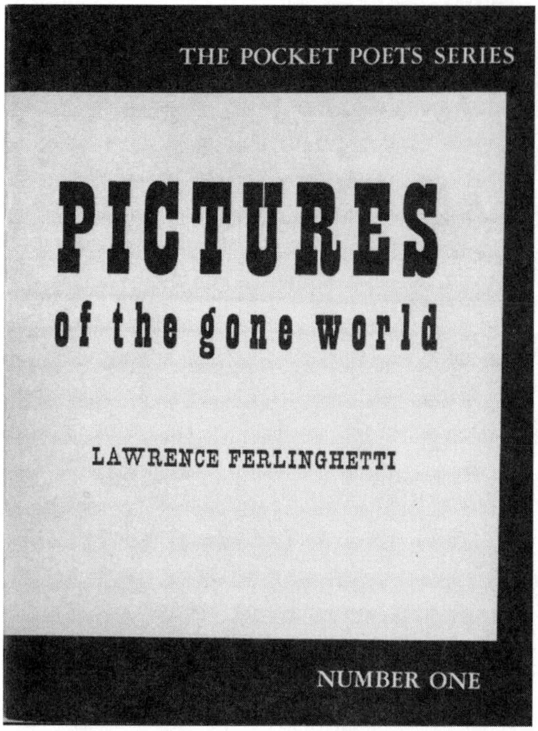

The first volume in the City Lights Books Pocket Poets Series, a collection of Ferlinghetti's poetry published in 1955 (left), and his best-known book of poetry, published by James Laughlin's New Directions in 1958

Ferlinghetti's Poetry

I am waiting for the day
that maketh all things clear
and I am awaiting retribution
for what America did
to Tom Sawyer
and I am waiting
for the American Boy
to take off Beauty's clothes
and get on top of her
and I am waiting
for Alice in Wonderland
to retransmit to me
her total dream of innocence
and I am waiting
for Childe Roland to come
to the final darkest tower
and I waiting
for Aphrodite
to grow live arms
at a final disarmament conference
in a new rebirth of wonder

–first stanza of "I Am Waiting,"
A Coney Island of the Mind, p. 4

Interviews

Ferlinghetti revealed his disdain for conventional biography in an interview.

Who's Who sent a questionnaire form and for several years I wrote "Fuck you!" on the *Who's Who* questionnaire, and sent it back to them. But they are very persistent people and they keep writing and they keep saying, "If you don't answer this, we will publish something about you which may not be correct–so you may as well correct this"–so you get involved correcting a column of type that they have written about you that they have scrounged from other sources. I make up a lot of things.

Was I probably born in 1919 or 1920 in either Paris or New York? Some days it's hard to tell. I really don't see the reason for giving a straight answer. For one thing, I enjoy putting on *Who's Who.* I have done this with a lot of different interviewers, since it is valid for a poet who considers himself a semi-surrealist poet.

If you are going to write in one manner and someone comes to you with some straight questions–why should you give them a straight answer?

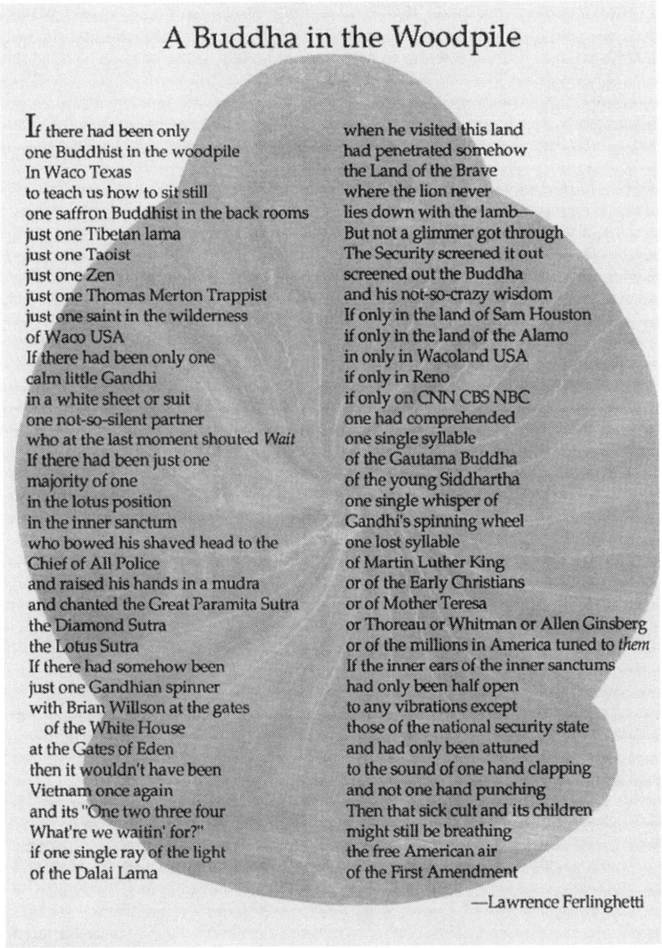

A Buddha in the Woodpile

If there had been only
one Buddhist in the woodpile
In Waco Texas
to teach us how to sit still
one saffron Buddhist in the back rooms
just one Tibetan lama
just one Taoist
just one Zen
just one Thomas Merton Trappist
just one saint in the wilderness
of Waco USA
If there had been only one
calm little Gandhi
in a white sheet or suit
one not-so-silent partner
who at the last moment shouted *Wait*
If there had been just one
majority of one
in the lotus position
in the inner sanctum
who bowed his shaved head to the
Chief of All Police
and raised his hands in a mudra
and chanted the Great Paramita Sutra
the Diamond Sutra
the Lotus Sutra
If there had somehow been
just one Gandhian spinner
with Brian Willson at the gates
  of the White House
at the Gates of Eden
then it wouldn't have been
Vietnam once again
and its "One two three four
What're we waitin' for?"
if one single ray of the light
of the Dalai Lama
when he visited this land
had penetrated somehow
the Land of the Brave
where the lion never
lies down with the lamb—
But not a glimmer got through
The Security screened it out
screened out the Buddha
and his not-so-crazy wisdom
If only in the land of Sam Houston
if only in the land of the Alamo
in only in Wacoland USA
if only in Reno
if only on CNN CBS NBC
one had comprehended
one single syllable
of the Gautama Buddha
of the young Siddhartha
one single whisper of
Gandhi's spinning wheel
one lost syllable
of Martin Luther King
or of the Early Christians
or of Mother Teresa
or Thoreau or Whitman or Allen Ginsberg
or of the millions in America tuned to *them*
If the inner ears of the inner sanctums
had only been half open
to any vibrations except
those of the national security state
and had only been attuned
to the sound of one hand clapping
and not one hand punching
Then that sick cult and its children
might still be breathing
the free American air
of the First Amendment

—Lawrence Ferlinghetti

Postcard of a Ferlinghetti poem, first published in Tricycle *magazine in 1993*

For instance, there was a very serious French professor from the Sorbonne who did a long serious book on American poets, and he interviewed me on tape. He asked me what my thesis was at the Sorbonne–what my doctor's thesis was there. I told him that it was the history of the pissoir in French literature. The interview was in French. And he wrote it all down and it came out in the book that my doctoral thesis at the Sorbonne was called *The History of the Pissoir in French Literature.* [The actual title was *The City as Symbol in Modern Poetry: In Search of a Metropolitan Tradition.*] He is really pissed now. He found out. They'll have to change the index cards in the Sorbonne where the damn thing is filed. Maybe the place will be burnt down in the next revolution. That would help.

–*The San Francisco Poets,* p. 152

Ferlinghetti commented on the writing voice of Kerouac and Ginsberg in Jack's Book.

I really didn't have a chance at publishing Kerouac's novels for quite a long time. Much later I could have published *Visions of Neal.* But we were such a small press that we didn't have the money to put out a great big book like that. I felt that really was out of our range.

But Jack was oriented to getting published in New York. We were just another little two-bit poetry press, printing a thousand copies or fifteen hundred copies of a little book of poetry. I read *Mexico City Blues* in manuscript and *San Francisco Blues,* too. By hindsight, now I can see there was a lot of opportunity to be a really big publisher right there, but we were struggling to have a bookstore.

I didn't used to think very highly of Jack's poetry. I had the manuscript of *Mexico City Blues* and could have published it, but it just didn't turn me on very much. I don't know why. I wasn't really tuned in to his voice enough. Now I can see it was all the same voice. I think he was a better novel writer than a poem writer. I'm putting it that way because it seems to me that the writing he did was all one, whether it was in the topography of poetry or in the topography of prose. It was the same kind of writing. If it were read aloud it sounded the same. It was poetry and vice versa. Right there the line between poetry and prose broke down.

It's the same with Ginsberg. On the manuscript of *The Fall of America,* when I was editing that, Allen wrote and said, "Do any of these poems strike you as poems that are not as good as the others, and some that are weaker than the others?" I wrote back and said, "Allen, once one starts digging your voice, no matter what comes out of your mouth, it's going to be as good as any other part because it's your whole voice that's coming across. If mind is comely, then everything that comes out of mind is going to be comely." When the mind is interesting, then anything that comes out of the mind is interesting. The trouble with so many poets that follow Ginsberg's poetics is that they don't have essentially very interesting minds, so it comes out really boring.

Later I got tuned into Jack's voice more, so that no matter what he said or wrote, it added up and sounded great.

–pp. 270–271

Ferlinghetti's autobiographical volume, published in 1960

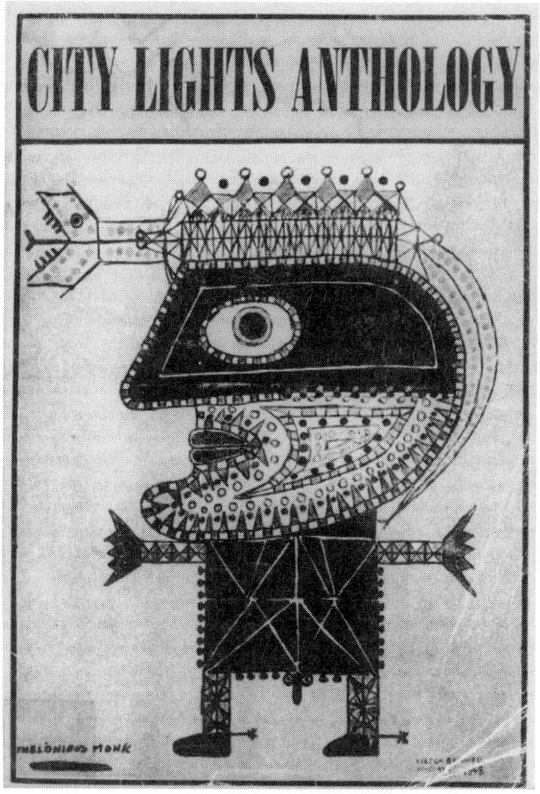

Cover for a 1974 collection including work by Ginsberg, Kerouac, Ferlinghetti, Diane di Prima, Jack Micheline, Charles Bukowski, Gary Snyder, Robert Creeley, Richard Brautigan, Michael McClure, Charles Upton, Jean Genet, and Arthur Rimbaud

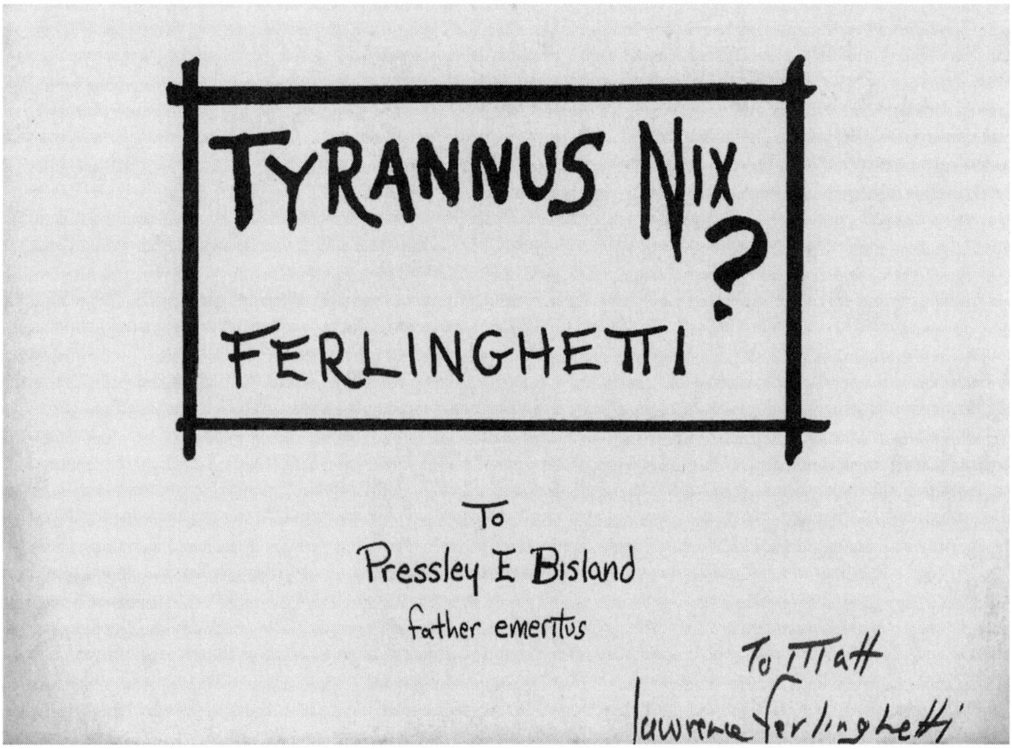

Signed title page for Ferlinghetti's 1969 book of poetry attacking President Richard M. Nixon (Collection of Matt Theado)

The Music of Kerouac and Cassady

In this letter to the Kerouac fan magazine Moody Street Irregulars *(Summer 1986), Carolyn Cassady agrees with a critic's negative response to the musical score for the movie* Heart Beat, *which was loosely based on her memoirs. In her letter she recounts the music that she, Neal, and Jack enjoyed.*

Dear Joel Scherzer,

I cheered your comments on the Jack Nitzsche score for the deplorable film, *Heart Beat.* Some of the fault must lie with John Byrum, I suspect, who mesmerized everyone into his interpretation of "my" story, except me and Mr. and Mrs. Jack Fisk.

When I first received the script and had recovered enough from the shock and dismay (to put it very mildly), I was compelled to send them scenes I set down from the true events which had dramatic effects–Alan Griesman having stated in print that "*No*body's real life is dramatic enough from cinema." Included with these scenes were suggestions for some of the musical numbers that not only had been an integral part of the events but would also enhance the sense of period and deepen the dramatic mood.

Some of them that come to mind are:

1. Anything by the younger Lester Young, for he was the cause of my meeting Neal in the first place.
2. Benny Goodman's "Sing, Sing, Sing" was played enthusiastically for me by Neal in a record booth on the day we met; neither of us ever forgot *that.*
3. "Peg O' My Heart," an accidental part of his wooing, not only of me but of my interest in auto racing.
4. Soon after meeting Jack in Denver, the record on the juke box we danced to, believe it or not, was "Too Close for Comfort."
5. Billie Holiday's "No Good Man" and the flip side, "Good Morning, Heartache," routinely played respectively night and morning when Neal was off on the first road.
6. Helen Hume's "He May Be Your Man But He Comes To See Me Sometimes." We didn't own

the record, but, whenever we'd hear it together we were both amused by the irony. I could be even that objective occasionally! One line in particular was all too apt: ". . . 'cause if he flags my train, I'm shore gonna let him ride."

7. Jack's crooning of "A Foggy Day in London Town" and "Funny Valentine" are among those that recall intimate moments between us.
8. When Jack and Neal would talk together in an excited way with rapid-fire glee, I equate the sound with Dizzy Gillespie's "Salt Peanuts."

Well-documented is Jack's taste in jazz which Neal shared, although I think Neal was more taken by the Bop style than was Jack. Both of them enjoyed a wide range of all kinds of music, but our radio was set at either Pat Henry on KJAZ or Jumpin' George on a station whose call letters I've forgotten. Rarely mentioned has been Stan Kenton, a great favorite, and by whose strains of "Artistry in Rhythm" and the others in that series I was taught the fine points of pot-smoking by Neal. Vocalists who warble consistently through my memory include, of course, Sinatra, Mel Torme, Ella, both Dinahs, Julie Christie, Al Hibler, Joe Williams, Pearl Bailey, Anita O'Day, and even Helen O'Connell's "Green Eyes," among the hosts of others less well-known. Soon after we got our first TV in 1954, I found it hard to credit Neal's insistence on tuning in Patti Page every evening, although I'm not convinced it was her singing alone that kept him on the edge of his seat.

Both Jack and Neal loved mambos, and we even managed to raise the price of a ticket and engineer a night out to go to a concert by our favorite, Prez Prado, the little jumping bean even more fun to watch.

Our children can better testify to Neal's favorites in the Chubby Checker, Buddy Holly eras and beyond, and, as often noted, Neal's tastes in later years were perhaps more varied than Jack's. If Neal had favorites or priorities, who knows; he said "yes" to almost everything.

Other musicians and performers and tunes lap at the shores of memory, and I'm sure I'll capture important ones as soon as I mail this, but from this vast pool what a wonderfully complementary score could have been selected for a film. Still, one thing to be said for Byrum's–it was consistent.

–Carolyn Cassady

In a telegram to Allen Ginsberg immediately after the "Six Gallery" reading, Lawrence Ferlinghetti echoes Ralph Waldo Emerson's words to Walt Whitman after reading Leaves of Grass *one hundred years earlier.*

I greet you at the beginning of a great career. When do I get the manuscript?

The San Francisco Scene

Poet Richard Eberhart wrote an overview of the San Francisco poetry scene that brought notice of Ginsberg and the other poets to readers in New York–as well as across the country.

West Coast Rhythms
Richard Eberhart
New York Times Book Review, 2 September 1956

The West Coast is the liveliest spot in the country in poetry today. It is only here that there is a radical group movement of young poets. San Francisco teems with young poets.

Part of this activity is due to the establishment of the Poetry Center at San Francisco State College three years ago. Its originator and moving spirit is Ruth Witt-Diamant, who began by offering readings by local poets and progressed to importing older poets from the East. She hopes next to stimulate the writing of verse drama.

Part of the activity of the young group has been inspired by Kenneth Rexroth, whose presence in San Francisco over a long period of time, embodying his force and convictions, creates a rallying point of ideas, interest and informal occasions. The influence of Kenneth Patchen is also felt by this group. Robinson Jeffers looms as a timeless figure down the Coast. . . .

In the Bay region there are several poetry readings each week. They may be called at the drop of a hat. A card may read "Celebrated Good Time–Poetry Night. Either you go home bugged or completely enlightened. Allen Ginsberg blowing hot; Gary Snyder blowing cool; Philip Whalen puffing the laconic tuba; Mike McClure his hip highnotes; Rexroth on the big bass drum. Small collection for wine and postcards . . . abandon, noise, strange pictures on walls, oriental music, lurid poetry. Extremely serious. Town Hall theatre. One and only final appearance of this apocalypse. Admission free."

Hundreds from about 16 to 30 may show up and engage in an authentic, free-wheeling celebration of poetry, an analogue of which was jazz thirty years ago. The audience participates, shouting and stamping, interrupting and applauding. Poetry here has become a tangible social force, moving and unifying its auditors,

Chinatown in San Francisco, where the Six Gallery poets gathered after their reading to celebrate the event

releasing the energies of the audience through spoken, even shouted verse, in a way at present unique to this region. . . .

The most remarkable poem of the young group, written during the past year, is "Howl," by Allen Ginsberg, a 29-year-old poet who is the son of Louis Ginsberg, a poet known to newspaper readers in the East. Ginsberg comes from Brooklyn; he studied at Columbia; after years of apprenticeship to usual forms, he developed his brave new medium. This poem has created a furor of praise or abuse whenever read or heard. It is a powerful work, cutting through to dynamic meaning. Ginsberg thinks he is going forward by going back to the methods of Whitman.

My first reaction was that it is based on destructive violence. It is profoundly Jewish in temper. It is Biblical in its repetitive grammatical build-up. It is a howl against everything in our mechanistic civilization which kills the spirit, assuming that the louder you shout the more likely you are to be heard. It lays bare the nerves of suffering and spiritual struggle. Its positive force and energy come from a redemptive quality of love, although it destructively catalogues evils of our time from physical deprivation to madness.

. . . .

It is certain that there is a new, vital group consciousness now among young poets in the Bay region. However unpublished they may be, many of these young poets have a numerous and enthusiastic audience. They acquire this audience by their own efforts. Through their many readings they have in some cases a larger audience than more cautiously presented poets in the East.

They are finely alive, they believe something new can be done with the art of poetry, they are hostile to gloomy critics, and the reader is invited to look into and enjoy their work as it appears. They have exuberance and a young will to kick down the doors of older consciousness and established practice in favor of what they think is vital and new.

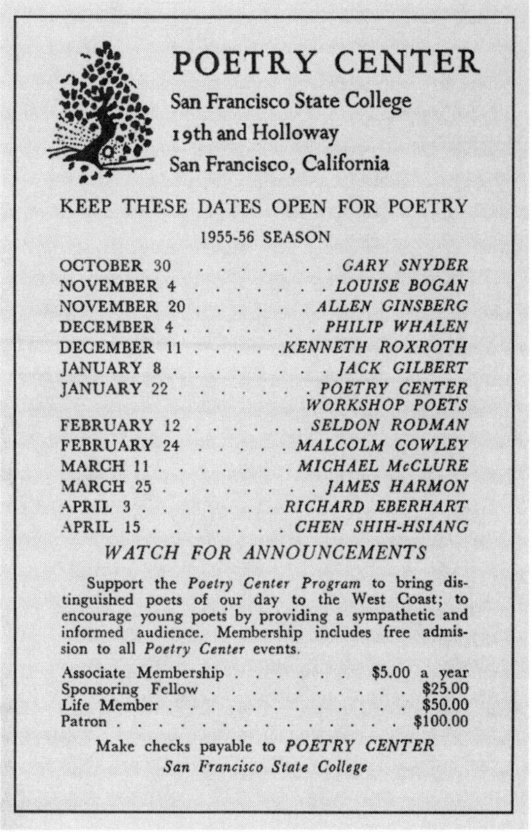
POETRY CENTER
San Francisco State College
19th and Holloway
San Francisco, California

KEEP THESE DATES OPEN FOR POETRY

1955-56 SEASON

OCTOBER 30	*GARY SNYDER*
NOVEMBER 4	*LOUISE BOGAN*
NOVEMBER 20	*ALLEN GINSBERG*
DECEMBER 4	*PHILIP WHALEN*
DECEMBER 11	*KENNETH ROXROTH*
JANUARY 8	*JACK GILBERT*
JANUARY 22	*POETRY CENTER WORKSHOP POETS*
FEBRUARY 12	*SELDON RODMAN*
FEBRUARY 24	*MALCOLM COWLEY*
MARCH 11	*MICHAEL McCLURE*
MARCH 25	*JAMES HARMON*
APRIL 3	*RICHARD EBERHART*
APRIL 15	*CHEN SHIH-HSIANG*

WATCH FOR ANNOUNCEMENTS

Support the *Poetry Center Program* to bring distinguished poets of our day to the West Coast; to encourage young poets by providing a sympathetic and informed audience. Membership includes free admission to all *Poetry Center* events.

Associate Membership	$5.00 a year
Sponsoring Fellow	$25.00
Life Member	$50.00
Patron	$100.00

Make checks payable to *POETRY CENTER*
San Francisco State College

Flier for reading schedule featuring several Beat writers

Avant Garde at the Golden Gate
George Baker
The Saturday Review, August 1957, p. 10

This summer, to the delight of those who have bemoaned the disappearance of the old Greenwich Village, a rousing communique is being broadcast through the pages of several literary quarterlies. Its message: "Listen, you squares, the avant garde isn't dead. In fact, it's jumping." It went on to explain that in San Francisco, a city to which they have been attracted by both geographical and spiritual climate, a new group of young writers from all parts of the U.S. has found temporary haven and dubbed itself the "Beat Generation." The proof of the group's vitality is three-fold: 1) a novel entitled "On the Road," by thirty-five-year-old Massachusetts-born Jack Kerouac, who has become one of the group's brightest stars, is being prepared for publication in September by Viking Press; 2) a new quarterly paperback review entitled "The Evergreen Review" (Grove Press, $1) has now devoted its second issue to writings by the San Francisco group; and 3) the group's high priest and spokesman (and at fifty-two one of its oldest members), writer-critic Kenneth Rexroth has recently commandeered considerable space in "New Directions #16" (New Directions, $2.50; paperbound $1.35) and in "New World Writing #11" (New American Library, $0.50).

Of the novel "On the Road" little can properly be said before its publication date. But of the views and goals of the whole movement writer-critic Rexroth was expatiating at length. "After the Second War," he wrote in "The Evergreen Review," "there was a convergence of interest–the Business Community, military imperialism, political reaction, the hysterical, tear and mud-drenched guilt of the ex-Stalinist, ex-Trotskyite American intellectuals, the highly organized academic and literary employment agency of the Neoantireconstructionists–what might be called the meliorists of the White Citizens' League, who were out to augment the notorious budgetary deficiency of the barbarously miseducated Southron male schoolmarm by opening up jobs 'up N'oth.' This ministry of all the talents formed a dense crust of custom over American cultural life–more of an ice pack. Ultimately the living water underneath just got so damn hot the ice pack has begun to melt, rot, break up and drift away into Arctic oblivion."

The characteristics of the Beat Generation, (which, of course, has broken through the ice pack) are, according to Rexroth, a respect for jazz, anarchy (though not political anarchy), William Carlos Williams (whom Rexroth considers the greatest living poet), Apollinaire, Henry Miller (who now lives in California within a stone's throw of the group), Gertrude Stein, and "the post-Hemingway detective story writers." The group's pet peeves: Henry James, T. S. Eliot and "the Social Lie" (which in Rexroth's mind seems to be a combination of all the forces he somehow manages to castigate in the long quotation above.) However, Rexroth cautions, it is possible to feel beaten in the manner of the Beat Generation without losing one's sense of humor. "It is," he insists in one of his more graphic descriptions of the aims of the group, "possible to bite the butt of the eternal Colonel Blimp with the quiet, penetrating tenacity of an unperturbed bull dog."

As proof of these characteristics "The Evergreen Review" offers such selections as these by the Beat Generation: Thirty-one-year-old New Jersey-born poet Allen Ginsberg's "The Howl" ("I saw the best minds of my generation destroyed by madness, starving hysterical naked. . ."); New York-born Ralph J. Gleason's "San Francisco Jazz Scene" ("San Francisco has always been a good-time town . . . And no matter how tight they close the lid and no matter the 2 A.M. closing mandatory in California, it is still a pretty wide-open town"); and an offering by novelist Kerouac himself entitled "October in the Railroad Earth" ("There was a little alley in San Francisco back of the Southern Pacific station at Third and Townsend . . ."). To such works as these critics will this summer and autumn undoubtedly have mixed reactions, but of one thing the

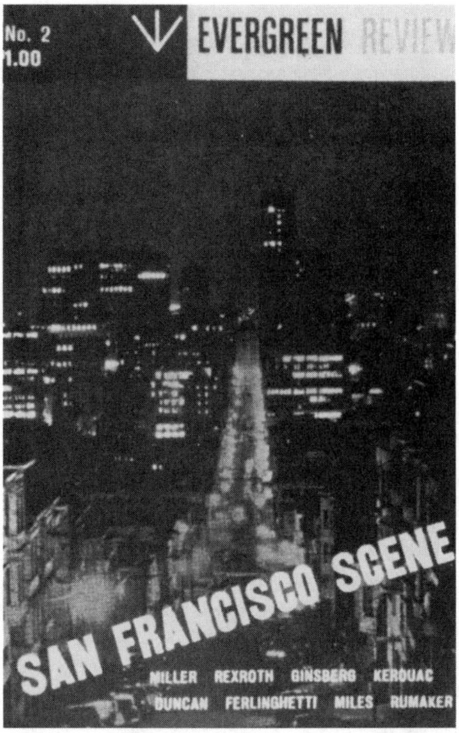

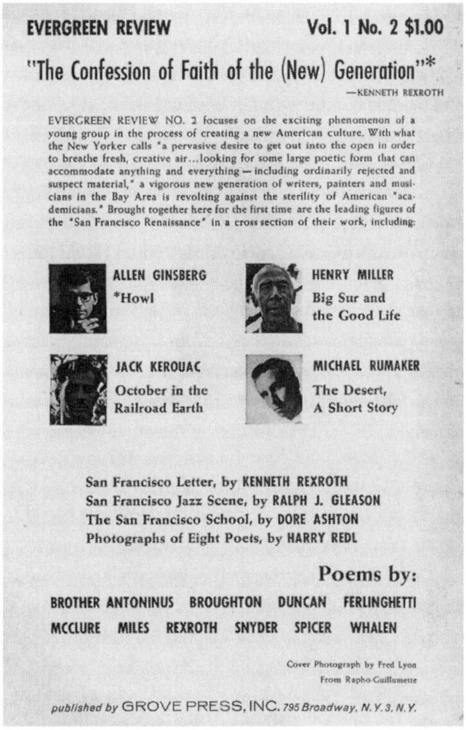

EVERGREEN REVIEW Vol. 1 No. 2 $1.00

"The Confession of Faith of the (New) Generation"*

—KENNETH REXROTH

EVERGREEN REVIEW NO. 2 focuses on the exciting phenomenon of a young group in the process of creating a new American culture. With what the New Yorker calls "a pervasive desire to get out into the open in order to breathe fresh, creative air…looking for some large poetic form that can accommodate anything and everything — including ordinarily rejected and suspect material," a vigorous new generation of writers, painters and musicians in the Bay Area is revolting against the sterility of American "academicians." Brought together here for the first time are the leading figures of the "San Francisco Renaissance" in a cross section of their work, including:

ALLEN GINSBERG
*Howl

HENRY MILLER
Big Sur and the Good Life

JACK KEROUAC
October in the Railroad Earth

MICHAEL RUMAKER
The Desert, A Short Story

San Francisco Letter, by KENNETH REXROTH
San Francisco Jazz Scene, by RALPH J. GLEASON
The San Francisco School, by DORE ASHTON
Photographs of Eight Poets, by HARRY REDL

Poems by:

BROTHER ANTONINUS BROUGHTON DUNCAN FERLINGHETTI
MCCLURE MILES REXROTH SNYDER SPICER WHALEN

Cover Photograph by Fred Lyon
From Rapho-Guillumette

published by GROVE PRESS, INC. *795 Broadway, N. Y. 3, N. Y.*

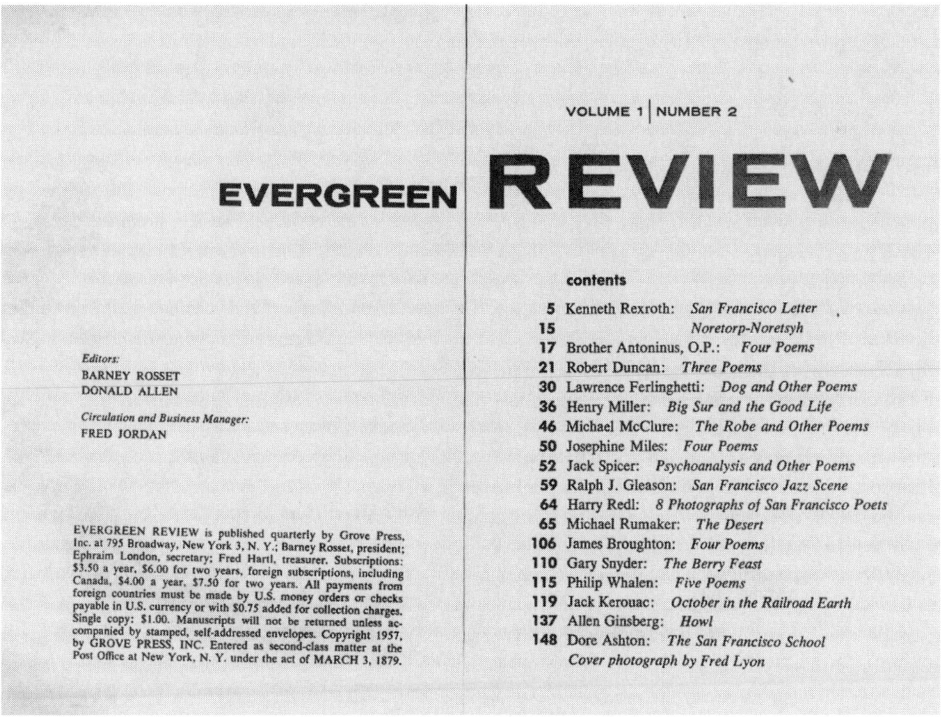

VOLUME 1 | NUMBER 2

EVERGREEN REVIEW

Editors:
BARNEY ROSSET
DONALD ALLEN

Circulation and Business Manager:
FRED JORDAN

EVERGREEN REVIEW is published quarterly by Grove Press, Inc. at 795 Broadway, New York 3, N. Y.; Barney Rosset, president; Ephraim London, secretary; Fred Hartl, treasurer. Subscriptions: $3.50 a year, $6.00 for two years, foreign subscriptions, including Canada, $4.00 a year, $7.50 for two years. All payments from foreign countries must be made by U.S. money orders or checks payable in U.S. currency or with $0.75 added for collection charges. Single copy: $1.00. Manuscripts will not be returned unless accompanied by stamped, self-addressed envelopes. Copyright 1957, by GROVE PRESS, INC. Entered as second-class matter at the Post Office at New York, N. Y. under the act of MARCH 3, 1879.

contents

Cover, contributors' page, and table of contents for the second issue of the magazine started by Grove Press publisher Barney Rosset and editor Donald Allen

Beat Generation can be sure: No matter how much the avant garde may have seemed to change in its new Western surroundings, there will always be those (even back East) who will be glad to know that it is still alive–and jumping.

The Beats Receive National Attention

In his novel Desolation Angels *(1965) Kerouac describes his reaction to the sudden attention he and his Beat colleagues began to receive in the fall of 1956. In this passage Gregory Corso is fictionalized as Raphael, Allen Ginsberg as Irwin Garden, and Philip Whalen as Ben Fagan.*

Tonight is the night we're going to have our pictures taken by the magazine so Raphael yells at me "Dont comb your hair–leave your hair uncombed!"

It had been his girl Sonya had just said, "Arent you wearing the Cross anymore?" and in such a nastified tone of voice as to indicate, *it was wearing the weary cross living with me?*–"Don't you comb your hair," says Raphael to me, and he has no money–"I dont believe in money."–The man on the bed in the bedroom hardly knows him, and he's moved in, and's playing his piano–

In between those two sonatas we'd had our bloody pictures taken and had got drunk all as who would stay sober to have his picture taken and to be called "Flaming-Cool Poets"–Irwin and I'd put Raphael between us, at my suggestion, my saying "Raphael is the shortest, should be in the middle" and thus arm in arm all three we'd posed for the world of American Literature, someone saying as the shutters pop: "What a threesome!" like talking 'bout one of them Million Dollar Outfields–There I am the left fielder, fast, brilliant runner, baserunner, bagger of long flies, some over my shoulder, in fact I'm a wallcrasher like Pete Reiser and am all bruised up, I'm Ty Cobb, I hit and run and steal and flape them bases with sincere fury, they call me The Peach–But I'm crazy, nobody's ever liked my personality, I'm no Babe Ruth Beloved–In centerfield is Raphael the fair haired DiMag who can play faultless ball without appearing to try or strain, that's Raphael–the rightfielder is serious Lou Gehrig, Irwin, who hits long homeruns left-handed in the windows of the Harlem River Bronx–Later on we pose with the greatest catcher of all time, Ben Fagan, squat-legged ole Mickey Cochrane is what he is, Hank Gowdy, he dont have no trouble putting on and removing those shin guards and mask between innings–

–*Desolation Angels,* pp. 196–197

Norman Podhoretz, a fierce critic of the Beats who was a contemporary of Ginsberg's at Columbia University

Norman Podhoretz, who had been a schoolmate of Ginsberg's at Columbia, wrote the first extensive condemnation of the Beats. Podhoretz writes that the "primitivism of the Beat Generation serves first of all as a cover for an anti-intellectualism so bitter that it makes the ordinary American's hatred of eggheads seem positively benign." He charges that the Beats' "primitivistic vitalism" leads to acceptance, if not enthusiasm for, violence.

The Know-Nothing Bohemians
Norman Podhoretz
Partisan Review, Spring 1958, pp. 305–318

Allen Ginsberg's little volume of poems, *Howl,* which got the San Francisco renaissance off to a screaming start a year or so ago, was dedicated to Jack Kerouac ("new Buddha of American prose, who spit forth intelligence into eleven books written in half the number of years . . . creating a spontaneous bop prosody and original classic literature"), William Seward Burroughs ("author of *Naked Lunch,* an endless novel which will drive everybody mad"), and Neal Cassady ("author of *The First Third,* an autobiography. . . . which enlightened Buddha"). So far, everybody's sanity has been spared by the inability of *Naked Lunch* to find a publisher, and we may never get the chance to discover what Buddha learned from Neal Cassady's autobiography, but thanks to the Viking and Grove Presses, two of Kerouac's original classics, *On the Road* and *The Subterraneans,* have now been revealed to the world. When *On the Road* appeared last year, Gilbert Millstein commemorated the event in the New York *Times* by declaring it to be "a historic occasion" comparable to the publication of *The Sun Also Rises* in the 1920's. But even before the novel was actually published, the word got around that Kerouac was the spokesman of a new group of rebels and Bohemians who called themselves the Beat Generation, and soon his photogenic countenance (unshaven, of course, and topped by an unruly crop of rich black hair falling over his forehead) was showing up in various mass-circulation magazines, he was being interviewed earnestly on television, and he was being featured in a Greenwich Village nightclub where, in San Francisco fashion, he read specimens of his spontaneous bop prosody against a background of jazz music.

Though the nightclub act reportedly flopped, *On the Road* sold well enough to hit the best-seller lists for several weeks, and it isn't hard to understand why. Americans love nothing so much as representative documents, and what could be more interesting in this Age of Sociology than a novel that speaks for the "young generation?" (The fact that Kerouac is thirty-five or thereabouts was generously not held against him.) Beyond that, however, I think that the unveiling of the Beat Generation was greeted with a certain relief by many people who had been disturbed by the notorious respectability and "maturity" of post-war writing. This was more like it–restless, rebellious, confused youth living it up, instead of thin, balding, buttoned-down instructors of English composing ironic verses with one hand while changing the baby's diapers with the other. Bohemianism is not particularly fashionable nowadays, but the image of Bohemia still exerts a powerful fascination–nowhere more so than in the suburbs, which are filled to overflowing with men and women who uneasily think of themselves as conformists and of Bohemianism as the heroic road. The whole point of *Marjorie Morningstar* was to assure the young marrieds of Mamaroneck that they were better off than the apparently glamorous *luftmenschen* of Greenwich Village, and the fact that Wouk had to work so hard at making this idea seem convincing is a good indication of the strength of prevailing doubt on the matter.

On the surface, at least, the Bohemianism of *On the Road* is very attractive. Here is a group of high-spirited young men running back and forth across the country (mostly hitch-hiking, sometimes in their own second-hand cars), going to "wild" parties in New York and Denver and San Francisco, living on a shoe-string (GI educational benefits, an occasional fifty bucks from a kindly aunt, an odd job as a typist, a fruit-picker, a parking-lot attendant), talking intensely about love and God and salvation, getting high on marijuana (but never heroin or cocaine), listening feverishly to jazz in crowded little joints, and sleeping freely with beautiful girls. Now and again there is a reference to gloom and melancholy, but the characteristic note struck by Kerouac is exuberance:

> We stopped along the road for a bite to eat. The cowboy went off to have a spare tire patched, and Eddie and I sat down in a kind of homemade diner. I heard a great laugh, the greatest laugh in the world, and here came this rawhide oldtimes Nebraska farmer with a bunch of other boys into the diner; you could hear his raspy cries clear across the plains, across the whole gray world of them that day. Everybody else laughed with him. He didn't have a care in the world and had the hugest regard for everybody. I said to myself, Wham, listen to that man laugh. That's the West, here I am in the West. He came booming into the diner, calling Maw's name, and she made the sweetest cherry pie in Nebraska, and I had some with a mountainous scoop of ice cream on top. "Maw, rustle me up some grub afore I have to start eatin myself or some damn silly idee like that." And he threw himself on a stool and went hyaw hyaw hyaw hyaw. "And throw some beans in it." It was the spirit of the West sitting right next to me. I wished I knew his whole raw life and what the hell he'd been doing all these years besides laughing and yelling like that. Whooee, I told my soul, and the cowboy came back and off we went to Grand Island.

Kerouac's enthusiasm for the Nebraska farmer is part of his general readiness to find the source of all vitality and virtue in simple rural types and in the dispossessed urban groups (Negroes, bums, whores). His idea of life in New York is "millions and millions hustling forever for a buck among themselves . . . grabbing, taking, giving, sighing, dying, just so they could be buried in those awful cemetery cities beyond Long Island City," whereas the rest of America is populated almost exclusively by the true of heart. There are intimations here of a kind of know-nothing populist sentiment, but in

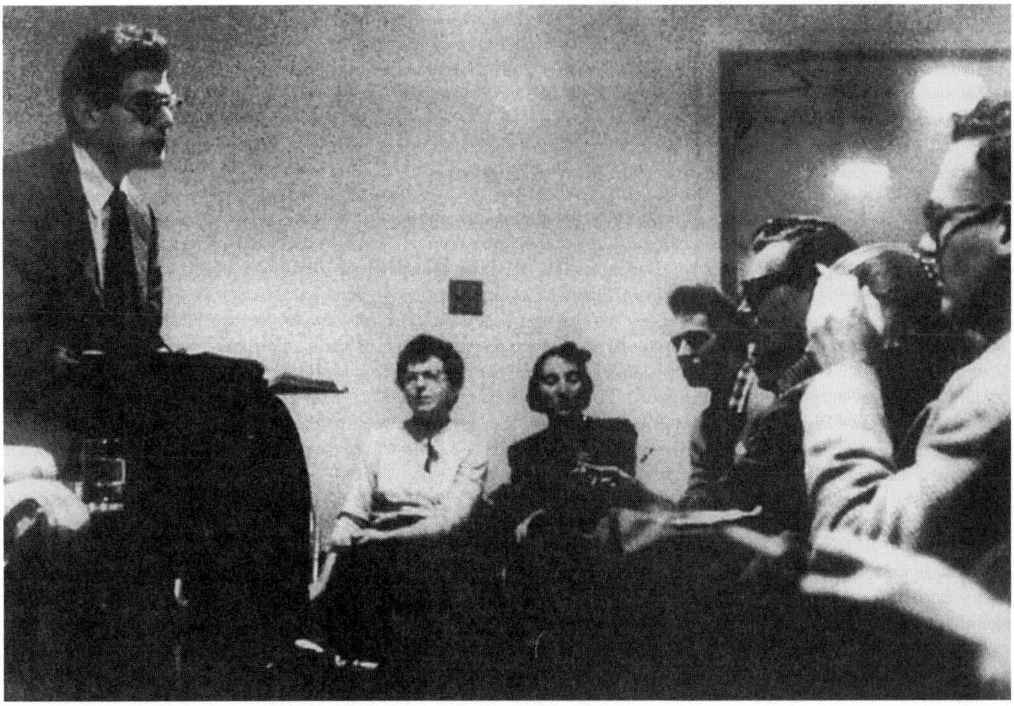

Ginsberg reading in San Francisco, circa 1956

other ways this attitude resembles Nelson Algren's belief that bums and whores and junkies are more interesting than white-collar workers or civil servants. The difference is that Algren hates middle-class respectability for moral and political reasons–the middle class exploits and persecutes–while Kerouac, who is thoroughly unpolitical, seems to feel that respectability is a sign not of moral corruption but of spiritual death. "The only people for me," says Sal Paradise, the narrator of *On the Road,* "are the mad ones, the ones who are mad to live, mad to talk, mad to be saved, desirous of everything at the same time, the ones who never yawn or say a commonplace thing, but burn, burn, burn like fabulous yellow roman candles exploding like spiders across the stars. . . ." This tremendous emphasis on emotional intensity, this notion that to be hopped-up is the most desirable of all human conditions, lies at the heart of the Beat Generation ethos and distinguishes it radically from the Bohemianism of the past.

The Bohemianism of the 1920's represented a repudiation of the provinciality, philistinism, and moral hypocrisy of American life–a life, incidentally, which was still essentially small-town and rural in tone. Bohemia, in other words, was a movement created in the name of civilization: its ideals were intelligence, cultivation, spiritual refinement. The typical literary figure of the 1920's was a midwesterner (Hemingway, Fitzgerald, Sinclair Lewis, Eliot, Pound) who had fled from his home town to New York or Paris in search of a freer, more expansive, more enlightened way of life than was possible in Ohio or Minnesota or Michigan. The political radicalism that supplied the characteristic coloring of Bohemianism in the 1930's did nothing to alter the urban, cosmopolitan bias of the 1920's. At its best, the radicalism of the 1930's was marked by deep intellectual seriousness and aimed at a state of society in which the fruits of civilization would be more widely available–and ultimately available to all.

The Bohemianism of the 1950's is another kettle of fish altogether. It is hostile to civilization; it worships primitivism, instinct, energy, "blood." To the extent that it has intellectual interests at all, they run to mystical doctrines, irrationalist philosophies, and left-wing Reichianism. The only art the new Bohemians have any use for is jazz, mainly of the cool variety. Their predilection for bop language is a way of demonstrating solidarity with the primitive vitality and spontaneity they find in jazz and of expressing contempt for coherent, rational discourse

a novel
by Jack
Kerouac
ON
THE
ROAD
"The hot pursuit
of pleasure
enables Mr. Kerouac to serve up the great, raw slices of America that give his book a descriptive excitement unmatched since the days of Thomas Wolfe. . . . As a portrait of a disjointed segment of society acting out of its own neurotic necessity, On the Road is a stunning achievement."
–DAVID DEMPSEY, N. Y. Times Book Review
"The most beautifully executed, the clearest and the most important utterance yet made by the generation Kerouac himself named years ago as 'beat'. . . . There are sections of On the Road in which the writing is of a beauty almost breathtaking. There is a description of a cross-country automobile ride fully the equal, for example, of the train ride told by Thomas Wolfe in Of Time and the River. There are the details of a trip to Mexico (and an interlude in a Mexican bordello) that are, by turns, awesome, tender and funny. And, finally, there is some writing on jazz that has never been equaled in American fiction, either for insight, style or technical virtuosity. On the Road is a major novel."
–GILBERT MILLSTEIN,
N. Y. Times
by JACK
KEROUAC
At all bookstores $3.95
THE VIKING PRESS • New York 22

Publisher's advertisement using the photograph that initially appeared in Mademoiselle. *It became the image most closely associated with Kerouac and the Beat Generation as* On the Road *climbed up the best-seller lists.*

In a 17 September 1956 letter to his agent, Sterling Lord, Kerouac mentioned that he wore a crucifix when posing for pictures for Mademoiselle.

Dear Sterling

The other night *Mademoiselle* magazine took our pictures (me and poet buddies Ginsberg and Corso) for a spread, which was already written before the pictures were taken, before we met and could talk to the writer: title: Flaming Cool Youth of San Francisco Poetry–

. . . .

I had my picture taken with a silver cross around my neck. . . .

–*Jack Kerouac: Selected Letters 1940–1956,* p. 586

Before she was his girlfriend, Joyce Johnson saw Kerouac's picture in Mademoiselle. *She remarked on the impact of the photograph in her book* Minor Characters: A Young Woman's Coming-of-Age in the Beat Orbit of Jack Kerouac (1983).

He looked wild and sad in a way that didn't seem appropriate to the occasion. This was Jack Kerouac, whose reputation was underground. Like the others, he was said to frequent North Beach, a run-down area where there were suddenly a lot of new coffee shops, jazz joints, and bars, as well as an excellent bookstore called City Lights that was the center of activity for the poets. Thus several thousand young women between fourteen and twenty-five were given a map to a revolution.

which, being a product of the mind, is in their view a form of death. To be articulate is to admit that you have no feelings (for how can real feelings be expressed in syntactical language?), that you can't respond to anything (Kerouac responds to everything by saying "Wow!"), and that you are probably impotent.

At the one end of the spectrum, this ethos shades off into violence and criminality, main-line drug addiction and madness. Allen Ginsberg's poetry, with its lurid apocalyptic celebration of "angel-headed hipsters," speaks for the darker side of the new Bohemianism. Kerouac is milder. He shows little taste for violence, and the criminality he admires is the harmless kind. The hero of *On the Road,* Dean Moriarty, has a record: "From the age of eleven to seventeen he was usually in reform school. His specialty was stealing cars, gunning for girls coming out of high school in the afternoon, driving them out to the mountains, making them, and coming back to sleep in any available hotel bathtub in town." But Dean's criminality, we are told, "was not something that sulked and sneered; it was a wild yea-saying overburst of American joy; it was Western, the west wind, an ode from the Plains, something new, long prophesied, long a-coming (he only stole cars for joy rides)." And, in fact, the species of Bohemian that Kerouac writes about is on the whole rather law-abiding. In *The Subterraneans,* a bunch of drunken boys steal a pushcart in the middle of the night, and when they leave it in front of a friend's apartment building, he denounces them angrily for "screwing up the security of my pad." When Sal Paradise (in *On the Road*) steals some groceries from the canteen of an itinerant workers' camp in which he has taken a temporary job as a barracks guard, he comments, " I suddenly began to realize that everybody in America is a natural-born thief"–which, of course, is a way of turning his own stealing into a bit of boyish prankishness. Nevertheless, Kerouac is attracted to criminality, and that in itself is more significant than the fact that he personally feels constrained to put the brakes on his own destructive impulses.

Sex has always played a very important role in Bohemianism: sleeping around was the Bohemian's most dramatic demonstration of his freedom from conventional moral standards, and a defiant denial of the idea that sex was permissible only in marriage and then only for the sake of a family. At the same time, to be "promiscuous" was to assert the validity of sexual experience in and for itself. The "meaning" of Bohemian sex, then, was at once social and personal, a crucial element in the Bohemian's ideal of civilization. Here again the contrast with Beat Generation Bohemianism is sharp. On the one hand, there is a fair amount of sexual activity in *On the Road* and *The Subterraneans.* Dean Moriarity is a "new kind of American saint" at least partly because of his amazing sexual power: he can keep three women satisfied simultaneously and he can make love any time, anywhere (once he mounts a girl in the back seat of a car while poor Sal Paradise is trying to sleep in front). Sal, too, is always on the make, and though he isn't as successful as the great Dean, he does pretty well: offhand I can remember a girl in Denver, one on a bus, and another in New York, but a little research would certainly unearth a few more. The heroine of *The Subterraneans,* a Negro girl named Mardou Fox, seems to have switched from one to another member of the same gang and back again ("This has been an incestuous group in its time"), and we are given to understand that there is nothing unusual about such an arrangement. But the point of all this hustle and bustle is not freedom from ordinary social restrictions or defiance of convention (except in relation to homosexuality, which is Ginsberg's preserve: among "the best minds" of Ginsberg's generation who were destroyed by America are those "who let themselves be----- in the---- by saintly motorcyclists, and screamed with joy, / who blew and were blown by those human seraphim, the sailors, caresses of Atlantic and Caribbean love"). The sex in Kerouac's books goes hand in hand with a great deal of talk about forming permanent relationships ("although I have a hot feeling sexually and all that for her," says the poet Adam Moorad in *The Subterraneans,* "I really don't want to get any further into her not only for these reasons but finally, the big one, if I'm going to get involved with a girl now I want to be permanent like permanent and serious and long termed and I can't do that with her"), and a habit of getting married and then duly divorced and re-married when another girl comes along. In fact, there are as many marriages and divorces in *On the Road* as in the Hollywood movie colony (must be that California climate): "All those years I was looking for the woman I wanted to marry," Sal Paradise tells us. "I couldn't meet a girl without saying to myself, What kind of wife would she make?" Even more revealing is Kerouac's refusal to admit that any of his characters ever make love wantonly or lecherously–no matter how casual the encounter it must always entail sweet feelings toward the girl. Sal, for example, is fixed up with Rita Bettencourt in Denver, whom he has never met before. "I got her in my bedroom after a long talk in the dark of the front room. She was a nice little girl, simple and true [naturally], and tremendously frightened of sex. I told her it was beautiful. I wanted to prove this to her. She let me prove it, but I was too impatient and proved nothing. She sighed in the dark. 'What do you want out of life?' I asked, and I used to ask that all the time of girls." This is rather touching, but only because the narrator is really just as frightened of sex as that nice little girl was. He is frightened of failure and he worries about his performance. For *performance* is the point–performance and "good orgasms," which are the first duty of man and the only duty of woman. What seems to be involved here, in short, is sexual anxiety of enormous proportions–an anxiety that comes out very clearly in *The Subterraneans,* which is about a love affair between the young writer, Leo Percepied, and the Negro girl, Mardou Fox. Despite its protestations, the book is one long agony of fear and trembling over sex:

> I spend long nights and many hours making her, finally I have her, I pray for it to come, I can hear her breathing harder, I hope against hope it's time, a noise in the hall (or whoop of drunkards next door) takes her mind off and she can't make it and laughs–but when she does make it I hear her crying, whimpering, the shuddering electrical female orgasm makes her sound like a little girl crying, moaning in the night, it lasts a good twenty seconds and when it's over she moans, "O why can't it last longer," and "O when will I when you do?"–"Soon now I bet," I say, "you're getting closer and closer"–

Very primitive, very spontaneous, very elemental, very beat.

For the new Bohemians interracial friendships and love affairs apparently play the same role of social defiance that sex used to play in older Bohemian circles. Negroes and whites associate freely on a basis of complete equality and without a trace of racial hostility. But putting it that way understates the case, for not only is there no racial hostility, there is positive adulation for the "happy, true-hearted, ecstatic Negroes of America."

> At lilac evening I walked with every muscle aching among the lights of 27th and Welton in the Denver colored section, wishing I were a Negro, feeling that the best the white world had offered was not enough ecstasy for me, not enough life, joy, kicks, darkness, music, not enough night. . . . I wished I were a Denver Mexican, or even a poor overworked Jap, anything but what I was so drearily, a "white man" disillusioned. All my life I'd had white ambitions. . . . I passed the dark porches of Mexican and Negro homes; soft voices were there, occasionally the dusky knee of some mysterious sensuous gal; and dark faces of the men behind rose arbors. Little children sat like sages in ancient rocking chairs.

It will be news to the Negroes to learn that they are so happy and ecstatic; I doubt if a more idyllic picture of Negro life has been painted since certain Southern ideologues tried to convince the world that things were just as fine as fine could be for the slaves on the old plantation. Be that as it may, Kerouac's love for Negroes and other dark-skinned groups is tied up with his worship of primitivism, not with any radical social attitudes. Ironically enough, in fact, to see the Negro as more elemental than the white man, as Ned Polsky has acutely remarked, is "an inverted form of keeping the nigger in his place." But even if it were true that American Negroes, by virtue of their position in our culture, have been able to retain a degree of primitive spontaneity, the last place you would expect to find evidence of this is among Bohemian Negroes. Bohemianism, after all, is for the Negro a means of entry into the world of the whites, and no Negro Bohemian is going to cooperate in the attempt to identify him with Harlem or Dixieland. The only major Negro character in either of Kerouac's two novels is Mardou Fox, and she is about as primitive as Wilhelm Reich himself.

The plain truth is that the primitivism of the Beat Generation serves first of all as a cover for an anti-intellectualism so bitter that it makes the ordinary American's hatred of eggheads seem positively benign. Kerouac and his friends like to think of themselves as intellectuals ("they are intellectual as hell and know all about Pound without being pretentious or talking too much about it"), but this is only a form of newspeak. Here is an example of what Kerouac considers intelligent discourse–"formal and shining and complete, without the tedious intellectualness":

> We passed a little kid who was throwing stones at the cars in the road. "Think of it," said Dean. "One day he'll put a stone through a man's windshield and the man will crash and die–all on account of that little kid. You see what I mean? God exists without qualms. As we roll along this way I am positive beyond doubt that everything will be taken care of for us–that even you, as you drive, fearful of the wheel . . . the thing will go along of itself and you won't go off the road and I can sleep. Furthermore we know America, we're at home; I can go anywhere in America and get what I want because it's the same in every corner, I know the people, I know what they do. We give and take and go in the incredibly complicated sweetness zigzagging every side.

You see what he means? Formal and shining and complete. No tedious intellectualness. Completely unpretentious. "There was nothing clear about the things he said but what he meant to say was somehow made pure and clear." *Somehow.* Of course. If what he wanted to say had been carefully thought out and precisely articulated, that would have been tedious and pretentious and, no doubt, *somehow* unclear and clearly impure. But so long as he utters these banalities with his tongue tied and with no comprehension of their meaning, so long as he makes noises that come out of his soul (since they couldn't possibly have come out of his mind), he passes the test of true intellectuality.

Which brings us to Kerouac's spontaneous bop prosody. This "prosody" is not to be confused with bop language itself, which has such a limited vocabulary (Basic English is a verbal treasure-house by comparison) that you couldn't write a note to the milkman in it, much less a novel. Kerouac, however, manages to remain true to the spirit of hipster slang while making forays into enemy territory (i.e., the English language) by his simple inability to express anything in words. The only method he has of describing an object is to summon up the same half-dozen adjectives over and over again: "greatest," "tremendous," "crazy," "mad," "wild," and perhaps one or two others. When it's more than just mad or crazy or wild, it becomes "really mad" or "really crazy" or "really wild." (All quantities in excess of three, incidentally, are subsumed under the rubric "innumerable," a word used innumerable times in *On the Road* but not so innumerably in *The Subterraneans.*) The same poverty of resources is apparent in those passages where Kerouac tries to handle a situation involving even slightly complicated feelings. His usual tactic is to run for cover behind cliché and vague signals to the reader. For instance: "I looked at him; my eyes were watering with embarrassment and tears. Still he stared at me. Now his eyes were blank and looking through me . . . . Something clicked in both of us. In me it was suddenly concern for a man who was years younger than I, five years, and whose fate was wound with mine across the passage of the recent years; in him it was a matter that I can ascertain only from what he did afterward." If you can ascertain what this is all about, either beforehand, during, or afterward, you are surely no square.

In keeping with its populistic bias, the style of *On the Road* is folksy and lyrical. The prose of *The Subterraneans,* on the other hand, sounds like an inept parody of Faulkner at his worst, the main difference being that Faulkner usually produces bad writing out of an impulse to inflate the commonplace while Kerouac gets into trouble by pursuing "spontaneity." Strictly speaking, spontaneity is a quality of feeling, not of writing: when we call a piece of writing spontaneous, we are registering our impression that the author hit upon the right words without sweating, that no "art" and no calculation entered into the picture, that his feelings seem to have spoken themselves, seem to have sprouted a tongue at the moment of composition. Kerouac apparently thinks that spontaneity is a matter of saying whatever comes into your head, in any order you happen to feel like saying it. It isn't the *right* words he wants (even if he knows what they might be), but the first words, or at any rate the words that most obviously announce themselves as deriving from emotion rather than cerebration, as coming from "life" rather than "literature," from the guts rather than the brain. (The brain, remember, is the angel of death.) But writing that springs easily and "spontaneously" out of strong feelings is *never* vague; it always has a quality of sharpness and precision because it is in the nature of strong feelings to be aroused by specific objects. The notion that a diffuse, generalized, and unrelenting enthusiasm is the mark of great sensitivity and responsiveness is utterly fantastic, an idea that comes from taking drunkenness or drug-addiction as the state of perfect emotional vigor. The effect of such enthusiasm is actually to wipe out the world altogether, for if a filling station will serve as well as the Rocky Mountains to arouse a sense of awe and wonder, then both the filling station and the mountains are robbed of their reality. Kerouac's conception of feeling is one that only a solipsist could believe in–and a solipsist, be it noted, is a man who does not relate to anything outside himself.

Solipsism is precisely what characterizes Kerouac's fiction. *On the Road* and *The Subterraneans* are so patently autobiographical in content that they become almost impossible to discuss as novels; if spontaneity were indeed a matter of destroying the distinction between life and literature, these books would unquestionably be It. "As we were going out to the car Babe slipped and fell flat on her face. Poor girl was overwrought. Her brother Tim and I helped her up. We got in the car; Major and Betty joined us. The sad ride back to Denver began." Babe is a girl who is mentioned a few times in the course of *On the Road;* we don't know why she is overwrought on this occasion, and even if we did it wouldn't matter, since there is no reason for her presence in the book at all. But Kerouac tells us that she fell flat on her face while walking toward a car. It is impossible to believe that Kerouac made this detail up, that his imagination was creating a world real enough to include wholly gratuitous elements; if that were the case, Babe would have come alive as a human being. But she is only a name; Kerouac never even describes her. She is in the book because the sister of one of Kerouac's friends was there when he took a trip to Central City, Colorado, and she slips in *On the Road* because she slipped that day on the way to the car. What is true of Babe who fell flat on her face is true of virtually every incident in *On the Road* and *The Subterraneans*. Nothing that happens has any dramatic reason for happening. Sal Paradise meets such-and-such people on the road whom he likes or (rarely) dislikes; they exchange a few words, they have a few beers together, they part. It is all very unremarkable and commonplace, but for Kerouac it is always the greatest, the wildest, the most. What you get in these two books is a man proclaiming that he is *alive* and offering every trivial experience he has ever had in evidence. Once I did this, once I did that (he is saying) and by God, it *meant* something! Because I *responded!* But if it meant something, and you responded so powerfully, why can't you explain what it meant, and why do you have to insist so?

I think it is legitimate to say, then, that the Beat Generation's worship of primitivism and spontaneity is more than a cover for hostility to intelligence; it arises from a pathetic poverty of feeling as well. The hipsters and hipster-lovers of the Beat Generation are rebels, all right, but not against anything so sociological and historical as the middle class or capitalism or even respectability. This is the revolt of the spiritually underprivileged and the crippled of soul—young men who can't think straight and so hate anyone who can; young men who can't get outside the morass of self and so construct definitions of feeling that exclude all human beings who manage to live, even miserably, in a world of objects; young men who are burdened unto death with the specially poignant sexual anxiety that America—in its eternal promise of erotic glory and its spiteful withholding of actual erotic possibility—seems bent on breeding, and who therefore dream of the unattainable perfect orgasm, which excuses all sexual failures in the real world. Not long ago, Norman Mailer suggested that the rise of the hipster may represent "the first wind of a second revolution in this century, moving not forward toward action and more rational equitable distribution, but backward toward being and the secrets of human energy." To tell the truth, whenever I hear anyone talking about instinct and being and the secrets of human energy, I get nervous; next thing you know he'll be saying that violence is just fine, and then I begin wondering whether he really thinks that kicking someone in the teeth or sticking a knife between his ribs are deeds to be admired. History, after all—and especially the history of modern times—teaches that there is a close connection between ideologies of primitivistic vitalism and a willingness to look upon cruelty and blood-letting with complacency, if not downright enthusiasm. The reason I bring this up is that the spirit of hipsterism and the Beat Generation strikes me as the same spirit which animates the young savages in leather jackets who have been running amuck in the last few years with their switch-blades and zip guns. What does Mailer think of those wretched kids, I wonder? What does he think of the gang that stoned a nine-year-old boy to death in Central Park in broad daylight a few months ago, or the one that set fire to an old man drowsing on a bench near the Brooklyn waterfront one summer's day, or the one that pounced on a crippled child and orgiastically stabbed him over and over and over again even after he was good and dead? Is that what he means by the liberation of instinct and the mysteries of being? Maybe so. At least he says somewhere in his article that two eighteen-year-old hoodlums who bash in the brains of a candy-store keeper are murdering an institution, committing an act that "violates private property"—which is one of the most morally gruesome ideas I have ever come across, and which indicates where the ideology of hipsterism can lead. I happen to believe that there is a direct connection between the flabbiness of American middle-class life and the spread of juvenile crime in the 1950's, but I also believe that juvenile crime can be explained partly in terms of the same resentment against normal feeling and the attempt to cope with the world through intelligence that lies behind Kerouac and Ginsberg. Even the relatively mild ethos of Kerouac's books can spill over easily into brutality, for there is a suppressed cry in those books: Kill the intellectuals who can talk coherently, kill the people who can sit still for five minutes at a time, kill those incomprehensible characters who are capable of getting seriously involved with a woman, a job, a cause. How can anyone in his right mind pretend that this has anything to do with private property or the middle class? No. Being for or against what the Beat Generation stands for has to do with denying that incoherence is superior to precision; that ignorance is superior to knowledge; that the exercise of mind and discrimination is a form of death. It has to do with fighting the notion that sordid acts of violence are justifiable so long as they are committed in the name of "instinct." It even has to do with fighting the poisonous glorification of the adolescent in American popular culture. It has to do, in other words, with being for or against intelligence itself.

LeRoi Jones responded to Podhoretz's article in a letter to the editor published in the summer 1958 issue of Partisan Review.

Sirs:

It would seem that Norman Podhoretz, in his article "The Know-Nothing Bohemians," objected more violently to certain instances of socio-ethical non-conformity in the Beat Generation than to its paucity of erudition, as the title of his essay states. It would also seem that his essay was less an attempt at objective literary criticism than it was a kind of ill-concealed rant .... Can it be that the Beat Generation's biggest would-be detractors are so taken up by the "violence and madness" which they seem to point out so readily as the exclusive content of Beat literature, that they find no room for the normal functions of literary criticism? ...

If any of the so-called criticism of the so-called "Beat Generation" needs a rebuttal (or at least an examination of motives) it is Mr. Podhoretz's claim that this whole movement made him nervous. ... "Next thing you know," Mr Podhoretz says, "he'll be saying that violence is just fine." Well, that's just it. Violence *is* just fine. I don't mean that someone ought to walk up to Mr. Podhoretz and smack him down, but that this generation of writers must resort to violence in literature, a kind of violence that has in such a short time begun to shake us out of the woeful literary sterility which characterized the '40's, to pull us out of what Dudley Fitts called (in his review of William Meredith's new book of verse) "an impoverished time, so far as poetry is concerned."

... I have read a great many of these scathing rants that are being palmed off as objective critical studies of the "New Bohemianism," and almost without exception they have come from the small coterie of quasi-novelists or *New Yorker* suburban intellectual types of the late '40's and early '50's which represents so much of what Beat is a reaction against. It seems to me that Beat is less a movement than a reaction. It is a reaction against, let us say to start, fifteen years of sterile, unreadable magazine poetry: poetry, as Mr. Fitts said so well, that is "neogeorgian, preserved from the almost obligatory dullness of the Georgians by a mild freshness of invention and an agreeably disturbing wit." To my mind, this is not what poetry ought to be. And Beat is also a reaction against what Randall Jarrell calls "The Age of Criticism."

... There was neither Bohemianism nor any great intellectual rebellion in the '40's, and there was no poetry to speak of. (Poor Dylan Thomas carried the ball all by himself in England, and we all know what happened when eventually he did get to America.) The only persons that caused even a semblance of a literary stir were a few addlebrained individuals mumbling under their breaths something about "creative criticism." There was nothing but one great big void.

LeRoi Jones, the poet who later changed his name to Amiri Baraka, took issue with Podhoretz's criticism of the Beats

I respect Randall Jarrell, Robert Lowell, Karl Shapiro, Delmore Schwartz, John Berryman, Peter Viereck, George Barker, Stephen Spender, Louis Macniece, and others who were so representative of what poetry was in the '40's, as well as Eberhart, Wilbur, Meredith, Merwin, Bishop, the Pack-Simpson bunch, etc., who represent the academically condoned poetry of the '50's. But I wish to say emphatically that from this entire group of poets (which represents almost twenty years of poetry) we have about five poems of note. ...

The Beat Generation, while not a movement as such, is a definite reaction to the void [of the '40's]. To deny the obvious immaturity and ingenuous quality of a good bit of the literature of this reaction would be absurd, just as it would be to say that all the art of such a parallel movement as Dada was purposeful and valid. ... As with Dada, Beat represents a line of departure rather than a concrete doctrine. And even if this departure never produces another poem as influential or controversial as Allen Ginsberg's "Howl," there is no doubt in my mind that it will produce better ones. The same is true of Kerouac's *On the Road.* It breaks new ground, and plants new seeds . . .

[Podhoretz] shows an ignorance about the whole of the Beat reaction. . . . Statements like "Kerouac's 'bop prosody' is not to be confused with bop language itself, which has such a limited vocabulary you couldn't write a note to the milkman in it, much less a novel" show not only a basic ignorance . . . of the role of bop language in our society, but also a complete inability to see its possible function in literature per se. To write a novel in bop language is not the point, no more than it was Shakespeare's *point* to write his plays in Elizabethan English. A novel, play, etc. is about people, the ideas of people, not about language. . . . Of course *On The Road* is unthinkable without bop language, just as *Hamlet* is unthinkable without Elizabethan English. If one thinks the hipster's language meaningless, perhaps it is not entirely the hipster's fault. . . . The point is that the language can be extended and enlivened by just such prosody as Kerouac's if we are not too snobbish to accept it.

Another of Mr. Podhoretz's misconceptions is his rather early-'30's middle class assumption that "Bohemianism, after all, is for the Negro a means of entry into the world of the whites, and no Negro Bohemian is going to cooperate in an attempt to identify him with Harlem or Dixieland": Harlem is today the veritable capitol city of the Black Bourgeoisie. The Negro Bohemian's flight from Harlem is not a flight from the world of color but the flight of any would-be Bohemian from what Mr. Podhoretz himself calls "the provinciality, philistinism and moral hypocrisy of American life." Dixieland. . . .is to traditional jazz what Rock and Roll is to Blues, or Rhythm and Blues–a cheap commercial imitation. The Negro intellectual certainly has no responsibility either for or to it.

Finally, a statement like "The only art the new Bohemians have any use for is jazz". . . .borders on back alley polemics, not at all in the tradition of the "coherent, rational discourse" Mr. Podhoretz says he cherishes. . . .

–pp. 472–473

Bruce Cook notes the effect of the popular media as a complicating factor in assessing the reputation of the Beats.

During their moment in the spotlight they received the full treatment from the media–coverage in the news magazines, special attention in *Life,* lots of time on the talk shows, and even a television documentary or two devoted to them. And now, although nearly all the writers who emerged from the movement are still being published, the Beat Generation, if remembered at all today, is recalled as some distant phenomenon, an isolated cultural event of the 1950s. And those of the present generation who have inherited so much from them have only the haziest notion of the Beat Generation, why, what, or even who it was.

All right, *who* were the Beats? Were they truly, as they called themselves, a generation? A movement? Or were they merely–as was said so often of them by members of the literary establishment of the day–a fad, a phenomenon of publicity, a creation of the Luce publications?

–*The Beat Generation,* p. 5

The following three articles are typical of the patronizing treatment that Time *magazine accorded the Beats in the 1950s during the Beat heyday.*

The first is a review of an anthology titled The Beat Generation and the Angry Young Men *(1958). Editors Gene Feldman and Max Gartenberg called the Beats in the U.S. and the "Angry Young Men" in Britain "the two most talked-about literary movements of the late '50s."*

Disorganization Man

Time, 9 June 1958, pp. 98, 102

The merit of the new anthology, edited by TV producer Gene Feldman, 37, and Literary Agent Max Gartenberg, 32, is that it answers this question better collectively than any one of the semi-articulate Beats and Angries has done on his own. The editors have culled the best from both schools (the U.S.'s Jack Kerouac, Allen Ginsberg, Clellon Holmes; Britain's Kingsley Amis, John Wain, John Osborne) and leavened the lot with sharp-eyed critical commentaries from both sides of the water. U.S. readers will find the Beat section more interesting, if only because it helps to illuminate such post-war phenomena as the James Dean cult, the Elvis Presley and rock-'n'-roll crazes, and the gratuitous ferocity of juvenile delinquency.

Jungle Waif. The central beat character that unintentionally emerges is a model psychopath. The hipster has a horror of family life and sustained relationships.

. . . .

The hipster is also estranged from nature. In George Mandel's *The Beckoning Sea,* the suicide-bent hero runs screaming along a beach, and "with a roar the ocean came up and bit at him with its foam-teeth."

Even when he is not being bitten by foam-teeth, the hipster is a chronic manic-depressive ("Crazy, man!"; "Everything drags me now"). A kind of urban waif in the asphalt jungle, he regularly tastes despair, or what Kerouac calls "the pit and prunejuice of poor beat life itself in the god-awful streets of man." Sometimes he "flips," *i.e.,* goes mad. Allen Ginsberg, 32, the discount-house Whitman of the Beat Generation, begins his dithyrambic poem *Howl* (which the New York *Times's* Critic J. Donald Adams has suggested should be retitled *Bleat*) with the lines: "I saw the best minds of my generation destroyed by madness, starving hysterical naked, dragging themselves through the negro streets at dawn looking for an angry fix . . ."

A good mind is hard to find among the Beats, but the leading theoreticians of hipdom are probably Jack Kerouac and Clellon *(Go)* Holmes. Each insists that the Beat Generation is on a mystic search for God. To be beat, argues Holmes in a recent *Esquire,* is to be "at the bottom of your personality looking up." Says Kerouac: "I want God to show me His face." This might be more convincing if Kerouac's novels did not play devil's advocate by preaching, in effect, "Seek ye first the Kingdom of kicks," *e.g.,* drink, drugs, jazz and chicks.

* * *

Bang Bong Bing

Time, 7 September 1959, p. 80

Those unwashed minstrels of the West, the beatniks of San Francisco's North Beach and Los Angeles' Venice West, make much of their loud vows of poverty. To be poor, yak the shirtless ones as they sit scratching in store-front espresso halls, is to be holy, man, holy. But last week, the mendicants of marijuana and mad verse were in the somewhat embarrassing position of monks whose liqueur sells too well. Tourists were snapping up their stuff like Chinese back-scratchers, and the beatniks were starting to rake in the dough.

On North Beach's Columbus Avenue, a dozen customers once constituted an oxygen problem at the City Lights bookstore, run by Lawrence Ferlinghetti, 40, as a combination Beat Haven and publishing house. Now the crush is so great that the bookstore has been expanded, and Ferlinghetti's only slightly offbeat *A Coney Island of the Mind* (New Directions) has sold a surprising 15,000 copies. The really far-out beatniks do even better. Allen Ginsberg's effete epic, *Howl,* published by Ferlinghetti, is up to 40,000 copies in print, and Fantasy Records is preparing a disk of Ginsberg reading Ginsberg, including some passages too naughty to print. Jack Kerouac's soapless saga, *The Subterraneans,* is doing so well (over 40,000 sold, not counting paperbound reprints) that M-G-M advance agents are prowling San Francisco's Beatland for material for a film. Latest beatnik hit, published last month: a murky outpouring called *Second April* ("O man, thee is onion-constructed in hot gabardine") by a scraggly bard named Bob Kaufman–2,500 copies already in print.

Why the popularity? The beat blather certainly is not literature. But it can be amusing, and at its best, more fun to recite in the bathtub than anything since Vachel Lindsay's *The Congo.*

* * *

Fried Shoes

Time, 9 February 1959, p. 16

The cocktail party was buzzing as only Chicago cocktail parties can buzz. In the richly appointed Lake Shore Drive apartment of Chicago Financier Albert Newman, the guests chatted animatedly, gazed at the original Picasso on the wall, and the Monet, the Jackson Pollock. On tables and shelves stood Peruvian fertility symbols, jade bracelets, sculptures that looked like the superstructure of a Japanese battleship. The heavy air clinked with philosophy, culture and sensitivity:

Do you realize we're sitting right in front of an original Jackson Pollock? It makes me want to cry. Why did he have to die?. . .

America is a gaudy place. It gives you a chance to do anything or to not do anything. . .

Spinoza understood because of all that suffering he went through in–where was it?– Rotterdam?. . .

You can sell, Jim. Sure you can sell. Anybody can sell . . .

Yes, but Bartok scores the gaps. That's the difference . . .

Tears from a Hydrant. This chatter was only a way of passing the time, for the guests had come for something more important than Scotch and Spinoza. They had come to meet 32-year-old Allen Ginsberg of Paterson, N. J., author of a celebrated, chock-full catalogue called *Howl* (*I saw the best minds of my generation destroyed by madness, starving hysterical naked*), recognized leader of the pack of oddballs (TIME, June 9) who celebrate booze, dope, sex and despair and who go by the name of Beatniks.

At length Poet Ginsberg arrived, wearing blue jeans and a checked black-and-red lumberjacking shirt with black patches at the elbows. With him were two other shabbily dressed Beatniks. One was Ginsberg's intimate friend, a mental-hospital attendant named Peter Orlovsky, 25, who writes poetry (*I talk to the fire hydrant, asking: "Do you have bigger tears than I do?"*); the other was Gregory

Corso, 28, a shaggy, dark little man who boasts that he has never combed his hair–and never gets an argument. Corso, also a poet, will be remembered for his lines:

But nothing would rid me of Dandruff.
Vitalis, Lucky Tiger, Wildroot, Brilliantine, nothing.

Hollyhocks & Daisies. The trio was an instant hit with the literary upper crust. There was in fact only one unbeliever in the crowd, one William Haskins, instructor in English at Northwestern University. Demanded Corso: "Man, why are you knocking the way I talk? I don't knock the way you talk. You don't know about the hollyhocks." Replied Haskins: "If you're going to be irrelevant, you might as well be irrelevant about hollyhocks." Countered Corso: "Man, this is a drag. You're nothing but a creep–a creep! But I don't care. I can still laugh and I can still cry. That's the way to be."

"The hell it is," snorted Haskins. "What kind of expression is that?" shouted Corso. "Don't you know that hell is passé?"

Then, as the formalities began, somebody shoved a microphone in view.

"I'm Peter Orlovsky," said Peter Orlovsky. "I'm very fine and happy and crazy as a wild flower."

"I'm Allen Ginsberg," said Allen Ginsberg, "and I'm crazy like a daisy."

"I'm Gregory Corso," said Gregory Corso, "and I'm not crazy at all."

Would they like to make any comment? "Yes," said Corso. "Fried shoes. Like it means nothing. It's all a big laughing bowl and we're caught in it. A scary laughing bowl." Added Gregory Corso, with the enigmatic quality of a true Beatnik: "Don't shoot the wart hog." Chimed in Allen Ginsberg: "My mystical shears snip snip snip."

Paul O'Neil argues that "the enormous difference" between the Beats and the "convocations of those crackpots and screwballs" that preceded them is notoriety: "While most of the forerunners of Beatdom were ignored by the general populace, the Beat Generation itself has attracted wide public attention and is exerting astonishing influence."

The Only Rebellion Around
Paul O'Neil
Life, 30 November 1959, pp. 114–130

If the U.S. today is really the biggest, sweetest and most succulent casaba ever produced by the melon patch of civilization, it would seem only reasonable to find its surface profaned–as indeed it is–by a few fruit flies. But reason would also anticipate contented fruit flies, blissful fruit flies–fruit flies raised by happy environment to the highest stages of fruit fly development. Such is not the case. The grandest casaba of all, in disconcerting fact, has incubated some of the hairiest, scrawniest and most discontented specimens of all time: the improbable rebels of the Beat Generation, who not only refuse to sample the seeping juices of American plenty and American social advance but scrape their feelers in discordant scorn of any and all who do.

. . . .

Beat philosophy seems calculated to offend the whole population, civil, military and ecclesiastic–particularly and ironically those radicals of only yesterday who demanded a better world for the ill-fed, ill-clothed and ill-housed of the Great Depression and who still breathe heavily from proclaiming man's right to work and organize. Hard-core Beats want freedom to disorganize and thus ensure full flowering of their remarkable individualities. They are against work and they are often ill-fed, ill-clothed and ill-housed by preference. The Negro, it is true, is a hero to the Beat (as are the junkie and the jazz musician), and he is embraced with a fervor which San Francisco's anarchist poet Kenneth Rexroth sardonically defines as "crow-jimism." But it seems doubtful that antisegregationists or many Negroes could take comfort in this fact. The things the Beat treasures and envies in the Negro are the irresponsibility, cheerful promiscuity and subterranean defiance which were once enforced in him during his years of bondage. A middle-class Negro would be hopelessly square. Novelist Norman Mailer, a devoted follower of hipsterism, calls the Beat movement the cult of the White Negro and glibly suggests that its members seek the "constant humility" of Negro life in order to emulate its "primitive . . . joy, lust, and languor. . . ." But the Beat Generation can be much more accurately described as a cult of the Pariah. It yearns for the roach-guarded mores of the skid road, the flophouse, the hobo jungle and the slum, primarily to escape regimentation. It shares these with Negroes, when it does, only by coincidence.

. . . .

A hundred million squares must ask themselves: "What have we done to deserve this?"

Reading to Jazz

One of the contributions of the Beats to poetry was the introduction of reading to jazz accompaniment. The flavor of the music perfectly suited the words and often produced an exciting aura of spontaneity. The following articles concern the use of jazz as a background for readings.

The Cool, Cool Bards

Time, 2 December 1957, p. 71

The poet and the jazzman met in a San Francisco basement, aptly named The Cellar, to discuss a fusion of the arts. "In *Now with Winter,*" said the poet, "we try something slow and soft. In *Artifacts* we want a sax solo, like the thrill is gone."

"You mean," said the jazzman, pointing to the text, "we goof around here."

"Yeah." said the poet. "Have a ball." Then the combo climbed onto the bandstand and gave out with a rippling accompaniment while the poet chanted into the mike. His name was Kenneth Ford, and he writes the kind of poetry the hip set digs. Sample lines, dedicated to Saxophonist Judy Tristano, separated wife of famed Jazz Pianist Lennie Tristano:

There was a grief, clearly heard,
Such lover's grief,
And your ax in the form of your sax,
Sounded like the sounds of a dying bird.

In downtown San Francisco and all along the Bohemian strip known as North Beach other poets and hipsters were giggling together to the raucous applause of the city's beard-and-sandal set. The poetry was usually poor and the jazz was worse, but nobody seemed to care. Record business was being done by dim little jazz spots such as the Sail'N and the Black Hawk–the Taj Mahal of West Coast jazz, where Dave Brubeck blew himself to fame. And at the Tin Angel, on the waterfront, Trumpeter Dick Mills and his combo were playing with the man who started the poetry-and-jazz trend, Poet Kenneth Rexroth, decked out in red shirt, olive green corduroy suit and black string tie. "Lord! Lord! Lord!" cried Rexroth happily. "Look how it packs them in!"

Yawps & Whimpers. Since the mid-40s, Poet Rexroth, now 52, has presided over a circle of San Francisco writers he describes as "mature Bohemians." Their characteristic literary theme is the decline and fall of practically everybody, delivered in a tone that wavers between a yawp and a whimper. At the GHQ of the San Francisco poets, a tiny joint on Grant Avenue known simply as The Place, the non-squares were invited to gather on Sunday afternoons to "snarl at the cosmos, praise the unsung, defy the order." Poet Rexroth first carried the snarls into the jazz clubs last winter. "Poetry," he argued, "is a dying art in modern civilization. Poetry and jazz together return the poet to his audience."

A longtime jazz buff, Rexroth got together with Saxophonist Bruce Lippincott and worked out a sketchy jazz accompaniment for his new poem, *Thou Shalt Not Kill,* a lengthy dirge for long-lost friends, mostly poets: "What happened to Robinson who used to stagger down Eighth Street, dizzy with solitary gin? . . . Where is Leonard who thought he was a locomotive? . . . What became of Jim Oppenheim? . . . Where is Sol Funaroff? What happened to Potamkin? . . . One sat up all night talking to H. L. Mencken and drowned himself in the morning." Then the Rexroth verse turns to a super Bohemian and a man who was also a good poet: Dylan Thomas. When Rexroth first read the poem, 500 fans stormed The Cellar (seating capacity: 43) to hear him.

Beat Generation Dead as Davy Crockett Caps, Says Rexroth, Passing Through

Kenneth Rexroth

The Village Voice Reader, pp. 337–339

The other day Kenneth Rexroth, in town for some jazz-poetry readings at a local bar, dropped by these offices for a chat. Urged to commit his remarks to paper, he said he would write The Voice *a letter. Here it is:*

Pursuant, as they say, to our conversation, the Village hasn't changed much. I grew up in high chairs at the Brevoort and Lafayette. There's more of it, and it's sharper. I don't think there's much doubt, for instance, that The Voice is a more civilized organ than Bruno's Weekly. The place is full of uptowners; it always was. It is expensive; it was in 1920. As a way of life, it goes on unchanged, amongst the call girls, customers' men, aboriginal Italians and Irish. But where one girl wore colored stockings in 1905, thousands wear them today. Where Floyd Dell read Nietzsche, untold numbers read Beckett in the dim light of cold-water walk-ups.

As for the Beat Generation. Let's all stop. Right now. This has turned into a Madison Avenue gimmick. When the fall book lists come out, it will be as dead as Davy Crockett caps. It is a pity that as fine an artist as Jack Kerouac got hooked by this label. Of course it happened because of Jack's naivete–the inno-

Rexroth in 1969 (photograph by Ann Charters)

cence of heart which is his special virtue. I am sure he is as sick of it as I am. I for one never belonged to it. I am neither beatified nor pummelled. I'm getting on, but I've managed to dodge the gimmick generations as they went past; I was never Lost nor Proletarian nor Reactionary. This stuff is strictly for the customers.

As for Jack himself. Yes, I threw him out. He was frightening the children. He doesn't frighten me, though when he gets excessively beatified he bores me slightly. I think he is one of the finest prose writers now writing prose. He is a naive writer, like Restif de la Bretonne or Henry Miller, who accurately reflects a world without understanding it very well in the rational sense. For that, Clellan Holmes is far better on the same scene, shrewd and objective; but, as I am pretty sure he himself would be the first to admit, not the artist Jack is, and lacking, because of his very objectivity, Jack's poignancy and terror. One thing about Jack and Allen Ginsberg, who, I might remind you, are Villagers, and only were temporarily on loan to San Francisco: I had to come back to New York to realize how good they are. They have sure as hell made just the right enemies.

Now about jazz poetry. Let anybody who wants to have started it go right ahead and have started it. I'm pretty sure I didn't. But Lawrence Ferlinghetti and I did first start it off as public entertainment before concert and club audiences. For better or worse, I guess we started the craze. It is a lot more than a craze as far as I am concerned. I am not interested in a freak gig. I think the art of poetry in America is in a bad way. It is largely the business of seminars, conducted by aging poets for five or six budding poets.

Jazz poetry gets poetry out of the classrooms and into contact with large audiences who have not read any verse since grammar school. They listen, they like it, they come back for more. It demands of poetry, however deep and complex, something of a public surface, like the plays of Shakespeare that had stuff for everybody, the commonalty, the middle class, the nobility, the intellectuals.

Jazz gives poetry, too, the rhythms of itself, so expressive of the world we live in, and it gives it the inspiration of the jazz world, with its hard simple morality and its direct honesty–especially its erotic honesty. Fish or cut bait. Poetry gives modern jazz a verbal content infinitely superior to the silly falsities of the typical Tin Pan Alley lyric. It provides people who do not understand music technically something to hook onto–something to lead them into the complex world of modern jazz–as serious and as artistically important as any music being produced today. And then, the reciting, rather than singing voice, if properly managed, *swings* more than an awful lot of vocalists. As you may know, most jazz men like two singers–Frankie and Ella. With a poet who understands what is going on, they are not at the mercy of a vocalist who wants just to vocalize and who looks on the band as a necessary evil at best. Too, the emotional complexity of good poetry provides the musician with continuous creative stimulus, but at the same time gives him the widest possible creative freedom.

All this requires skill. Like if you just want to blow a lot of crazy words, man, if you think jazz is jungle music while the missionary soup comes to a boil, if you believe in the jazz myth of the hipster, you are going to fall on your face. Charlie Parker, or many younger men, are just as sophisticated artists as T. S. Eliot, and in some cases better, and have a lot more kinship with Couperin than with the King of the Cannibal Isles. And the combination of jazz and poetry requires good poetry, competent recitation, everybody in the group really digging what everybody else is doing, and, of course, real tasty music. Then it's great, and everybody loves it, specially you, baby.

Rexroth discussed the popularity of combining poetry and jazz in an interview with David Meltzer for a 1971 book on the poetry scene in San Francisco.

See, the great problem, is that to do a thing really well in the first place, the poet has to know a great deal about music, either play an instrument or be able to write music or both. He should have some idea about what is happening. Then the band has to rehearse. You don't just get up and blow. And if you lived in San Francisco, the better bands were not available because they were on tour. The musicians were moving around all the time. That's why we started in The Cellar, because the owners were the band. The piano player (Bill Weisjahn) and the drummer (Sonny Wayne) were the owners. And Bruce Lippincott on tenor . . . they were the house band. Other musicians came and went and played with the band. (Mingus and I did something a long time ago in The Black Cat during the war, just for fun one night.) As soon as Ferlinghetti did it, then Patchen brought out his record with a highly trained group. Mingus and Langston Hughes played the Five Spot in New York after I did, and I understand it was very successful. . . .Well, this started a thing so that in every Greenwich Village coffee shop and bar for about two years, all kinds of bums with pawnshop saxophones put together with scotch tape, and some other guy with something called poetry, were, like, you know, blowing poetry, man, dig? And it was absolutely unmitigated crap. It killed the whole thing. It had a terribly bad effect. There wasn't anything like it in San Francisco because we had done the thing in San Francisco . . . People knew it, people knew all about it, even though there was an awful lot of trash at the Coffee Gallery, but by and large the music was better and the poetry was better too. But the stuff in New York was ridiculous, and of course it's that whole New York commercial scene. That was all it was for. To make the tourist go to Greenwich Village. You went down there where the first miniskirts were worn, and the miniskirted chicks were waitresses, and you got yourself a free grope, and you listened to free jazz and poetry done by a couple of stumblebums who weren't being paid anything, and it killed the whole thing. Then Lipton in Southern California staged the first big show. It was very successful, Shorty Rogers heading one group with me and Freddy Katz heading the other. Lipton, Stu Perkoff, and some others. This was quite a show. And it ran for weeks and drew all kinds of people

Poster for a poetry reading in San Francisco

and made all kinds of bread. The musicians were top musicians.

I was always luckier than anybody else because I knew more about what I was doing. I got top musicians. The people I had working with me at the Five Spot were part of the Blakey organization: Bobby Timmons, Doug Watkins, and the star of those days, Donald Byrd, and Elvin Jones on drums, and then Pepper Adams on baritone. The same in Chicago. The band I worked with up and down the coast was built around Brew Moore, who was a Lester Young-type tenor. He was very good for Kansas City soul. An awful lot of work went into this, long rehearsals. I always worked with head-arrangements. Patchen worked with stuff that was all written down.

—*The San Francisco Poets,* pp. 24–25

Race, Jazz, and the Beats

Kerouac, Neal Cassady, and others read jazz musician Mezz Mezzrow's Really the Blues. *Mezzrow tells the story of growing up in Chicago and other cities and how he became a successful jazz musician with the "in" crowd. In this excerpt, he discusses jazz talk–"jive."*

Another well-known author and journalist, Earl Conrad, talks about jive as a kind of caricatured twist the Negro gives to the language that was foisted on him. "White America perpetrated a new and foreign language on the Africans it enslaved. Slowly, over the generations, Negro America, living by and large in its own segregated world, with its own thoughts, found its own way of expression, found its own way of handling English, as it had to find its own way in handling many other aspects of a white, hostile world. Jive is one of the end-results. . . . Jive talk may have been originally a kind of 'pig Latin' that slaves talked with each other, a code–when they were in the presence of whites. Take the word 'ofay.' Ninety million white Americans right now probably don't know that that means 'a white,' but Negroes know it. Negroes needed to have a word like that in their language, needed to create it in self-defense." *Ofay,* of course, is pig Latin for *foe.*

Conrad's right a hundred times over, but I think you have to make a big distinction between the Southern Negro's strictly cautious and defensive private lingo and the high-spirited, belligerent jive of the younger Northern Negroes. Down South, before the Civil War and for long decades after it, right up to today, the colored folks had to nurse their wounds in private, never show their hurts and resentments, and talk among themselves in conspiratorial whispers. The language was mostly a self-protective code to them, and so it wasn't very elaborate or full of bubbling energy and unshackled invention; it was the tongue of a *beaten* people. But once the big migration got under way and the more adventurous Negroes started trekking northward up the Mississippi, a lot of their pent-up feelings busted out and romped all over the place. They brought their New Orleans music North with one hell of a roar. And their talk got more explosive, too, and more animated, filled with a little hope and spirit. That's when jive as we know it today really got going.

I first heard the jive language in its early stages, when I was hanging around the South Side in Chicago. It was the first furious babbling of a people who suddenly woke up to find that their death-sentence had been revoked, or at least postponed, and they were stunned and dazzled at first, hardly able to believe it. Then came the full exuberant waking up, the full realization that the bossman, at least the peckerwood kind with a bullwhip in his hand, was gone. The music got wilder and wilder. The excited rush of talk on street corners, and in poolrooms and ginmills, swelled up to a torrent. That was the first real jive–the lingo of prisoners with a temporary reprieve. When I got to Harlem I found it had spread to the East, and really come of age. These Harlem kids had decided they wouldn't be led back to jail nohow. They spieled a mile a minute, making that clear.

– *Really the Blues,* pp. 216–217

Debating the Significance of the Beats

The Innocent Nihilists Adrift in Squaresville
Eugene Burdick
The Reporter, 3 April 1958, pp. 30–33

The "Beat Generation" is really a private vision. The "originals"–Jack Kerouac (*On the Road),* John Clellon Holmes ("Go!"), and Allen Ginsberg ("Howl")–dreamed of a ". . . generation of crazy illuminated hipsters suddenly rising and roaming America, serious, curious, bumming and hitchhiking everywhere, ragged, beatific, beautiful in an ugly graceful new way. . . *beat,* meaning down and out but full of intense conviction." The "beat" man was in a muted, low-pitched, inarticulate revolution, but disenchanted enough to know that political action was not the way out. The trick was to stay free; stay poor; stay hallucinated; dig Ezra Pound, but not loudly or pretentiously; dig friends, but, man, really dig them deep and true; with strangers use the implacable cruel language of the hipster and you're safe; and, above all, keep "them" away from you, keep that big, safe, fat, efficient, cold world away from you.

Lately the vision has been invaded, mauled, overstudied, imitated. The ring of bemused spectators has pressed in close with the inevitable result: the vision has suffocated.

. . . .

The battle between generations has always existed. What makes the hipster different is that he knows the battle is hopeless, that he is bound to lose, and that by fighting he merely exhausts himself and gives the squares comfort. This is what the calm, icy imperturbability of juvenile delinquents means when they put their faces under the bright lights for a police line-up. They don't get hysterical or shout or try to explain. Why explain that their marijuana "tea parties" and kicks in a stolen car and sexual indulgences are little things compared to the barely controlled violence of adults who allowed a world war, a cold war, and Korea? They see the adult world as senseless, hypocritical, violent, and essentially beyond redemption. You don't try to convert the square world, you don't enter into that sick rationality, you just ignore "them." Parents who have seen that opaque nonlistening look go over the faces of their teen-age children are being exposed to the most shared sentiment of the beat generation.

The Beat Debated–Is it or Is It Not?
Marc D. Schleifer
The Village Voice, 19 November 1958, pp. 1, 3

"Let the cats in," someone shouted, while an overflow crowd of hundreds pushed against doors barred by anxious college girls. The place was Hunter College Playhouse on November 6, [1958,] where there was a debate scheduled on the theme, "Is There a Beat Generation?"

Sponsor of the affair was Brandeis University, whose dean, Joseph Kauffman, peered at the audience and looked uncomfortable, glanced at guests Kingsley Amis, Ashley Montagu, James Wechsler, and then looked more uncomfortable. When the evening's festivities of hoots, cheers, insults, and poetry were over, Dean Kauffman's discomfort was so great that I feared for his supper. *But he was still smiling.* And after all, isn't discomfort a small price for enlightened academicians to pay when they carry the creative process into lecture-hall operating rooms on a stretcher and then dissect it as they would a bloodless corpse?

Thoughts, somewhat excerpted, in order of their appearance:

KEROUAC (dashing offstage a dozen times, clowning with a hat to the final stumble and wild dragging of poet Allen Ginsberg onstage toward the end of the "debate"): "Live your lives out, they say; nah, love your lives out, so when they come around and stone you, you won't be living in any glass house–only a glassy flesh. What is called the "beat generation" is really a revolution in manners . . . being a swinging group of new American boys intent on life. James Dean was not the first to express this. Before him there was Bogart and the private eyes. Now college kids have started to use the words 'hung up.' . . . I'm hung up, you know–words I first heard on Times Square in the '40s. Being beat goes back to my ancestors, to the rebellious, the hungry, the weird, and the mad. To Laurel and Hardy, to Popeye, to Wimpy looking wild-eyed over hamburgers, the size of which they make no more; to Lamont Cranston, the Shadow, with his mad heh-heh-heh knowing laugh. And now there are two types of beat hipsters–the Cool: bearded, sitting without moving in cafes, with their unfriendly girls dressed in black, who say nothing; and the Hot: Crazy, talkative, mad shining eyes, running from bar to bar only to be ignored by the cool subterraneans. I guess I'm still with the hot ones. When I walk into a club playing jazz, I still want to shout: 'Blow, Man, Blow.'"

KINGSLEY AMIS (author of *Lucky Jim,* wearing a conservative light brown suit, perplexed by the mad audience, but in a friendly way trying to understand the madness): "There is a general impression that the beat generation has opened a branch in England, or at least made an alliance with a group called 'the Angry Young Men.' Thus a Detroit critic says: 'America's angry young men are called the beat generation.' Is there a group of young English writers united and unique in protesting about creative stagnation in contemporary life? No, emphatically, no. 'The Angry Young Men' is an invention of literary middlemen, desperate journalists who thrive on classifications and clichés, who put writers in pigeonholes and save people the trouble of reading. This nonsense can also be traced to the Anglo-American cult of youth. In England, anybody who writes and is under pensionable age is put under the title of AYM. Any day I expect to see Boris Pasternak so labeled. Yes, Osborne *is* angry, that's his privilege. But all the English writers who have been so categorized are doing what writers have always done–they are going about the job of writing. There is no Angry Young Men movement. There may be a beat generation, but I doubt it."

JAMES WECHSLER (editor of the *New York Post* and author of *Revolt on the Campus,* looking angry if not young, vigorously chewing his gum with open-mouthed liberal sincerity, staring at Kerouac with incomprehension whenever Jack mentioned God, Poetry, or the Cross): "I am one of the few unreconstructed radicals of my generation. Much of what has happened in the past 20 or so years has challenged my basic beliefs, but I still adhere to them. *[Turning to Kerouac]* Life is complicated enough without having to make it into a poem. I am convinced that ethical values will reemerge. What gives meaning to life is the survival of these values. It is a sad thing for America that this beat generation is supposed to represent rebellion and unorthodoxy. After listening to Kerouac I understand less about what they stand for than before. I see no virtue in organized confusion. The beat generation as a symbol is sort of a joke. The issue is not whether there is a beat generation, but whether civilization will survive. There is no valor in their [the beats'] kind of flight and irresponsibility."

ASHLEY MONTAGU (Princeton anthropologist, author of *Immortality and Man: The First Millon Years,* white-haired, calm, slightly amused, and slightly sleepy-looking just the way the Ladies League thinks a professor should look): "James Dean symbolized the beat generation. His death was consistent with the BG philosophy–life is like Russian Roulette. Their only conformity is nonconformity. The beats give personal testimony to the breakdown of Western values. These are the children who were failed by their parents. Compassion, not condemnation, is called for. The BG is the ultimate expression of a civilization whose moral values have broken down. While not everybody born in the past 30 years is beat, and while there were beat people born more than 30 years ago, the beat writers are describing this generation."

Ginsberg, Corso, and Orlovsky gave a reading at Columbia University on 5 February 1969. A week after the occasion Ginsberg wrote to Ferlinghetti: "It's my old school I was kicked out of so I suppose I'm hung up on making it there and breaking its reactionary back." Ginsberg's return to the university prompted the wife of Lionel Trilling, his former professor, to examine her own reaction to the poet, his reputation, and his appearance.

The Other Night at Columbia:
A Report from the Academy

Diana Trilling

Partisan Review, Spring 1959, pp. 223–230

The "beats" were to read their poetry at Columbia on Thursday evening and on the spur of the moment three wives from the English department had decided to go hear them. But for me, one of the three, the spur of the moment was not where the story had begun. It had begun much farther back, some twelve or fourteen years ago, when Allen Ginsberg had been a student of my husband's and I had heard about him much more than I usually hear of students for the simple reason that he got into a great deal of trouble which involved his instructors, and had to be rescued and revived and restored; eventually he had even to be kept out of jail. Of course there was always the question, should this young man be rescued, should he be restored? There was even the question, shouldn't he go to jail? We argued about it some at home but the discussion, I'm afraid, was academic, despite my old resistance to the idea that people like Ginsberg had the right to ask and receive preferential treatment just because they read Rimbaud and Gide and undertook to be writers themselves. Nor was my principle, if one may call it that, of equal responsibility for poets and shoe clerks so firm that I didn't need to protect it by refusing to confront Ginsberg as an individual or potential acquaintance. I don't mean that I was aware, at the time, of my motive for disappearing on the two or three occasions when he came to the house to deliver a new batch of poems and report on his latest adventures in sensation-seeking. If I'd been asked to explain, then my wish not to meet and talk with this disturbing young man who had managed to break through the barrier of student anonymity, I suppose I'd have rested with the proposition that he made life too messy, although then I'd have had to defend myself against the charge, made in the name of art, of a strictness of judgment which was too little tolerant of deviation from more usual and respectable standards of behavior. But ten, twelve, fourteen years ago, there was still something of a challenge in the "conventional" position; I still enjoyed defending the properties and proprieties of the middle class against friends who persisted in scorning them. Of course, once upon a time–that was in the thirties–one had had to defend even having a comfortable chair to sit in, or a rug on the floor. But by the forties things had changed; one's most intransigent literary friends had capitulated by then, everybody had a well-upholstered sofa and I was reduced to such marginal causes as the Metropolitan Museum and the expectation that visitors would put their ashes in the ashtray and go home by 2:00 A.M. Then why should I not also defend the expectation that a student at Columbia, even a poet, would do his work, submit it to his teachers through the normal channels of classroom communication, stay out of jail, and, if things went right, graduate, start publishing, be reviewed, and see what developed, whether he was a success or failure?

Well, for Ginsberg, things didn't go right for quite a while. The time came when he was graduated from Columbia and published his poems, but first he got into considerable difficulty, beginning with his suspension from college and the requirement that he submit to psychiatric treatment, and terminating–but this was quite a few years later–in an encounter with the police from which he was extricated by some of his old teachers who knew he needed a hospital more than a prison. The suspension had been for a year, when Ginsberg had been a senior; the situation was not without its grim humor. It seems that Ginsberg had traced an obscenity in the dust of a dormitory window; the words were too shocking for the Dean of Students to speak, so he had written them on a piece of paper which he pushed across the desk to my husband: "Fuck the Jews." Even the part of Lionel that wanted to laugh couldn't; it was too hard for the Dean to have to transmit this message to a Jewish professor—this was still in the forties when being a Jew in the university was not yet what it is today. "But he's a Jew himself," said the Dean. "Can you understand his writing a thing like that?" Yes, Lionel could understand; but he couldn't explain it to the Dean. And anyway, he knew that to appreciate why Ginsberg had traced this particular legend on the window required more than an understanding of Jewish self-hatred, and also that it was not the sole cause for administrative uneasiness about Ginsberg and his cronies. It was ordinary good sense for the college to take protective measures with Ginsberg and for him.

I now realize that even at this early point in his career I had already accumulated a fund of information about young Ginsberg which accurately forecast his later talent for self-promotion although it was surely disproportionate to the place he commanded in his teacher's mind and quite failed to jibe with the physical impression I had caught in opening the door to him when he came to the apartment. He was middling tall, slight, dark, sallow; his dress suggested shabby gentility, poor brown tweed gone threadbare and yellow. The description would have fitted any number of undergraduates of his or any Columbia generation; it was only the personal story that set him acutely apart. He came from New Jersey, where his father was a schoolteacher, or perhaps a principal, who wrote poetry too—I think for the *Saturday Review,* which would be as good a way as any of defining the separation between father and son. His mother was in a mental institution, and she had been there, off and on, for a long time. This was the central and utterly persuasive fact of the young man's life; I knew this because I was told it in poetry at Columbia the other night, and doubtless it was this knowledge that at least in some part accounted for the edginess with which I responded to so much as the mention of Ginsberg's name. Here was a boy on whom an outrageous unfairness had been perpetrated: his mother had fled from him into madness and now whoever crossed his path became somehow responsible, caught in the impossibility of rectifying what she had done. It was an unjust burden for Ginsberg to put, as he so subtly did, on those who were only the later accidents of his history and it made me defensive instead of charitable with him. No boy, after all, could ask anyone to help him build a career on the terrible but gratuitous circumstance of a mad mother; it was a justification for neither poetry nor prose nor yet for "philosophy" of the kind young Ginsberg liked to expound to his teacher. In the question period which followed the poetry-reading the other night at Columbia, this matter of a rationale for the behavior of Ginsberg and his friends came up: someone asked Ginsberg to state his philosophy. It was a moment I had been awaiting and I thought: "Here we go; he'll tell us how he's crazy like a daisy and how his friend Orlovsky is crazy like a butterfly." I had been reading *Time;* who hadn't? But, instead of repeating the formulations of earlier interviews, Ginsberg answered that he had no philosophy; he spoke of inspiration, or perhaps it was illumination, ecstatic illumination, as the source of his poetry, and I was more than surprised; I was curiously pleased for him because I took it as a considerable advance in self-control that he could operate with this much shrewdness and leave it, if only for this occasion, to his audience to abstract a "position" from his and his friends' antics while he himself moved wild, mild, and innocent through the jungle of speculation. Back in the older days, it had always been my feeling that so far as his relationship with his teacher was concerned, this trying to formulate a philosophy must reveal its falseness even to himself; his recourse to it was somehow beneath his intelligence. Apart from the need to force a recognition of his personal suffering upon certain figures who, in his mind, stood for society, two motives, it seemed to me, impelled him then: the wish to shock his teacher, and the wish to meet the teacher on equal ground. The first of these motives was complicated enough, involving as it did the gratifications of self-incrimination and disapproval, and then forgiveness; but the second was more tangled still. To talk with one's English professor who was also a writer, a critic, and one who made no bones about his solid connection with literary tradition, about one's descent from Rimbaud, Baudelaire or Dostoevsky was clearly to demonstrate a good-sized rationality and order in what was apparently an otherwise undisciplined life. Even more, or so I fancied, it was to propose an alliance between the views of the academic and the poet-rebel, the unity of a deep discriminating commitment to literature which must certainly one day wipe out the fortuitous distance between boy and man, pupil and teacher. Thus, Ginsberg standing on the platform at Columbia and refusing the philosophy gambit might well be announcing a new and sounder impulse toward self-definition for which one could be grateful.

But I remind myself: Ginsberg at Columbia on Thursday night was not Ginsberg at Chicago—according to *Time,* at any rate—or Ginsberg at Hunter either, where Kerouac ran the show, and a dismal show it

Cover and paired cartoons from a 1959 paperback book

must have been, with Kerouac drinking on the platform and clapping James Wechsler's hat on his head in a grand parade of contempt–they were two of four panelists gathered to discuss "Is there such a thing as a beat generation?"–and leading Ginsberg out from the wings like a circus donkey. For whatever reason–rumor had it he was in a personal crisis–Kerouac didn't appear on Thursday night, and Ginsberg at Columbia was Ginsberg's own man, dealing with his own history, and intent, it seemed to me, on showing up the past for the poor inaccurate thing it so often is: it's a chance we all dream of but mostly it works the other way around, like the long-ago perhaps-apocryphal story of the successful theater director coming back to Yale and sitting on the fence weeping for a youth he could never rewrite no matter how many plays of Chekhov he brought to Broadway, no matter how much money he made. I suppose I have no right to say now, and on such early and little evidence, that Ginsberg had always desperately wanted to be respectable, or respected, like his instructors at Columbia, it is so likely that this is a hindsight that suits my needs. It struck me, though, that this was the most unmistakable and touching message from platform to audience the other night, and as I received it, I felt I had known something like it all along. Not that Ginsberg had ever shown himself as a potential future colleague in the university; anything but that. Even the implied literary comradeship had had reference, not to any possibility of Ginsberg's assimilation into the community of professors, but to the professor's capacity for association in the community of rebellious young poets. Still, it was not just anyone on the campus to whom Ginsberg had come with his lurid boasts which were also his confession; it was Lionel, it was Mark Van Doren; if there was anyone else it would very likely be of the same respectable species, and I remember saying, "He wants you to forbid him to behave like that. He wants you to take him out of it, or why does he choose people like you and Mark Van Doren to tell these stories to?" To which I received always the same answer: "I'm not his father," a response that of course allowed of no argument.

And yet, even granting the accuracy of this reconstruction of the past, it would be wrong to conclude that any consideration of motive on Ginsberg's part was sufficiently strong to alter one's first and most forceful image of Ginsberg as a "case"–a gifted and sad case, a guilt-provoking and nuisance case, but, above all, a case. Nor was it a help that my husband had recently published a story about a crazy student and a supposedly normal student in which the author's affection was so plainly directed to the former; we never became used to the calls, often in the middle of the night, asking whether it wasn't the crazy character who was really sane. Allen Ginsberg, with his poems in which there was never quite enough talent or hard work, and with his ambiguous need to tell his teacher exactly what new flagrancy had opened to his imagination as he talked about Gide with his friends at the West End Café, had at any rate the distinction of being more crudely justified in his emotional disturbance than most. He also had the distinction of carrying mental unbalance in the direction of criminality, a territory one preferred to leave unclaimed by student or friend.

Gide and the West End Café in all its upper-Broadway dreariness: what could the two conceivably have in common except those lost boys of the forties? How different it might have been for Ginsberg and his friends if they had come of age ten or fifteen years sooner was one of the particular sadnesses of the other evening; it virtually stood on the platform with them as the poets read their poems, whose chief virtue, it seemed to me, was their "racial-minority" funniness, their "depressed-classes" funniness of a kind which has never had so sure and live a place as it did in the thirties, the embittered fond funniness which has to do with one's own impossible origins, funniness plain and poetical, always aware of itself, of a kind which would seem now to have all but disappeared among intellectuals except as an eclecticism or a device of self-pity. It's a real loss; I hadn't quite realized how much I missed it until Thursday night when Ginsberg read his poem "The Ignu," and Corso read his poem "Marriage" (a compulsive poem, he called it, about a compulsive subject), and they were still funny in that old racial-depressed way but not nearly as funny and authentic as they would have been had they been written before the Jews and the Italians and the Negroes, but especially the Jews, had been awarded a place as Americans-like-everyone-else instead of remaining outsiders raised in the Bronx or on Ninth Avenue or even in Georgia. The Jew in particular is a loss to literature and life–I mean the Jew out of which was bred the Jewish intellectual of the thirties. For a few short years in the thirties, as not before or since, the Jew was at his funniest, shrewdest best; he perfectly well knew the advantage he could count on in the Gentile world, and that there was no ascendancy or pride the Gentile comrades could muster against a roomful of Jewish sympathizers singing at the tops of their voices, "A SOCialist union is a NO good union, is a COM-pan-y union of the bosses," or against Michael Gold's mother, who wanted to know did her boy have to write books the whole world should know she had bedbugs. If Ginsberg had been born in an earlier generation it would surely have been the Stewart Cafeteria in the Village that he and his friends would have frequented instead of the West End, that dim waystation of undergraduate debauchery on Morning-

Poetry reading at Columbia University: Peter Orlovsky, Corso, and Ginsberg being introduced by Professor F. W. Dupee (photograph © by Fred W. McDarrah)

side Heights–and the Stewart Cafeteria was a well-lighted place and one of the funniest places in New York; at least, at every other table it was funny, and where it was decadent or even conspiratorial, that had its humor too, or at least its robustness. As for Gide–the Gide of the thirties was the "betrayer of the Revolution," not the Gide of the *acte gratuite* and homosexuality in North Africa. One didn't use pathology in those days to explain or excuse or exhibit oneself and one never had to be lonely; there was never a less lonely time for intellectuals than the Depression, or a less depressed time–unless, of course, one was recalcitrant, like Fitzgerald, and simply refused to be radicalized, in which stubborn case it couldn't have been lonelier. Intellectuals talk now about how, in the thirties, there was an "idea" in life, not the emptiness we live in. Actually, it was a time of generally weak intellection–or so it seems to me now–but of very strong feeling. Everyone judged everyone else; it was a time of incessant cruel moral judgment; today's friend was tomorrow's enemy; whoever disagreed with oneself had sold out, God knows to or for what; there was little of the generosity among intellectuals which nowadays dictates the automatic "Gee, that's great" at any news of someone else's good fortune. But it was surely a time of quicker, truer feeling than is now conjured up with marijuana or the infantile camaraderie of Kerouac's *On the Road*. And there was paradox but no contradiction in this double truth, just as there was no contradiction in the fact that it was a time in which the neurotic determination of the intellectual was being so universally acted out and yet a time in which, whatever his dedication to historical or economic determinism, personally he had a unique sense of free will. In the thirties one's clinical vocabulary was limited to two words, escapism and subjectivism, and both of them applied only to other people's wrong political choices.

Well, the "beats" weren't lucky enough to be born except when they were born. Ginsberg says he lives in Harlem, but it's not the Harlem of the Scottsboro boys and W. C. Handy and the benign insanity of trying to proletarianize Striver's Row; their comrades are not the comrades of the Stewart Cafeteria nor yet of the road, as Kerouac would disingenuously have it, but pickups on dark morning streets. But they have their connection with us who were young in the thirties, their intimate political connection, which we deny at risk of missing what it is that makes the "beat" phenomenon something to think about. As they used to say on Fourteenth Street, it is no accident, comrades, it is decidedly no accident that today in the fifties our single overt manifestation of protest takes the wholly nonpolitical form of a group of panic-stricken kids in blue jeans, many of them publicly homosexual, talking about or taking drugs, assuring us that they are out of their minds, not responsible, while the liberal intellectual is convinced that he has no power to control the political future, the future of the free world, and that therefore he must submit to what he defines as political necessity. Though of course the various aspects of a culture must be granted their own autonomous source and character, the connection between "beat" and respectable liberal intellectual exists and is not hard to locate: the common need to deny free will, divest oneself of responsibility and yet stay alive. The typical liberal intellectual of the fifties, whether he is a writer or a sociologist or a law-school professor, explains his evolution over the last two decades–specifically, his current attitudes in foreign affairs–by telling us that he has been forced to accept the unhappy reality of Soviet strength in an atomic world, and that there is no alternative to capitulation–not that he calls it that–except the extinction of nuclear war. Even the diplomacy he invokes is not so much flexible, which he would like to think it is, as disarmed, an instrument of his impulse to surrender rather than of any wish to win or even hold the line. Similarly docile to culture, the "beat" also contrives a fate by predicating a fate. Like the respectable established intellectual–or the organization man, or the suburban matron–against whom he makes his play or protest, he conceives of himself as incapable of exerting any substantive influence against the forces that condition him. He is made by society, he cannot make society. He can only stay alive as best he can for as long as is permitted him. Is it any wonder, then, that *Time* and *Life* write as they do about the "beats"–with such a conspicuous show of superiority, and no hint of fear? These periodicals know what genuine, dangerous protest looks like, and it doesn't look like Ginsberg and Kerouac. Clearly, there is no more menace in "Howl" or *On the Road* than there is in the Scarsdale PTA. In the common assumption of effectlessness, in the apparent will to rest with social determination over which the individual spirit and intelligence cannot and perhaps even should not try to triumph, there merge any number of the disparate elements of our present culture–from the liberal intellectual journals to Luce to the Harvard Law School, from Ginsberg to the suburban matron.

But then why, one ponders, do one's most relaxed and non-square friends, alongside of whom one can oneself be made to look like the original object with four sides of equal length, why do one's most politically "flexible" friends, alongside of whom one's own divergence from dominant liberal opinion is regularly made to look so ungraceful, so like a latter-day sectarianism, feel constrained to dispute Columbia's judgment in giving the "beats" a hearing on the campus and my own wish to attend their poetry reading? Why, for instance, the dissent of Dwight MacDonald, whom I happened to see that afternoon; or of W. H. Auden, who, when I afterward said I had been moved by the performance, gently chided me, "I'm ashamed of you"; or of the editor of *Partisan Review,* who, while he consents to my going ahead with this article for his magazine, can't hide his editorial puzzlement, even worry, because I want to give the "beats" so much attention? In strict logic, it would seem to me that things should go in quite the other direction and that I, who insist upon at least the assumption of free will in our political choices, who insist upon what I call political responsibility, should be the one to protest a university forum for the irresponsibles whereas my friends whose politics are what I think of as finally a politics of passivity and fatedness, should be able to shrug off the "beats" as merely another inevitable, if tasteless, expression of a *Zeitgeist* with which I believe them to be far more in tune than I am. I do not mean, of course, to rule out taste, or style, as a valid criterion of moral judgment. A sense of social overwhelmment which announces itself in terms of disreputableness or even criminality no doubt asks for a different kind of moral assessment than the same emotion kept within the bounds of a generally recognized propriety. But I would simply point to the similarities which are masked by the real differences between the "beats" and those intellectuals who most overtly scorn them. Taste or style dictates that most intellectuals behave decorously, earn a regular living, disguise instead of flaunt any private digressions from the conduct society considers desirable; when they seek support for the poetical impulse or ask for light on their self-doubt and fears, they don't make the naked boast that they are crazy like daisies but they elaborate a new belief in the indispensability of neurosis to art, or beat the bushes for some new deviant psychoanalysis which will generalize their despair though of course without curing it. And these differences of style are undeniably important, at least for the moment. It is from the long-range view of our present-day cultural situation, which bears so closely upon our continuing national crisis, that the moral difference between a respectable and a disreputable acceptance of defeat seems to me to constitute little more than a cultural footnote to history.

But perhaps I wander too far from the other night at Columbia. There was enough in the evening that was humanly immediate to divert one from this kind of ultimate concern. . . .

It was not an official university occasion. The "beats" appeared at Columbia on the invitation of a student club–interestingly enough, the John Dewey Society. Whether the club first approached Ginsberg or Ginsberg initiated the proceedings, I don't know, but what had happened was that Ginsberg in his undergraduate days had taken a loan from the university–$200? $250?–and recently the Bursar's office had caught up with him in his new incarnation of successful literary itinerant, to demand repayment. Nothing if not ingenious, Ginsberg now proposed to pay off his debt by reading his poetry at Columbia without fee. It was at this point that various members of the English department, solicited as sponsors for the operation, had announced their rejection of the whole deal, literary as well as financial, and the performance was arranged without financial benefit to Ginsberg and without official cover; we three wives, however, decided to attend on our own. We would meet at 7:45 at the door of the theater; no, we would meet at 7:40 at the door of the theater; no, we would meet no later than 7:30 across the street from the theater: the telephoning back and forth among the three women was stupendous as word spread of vast barbarian hordes converging on Columbia's poor dull McMillin Theater from all the dark recesses of the city, howling for their leader. The advance warnings turned out to be exaggerated.

It was nevertheless disconcerting that Fred Dupee of the English Department had consented, at the request of the John Dewey Society, to be moderator, chairman, introducer of Ginsberg and his fellow-poets, for while it provided the wives of his colleagues with the assurance of seats in a section of the hall reserved for faculty, it was not without its uncomfortable reminder that Ginsberg had, in a sense, got his way; he was appearing on the same Columbia platform from which T. S. Eliot had last year read his poetry; he was being presented by, and was thus bound to be thought under the sponsorship of, a distinguished member of the academic and literary community who was also one's long-time friend. And indeed it was as Dupee's friend that one took a first canvass of the scene: the line of policemen before the entrance to the theater; the air of suppressed excitement in the lobbies and one's own rather contemptible self-consciousness about being a participant in the much-publicized occasion; the shoddiness of an audience in which it was virtually impossible to distinguish between student and camp-follower; the always-new shock of so many young girls, so few of them pretty, and so many blackest black stockings; so many young men, so few of them–despite the many black beards–with any promise of masculinity. It was distressing to think that Dupee was going to be "faculty" to such an incoherent assembly, that at this moment he was backstage with Ginsberg's group, formulating a deportment which would check the excess of which one knew it to be capable, even or especially in public, without doing violence to his own large tolerance.

For me, it was of some note that the auditorium smelled fresh. The place was already full when we arrived; I took one look at the crowd and was certain that it would smell bad. But I was mistaken. These people may think they're dirty inside and dress up to it. But the audience was clean and Ginsberg was clean and Corso was clean and Orlovsky was clean. Maybe Ginsberg says he doesn't bathe or shave; Corso, I know, declares that he has never combed his hair; Orlovsky has a line in one of the two poems he read–he's not yet written his third, the chairman explained–"If I should shave, I know the bugs would go away." But for this occasion, at any rate, Ginsberg, Corso and Orlovsky were all beautifully clean and shaven; Kerouac, in crisis, didn't appear, but if he had come he would have been clean and shaven too–he was entirely clean the night at Hunter; I've inquired about that. Certainly there's nothing dirty about a checked shirt or a lumberjacket and blue jeans; they're standard uniform in the best nursery schools. Ginsberg has his price, as do his friends, however much they may dissemble.

And how do I look to the "beats," I ask myself after that experience with the seats, and not only I but the other wives I was with? We had pulled aside the tattered old velvet rope which marked off the section held for faculty, actually it was trailing on the floor, and moved into the seats Dupee's wife had saved for us by strewing coats on them; there was a big gray overcoat she couldn't identify: she stood holding it up in the air murmuring wistfully, "Whose is this?"–until the young people in the row in back of us took account of us and answered sternly, "*Those* seats are reserved for faculty." If I have trouble unraveling undergraduates from "beats," neither do the wives of the Columbia English department wear their proper manners with any certainty.

But Dupee's proper manners, that's something else again: what could I have been worrying about, when had Dupee ever failed to meet an occasion, or missed the right style? I don't suppose one could witness a better performance than his on Thursday evening: its rightness was apparent the moment he walked onto the stage, his troupe in tow and himself just close enough and yet enough removed to indicate the balance in which he held the situation. Had there been a hint of betrayal in his deportment, of either himself or his guests–naturally, he had made them his guests–the whole evening might have been different: for instance, a few minutes later when the overflow audience outside the door began to bang and shout for admission, might not the audience have caught the contagion and become unruly too? Or would Ginsberg have stayed with his picture of himself as poet serious and triumphant instead of succumbing to what must have been the greatest temptation to spoil his opportunity? "The last time I was in this theater," Dupee began quietly, "it was also to hear a poet read his works. That was T. S. Eliot." A slight alteration of inflection, from irony to mockery, from wit to condescension, and it might well have been a signal for near-riot, boos and catcalls and whistlings; the evening would have been lost to the "beats," Dupee and Columbia would have been defeated. Dupee transformed a circus into a classroom. He himself, he said, welcomed the chance to hear these poets read their works–he never once in his remarks gave them their name of "beats" nor alluded even to San Francisco–because in all poetry it was important to study the spoken accent; he himself didn't happen especially to admire those of their works that he knew; still, he would draw our attention to their skillful use of a certain kind of American imagery which, deriving from Whitman, yet passed Whitman's use of it or even Hart Crane's. . . . It was Dupee speaking for the Academy, claiming for it its place in life, and the performers were inevitably captive to his dignity and self-assurance. Rather than Ginsberg and his friends, it was a photographer from *Life,* exploding his flashbulbs in everybody's face, mounting a ladder at the back of the stage the more effectively to shoot his angles, who came to represent vulgarity and disruption and disrespect; when a student in the audience disconnected a wire which had something to do with the picture-taking, one might guess that Ginsberg was none too happy that his mass-circulation "story" was being spoilt but it was the photographer's face that became ugly, the only real ugliness of the evening. One could feel nothing but pity for Ginsberg and his friends that their front of disreputableness and rebellion should be this vulnerable to the seductions of a clever host. With Dupee's introduction, the whole of their armor had been penetrated at the very outset.

Diana Trilling, the wife of Columbia professor Lionel Trilling, who taught Ginsberg

Pity is not the easiest of our emotions today; now it's "understanding" that is easy, and more and more–or so I find for myself–real pity moves hand in hand with real terror; it's an emotion one avoids because it's so hard: one "understands" the crippled, the delinquent, the unhappy so as not to have to pity them. But Thursday night was an occasion of pity so direct and inescapable that it left little to the understanding that wasn't mere afterthought–and pity not only for the observed, the performers, but for us who had come to observe them and reassure ourselves that we were not implicated. One might as readily persuade oneself one was not implicated in one's children! For this was it: these *were* children, miserable children trying desperately to manage, asking desperately to be taken out of it all, so that I kept asking myself, where had I had just such an experience before, and later it came to me: I had gone to see O'Neill's *Long Day's Journey into Night,* and the play had echoed with just such a child's cry for help; at intermission time all the mothers in the audience were so tormented and anxious that they rushed in a body to phone home: was the baby really all right, was he really well and warm in his bed; one couldn't get near the telephone booths. A dozen years ago, when Ginsberg had been a student and I had taxed Lionel with the duty to forbid him to misbehave, he had answered me that he wasn't the boy's father, and of course he was right. Neither was Mark Van Doren the boy's father; a teacher is not a father to his students and he must never try to be. Besides, Ginsberg had a father of his own who couldn't be replaced at will: he was in the audience the other night. One of the things Ginsberg read was part of a long poem to his mother, who, he told us, had died three years ago, and as he read it, he choked and cried; but no one in the auditorium tittered or showed embarrassment at this public display of emotion, and I doubt whether there was a young Existentialist in the audience who thought, "See he has existence: he can cry, he can feel." Nor did anyone seem very curious when he went on to explain, later in the evening, that the reason he had cried was because his father was in the theater. I have no way of knowing what Ginsberg's father felt the other night about his son being up there on the stage at Columbia (it rather obsesses me), but I should guess he was proud; it's what I'd conclude from his expression at the end of the performance when Ginsberg pressed through the admirers who surrounded him to get to his father as quickly as he could: surely that's nice for a father. And I should suppose a father was bound to be pleased that his son was reading his poems in a university auditorium: it would mean the boy's success, and this would be better than a vulgarity; it would necessarily include the chairman's critical gravity and the fact, however bizarre, that T. S. Eliot had been the last poet in this place before him. In a sense, Orlovsky and Corso were more orphans than Ginsberg the other night, but this was not necessarily because they were without fathers of their own in the audience; I should think it would go back much farther than this, to whatever it was that made them look so much more masked, less openly eager for approval; although they were essentially as innocent and childlike as Ginsberg, they couldn't begin to match his appeal; it was on Ginsberg that one's eye rested, it was to the sweetness in his face and to his sweet smile that one responded; it was to him that one gave one's pity and for him one felt one's terror. Clearly, I am no judge of his poem "Lion in the Room," which he announced was dedicated to Lionel Trilling; I heard it through too much sympathy, and also self-consciousness. The poem was addressed as well as dedicated to Lionel; it was about a lion in the room with the poet, a lion who was hungry but refused to eat him; I heard it as a passionate love-poem; I really can't say whether it was a good or a bad poem, but I was much moved by it, in some part unaccountably. It was also a decent poem, and I am willing to admit this surprised me; there were no obscenities in it as there had been in much of the poetry the "beats" read. Here was something else one noted about the other evening: most of the audience was very young, and Ginsberg must have realized this because when he read the poem about his mother and came to the place where he referred to the YPSLs of her girlhood, he interposed his only textual exegesis of the evening; in an aside he explained, "Young People's Socialist League"–he was very earnest about wanting his poetry to be understood. And it wasn't only his gentility that distinguished Ginsberg's father from the rest of the audience; as far as I could see, he was the only man in the hall who looked old enough to be the father of a grown son; the audience was crazily young, there were virtually no faculty present: I suppose they didn't want to give this much sanction to the "beats." For this young audience the obscenities read from the stage seemed to have no force whatsoever; there was not even the shock of silence, and when Ginsberg forgot himself in the question period and said that something or other was bull-shit, I think he was more upset than his listeners; I can't imagine anything more detached and scientific outside a psychoanalyst's office, or perhaps a nursery school, than this young audience at Columbia. And even of Corso himself one had the sense that he mouthed the bad word only with considerable personal difficulty: this hurts me more than it hurts you.

Obviously, the whole performance had been carefully planned as to who would read first and what, then who next, and just how much an audience could take without becoming bored and overcritical: it would be my opinion we could have taken a bit more before the question period, which must have been an anti-climax for anyone who had come to the reading as a fellow-traveler. I've already reported how Ginsberg dealt with the philosophy question. There remains, of the question period, only to report his views on verse forms.

I don't remember how the question was put to Ginsberg–but I'm sure it was put neutrally: no one was inclined to embarrass the guests–which led him into a discussion of prosody; perhaps it was the question about what Ginsberg as a poet had learned at Columbia; but anyway, here, at last, Ginsberg had a real classroom subject: he could be a teacher who wed outrageousness to authority in the time-honored way of the young and lively, no-pedant-he performer of the classroom, and suddenly Ginsberg announced firmly that no one at Columbia knew anything about prosody; the English department was stuck in the nineteenth century, sensible of no meter other than the old iambic pentameter, whereas the thing about him and his friends was their concern with a poetic line which moved in the rhythm of ordinary speech; they were poetic innovators, carrying things forward the logical next step from William Carlos Williams. And now all at once the thing

Lionel Trilling, to whom Ginsberg dedicated his poem "The Lion for Real" at the Columbia reading. Trilling did not attend the Columbia reading.

about Ginsberg and his friends was not their social protest and existentialism, their whackiness and beat-upness: suddenly it had become their energy of poetic impulse that earned them their right to be heard in the university, their studious devotion to their art: Ginsberg was seeing to that. Orlovsky had made his contribution to the evening; he had read his two whacky uproarious poems, the entire canon of his work, and had won his acclaim. Corso had similarly given his best, and been approved. The question period, the period of instruction, belonged to Ginsberg alone, and his friends might be slightly puzzled by the turn the evening had taken, the decorousness of which they suddenly found themselves a part–Corso, for instance, began to look like a chastened small boy who was still determined, though his heart was no longer in it, to bull his way through against all these damned grown-ups–but they had no choice except to permit their companion his deviation into high-mindedness. And thus did one measure, finally, the full tug of something close to respectability in Ginsberg's life, by this division in the ranks; and thus, too, was the soundness of Dupee's reminder, that there is always something to learn from hearing a poet read his poems aloud, borne in on one. For the fact was that Ginsberg, reading his verse, had naturally given it the iambic beat: after all, it is the traditional beat of English poetry where it deals with serious subjects, as Ginsberg's poems so often do. A poet, one thought–and it was a poignant thought because it came so immediately and humanly rather than as an abstraction–may choose to walk whatever zany path in his life as a man; but when it comes to mourning and mothers and such, he will be drawn into the line of tradition; at least in this far he is always drawn toward "respectability."

The evening was over, we were dismissed to return to our homes. A crowd formed around Ginsberg; he extricated himself and came to his father a few rows ahead of us. I resisted the temptation to overhear their greeting. In some part of me I wanted to speak to Ginsberg, tell him I had liked the poem he had written to my husband, but I didn't dare: I couldn't be sure that Ginsberg wouldn't take my meaning wrong. Outside, it had blown up a bit–or was it just the chill of unreality against which we hurried to find shelter?

There was a meeting going on at home of the pleasant professional sort which, like the comfortable living room in which it usually takes place, at a certain point in a successful modern literary career confirms the writer in his sense of disciplined achievement and well-earned reward. It is of course a sense that all writers long for quite as much as they fear it; certainly it is not to be made too conscious, nor ever to be spoken of except without elaborate irony, lest it propose a life without risk and therefore without virtue. I had found myself hurrying as if I were needed, but there was really no reason for my haste; my entrance was an interruption, even a disturbance of the orderly sense, not the smallest part of whose point for me lay, now, in the troubling contrast it made with the world I had just come from. Auden, alone of the eight men in the room not dressed in a proper suit but wearing a battered old brown leather jacket, was first to inquire about my experience. I told him I had been moved; he answered gently that he was ashamed of me. In a dim suffocated effort of necessary correction, I said, "It's different when it's human beings and not just a sociological phenomenon," and I can only guess, and hope, he took what I meant. Yet as I prepared to get out of the room so that the men could sit down again with their drinks, I felt there was something more I had to add–it was so far from enough to leave the "beats" as no more than human beings–and so I said, "Allen Ginsberg read a love-poem to you, Lionel. I liked it very much." It was an awkward thing to say in the circumstances, perhaps even a little foolish as an attempt to bridge the unfathomable gap that was all so quickly and meaningfully opening up between the evening that had been and the evening that was now so surely reclaiming me. But I'm certain that Ginsberg's old teacher knew what I was saying, and why I was impelled to say it.

This article concerns a scientific approach to the question of Beatniks.

Beatniks Just Sick, Sick, Sick
Science Digest, July 1959, pp. 25–26

The "beat" generation is not necessarily rebelling against society. It is instead "acting-out internal conflicts and needs." "Beatniks" are not necessarily sick of life, but "like any group of sick people they want to be left alone."

This explanation of beat behavior comes from Dr. Francis Rigney, staff psychiatrist for the Veterans Administration Hospital at San Francisco, Calif. Dr. Rigney spent more than 100 nights in beatnik dens and dives in the interests of science. He gave personality tests to about 150 persons, whom he considers to represent about one-fourth of the hard core of beatniks residing in San Francisco.

About two-thirds of the beatniks Dr. Rigney tested classified themselves as creative persons–writers, musicians, painters. The study revealed "a wide spectrum of behavior–happy, sick, tragic, creative and just plain no-good," Dr. Rigney says.

The male beatnik averaged about 30 years of age, while the women averaged 23 years. The educational level was two years of college.

Although San Francisco is considered the U.S. capital of beatism, 50 percent of the beatniks tested came from the East coast, 10 percent of them from New York City.

Lawrence Lipton's focus on Venice, California, in The Holy Barbarians *(1959), which was advertised as "the first complete inside look at the Beat Generation," angered many of the residents of the community.*

Heat on the Beatniks
Newsweek, 17 August 1959, p. 36

For about three years, a handful of shaggy, arts-dedicated beatniks lived in harmonious togetherness among the property owners of Venice, Calif. (population: about 40,000). A real-estate development (in the early 1900s) patterned on canal-crossed Venice, Italy, the community was somewhat the worse for wear after an influx of pensioners, low-income workers, and winos who reveled in low rents, sunshine, and the beach.

Then writer-resident Lawrence Lipton, balding but beat middle-aged former husband of the late mystery-tale-spinner Craig Rice, broke the peace with a book. Last week the property-owning solid citizens got hot under the collar and the bearded, poetry-spouting minority (an estimated 500 to 1,000) tried to play it cool. (Collars and ties are anathema to the beatnik creed.)

What bugged the squares: Lipton's description of their fair city in his book "The Holy Barbarians" as a "horizontal jerry-built slum by the sea . . ." Still worse, the book's publication in June touched off a migration of hundreds of the beat and near-beat into the community, a part of sprawling Los Angeles.

While beatniks clustered in the Gas House, a former Bingo parlor converted six weeks ago into an artsy-craftsy coffeehouse (instant coffee poured, no espresso), Alfred S. Roberts, Venice Civic Union president, told irate property owners: "We've got to get on our feet and scream and get these people out of here."

'Funky Blues': In retaliation, the beatniks sought to sell themselves to the public at a Gas House open house. But about 2,000 of the curious public were barred. Police, declaring that the establishment had no entertainment license, ruled that only a private meeting could be held. Lipton wasn't allowed to read his special poetry, either. The cops said it was "entertainment." So Lipton ran off a tape recording entitled "Funky blues for all squares, creeps, and cornballs." The property-owning public got the point.

Police later closed down the Gas House, pending a hearing whose date will be set Aug. 12 by the Los Angeles Police Board of Commissioners. Although the battleline was pretty well drawn last week between haves and have-nots, one property owner, hefty, free-lance writer Robert Chatterton, sided with the beatniks. Chatterton formed the Venice Citizens and Property Owners Committee for Cultural Advancement, pledged to combat the unbeat Civic Union.

Soft-pedaling beards, open shirts, and wild parties, Chatterton's committee stressed the potential contribution of the intellectuals to the community. Civic-minded beatniks even offered to paint Venice's dented, back-alley garbage cans, for the sake of beauty.

But culture didn't sell too well. "They're a dirty bunch of people," said Mrs. Millie Rieber, manager of a Venice hotel. "They drink and every night is debauchery. They make free love practically in the streets, play bongo drums, and none of us can get any sleep at all after 2 a.m."

The reviewer for The Nation *considered Allen Churchill's* The Improper Bohemians; A Re-creation of Greenwich Village in its Heyday *(1959) and Lipton's* Holy Barbarians *in the same essay to constrast the bohemians of the 1920s with those of the 1950s.*

Beatniks Then and Now
Gene Baro
The Nation, 5 September 1959, pp. 115–117

Mr. Lipton's encomium of today's Beat Generation and Mr. Churchill's account of the Village in the "heyday" of the twenties are books related in substance and spirit. Both volumes celebrate a knowledge presumed unavailable in Scarsdale or Oak Park. Both detail eccentric lives of nervous irascibility, poverty, sexual license and alcoholism. Both denigrate contemporary civilization and support promiscuous individual freedom at the expense of social regularity. Both praise creativeness for its own sake, without applying any sound standard to what is created.

Mr. Churchhill's book is somewhat the less pretentious. There is also less in it that merits serious consideration. It is a compendium of anecdotes gathered from many sources. Not much is fresh in viewpoint or expression. . . .

What insight develops from this book is incidental to its purpose. One comes to realize how little the Village figured as a source or center of the important American writing of the twenties. A "heyday" there may have been, but it did not include T. S. Eliot, Robert Frost, Ernest Hemingway, Marianne Moore, Ezra Pound, Gertrude Stein, F. Scott Fitzgerald, William Carlos Williams, or William Faulkner. For that matter, it did not include, except in a technical sense, Theodore Dreiser, Sherwood Anderson, Willa Cather, or Sinclair Lewis. These writers owed little or nothing to the Village. Even Eugene O'Neill's debt is hardly a spiritual one. What literature the Village produced was largely second-rate.

A "NEW" Village is discovered in Mr. Lipton's book. Venice, California, is the Village of the West, the beatnik paradise. Another vocabulary, more elaborate and ironic, celebrates virtually the same phenomena. The "square" might as well be the man from above Fourteenth Street. The Bohemian has become the Cat.

The Holy Barbarians differ from the Improper Bohemians in that their mythology is still in the making. (The Village mythology was made from politics and nothing is staler than political attitudes a few decades old.) The beatniks are anti-political and, while their rejection of society is accomplished by traditional means–by sex, drinks, drugs and the arts of self-expression–the rationale of their behavior is exotic and sophisticated, a matter of mysticism, philosophical solipsism and natural religion. The beatnik apologists have raided all cultures for tags in support of not very precise attitudes; sensations, after all, are hard to intellectualize, especially as sensations are The Thing. The beatniks talk too much to be Zen philosophers. Their failure to find a vocabulary reasonably sufficient to their states of being has given so much beatnik literature its rather wordy, scrambled, egghead character. Whether beatnik literature can ever be more than Village second-rate depends really upon how coherent a view of the world it can give and how it overcomes its ignorance of tradition and discovers a connection with the literary past. As it is, writers like Kerouac make mistakes as if they were discoveries.

Reports of the Beat Generation's demise circulated soon after the Beat Generation achieved nationwide notice. The principle Beats had established a presence in bohemian neighborhoods on both coasts (New York's Greenwich Village and San Francisco's North Beach), yet they were never in one place for long. The slipperiness of the primary figures added to the general notion that the Beat Generation was fading in prominence, if, in fact, it had existed at all.

The Old Beat Gang Is Breaking Up
Michael Grieg
San Francisco Examiner, 28 September 1958, p. 18

Locally at least, the Beat Generation can almost be said to be dead beat.

Down on Grant Ave. these days you'll have a difficult time finding what some one called "that generation of rag pickers' looking for mystery, magic and God in a bottle, a needle, a horn."

Yes, the hard core of the old beat gang is breaking up. They're fleeing the scene. They're leaving it to the police reinforcements, the tourists from the Sunset, juvenile delinquents, old fashioned bohemians and magazine staffers in search of colorful copy.

Sure, there may be a few left who don't have the fare to go elsewhere. There may be others who pretend beatness to cadge a drink from a tourist. Appearing beat also profits certain pastrami sandwich merchants and gains others a place in the night club spotlight or the gossip columns.

But don't go rubbernecking for those who put the Beat Generation on the San Francisco map.

Jack Kerouac, handsome magus of the mindless, recently bought a house in a New York suburb where he lives with his mother, a charming matron who prefers TV to her son's hectic works. Allen Ginsberg went to Europe even before his book of poems, "Howl," became the judicial cause celebre last year of the Beat Generation. In Europe, too, are Tarzan-like poet Gregory Corso and Kenneth Rexroth, elder statesman of the group. (Before leaving, Rexroth–now disenchanted with the whole beat shebang–said in a broadcast that the Beat Generation was an old story, only in his day they were called "punks.")

Another member of the original group, poet Gary Snyder, has been living in a Japanese Buddhist monastery. Philip Lamantia, a surrealist turned hipster, has settled for a while in Greenwich Village. Not quite so far away are poet Philip Whalen, now of Berkeley, and bookseller-satirist Lawrence Ferlinghetti, a wary patron of the hipsters, who has retired to Potrero Hill.

It would be difficult, granting them a return to Grant Ave., to recognize the original hipsters. Contrary to popular opinion or police intelligence, beards were never as popular with the old beat gang as they were with Gold Rush miners and business men of Victorian England. As far as any one can remember, clean shaven Kerouac never did own a black turtleneck sweater or a pair of sandals.

. . . .

Kerouac and his fellows may have been looking for peace, but they found something much more disquieting–success. This is an embarrassment of riches to an authentic hipster looking eastward to a Buddhist victory over worldly success.

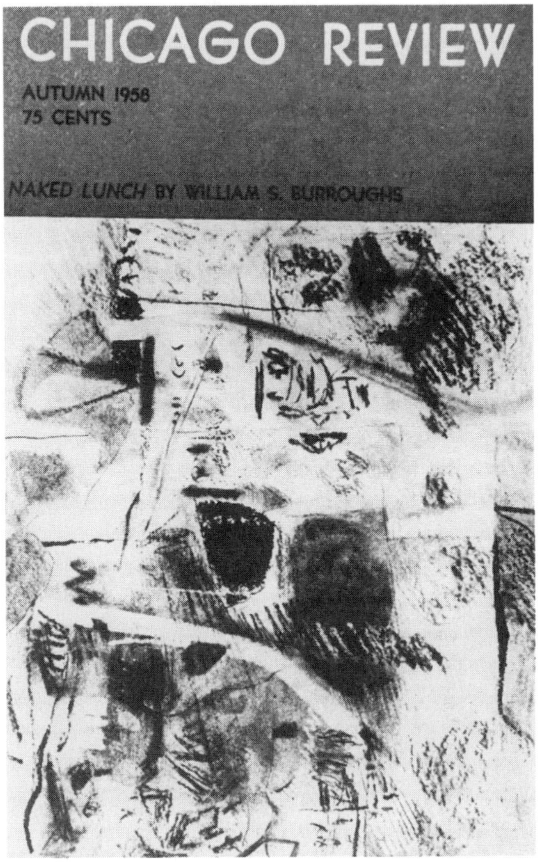

Cover for the magazine issue that sparked a censorship debate

The Chicago Review and a Case of Censorship

When The Chicago Review, *published under the aegis of the University of Chicago, was attacked by a newspaper columnist for the vulgarity of the contents of its Autumn 1958 issue that included excerpts of William Burroughs's* Naked Lunch, *university officials told editor Irving Rosenthal that he could not publish work by Kerouac and Burroughs in the subsequent Winter issue. In November 1958 Rosenthal and other editors, including Paul Carroll, resigned their positions; Rosenthal and Carroll then decided to found* Big Table.

In the introduction to the first issue of Big Table, *Rosenthal explained the circumstances that led to the birth of the new magazine.*

On October 25, 1958, Jack Mabley, a columnist in the Chicago *Daily News,* attacked the Autumn 1958 *Chicago Review* under the banner "Filthy Writing on the Midway." His column ends: "But the University of Chicago publishes the magazine. The trustees should take a long hard look at what is being circulated under this sponsorship." I have heard that a number of trustees called on the

Titling *Big Table*

When editor Paul Carroll was searching for a title for the journal he and Irving Rosenthal were beginning, he wrote to Kerouac, who was reputed to have titled Ginsberg's *Howl* and Burroughs's *Naked Lunch.* Kerouac sent him a telegram, suggesting "Big Table." Carroll relates the exchange: "I was reading the telegram while riding a cab through Lincoln Park and I thought, my God, he's right; the name is midwestern, and it says everybody's welcome. I talked to Irving [Rosenthal] and he agreed it was just right and so it was. A month later I asked Kerouac how he found that name. He said he had had a note on his writing desk in Long Island, 'GET A BIGGER TABLE.' I never regretted that title. It was perfect for what we were doing."

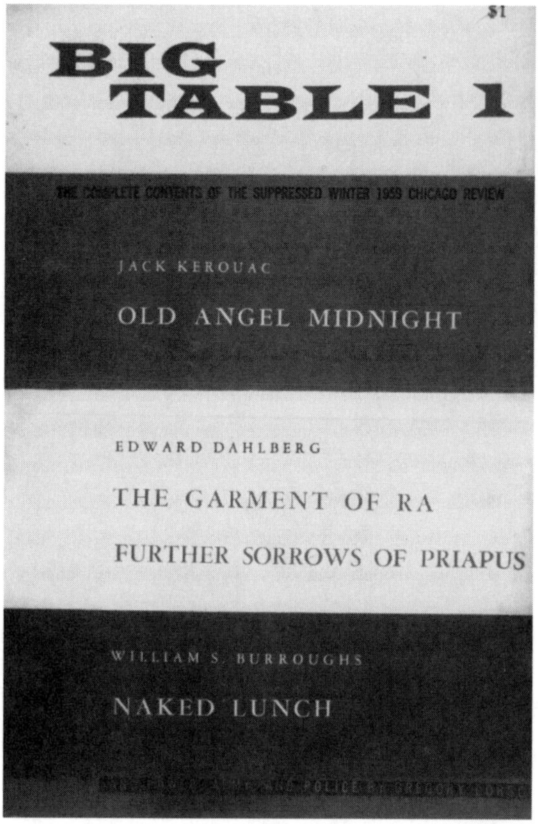

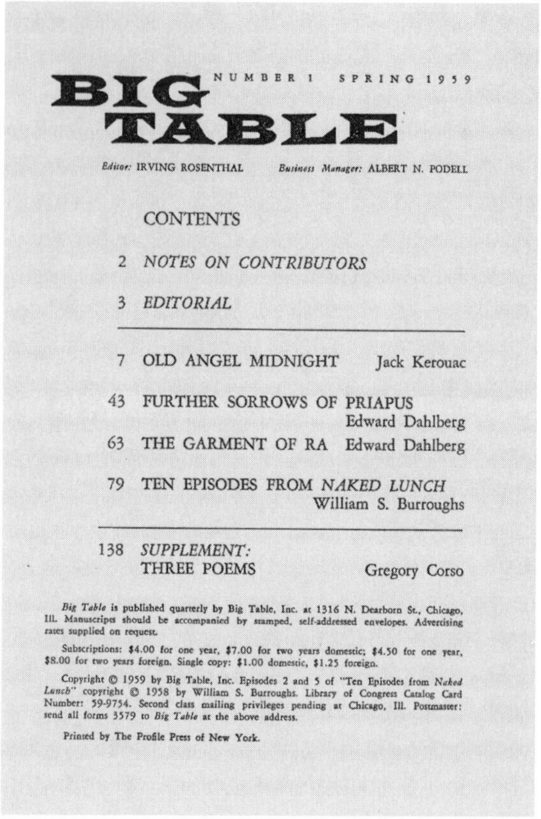
BIG TABLE NUMBER 1 SPRING 1959

Editor: IRVING ROSENTHAL *Business Manager:* ALBERT N. PODELL

CONTENTS

Big Table is published quarterly by Big Table, Inc. at 1316 N. Dearborn St., Chicago, Ill. Manuscripts should be accompanied by stamped, self-addressed envelopes. Advertising rates supplied on request.

Subscriptions: $4.00 for one year, $7.00 for two years domestic; $4.50 for one year, $8.00 for two years foreign. Single copy: $1.00 domestic, $1.25 foreign.

Copyright © 1959 by Big Table, Inc. Episodes 2 and 5 of "Ten Episodes from *Naked Lunch*" copyright © 1958 by William S. Burroughs. Library of Congress Catalog Card Number: 59-9754. Second class mailing privileges pending at Chicago, Ill. Postmaster: send all forms 3579 to *Big Table* at the above address.

Printed by The Profile Press of New York.

Cover and table of contents for the first issue of the magazine that published material by Kerouac and Burroughs censored from the Chicago Review

Chancellor, Mr. Lawrence A. Kimpton, who in any case took the position of expediency: Between November 3 and November 18, about six conferences took place between Mr. Napier Wilt, Dean of the Division of Humanities, and me, in my capacity as editor of the *Chicago Review*. At first I was told flatly that the *Review* would be discontinued. Then I was told that the magazine had a chance to survive if the coming Winter Issue were "toned down," but Mr. Wilt was unable to tell me exactly what "toning down" the Chancellor had in mind. At this time I think Mr. Wilt and I assumed that at worst I would have to substitute asterisks for any four-letter words. On November 7, just before I brought the manuscript of the Winter Issue to Press, I called Mr. Wilt and asked him if I should read the manuscript for four-letter words, and asterisk them. I told him that I was willing to go this far, if it would insure the continuation of the magazine. He said he thought it was a puerile thing to do, and "let's not do it unless we have to." I assumed that the prospects both for saving the magazine and for Mr. Kimpton's keeping his hands off my Winter Issue were good ones.

I brought the manuscript to the University of Chicago Press; within an hour (I learned later) it had been delivered to "someone in the Administration Building." It was returned three days later. I recovered the manuscript, added some material which had come in late, and delivered the manuscript myself to the foreman of the printing department. A week later it was gone from the printing department, and this time I found it in the possession of the Press office manager, who returned it to me from the safe behind his desk.

Meanwhile, back in Dean Wilt's office, I learned on one day that I absolutely could not publish Kerouac or Burroughs in the Winter Issue, though I could publish Dahlberg, and I could publish a note saying that I had planned to publish Kerouac and Burroughs in this issue, "but was unable to do so"–nothing stronger. On the next day Mr. Wilt added Dahlberg to my Index and told me there could be no prefatory note at all. He said that the Winter Issue must be *"completely* innocuous," and that the manuscript would have to be read by him before it was taken to Press. He urged me to put together a new Winter Issue, and asked me what manuscripts I had on hand. I told him we had been planning a German Expressionist number–"German Expressionism would be too strong," he said. On November 17 I had my last conference with him. I told him that I could not edit a magazine under the conditions he gave me. On November 18 six of the seven staff-members who held the rank of editor resigned; the seventh is my successor. The editors who left with me are Paul Carroll, Charles Horwitz, Eila Kokkinen, Doris Nieder, and Barbara Pitschel.

The suppression was a bad administrative mistake of the Chancellor's, and I hope he never lives it down. A few faculty members spoke up privately against the breach of academic, or in this case artistic, freedom, but the faculty position which appeared in print was to deny that any censorship or suppression had taken place, and finally, to pretend that I was asked to modify the Winter Issue because of my narrow and irresponsible editorial policies. The faculty spokesmen so quick to protect the administration were Richard G. Stern and Joshua Taylor. Both of these men earn their bread by teaching literature and the arts.

A careful and well-documented account of the suppression has just been published by the Student Government of the University of Chicago (Chicago 37, Illinois) as "Report of the Special Committee of the Student Government In Re: The Chicago Review." It is well worth the attention of anyone interested in censorship problems (or administrative skulduggery). In the event that the report is suppressed by Chancellor Kimpton, it will be made available by *Big Table*. The only fault I find in it is that Mr. Stern, from a few quotations, emerges as a kind of champion of the freedom of literary expression; nothing could be further from the truth. After the suppression had been accomplished he was zealous in his support of it, and his justification in the *Maroon* of December 12, 1958 is composed of lies.

Another account of the suppression will appear in the second issue of the *San Francisco Review*. I have read it and think it offers several very interesting speculations about what Mr. Kimpton hoped to accomplish in suppressing the *Chicago Review*. His act was rigidly consistent with his program to placate the trustees by "normalizing" the University–to increase the endowment at the expense of everything that a university in a free society is supposed to support (and seldom does). Mr. Kimpton does not want free expression at the University of Chicago; he wants money.

The editors who resigned determined first of all to publish what would have been our Winter Issue, and secondly to form a literary magazine in Chicago which would not be subject to the review of a Chancellor loyal to the philistines. Thanks to the hard work and financial support of a large number of people, it has been possible for us to do both. I especially want to thank John Fles, who flew to Chicago from California when he heard of my trouble, to put himself at my disposal; Allen Ginsberg and Gregory Corso, who promised the first financial backing for the magazine by offering to read for us free; and Bill Smith, who introduced us to our first patron. It was the promise of a donation by this patron, Jac Worth, and a donation from William E. Hartmann which brought the magazine into the realm of printer's estimates and cover planning. Barbara Siegel made sure that everybody in Chicago knew that Allen Ginsberg and Gregory Corso were going to read poems on January 29. The Shaw Society of Chicago sponsored the reading, and during the week that the poets were in town, Mr. and Mrs. Albert H. Newman and Mr. and Mrs. Leonard Solomon helped us in a hundred ways. In all matters technical and legal we had the help of Lewis Manilow.

A non-profit corporation has been formed, and so we have launched *Big Table*. Paul Carroll will be its editor, and I can hardly wait to see his first issue. For I have stolen number *1* from him to fulfil what I wish to be my last editorial responsibility.

Poet John Ciardi considered the charge of obscenity in relation to the work of the Beat writers.

The Book Burners and Sweet Sixteen
John Ciardi
Saturday Review, 27 July 1959, p. 22

The Chicago Review is a literary quarterly published by the University of Chicago. Last fall, as the editors were preparing their winter issue, a columnist on one of the Chicago newspapers attacked the fall issue as "filthy." The charge called forth a prompt reaction from Chancellor Lawrence A. Kimpton. In a memorable blow for academic freedom, Chancellor Kimpton summoned then Editor-in-Chief Rosenthal and announced that the material submitted for the winter issue was definitely not to be published. The issue, as Rosenthal reports the Chancellor's instructions, was to be completely "innocuous and noncontroversial" and it must contain "nothing which [sic] would offend a sixteen-year-old girl."

When has the true role of the American university been more profoundly enunciated? Its intellectual content is to be harmless and innocuous; its final test of moral values is to reside in the sensibilities of a sixteen-year-old girl. The petty-minded may insist that there is still some question as to exactly which sixteen-year-old girl Chancellor Kimpton may have had in mind, but in general, all men of learning and good will must certainly be grateful to Chancellor Kimpton for the depth and courage of his intellectual leadership.

The student editors of the *Review,* however, showed no sign of gratitude, as six out of seven of them promptly resigned over so trivial a matter as intellectual freedom. Some of the six thereupon managed to raise private funds, and founded a new magazine called *Big Table,* the first issue of which published intact the material suppressed by Chancellor Kimpton.

Now, as if to confirm Chancellor Kimpton's standing in the company of men of taste and learning, the scholar-inspectors of the Post Office Department have entered the picture by seizing 400 copies of *Big Table #1.* A hearing scheduled for early June will already have been held by the time this issue reaches the newsstands, and the charge will in all probability have been that there exists obscenity in two of the works featured in *Big Table #1,* specifically, in "Old Angel Midnight," by Jack Kerouac, and in "Ten Episodes from Naked Lunch," by William S. Burroughs. The third featured author, Edward Dahlberg, will probably not have been charged.

The immediate issue, therefore, is the charge of obscenity brought against two specified works.

There have been many court rulings on obscenity in the last two decades, and the tests are by now clearly established. Obscenity cannot be determined by any isolated word or passage but only by the total intent of a particular work. That total intent cannot be found to be obscene unless there is reasonable likelihood that it will stimulate to lewd and lustful excitement a man of average sexual instincts—*l'homme moyen sensuel,* as Judge Woolsey labeled him in the 1933 decision that cleared Joyce's "Ulysses" of the charge of obscenity.

Jack Kerouac often disassociated himself from the term beatnik.

Do you know what a beatnik is? Usually some guy who says, "I hate my father. I hate my mother." So they leave home in Indiana and they come to New York. They write a line of poetry, type it up in a great big expensive five dollar binding book, put it under their arm, put on sandals, grow a little goatee, walk down the street and say they're poets. It's just kind of a fad. It was invented by the press. Listen, I'm a railroad brakeman, merchant marine deckhand in war time. Beatniks don't do those things. They don't work. They don't get jobs.

—*New York Herald Tribune,* 22 September 1957, p. 2

A further test of obscenity is in the social importance of the work. As Judge Horn ruled in 1957 in clearing Allen Ginsberg's "Howl": "If the material has the slightest redeeming social importance it is not obscene because it is protected by the First and Fourteenth Amendments of the United States Constitution." Various other tests have been applied by the courts, but the legal ground is substantially covered by these three principles: total intent, *l'homme moyen sensuel,* and "the slightest redeeming social importance."

I am no admirer of Kerouac's assaults on near-prose. But the issue here is legal and not esthetic, and to argue an esthetic disagreement cannot imply in any remotest legal sense that Kerouac's writing is not immensely serious in its conceived intent, and that it is in fact a life-consuming attempt to describe what the writer sees as the place of value in a world fractured by disorder. Nor, in either a legal or an esthetic sense, could one argue that Kerouac is not a writer of substantial gift, however much the gift may be smothered by indiscipline.

The impulse toward censorship can only arise from failure to understand the intent. True, an excessively literal-minded man may easily become suspicious of the surfaces of Kerouac's writing. Nor is it hard to imagine that excessive literal-mindedness is a survival characteristic in Post Office bureaucracy. But the test of literature cannot reside in men of such mind, neither in the esthetic nor legal sense.

Beatniks in a Hollywood coffeehouse in November 1958

"Beatsploitation"

Once the Beat Generation became part of popular culture, the perceived excesses of the "Beatniks" became the fodder for exploitative works. Although the covers of paperback original The Girl in the Gold Leather Dress *(1961) mentions Kerouac and Ginsberg, there was little in style or substance to link the "emotionally charged story of a beat coed" or other such tales to the work of the original writers. Much of what was written to cash in on the fad was moralistic as well as sensational, such as the cover story of the March 1961 issue of* Startling Detective, *"My Life as a Beatnik: Exposing the Weird Cult that Confuses Sin With Art."*

Coffeehouses

William Burroughs once said that Jack Kerouac was responsible for selling a million cups of espresso. As was asserted in the 13 August 1960 issue of Business Week, *"In the past five years, coffee houses and espresso shops have sprung up all across the country–from New York's Greenwich Village to Hollywood's Sunset Strip." Certainly the beatniks, who were famous for hanging out in coffeehouses, contributed to the popularity. According to the magazine, the fad was over and at least one coffeehouse owner blamed the too close association with the beatniks. In Greenwich Village, though, the owner of an espresso shop was still doing good business: "These out-of-towners have all heard about the beatniks down here, so we don't disappoint them. We get some characters up on a stage to read beat poetry and the tourists flock in to absorb the atmosphere. At the same time, we make sure that they absorb enough coffee–at premium prices–to turn a neat profit."*

Covers for a few of the many paperbacks that were published from the late 1950s to the mid 1960s to cash in on the interest in beatniks

ACE DOUBLE BOOKS
TWO BOOKS IN ONE 35c
JUNKIE
Confessions of an Unredeemed Drug Addict
An ACE Original
WILLIAM LEE
S-87
ACE
25¢
BOOKS
WHY I AM SO
beat
"NOT FOR THE EASILY SHOCKED . . ."
NOLAN MILLER
Complete and Unabridged
A GLIMPSE INTO THE LIVES OF OUR LOST GENERATION
Reefer Club
35¢
MAXWELL BODENHEIM
My Life and Loves in
GREENWICH VILLAGE
COMPLETE AND UNCENSORED
231
35¢

Many of the jacket blurbs for paperbacks that exploited the Beat phenomenon focused on its presumed depravity.

"Mystery and murder in a beatnik bar."

–*The Madhouse in Washington Square* (1961)

"I'll take a clean-cut homicidal maniac next to a bearded bard in a dirty sweatshirt or a doped-up dame who'll wiggle out of her leotard at the drop of a beret."

–*Epitaph for a Dead Beat* (1961)

"By day he was a ruthless executive, by night a free-wheeling beatnik . . ."

–*Uptown Downtown* (1963)

"Banned in court, burned in Greenwich Village, *What's Happening?* dares to tell the shocking truth about today's far-out generation . . . its rebels, its outcasts, its morally confused and sexually misguided and their frantic, never-ending search for brand-new kicks and off-beat thrills!"

–*What's Happening?* (1964)

"Rusty Meaghan had been a successful sportsman in college, and was a talented musician. But suddenly he went on a mental bender in a 'beat' world of drugs, orgiastic parties, promiscuity–and tragedy."

–*The Gods of Our Time* (1964)

"These village cats lived a loose life of depraved immorality."

–*Bohemian Stud Bums* (1966)

Twenty-year-old novelist Mitchner argued that the Beat Generation had become a commercialized fad.

Those Phony Beatniks!
Stuart Mitchner
Chicago Sunday Tribune Magazine, 8 November 1959, pp. 46, 48

If the Beat Generation is a label for our time, I'll not submit to it. To accept such an epithet would be like taking part in a farce that you know will make a fool of you. The Beat Generation is a by-product of the war ridden thirties and forties and fifties–it's akin to a radiation freak left by the atom bomb explosions.

You've heard children pound dissonant nonsense on the piano. They have no ear, no sense of rhythm, yet they pound on and it pleases them. But no one offers them a recording date.

Most of the poets and writes who consider themselves beat make the same nonsense on a typewriter, create worthless literary dissonance–*and get away with it!* They are published, and they are cheapening literature.

In my novel, "Let Me Be Awake," I worked off some anger in a parody of the Beat Generation, specifically of the ritual of reading poetry to jazz (which, I've learned since, can be entertaining if it's *good* poetry and *good* jazz). The trouble is that most beat writing is so bad it parodies itself and leaves no room for satire.

We shouldn't condemn the Beat Generation because of their dress or interests or, especially, their language. *Real* hippy talk is a most expressive and exciting language.

The Beat Generation does not mean crime to me. Nor does it mean immorality or delinquency. Nor does it mean writing, nor is it an echo of the days of "old American whoopee," mentioned by a

Blurbs for beatsploitation novels often emphasized sexual immorality, particularly among young women.

"These bawdy bohemian babes knew what they wanted . . ."

–*Girls Afire* (1962)

"Follow Basil Crowe, super-hipster just off the passion road, as he roams the streets and alleys where wine, pot and lust flow like water and a beard is your ticket to a torrent of passion . . ."

–*Sin Hipster* (1963)

"If you're a Beat chick with hip ways . . . there are plenty of wine-guzzling, passion-talking, pot-blowing studs around to show you a thousand different sin-ways to be a wanton."

–*Lust Pad* (1963)

"A love-hungry young girl looked for excitement among the Beat and found degradation and terror."

–*Long Night in Hell* (1966)

major spokesman, Jack Kerouac, in a recent magazine article. To tell the truth, the Beat Generation means nothing to me.

But what Kerouac *says,* in his article on the origins of the Beat, *does* mean something to me because I like his concept of the glory and pathos and sweet richness of the American names, from Krazy Kat to Fay Wray to Jiggs and Maggie to Clark Gable to Ted Williams. What he says is honest, in terms of himself.

The Beat Generation seems to have an all-consuming interest in topical allusions and actual names.

Even in his relatively short article, Kerouac manages to mention around 70 names, all of famous people or imaginary or legendary figures or comic strip characters. In much of the "beat" poetry there is a great deal of literary name dropping.

. . . .

I think this talk of names is relevant because the literature of the Kerouac segment of the Beat Generation seems to be founded on this love of names of our time, and I think that's fine.

. . . .

The Beat Generation is a handful of nothing. It's a freak and (because we thrive on freaks in America) it has become that common commercial thing: The Fad. Like the hula hoop, like Davy Crockett, it is a fad, distorted beyond all honest shape or meaning.

A movement starts (consciously or unconsciously) with a few close friends who understand what you are trying to do, what you are trying to express, and what you feel and think. But as soon as your "movement" gets attention in the newspapers, as soon as one novel is written and the slogan catches on, the "movement" is taken over by people who have no conception of its intention.

The circle of good friends–the core of the movement–shrinks away. What the core began has become something false: it is no longer theirs. The intruders are squares, fools with no sense of human rhythm, freaks, loafers, and zombies, all looking for some wagon to jump.

So, Jack Kerouac (or anyone else who was there at the "beginning") why don't you forget the monster you seem to have inspired? Why don't you shame it and stand above it?

You all speak of your holy individuality, yet if you (Jack Kerouac) cling to that label (the Beat Generation) you've branded yourself the king of all conformists. Standing alone, you and a few others who have genuine talent might at last, some day, prevail above the rubble and waste of the movement you began.

Whether you admit it or not, Kerouac, there is hatred and bitterness and ugliness in this thing called the Beat Generation. People without talent or ambition (hating at the same time those who do have talent) cluster under your wing for inspiration (for what?) and protection (from what?).

But you, Kerouac, seem to have that greatest of all things–*soul*–and I don't think you're phony. But if there is one thing on the earth in this year 1959 that *is* cheap and phony, it's the cancer called the Beat Generation.

–*Chicago Sunday Tribune Magazine,* p. 48

The Subterraneans as a Movie

Kerouac's chance to break into the big-time movie business came when movie rights to his book, The Subterraneans, *were sold shortly after the publication of the book in 1958. No one, including Kerouac, was happy with the movie that resulted. The black woman in the book was changed to a white woman for the movie, played by Leslie Caron, who starred with George Peppard.*

As Tony Floyd notes in the Kerouac newsletter Moody Street Irregulars *(Winter 1989–1990), the movie* The Subterraneans *did not live up to expectations.*

Metro Goldwyn Mayer purchased the film right to *The Subterraneans* in early 1958–right after the book was published–for fifteen thousand dollars, but the film wasn't released until two years later, when it was previewed at the studio on June 15, 1960 and then later premiered on June 23. The film was produced by Arthur Freed, who had been responsible for such musicals as *On the Town, An American in Paris, Singin' in the Rain* and *Band Wagon,* and directed by Ronald MacDougall, an ex-screenwriter and cowriter of *The Naked Jungle,* memorable for its scenes of African soldier ants on the march. With Andre Previn in charge of the music and the cinematography by four-time Academy Award winner Joseph Ruttenberg, *The Subterraneans* was certainly intended by MGM to be a prestigious production. However, its reception upon release was tepid, to say the least.

Poster for the 1960 movie based on Kerouac's third novel

Three reviews of the movie version of The Subterraneans *that found little to praise.*

Freed MacDougall Pic Lacks Drama
James Powers
Hollywood Reporter, 21 June 1960

As a story of the Beat Generation, filmed largely in the lair of the New Bohemians, the film lies outside both points of view (i.e. being neither beat nor square). Kerouac's book must have been a headbuster to screenplay, but even though it was rambling in storyline, it had good characters, some flashes of perception, a certain loony humor and an accurate statement of what the Beat Generation means. The Beats may be annoying to a great many of their fellow citizens, but they form a vital movement of social protest, and are having an impact. . . . The finished film gives the impression that the Beats are just another younger generation, sowing a few wild oats, and settling down to life on the installment plan in a romantic story in which the hazards of Bohemia are just another roadblock in the path of true love.

* * *

Review of *The Subterraneans*
Variety, 22 June 1960

Those who have suspected all along that beatniks are dull, have proof in Metro's *The Subterraneans.* How [it] will fare depends to a great extent on whether beatnikism has sustained enough of its initial attention. Odds are that even young people will find this version unappealing and uninteresting. Since youth appears to be the prime audience target, both the film and the fad seem headed for ho-humsville. . . . Robert Thom's screenplay . . . dredges up some bargain basement philosophy, B(eat) girls and bed ruminations. Its hero (George Peppard) . . . beats it when his mom chants the square cliche, "You need a nice girl."

Cruising around the Bay Area in search of meaning, he finds his home-away-from-home with the local coffee-house colony, promptly develops a crush on its most mixed-up member (Leslie Caron), an analyst's darling whose Freudian slip shows every time she submits frigidly to the sexual advances of her pals. Warming up to Peppard's amorous attentions, she is promptly with child, leading to a happy ending in which both decide to "go straight."

* * *

Review of *The Subterraneans*
Time, 20 June 1960, p. 66

The bushy-bearded Beat Generation is a collective hair farm that the average solid citizen does not dig. Nevertheless, in this picture, which bears about as much relationship to Jack Kerouac's novel as Hollywood does to Endsville, producer Arthur Freed attempts to sell the beatniks back to the mass culture they are desperately and often comically trying to escape. He shaves them down, scrubs them up and presents them, in deadly earnest, as pioneers in the great American tradition, as "the Young Bohemians . . . the makers of the future." Unhappily, the notion is so translucently ludicrous and the picture so poorly put together that in box-office terms all this cold water flattery will probably get the movie-makers nowhere.

The story is set in San Francisco, the holy city of hip, and describes how a young cube, who lives with his ever-loving mother and writes nothing novels, sees something sweet where the beat meet to eat. In the book she is a pretty Negro, but in the film she is Leslie Caron. "I want every bit of life," he announces. So they go to her pad and really make the scene, and in the morning he drives her over to see her analyst. Soon they are sharing the same toothbrush, but he wants to write, and one night he flobs off to somebody else's pad. She flips but good, and goes ankling down the main drag with nothing on but her epidermis. In the end, though, she announces that she is pregnant, and he promises to marry her, get a job, straighten up and fly right back to bourgeois respectability.

In short, the film is basically just a remake of *La Boheme* with a happy ending and bop instead of Puccini. And though it is at no time authentically beat, it has one thing in common with the beats: dullness.

Set of lobby cards

The lure of Gerry Mulligan's saxophone fires Janis Rule into a dance of poetry and passion.
M-G-M Presents
An Arthur Freed Production
"THE SUBTERRANEANS"
In CinemaScope and METROCOLOR
60-29

M-G-M Presents
An Arthur Freed Production
"THE SUBTERRANEANS"
In CinemaScope and METROCOLOR
60-29

In that wild, strange life of the new Bohemians a fine love was born. (George Peppard, Leslie Caron)
M-G-M Presents
An Arthur Freed Production
"THE SUBTERRANEANS"
In CinemaScope and METROCOLOR
60-29

They called themselves sophisticates, but they were explosively primitive in their loves and hates.
M-G-M Presents
An Arthur Freed Production
"THE SUBTERRANEANS"
In CinemaScope and METROCOLOR
60-29

Poster for 1959 movie marketed as an exposé of the subculture inspired by the Beat writers

The End of an Era

Begone, Dull Beats
Ralph Gleason
New Statesman, 2 June 1961

A full U. S. Grant beard, luxurious and flocked with gray, provided Bill the Beatnik with a supplementary income during his several years in San Francisco's North Beach neighborhood, home of the original Beats.

Photographed–for a fee–by a tourist against the wall of the Co-Existence Bagel Shop, the Coffee Gallery or any telephone pole on Grant Avenue, Bill was the living symbol of modern American urban dissent, proof positive to the folks back home that the tourist had seen a Beatnik in the flesh.

Last year Bill went to Veterans Hospital for repairs. He came back to the Beach this spring, his beard a hospital casualty. But it didn't matter really because, for Bill, North Beach is now a strange and lonely land. The tourists still throng the streets, but the regulars have gone like the ferries from the Bay. 'What happened? Everybody's split,' Bill complained on his first night back On the Scene: 'All the joints are closed. Where's everybody?' Now beardless, Bill is no longer even in demand as a model. 'There's nothing to do but sit in somebody's car and dig the tourists,' he says resignedly.

Bill's dilemma symbolises what has happened to North Beach, locale of Beat Generation literature from Kerouac and Ginsberg to *The Connection.* The Beatnik in his native form has all but disappeared from its alleys and cafes, like the Model T Ford from the roads of the U.S.

25¢
THE BEAT GENERATION
The shocking and revealing novel of a generation gone wild based on the sensational MGM motion picture release
BY ALBERT ZUGSMITH
A BANTAM BOOK

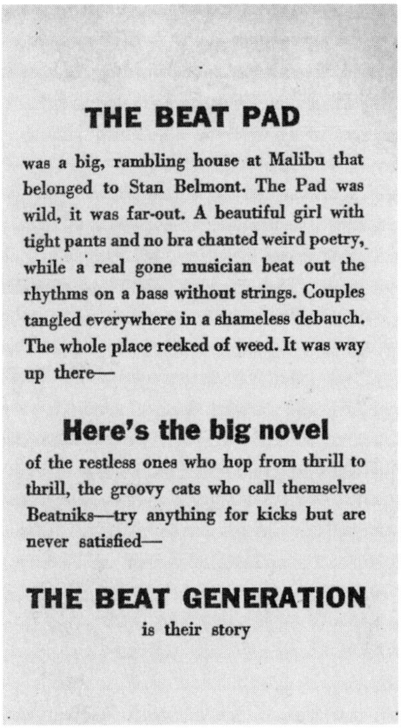

THE BEAT PAD

was a big, rambling house at Malibu that belonged to Stan Belmont. The Pad was wild, it was far-out. A beautiful girl with tight pants and no bra chanted weird poetry, while a real gone musician beat out the rhythms on a bass without strings. Couples tangled everywhere in a shameless debauch. The whole place reeked of weed. It was way up there—

Here's the big novel

of the restless ones who hop from thrill to thrill, the groovy cats who call themselves Beatniks—try anything for kicks but are never satisfied—

THE BEAT GENERATION

is their story

THE BEAT GENERATION
is the searing story of the restless, jaded men and women, with no aim in life except a new sensation—drugs, "way-out" jazz, perverted sex, actual crime.
THE BEAT GENERATION
is especially the story of rich, young Stan Belmont, who had known every thrill. Now his only kick was—rape.
THE BEAT GENERATION
is an MGM release, a spectacular Albert Zugsmith production starring Steve Cochran, Mamie Van Doren, Ray Danton, Fay Spain, Maggie Hayes, Jackie Coogan, and Louis Armstrong and his All-Stars.

Front cover, back cover, and promotional page of Albert Zugsmith's 1959 novel that was based on the movie of the same title that he produced

Cover for a magazine that supposedly reveals the excesses of the Beat Generation

When you see a Model T now, it's owned by a vintage car club member. Any surviving Beatnik on the Beach belongs to the entrepreneurial minority making a living off the tourists, selling sandals or running guided tours for Little Old Ladies from Dubuque. Or they are amateur Beats, fleeing part-time a dull office. . . .

Kerouac and Ginsberg had already left by the time the tourists and the amateurs took over (though both returned for brief visits in 1960). Bob Kaufman, known as Bomkauf and author of the Abominist Manifesto, went to New York; Pierre de-Lattre, the Beatnik priest, whose Bread-and-Wine Mission was a landmark but is now a laundromat (Pierre got tired of being a housemother to the Beats, on call any hour of the night), went to the country to write a novel. Grant Avenue now is as dark and lonesome at night as any neighbourhood street. The Cassandra (Zen soup–20 cents) is a record store; The Place is an art-goods shop; the Coffee Gallery is open only occasionally ('They have events now,' an old-timer says disgustedly); the CoExistence Bagel Shop is a sandals-and-jewelry shop, and the Jazz Cellar is dark and empty.

The end was really heralded when the whole of Grant Avenue burst into brief flame last year with a series of tourist traps. The Surplus Store added berets and turtle-neck sweaters to its staples of sweatshirts, blue jeans and GI clothing. A leather-goods shop offered 'sandals for beat-nik dogs'. . . .

Mike Wallace Asks Jack Kerouac
"What Is the Beat Generation?"
New York Post, 21 January 1958, p. 16

Mike Wallace: *What sort of mysticism is it? What do the Beat mystics believe in?*

Jack Kerouac: Oh, they believe in love. They love children . . . and I don't know, it's so strange to talk about all this. They love women, they love animals, they love everything.

MW: *Why is jazz so important to this new mystique?*

JK: Jazz is very complicated. It's just as complicated as Bach. The chords, the structures, the harmony and everything. And then it has a tremendous beat. You know, tremendous drummers. They can drive it. It has just a tremendous drive. It can drive you right out of yourself.

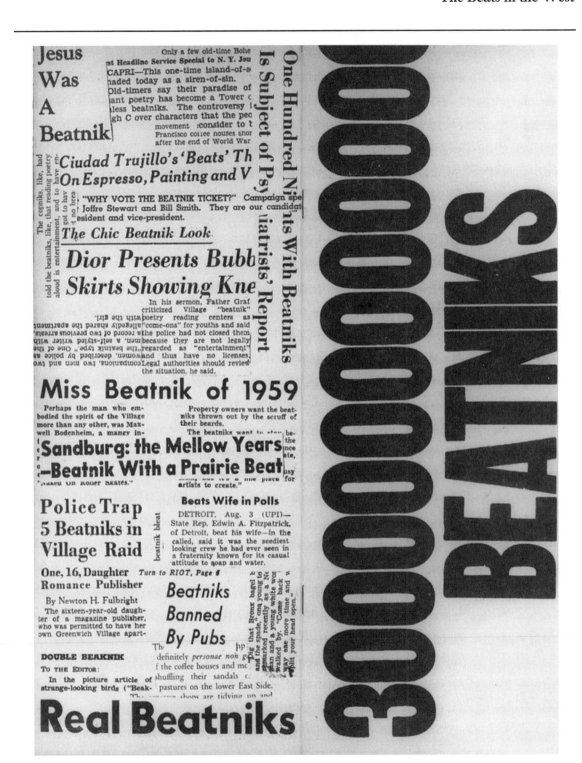

Cover of 1961 booklet put together by beat writer Tuli Kupferberg, who decried "the war against the Beats"

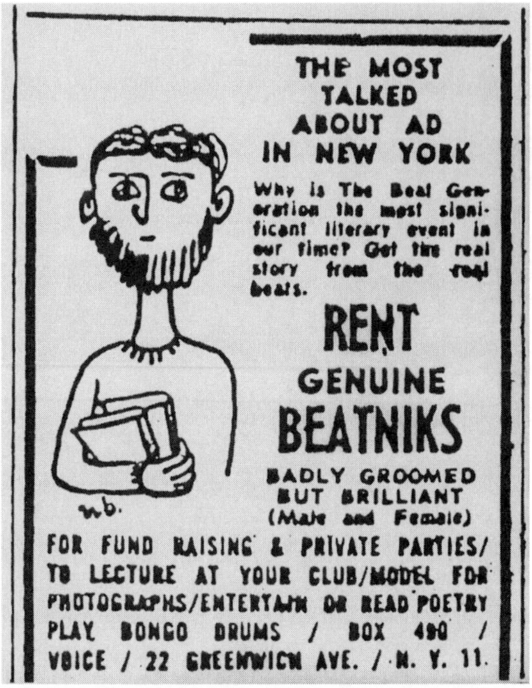

Advertisement placed in The Village Voice *by Fred McDarrah, a photographer of the Beat scene. This spoof received serious responses.*

MW: *What is the basis of your mysticism?*
JK: What I believe is that nothing is happening.

MW: *What do you mean?*
JK: Well, you're not sitting here. That's what you think. Actually, we are great empty space. I could walk right through you . . . you know what I mean, we're made out of atoms, electrons.

We're actually empty. We're an empty vision . . . in one mind.

MW: *In what mind–the mind of God?*
JK: That's the name we give it. We can give it any name. We can call it tangerine . . . god . . . tangerine. But I do know we are empty phantoms, sitting here thinking we are human beings and worrying about civilization. We're just empty phantoms. And yet, all is well.

MW: *All is well?*
JK: Yeah. We're all in Heaven, now, really.

MW: *You don't sound happy.*
JK: Oh, I'm tremendously sad. I'm in great despair.

MW: *Why?*
JK: It's a great burden to be alive. A heavy burden, a great big heavy burden. I wish I were safe in Heaven, dead.

Holmes wrote this essay in 1965.

The Game of the Name
John Clellon Holmes
Beat Reader, pp. 615–622

Spiritual quests to the contrary, after the initial furor about the Beat Generation in the late fifties, the public, the Media, and the critics decided that when you spoke of "beatness" you were referring exclusively to the folkways of a group of urban Thoreaus who lived in those limbo-neighborhoods where the nation's Bohemias shelved off into the nation's slums. In other words, the so-called Beatniks.

That sneering diminutive, which is about all that is left of the Beat Generation today ("Among the sit-ins was the usual sprinkling of beatniks," "The moral contagion represented by juvenile delinquents, racial malcontents, and beatniks," "I certainly don't intend to support my son if he wants to be a beatnik"), was originally coined by Herb Caen, a facetious columnist in San Francisco, to describe the bearded, sandaled coffeehouse loungers of the North Beach Bohemia, but it was immediately adopted by the mass media as a handy caricature for everyone associated with Beatness, and thereby quickly entered the smear-vocabularies of all those perceptive people who like to call intellectuals "eggheads." And for the same perceptive reason: if you can't understand them, brand them.

The notion (which became universal) that when you talked about the Beat attitude you were speaking of Caen's idea rather than Kerouac's, had the paradoxical effect of at once making the Beat Generation briefly notorious in the popular mind as a species of hip Amish, and more or less permanently obscuring the wider, and deeper, implications of the term. In my not-unprejudiced view, the Beatniks and the Mass Media,

In September 1968 Kerouac appeared on the television program Firing Line *with William F. Buckley.*

A lot of hoods and communists jumped on my back and turned the idea that I had that the Beat Generation is a generation of beatitude and pleasure in life and tenderness. In the papers they called it "beat mutiny" and "beat insurrection," words I never used. Being a Catholic, I believe in order, tenderness, and piety.

Early 1960s advertisement

between them, succeeded in the beclouding most of what was unsettling, and thereby valuable, in the idea of Beatness, and I might as well deal with this aspect of the matter before discussing the more serious critical appraisals of that idea.

The Beaniks were (and, I suppose, still are) essentially Bohemians–that is, *artistes manqués,* colony-establishers, citified Trobriand Islanders. On the run from the ant heaps of the industrial revolution, in flight from its moral cul-de-sacs, they gathered into seedy enclaves on the margins of the arts, where they immediately went about setting up a kind parody of the society they had fled. The life-style described in *On the Road,* "Howl," and other works gave a direction to their withdrawal, but their dominant preoccupations remained nest-building and Square-baiting. They talked so incessantly about "the rat race" and their own group identity that, with a few changes of reference, they would have almost gone unnoticed in Levittown.

Of course, Bohemians have always, drearily, derived most of their behavior patterns from attentively watching the bourgeoisie and then doing the opposite, but the Beatniks, unlike most Bohemians, could admit that their need to shock the Squares was only the obverse side of the Squares' need to *be* shocked, and this led to such sure-fire merchandising schemes as the Rent-a-Beatnik fad, and the Do-It-Yourself Beatnik Kit. It also led to a rigorous uniformity of language, dress, tastes, attitudes, and values that was almost a mirror image of the very conformity against which they were in revolt. The only difference was that the Beatniks were obsessed with the Squares, while the Squares were not obsessed with them, and a far better gimmick would have been an agency from which one could Rent-a-Square, because every pad needed one if it wanted to really swing. . . .

As should be wearisomely clear by now, a confusion of terminology has plagued the naming of this generation, as it did those of biblical times, and Mailer's vote would probably go to "Hip." I am sure all of us by now would cordially be rid of labels altogether. Certainly I have no fondness for the one with which I am associated, and am only interested in the New Con-

Bob Denver played beatnik Maynard G. Krebs and Dwayne Hickman the title character in the television situation comedy The Many Loves of Dobie Gillis *(1959–1962)*

sciousness for which it is a crude and perhaps misleading adjective, but nevertheless Mailer, and Hip, deserve a brief look.

As has been seen, I consider *The White Negro* to be a prisoner exploration of this New Consciousness, a document fully as important to the secret history of this age as *Notes from Underground* was to the Europe of its time. In a footnote to *The White Negro* (written somewhat later), Mailer says, "The Beat Generation is probably best used to include hipsters and beatniks"; he then goes on to detail with fine precision the differences between the two. The Beatniks are more intellectual, less sexy; they are mystic, pacifist, and neurotic, whereas "the hipster is still in life; strong on his will, he takes on the dissipation of the drugs in order to dig more life for himself, he is wrestling with the destiny of his nervous system, he is Faustian." I find little of importance to disagree with in this, as my views of the Beatniks may have made clear. But it is on this matter of "the destiny of the nervous system" where Mailer and I diverge, just as Hipness and Beatness (as I mean it) ultimately reach a crossroads of the consciousness, and must go their different ways.

Mailer's hipster goes back into the jungle of the world, where Power is the prize, and Ego is the weapon, and Hip the sight through which you aim. But the destiny of the nervous system, accumulating Sensation the way Faust's mind accumulated Knowledge, is inexorably violence, just as surely as Faust's destiny was damnation, for neither the mind *nor* the nervous system is a large enough channel for the whole of Consciousness. And it is our consciousness of *more* than either our nerves or our minds can contain by themselves that is the primary fact of this half of the twentieth century.

I have always thought that Mailer stubbed his toe on God. He is a metaphysician snagged in the data of the senses. I do not mean to say that he is immodest when I say that he cannot seem to endure the ego-loss toward which all his finest perceptions are driving him. There is something about the "merging" that all states of heightened Consciousness precipitate that revulses him. And yet he knows, he knows–for in sex, where the dissolving of the ego is most imminent and most intense, his vision comes perilously close to a drunken fusion of the insights of Sade and Swedenborg (if that can be imagined), only to draw back at the final moment when the character armor begins to melt, and insist on once again confusing the Ego with the Self.

His version of Beat (call it what you will) is decidedly "of this world," and, as such, it has proved more comprehensible, and more attractive, than any other version. It has even succeeded in establishing a point of

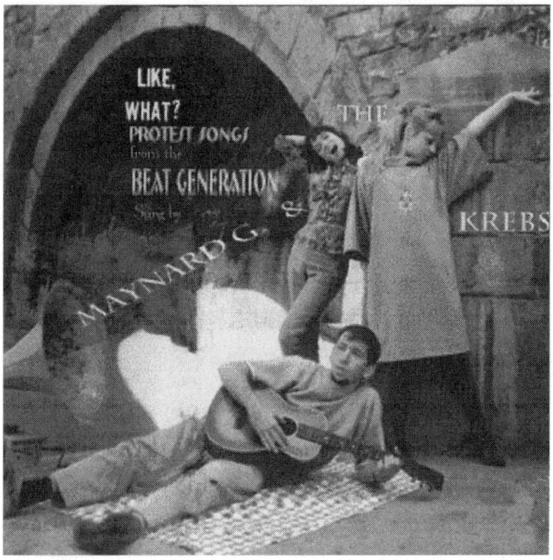

Album cover, 1962

Ginsberg in 1991 looking at a photo of Kerouac that was taken shortly before Kerouac's death in 1969

re-entry into the public world (what he has dubbed "existential politics") that a serious man can take seriously, and the consequences of which are as yet incalculable. . . .

It is clear that my conception of Beatness was just that–mine; or at best a conception shared to one degree or another by my *crowd*–Kerouac, Ginsberg, Burroughs, Corso, and a few others, like Snyder and Whalen, who turned up on the West Coast. What I was projecting were my own bankruptcies and aspirations, just as Jack projected his in all his novels. But it was the blasting, beering, and bumming in our work, the restless, energetic surface of the life described, and *not* the world-and-mind weariness, the continual moulting of consciousness, and the spirit's arduous venture toward its own reconciliations, that caught whatever fancies–Square *or* Beatnik–that were eventually caught.

Finally, *my* Beat Generation, like the Lost Generation before it, was primarily a literary group, and not a social movement; and probably all that will last out of our Beat years are a rash of vaporous anecdotes, and the few solid works that were produced. We have paid for the audacity of daring to label ourselves a "generation" by being continually ticketed with attitudes of mind and styles of behavior that were not necessarily ours, and having our work dismissed as these attitudes and styles became moribund. But thankfully a book is not as ephemeral as a beard, and, if it is a good book, it will outlast whatever quick-fading labels are attached to it. Time will tell, and not too quickly.

For the rest of it, it seems to me, the Beat Generation (and even the sorriest of the Beatniks) made contributions to the scene which deserve to be assessed–if only because they are in danger of being forgotten now, so radically has that scene changed in the last years.

Culturally, America has gone through something of a "thaw" since 1960. Part of this can be attributed to the fact that we had a president, albeit briefly, for whom culture, if it did not mean Charlie Parker, at least meant more than Lawrence Welk; a man in whose mouth the names of Faulkner and Hemingway did not sound ghost-written; a man who could speak of the inner life without somehow suggesting the digestive process. But whatever the reason, the atmosphere has changed. Among other things, the old puritan structure of censorship has been dismantled, idiocy by idiocy,

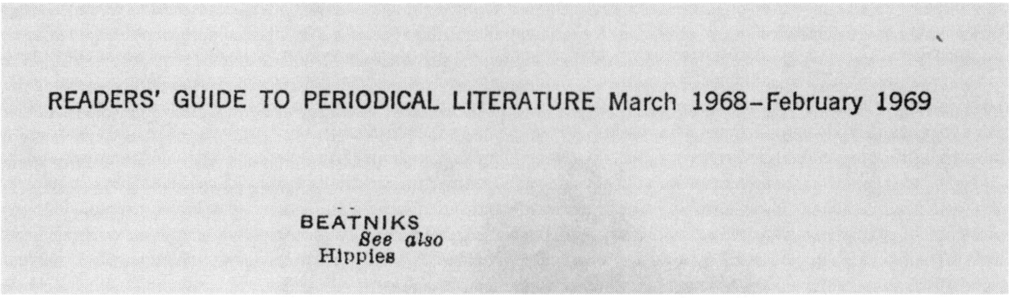
READERS' GUIDE TO PERIODICAL LITERATURE March 1968–February 1969

BEATNIKS
See also
Hippies

As this reference listing shows, the phenomenon of the Beatniks was seen as closely linked to their more politically active successors, the hippies

and the clammy hand of Academia has been returned to the exhumation of dead works, rather than the murder of living ones. It is assumed, once more, that poetry *can* make something happen–other than plague of exegetics, spreading through the "little magazines" like African sleeping sickness. Novels are published now that couldn't even have been written a few scant years ago. John Cage is no longer spoken of as a demented piano tuner; De Kooning is welcomed in the White House; even Iowa City has its Bergman Festival.

Off-Broadway, LSD, Ornette Coleman; the Frug, Genet, Buñuel–for the first time, the avant-guard is fashionable, experimentation is news, the far-out style is the chic style. Much of this is a mixed blessing at best, for much of it suggests the supermarket gourmand ("More, more! New, new!"), rather than the specialty-shop gourmet ("This, and this, but not that"). Still, it is a more open culture now, a culture at least trying to relate to a real and specific world, a culture in which strongly individual voices can be heard over the mindless din of the entertainment factories.

The poets, playwrights, and novelists, who might be loosely associated with the Beat attitude, were among the first of these voices to be heard, and their insistence on talking in loud, personal terms (whose very negation of certain values was an implicit affirmation of others) provoked those, who were not specifically "beat" themselves, into speaking up as well. The basic *tone* of the culture has changed from the caution, irony, and impersonality of the critical intellectual to the daring, commitment, and diversity of the creative artist, and the Beats certainly deserve a sizable part of the credit for this.

Socially, also, America is different land. If there has been a new tide running in the nation these past years–a tide of dissent, activism, and involvement (in civil rights, disarmament, poverty, and freedom of speech); a tide that bluntly calls into question the quality of our life here at home, and challenges mere anticommunism as a sane foundation for our policy abroad; a tide that has noisily erupted in the universities, the magazines, the public forums and the streets themselves–this tide is urged on by a new generation, which grew to awareness in the last half of the fifties, and was exposed to the example of a fragment of my generation, whose fixation with the idea that the emperor had no clothes led it to proclaim the bald and unruly "No!," without which the Free Speechers, and the Ban-the-Bombers, and the white (at least) Sit-ins might not have been able to say the challenging "Yes!" we are hearing at last in the land. For if politics are back "in" among the young, they are a very different sort of politics than those of the thirties or the forties–a much tougher-minded, pragmatic, lifegrounded politics, a politics of personal witness and nonviolence, a politics that tries to replace bloodless ideology with the living body interposed between the finger of the Establishment and the various buttons of the Society. All in all, it is time of possibilities again, for which the Beat revolt is not a little responsible.

Perhaps because of all this, the fever for naming generations may be dying out of our culture at last. Perhaps the future holds no single occurrence that will prove so forming that an entire age group can be characterized by a single term. Sometimes I find myself wondering if this happened, in actual fact, in our case. But deluded though we may have been, it *was* a generation we sought to describe, and not simply a minority group and its exotic mores; it was a unique phenomenon-of-mind in all of us, and not only the eccentric behavior patterns in a few, that we felt impelled to name. And if we were wrong, it was not because we were electric. For myself, I believe that we perceived the new sort of consciousness that distinguished us from our elders with a clarity the intervening years have not seriously blurred.

But I cannot leave this matter of the Beat attitude without a word about the generation that has come along since mine. If, as I believe, some of its achievements, and a lot of its style, have flourished on the ground we cleared, nevertheless the differences between us may yet prove to be greater than the similarities. Existentialism, as an example, exerts a powerful influence on both generations, and probably constitutes the only philosophic point of view

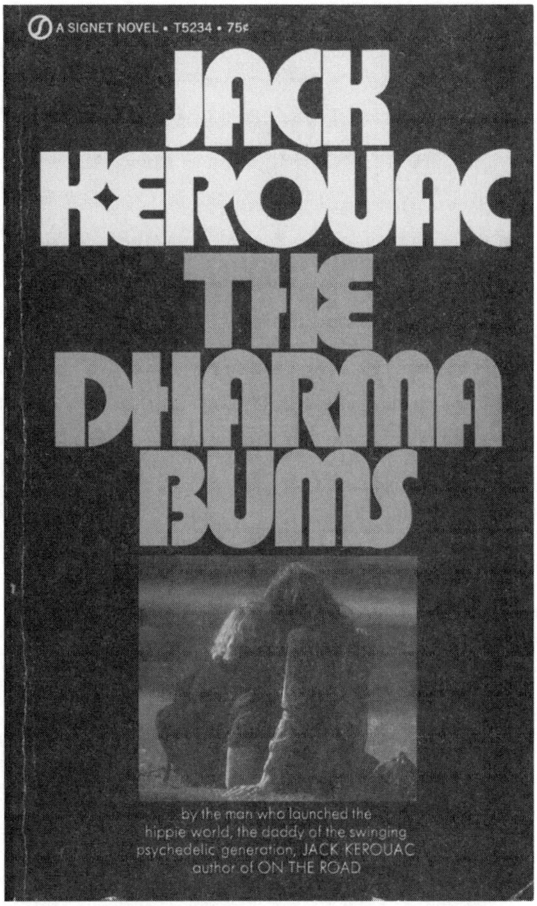

Covers for the first and seventh printings of the paperback edition of Kerouac's fourth novel, showing the change in marketing from the late 1950s to the 1960s as the Beat couple is replaced by a hippie couple

that is broadly typical of this time. But whereas it was existentialism's conception of the nature of man that spoke so clearly to *us,* it is existentialism's engagement in the community of men that most appeals to *them.* Nonviolence, pacifism, and reverence for life are mostly means of social action to young people today, whereas, to us, they were ends in themselves: you were nonviolent not because it was one way of changing institutions, but because it was the only way of remaining a human being. . . .

Perhaps these are inevitable reactions to a world that twenty years of Cold War have brought closer to insanity than to sense, but if that world is ever to be diverted from its present collision course with the fatality inherent in its own history (an onerous task that will fall on people who are under twenty-five today), my generation's stubborn choice of man over society, the Self over the Ego, and the spirit over psychology may have to be made all over again by those to whom we honestly thought we had bequeathed it already.

But then growing up in America has always been arduous. Our maturation rites are compounded of equal parts of nihilism and idealism, and we have always smashed our icons with other icons. Young Americans have immemorially been an uncritical in their surrender to the present as they are ruthless in their repudiation of the past, and a disorderly, eruptive process of individuation, whose first requirement seems to be a weaning-by-excess, is a tradition so unbroken and so peculiar to us that America's senescence may only be said to have arrived when it no longer produces successive generations-in-revolt.

For my own part, I am weary of labels. Whatever lies ahead for my generation will certainly make them less and less applicable to our experience, for an inevitable part of aging seems to be that one relentlessly becomes less representative of one's times, and more representative of oneself. Something like this, it seems to me, is happening to all of us who shared the Beat years–which, of course, was precisely what the Beat Generation was all about.

Poster for the 1987 movie

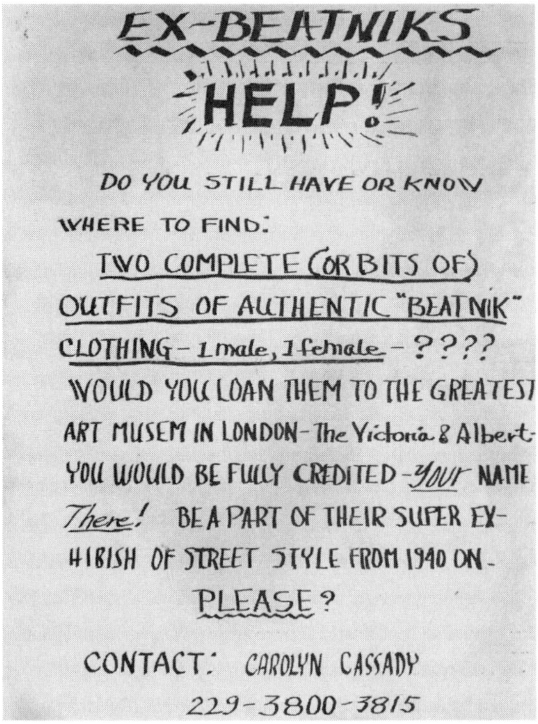
EX-BEATNIKS

HELP!

DO YOU STILL HAVE OR KNOW WHERE TO FIND:

TWO COMPLETE (OR BITS OF) OUTFITS OF AUTHENTIC "BEATNIK" CLOTHING - 1 male, 1 female - ????

WOULD YOU LOAN THEM TO THE GREATEST ART MUSEM IN LONDON - The Victoria & Albert - YOU WOULD BE FULLY CREDITED - your NAME There! BE A PART OF THEIR SUPER EX-HIBISH OF STREET STYLE FROM 1940 ON - PLEASE?

CONTACT: CAROLYN CASSADY

229-3800-3815

Notice posted by Neal Cassady's widow

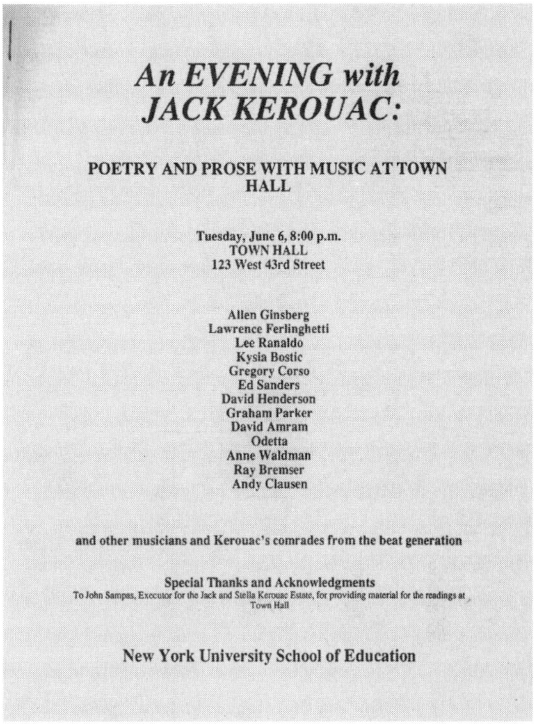
An EVENING with JACK KEROUAC:

POETRY AND PROSE WITH MUSIC AT TOWN HALL

Tuesday, June 6, 8:00 p.m.
TOWN HALL
123 West 43rd Street

Allen Ginsberg
Lawrence Ferlinghetti
Lee Ranaldo
Kysia Bostic
Gregory Corso
Ed Sanders
David Henderson
Graham Parker
David Amram
Odetta
Anne Waldman
Ray Bremser
Andy Clausen

and other musicians and Kerouac's comrades from the beat generation

Special Thanks and Acknowledgments
To John Sampas, Executor for the Jack and Stella Kerouac Estate, for providing material for the readings at Town Hall

New York University School of Education

First page of a 1994 program based on Kerouac's writing

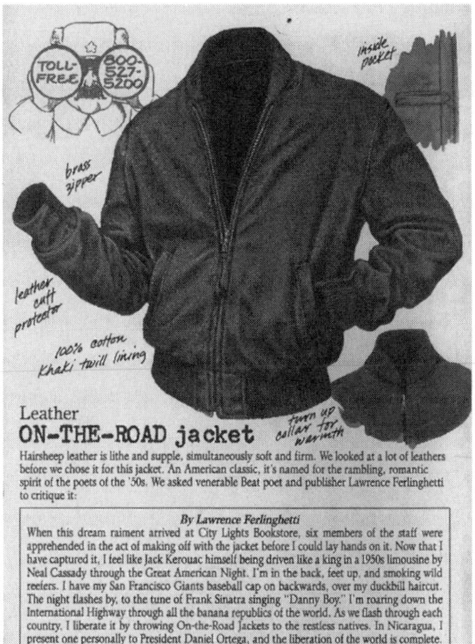

Advertisement for a jacket, exploiting title of Kerouac's first novel

NYU News

Press Office
New York University
25 West Fourth Street
New York, N.Y. 10012-1199

For Immediate Release

Contact: Elisa Guarino
212-998-6871

MAJOR CONFERENCE ON THE BEAT GENERATION TO BE HOSTED BY THE NEW YORK UNIVERSITY SCHOOL OF EDUCATION MAY 17 - 22, 1994

ALLEN GINSBERG, DAVID AMRAM, LAWRENCE FERLINGHETTI, AND GREGORY CORSO AMONG BEAT MOVEMENT LEADERS TO SPEAK AT NYU

Art Exhibits, Lectures, Concerts, Poetry Readings, Theater, and Film Are Among Beat Week Activities

Press Coverage Invited

Allen Ginsberg, David Amram, Lawrence Ferlinghetti and Gregory Corso are among the many legendary Beat figures who will participate in a major conference on the Beat movement hosted by the New York University School of Education from May 17 through May 22, 1994.

The conference, entitled "The Beat Generation: Legacy and Celebration," will examine the movement's impact on literature, art, culture, and society, with a special focus on educational issues as Beat literature enters the school and college curriculum. Various concerts, lectures, poetry readings, and other events will be held at NYU in Greenwich Village, the American bohemia which first provided the Beats with an atmosphere of tolerance, creativity, and artistic ferment that fostered the development of their work.

"The Beat conference is significant not only for the number of artists and academics attending, but especially because it is the first to take a critical look at the issues and challenges Beat literature presents to teachers and professors," said Ann Marcus, dean of the NYU School of Education. "The conference will also provide an opportunity to examine the impact of the Beats on "Generation X," the youth of the nineties."

Highlights of the week-long celebration are described below. *Members of the public wanting complete information about the conference and other activities should contact Helen Kelly at the NYU School of Education, 212-998-5090. Members of the press should contact Elisa Guarino at 212-998-6871.*

- more -

Press release for a 1994 academic conference on the Beat Generation

Chapter 3
Jack Kerouac

(12 March 1922–21 October 1969)

See also the Kerouac entries in *DLB 2: American Novelists Since World War II; DLB 16: The Beats: Literary Bohemians in Postwar America;* and *DS 3: Saul Bellow, Jack Kerouac, Norman Mailer, Vladimir Nabokov, John Updike, Kurt Vonnegut.*

The man who signed "John Kerouac" to his first novel, The Town and the City *(1950), and who went on to fame and notoriety as Jack Kerouac, the King of the Beats, was born Jean Louis Lebris de Kerouac in Lowell, Massachusetts, on 12 March 1922, the third and last child of Leo and Gabrielle Mémêre Kerouac. His parents were French Canadians whose families had immigrated to the United States, and French remained the language of the Kerouac household. Kerouac did not begin to learn English until he entered school, and he later recalled that as late as junior high school he was not completely confident in English. Kerouac's life was profoundly influenced by the circumstances of his childhood–especially his growing up in the working-class tenements of a mill town during the Depression and his attending Catholic parochial schools. A standout high-school athlete in baseball, football, and track, Kerouac earned a scholarship to attend Columbia University. Even more important to his future was his early determination to become a writer. As is frequently the case with young artists, he faced the resistance of his parents, who forecast a more predictable and prosperous life for their son. Nevertheless, Kerouac wrote prodigiously, and his ambition was to be a great writer–indeed, to rise as America's greatest writer and poet.*

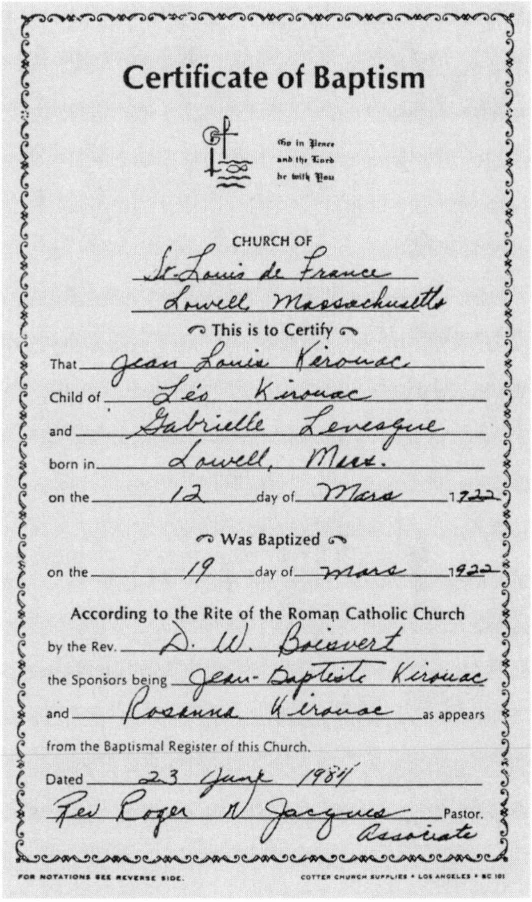

Certificate of Baptism

Go in Peace and the Lord be with You

CHURCH OF
St-Louis de France
Lowell Massachusetts

This is to Certify

That Jean Louis Kirouac
Child of Léo Kirouac
and Gabrielle Levesque
born in Lowell, Mass.
on the 12 day of Mars 1922

Was Baptized

on the 19 day of mars 1922

According to the Rite of the Roman Catholic Church

by the Rev. D. W. Boisvert
the Sponsors being Jean-Baptiste Kirouac
and Rosanna Kirouac as appears
from the Baptismal Register of this Church.

Dated 23 June 1984
Rev Roger N Jacques Pastor. Associate

FOR NOTATIONS SEE REVERSE SIDE. COTTER CHURCH SUPPLIES • LOS ANGELES • BC 101

Certificate from the Parish of St. Louis de France in Lowell. Kerouac remained a lifelong Catholic (Ellis Amborn, The Subterranean Kerouac, *p. 212).*

Growing up in Lowell and New York City

Kerouac described the day of his birth in a 28 December 1950 letter to Neal Cassady that he called "a full confesion of my life."

March 12, 1922, at five o'clock in the afternoon, in Lowell, Mass. was the day of the first thaw. I was born on the second floor of a wooden house on Lupine Road, which to this day sits on top of a

Kerouac's birthplace at 9 Lupine Road in Lowell, Massachusetts. The Kerouacs lived on the first-floor apartment for the first three years of the writer's life.

Lowell High School clock, a gift provided in part by Kerouac's graduation class. He mentions this clock anachronistically in Maggie Cassidy *(1959), a novel of high-school romance (photograph by Matt Theado).*

hill overlooking Lakeview Avenue. From this house my mother, God bless her dear heart, lay listening to the distant roar of the Pawtucket Falls a mile away; she has told me all this. Besides of which it was a strange afternoon, red as fire; 'noisy with a lyrical thaw,' as I said in my fictions of the past.

. . . .

I remember it, I remember the day of my birth. I remember the red air and the sadness–the strange red afternoon light Wolfe also was hung on–

–*Jack Kerouac: Selected Letters, 1940–1956,* pp. 248–249

In preparation for his matriculation to Columbia University, Kerouac attended the Horace Mann School for Boys, a private school in New York City, for one year after graduating from Lowell High School. The caption for his photo in the Horace Mannikin *(1940), the school's yearbook, shows the impression he made upon his fellow students.*

> John. L. Kerouac: Brains and brawn found a happy combination in Jack, a newcomer to school this year. A brilliant back in football, he also won his spurs as a *Record* reporter and a leading *Quarterly* contributor. Was outfield on the Varsity nine.

Kerouac's move to New York City was crucial because there he later met Allen Ginsberg, William Burroughs, and Neal Cassady, the core figures of what would become the Beat Generation.

Sebastian Sampas, one of Kerouac's closest friends in Lowell, infected young Kerouac with his enthusiasm for popular author William Saroyan (1908–1981). Probably in fall 1942, Sampas wrote to Saroyan, requesting that he send a postcard to Kerouac, who was then a student at Columbia University. Sampas was wounded in Italy during World War II and died in March 1944. For Kerouac's perspective on some of the incidents Sampas relates, see "We Thronged," in Atop an Underwood: Early Stories and Other Writings *(1999) and the opening of chapter 3 of* The Town and the City *(1950).*

My dear Mr. Saroyan,

This is a letter I was never going to write but somehow brooding here in the middle of the night I find myself perplexed by many things. Also I find that there are so many things I must tell you. You see October's here. I just left college. I'm 1-A in the Draft . . . . My friends are gone. But let me tell you about my friends Bill, because it was enthusiasm of your works and your ideals that bound us in comradeship.

Three years ago Billy Chandler, a friend of mine came up my house and asked me to read *The Daring Young Man on the Flying Trapeeze* . . . . and I remember it–

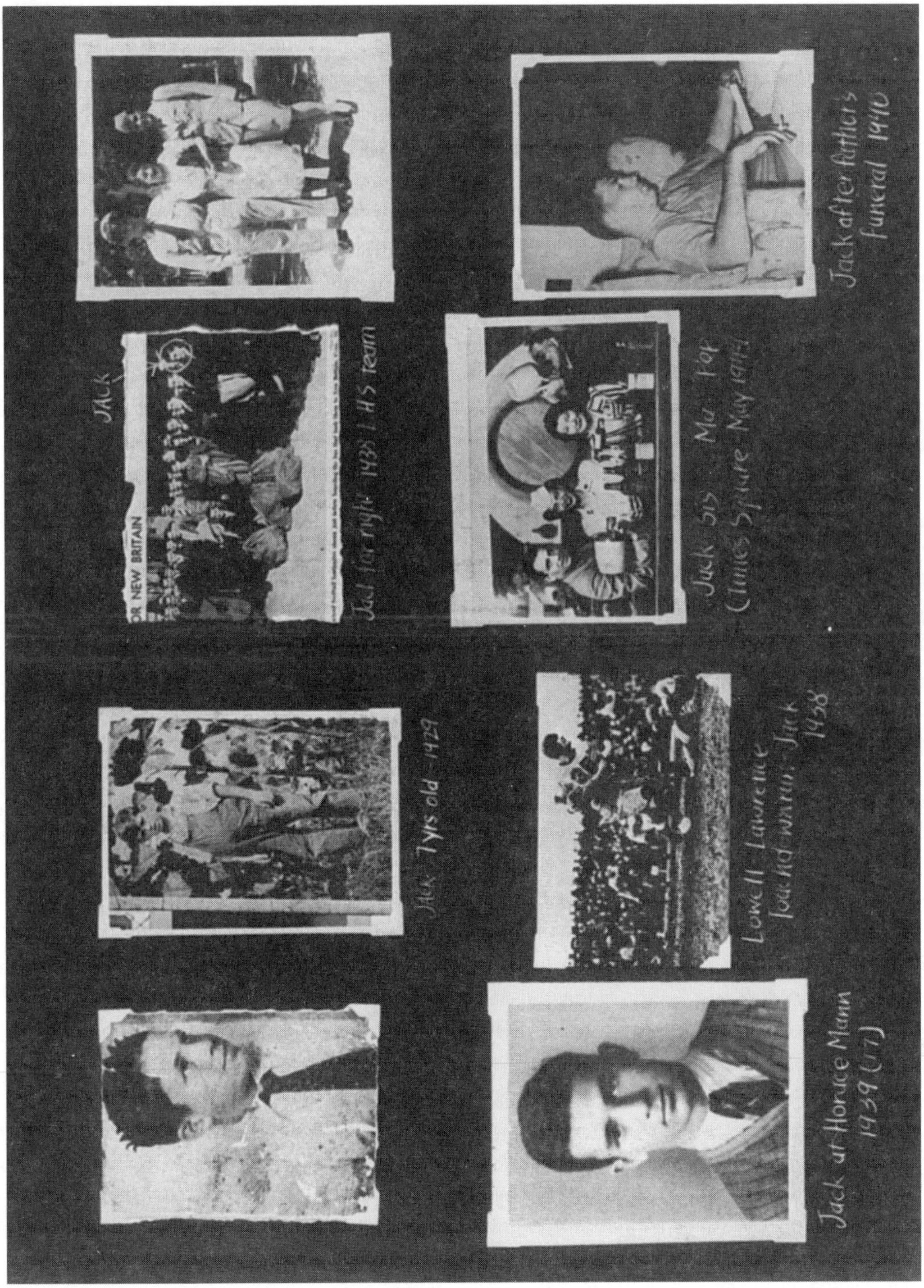

Endpapers for Kerouac's 1968 autobiographical novel Vanity of Duluoz: An Adventurous Education 1935–46

Kerouac in football uniform of the Horace Mann School for Boys

"Horizontal awakening . . . . . (Oh! That's not quoted correctly but you get the point)

That night Billy Chandler & Jack Kerouac, another young man nurtured in the Saroyan humanism, and I went to see the sun-rise–We stayed up all night Bill, discussing our ideals, life, & all humane matters–

Jack Kerouac, Billy Chandler & I had a wonderful summer back in '39. O! I'm not saying what I want to say. I can't project the enthusiasm, the fire, the burning zeal for Truth. Anyhow Billy joined the U.S. Army that summer & was shipped to the Philipinnes. Where is Billy now? Jackie went to Columbia, & I continued my own schooling–

Bill, do you see what I'm driving at! It isn't my fault that I wake up in the night with half-a-million broken dreams!

Well, we read all your plays & all your stories and we were enteared with happiness the next summer when you made that statement regarding Thomas Wolfe–

Last spring Jack joined the Merchant Marine & after one trip he went back to Columbia. He is playing foot-ball there–I have reams and reams of letters Jackie sent me & one short story in which he meets Billy Saroyan–That kid really is a great writer.–

Anyhow we have followed your career very closely and admire you very much. It's so hard to make this statement. I guess it's the American tradition on frowning on emotions.

I went down to see Jack 3 weeks ago & caught your play *Hello, Out There* & we got tight along with 2 females & we went down the Village exhorting mankind to seek Truth with the words *Hello, Out There*

Later, that week, while Jack & I were discussing, well here's what Jack said

"I wish we could talk to Billy Saroyan & tell him how much he means to us." But there was such a sad look on his face when he said that Bill–

God! if only you could read his manuscripts to see the stuff he has got–Look, my main reason for writing this letter was just to tell you all this. Tell you how we were moved to tears when your plays folded on Broadway & how awful you must have felt because we both knew it was a defeat hard for you to take–

Do me this favor Bill. It means a lot. Drop a postal card or a letter (I know how pressed you are for time) to John Kerouac, 209 Livingston Hall, Columbia University, New York City–and write him a few lines–anything–It would mean so much to him–I'll finish this letter with one of Jack's paragraphs.

"If tears alone shall wash away, the cruelty of the years, and nourish the white flower that grows in our black & broken hearts and teach us that life is not long & foolish, but brief & lovely, if tears alone must serve then let it be with tears"

Fraternally yours,
Sebastian Sampas
–Saroyan Estate

In spring 1942 Kerouac joined the U.S. Merchant Marine, sailing aboard the S.S. Dorchester. *On 7 April 1943 the twenty-one-year-old Kerouac wrote to his childhood friend G. J. Apostopolous of a split within his personality. With G. J., Kerouac had been an athlete, a beer drinker, a chaser of women—a man's man. With Sampas, however, he had shown his "introverted, scholary side."*

One of the reasons for my being in a hospital, besides dementia praecox, is a complex condition of my mind, split up, as it were, in two parts, one normal, the other schizoid.

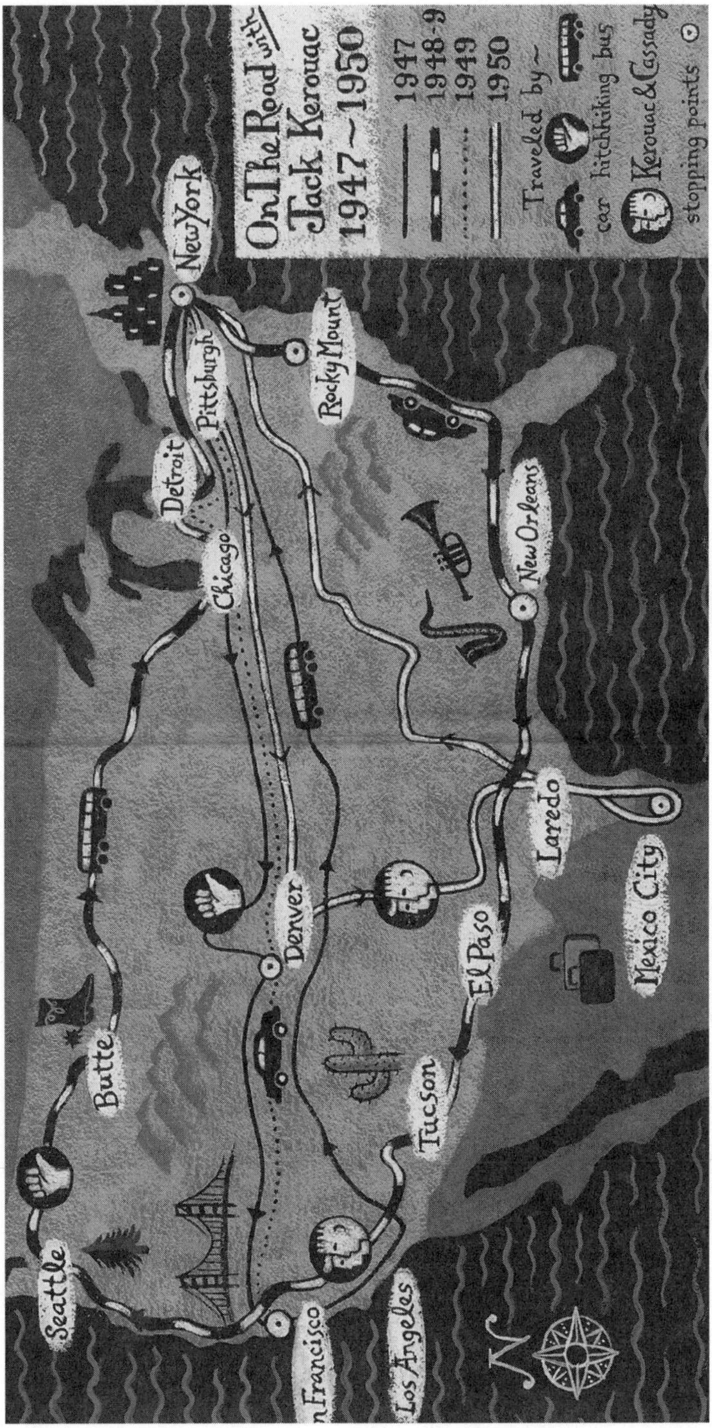

Endpapers diagramming Kerouac's travels (from Steve Warson, The Birth of the Beat Generation: Visionaries, Rebels, and Hipsters, 1944–1960 *[1995])*

Kerouac (front row, second from left) and the Horace Mann baseball team

My schizoid side is the Raskolnikov-Dedalus-George Webber-Duluoz side, the bent and brooding figure sneering at a world of mediocrities, complacent ignorance, and bigotry exercised by ersatz Ben Franklins; the introverted, scholarly side; the alien side.

My normal counterpart, the one you're familiar with, is the halfback-whoremaster-alemate-scullion-jitterbug-jazz critic side, the side in me which recommends a broad, rugged America; which requires the nourishment of gutsy, redblooded associates; and which lofts whatever guilless laughter I've left in me rather than that schizoid's cackle I have of late.

And, all my youth, I stood holding two ends of rope, trying to bring both ends together in order to tie them. Sebastian was at one end, you on the other, and beyond both of you lay the divergent worlds of my dual mind, and both of you the clearest symbols I could see. I pulled–had a hell of a time trying to bring these two worlds together–never succeeded actually; but I did in my novel "The Sea Is My Brother," where I created two new symbols of these two worlds, and welded them irrevocably together.

–*Jack Kerouac: Selected Letters, 1940-1956,* p. 60

Traveling

Between 1947 and 1950, Kerouac traveled extensively around the United States and into Mexico. His adventures provided the material for On the Road. *On one trip Luanne Henderson traveled with Cassady and Kerouac from New York City to William Burroughs's farm in Louisiana. In her interview for* Jack's Book *she describes her experience there and on the subsequent trip to San Francisco.*

I didn't really have any opportunity to get well acquainted with Burroughs at that time. I don't think even Neal and Jack got too much of a chance. Jack, more than Neal, was talking with Burroughs, and kind of in need of Burroughs at the time. The fact that we were going down by Burroughs really meant a great deal to Jack. When we would talk or anything, Burroughs was very much a part of him, like a teacher. He always found a way to take Burroughs aside and talk with him.

Neal kind of avoided Burroughs for some reason. I think Bill was a little unhappy with Neal at that point. I wasn't really too sure why, what the whole thing was about, but I got the definite impression that Burroughs wasn't all that pleased about seeing Neal. It kind of put me in a position of holding back.

Joan was really involved in speed, that inhaler trip. We cleaned Algiers out and then had to start going over

Luanne Henderson

aking trips to every drugstore in at that time– I'm not positive– she ubes a day.

leep. I don't care what time I got up or came home or anything, Joan was up, either with the broom or rake, scraping lizards off the tree, in the kitchen washing walls, continuously scrubbing.

There were several evenings that we all sat around Burroughs' feet, him in his rocking chair. I don't think I ever saw Bill out of that rocking chair all the time we were there, except a few times outside with Jack. Listening to Bill was very interesting.

He was directing most of his conversation to Jack, more than Neal or I, concerning things in New York, and Jack's writing. And I think Neal felt all that deeply, and proceeded to agitate or irritate Bill further by some of his antics, which Neal had a tendency to do when he felt inadequate around someone. It would speed him up even more, and then he would get into things that normally weren't part of him.

After we left Algiers for California we were going through the bayous. It was midnight on this spooky little road with all the willow trees hanging down, and Jack proceeded to tell the story of the death of David Kammerer, just like we were listening to a version of *The Shadow*.

It was really wild. He had me just with shivers up and down, and he was talking in that kind of voice deliberately. We'd been listening on the radio, 'cause at that time, all our spook stories were on, like *The Shadow* and some other old-time radio shows, and that's just how Jack related it. Speaking in a low, mysterious voice, and picturing the whole thing of the river, the darkened streets. He really went into vivid detail, and I felt like I was there, and I got the shivers. Jack and Neal, of course, were giggling like they were telling ghost stories.

Then we all took our clothes off when we were going across Texas. Jack went through that thing in *On the Road,* saying I smeared them with cold cream, and all that, which was totally unreal. We did take our clothes off, because it was sweltering hot. I mean, we were just dying. We didn't have any cold cream. I would have loved to have had some. Any kind of cream.

But the most memorable part Jack didn't go into much description of. We stopped at some ruins and all of us went over there and for miles around you couldn't see a thing. You could see a car coming for a hundred miles down the road, and we were all cavorting naked through the ruins and we saw a car approaching, which we all proceeded to ignore until it was just a few hundred feet away. Then Jack and I sprinted across the highway to get back in the car. Neal struck this magnificent pose up on one of these concrete platforms. You could see the car slowing down, this elderly couple coming by. You could see this old woman on the passenger side pointing, and Jack and I were discussing exactly what she was saying. "Isn't that amazing?" Because Neal did have a beautiful body. "Isn't that a magnificent statue? And the way it's held up through the years when all this deterioration was around it." There wasn't a finger out of place. He must have stood there in that hot sun for a long while, because they just slowed down to a crawl. And of course Jack and I were getting lower and lower in the car. I guess now when I look back on it. We really were lucky none of us was ever arrested.

The ending of the trip was so abrupt, and so cold.

Neal left Jack and I on the street in San Francisco. Neal just drove away, and there was Jack and I without penny one, without anything except a lousy suitcase and each other. We just stood there looking at each other and thought, "Where do we go from here?"

It had been such a happy trip, but, of course, with nobody thinking about tomorrow.

We didn't have anything when we got to San Francisco. I think at that point, whatever Jack had, he had given to Neal for gas and food and such. He might have given Burroughs something for the food.

There had been a point when we were in New York, close to the time when we were leaving, and Neal was feeling kind of panicky, and I recognized it. I don't really know if Jack did at that time. I know he wouldn't have discussed it with me if he had. But Neal was kind of trying to push Jack and I together, which would have eased things off for him as far as I was concerned. That would have gotten one problem out of the way.

That's the way it was going, because at this point I felt a definite attraction to Jack, and I felt that he did to me. There really was no need for pushing on Neal's part, but Al said that if Neal was aware of that, he would have been very unhappy. He was later, when he found out I was really attracted to Jack, and it wasn't Neal's idea but Jack's and mine also. He was very unhappy about the situation, and he tried to reverse it, which wasn't that easy to do.

But then when Jack and I got to San Francisco we had no money for food, and I went over to this other hotel about a block from the one where Jack and I were staying. This was a girl that I had stayed with previously, and we had learned to use this iron upside down to cook on. You sit it on a wastepaper basket and turn the iron upside down. They didn't allow hot plates or anything, and the manager used to go crazy smelling coffee or food.

One of her recipes that we loved by was boiling noodles and opening a can of cream of chicken soup and just mixing it up. It was great.

I also had a problem because, as you remember, before I left I was going to be married. It was only about two weeks and he was due home in San Francisco. And here I am and I really didn't know what to do. Not only because Jack was there alone, but the thing was that I knew Jack would go to Neal, and I was very confused at that point about how I felt.

I was involved with Jack and cared a great deal about him. To me, at that time, three months was like three years, and so much had happened in the three months since my fiancé was gone, I really didn't have any idea how I felt about him any more. I'd even forgotten what he looked like, but I did know that the letters were still coming in and he was still expecting me to be writing. I had an obligation to at least give him an explanation of what was happening. He had no idea I'd been to New York.

I went over to a hotel about a block and a half away from the hotel that Jack and I had been staying at, where this girl stayed. She was a hooker, a very, very young girl that I had met when I first came out to San Francisco. I ran into her in the bar that was downstairs from the girl with the iron, and she was living with a guy that owned a bar on Turk Street. I told her I had just gotten back, and that I didn't have any money or anything and I wanted to get a job at the bar–except that I was underage. She was underage, too, but she was living with the owner, so I thought maybe she might be able to help me through him. So she said why don't I go out for dinner with him and her and the bartender? I realized they were setting me up, but I didn't care about that. And she also said she would give me some money, which she did. Anyway, I went out to dinner with them. I didn't get the job. I didn't know a damn thing about hustling or anything at all, and I thought she's being my friend, working with me, but it was the other way around. She was with them and trying to use me. It didn't work out at all.

Jack called Neal the day before I left for Denver. Neal told him that he would pick him up, and that was all settled and straight. Jack and I spent that whole night talking about he and I, and we both agreed that I had to do something as far as the man I was to marry was concerned–do something one way or the other. And then I was supposed to get in touch with Jack afterward and go on from there.

As it turned out I got married, and I didn't see Jack or Neal.

I had seen Jack in relationships with other women, but naturally I had no idea whether he was the same with them as he was with me. With me, Jack reverted to a little-boy type of thing. He needed mothering. He was extremely lovable and beautiful, but I think Jack had a need for being taken care of.

But at the time, so did I. I needed someone–not necessarily to take care of me financially, but I wasn't emotionally strong enough. At least I didn't think I was. I just didn't feel secure. Since we didn't go on with it, I don't know if things would have changed. But I felt like Jack leaned on me more that I leaned on him. And that was a scary time, and I was the one who would have to make all the decisions or all of the moves, and I wasn't quite sure I was ready to make all the right ones. I wanted help.

After I got older and I saw Jack, as I did, through the years, I think that made me sadder than anything, that Jack couldn't get away from the hang-up with his mother, the relationship with his mother, and not being able to find a good, stable relationship with a woman. He just never was able to pull himself out of that.

Neal was very, very jealous of Jack, but I don't think Jack was appreciative enough of that. I tried to tell him. I really thought it would help Jack to realize that Neal was very jealous of him as a man, because Jack always acted as though the women around would only turn to him as second-best, if Neal didn't want them. I tried to tell him it wasn't that way at all, but I don't think he ever really realized it. He thought I was just saying it to make him feel good, which I was, but not for the reasons that he thought.

I think that Neal tried to prove to himself that even if he gave his women away, he would win in the end. He had the doubt about women and everything else concerning himself, but because nobody else had that doubt, he had to live up to it. Jack wouldn't expect him to have any kind of worry concerning himself. You know, "Why worry about me with the woman? You know you can have her back anytime you want." But Neal wasn't that sure of it.

This was a pattern of Neal's with most of those who cared for him. They found themselves being left a great many times. I think Neal would feel pressure when he felt someone was relying on him that much. Neal would get panicky, too. I think all of us had a tendency to think that Neal was strong enough and infallible enough to accept anything. When someone would be depending on him a great deal, he would get panicky, not necessarily showing it as panic, but just suddenly splitting from the scene. That way he didn't have to face up to the responsibility of whatever people were expecting of him.

. . . .

It was kind of a shock when I found out that *On the Road* had become a pattern for young people.

A friend of mine, a young boy about twenty-two years old, I guess, come up from Los Angeles with these two young girls, about eighteen–in their late teens–and this woman that was a friend of the boy, she had lived with me. She had told him about *On the Road*, and so forth. I'd never even talked to him about it at all, but he had related all this to these girls, and they had to come to meet me, so he brought them up to the house.

They were on their way to Denver to recreate the trip back to New York, and I couldn't believe that. How could anybody? It was just totally insane to me. You know, here are these two well-heeled young women from upper-middled-class families, money in their pockets and beautiful clothing, and they were going to Denver and go through with this. I don't care what they did, but I just couldn't imagine young people trying to recreate something out of a book like that. It was really a shock to me to find out what impact Jack's books were having on the younger generation.

Of course, I loved the book, but I guess in living it and being around Jack and Allen and all of them I didn't think about it as material for a book. I was quite convinced that John [Holmes] would finish his book, because they were all dedicated and disciplined. They weren't fly-by-night, you know, running around not getting anything accomplished. I just never thought of Jack as being famous, or Allen as being famous. We were all just doing a thing, and that was the extent of it.

–*Jack's Book,* pp. 136–141, 317–318

Getting a First Novel Published

Kerouac was married to Edie Parker, an art student at Columbia, on 22 August 1944 and lived briefly in Gross Pointe, Michigan, but the marriage ended quickly and he returned to New York City in October 1944.

After his father's death of stomach cancer in 1946, Kerouac focused on producing the Great American Novel, an effort that he later claimed was designed to "explain everything to everybody." The result was an eleven-hundred-page typescript that was pared down and published by Harcourt, Brace in 1950 as The Town and the City.

In his novel Kerouac explored the split in his personality, contrasting the "guileless laughter" of his town characters with the "schizoid's cackle" of the city characters such as those based on Allen Ginsberg and William Burroughs. Kerouac and Columbia schoolmate Hal Chase later divided the core Beat Generation members into the "Wolfeans," the all-American boys who were influenced by of Thomas Wolfe's novels, and the "non-Wolfeans," or black priests Ginsberg and Burroughs, who were decadent and possessed of immoral lust. His large cast of characters in his novels can frequently

Kerouac in New York City, circa 1945 (Kerouac Estate)

be divided into these broad categories, particularly his first-person narrators, as critic Warren French has noted in Jack Kerouac: Novelist of the Beat Generation (1986).

After Kerouac finished writing The Town and the City, *Ginsberg suggested that Kerouac take it to Mark Van Doren, who had been one of their English professors at Columbia. From the start, Ginsberg acted as an agent for Kerouac's work and also for the work of other friends. Ginsberg tirelessly carried his friends' manuscripts around New York City. Their choice of Van Doren as a champion for their cause is also worth noting. The all-male circle of Beat writers were, in their early stages, seeking father figures in the academic and publishing worlds. This search led them not only to Van Doren but also to William Carlos Williams, Kenneth Rexroth, and Malcolm Cowley, among others.*

In an April 1948 letter to Ginsberg, Kerouac discusses the plan to have Van Doren read his novel; he also refers to Neal Cassady, the "young jailkid shrouded in mystery" they had known for over a year at this point, and to Hal Chase.

I wonder if you were right about my taking "Town & City" to Van Doren instead of a publisher. Tell me what you think about that in your considered well-groomed Hungarian Brierly-in-the-bathrobe opinion. It seems to me perhaps that if I took my novel to publishers they would glance at it with jaundiced eyes knowing that I am unpublished and unknown, while if Van Doren approved of it, everything would be quite different. I imagine that's what you think, too. We creative geniuses must bite fingernails together, or at least, we should, or perhaps, something or other.

Have you heard from Neal? Reason I ask, if I go to Denver on June 1st to work on farms out there I'd like to see him. It's strange that he doesn't right (write)–and as I say, he must be doing ninety days for something, only I hope it's not ninety months, that's what I've been really worrying about.

Hal has been reading my novel and he said it was better than he thought it would be, which everybody says. As a matter of fact I don't know much about it myself since I never read it consecutively if at all.

. . . .

So when you see Van Doren–tell him I plan to take my novel (380,000 words) to him, tell him I *will* take it to him in the middle or end of May, completed novel: tell him it's the same one I told him about 2-1/2 years ago and go and tell him that I have laboured through poverty, disease, and bereavement and madness, and the novel hangs together no less. If that isn't the pertinacity or the tenacity or something of genius I don't know what is. Go tell him that I have been consumed by mysterious sorrowful time yet I have straddled time, that I have been saddest and most imperially time-haunted yet I have worked.

–*Jack Kerouac: Selected Letters, 1940–1956,* pp. 146–147

In the 17 April 1949 entry in his journal, Kerouac pondered working with Harcourt, Brace editor Robert Giroux on his first published novel, The Town and the City:

I like the idea that we're going to "work in his office in the evenings"–with its hints of coffee in cartons; in shirt sleeves (good Arrow shirts); maybe a pint of whiskey; the big city night of April and May outside the windows of Harcourt, Brace, and the thought of ships and women, and of Broadway glowing.

Robert Giroux, the editor at Harcourt, Brace who worked with Kerouac on his first novel

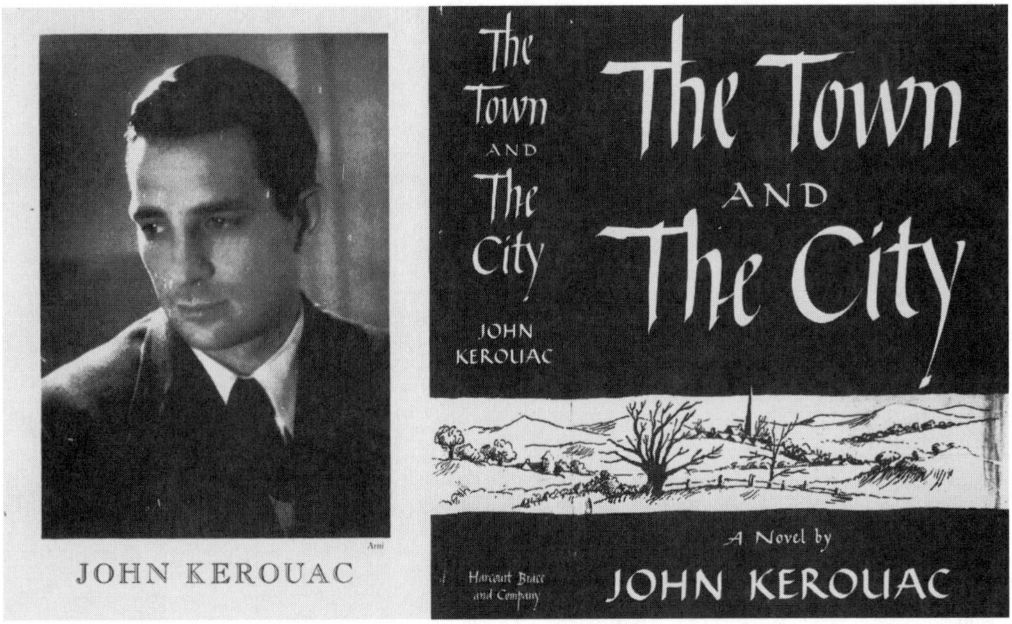

Dust jacket for Kerouac's first novel, which received mixed reviews; approximately five thousand copies were sold. The author's advance was $1,000.

John Clellon Holmes, whose friendship with Kerouac began in 1948, recalled Kerouac's acquiescent attitude with editor Giroux as the two men worked to bring The Town and the City *to publication.*

In the months after the editing process was through Jack was very defensive about the editing, with his buddies who knew the book, anyway. I said, "Oh, God damn it, you didn't cut that out!" And he said, "No, Giroux knows." Jack was of two minds all the time. He wanted to get published. He was flattered and pleased and relieved by the fact that Giroux thought he was a marvelous, young new writer. So even against his better instincts–I choose to believe–he accepted all kinds of cuts in that book that I think he personally felt were wrong. He was sorry to lose whole sections, but still, he was feeling very, very upbeat.

He was waiting for publication the way you do, the first book. God, you feel you've crossed over. You've suddenly gotten to someplace. He was feeling full of beans about the next book. He was trying to be responsible, the way everybody does. He was very close to Giroux. He tended to idolize Giroux in the old sort of Fitzgerald-Hemingway-Perkins kind of thing. "I've now found my father," in effect, "the guy who will get me through all of this madness."

–*Jack's Book,* p. 79

Much of Kerouac's The Town and the City *re-creates his hometown, Lowell, depicting the town and its citizens much as Thomas Wolfe had done for Asheville, North Carolina, in* Look Homeward, Angel *(1929). Kerouac's novel, though, is structured on contrast. The Martin family, whose story is at its core, moves to New York City, and there Peter Martin, based on Kerouac, meets the hipsters and other denizens of the city. In these two excerpts, which show the hipster influence in Kerouac's story as well as his interest in their language, Junkey is based on Herbert Huncke; Dennison is based on William Burroughs; "Beckwell's cafeteria on the Square" is Bickford's on Times Square; and "shiazit" is hipster slang for marijuana.*

"Well, man," greeted Junkey, with his somnolent gaze of dry reproach, "I was wondering when you'd come in and say hello." He had a crooked, pathetic way of grinning. "I've got no place to sleep," he went on. "I was up all last night in Beckwell's cafeteria on the Square waiting for a guy to show up with some shiazit. Don't you know, I'm beat and I need some sleep if I'm also going to score with the doctors for everybody around here." He continued with the bulbs in a dark ruminative chore. The purpose of the blue bulbs, he said, was to give the room a "weird, soothing effect" in the evenings. It was one of Junkey's many rudimentary decorations intended to ward off the stark street world he always had to live in. He hoped he could sleep in Dennison's that night.

. . . .

Liz and her husband Buddy were "just friends" now. There was a certain kick in their new relationship, a "cool kick"–Buddy was Liz's "mother." He came around every now and then to talk to her awhile, to swap news about happenings all the way from Los Angeles to Boston, from Miami to Seattle, news of other "cats" and "chicks" like themselves connected in some way with jazz music, nightclubs and show business, and after that he kissed her on the cheek and coolly slouched off back to his jazz music, that was all.

In New York Liz held down various types of jobs, singing in small clubs at times, at other times standing around showing her legs in second-rate floorshows, at other times wandering "beat" around the city in search of some other job or benefactor or "loot" or "gold." When you were loaded with loot and having your kicks, that was living; but when you were hung up without gold and left beyond the reach of kicks, that was a drag.

–*The Town and the City,* pp. 402, 450–45

The most notable critic to review The Town and the City *was Howard Mumford Jones, Harvard professor and distinguished scholar.*

Back to Merrimac

Howard Mumford Jones

Saturday Review of Literature, 11 March 1950, p. 18

In the present amorphous state of book reviewing this will likely be hailed as a novel displaying great life, energy, and realism. Life, energy, and realism of a kind it certainly has. It belongs to the category of the "big" novel–the lengthy book, in which a prodigious splashing about, general emotional appeals in the "lost, lost, lost" cadence of Thomas Wolfe, and a rather simple notion of what constitutes fictional characters are supposed to compensate for radical deficiencies in structure and style.

. . . .

That classic stylist Willa Cather some years ago made a plea for the novel *démeublé*–the novel from which all the unnecessary furniture of realism, both words and things, had been removed, so that writer and reader might confront theme and character and so discover the graver issues of the tale. It is Mr. Kerouac's failure to throw the furniture out that leads to his confusion. A drive for "bigness" overcomes structure. There seems to be no special reason why the novel is as long as it is, none why it should not be half as long, none why it should not be the first of a series of novels quite as "big," following the Martins as far as Mr. Kerouac wants to go. But the pattern, the shape, the spire of meaning is here so overlaid one isn't sure whether even this would be his long-run intent.

One infers from the title that the conflict between town and city is to determine fate and perhaps character. The elements of the conflict are loose in the book, but the issue is never honorably joined. The Merrimac Valley opening is excellent writing but it remains merely excellent writing. There come whole rows of scenes elsewhere including some queer ones laid in New York City and written with naive power, but these are so loosely integrated with the conflict (is there conflict?) one doesn't quite know how to take them. Time goes by in a series of jerks, but time as development (essential to the family novel, as in "Buddenbrooks") isn't there.

I suspect that if the unnecessary furniture of realism were removed, Mr. Kerouac would have seen what is wrong. But there are so many people, all motivated by a rather elementray notion of emotional drives, there are so many scenes presented in a kind of good-humored scramble, that the lives of the one are in many cases indistinguishable, and the purpose of the other never comes

Excerpts From Reviews of *The Town and the City*

There is an unremitting emphasis in the following of each personal life, there is a lyrical rhythm to the writing, a certain control in the handling, that keeps alive interest in what might have been an overlong novel whose reality is neither forced nor raw.

Kirkus Reviews, 1 February 1950, p. 69

A first novel of moral strength. Recommended, but not for the faint-hearted.

Library Journal, 15 February 1950, p. 318

Mr. Kerouac's boundless capacity for sincerity, unmixed with humor, grows very tiresome after a short time, and his habit of using ten words where one would do inclines the reader to put this book aside until some day when there is absolutely nothing else around to read.

–*The New Yorker,* 25 March 1950, p. 115

An incoherent novel adolescent in its philosophy, that could stand stern editing.

Catholic World, April 1950, p. 72

cleanly through this energetic prose. I think Mr. Kerouac has many of the essential attributes of the practising novelist–fecundity, invention, a kind of abundance (yet unchanneled)–but they do not here fuse into unity.

Writing *On the Road*

Kerouac married Joan Haverty, his second wife, on 17 November 1950. Although the marriage did not endure, the couple did have a daughter, Jan Michelle, born 16 February 1952. After the mild success of his first novel, Kerouac's subsequent novels remained unpublished until 1957, when Viking brought out the best-seller On the Road. *During these years of struggle, fellow writer John Clellon Holmes proved to be his solid supporter, sending him long, encouraging letters. After the publication of* The Town and the City, *Kerouac had difficulty getting started on his next book in which he planned to treat his road adventures with Neal Cassady. In his 27 December 1950 letter to Kerouac, Holmes addresses the trials of putting into acceptable form what his friend called his "daily heap" of words.*

And now, about your predicament, which I hope I am not wrong in mentioning. In *T&C* the form was implicit in the material. Perhaps you did not worry overmuch about it. Perhaps you let the great flood of material simply take you and find and form itself. You told me, one of the first times I met you, "You know, John, I haven't *got* form really. But I think my book has *deep* form." That stuck in my craw, and I think it is true of you, and true of many American writers. Those that have plagued their minds with form have produced but stunted garden flowers that have no magnificence, not of that exultant always-blooming burst and power of really great American writing. But, now, in "On the Road," you are struggling with the difficulties of form and mould. Where to put all this vast heap of material? How shape the mountain to a hill the eye can contain? How domesticate the wild and majestic elephant? I have seen you attack your great lump of clay with eager, desperate, and facile hands. But always, though it may have satisfied me or someone else, it did not settle your mind. Something had been stripped away, or you had not gotten the perspective right. You began again. No one could say you have not been tireless, patient, persevering. But it has resisted your head.

Well, I am no one to add a word on this. I have myself had too many false starts (far more than you). I myself have produced too little that can withstand any public wind. I myself have brought into the world too many abortions and thought them alive to think I have any concession on speech here. And yet I have thought deeply upon you this last day, and upon this problem, that may be your present dilemma. You have started so many times, tried so hard, and yet found it still not right. Well, perhaps some of what I have said about Goodman [Holmes had described a Benny Goodman concert recording] will strike you. I know that it takes little view of the huge technical hangups that writing entails, the endless taking of pains and blows that getting a book out of mind demands. But nevertheless I think you should get your vision straight. Do not forget what it is you are trying to give to the people. Do not despair.

I have tacked upon my working heart one of [the] things you told me after reading some of my twisted scenes toward the beginning of this book. You had read them sympathetically, at length, considering, and you turned to me and said: "The daily heap! The daily heap is everything!" And that I pinned upon my laboring heart, because I knew for a certainty that it was right. There were other things you told me: about simply saying what I had to say, and saying simply what I had to say. About the "angel-author" (oh, these were words of clarity for so muddled a battler as myself!), and about "the sincere tone." I have never forgotten these things, and much that I have done in this book (most of what in it is worthwhile) is the result of a painstaking scrutiny of these maxims. Now I say that you must take heart as well. Fill with that sure compassion out of which I know your best work has come.

Remember all the madness, the Fellaheen people on the dark roads, those strange apocalyptic moments with Neal, and all the other crazy things you know better than anyone else. Go back to the moment (if this can be done) when "On the Road" came to you out of nowhere. Go back to that instant, and remember it in all the naked excitement it possessed then. Do not think about the ulcers that twitter and scribble in the Rockefeller Centers of the world, or the long-nosed and petulant editors who browse and yawn over the terrible children that writers of the past have brought forth in pain and faith. Think only of your own feelings and believe in them. Turn neither to right nor to left! Start writing some night, in this reverant mood, and go on. Fill your head (and page) with everything you can think of, in its natural order, in the beauty of its happening, and then worry later about the rest. You have so much that must come out. Do not forget that each year for the rest of your life there will be other books. One cannot build a universe in one year, or one book. The writer struggles and hurries to push forth as much of himself as one lifetime upon the earth will allow. I learned that one cannot wager the whole of life upon one book, that words get tougher and most resistent the longer one pauses over them. They begin to loom large, to bare teeth, and to thrust their feet into the earth and refuse to budge. You hold the whip that sends them forth in shimmering battalions to amaze and alarm the waiting people. Moments of poetry are in your soul, Jack, and, yes, and foolishness too. A writer can only hope to facilitate the appearance of the first and keep the second chained in the dungeons of his guts. He can't do away with foolishness, with vain belief and stupid faith. These are his reservations in the human race, and in him they grow fat on the relentless pursuit of his very blood after the perfection of his works. Perfection has eluded every man who toiled upon a stone. Let us only be perfect in our imperfections.

The world will neither bow to you as a result of "On the Road," nor will it necessarily send a posse out after you. You would have come closer to what you intend if it does the latter, but no matter. Amaze and astound yourself, and that is the most that you can expect. I seem to know these things with a certainty today. Our own moment of triumph, and I think it comes in its most pure and nearly angelic wonder at the moment that we create its expression, must be enough for a little while. Write, with that earnest hurry of Balzac, that huge urgent intensity of Dostoyevski, that simple long-shoreman faith of Melville (and his nerve, his daring to say grandly grand things), and write with that love of self and world and life that I find in Cervantes, Shakespeare and all the others who have given man his deepest tributes. But write. Labor in your vineyard simply and with faith.

Remember the children that roam your roads, perfect yourself only insofar as your heart is not wounded. Do not cogitate the effect of your work, do not plumb the undecipherable and incalculable mysteries of the world which will choose or reject you. There is some truth in the statement that we cannot know its ways. We can only do our best, amaze and astound ourselves. Keep simple and lonely faith with yourself, Jack. In no one's eyes, but in your own inner, secret eyes, seek to shine. I know your genius. Often I tend to flatter myself that I know it better than most. I know that you are like that iceberg (the favorite of all analogy-makers), and that what there is on the surface is only a bare shadow. But, you see, that is what we must most strive to do, that thing that Dante said: "Make of shadows substantial things." I know that there is much inside you, and I worry, fret and feel a strange, personal gnaw when you have trouble with it. Make your book as defiant, pure, dastardly, sweet or crazy as you will. If the tone is right we'll weep when you tell us. It is not that readers are slavish, but that they are like you and when you hold up your picture it will be a mirror to them. Your note of triumph cannot help but be heard. Fill your book with everyone who lives in your head, make them live and readers will commend you and buy. I seem to know these things, as I have said. Forgive my strange advice; concern and love brings it forth. There are few enough writers today who would be worth saving even if one could do so, and I count you on the first team of those that deserve preservation from the vantage-point of the future. You know, the years pass all too quickly, and I am reminded of another thing you said to me (on a horrible and grim and fateful night of life!). You said: "Writers don't work enough today. They turn out a few little, tidy books and that's all!" (Or words to that effect). It stuck with me, because that night, later, after I had left you, another part of my life collapsed, and I knew that what you had said was true of more things than writing. But we have short time and so much to do.

John

–*The Beat Diary,* pp. 122–124

Ann Charters quoted Kerouac's description of the circumstances of the composition of On the Road *in her 1973 biography.*

[My wife Joan] would come home from her four-hour waitress job and she'd always want to know all about Neal and what we'd done. 'What did you and Neal really do?' she'd ask, and I'd write it for her and she'd come home and laugh at what I'd written. I'd sit behind a big screen and yell, 'Coffee!' and her hand would come around the corner holding a cup.

–*Kerouac, A Biography,* pp. 133–134

After writing the confessional letters to Cassady, Kerouac turned again to writing the book of his road adventures, which he had been calling "On the Road." Holmes describes Kerouac's sudden determination to produce the book and the manner in which he did it.

He wanted to break loose and he didn't want to have to pause for anything, so he wrote *On the Road* in one long paragraph about 120,000 words long. It was unparagraphed, using all the original names and everything.

He just flung it down. He could disassociate himself from his fingers, and he was simply following the movie in his head.

Jack was a lightning typist. Once, Jack said, "Let's write a letter to Alan Harrington." And I said, "What do you mean?" He said, "Well, you do the

Dec.28,50

Dear Neal,

The time has come for me to write a full confession of my life to you. So many things have to be discussed by me before I can even begin with what I know of the moment of my birth and its relation to the chief points of my confession, that of course I don't know where to start. In the first place there is the matter of motives: why a man should write the confession of his life to a buddy and yet have the temerity to try to claim that he does not harbor the tiniest wish to publish for money and profitable fame; a writing-man at that, a previously published writer. Then shall I say, Neal, I hereby renounce all fiction; and say further, dear Neal, this confession is for YOU, and through you to God, and through God back to my life, and wife, whatever and what-all. I urge you to consider my motives carefully; I hope I will become more interesting and less literary as I go along and proceed into the actual truth of my life. This: burn these things if you feel that the time has come for me to renounce the world; or keep them, to hand, personally, to Giroux the editor of Harcourt-Brace. I already assume that you'll not burn, but turn in, my work; but this is temerity. So many things!---I feel it will never get underway. A final statement in this poor preambling paragraph: that I wish to write the confession of my entire life to you, Neal Cassady, and send, by mail, in installments three thousand two hundred miles across the continent we knew so well, through wind,rain,hail,sleet and snow, at risk of loss, in hopes of <u>some</u> loss, in fear of total loss, in trembling of loss, for gain of your friendship and the respect of the Lord. It has been written in the Bible, "God is light and truth." Nor will I make further talk about truth; simply to say, in this confession I will travel again the experiences already written by me for the fiction-work (T&C) and tear them down systematically; have come to believe, like you, bullshit is bullshit. Everything's got to go this time. No one can take it but you. From the very start we were brothers. Now that I have read your great work---the letter dated Dec.23 dealing with Joan Anderson and Christmas of 1946 Denver---I feel that no one in the world, and in history, could have the strength and holy will to read in its total mass everything I have to say about my sins in the "bleakness of this mortal realm;" that, briefly, no one is as great as you, nor humbler.

Neal, harken to my plea as I grow more natural and make real confessions that are designed & aimed to your <u>knowing</u> that which I know, and understand the difficulty of the undertaking. In the first place there's the feeling that you and I both know the falseness of the first and above paragraph; the stiff, necessary, opening preamble, written with the mysterious outside reader, who is certainly not God, bending over my shoulder; even the neatness of the page, not a correction, not an X, not a blot; and the fact that I write this, as you know, almost and certainly more than almost in direct challenge to your colossal achievements of the past two months (the letters, your own confession in non-chronological fragments, something I do not hope to best, but equal); the fact that we are now contending technicians in what may well be a little American Renaissance of our own and perhaps a pioneer beginning for the Golden Age of American Writings. God, God, how I'm haunted by the feeling that I am false; I can never forget that eminent gent Lucien telling me I was a sly old French storekeeper with a bag of tricks, bottom ones rotten; meaning, I've my eye too much on the last dribble-dreg of subtlest advantage. Enough, though, preambles may last forever. Only this: and if only the THIS were simpler: the opening confession shall end the preamble: I am writing the confession of my entire life, limited only by the selectivity that eliminates the obvious we both know, simpler to say, those things we both know are of course unnecessary and if the "mysterious reader" (providing you do not burn the manuscripts) fails to understand the level of our

First page of a Kerouac letter to Neal Cassady in which he declares his intention to write "a full confession" of his life. Working nearly every night for the next two weeks, Kerouac produced long letters that served as the essential material of the autobiographical Duluoz Legend. The full text of this letter is published in Jack Kerouac: Selected Letters, 1940–1956 *(pp. 246–263).*

first page, dictate to me, and I'll take it down on the typewriter, and then I'll do the same with you." And literally–and I was talking much faster than I'm talking now–he took it down, just as I talked to him. I tried to do it–I'm a very fast but inexact typist–and I couldn't come anywhere close.

He wrote *On the Road* in the spring of '51 when he was living with [his second wife] Joan in Chelsea. They had split by that point and he was then living with Lucien, or he'd moved his desk into Lucien's apartment, and he was typing it up. Typing to Jack–in Jack's career–meant rewriting. That's how he rewrote.

I remember going down there. Allan Temko was there, Lucien's then-girl, Liz Lerman was her name, was there. Lucien was there, and we were all waiting to go out and do something, and Jack had to finish typing up this chapter. It was noon. So it must have been a week after that that he finished and took it to Giroux and Harcourt, Brace.

How much longer it was after that that they rejected it, I can't remember. But it wasn't too long. Two weeks maybe. He never told me the details. He just told me that Giroux had rejected it and said that this isn't what we wanted. We wanted another novel like *The Town and the City.*

Here he was, after all the difficulty of writing the book, all the false starts, he thought he had something. So he delivered it to Big Daddy, and then when Big Daddy said no, he was both angry–he was angry on the surface–but I think much more important, he was confused.

I read *On the Road.* I read the roll, and I read it–I can't remember exactly, but it was no more than a week after he had finished it. He had not even read it. He brought it to me and it was a roll like a big piece of salami. And he was so confused and exhausted when he was finished.

It was much longer than the book is now, about a third longer, and it went on and on and on. It took me a whole day to read it. I read it like a Chinese scroll. And it was one paragraph! Of 120,000 words, with the names unchanged. We all used to do that then.

I knew it was good. I knew it was something. His work always changed my days, whenever I read anything. His enormous capacity for sense impressions and his gift for catching them on the fly somehow, always changed my reality whenever I read his stuff.

– *Jack's Book,* pp. 156–158

Kerouac's close friend Lucien Carr lived near the Kerouacs in Morningside Heights. During the final stages of the composition of the On the Road *scroll, Kerouac stayed with Carr, who recalled that his friend wrote "absolutely constantly."*

I remember I was working days at the time [at the Associated Press]. I'd get up in the morning to the sound of him at the typewriter, come in at night and he would still be at it, and when I went to bed he would be going strong. I suppose he must have stopped some times to eat and sleep, but you couldn't prove it by me.

– *The Beat Generation,* p. 74

The original typescript of On the Road *on display at the New York Public Library in 1995 (photograph by James T. Jones)*

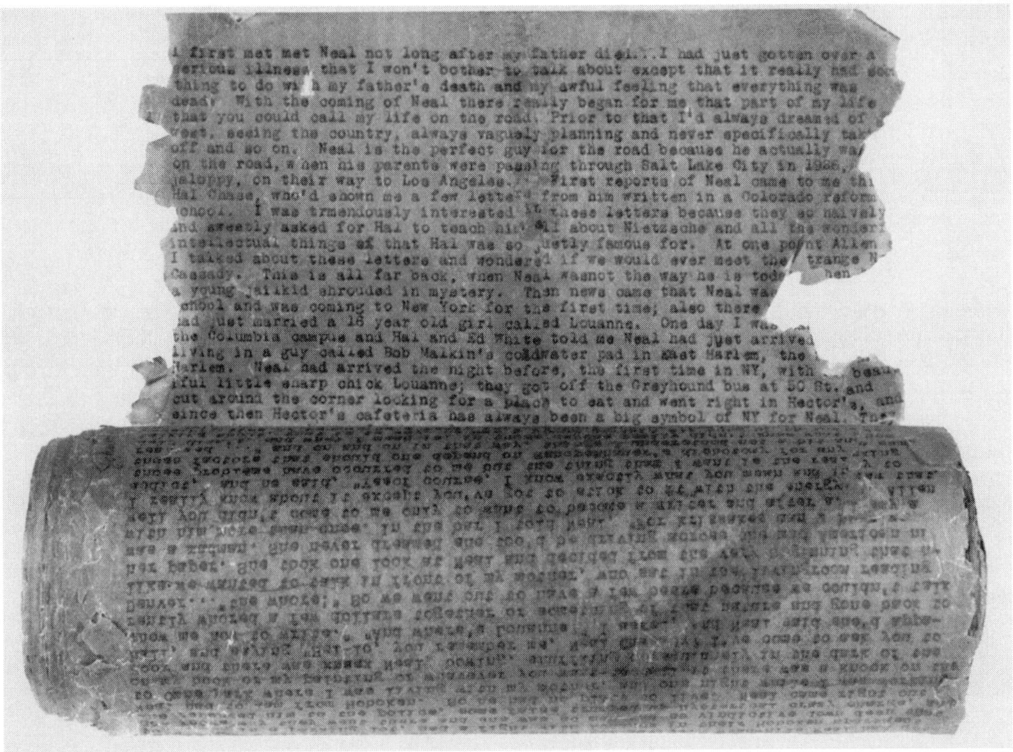

Close-up of the On the Road *scroll*

Rejecting *On the Road*

Every publisher who examined Kerouac's novel between 1951 and 1954 rejected it. The 27 December 1954 rejection memo of Joseph Fox, a senior editor at Knopf, presented some of the reasons On the Road *was turned down by publishers for six years. Alfred Knopf Jr. agreed with the editor: "I don't dig this one at all. Not my dish of tea, and after 75 pages I was too breathless to go on. JMF is absolutely right. Reject."*

I finished this over a week ago and have been procrastinating on it ever since. It is a novel I feel sure we should turn down; the vitality–gargantuan–the very special and somewhat appalling joie de vivre of almost all characters, the scope and breathlessness of it all, and the very real insight into a minute cross-section of the post-war generation does not hide the fact that this is a badly misdirected talent and that this huge, sprawling and, *au fonde,* inconclusive novel would probably have small sales and sardonic, indignant (with some justice) reviews from every side except that embattled one commanded by

Publishers that Rejected *On the Road*

Harcourt, Brace

Ace Books

Criterion

Bobbs, Merrill

Scribners

Viking

Ballantine

Little, Brown

Dutton

Knopf

Dodd, Mead

After Viking editors changed their minds and published On the Road *in 1957, it became a best-seller. Kerouac's second novel has never gone out of print and currently sells more than 100,000 copies per year.*

Vance Bourjaily, John Holmes, John Aldrich and Brossard.

To describe the plot of this is quite impossible. The narrator of the story, if it can be called a story, is one Sal Paradise, intermittent college student, traveller and novelist. The protagonist, a fantastic creation of the author's and something of a tour de force, is a perennial juvenile delinquent named Dean Moriarty; he has tremendous endurance, drive and restlessness, is insatiable in his curiosity, appetites and sexuality; he is incredibly selfish, ego-ridden, ridiculous, highly neurotic, despicable, sometimes insane, diseased in his compulsions; withal I found him a touching and curiously attractive character. There are dozens of other actors here; all make more or less meaningless entrances, exits and re-entrances. But what does this huge cast do, for all its frenetic activity? Almost nothing and almost everything. All of the action stems from the wild trips across the country undertaken by various members of this motley crew; there are literally 10 or 12 of these jaunts,[33] most of them in battered cars travelling at wild speeds, 3000-mile trips undertaken for no other reason that [sic] restlessness and the urge to move on has set in. Grotesque adventures occur to these bopster-pilgrims in every section of the country–New Orleans, Texas, Denver, San Francisco, Chicago, Virginia, New York, Los Angeles, Mexico. But it is all meaningless activity for its own meaningless sake. There is no goal to the pilgrimage and no end to it save the complete physical exhaustion of its members.

In his style and in his absorption with variability of country, custom and people, Kerouac bears more than a faint resemblance to Saul Bellow. Unfortunately, in the things that count for a novelist–what he is trying to say and technical organization of how he says it–he has gone way off base even from THE TOWN AND THE CITY, his first novel published by Harcourt in 1950 which sold almost 5000 copies. Ordinarily I might ask for a second reading on a book like this. But since Kerouac and Lord want a decision before the author leaves for Mexico at the end of the month, because I am perfectly sure that no other reader here will find this half as worthy of consideration as I have–I feel myself that I have taken far too much time, space and trouble over it–and because I gather that Kerouac personally is almost impossible to deal with–evidently he refuses to change this in any way, and it would have to be changed–I do not recommend that any further time be spent on this. REJECT

JMF 12/27/54

–Harry Ransom Humanities Research Center, University of Texas, Austin

---

Life with the Cassadys

In 1951, after Kerouac had completed the scroll version of On the Road, *Neal Cassady wrote to him from San Francisco, urging him to come west and live with him and his wife, Carolyn, in their home in Russian Hill. As Gerald Nicosia reports in* Memory Babe: A Critical Biography of Jack Kerouac *(1983), Cassady played up to Kerouac's conviction that they both would be famous writers one day: "If we're so all-fired good, then think of the funny times historians of the future will have in digging up period in last half of 1951 when K lived with C, much like Gauguin and Von Gogh, or Neitche [sic] and Wagner, or anybody and how, during this time of hard work and reorientation C learned while K perfected his art and how under the tutoring of the young master K, C ironed out much of his word difficulties and in the magnificent attic K did his best work. . . ." Kerouac would later remember that he did in fact do much of his best writing there in the Cassady attic.*

In A Bibliography of Works by Jack Kerouac *(1967), Ann Charters quotes the author on his time with the Cassadys.*

I wrote *Visions of Cody* from October, 1951, to May, 1952, beginning in Long Island and then in Cassady's attic in San Francisco. I had a bed there. That was the best place I ever wrote in. It rained every day, and I had wine, marijuana, and once in a while his wife would sneak in.

–p. 19

Cassady's Russell Street house in San Francisco (photograph by Matt Theado)

Carolyn Cassady in 1946 (Collection of Carolyn Cassady)

In Off the Road: My Years With Cassady, Kerouac, and Ginsberg *(1990) Carolyn Cassady describes Kerouac's arrival in San Francisco in January, 1952. Kerouac describes these times in* Visions of Cody *(1972).*

The first few weeks I didn't see much of Jack. He'd go with Neal, wander off on his own or stay in his room reading or writing. The attic worked well for him. He settled in and carefully arranged the few precious books and papers he needed to make him feel at home. As Neal had told him, I had found a huge piece of plywood and, with the aid of orange crates (which also served to hold books), constructed a great desk, the surface smoothed with several coats of dark green enamel. It could hardly fail to inspire a writer, I felt.

Only half the attic was 'finished,' but Jack preferred it that way. The rough, bare other half lent a barn effect and satisfied his craving for the natural and simple. The end he occupied was far from complete or decorated, but it was cozy and snug. A box spring and mattress made a low 'pad' and was covered with a paisley spread. The one window with its dark green shade was softened somewhat by burlap curtains. One square

Kerouac in 1952 (photograph by Carolyn Cassady)

striped rug covered the bare floor boards and added a touch of color and warmth. He was gratifyingly enthusiastic. The only uncomfortable aspect for Jack was that the sole access to and from his lair was through a door in Neal's and my bedroom . . . as was the only route to the bathroom. It surprised me to find him so shy, old-fashioned and modest about personal physical needs or habits, but he used the bathroom only when

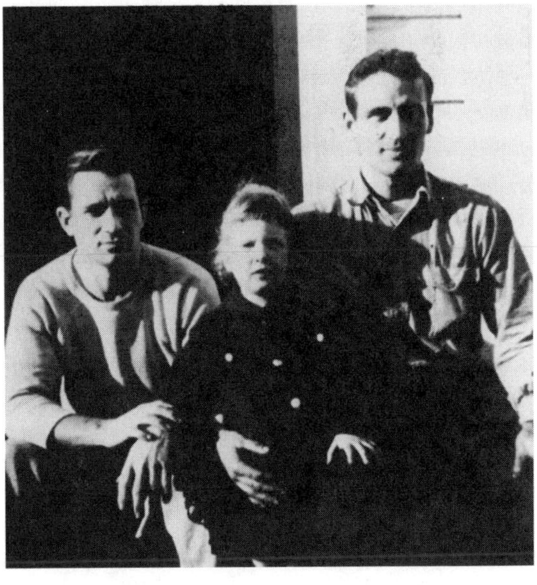

Kerouac with Neal Cassady and the Cassadys' first child, Cathleen Joanne Cassady, 1952

Seven notebooks labeled "SK" that include Kerouac's sketches. In October 1951 the author had begun his habit of in-the-street "sketching"–a kind of rapid, stream-of-consciousness writing done on the scene, as a painter might sketch a view. He used several dozen of these sketches in the opening section of Visions of Cody. *Throughout his life Kerouac wrote in pocket-sized notebooks, using them to compose novels such as* Maggie Cassidy, Desolation Angels, *and* Satori in Paris *(New York Public Library).*

no one was around and made arrangements elsewhere whenever possible. We all tried to cater to his embarrassment, though it was somewhat difficult with small children, and I had to be careful to be fully clothed at all times.

He had arrived at the worst time for hiring out as a brakeman, but after a few weeks Neal managed to get him a job in the baggage room at the depot. This eased things a bit, as Jack was forever fearful of imposing on us; this way he felt more independent. Neal's work was slower now, and they were able to spend more time together.

–*Off the Road,* p. 153

Kerouac called Neal Cassady late on the night of Neal's twenty-sixth birthday, 8 February 1952, with a story that he was in jail and needed help. Kerouac was drunk, and the call was a ruse to lure Neal out of his house. The two men returned hours later, with Kerouac escorting a prostitute to his attic room. Carolyn discovered the situation and a scene followed. Carolyn described the aftermath in her memoir.

When I returned home [from a doctor's appointment the next morning], I noticed a book on the dressing table that had not been there when I had left. I picked it up and saw it was *The Town and the City,* the copy Jack had sent when it was published. I opened the cover and beneath Jack's original inscription was a note: "With the deepest apologies I can offer for the fiasco, the foolish tragic Saturday of Neal's birthday–all because I got drunk–Please forgive me, Carolyn, it'll never happen again."

So that was why he'd stayed upstairs: suffering with guilt and remorse. I was deeply touched, uplifted and eager to show him all was forgiven. A thought flashed through my mind: "Not like Neal." Why could

I look forward with pleasure to righting a situation like this with Jack but not with Neal? Was it because I believed Jack when he said it wouldn't happen again?

. . . .

When I'd reread the message several times, I took the book downstairs to show Neal. After reading the note himself he bounded upstairs and in wild jocularity released Jack from his prison with promises of total absolution from my hands. They came giggling down to the kitchen, Jack and I smiling shyly. Neal became master of ceremonies, opened the beer and wine, and we eagerly gave up any thoughts of sorrow or condemnation in our efforts to restore a state of mutual comradeship, even racing out into the street to take photos of us all.

That evening after dinner there was no mention of going out. They got high, talked and laughed into the tape recorder and were careful to include me in their conversation and reminiscences. Wisely, I let sleeping dogs lie.

—*Off the Road,* p. 160

Cover for the paperback edition of Carolyn Cassady's memoirs. A feature film, Heartbeat, *starring Sissy Spacek, Nick Nolte, and John Hurt (as Carolyn, Neal, and Jack, respectively) was based on this book. Cassady produced a more thorough memoir,* Off the Road, *published in 1990.*

In a 1992 interview Carolyn Cassady discusses her memoir.

Off the Road and on the Record

Kelly Reynolds

Organica, Autumn 1992, pp. 12–13

Carolyn Cassady: Soon after Jack Kerouac died in October of 1969, Doubleday commissioned me to write my memories of my marriage to Neal which included our relationship with Kerouac and other writers we had known. I began writing in January of 1970 and finished in July of 1971. We were unable to obtain permission from Jack's widow to publish his letters, so the project was put aside. Years went by.

Then, in 1975, a small Berkeley press, Creative Arts, published a 92-page excerpt from it, under a title meant to indicate the love interest of the "Beat" individuals involved, *HEART BEAT*. But nobody ever seems to have gotten it—oh, well.

In 1976 I was approached by a young would-be producer claiming to be with a group that had made documentaries for Public Television that I regarded as exceptional and excellent. So I said "goody," only reading later, after I had signed the contract, that the group had disbanded before he had even approached me. This Michael Shamberg wanted to make a "major motion picture" from my entire manuscript. I believe he was sincere in the beginning in spite of the deception, and everyone hired for the film, actors and crew alike, were excellent choices. It was only when he found shut doors at the studios and hired a writer to be director of the film, who already had a foot in those doors, that the damage was done.

From there the exploitation mushroomed. All I could ask in recompense was to tag along and watch a film being made, a demand they reluctantly granted.

Organica: You kept working on the original manuscript, though?

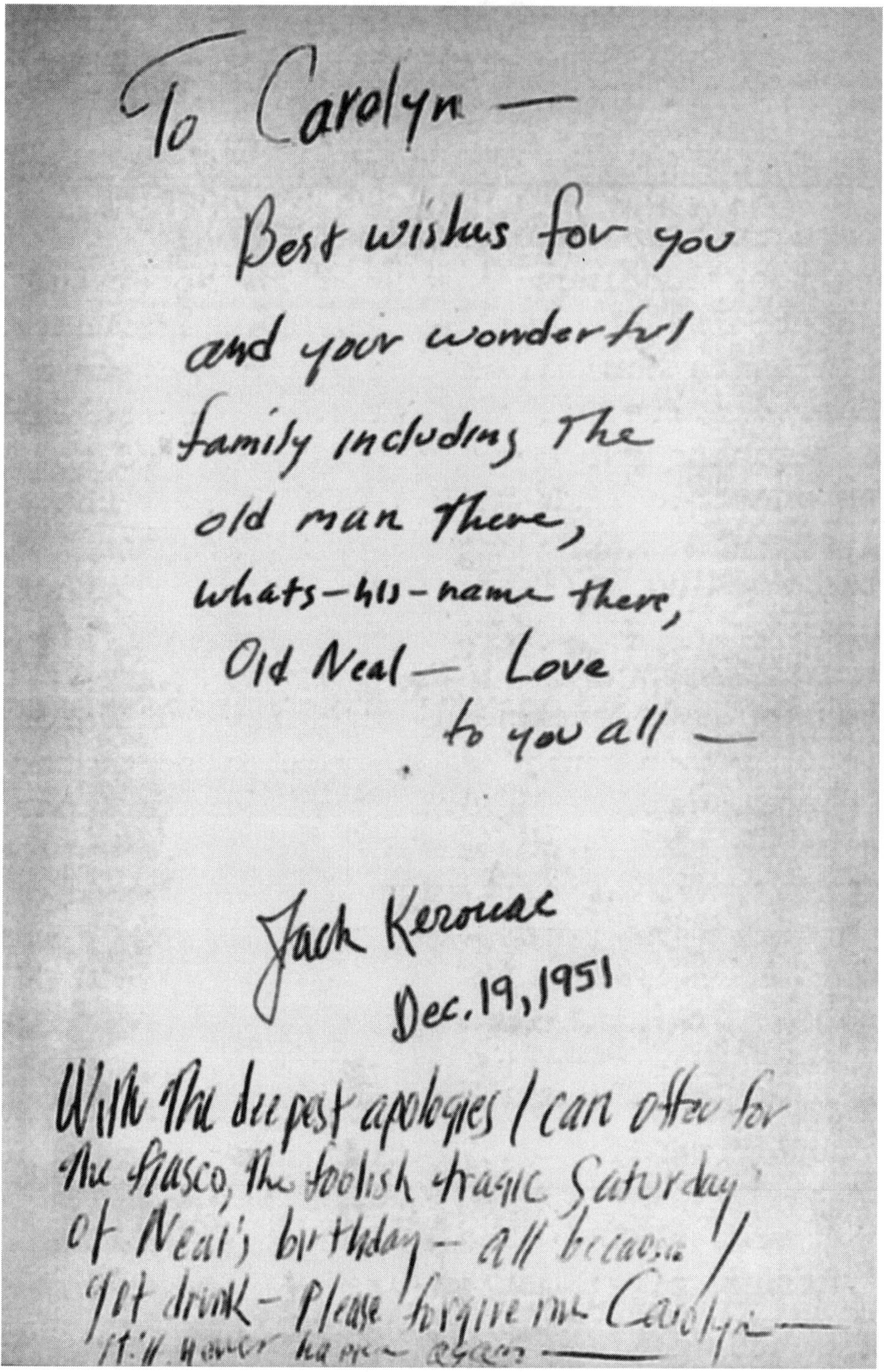

To Carolyn —

Best wishes for you
and your wonderful
family including the
old man there,
whats-his-name there,
Old Neal — Love
to you all —

Jack Kerouac
Dec. 19, 1951

With the deepest apologies I can offer for
the fiasco, the foolish tragic Saturday
of Neal's birthday — all because I
got drunk — Please forgive me Carolyn —
It'll never happen again —

Kerouac's inscription to Carolyn Cassady in The Town and the City *(Collection of Carolyn Cassady)*

C.C.: The 1,143 pages I had written were never edited at Doubleday. Over the years I tried editing them myself but found I couldn't be sufficiently objective. Several other editors were interested. But, by then, publishers only accepted polished manuscripts which did not require the line-by-line editing formerly available to unknown authors like myself. Finally, in 1990, a much-edited book was published in England by Black Springs Press as *Off the Road.* Then William Morrow published the American edition.

O: There's an almost aggressive feel to the title, *Off.* It suggests that we're going to be reading–I don't know–a kind of expose. What sort of feelings did you have when you were doing the writing? That you had an axe to grind?

C.C.: I did not feel defensive or aggressive, and certainly not, as you put it, "axe-to-grind." The media was describing men I did not know. I was merely hoping to reveal aspects of these men's characters I thought had been misunderstood and misrepresented.

O: When you bring up misrepresentation, I have to wonder about the problem of versions. Here's the way that Jack Kerouac described the importance of his versions to an interviewer in 1962: "Everything I've written is the pure, undiluted truth. Once God moves this hand, it doesn't turn back." For a lot of people who are going to read your book, I'm not kidding, this is Gospel.

C.C.: Kerouac had fictionalized his adventures with Neal "on the road," and I wrote about what was really happening behind the scenes or between the trips and their attitudes and involvements with home and family life, just as Jack had done with their single-male escapades.

O: Well, take for instance the scene where Neal moved into your hotel room in Denver and everything got started. It seems to me, by comparison, that Jack glamorized that very considerably, and in a very charming way, in *On the Road.* To the general public, what's the advantage of the real story?

C.C.: I disagree with you that Jack "glamorized" my relations with Neal in Denver in a "charming" way! But the fictional distortion is akin to the other distortions in *On the Road*–such as the way Dean and Camille met and behaved. Unfortunately, most readers do take all he wrote as fact, and those

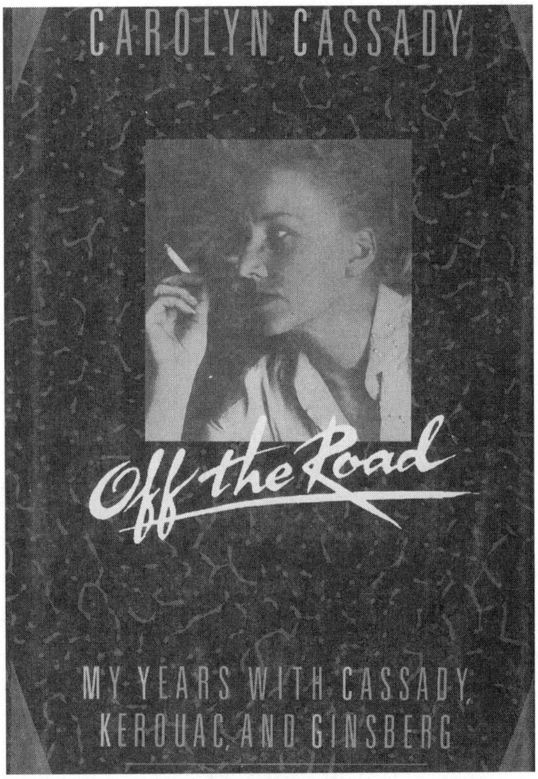

Dust jacket for Cassady's 1990 memoir

"facts" are now considered history. I had hoped that my telling of the real facts might dispel some of the myths and distortions. Then Jack Kerouac might be better understood as a man–since most critics also judged him to be as irresponsible as Sal Paradise.

So far my attempt has been just that, an attempt, because those who believe the myths prefer them to the truths. And the rest of us involved in the mythology have been similarly judged, and it is most distressing, I can tell you. For Jack the distress was severe enough to cause him to resolve to drink himself to death–which he did.

***O*:** From your experience it often sounds as if *Off the Road* could mean "Down to Earth." *On the Road* then would be on the order of escapism, the idea of living in the clouds, of doing every form of "up" except growing up. And certainly that book did as much as anything of its time to promote the idea, "Get high and stay high." Now this idea has become a steadily more awesome force to oppose and yet you've opposed it in two ways. First, in your personal life by trying to save Jack and Neal from the lifestyle and intoxicants that ultimately killed them. But simply by writing about that struggle, you're delivering the message to everybody: "Get off the road." How do you feel about your struggle to keep this message alive today?

C.C.: I have ceased "struggling" to keep my views alive, because I have already stated them sufficiently. Frankly, I think that those who are reading Jack for the glamour–for the myth–could use a little reality, in their reading, to begin with. Particularly in dramatic terms, they'd have a deeper understanding of his books.

But I can do no more than I already have and I do not wish to. After all, my involvement with the manuscript of *Off the Road* lasted about 20 years. I would much rather look forward rather than constantly backward. "It came to pass," that's all.

***O*:** Yes, but there's much more to *Off the Road* than just a kind of antidote to this whole hyping-up and ultimate commercialization of a lifestyle myth. It even seems to me that to concentrate on the boys–as I've certainly been guilty of right here–is part of the problem. The book is primarily about yourself, about your family, and you have many important things to say that are uniquely your own.

C.C.: If there is a main message in my book that I hope might be grasped, it's that effort and even suffering are necessary for the evolution of human nature. Growth–enlightenment–change–these amount to the purpose of life, not "happiness," which can be self-defeating and self-destructive.

***O*:** But a lot of young people are going to say–and I've had this put to me as a parent–"You've had your fun. Now it's our turn to do the same thing." How do you answer this? What should young people do with their lives?

C.C.: In the first place, I'd be very surprised that anybody who reads my book is going to accuse me of having "had my fun!" As to what young people should do with their lives, I support education. Education, education, and more education to develop the mind and all its powers and faculties for a selfless goal. There are no shortcuts and you can't expect good from evil causes.

O: What's unique about your perspective is that you have been the direct witness to a great waste of energy and talent. Nonetheless from the public perspective this waste is seen as a glorious thing. It's marketed as a glorious thing. Why is this?

C.C.: Beats me! (laughter) I think some day cycles of light/dark, day/night, life/death, construction/destruction, common to life on all levels, will fit the 50s and 60s into a recognizable universal scheme. Gregory Stephenson has already made a good start on helping us see this in his book *The Daybreak Boys.*

I'm sure there's some reason for it all, but the different journeys–my own and others'–tell me that we must hold a firm faith in a universal order and the powers within ourselves. I don't know any other "Beats" who have such a faith. Many, like Bill Burroughs, think that with enough willpower they can go to the depths of man's possible experiences and come back in one piece every time–that they can confront evil and transform it into good. I have no evidence that this can really be so, and certainly the glorification of the debasement and destruction of your mental and physical equipment in the process makes no sense to me. After all, what talent, what originality does debasement or destruction require? As Henry Miller once told me–"spontaneity" only has value when the underlying mind has something to offer.

So I repeat, anything worthwhile is achieved only when we take charge of our life, direct our will, and even "suffer"–although not for its own sake.

Carolyn Cassady

O: A while back, when I was introducing myself as someone who'd read both *On the Road* and *Off the Road,* you said something in this regard that's been hard to forget. "Human nature can–indeed, must–change." Is that what you mean, finally?

C.C.: That's what I mean. Human nature can–indeed, must–change.

O: How about your life since *Off the Road?* Any new directions?

C.C.: I've been wallowing in theatre, galleries, artists, writers, music, and the beautiful scenery Britain has to offer. And some good trips just recently to Russia and Germany. Right now, though, I would like to concentrate on relearning to paint. But there's been a lot of hoopla because the book's come out in paperback. Then I hope to get down to it–the new painting–and the stacks of books waiting to be read. Can't give up the theatre or friends, however. There is so little time!

Moving and Writing, 1952–1957

After leaving the Cassadys, Kerouac went to live for a time in Mexico City with William Burroughs, where he believed his impoverished condition would not hinder him so severely as it did in the United States. His desire was to live cheaply and to write.

In subsequent years Kerouac kept on the move, taking odd jobs, staying for periods in North Carolina, where his mother was living with his sister, Caroline; in Manhattan; and on the West Coast. Between 1952 and the publication in 1957 of On the Road, *Kerouac drafted "Doctor Sax," "Maggie Cassidy," "The Subterraneans," "Mexico City Blues," "Tristessa," "Visions of Gerard," and the first part of "Desolation Angels," though he often had little hope that his work would ever be published.*

In this 17 June 1952 letter, written from Mexico City to Holmes, Kerouac refers in this letter to his wife, Joan, whom he had left and would divorce, and their daughter, Jan, born earlier that year. At the time he was composing what was later published as Doctor Sax: Faust Part Three *(1959).*

I am starving to death. I have no more money, not a red cent. I weigh 158 lbs. instead of 170. Bill thinks I'm mad at him because I was writing when he got up and retired to the bathroom with my tea and pencil pads, so he's gone, has only money, nothing to eat in house, it's cold . . . I sit here yearning to get back to food and drink and regular people . . . I'll personally return this copy of Walden Blue to you this summer. . no money to mail it back, of course. I've had to resort to writing to Neal for money for traveling back to a job–I simply am destitute. I hate to bother poor Neal, especially since he's right, all I have to do is go to Frisco and earn and save $2000 on the railroad before Xmas – but I've got other things to do–other places to work.

. . . .

What have I got? I'm 30 years old, broke, my wife hates me and is trying to have me jailed, I have a daughter I'll never see, my old mother after all this time and work and worry and hopes is STILL working her ass off in a shoe shop; I have not a cent in my pocket for a decent whore. Goddamn sonofabitch sometimes I think the only thing that's ready to accept me is death, nothing in life seems to want me or even remembers me. John, you know how I feel about this lousy life. . lyric epic novels aside, and all things, and my talent if any exists, I still know that there's nothing but doom and despair on all sides waiting for everybody and especially for me who am so alone . . . I'm the loneliest writer in America and I'll tell you why . . . it's because I have written exactly three full-length novels since March 1951 or less almost less than a year ago and not one is wanted now . . .

. . . .

–probably the greatest living in America writer today–and the most despised bum, you realize don't you that Giroux not only feels that I am irresponsible and "uncooperative" but also that if I could write a great book still I wouldn't do it out of sheer irresponsible spite and no-goodness. This is what my contemporaries think of me. Paste it on yr hatbrim and study it–

–*The Beat Diary,* pp. 128–138

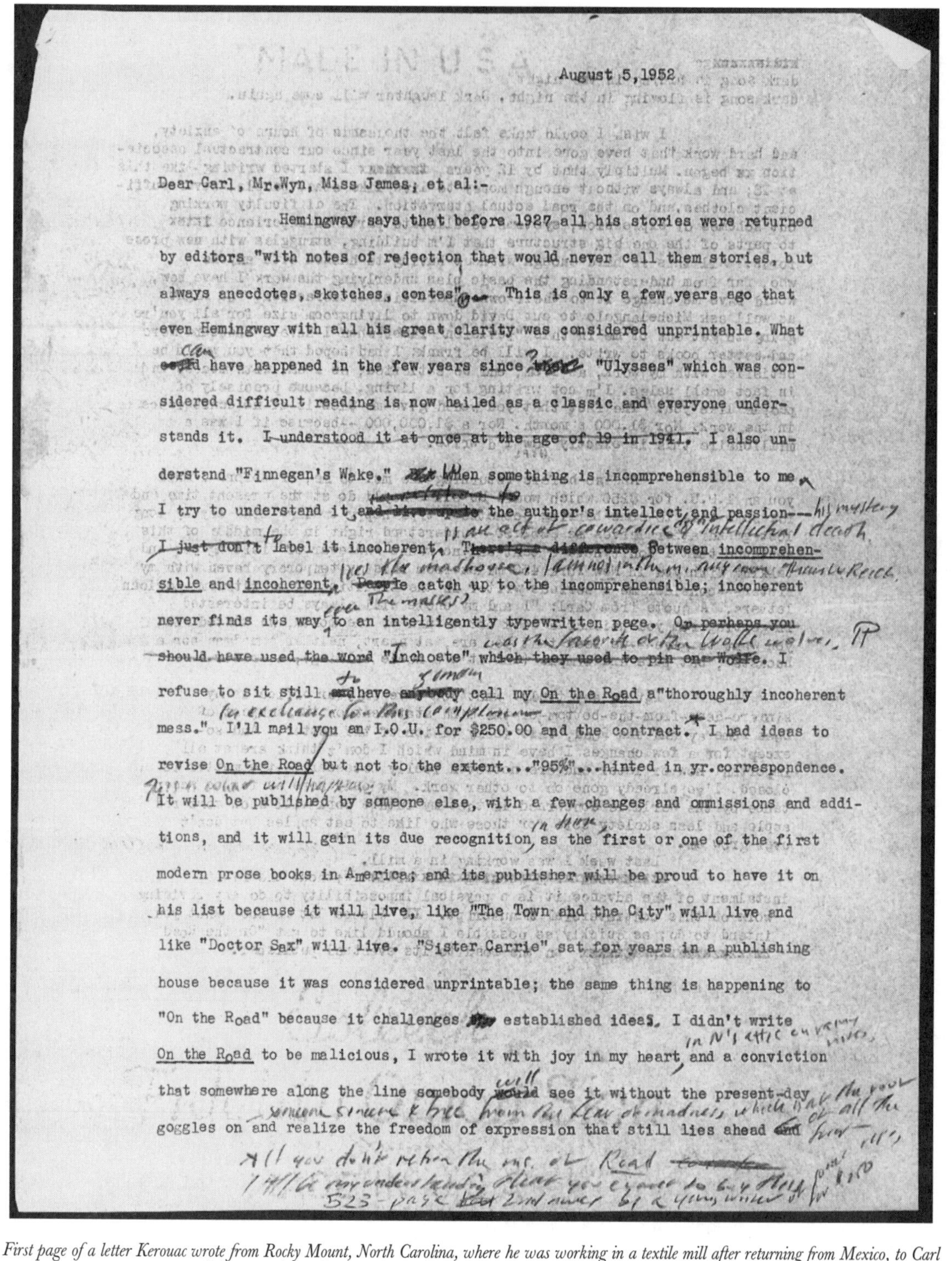

August 5, 1952

Dear Carl, Mr. Wyn, Miss James, et al:-

Hemingway says that before 1927 all his stories were returned by editors "with notes of rejection that would never call them stories, but always anecdotes, sketches, contes". This is only a few years ago that even Hemingway with all his great clarity was considered unprintable. What can have happened in the few years since "Ulysses" which was considered difficult reading is now hailed as a classic and everyone understands it. I understood it at once at the age of 19 in 1941. I also understand "Finnegan's Wake." When something is incomprehensible to me I try to understand it the author's intellect and passion--- I just don't label it incoherent. Between incomprehensible and incoherent, catch up to the incomprehensible; incoherent never finds its way to an intelligently typewritten page. Or perhaps you should have used the word "Inchoate" which they used to pin on Wolfe. I refuse to sit still and have anybody call my On the Road a "thoroughly incoherent mess." I'll mail you an I.O.U. for $250.00 and the contract. I had ideas to revise On the Road but not to the extent..."95%"...hinted in yr. correspondence. It will be published by someone else, with a few changes and ommissions and additions, and it will gain its due recognition as the first or one of the first modern prose books in America; and its publisher will be proud to have it on his list because it will live, like "The Town and the City" will live and like "Doctor Sax" will live. "Sister Carrie" sat for years in a publishing house because it was considered unprintable; the same thing is happening to "On the Road" because it challenges established ideas. I didn't write On the Road to be malicious, I wrote it with joy in my heart and a conviction that somewhere along the line somebody will see it without the present-day goggles on and realize the freedom of expression that still lies ahead

First page of a letter Kerouac wrote from Rocky Mount, North Carolina, where he was working in a textile mill after returning from Mexico, to Carl Solomon and the editors at Ace Books in New York City (New York Public Library)

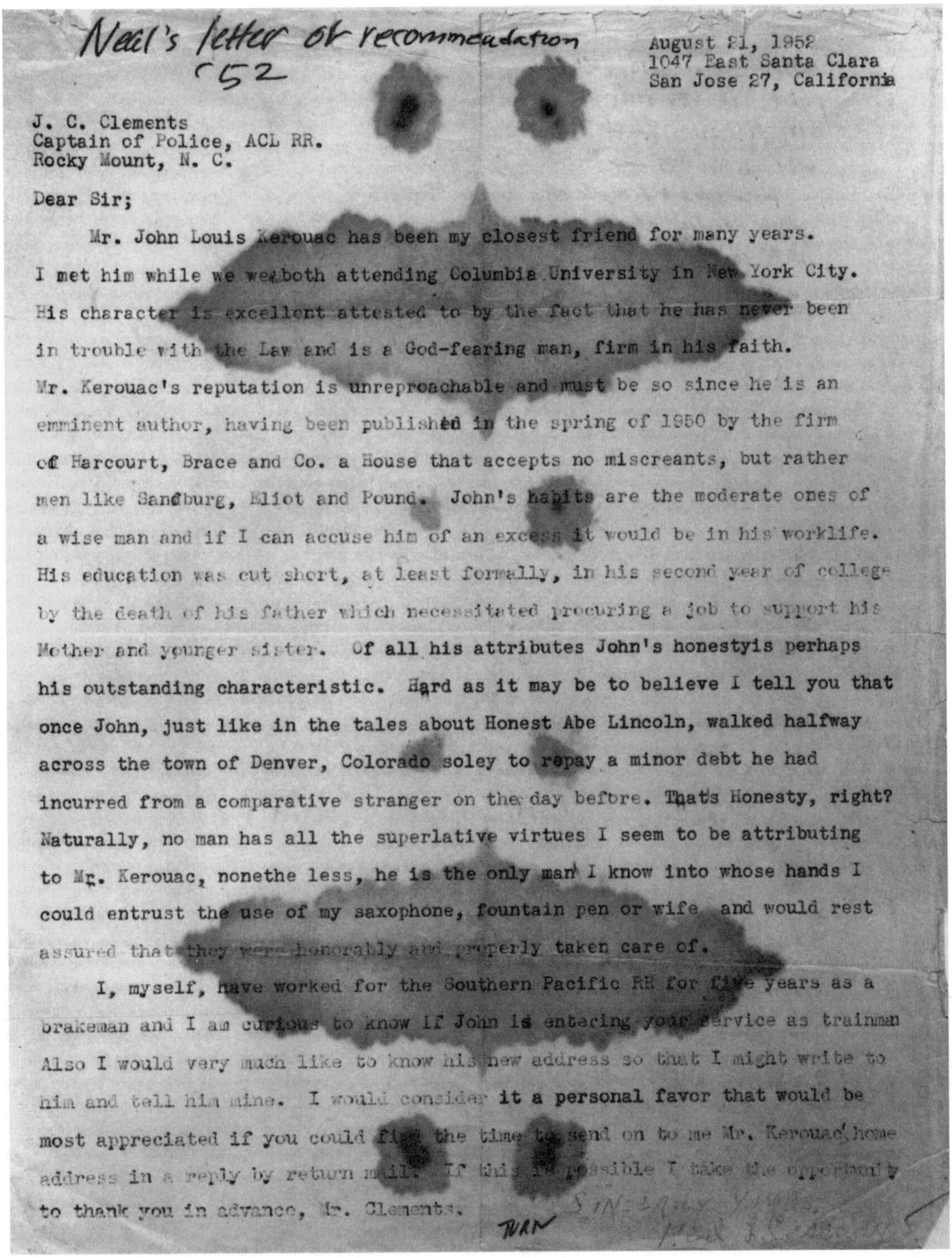

Neal's letter of recommendation '52

August 21, 1952
1047 East Santa Clara
San Jose 27, California

J. C. Clements
Captain of Police, ACL RR.
Rocky Mount, N. C.

Dear Sir;

Mr. John Louis Kerouac has been my closest friend for many years. I met him while we were both attending Columbia University in New York City. His character is excellent attested to by the fact that he has never been in trouble with the Law and is a God-fearing man, firm in his faith. Mr. Kerouac's reputation is unreproachable and must be so since he is an emminent author, having been published in the spring of 1950 by the firm of Harcourt, Brace and Co. a House that accepts no miscreants, but rather men like Sandburg, Eliot and Pound. John's habits are the moderate ones of a wise man and if I can accuse him of an excess it would be in his worklife. His education was cut short, at least formally, in his second year of college by the death of his father which necessitated procuring a job to support his Mother and younger sister. Of all his attributes John's honestyis perhaps his outstanding characteristic. Hard as it may be to believe I tell you that once John, just like in the tales about Honest Abe Lincoln, walked halfway across the town of Denver, Colorado soley to repay a minor debt he had incurred from a comparative stranger on the day before. Thats Honesty, right? Naturally, no man has all the superlative virtues I seem to be attributing to Mr. Kerouac, nonethe less, he is the only man I know into whose hands I could entrust the use of my saxophone, fountain pen or wife and would rest assured that they were honorably and properly taken care of.

I, myself, have worked for the Southern Pacific RR for five years as a brakeman and I am curious to know if John is entering your service as trainman Also I would very much like to know his new address so that I might write to him and tell him mine. I would consider it a personal favor that would be most appreciated if you could find the time to send on to me Mr. Kerouac's home address in a reply by return mail. If this is possible I take the opportunity to thank you in advance, Mr. Clements.

TURN

First page of Neal Cassady's letter of recommendation for Kerouac (Harry Ransom Humanities Research Center, University of Texas, Austin)

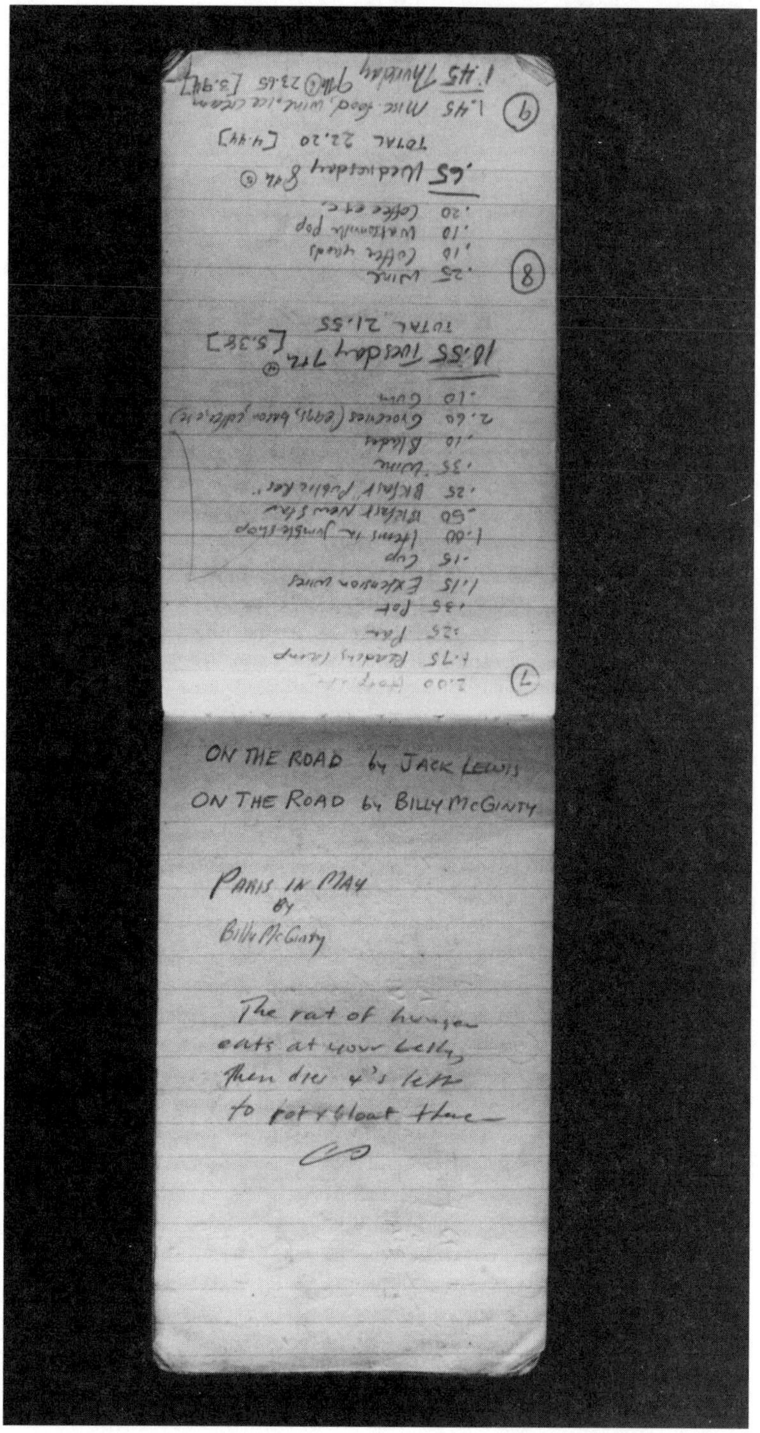

Pages from Kerouac's notebook from October 1952, when he was living in a San Francisco skid-row hotel, the Cameo, near Third and Howard Streets, and working as a brakeman on the Southern Pacific Railroad (New York Public Library)

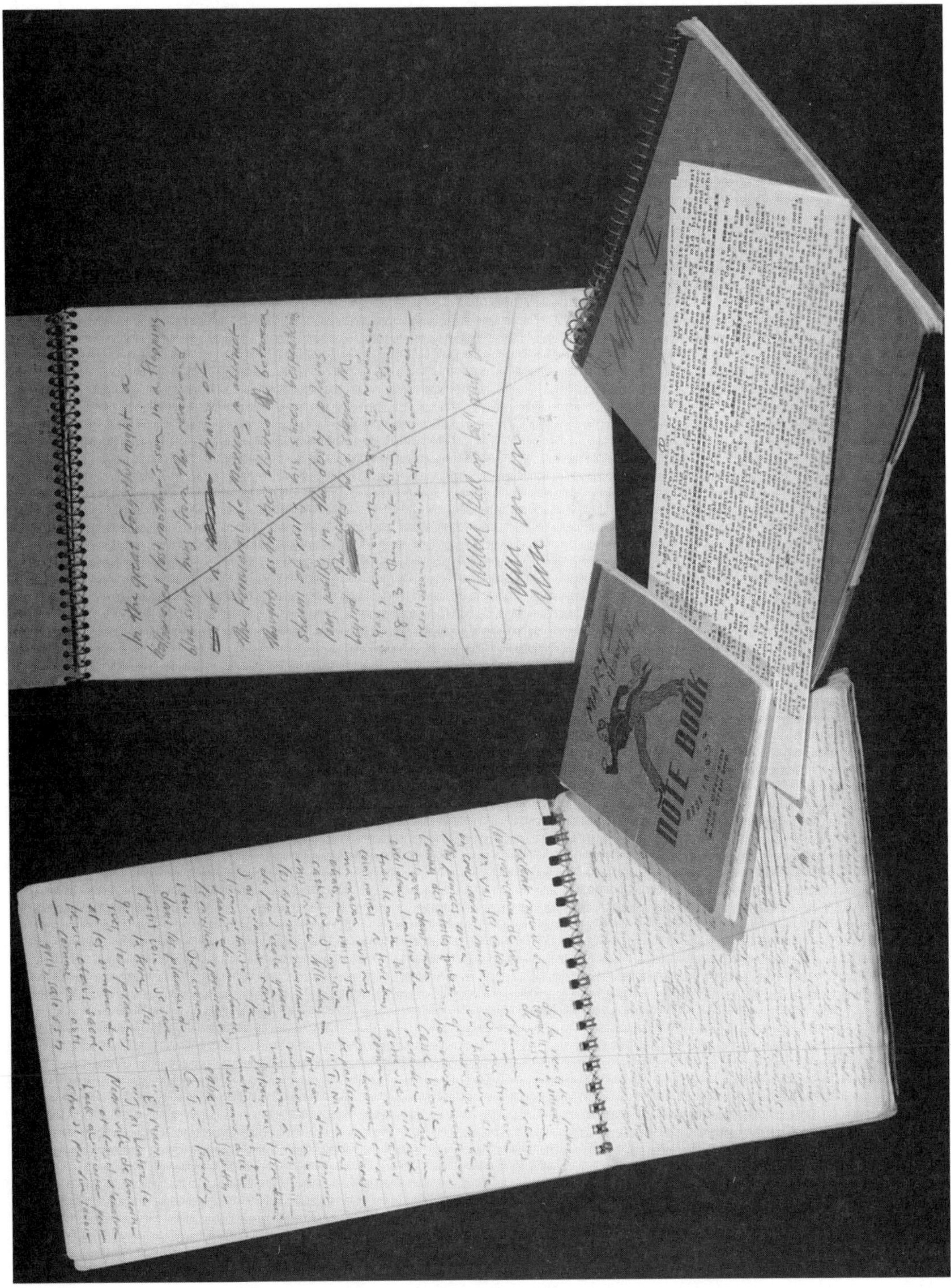

Notebooks in which Kerouac, living in New York in 1953, drafted Maggie Cassidy. *His working title was "Springtime Mary," thus the title "Mary." The open pages of the top notebook are written in French. In the small center notebook Kerouac also wrote "History of Bop" (New York Public Library).*

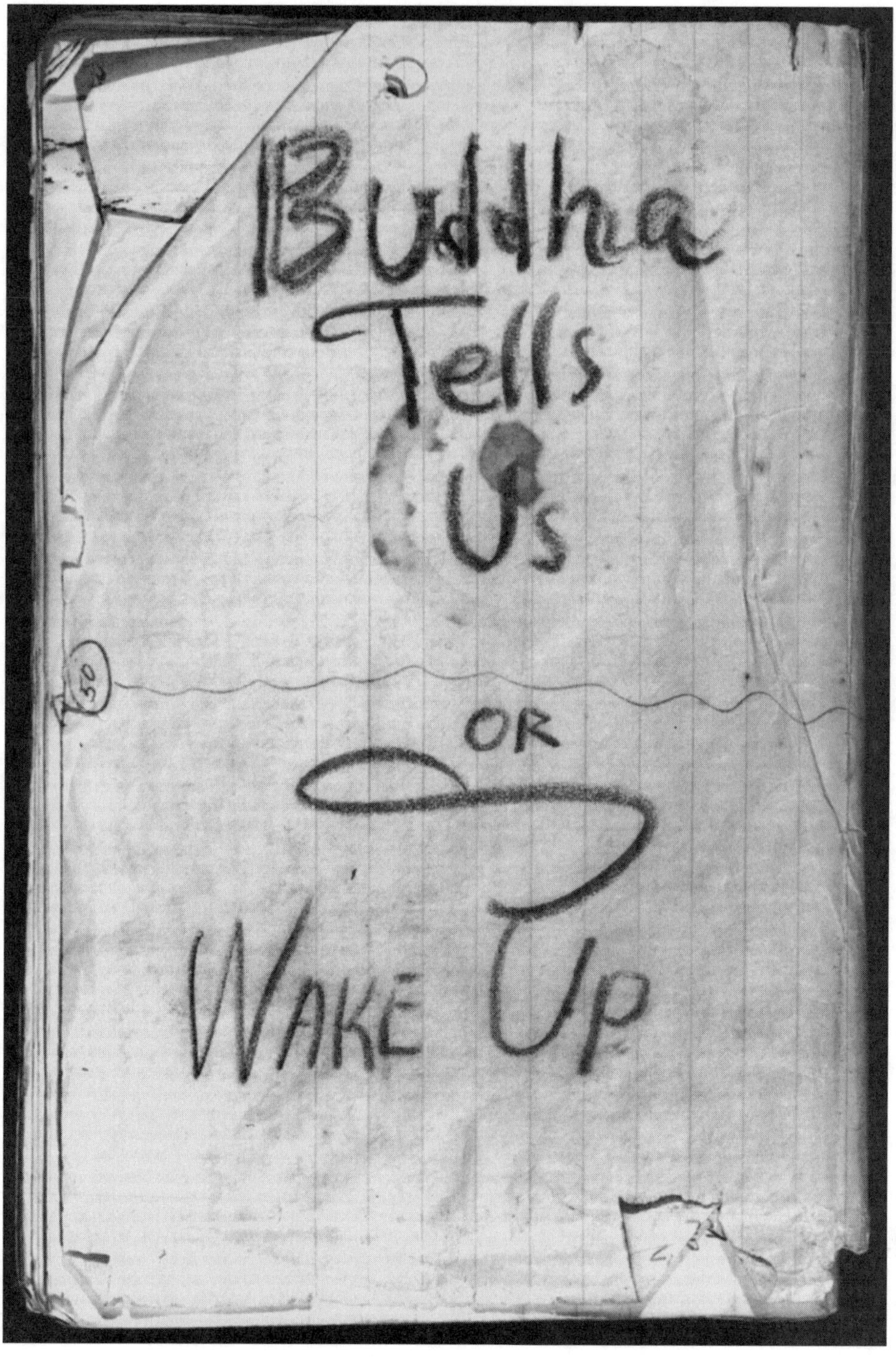

Kerouac's title page for his version of the life of Gotama Buddha. Kerouac began his serious study of Buddhism in New York and California in 1954 (New York Public Library).

Viking Deliberates

While Kerouac continued to write new material, the works he submitted to publishers were being reviewed. For a time in early 1953, Phyllis Jackson of MCA Management, was Kerouac's literary agent. In a letter dated 12 May 1953, she responds to Malcolm Cowley, a literary advisor at Viking Press and author of Exiles' Return *(1934; revised, 1951), who was interested in publishing some excerpts from the rejected* On the Road.

Dear Mr. Cowley:

You ask about Kerouac and if he broke with me as well as with Viking. I wish I could answer that. There was no overt break; he simply went away muttering that he didn't want to be published by anyone.

I have had one note from him. He did leave an address which is his mother's, and I will be glad to forward anything to him that you may want to send.

I am wondering about the short piece. I asked him about it and he said he didn't think he wanted that or anything else published. I will wait to hear from Mr. West; if he does want to use it, I will get in touch with Kerouac.

I had quite a long talk with John Clellon Holmes who has known Kerouac long and well, and he says that he agrees with me that there is nothing to do at this point but wait. Holmes is of the opinion that Kerouac will change his mind back just as suddenly as he made his first rash decision. We'll see.

–Malcolm Cowley Papers, Newberry Library

Viking Press interoffice memos show that the editors were quite interested in On the Road, *which for a time was being called "The Beat Generation." Despite the positive responses of editors, the book was not published for another four years. The reasons for the long delay are unclear. It is possible that Kerouac refused to let the book be published because he was unwilling to make suggested changes.*

Probably in summer 1955, Viking editor Evelyn Levine responded enthusiastically to Kerouac's novel.

(1) The novel must be and will be published eventually. (2) Jack Kerouac is a fresh, new (and fascinating) talent. (3) The manuscript still needs a lot of work. (4) The novel must be published even if it is a literary and financial failure.

THE BEAT GENERATION is not a new look at F. Scott Fitzgerald's 20's generation (with a 1950's theme), or any other decade's flaming youth brought up to date. I think it's essentially about young people trying to find their identity (and true, a subject of many past and current novels). What I think the author is trying to say–is that Dean Moriarty does not (and probably never will) find his identity and that his friend, Sal, does in the end. But he tries to prove this too hastily and unconvincingly for me–and it's a kind of sloppy ending–just to have Sal live happily ever after and settle down. He doesn't back up his last chapter–or establish proof (for Sal's settling down) in the beginning (and maybe that's where it should be done). (Also, the section where Sal finds "the old gentleman" with the answer he's [been searching] for. [The] author must explain further.)

All the male characters are for me–very well drawn and convincing–Dean and Sal, Ed Dunkel, Carlo Marx, Bull Lee . . . I dug 'em all (e.g. I understood them and liked the portraits Kerouac painted–good and bad). The girls in the story–are another thing–almost none of them are real . . . Marylou, Camille . . . perhaps Jane, Bull's wife, fares better than the rest and becomes a person . . . and maybe Terri–the Mexican girl Sal loves, is good–but even she is not convincing.

So here are these characters–in search of their identity–and the way they must do it–is by driving all over the U.S.–and the way they are really doing it is by "feeling" life down to its very roots. And they search from plain to city to city (Incidentally–there are [too] many trips–and I was finally going around circles with all of them–perhaps some of the material from these trips could be condensed in the main ones. I loved Kerouac's poetic style, and the sense of poetic rhythm in the prose; as they're driving thru the country you can really feel the U.S. passing by, feel the actual speed of the car; throughout there is a Whitman-esque style of expression for the U.S., a feeling that Kerouac communicated–the poetry of the U.S. He also tries to communicate to the reader the feeling of the various cities, Denver, San Francisco, Chicago, N.Y., the California country–with apologies to Steinbeck. The chapter about jazz–reprinted in New World Writing–in this the style of the prose adds to the descriptive passages about jazz because it sounded exactly like bop music. I don't know if this [is] great writing–but I loved it.

So here's another lost generation–but this one doesn't run away to Paris–they stay right here–and try to find themselves. There is a great deal of (what might be called) immorality in the book–use of narcotics, drinking, immoral sexual relationships. I don't think that author is exaggerating too much–in search for their identity, they're also trying to live to the fullest; protesting against the older generations and society's rules. In other periods, the young people exiled themselves in Paris, participated in revolutions, became radicals, etc. The Beat Generation searches thru the United States via fast cars.

The six notebooks that contain Kerouac's work on Mexico City Blues, *which he wrote in 1955 while living in that city. This was his first extended use of Buddhism in a work. The long poem consists of 242 individual units, called "choruses," limited in length by the size of the notebook page (New York Public Library).*

Kerouac, Ginsberg, Peter Orlovsky (standing), Gregory Corso, and Lafcadio Orlovsky (kneeling) in the Prado, Mexico City, 1956

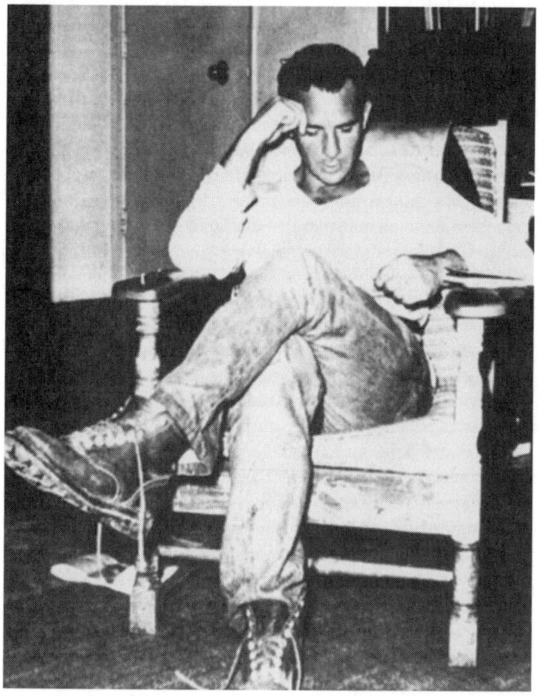

Kerouac at Neal and Carolyn Cassady's home, Los Gatos, California, 1954 (photograph by Carolyn Cassady)

Kerouac later evoked the photograph of him, Ginsberg, Corso, and Peter and Lafcadio Orlovsky in his fiction.

And that was the really great day when we all went to the Pyramids of Teotihuacan–First we had our picture taken by a photographer in the park downtown, the Prado–We all stand there proud, me and Irwin and Simon standing (today I'm amazed to see I had broad shoulders then), and Raphael and Laz kneeling in front of us, like a Team.

Ah sad. Like the old photographs all brown now of my mother's father and his gang posing erect in 1890 New Hampshire–Their mustaches, the light on their heads–or like the old photographs you find in abandoned Connecticut farmhouse attics showing an 1860 child in a crib, and he's already dead, and *you're* really already dead–The old light of 1860 Connecticut enough to make Tom Wolfe cry shining on the little baby's proud be-bustled brown lost mother–But our picture really resembles the old Civil War Buddy Photographs of Thomas Brady, the proud captured Confederates glaring at the Yankees but so sweet there's hardly any anger there, just the old Whitman sweetness that made Whitman cry and be a nurse–

–*Desolation Angels,* pp. 240–241

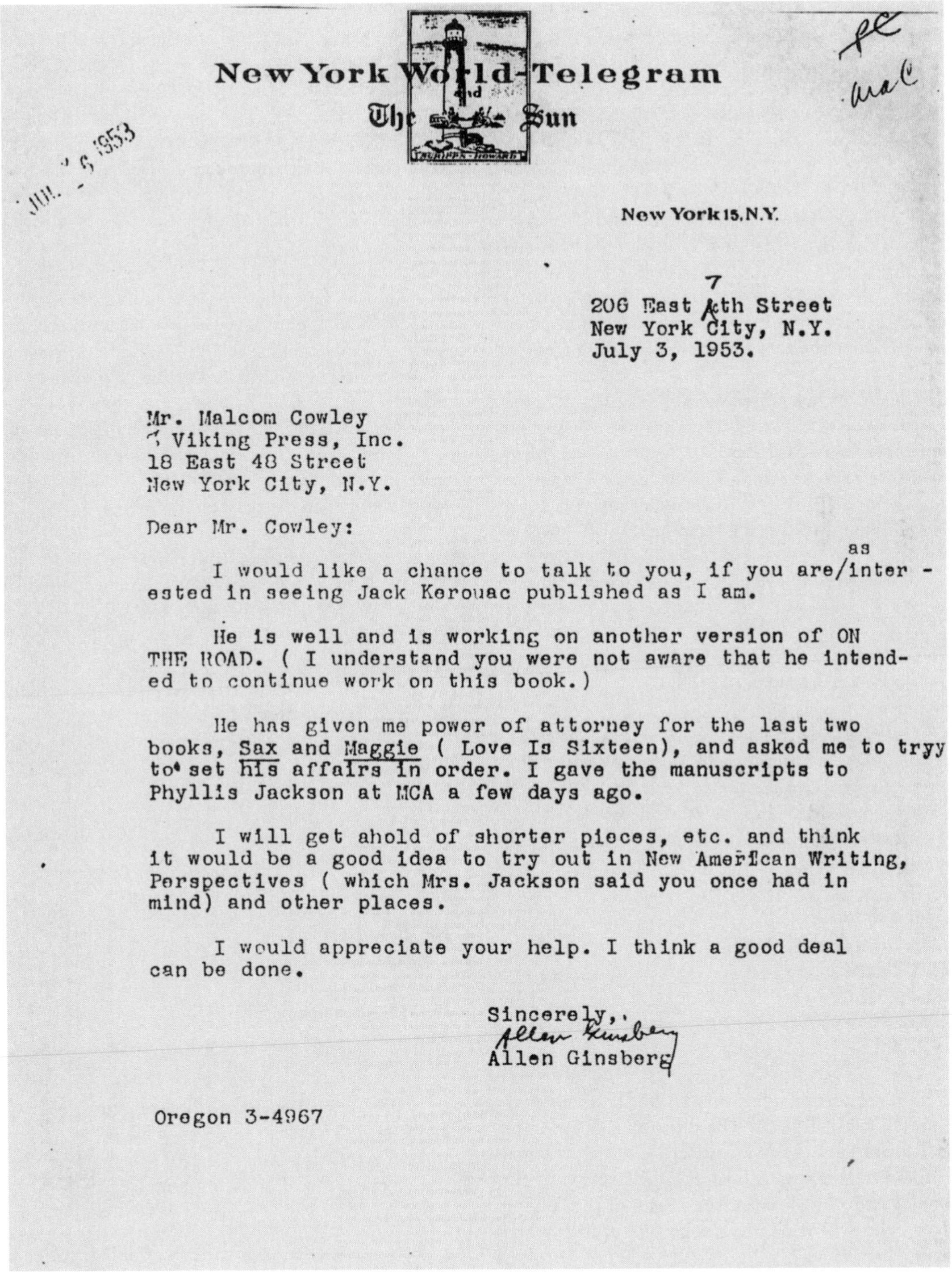

New York World-Telegram and The Sun

New York 15, N.Y.

JUL 6 1953

206 East 7th Street
New York City, N.Y.
July 3, 1953.

Mr. Malcom Cowley
The Viking Press, Inc.
18 East 48 Street
New York City, N.Y.

Dear Mr. Cowley:

I would like a chance to talk to you, if you are as interested in seeing Jack Kerouac published as I am.

He is well and is working on another version of ON THE ROAD. (I understand you were not aware that he intended to continue work on this book.)

He has given me power of attorney for the last two books, Sax and Maggie (Love Is Sixteen), and asked me to tryy to set his affairs in order. I gave the manuscripts to Phyllis Jackson at MCA a few days ago.

I will get ahold of shorter pieces, etc. and think it would be a good idea to try out in New American Writing, Perspectives (which Mrs. Jackson said you once had in mind) and other places.

I would appreciate your help. I think a good deal can be done.

Sincerely,.
Allen Ginsberg
Allen Ginsberg

Oregon 3-4967

Letter in which Ginsberg acts as Kerouac's intermediary. Kerouac had rejected earlier suggestions that he publish short works in journals such as New American Writing *or* Perspectives *(Malcolm Cowley Papers, Newberry Library).*

I like the episode in Mexico, also the episode with Terri in California, right now I can't remember some of the others I liked so much.

Kerouac is not trying for sensationalism–and I think it's a true picture of a some [sic] people, odd as they may seem.

Kerouac is a jived up Walt Whitman–and I loved his picture of America (if you omit the plot of the novel) and I think it's a novel of protest–but I'm not sure what he's protesting about–but that doesn't matter. It is not a picture of the younger generation as we know it–but neither are they juvenile delinquents.

This isn't really what I wanted to say–I'm at a loss trying to write this 3 weeks after reading the ms. but I remember Dean Moriarty, I remember Dean Moriarty. In some ways–I think Kerouac is a more honest writer than Saul Bellow (in Augie) maybe that's cause he's younger–I don't mean he's a better writer, though. . . .

–Malcolm Cowley Papers, Newberry Library

A Question of Libel

Cowley advised Kerouac on clearing up potentially libelous depictions in On the Road. *In his 12 October 1955 letter Cowley stressed that since the scenes and characters in the novel corresponded closely to those of real life, certain changes would have to be made in the book to assure its status as a work of fiction.*

Mr. John Kerouac
c/o Mr. Allen Ginsberg
1624 Milvia Street
Berkeley, California

Dear Jack:

We are still thinking very seriously about publishing ON THE ROAD. The difficulties are still the ones I mentioned in my last letter, and the principal difficulty is the danger of libel. For the last two weeks the manuscript has been in the hands of the Viking lawyer, who will mark the dangerous passages and submit a brief to us.

I'd better warn you again that this question of libel is serious. The great difficulty is that ON THE ROAD is primarily a record of experiences. Just changing the names of the characters and changing a few of their physical characteristics aren't enough to prevent a libel suit if the character can still be recognized by the details that we name–especially if he can claim in court that the narrative holds him up to shame or ridicule. The passage about Denver D. Doll is clearly libelous if the man wants to bring suit. The changes that you mentioned in your letter aren't nearly enough. You had better be thinking of some further changes that would keep him from bringing suit.

There are other characters like Moriarty who play such a big part in the story that it would be difficult to change them. In that case, the safest course might be to get the original of the character to sign a release, saying that he had read the passages that portrayed a character who might be taken to resemble himself, and was satisfied to have them published as they stood. Later on I'll get for you the exact wording of such a release.

You'll be hearing from me again as soon as the lawyer submits his brief. There are serious difficulties in the way of publishing ON THE ROAD, as you can see, but we we all work together I do hope we can get them ironed out and sign a contract. In any case the decision will take time. Good luck to you and let me know where you are.

–Malcolm Cowley Papers, Newberry Library

In his 8 November 1955 letter Cowley cites lawyer Nathaniel Whitehorn, of Hays, Sklar, Epstein, and Herzberg, a New York City firm.

Mr. John Kerouac
c/o Allen Ginsberg
1624 Milvia Street
Berkeley, California

Dear Jack:

The lawyer spent a long time going over your manuscript and that explains why I have been so slow in answering your last two letters. He is considerably exercised about the danger of libel suits. He says, in part:

> You must remember that in a book of this type every character starts out with two fixed points of reference and identification. Each one of them is a friend of the author or has had some contact with him in the manner reflected in the book, and each of them is also a friend or acquaintance of Dean. In addition, each of them is a friend of one or more of the other charac-

for MAC from HKT 10/22/53

ON THE ROAD by John Kerouac

I heartly agree with your feeling that this is a "classic of our times." I hope that we will get a book out of it that we will publish quietly and ~~xxxxxxx~~ conviction.

Since I won't see you to talk to Tuesday, I'll make this ~~a~~ conversation piece rather than an editorial report.

The book stirred me for two sets of reasons, operating concurrently. First, Kerouac's bold writing talent: it's lavish, reckless, but for all its rapid-jitters and seeming carelessness, it is almost always effective. Moreover, the effectiveness does not lessen, but builds an energy of its own that is all-pervasive by the end of the book. The writing is a torrential force that comes directly out of the material, instead of being applied to it. It is almost as if the ~~/~~ author did not seem to exist as an outside agency of creation.

Secondly, the book is a piece of raw sociology. I am not shocked by this portrayal of the hipster generation as a portrayl, but by the fact that the generation exists, and was constantly forced to think of the why of it. I don't say this in the voice of the YMCA, nor view the book as a piece of exposure. It is a life slice so raw and bleeding that it makes me terribly sad. It's the quintessence of everything that is bad and horrible about this otherwise wonderful age we live in. The trickles of evil run small and unnoticed throughout the pattern of life today, and here they come together in a flood, in a bunch of young people who are irretrievably gone in the literal sense of the word. There is no redemption for these psychopaths and hopeless neurotics, for they don't want any. They believe that the forebrain is subservient to and learns from the violences of sensation. You don't change such people, but you reflect on the small evils that have compounded this great human waste.

The figure of Dean is a gargantuan ~~/~~ but believably pitiful "hero" viewed in these tersms. The terms are unstated, of course, but are implicit extensions from the whole crazy mass of the book.

It's one of those books that "just is." Except for some large-~~xxxxx~~ chunk cutting (for it is too long) it needs only the lightly touching pencil, for refinement has no place in this prose. It might be a time-consuming job, but not a difficult one. I am not too much worried about the obscenity. I'm sure the whorehouse scene can get by practically in toto. Not that people won't think it's a dirty book. It's a question of publishing it quietly for the discerning few, with no touting, pre-viewing, or advance quotes from run-of-the-mill names. Not easy, but ~~/~~ very challenging.

Vetting report from Viking editor Helen K. Taylor, who later edited On the Road, *to Malcolm Cowley (Malcolm Cowley Papers, Newberry Library)* ters. As a result, it takes but a little more definite reference to identify any particular character. . . .

In my notes I have, I think, mentioned the Windsor Hotel, and this can serve as an example of the difficulty of disguising a person or place. I am sure the author had changed the name of the hotel. Nevertheless, it is easily identifiable by the fact that Lucius Beebe visits it once a year. Probably everybody in the area is well aware of Beebe's visit to a hotel. The fact that another name is used would not be sufficient disguise.

I will send you his complete report after I have had time to compare it with the manuscript. He is chiefly worried about the Denver section, because apparently several respectable or near respectable people are involved in that part of the story, and they are the sort most likely to bring suit. The lawyer also says that without signed releases from Dean Moriarty and Carol Marx–to give their names in the story–he thinks it would be impossible to make the book libel-proof. Accordingly I am sending you two of the release forms which he had typed out for us. Do you think you can get those two signatures?

Mrs. Cowley and I are going to be in Palo Alto beginning about January 2, and of course I plan to see you then if you are still in San Francisco.

–Malcolm Cowley Papers, Newberry Library

Frustrated by the seeming inability of publishers to come to a decision regarding his work, Kerouac on 23 January 1956 wrote to his agent Sterling Lord requesting the return of his manuscripts. In his letter he included a chart showing his understanding of the disposition of his work. Lord was able to dissuade the author from this course.

Dear Sterling,

I think the time has come for me to pull my manuscripts back and forget publishing. Clearly, publishing is now in a flux of commercialism that began during World War II; for instance I wonder if Thomas Wolfe's wild huge books would be published today if he was just coming up, like me. But they'll swing back to the ardor of the Thirties, maybe in 1960. Meanwhile I get nothing out of it but headache and the uneasy feeling that there's too much arbitrary free reading of my hard-worked manuscripts. So I want them back, all of them, including "Beat Generation," and will hold them myself and not release them except on option of at least $100, a better situation than now exists with these "realistic" publishers sentimentalizing for free over my pages and not even realizing their own minds, i.e., if the manuscripts were unpublishable they wouldnt read them through and make such passionate nays after they've had their kicks of finding out what happens. If Dutton wants to go on perusing Beat G. tell them I want $100 option now, or nothing.

–*Jack Kerouac: Selected Letters, 1940–1956,* p. 466

MS	COPIES	DATA
1. *Doctor Sax* (203p.) a Novel	2 copies	Rejected by A. A. Wyn, Viking and New Directions
2. *Mary Cassidy* (185p.) a Novel	2 copies	Rejected by A. A. Wyn, Viking and New Directions
3. *On the Road* (297p.) a Novel	2 copies	Rejected by Harcourt Brace, Farrar Straus & Viking–now at Ballantine, Little, Brown Vanguard
4. *The Town and the City* (499p.) a Novel	Rights	Not yet reprinted–Bantam Reprint undecided because of length–now at Pocketbooks, Inc.
5. *History of Bop* (11p.) An Article	1 copy	No information of record or whereabouts given
6. *"Well The Snake"* (8p.) A Short Story Roll-Faw-Log	1 copy	Whereabouts unknown
7. *The Subterraneans ~~Are Cool~~* A Novel (173p.)	1 copy	Unread (Malcolm Cowley reading it)
8. *Vision of Neal* (512p.) A Novel	1 copy	"Unpublishable"–rejected by A. A. Wyn, Viking
9. ~~Gray~~ Book of Dreams	1 copy	Unread, in my possession

Table that Kerouc included in his 23 January 1956 letter to Sterling Lord (Jack Kerouac: Selected Letters, *pp. 467–468)*

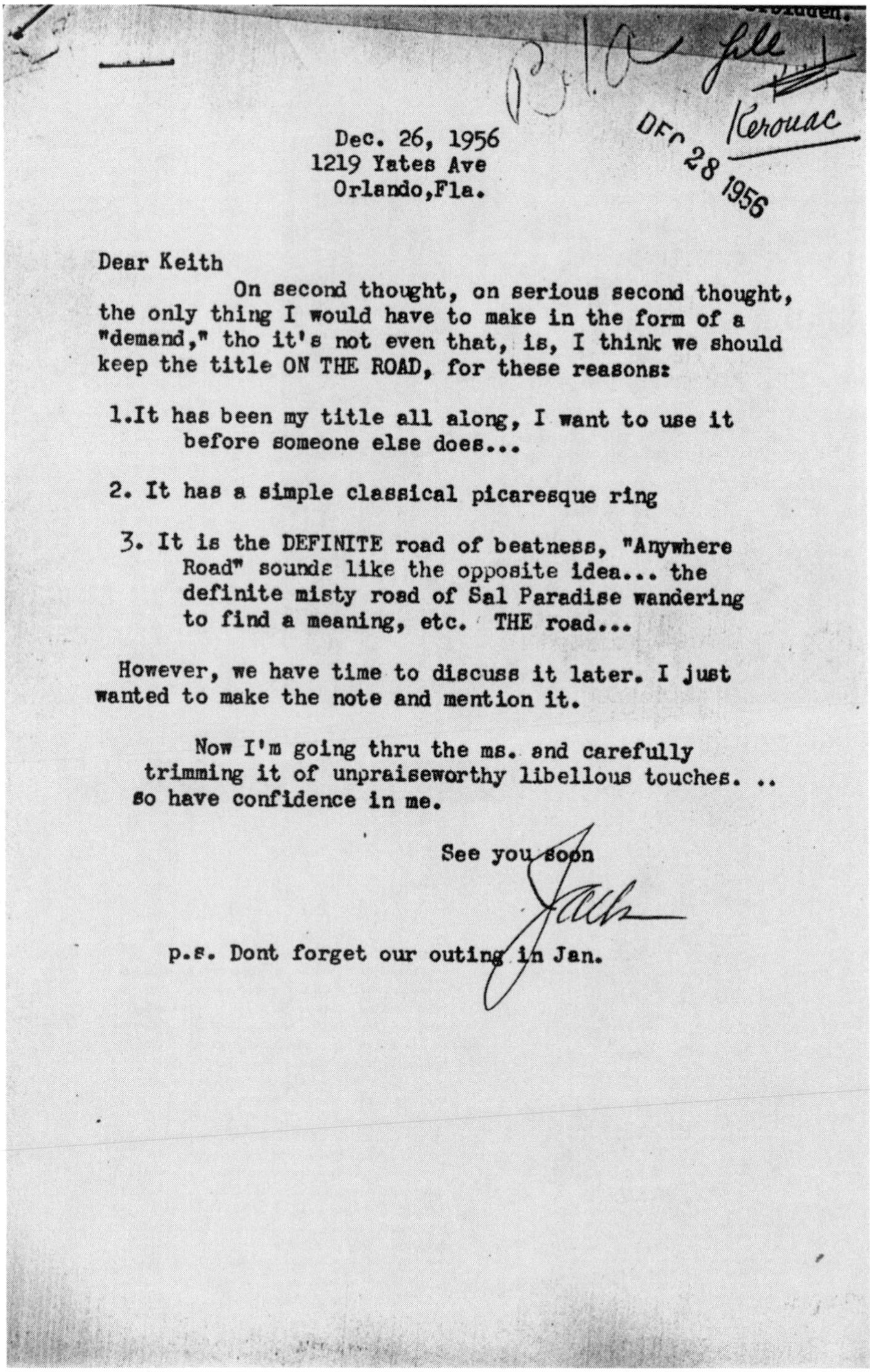

DEC 28 1956

Dec. 26, 1956
1219 Yates Ave
Orlando, Fla.

Dear Keith

On second thought, on serious second thought, the only thing I would have to make in the form of a "demand," tho it's not even that, is, I think we should keep the title ON THE ROAD, for these reasons:

1. It has been my title all along, I want to use it before someone else does...

2. It has a simple classical picaresque ring

3. It is the DEFINITE road of beatness, "Anywhere Road" sounds like the opposite idea... the definite misty road of Sal Paradise wandering to find a meaning, etc. THE road...

However, we have time to discuss it later. I just wanted to make the note and mention it.

Now I'm going thru the ms. and carefully trimming it of unpraiseworthy libellous touches. .. so have confidence in me.

See you soon

Jack

p.s. Dont forget our outing in Jan.

Kerouac's letter to Viking editor Keith Jennison, in which he states his preference for the title "On the Road." He wrote the letter from his sister's new home in Florida (Malcolm Cowley Papers, Newberry Library).

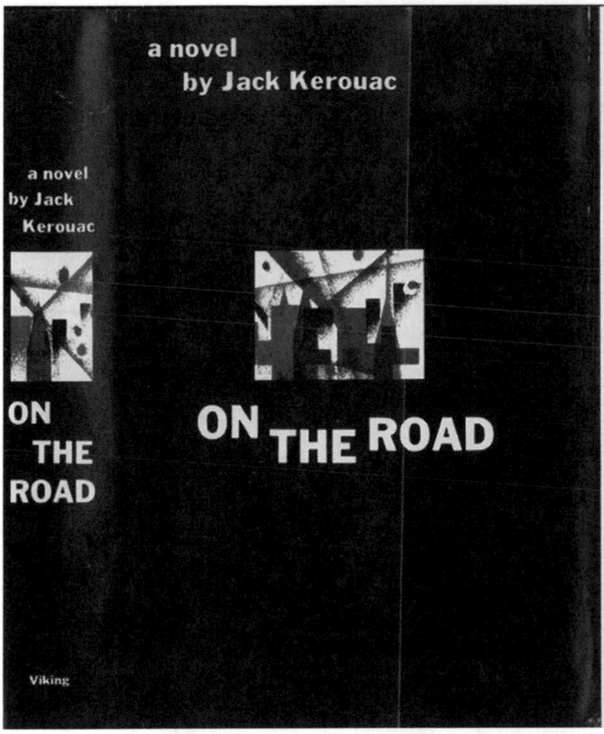

On the Road $3.95

After World War I a certain group of restless, searching Americans came to be called "The Lost Generation." This group found its truest voice in the writings of the young Hemingway. For a good many of the same reasons after World War II another group, roaming America in a wild, desperate search for identity and purpose, became known as "The Beat Generation." Jack Kerouac is the voice of this group and this is his novel.

On the Road is about Sal Paradise, Dean Moriarty, and their friends – one moment savagely irresponsible and the next touchingly responsive and gentle. The narrative of life among these wild bohemians carries us back and forth across the continent, down to New Orleans and Mexico. The characters buy cars and wreck them, steal cars and leave them standing in fields, undertake to drive cars from one city to another, sharing the gas; then for variety they go hitch-hiking or sometimes ride a bus. In cities they go on wild parties or sit in joints listening to hot trumpets. They seem a little like machines themselves – machines gone haywire – always wound to the last pitch, always nervously moving, drinking, making love, determined to say Yes to any new experience. The writing at its best is deeply felt, poetic, and extremely moving. Again at its best this book is a celebration of the American scene in the manner of a latter-day Wolfe or Sandburg. The story itself has a steady, fast, unflagging movement that carries the reader along with it.

Jack Kerouac's first novel, *The Town and the City*, was greeted with high praise by the critics. Three short sections from *On the Road* which appeared in *The Paris Review*, *New World Writing*, and *New Directions* attracted considerable attention; through these selections, and through numerous comments in magazines and newspapers, *On the Road* has achieved a certain pre-publication fame. The appearance of the complete work in book form is a publishing event of no small interest.

JACKET DESIGN BY BILL ENGLISH

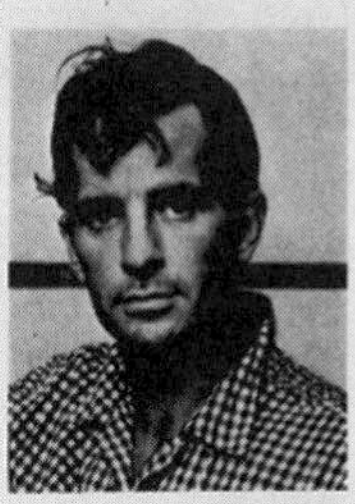

Photo by William Eichel,
Courtesy *Mademoiselle*

JACK KEROUAC

Of French-Canadian extraction, Jack Kerouac was born thirty-five years ago in Lowell, Massachusetts. His remarkable prowess as a high-school football player landed him at Horace Mann School in New York to prepare for an academic-sporting career at Columbia College. He made the varsity squad, all right, as a sophomore; then suddenly and astonishingly quit. Why? Lou Little told the newspapers, "Kerouac is tired." He was: tired and *beat*.

After his hitch in the Merchant Marine was over, Kerouac took up a peripatetic existence: exploring the U.S. and Mexico by foot, bus, and car; laboring at miscellaneous jobs; and writing. His first novel, *The Town and the City*, appeared in 1950, prompting critics to comparisons with Joyce, Dreiser, Wolfe, Hemingway, and Sandburg. Since then he has continued traveling, but has exchanged New York for the Far West as his home base.

THE VIKING PRESS
Publishers of The Viking Portable Library
625 Madison Avenue, New York 22, N. Y.

PRINTED IN U.S.A.

F·E·L

FROM

ON THE ROAD:

"They rushed down the street together, digging everything in the early way they had, which later became so much sadder and perceptive and blank. But then they danced down the streets like dingledodies, and I shambled after as I've been doing all my life after people who interest me, because the only people for me are the mad ones, the ones who are mad to live, mad to talk, mad to be saved, desirous of everything at the same time, the ones who never yawn or say a commonplace thing, but burn, burn, burn like fabulous yellow roman candles exploding like spiders across the stars and in the middle you see the blue centerlight pop and everybody goes 'Awww!' What did they call such young people in Goethe's Germany? Wanting dearly to learn how to write like Carlo, the first thing you know, Dean was attacking him with a great amorous soul such as only a con-man can have. 'Now, Carlo, let *me* speak – here's what *I'm* saying . . .' I didn't see them for about two weeks, during which time they cemented their relationship to fiendish allday-allnight-talk proportions.

"Then came spring, the great time of traveling, and everybody in the scattered gang was getting ready to take one trip or another. I was busily at work on my novel and when I came to the halfway mark, after a trip down South with my aunt to visit my brother Rocco, I got ready to travel West for the very first time."

Dust jacket for Kerouac's 1957 novel that defined the beat generation

In an internal 21 March 1957 memorandum to "MAB" from "HKT" (Helen K. Taylor), Viking editors discussed the potential for libel that still existed for the company.

Kerouac's ON THE ROAD – The Libel Reading

Whitehorn called this morning to say that the book was clean now, in his opinion, except that two of Dean's wives (we have a release from Dean himself) could not be considered entirely safe. Their characteristics and names changed, but by the marriage connection they could, if they wished, identify themselves. I know nothing of these girls and where they are now. Keith does not, and if Malcolm does (and he may) he's left no notes about it. He conducted a good deal of this libel stuff with Kerouac.

This doesn't worry me, though Tanny is right to point it out. If the women are respectable now (dubious), they would hardly sue. If they are not, they are hopheads or otherwise so unrespectable that they would not sue. It was stated at the outset of this project that we could never be entirely safe from a nuisance suit, and this is quite true. Therefore it becomes a company decision that we take this risk, which I honestly consider minor.

Tanny mentioned one other character, Stan Shepherd, who goes on the trip to Mexico. He too has been changed as to family relationships, name, etc. Except for visiting a whorehouse in Mexico and smoking a bit of tea there, he does nothing disgraceful nor is he made to look ridiculous.

At to Stan, and to all the people in the book, we've got to remember that, in all the editors' opinions who've been connected with it, they will consider it a privilege and an honor to be in this document, if they recognize themselves.

This may not apply to the two wives, but then again it may. I'm for going ahead.

–Malcolm Cowley Papers, Newberry Library

Reception of *On the Road*

On the Road *was published by Viking Press on 5 September 1957; it was hailed as a major novel the same day in* The New York Times.

Review of *On the Road*
Gilbert Millstein
The New York Times, 5 September 1957

On the Road is the second novel by Jack Kerouac, and its publication is a historic occasion in so far as the exposure of an authentic work of art is of any great moment in an age in which the attention is fragmented and the sensibilities are blunted by the superlatives of fashion (multiplied a millionfold by the speed and pound of communications).

This book requires exegesis and a detailing of background. It is possible that it will be condescended to by, or make uneasy, the neo-academicians and the "official" avant-garde critics, and that it will be dealt with superficially elsewhere as merely "absorbing" or "intriguing" or "picaresque" or any of a dozen convenient banalities, not excluding "off-beat." But the fact is that *On the Road* is the most beautifully executed, the clearest and the most important utterance yet made by the generation Kerouac himself named years ago as "beat," and whose principal avatar he is.

Just as, more than any other novel of the Twenties, *The Sun Also Rises* came to be regarded as the testament of the "Lost Generation," so it seems certain that *On the Road* will come to be known as that of the "Beat Generation." There is, otherwise, no similarity between the two; technically and philosophically, Hemingway and Kerouac are, at the very least, a depression and a world war apart.

THE "BEAT" BEAR STIGMATA

Much has been made of the phenomenon that a good deal of the writing, the poetry and the painting of this generation (to say nothing of its deep interest in modern jazz) has emerged in the so-called "San Francisco Renaissance," which, while true, is irrelevant. It cannot be localized. (Many of the San Francisco group, a highly mobile lot in any case, are no longer resident in that benign city, or only intermittently.) The "Beat Generation" and its artists display readily recognizable stigmata.

Outwardly, these may be summed up as the frenzied pursuit of every possible sensory impression, an extreme exacerbation of the nerves, a constant outraging of the body. (One gets "kicks"; one "digs" everything, whether it be drink, drugs, sexual promiscuity, driving at high speeds or absorbing Zen Buddhism.)

Inwardly, these excesses are made to serve a spiritual purpose, the purpose of an affirmation still unfocused, still to be defined, unsystematic. It is markedly distinct from the protest of the "Lost Generation" or the political protest of the "Depression Generation."

The "Beat Generation" was born disillusioned; it takes for granted the imminence of war, the barrenness of politics and the hostility of the rest of society. It is not even impressed by (although it never pretends to scorn) material well-being (as distinguished from

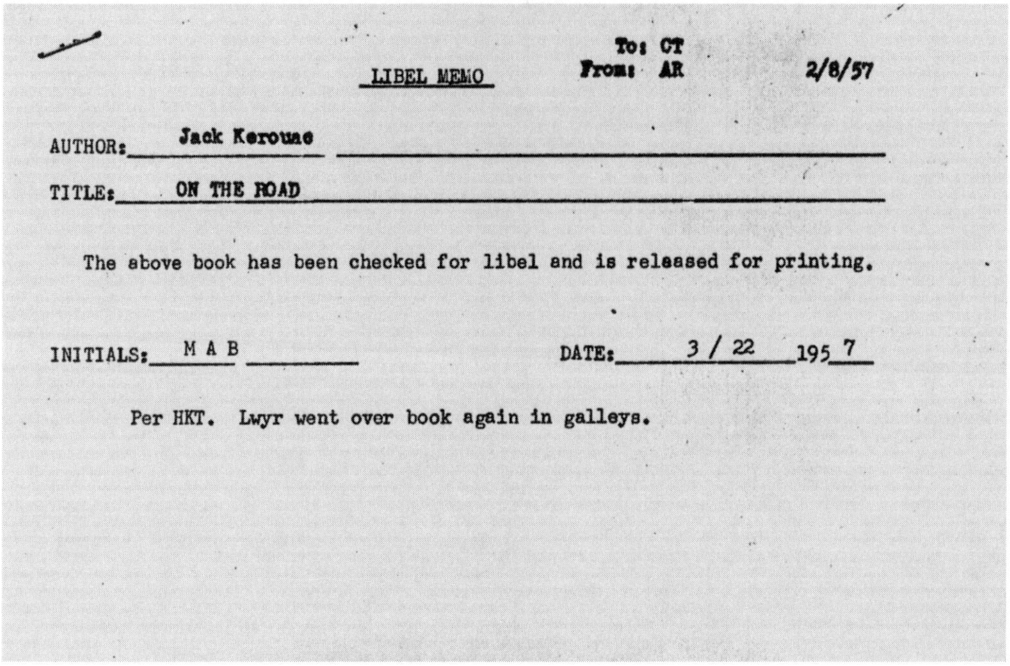

LIBEL MEMO — To: CT From: AR 2/8/57

AUTHOR: Jack Kerouac

TITLE: ON THE ROAD

The above book has been checked for libel and is released for printing.

INITIALS: M A B DATE: 3 / 22 1957

Per HKT. Lwyr went over book again in galleys.

Viking memo clearing On the Road *for publication (Malcolm Cowley Papers, Newberry Library)*

materialism). It does not know what refuge it is seeking, but it is seeking.

As John Aldridge has put it in his critical work, *After the Lost Generation,* there were four choices open to the post-war writer: novelistic journalism or journalistic novel-writing; what little subject-matter that had not been fully exploited already (homosexuality, racial conflict), pure technique (for lack of something to say), or the course I feel Kerouac has taken–assertion "of the need for belief even though it is upon a background in which belief is impossible and in which the symbols are lacking for a genuine affirmation in genuine terms."

Five years ago, in the Sunday magazine of this newspaper, a young novelist, Clellon Holmes, the author of a book called *Go*, and a friend of Kerouac's, attempted to define the generation Kerouac had labeled. In doing so, he carried Aldridge's premise further. He said, among many other pertinent things, that to his kind "the absence of personal and social values . . . is not a revelation shaking the ground beneath them, but a problem demanding a day-to-day solution. *How* to live seems to them much more crucial than *why.*" He added that the difference between the "Lost" and the "Beat" may lie in the latter's "will to believe even in the face of an inability to do so in conventional terms"; that they exhibited "on every side and in a bewildering number of facets a perfect craving to believe."

THOSE WHO BURN, BURN, BURN

That is the meaning of *On the Road.* What does its narrator, Sal Paradise, say? ". . . The only people for me are the mad ones, the ones who are mad to live, mad to talk, mad to be saved, desirous of everything at the same time, the ones who never yawn or say a commonplace thing, but burn, burn, burn like fabulous yellow roman candles. . . ."

And what does Dean Moriarty, Sal's American hero-saint say? "And of course no one can tell us that there is no God. We've passed through all forms. . . . Everything is fine, God exists, we know time. . . . God exists without qualms. As we roll along this way I am positive beyond doubt that everything will be taken care of for us–that even you, as you drive, fearful of the wheel . . . the thing will go along of itself and you won't go off the road and I can sleep."

The search of affirmation takes Sal on the road to Denver and San Francisco; Los Angeles and Texas and Mexico; sometimes with Dean, sometimes without; sometimes in the company of other beat individuals

DATE: 4-8-57

Please Push Along for Wednesday's Meeting

SPONSOR: MaC/KWJ

MANUSCRIPT ACCEPTANCE REPORT

AUTHOR: ~~John~~ Jack Kerouac

TITLE: ON THE ROAD

CLASSIFICATION: Fiction

AGENT: Sterling Lord

FINAL MS. DATE: Received

TRANSLATOR:

BASIC CONTRACT: 10% retail 10M, 12½% 12½M, 15% thereafter. Adv. $1000.

SUBSIDIARY RIGHTS: 10% film rights if sold within 90 days after publication. 2d serial.

TERRITORY: US, Canada, OBE.

LENGTH: about 100,000 words

INDEX?: None

ILLUSTRATIONS: None

OTHER SPECIAL FEATURES: None

FURTHER EDITORIAL WORK REQUIRED: None

SUMMARY AND DESCRIPTION:

This is a narrative of life among the wild bohemians of what Kerouac was the first to call "the beat generation." It carries us from New York to Denver, from Denver to San Francisco, then back to New York (with a detour through the Mexican settlements of the Central Valley)--then New York, New Orleans, San Francisco, Denver again, Chicago in seventeen hours in a borrowed Cadillac, Detroit, New York, Denver once more, and a Mexican town--the characters are always on wheels. They buy cars and wreck them, steal cars and leave them standing in fields, undertake to drive cars from one city to another, sharing the gas; then for variety they go hitch-hiking or sometimes ride a bus. In cities they go on wild parties or sit in joints listening to hot trumpets. They seem a little like machines themselves, machines gone haywire, always wound to the last pitch, always nervously moving, drinking, making love, with hardly any emotions except a determination to say Yes to any new experience. The writing at its best is deeply felt, poetic, and extremely moving. Again at its best this book is a celebration of the American scene in the manner of a latter-day Wolfe or Sandburg. The story itself has a steady, fast, unflagging movement that carries the reader along with it, always into new towns and madder adventures, and with only one tender interlude, that of the Mexican girl. It is real, honest, fascinating, everything for kicks, the voice of a new age.

It has an interesting history. It was written in 1950 (incidentally on a continuous roll of Japanese drawing paper) and was, with some regret, rejected at the time by Harcourt, Brace, who had published Kerouac's first naturalistic novel (The Town and the City) with moderate success. It first came into our hands

Viking report, 8 April 1957, prepared by Malcolm Cowley and Keith Jennison (Malcolm Cowley Papers, Newberry Library)

ON THE ROAD, by John Kerouac - 2 - April 8, 1957

about two years ago—or was it three?—and was rejected at the time, but with the proviso that we'd like to see it again. When we did see it again, we decided to work on it to remove the two great problems of libel and obscenity. But while we held on to it, prevented from working on it by other projects that might take less time, Kerouac began amassing quite a reputation. The episode of the Mexican girl was printed in Paris Review, a jazz passage was used to lead off one issue of New World Writing, and a Mexican cathouse episode was accepted by New Directions, so that more of a groundwork seemed to be laid for publication of the book. Moreover, Kerouac changed the story to avoid most of the libel danger (as well as getting signed releases from four characters), and Helen Taylor went over it taking out the rest of the libel, some of the obscenity, and tightening the story.

The book, I prophesy, will get mixed but interested reviews, it will have a good sale (perhaps a very good one), and I don't think there is any doubt that it will be reprinted as a paperback. Moreover it will stand for a long time as the honest record of another way of life.

Viking report (cont.)

whose ties vary, but whose search is very much the same (not infrequently ending in death or derangement; the search for belief is very likely the most violent known to man).

There are sections of *On the Road* in which the writing is of a beauty almost breathtaking. There is a description of a cross country automobile ride fully the equal, for example, of the train ride told by Thomas Wolfe in *Of Time and The River*. There are the details of a trip to Mexico (and an interlude in a Mexican bordello) that are, by turns, awesome, tender and funny. And, finally, there is some writing on jazz that has never been equaled in American fiction, either for insight, style or technical virtuosity. *On the Road* is a major novel.

It was actually OK to write like this! Who knew?

–Thomas Pynchon

Itching Feet
Carlos Baker
Saturday Review of Literature, 7 September 1957, pp. 19, 32

The seeing eye of Jack Kerouac's second novel "On the Road" is a young novelist named Salvatore Paradise who is filled with transcontinental dreams, will do anything for "kicks," has evidently read "The Adventures of Augie March" and "A Walk on the Wild Side," attends Columbia College, has a book partly done, and lives with his aunt in Paterson, N. J.

But Sal is restless. By page 37, he has reached Denver, 3200 miles from Paterson, and is staying with another writer named Roland Major, who lives in a "really swank apartment" belonging to someone else (all the artifacts in this book belong to someone else), and enjoys fine wines "just like Hemingway."

. . . .

Up in the Pecos Canyon country on the way home, they all take their clothes off and sit side by side in the front seat while Dean cries, "Yass, yass. . . . If I lived around here I'd go be an idjit in the sagebrush. . . . I'd look for pretty cowgirls–hee-hee-hee-hee! Damn! Bam!" For that is the way Dean talks, whether they are stumbling out of a bus in Detroit or getting high on marijuana in Old Mexico. It is said to be sad and blank when Dean's huge hunger for "life" begins to shows signs of appeasement.

But what is really sad and blank is Kerouac's American landscape. "On the Road" contains evidence that he can write when he chooses. But this dizzy travelogue gives him little chance but to gobble a few verbal goofballs and thumb a ride to the next town.

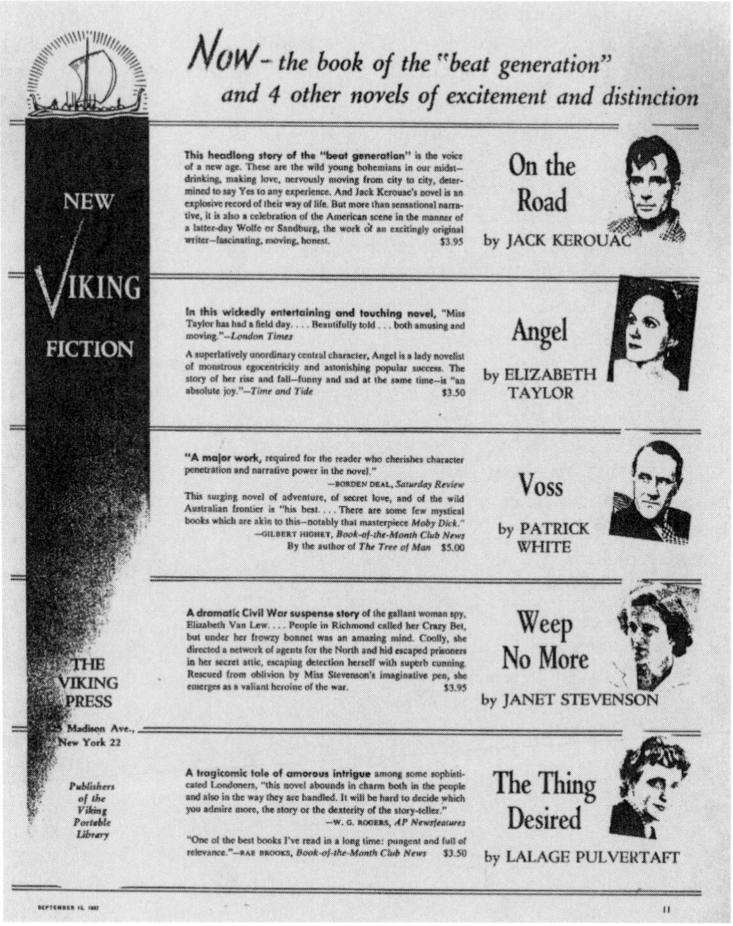

Advertisement that appeared in the 15 September 1957 issue of The New York Times Book Review

The Roughnecks
David Boroff
New York Post, 8 September 1957, p. 11

I recently talked with a girl friend of the late James Dean. She spoke reverently about his "soul," how all he wanted was for people to love each other. But I could only think of Dean in that projectile of a sports car, hurtling through the night at 90 miles per hour.

Now in Jack Kerouac's "On The Road" we have a testament of Dean's confreres, the beat generation–a curious amalgam of jazz and intellectualism, hoodlumism and tenderness, marijuana and the literary life.

* * *

The book jacket tells us that this is our era's equivalent of "The Sun Also Rises." However, "On The Road" makes Hemingway's characters seem about as mobile as your maiden aunt in her rocker. Kerouac's characters really go–with a dizzying velocity.

Moreover, unlike Hemingway's expatriates, Kerouac's characters are stubbornly provincial, wearing their T shirts like badges of allegiance and crooning Whitmanesque love songs to the sensuous body of America.

Hemingway's world is nihilistic, but there is also a sense of a redeeming discipline about his athletes and fighters. Kerouac's characters live at full throttle, incapable of control, leaping from peak to peak of intense experience.

They talk about writing, they plan like mad, but there is only the incessant motion. ("We were all delighted, we all realized we were leaving confusion and nonsense behind and performing our one and noble function of the time, move.")

* * *

Kerouac, who writes in a feverish, hot-rodding style, is no literary primitive. There is evidence of a ransacking of models. He often sounds like Sandburg, more often like Thomas Wolfe improbably using bop talk ("Now we must all get out and dig the river and the people and smell the world").

Kerouac is a talented writer but the world he creates with such uncompromising force gets in the way of our appreciation of his gifts. The sociology of his novel defeats it as literature. To be plain, "On the Road" is a frightening portrait. Overblown? Larger than life? Certainly! But the core of truth is there.

* * *

Part of the new generation is like this—bright, creative, but committed to a willful and narcissistic ethos. They are religious without a God; insurgent without a program; hell-bent on a self-transcendence which can find release only in speed and narcotics. Kerouac's crowd is the asocial fringe of the new generation which is conformist only because it couldn't care less about society.

In any event, Kerouac has given us a vivid evocation of a part of our time. Amid the bright glitter of togetherness and the new active leisure, this book should give us pause.

Review of *On the Road*

John K. Hutchens

New York Herald Tribune, 13 September 1957, p. 17

They called that other post-war generation "lost," when in fact it was nothing of the sort, but had a wonderful time thinking so. But the one Jack Kerouac is writing about in "On the Road," this latest post-war generation, is genuinely lost, and no Hemingway-Fitzgerald-Cafe Dome romance about it, see? It is also "beat," sad, crazy, and feverishly and forever on the move. But sad, especially. Very sad.

What Next?

Let's assume that every word of "On the Road" is true, in the sense that all honestly intended fiction is true—that it really is the portrait of a generation or a subdivision of it. Then "On the Road" becomes sadder still, and not simply because the people in it aren't members of an H. W. Longfellow fan club muttering about life being real and earnest. Nor is it because all they look ahead to is what they will do next for "kicks." The truly sad thing is that nothing they do means much to them for long. When Gertrude Stein told Ernest Hemingway *his* generation was lost, at least he could go to the bullfights and get some fun and a book out of it.

They—in "On the Road"—are the narrator, Sal Paradise, a young collegian and writer, and his friend Dean Moriarty, sometime reform-school kid, car thief and bop-music addict, and their sundry friends, male and female, hipsters, drunks and real-gone cats. What do they do? They pound across the country, coast to coast, at dazzling rates of speed, preferably in cars stolen or unpaid for, looking for something to believe in beyond the next bout with sex or benzedrine. They don't find it.

Meet a New Saint

Do they talk about anything very significant to the pathetic squares, perhaps you and certainly me, outside their frantic world? Hardly. Moriarty—in whom Sal finds the "tremendous energy of a new kind of American saint"—is given to rubbing his stomach and saying "Ah! Hmmm! Wow!" They talk bop-talk, which has a curious affinity with baby-talk ("you fine gone daddy you"), though sometimes they talk about God. Moriarty, the American saint whose halo would have to be made of reefer smoke, believes in Him.

"As we roll along this way," he tells Sal while they tear through the night, "I am positive beyond doubt that everything will be taken care of for us—that even you, as you drive, fearful of the wheel—the thing will go along of itself and you won't go off the road and I can sleep." To Sal this means that Moriarty is becoming a mystic. With his "bony mad face" and "slitted eyes," Sal reflects, his friend the saint "was BEAT—the root, the soul of Beatific."

Just possibly, at this point, Mr. Kerouac is announcing that a new religion is in the works, with its ecstasies induced by marijuana and "Mambo de Chattanooga" standing in for "Rock of Ages"? But you had better ask about that of the Kerouac cult now rapidly forming. From way over here, "On the Road" seems a neurotic newsreel with all its nerve-ends showing, populated by odd fauna vividly seen but dimly explained. For instance, just what is it that has made them as they are?

Anyhow, It Moves

What saves the newsreel from a mindless incoherence is that something does go on inside its narrator—and that Mr. Kerouac can write. When conversing with his fellow hipsters, Sal Paradise is as cretinous as the next one. When he is thinking of America, he is something else again. He dreams of it in the authentic, rolling rhythms of a Whitman or a Thomas Wolfe drunk with eagerness for life.

And his creator, Mr. Kerouac, not only knows his America, the loneliness of far corners, the excitement of cities, but conveys it in a nervous, driving style exactly suited to a documentary of frenzy. Which, when all is said and done, is what "On the Road" turns out to be. You may do a lot of groaning, and laugh in the wrong places, but you are apt to stay with it, probably for the reason that people seldom jump out of roller coasters. One trip, I must say, was enough for me, but I'm not sorry that I took it.

Review of *On the Road*
Arthur Oesterreicher
The Village Voice, 18 September 1957, p. 5

As you have no doubt already gathered by now, the public emergence of Jack Kerouac from the hipsters' underground into American literature is upon us, and is going to be THE big thing for quite a while. (Another of his books is being published by Grove Press later this season). The author of "On the Road" was on "Nightbeat" last week (looking and sounding remarkably like the late James Dean, incidentally), people are already leafing curiously through it in bookstores, toting it around the Village, hugging it under their arm as they ride the subway to work. I understand that, despite the complete and incompressible lack of publisher's advertising so far, the first printing sold out a week after publication.

A Voice

Some of us knew Kerouac's work before this–pieces of "On the Road" had appeared in New World Writing, New Directions, and the Paris Review, and another novel, "The Town and the City," was published in 1950. "On the Road" itself was written almost a decade ago; Malcolm Cowley was touting it as far back as 1951 or so, in his book "The Literary Situation." But now at last the news is out for good: Kerouac is not just a writer, not just a talent, but a *voice*, as Hemingway, Henry Miller, the early Gide were and are to those who are disposed to listen. Kerouac has taken the way he and his friends lived and felt about life in the years 1947–1950 and written a lusty, noisily lyrical, exuberantly overwritten book about it all. But more important than that, he offers a belief, a rallying point for the elusive spirit of the rebellion of these times, that silent scornful sit-down strike of the disaffiliated which has been the nearest thing to a real movement among the young since the end of World War II. "On the Road" is as crucial to the social history of the past 10 years in America as "The Lonely Crowd."

Inevitably "On the Road" suffers from the unevenness which is almost dictated by the scattered, episodic nature of the material. As an artist, Kerouac is all too frequently overcome by the sound of his own voice: there is a lot of mumbling mystical junk about "the wild American night" and the like. But the unforgettable scenes that stud the book (a tour of the San Francisco jazz joints stands out most vividly for this reader) more than make up for the hoarseness of Kerouac's cry. Sore throats are, after all, an occupational disease with rebels.

But what a lot of good things Kerouac has packed into this book! There are pages of hilarity, of despair, of tremendous excitement about merely being alive, of horror at being alive in today's America. It's an easy book to be cynical about because it is so thoroughly alive; academically literary fault-finders will have a holiday with it. (*Cf.* Carlos Baker's review in the Saturday Review.)

But man, like Kerouac's *got* it, really got it. And I'm happy that he has and that this book is finally here.

> Mr. Kerouac writes as if he had invented American slang.
>
> –*The New Yorker,* 5 October 1957, p. 198

Kerouac's "Beat Generation"
Ralph Gleason
The Saturday Review, 11 January 1958, p. 75

> "As he was the illegitimate son of the Lost Generation, the Hipster was really *nowhere*. And, just as amputees often seem to localize their strongest sensations in the *missing* limb, so the Hipster longed, from the very beginning, to be *somewhere*. He was like a beetle on its back; his life was a struggle to get *straight*. But the law of human gravity kept him overthrown, because he was always of the minority–opposed in race or feeling to those who owned the machinery of recognition."–Anatole Broyard, "Portrait of the Hipster" (*Partisan Review,* June 1948).

The central character in Jack Kerouac's "On the Road" (*SR* Sept. 7) is no hipster, even if the literary critics may call him one. That is, he is no hipster in the jazz musician sense. But he is a hipster in the Broyardian sense of trying to get somewhere. His motivation is the same and it carries with it the identification with jazz. The entire book is, on more than one level, the account of postwar youth trying madly to get somewhere, somehow.

And despite the fact that there is actually very little about jazz in this book—and where there is, it is usually a reflection of the European critical view of entrenched primitivism (*i.e.,* crow-jim)—it is still a jazz novel in that it reflects, immediately and vividly, to those who have been stricken with the jazz virus, a knowledge and expression of their own struggle to get straight, like Mr. Broyard's beetle.

We have had jazz novels before just as we have had a jazz generation. And, now that jazz is known to be something more than Paul Whiteman playing "San," it may be time to realize that the jazz generation of the Twenties, and the expression of its culture by F. Scott Fitzgerald, had as little to do with jazz as, indeed, did Paul Whiteman.

Kerouac's situation is different. He is of a generation that has acknowledged jazz as its voice, that identifies itself with jazz. In an early passage of "On the Road" Kerouac refers to "that sound in the night which bop has come to represent for all of us." This is the whole point. Faced with a society which he considers has rejected him (and the fact that he believes this makes it real, if not a fact), the young intellectual has come to identify himself in a great degree with jazz music because this is also the position of the jazz artist. It has aspects of a cult, to be sure. But it also has something much more than that. It has a culture. Put him down anywhere and the jazz fan finds himself at home as soon as he finds the inevitable brother jazz fan. (EDITOR'S NOTE: Kerouac's debut as a night-club "reader" to jazz in the background left him somewhat bereft of "brothers" during his year-end appearances at the Village Vanguard in New York's Greenwich Village.)

Kerouac writes from this point of view. His book assumes a knowledge of the language and litany of jazz. He is able, through adroit use of the jazz slang, to express ideas and situations which, if depicted in ordinary English prose, would raise the temperature in Boston and have him swung from the Golden Gate. But there is no profanity in the ordinary sense in this book. Instead there is the explicit, vivid vocabulary of jazz.

And since jazz has been, of necessity, a strong-limbed survivor of the Tenderloin, it has the clannishness, the in-group feeling and the special atmosphere of the underworld. Jazzmen—and some jazz fans—are in the underworld, though not of it, and some to think of themselves as outside society in the way many youths think they are. In addition, the jazz musician is homeless, in the ordinary sense. His life is a constant, roaring drag race from city to city, from one smoky night club to the same scene in another setting, alleviated occasionally by a concert's clean air and now and then celebrating the truth of his existence in the fertility rite of the jam session. As Jack Teagarden sings, "I started up to see Bud Freeman but I lost my way, and thought for a minute I was on the road for MCA."

Even though Kerouac himself—and many of his admirers—speaks of "the beat generation," this is not true. To be beat means to be "beat to the socks," down and out, discouraged and without hope. And not once in "On the Road," no matter how sordid the situation nor how miserable the people, is there no hope. That is the great thing about Kerouac's book and incidentally, this generation. They swing. And this, in the words of Father Kennard, a Catholic commentator on jazz, means to affirm. Kerouac himself points out (through the medium of his autobiographical character and narrator, Sal Paradise), "All my New York friends were in the negative, nightmarish position of putting down society—this can't go on all the time—all this franticness and jumping around. We've got to go someplace, find something."

Be somewhere, in other words.

Later in the book Kerouac asks, "What's your road, man? Holyboy road, madman road, rainbow road . . . it's an anywhere road for anybody, anyhow." And, unlike a member of a generation that is really beat, Kerouac leaves you with no feeling of despair, but rather of exaltation.

This is really the quality we get from jazz, even from the lowest of low-down blues. Ellington's lyric "The saddest tale on land or sea is the tale they told when they told the truth on me" has exaltation in it. And "On the Road" certainly has. Locked in the perpetual struggle against the formality of what has been accepted (just as jazz is struggling for its own tradition) the postwar generation can be "cool" or "beat" or whatever you want to call it. But it is only a passing stage. Like the character in Bernard Wolfe's "The Late Risers" who says, "Don't be fooled. I'm really not cool. I just don't know what else to be," the jazz generation is marking time, being cool, waiting, disengaged, if you must, looking for somewhere to be. Meanwhile, writers like Kerouac and music like jazz are its voice.

Dust jackets and paperback covers for fourteen editions of On the Road

As Kerouac was becoming the novelist of the Beat Generation, John Clellon Holmes was becoming its spokesperson. He was more willing–and perhaps more capable–of writing feature commentaries acceptable to the mainstream press and the public. His novel Go *(1952) was the first "Beat" novel, and his article "This Is the Beat Generation" had clarified the Beat aesthetic for readers of* The New York Times *in 1952, years before the publications of* Howl *and* On the Road.

The Philosophy of the Beat Generation
John Holmes
Esquire, February 1958, pp. 35–38

Last September a novel was published which *The New York Times* called "the most beautifully executed, the clearest and most important utterance" yet made by a young writer; a book likely to represent the present generation, it said, as *The Sun Also Rises* represents the twenties. It was called *On the Road,* by Jack Kerouac, and it described the experiences and attitudes of a restless group of young Americans, "mad to live, mad to talk, mad to be saved," whose primary interests seemed to be fast cars, wild parties, modern jazz, sex, marijuana, and other miscellaneous "kicks." Kerouac said they were members of a Beat Generation.

No one seemed to know exactly what Kerouac meant, and, indeed, some critics insisted that these wild young hedonists were not really representative of anything, but were only "freaks," "mental and moral imbeciles," "bourgeois rebels." Nevertheless, something about the book, and something about the term, would not be so easily dismissed. The book became the object of heated discussion, selling well as a consequence; and the term stuck–at least in the craw of those who denied there was any such thing.

. . . .

What differentiated the characters in *On the Road* from the slum-bred petty criminals and icon-smashing Bohemians which have been something of a staple in much modern American fiction–what made them *Beat*–was something which seemed to irritate critics most of all. It was Kerouac's insistence that actually they were on a quest, and that the specific object of their quest was spiritual. Though they rushed back and forth across the country on the slightest pretext, gathering kicks along the way, their real journey was inward; and if they seemed to trespass most boundaries, legal and moral, it was only in the hope of finding a belief on the other side. "The Beat Generation," he said, "is basically a religious generation."

"That's not writing, it's just . . . typing!"

Along with high praise, Kerouac and his book also were the targets of sometimes scathing criticism. In The Beat Generation, *Bruce Cook describes the occasion of the most memorable Kerouac criticisms.*

Norman Mailer proved a good friend to the Beats. An articulate and energetic defender of the faith, he appeared often on television talk shows and usually made a point of identifying himself with Kerouac, Ginsberg, and Burroughs and promoting their work. It was in such a context that Truman Capote's notorious put-down of Jack Kerouac was delivered. Mailer's version of the story is interesting because it adds a certain dimension to an anecdote that has now become almost legendary. "It was on a sort of panel discussion show on the Beats," Mailer remembers. "I was coming on long and hard for Kerouac–really talking too much, it's a habit of mine. At intermission, Truman turns to me and says, 'Damn you, Nawmin, youah *so* articulate.' He pots at you that way. He's a deceptively slight little guy, but under that swishy exterior, he's tough and hard. Well, I went on about Kerouac's rapid writing, how I think he's the best *rapid* writer in America today. And when I stopped just long enough to catch my breath, Truman comes in with 'Writing! That's not writing, it's just . . . *typing!*' Now this is a great put-down. And New York is a town for the one-line put-down. But Truman took it very hard when it was quoted all over, practically apologized. He said to me later, 'I shouldn't even have been on that show. I've got this *small* talent for ridicule.'"

–pp. 95–96

The Subterraneans

Grove Press published The Subterraneans *(1958) six months after* On the Road. *Although* On the Road *had been written quickly, its prose style was conventional.* The Subterraneans *was also written rapidly–in three nights–but it was the product of a new technique, which Kerouac called "spontaneous prose."*

Cried in the railyard sitting on an old piece of iron under the new moon and on the side of the old Southern Pacific tracks, cried because not only I had cast off Mardou whom now I was not so sure I wanted to cast off but the die'd been thrown, feeling too her empathetic tears across the night and the final horror both of us round-eyed realizing we part–but seeing suddenly not in the face of the moon but somewhere in the sky as I looked up and hoped to figure, the face of my mother–remembering it in fact from a haunted nap just after supper that same restless unable-to-stay-in-a-chair or on-earth day–just as I woke to some Arthur Godfrey program on the TV, I saw bending over me the visage of my mother, with impenetrable eyes and moveless lips and round cheekbones and glasses that glinted and hid the major part of her expression which at first I thought was a vision of horror that I might shudder at, but it didn't make me shudder–wondering about it on the walk and suddenly now in the railyards weeping for my lost Mardou and so stupidly because I'd decided to throw her away myself, it had been a vision of my mother's love for me–that expressionless and expressionless-because-so-profound face bending over me in the vision of my sleep, and with lips not so pressed together as enduring and as if to say, "*Pauvre Ti Leo, pauvre Ti Leo, tu souffri, les hommes souffri tant, y'ainque toi dans le monde j'va't prendre soin, j'aim'ra beaucoup t'prendre soin tous tes jours mon ange.*"– "Poor Little Leo, poor Little Leo, you suffer, men suffer so, you're all alone in the world I'll take care of you, I would very much like to take care of you all your days my angel."–My mother an angel too–the tears welled up in my eyes, something broke, I cracked–

– pp. 103–104

Kerouac opened a million coffee bars and sold a million pairs of Levi's to both sexes. Woodstock rises from his pages.

–William Burroughs

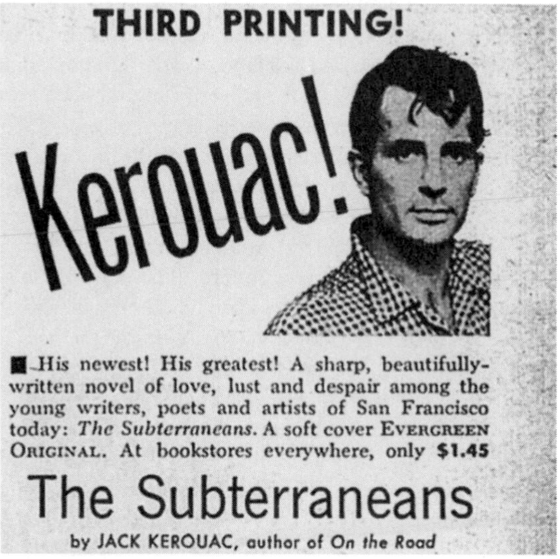
THIRD PRINTING!
Kerouac!
His newest! His greatest! A sharp, beautifully-written novel of love, lust and despair among the young writers, poets and artists of San Francisco today: The Subterraneans. A soft cover EVERGREEN ORIGINAL. At bookstores everywhere, only $1.45
The Subterraneans
by JACK KEROUAC, author of On the Road

Advertisement in The Saturday Review, *22 March 1958*

Boroff reviewed The Subterraneans *as a "social document" that sheds light on juvenile crime.*

Beatville, U.S.A.
David Boroff
New York Post, 23 February 1958, p. M11

A friend of mine often used the term, "uptown crowd," to describe people who lived outside the tight little island of Greenwich Village. It was the first hint of a separatist movement in our culture which has recently achieved full Baudelairean flower.

Its high priest is Allen Ginsberg, and its apostle to the Philistines is Jack Kerouac, whose "On The Road" induced both repugnance and tizzies of rapture among critics.

I refer, of course, to the Beat Generation, hipsterism, and, with Kerouac's new book, the subterraneans – synonyms all. Resist it though we might, with its self-dramatizing terminology and its disquieting links to hoodlumism, there is no escaping it.

It's a familiar of our time. And we find it all around us; in its chic uptown manifestations– the decorous interest in jazz and Buddhism–through the willfulness of the Actors Studio, right down to the hoods in their leather jackets–brothers in this new fraternity of the beat.

Fascinating in its evocation of the subterranean in his "pad," the book is a Baedeker of hipsterism–wild parties, Reichian analysis, existentialism, the literary idols, etc.

The style is revealing too. It is written in a kind of Actor's Studio prose–alternately slack and tense. In a stubborn monotone, the sentences uncoil their serpentine length, often limp and just as often caught up in an exciting burst of lyric energy.

At his best, Kerouac has a certain ingenuous grace, an incantatory force. But the sudden lift of language is usually brought to earth by an incongruous hipster phrase.

* * *

Ironically, by all hipster definitions, Kerouac is a rightwing conservative. Throughout the book, there is the wistful image of a normal life–boy and girl living quietly together while he gets his life's work done.

As a social document, "The Subterraneans" is important. It may provide a key to understand what is going on around us. (Consider for a moment how bewildered we are by juvenile crime, the bottom of the hierarchy of hip.)

As literature this novel strikes me as an unstable mixture of the genuinely poetic and the absurd. But this may well be a transition period, as a new idiom, a new language of desperation, is hammered out by these strange times.

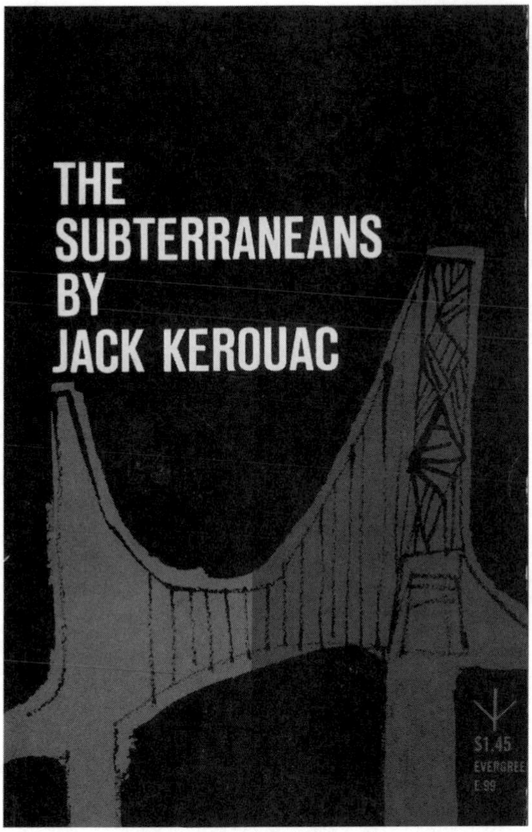

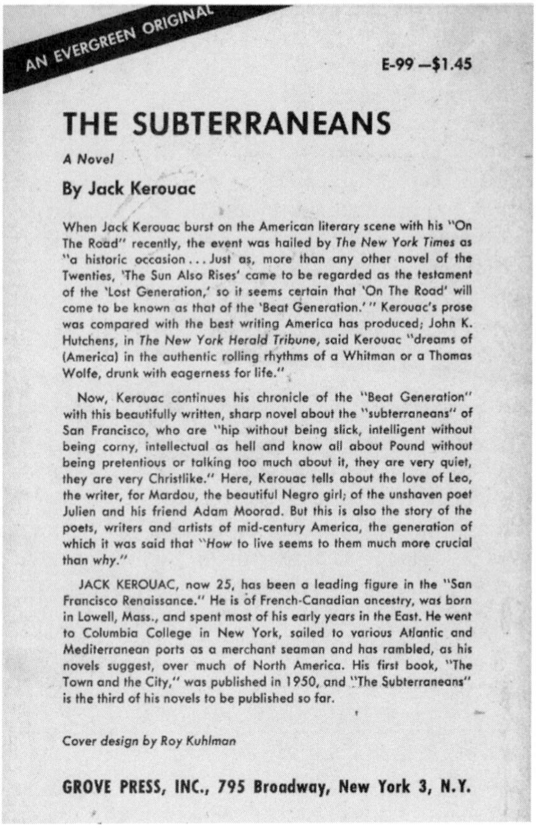

AN EVERGREEN ORIGINAL

E-99 —$1.45

THE SUBTERRANEANS

A Novel

By Jack Kerouac

When Jack Kerouac burst on the American literary scene with his "On The Road" recently, the event was hailed by *The New York Times* as "a historic occasion . . . Just as, more than any other novel of the Twenties, 'The Sun Also Rises' came to be regarded as the testament of the 'Lost Generation,' so it seems certain that 'On The Road' will come to be known as that of the 'Beat Generation.'" Kerouac's prose was compared with the best writing America has produced; John K. Hutchens, in *The New York Herald Tribune*, said Kerouac "dreams of (America) in the authentic rolling rhythms of a Whitman or a Thomas Wolfe, drunk with eagerness for life."

Now, Kerouac continues his chronicle of the "Beat Generation" with this beautifully written, sharp novel about the "subterraneans" of San Francisco, who are "hip without being slick, intelligent without being corny, intellectual as hell and know all about Pound without being pretentious or talking too much about it, they are very quiet, they are very Christlike." Here, Kerouac tells about the love of Leo, the writer, for Mardou, the beautiful Negro girl; of the unshaven poet Julien and his friend Adam Moorad. But this is also the story of the poets, writers and artists of mid-century America, the generation of which it was said that "*How* to live seems to them much more crucial than *why*."

JACK KEROUAC, now 25, has been a leading figure in the "San Francisco Renaissance." He is of French-Canadian ancestry, was born in Lowell, Mass., and spent most of his early years in the East. He went to Columbia College in New York, sailed to various Atlantic and Mediterranean ports as a merchant seaman and has rambled, as his novels suggest, over much of North America. His first book, "The Town and the City," was published in 1950, and "The Subterraneans" is the third of his novels to be published so far.

Cover design by Roy Kuhlman

GROVE PRESS, INC., 795 Broadway, New York 3, N.Y.

Front and back covers for first paperback edition of Kerouac's third novel. Because of an error by Grove Press, readers were informed that the thirty-six-year-old author was twenty-five in 1958, a misconception he referred to in Big Sur.

Hobohemian Thoreaus

Time, 24 February 1958

The Subterraneans celebrates that "systematic derangement of the senses" from which Rimbaud concocted his visions of hell. The difference is that Jack Kerouac, ex-merchant seaman, ex-railroad brakeman, is not Rimbaud but a kind of latrine laureate of Hobohemia. The story line of *The Subterraneans* is simple and stark: it concerns a short, manic-depressive love affair between a "big paranoic bum" and occasional writer named Leo Percepied and a near-insane Negro girl named Mardou Fox. Says Kerouac: "I wrote this book in three full-moon nights," and it reads that way. The details of the Leo-Mardou relationship are explicit and near pornographic. But *The Subterraneans* is not really about sex. It is about an oddball fringe of social misfits who conceive of themselves as "urban Thoreaus" in an existential state of passive resistance to society. "They are hip without being slick, they are intelligent without being corny, they are intellectual . . . without being pretentious or talking too much about it, they are very quiet."

For Leo, Mardou and their ambisextrous and hipsterical pals, the road to fulfillment leads through drink, drugs, jazz. Depending on the point of view, these are seen as evil escape mechanisms to evade reality, or accepted as strange techniques for intensifying reality. Primed with tea (marijuana) or benny (Benzedrine), the "kicks" of ecstasy become the "flips" of madness. Virtually all the characters in *The Subterrareans* flip. But Author Kerouac has known beat characters to do a reverse flip: "The hero of *On the Road* is now a normal settled-down adult. He's a railroad conductor with three kids. I've seen him put the kids to bed, kneel down and say the Lord's Prayer, and then, maybe he'll sit down and watch television."

"O Grayscreen Gangster." Author Kerouac is a cut-rate Thomas Wolfe, and he writes in vivid if not always lucid gushes and rushes, a style he attributes to the rambling reminiscences of his French Canadian mother.

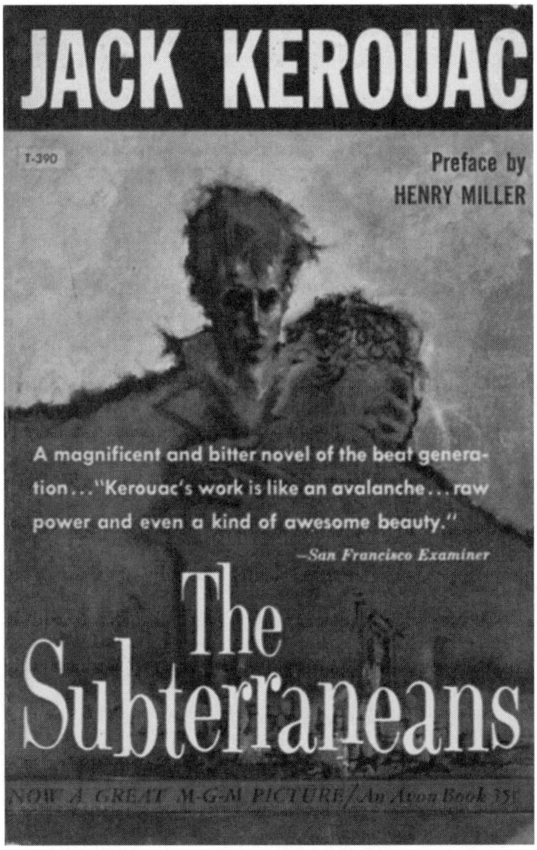

Cover for paperback first published in 1959

Love and Loss

Clyde S. Kilby

New York Herald Tribune Book Review, 23 February 1958, p. 4

This novel is the story of a brief passion between Leo Percepied, a writer, and Mardou Fox, a Negro girl ten years his junior. Leo describes himself as a bum, an egomaniac, a Baudelaire, and a continual sufferer from "beermares," hangovers and dope. His mother has supported him for years because he is not able to bear the normalities of life. Mardou, once ambitious and hopeful, has become a play doll of the Subterraneans, a group of young San Franciscans who are "hip without being slick . . . intelligent without being corny . . . intellectual as hell and know all about Pound without being pretentious or talking too much about it." Mardou is subject to fits of insanity, and when not in the hospital lives in Heavenly Lane, a gloomy, dark, and smelly tenement of twenty families. It is there that Leo spends his time with her.

The novel consists mainly of Leo's tortured realization of his inability to live without Mardou just at the moment when she is calmly dropping him for another man. It gives a penetrating look into the soul of a man greatly gifted yet somehow unable to capitalize on his gifts, unable even to evaluate his relation to Mardou in time to prevent his loss of her.

The most noteworthy quality of the novel is its coalescence of theme and style. The tumult in one is made comprehensible, and bearable, by the tumult in the other. Kerouac calls himself a jazz poet. There is no doubt about his great sensitivity to language. His sentences frequently move in tempestuous sweeps and whorls and sometimes they have something of the rich music of Gerard Manley Hopkins or Dylan Thomas.

Review of *The Subterraneans*

A. Lee

The Village Voice, 26 February 1958, p. 5

Mr. Kerouac's prose is at times graphic and reportorial, at best lyrical and exciting, at worst devoid of rhyme or reason. His assorted manuscripts have been written sitting high as a kite on latrines in Mexico, popping bennies in dim dark Long Island flats with the benefit of full moon, and while wandering Whitmanesquely across the U. S. A. One wishes he would stop playing Pied Piper to deadbeats, take a cool, cool shower, and come out writing about the real hot things in life.

There are some not-so-beat members of this generation who have a few reservations as to whether they want a junkie as their God, hipsterism as a religion, marijuana as their means to communicate, or, for that matter, Mr. Kerouac as a prophet.

New Revolution?

Mr. Kerouac's followers feel that his writing represents a new revolutionary literary style in America. I shudder to think of scores of American writers under this dispensation. After an era of Hemingways who have their own claims on beatness, are our senses now to be assaulted by long-winded tortuous accounts of erotic experience which verge on secondary self-masturbation?

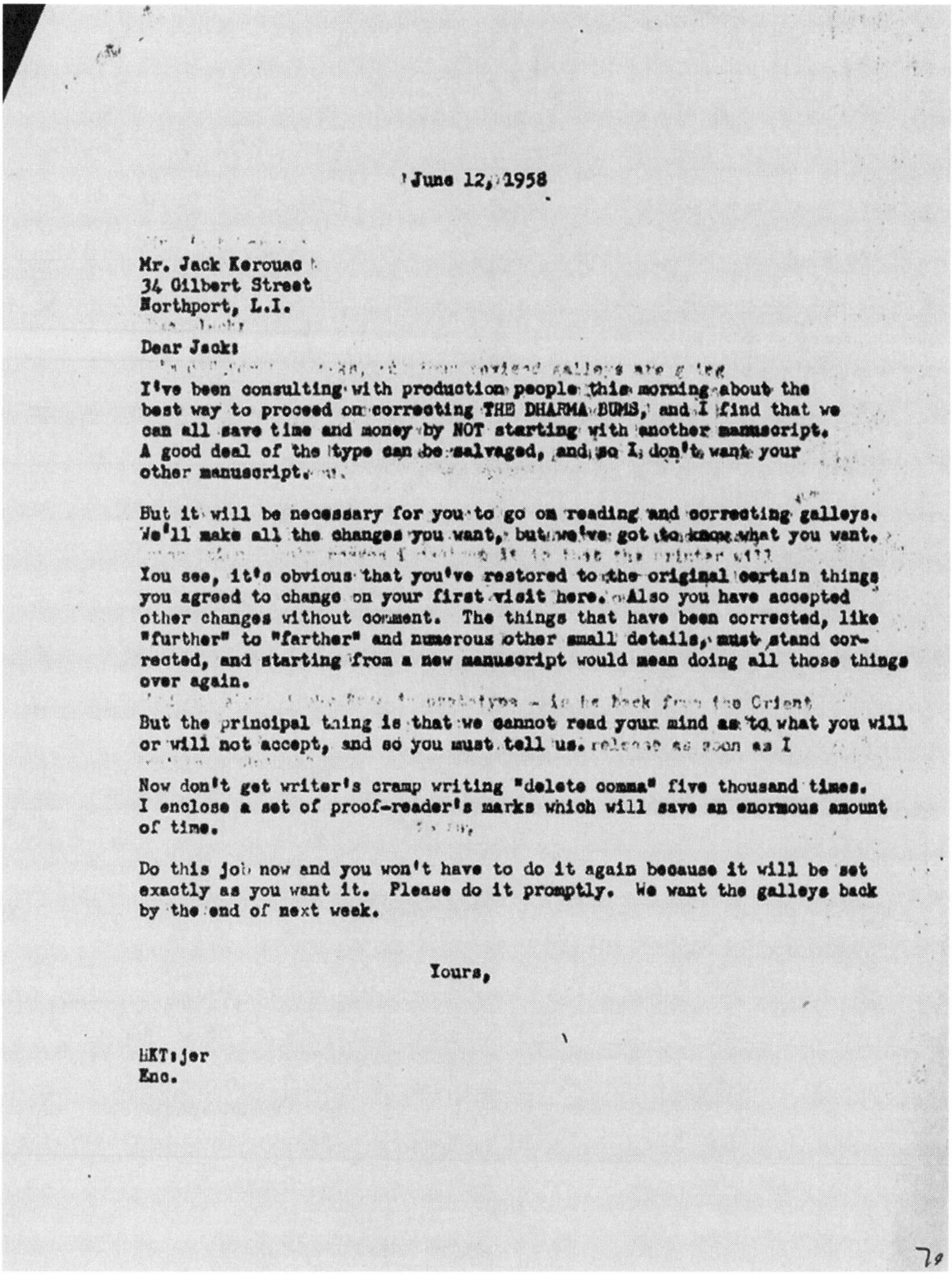

June 12, 1958

Mr. Jack Kerouac
34 Gilbert Street
Northport, L.I.

Dear Jack:

I've been consulting with production people this morning about the best way to proceed on correcting THE DHARMA BUMS, and I find that we can all save time and money by NOT starting with another manuscript. A good deal of the type can be salvaged, and so I don't want your other manuscript.

But it will be necessary for you to go on reading and correcting galleys. We'll make all the changes you want, but we've got to know what you want. You see, it's obvious that you've restored to the original certain things you agreed to change on your first visit here. Also you have accepted other changes without comment. The things that have been corrected, like "further" to "farther" and numerous other small details, must stand corrected, and starting from a new manuscript would mean doing all those things over again.

But the principal thing is that we cannot read your mind as to what you will or will not accept, and so you must tell us.

Now don't get writer's cramp writing "delete comma" five thousand times. I enclose a set of proof-reader's marks which will save an enormous amount of time.

Do this job now and you won't have to do it again because it will be set exactly as you want it. Please do it promptly. We want the galleys back by the end of next week.

Yours,

HKT:jer
Enc.

79

Letter from Viking editor Helen K. Taylor to Kerouac (Malcolm Cowley Papers, Newberry Library)

The Dharma Bums

The Yabyum Kid

Time, 6 October 1958, p. 94

Jack (On the Road) Kerouac might have called his latest novel *On the Trail,* or *How the Campfire Boys Discovered Buddhism.* The book is less frantic than *On the Road,* less sexy than *The Subterraneans,* but it reconfirms Kerouac's literary role as a kind of Tom Thumb Wolfe in hip clothing. Like other Kerouac novels, the book has the sound of jazzed-up autobiography, and the most fictional thing about it may well be the brand of Buddhism (ostensibly Zen) that the beat hero and his pals preach and practice.

Review of *The Dharma Bums*

The New Yorker, 1 November 1958, p. 175

Plodding through pages and pages of this breathless stuff is like listening to the steady flow from an adolescent passing through that phase in which everything which involves the speaker in any way seems momentous, essential, and exciting. How, the question poses itself, can a writer with Mr. Kerouac's obvious gifts bear to set such rubbish down? The question puts itself more insistently when Mr. Kerouac starts hosing his pages with smart neoBuddhist chitchat and takes his hero up a mountain for a Zen-type revelation. A possible answer suggests itself almost as insistently as the question; the suspicion grows with the turning of every trivia-crowded page that Mr. Kerouac occupies himself with this thin stuff because he has nothing else to write about, and that all this rattling of meaningless information has the sole function of concealing the absence of any true feeling or of real experience behind the book.

Beat–and Buddhist

Nancy Wilson Ross

The New York Times Book Review, 5 October 1958, pp. 5, 14

The novel by Jack Kerouac, "On the Road," was a chronicle of the hitch-hikers, hipsters, jazz fans, jalopy owners, drug addicts, poets and perverts of the Beat Generation. In the present book, however, not only are his "bums" considerably more respectable and articulate, but they are no longer merely moving for movement's sake. "Sitting" has even been discovered to possess possible virtue, for Kerouac and his restive pals–now in search of Dharma, or "Truth"–are trying to learn to meditate in Buddhist style, their new goal nothing less than total self-enlightenment, the *satori* of the Zen masters of Japan and China.

Kerouac's Dharma Bums–future Bodhisattvas one and all, by their own admission–are members of a "rucksack revolution." Carefree wanderers, they compare themselves to those Zen Lunatics immortalized in classic Japanese *sumi* painting, caught in swift brush strokes as they gaily loaf, or stroll about laughing fit to kill at the whole ephemeral world of illusory phenomena.

. . . .

Kerouac really comes close to the terse, equivocal, suggestive shorthand of Japanese poetry–which he has obviously been studying. The qualities found in *haiku* appear in other lines–"The bird of perfect balance on the fir point just moved his tail, then he was gone and distance grew immensely white." This writing is altogether different in tone from Kerouac's famous "Buddhist" poem, "The Wheel of the Quivering Meat Conception," and vastly unlike that aggressively unintelligible "spontaneous" or spray-gun type of expression favored in general by the San Francisco Group. Unfortunately, however, other passages in "The Dharma Bums," stemming perhaps from random reading in literal translations of Buddhist Scriptures, fall with awkward, even ludicrous, force on the ear: "'Let there be blowing out and bliss forevermore' I prayed in the woods at night."

Happily the higher life has not too greatly affected Ray Smith's robust sensory apparatus. Kerouac can describe a simple supper of pea soup and wild mushrooms, or even a spartan repast prepared from those little plastic bags of dried food carried by seasoned mountaineers, in a way to make your mouth water. He is at his very best in describing the smells, sounds, sights and general feeling of walking a Western trail.

In his often brilliant descriptions of nature one is aware of exhilarating power and originality, and again when he creates the atmosphere of lively gatherings for drinking, talking and horsing around in those simple but highly stylized dwellings of his Pacific Coast friends: rough wooden shacks in the forest, or sagging old houses on side streets, all with their *de rigueur* straw matting, burlap walls, bookshelves of orange crates, flowers in sake bottles, hi-fi sets. Here the entire cast of characters is presented with that not unrefreshing blend of naivete and sophistication that seems to be this author's forte.

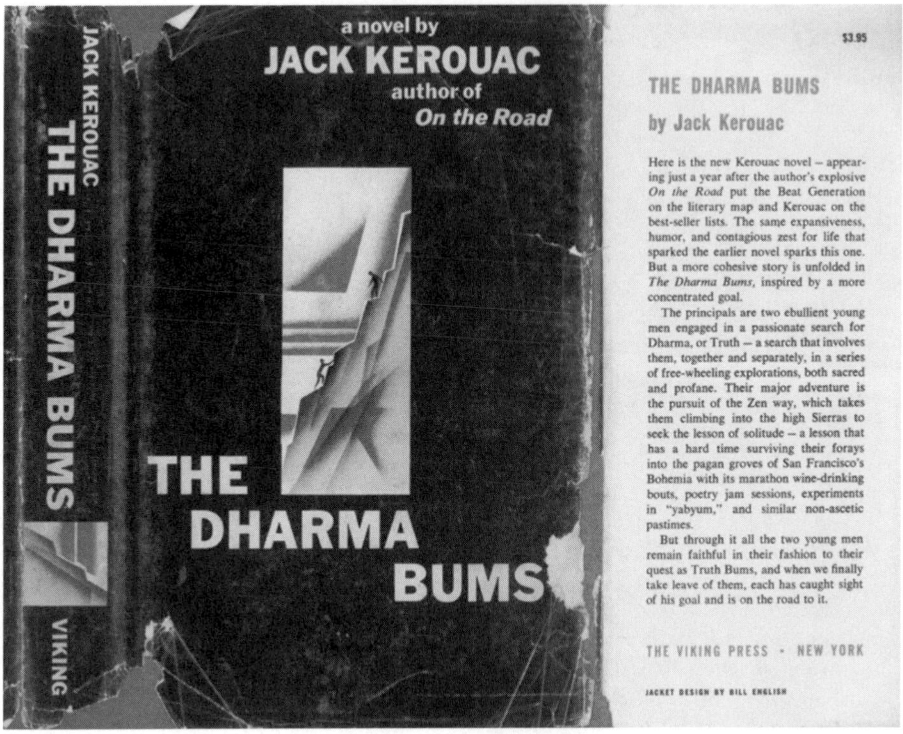

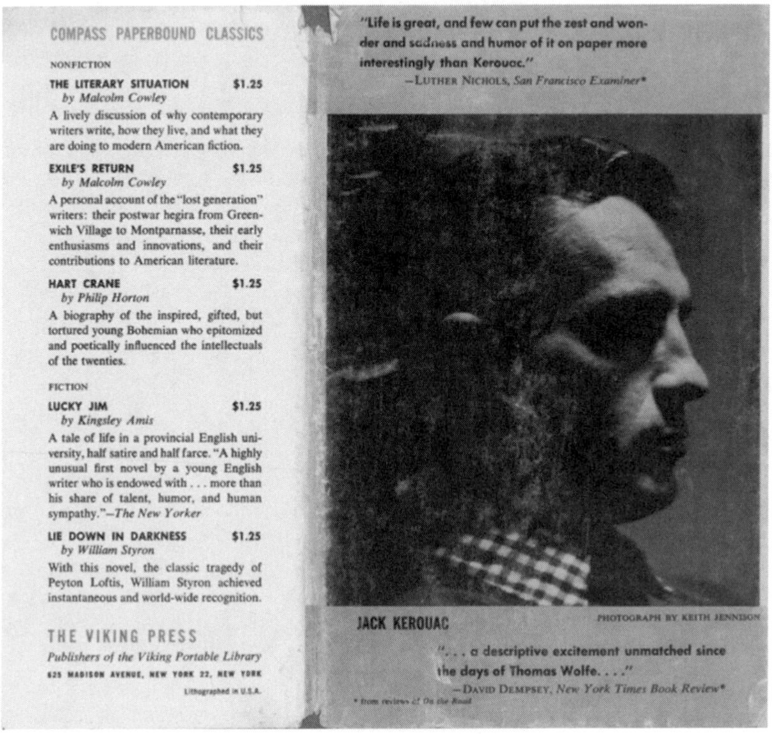

Dust jacket for Kerouac's fourth novel

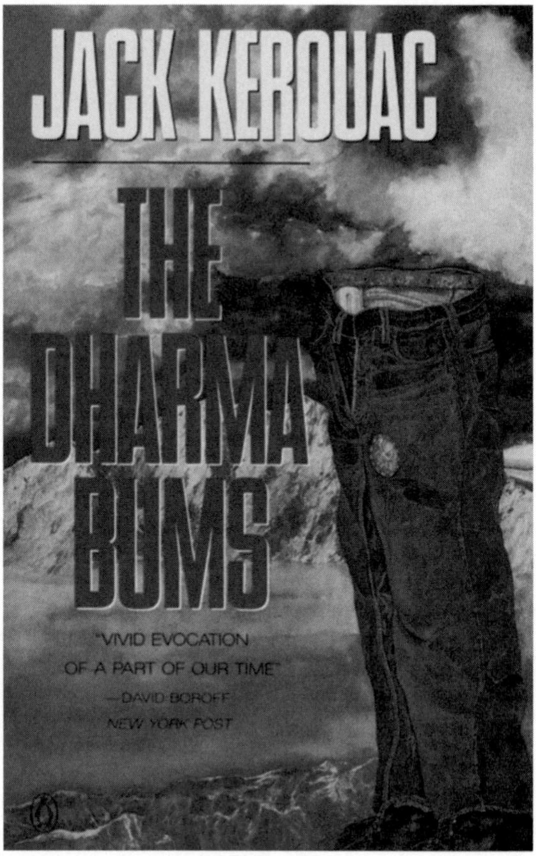

Covers for the 1959 and 1976 paperback editions for one of Kerouac's most popular novels

Review of *The Dharma Bums*
Allen Ginsberg
The Village Voice, 12 November 1958, pp. 3–5

A few facts to clear up a lot of bull. *On the Road* was written around 1950, in the space of several weeks, mostly on benny, an extraordinary project, sort of a flash of inspiration on a new approach to prose, an attempt to tell completely, all at once, everything on his mind in relation to the hero Dean Moriarty, spill it all out at once and follow the convolutions of the active mind for direction as to the "structure of the confession." And discover the rhythm of the mind at work at high speed in prose. An attempt to trap the prose of truth mind by means of a highly scientific attack on new prose method. The result was a magnificent single paragraph several blocks long, rolling, like the Road itself, the length of an entire onionskin teletype roll. The sadness that this was never published in its most exciting form–its original discovery–but hacked and punctuated and broken–the rhythms and swing of it broken–by presumptuous literary critics in publishing houses. The original mad version is greater than the published version, the manuscript still exists and someday when everybody's dead be published as it is. Its greatness (like the opening pages of Miller's *Cancer)*–the great spirit of adventure into poetic composition. And great tender delicacy of language.

The long lines of "Howl" are piddling compared to the sustained imagic rhythms of that magnificent endless paragraph. Some of the original, a lot of it, can be seen in the published version though. The book took 7-8 years to appear in mutilated form. By then K had disappeared down that road and was invisible, magic art car soul.

The conception for such prose came from the hero of the Road himself, Moriarty's prototype, who sent K a long wild introspective 40-singlespace-page letter. It's been lost, by me, I think.

The next step (after the rejection of the original *Road)* was to redo the subject, chronological account of the hero's life, in regular gothic-Melvillian prose.

That was started with one magic chapter about a Denver football field. But then K said, shove publishing and literary preconceptions, I want something I can *read,* some interesting prose, for my old age. *Visions of Neal* and *Dr. Sax* (1951–53) and another dozen subsequent books (prose, poetry, biography, meditation, translation, sketching, novels, nouvelles, fragments of brown wrapping paper, golden parchments scribbled at midnight, strange notebooks in Mexico and Desolation Peak and Ozone Park) follow.

Writing is like piano playing, the more you do it the more you know how to play a piano. And improvise, like Bach.

Not a mechanical process: the mechanical and artless practice would have been to go on writing regular novels with regular types form and dull prose. Well, I don't know why I'm arguing.

Too many critics (all incomplete because they themselves do not know how to write). Pound said not to take advice from someone who had not himself produced a masterpiece.

Am I writing for The Village Voice or the Hearing of God? In a monster mechanical mass-medium age full of horrible people with wires in their heads, the explanation is hard to make; after everybody's cash-conscious egotistical book-reviewing, trend-spotting brother has bespoke his own opinion.

It's all gibberish, everything that has been said. There's not many competent explainers. I'm speaking of the Beat Generation, which after all is quite an Angelic Idea. As to what non-writers, journalists, etc., have made of it, as usual–well, it's their bad poetry not Kerouac's.

Be that as it may, *The Subterraneans* (1953) and *The Dharma Bums* (1958) are sketchy evidence of the prose pilgrimage he's made.

The virtue of *The Subterraneans* was that it was, at last, published, completely his own prose, no changes.

An account of his method of prose (written 1953) about the time of the composition of *The Subterraneans* is reprinted in Evergreen Review, Vol. II, No. 8, from the No. 8 of the Black Mountain Review.

An excellent sample of the kind of sentence, the peculiar kind of rhythm, the appropriate alterations of square syntax, the juicy kind of imagery, the intimacy and juxtaposition of strange eternal detail, the very modernity of the thought, the very individuality (and therefore universality) of the specific sense perceptions, are to be found, for instance, in the long sentence that winds from the 6th line of p. 34 to the 13th line of p. 35 *(The Subterraneans).*

(Please quote this if you have room.)

[*Not that kind of room*–Ed.]

Spontaneous Bop Prosody, a nickname one might give to this kind of writing–that is to say, read aloud and notice how the motion of the sentence corresponds to the motion of actual excited talk.

It takes enormous art (being a genius and writing a lot) to get to that point in prose. (And trusting God.)

Bop because, partly, in listening to the new improvisatory freedoms of progressive musicians, one develops an ear for one's own actual sounds. One does not force them into the old rhythm. Unless one wishes to protect one's old emotions by falsifying the new one and making them fit the forms of the old.

Jack very concerned with the rhythm of his sentences, he enjoys that like he enjoys jazz, Bach, Buddhism, or the rhythm in Shakespeare, apropos of whom he oft remarks: "Genius is *funny*." The combinations of words and the rhythmic variations make masters laugh together (much as the two dopey sages giggling over a Chinese parchment–a picture in the Freer Gallery). All this ties in with the-half-century-old struggle for the development of an American prosody to match our own speech and thinking rhythms. It's all quite traditional actually you see. Thus W. C. Williams has preached the tradition of "invention."

All this is quite obvious except to those who are not involved with the radical problems of artistic form.

Dharma Bums is a late and recent book, he's weary of the world and prose. Extraordinary mystic testament, however, and record of various inner signposts on the road to understanding of the Illusion of Being.

The sentences are shorter (shorter than the great flowing inventive sentences of *Dr. Sax*), almost as if he were writing a book of a thousand *haikus*–Buddhist Visionary at times. He's had an actual religious experience over a prolonged period of time. This book puts it,

Kerouac responded to Ginsberg's Village Voice *review in a 19 November 1958 letter.*

Your Village Voice review best I ever got, of course, but Road was not written on benny, on coffee, and in 1951, (May), and wasnt onionskin teletype roll but Bill Canastra's drawing paper etc. we should have consulted somehow–I thought page 34 to page 25 a real silly maneouver–(by wiseguy editors who don't believe you anyway)–But you told them off–Next time you start an article say "Now to put an end to all this cowflop"

–Columbia University Rare Books Collection,
Allen Ginsberg Collection

for convenience, in the form of a novel about another interesting friend. The passages of solitary meditation are the best I'd say. The wildest sentence, perhaps:

"Suddenly came the drenching fall rains, all-night rain, millions of acres of Bo-trees being washed and washed, and in my attic millennial rats wisely sleeping."

Now that's a very strange sentence, an oddly personal associative jump in the middle of it to the eternal rats. Not many prose writers alive (Celine, Genet, a few others) would have the freedom and intelligence to trust their own minds, remember they made that jump, not censor it but write it down and discover its beauty. That's what I look for in K's prose. He's gone very far out in discovering (or remembering, or transcribing) the perfect patterns that his own mind makes, and trusting them, and seeing their importance–to rhythm, to imagery, to the very structure of the "novel."

In this, in the present American scene in prose, he is the great master innovator. There are others (Robert Creeley, maybe I don't understand what he's doing in prose though his poetry is perfect I know). And our legendary unpublished Wm. S. Burroughs.

A few other notes. The meditation in the woods, published originally in Chicago Review, Zen issue, is an excellent sincere long passage. Reading it one wonders how anybody but a boor can vision Kerouac as anything but a gentle, intelligent, suffering prose saint. The abuse he's taken is disgusting, and the technical ignorance of most of his reviewers both pro and con is scandalous.

There has not been criticism that has examined his prose purpose–nor his hip-beat insight and style–nor, finally, his holy content. It takes one to find one. Don't expect much understanding from academic journalists who, for all their pretense at civilization, have learned little but wicked opinion. (And you, Wicked Opinion–wrote Gregory Corso.)

I'm only vomiting up some of the horror of Literature. Hacks in every direction. And a nation brainwashed by hacks. I begin to see why Pound went paranoiac, if he did. It's the same situation as 1910. There is a great revolution, innovation, in poetry and prose and going on now–continuing. That the academies have learned so little in the meantime–I feel betrayed. I'll stop before I go mad.

Chapter 34, *Dharma Bums,* winds up with a great series of perfectly connected associations in visionary *haikus* (little jumps of the "freedom of eternity"). (Two images set side by side that make a flash in the mind.) Particularly pp. 241–2. Book ends with a great holy Blah! At last America has a new visionary poet. So let us talk of Angels.

Kerouac Taken Seriously

Tallman wrote the first extensive criticism of Kerouac's writing.

Kerouac's Sound

Warren Tallman

Tamarack Review, 11 (Spring 1959), pp. 58–74

It is always an implicit and frequently an explicit assumption of the Beat writers that we live, if we do at all, in something like the ruins of our civilization. When the Second World War was bombed out of existence in that long-ago '45 summer, two cities were in literal fact demolished. But psychically, all cities fell. And what the eye sees as intact is a lesser truth than what the psyche knows is actually in ruins. The psyche knows that the only sensible way to enter a modern city is Gregory Corso's way, very tentatively, "two suitcases filled with despair." This assumption that the cities which live in the psyche have all gone smash is one starting point of Beat.

But if our cities are in something like ruins, there have been survivors. Those have survived who had the least to lose, those whose psychic stance in face of modern experience had already been reduced to minimum needs: the angry Negro, the pathological delinquent, the hopeless addict. These outcasts had already fought and *lost* the battle each of us makes to establish his psyche within the social continuum. The Negro who feels that integration offers worse defeats than those already suffered at hands of the segregation to which he has long-since adjusted; the delinquent who realizes that continued irresponsibility is the only effective physician to the ills which previous irresponsibilities have brought upon him; the addict who knows that the extent to which he is hooked by his habit is as nothing alongside the extent to which he is hooked by the social purgatory he must endure in order to feed that habit–these advanced types of the social outcast have long since had to forgo the psychic luxuries available to those of us who are not outcasts. Crucially, they have had to give up that main staple of psychic continuity, Ego. Here, from Clellon Holmes's novel *Go,* is an addict evaluating the reaction of fellow passengers on a bus:

> they knew I was completely saturated with narcotics and had this disgusting skin disease and everything. . . . I realize they think I'm revolting, abhorrent . . . but not only that, I know *why* they think that . . . and more important, I *accept* the fact that they do. . . . They're disgusted because they've got to save their own egos, you see. But I haven't got one, I mean I don't care about all

> that anymore, so it doesn't matter to me . . . I just accept it so as not to get hung up.

The outcast knows that ego, which demands self-regard, is the enemy that can trap him into kinds of social commitment which his psyche cannot afford. Ego is for the squares. Let them be trapped. To be released from the claims of ego is to be released from the claims of others, a very necessary condition for survival if you happen to be an outcast. But the consequences can be devastating. For when ego vanishes, the continuity of one's existence is likely to vanish with it.

A most vivid instance of what can happen to a man when the continuity of his life is suddenly disrupted comes not from the Beat writers but from Conrad, in *Nostromo*. Decoud, isolated by circumstances, "dreaded the sleepless nights in which the silence, remaining unbroken in the shape of a cord to which he hung with both hands, vibrated with senseless phrases." The "senseless phrases" happen to be the names of the woman he loves, of the man with whom he is conspiring, and of the man against whom they conspire. Just because the most meaningful continuity in his life has been reduced by solitude to "senseless phrases," he begins to wish that the cord of silence to which he clings will snap; as, with his suicide, it does. The kinds of solitude from which the city-bred outcasts suffer are not as severe as Decoud's, doubtless, and the loss of continuity which follows from the abandonment of ego not as total. But what Decoud suffers in a total way is known in less intense but still devastating ways to all those outcasts who waken, without ego, to the consequent drift of their aimless day.

It is an axiom of the human spirit that whosoever wanders into purgatory will attempt to escape. With luck, with courage, with ingenuity, some succeed. The solution of the outcast who has given up a large part of his ego has been to fall back not upon the mercy of society–for society has long since been committed to the merciless proposition that only certain men are brothers–but upon, or rather into the moment. The moment becomes the outcast's island, his barricade, his citadel. Having lost his life in the social continuum, cast out and cyphered, he finds it again within the moment. But when the social outcast takes over the moment as his province, he is faced with yet another problem. He must make it habitable. How unsuccessful most such outcast efforts have been can best be seen in any skid-road district, where men come to their vacant pauses within what Ginsberg describes as "the drear light of Zoo." However, some of the animals in the skid road and slum zoos have long since rebelled. Up from the rhythms and intensities which animate the Negro, the delinquent, and the addict have risen the voices that dig and swing on the Beat streets in the North American night, a music and a language, Jazz and Hip.

First the language. Strictly speaking, a hipster is an addict and hip talk is the addict's private language. But it has become much more. Granting many exceptions in which addiction incurred accidentally, it is almost axiomatic that the addict is an outcast first and acquires his habit in an effort to escape from the psychic ordeal of being brotherless, unable to exert claims upon anybody's love. But once hooked, he is necessarily a man living from moment to moment, from fix to fix. The intervals between become a kind of purgatorial school in which one learns to care about less and less: not surroundings, not status, not appearance, not physical condition, not even crimes, but only for the golden island ahead where one can score, then fix, then swing. To swing is to enter into full alliance with the moment and to do this is to triumph over the squares who otherwise run the world. For to enter the moment, you must yield to the moment. The square person can never get the camel caravan of his ego-commitments through the eye of the needle which opens out upon hipster heaven. Excluded from the moment and consequently seeking it out ahead in a future which never has been and never will be, all that the square person can dig is his own grave. The hip person knows that the only promised land is Now and that the only way to make the journey is to dig everything and go until you make it and can swing.

Hip talk, then, is Basic English which charts the phases, the psychology, even the philosophy of those outcasts who live for, with, and–when they can–within the moment. It is in fact less a language than a language art in which spontaneity is everything. The words are compact, mostly monosyllabic, athletic: dig, go, make it, man, cat, chick, flip, goof, cool, crazy, swing. In his very suggestive essay, "The White Negro," Norman Mailer argues that the basic words of hip form a nucleus which charts and organizes the energies of the hipster into maximum mobility for his contentions with the squares, as indeed with other hipsters, for the sweets of this world. Mailer's emphasis upon the endless battle between hip and square is true, I think, but not true enough because less vital than is the hipster's even deeper need to establish a new continuity for his life. The most severe ordeal of his constantly emphasized isolation is not loss of the social sweets but loss of the moment. It is against this fate that he has evolved his cryptic language art. The talented hipster is as sensitive to the nuances and possibilities of his language as he necessarily is to the nuances and possibilities of his always threatened moment. Which is why the real hip cat who can dig and swing with the other cats in hip-land has such close affinities with the aristocrat among such outcasts, the jazzman.

Jazz swings in and with the moment. The universal name for a good group is "a swinging group," one in which each individual is attuned to all of the others so that improvisation can answer improvisation without loss of group harmony. Baby Dodds, who drummed with Louis Armstrong in the early jazz days, describes this process very clearly:

> Louis would make something on his horn, in an afterbeat, or make it so fast that he figured I couldn't make it that fast, or he'd make it in syncopation or in Charleston time, or anything like that for a trick. And I would come back with something on the snare drums and with an afterbeat on the bass drum or a roll or something. But I had to keep the bass drum going straight for the band. I couldn't throw the band . . . at all times I heard every instrument distinctly.

Jazz played in this way can be a spontaneous, swinging poem in which the group first creates the shape, the musical metrics of the given moment. Then individuals begin to improvise in the way Dodds describes or the talented soloist to move his sound out into the possibilities of the moment. When this happens the jazzman and the hip person who can swing with him experience release into the moment that is being created, as Kerouac notes, "so he said it and sang it and blew it through to the stars and on out." Since such release is the hip person's deepest need and desire, the jazzman becomes the hipster hero who has moved among the mountains of the moment and in so doing has conquered the most vindictive of their enemies, time. In jazz the moment prevails.

But sounds die out. And are replaced by other sounds. Where jazz was, factory whistles will be when Daddio Time turns on tic toc dawn to light the hipman and the jazzman home. And the square eye of morning tells both what each had been trying to forget, that when you fall out of the moment and happen to be an outcast you are back among the ruins in a world where only certain men are brothers. At which point the Beat writers appear on the scene, chanting Holy, Holy, Holy–but with a Bop beat.

BOP: In a conventional tune the melody moves along not quite like but something like an escalator, steadily and as the feet would expect, so that the good children of this world can keep their eyes fixed upward for the sign that says: TOYS. But the restless outcast children in the department store of this world know that the journey is NOW. As their jazz escalator goes at a syncopated beat from level to level, the outcast children dip into the toy shop of the moment and come up with little hops, skips, and jumps that are answered back by other hops, skips, and jumps, until, by the time the syncopated escalator reaches the top level, everybody is hopping and jumping about, together and as individuals, and this of course is improvisation–the life of jazz. However, this dual progression in which the syncopated beat of the melody escalator carries the spontaneous action of the improvisations from level to level has given way, with the advent of Bop, to a music which seems to travel from level to level on the improvisations alone. That is, the melody (the escalator) has been assimilated into the pattern of improvisations (hop, skip, jump) and the improvisations–always the life impulse of jazz–have dominated in this merger. At best Bop has freed jazz from the tedium of banal melodies. It has also given emphasis to a principle of spontaneous creative freedom which has been taken over by the Beat writers in ways likely to have a strong influence upon North American poetry and fiction.

In conventional fiction the narrative continuity is always clearly discernible. But it is impossible to create an absorbing narrative without at the same time enriching it with images, asides, themes and variations–impulses from within. It is evident that in much recent fiction–Joyce, Kafka, Virginia Woolf, and Faulkner are obvious examples–the narrative line has tended to weaken, merge with, and be dominated by the sum of variations. Each narrative step in Faulkner's work is likely to provoke many sidewinding pages before a next narrative step is taken. More, a lot of Faulkner's power is to be found in the sidewindings. In brief, what happens in jazz when the melody merges with the improvisations and the improvisations dominate, has been happening in fiction for some time now.

However, the improvisations of jazz are incomparably more fluent than have been the variations of fiction. The jazzman is free to move his sound, which is simply himself, where and as the moment prompts, "one mountain, two mountains, ten clouds, no clouds." But the fiction man has always had to move his style, which also is himself, into the present-day deviousness, the "messy imprecision" of words. The fiction man encounters deviousness and imprecision in our language because an evident fragmentation has overtaken meanings in our time. Empson's *Seven Types of Ambiguity,* the first work to *exploit* the plight of meanings in our time, may well turn out to have been the handwriting on the wall announcing the breakup of our camp, the only camp that truly signifies: the human one. For it is not, as Empson supposed, our language that is ambiguous. It is our relations with one another. Trust lacking, meanings become ambiguous. And when meanings become ambiguous language becomes imprecise, difficult, devious.

There have been a number of attempts, heroic in their singlemindedness, to confront with language the increasing ambiguity of meanings, notably those of Joyce and Eliot. But the result has been a fiction and poetry so circuitously difficult as to require years-long efforts of creation and explication–which is to communicate the slow way. The outcome for most persons has been a distinct breakdown of any vital connection with our best literature. To the fact of this breakdown the Beat writers bring a new solution.

Their solution is to be Beat. To be Beat is to let your life come tumbling down into a humpty-dumpty heap, and with it, into the same heap, the humpty-dumpty meanings which language attempts to sustain. There are fewer things beneath heaven and earth than our present-day multiple-meaning philosophers would have us believe. From the ruin of yourself pick up yourself (if you can) but let old meanings lie. Now cross on over to the outcast side of the street to where the hip folk and the jazz folk live, for the way your life is now is the way their lives have been for years. Step right in through the Open Door to where the tenor man is crouching with the bell mouth of his horn down in the basement near his feet, reaching for the waters of life that come rocking up through the debris of the day that dawned over Hiroshima everywhere long 1945 ago. The sound you hear is life, "the pit and prune juice of poor beat life itself in the god-awful streets of man." And life is Holy. And this is the meaning of words. Life is holy, and the journey is Now. Say it with a Bop beat.

KEROUAC'S SOUND

Kerouac's sound starts up in his first novel, *The Town and the City,* and anyone who grew up with or remembers the sentimental music of the 1930s will recognize what he is doing. The New England nights and days of his childhood and youth are orchestrated with slow violins, to which sound the children whose lives he chronicles are stirred into awareness as the stars dip down and slow breezes sweep along diminishing strings towards soft music on a farther shore. It is the considerable achievement of the novel that Kerouac is able to sustain the note of profound sentimentality his style conveys even as he is tracing, with remorseless intelligence, the downfall of the New England family, the Martins, who try to sustain their lives on this tone. The sound bodies forth their myth–soft music on a farther shore–while the action brings both myth and sound down in ruins.

The protagonist is George Martin, one version and a good one of the mythical American–big, outgoing, direct–who sustains his life, his certainties, his soul on the music Kerouac builds in around him: at the rim of all things, violins. He rises at dawn, splashing, coughing, spluttering, and plunges into the day like a playful porpoise, rolling in the life element. But his cough is cancer, and the novel concerns the downfall of this man. His career carries from the town, where he was known to every man, to New York City where he has no acquaintances at all. He ends his life on a mean Brooklyn street in a mean apartment with only a direct if ravaged love for his dispersed and tormented children to see him through disease into silence.

A main sign of Kerouac's control over the melody he projects is to be seen in the variety of fates to which he sends the Martin children. One son goes via books to success at Harvard and then on into the books and the sterility of a quasi-homosexual existence. Another son heads for adventure on the big trucks that whirr across the North American night only to discover that the whirring of trucks is a nothing song for a nowhere journey. Another son ends at Okinawa. The principal son goes via a football scholarship to Pennsylvania and early stardom. But just as he is about to become Saturday's hero and thus confirm his father's belief in the rightness of his myth, the son rebels in order to destroy the myth; and so helps destroy his father's life; and so his own. One daughter elopes with a jazzman and ends divorced in bohemian New York, singing at a second-rate bar. Another daughter disperses to Los Angeles. Another to Seattle. All of the children plunge like the playful porpoises their father had taught them to be into the swaying waters of the myth he created, soft music on a farther shore. All drown. The football-playing son who manages to break the myth, and with it his own life, swims for love of the father back to shore. He is seen at the last on a rainy roadway, hitchhiking west and known to no man–but with no more violins.

I think it is evident that in creating this testimonial to a gone childhood, Kerouac is also breaking with the mood of that era. How decisively he does break becomes plain in his second published novel, *On the Road,* where the sounds become BIFF, BOFF, BLIP, BLEEP, BOP, BEEP, CLINK, ZOWIE! Sounds break up. And are replaced by other sounds. The journey is NOW. The narrative is a humpty-dumpty heap. Such is the condition of NOW. The ruins extend from New York City, down to New Orleans, on down to Mexico City, back up to Denver, out to San Francisco, over to Chicago, back to New York–six cities at the end points of a cockeyed star. The hero who passed from star-point to star-point is Dean Moriarty, the mad Hamlet of the moment, shambled after by Sal Paradise, who tells the story. And all that Sal can say is, "Yes, he's mad," and "Yes, he's my brother." Moriarty is the hero-prince of all Beat people, a "madman angel and bum" out to con the North American nightmare of a chance for his soul to live. Nothing that his tormented hands reach for will come into his hands except the holiness which comes rocking up direct from the waters of life upon the jazz rhythms with which Kerouac pitches his cockeyed star of wonder about.

Moriarty is a Denver jailkid who does not have to wait for his life to come down in ruins. It begins that way. His mother "died when Dean was a child" and his wino father is so indistinguishable from all the other winos in all the skid-road districts where Dean thinks he may find him that "I never know whether to ask." Kerouac provides only enough details about "all the bitterness and madness" of Dean's Denver childhood to make it clear that the social forms to which all good children go for their bread of life (or so they think) were made forbidden areas for Dean by reason of rejection, guilt, shame, rage, hatred–the dreadful emotions likely to orchestrate the secret lives of children who one day wake up Beat. Hence the car-stealing frenzies in which he turns himself into a car so that his thwarted energies can come "blasting out of his system like daggers." On the maddest night of the novel he climaxes one such (five-car) binge by stealing a police detective's auto (inviting punishment) which he abandons in front of the house where he then passes out in peace and calm of mind–drunk–all passion spent.

An even more definite sign of Moriarty's inability to live within existing social forms consists in the insane doubling-up of those relationships from which he does seek satisfaction, brotherhood, love. No sooner does he dig Sal Paradise the very most than he must rush into an even more intense relationship with Paradise's friend, Carlo Marx. No sooner does he set up housekeeping with his first wife, Marylou, than he must arrange an elaborate time-schedule in order to set up parallel housekeeping with his second, interchangeable wife, Camille. The Denver Bohemia must be matched by bohemian San Francisco. His life on the West Coast is a process of creating the complications which will be resolved by flight to the East Coast. Tormented by almost complete inability to live within even the relaxed bohemian life-forms, Moriarty turns again and again to the one form in which his energies find something like release and fulfilment–the road.

In a car on the road, surrounded by darkness, the existing forms vanish and with them vanishes the distraught, guilt tormented self. Speed, strangeness and space, dark forests, heavy-shouldered mountains and open prairies bring new transient forms, semi-forms, even formless forms, rushing into place. All of these are fleetingly familiar, for all of these are life. And because life is holy, the soul moves in behind the wheel and "every moment is precious" as the mad city Hamlet gives way to a road-going Quixote who cares only for the soul's journey, the one sweet dreadful childhood could not steal from him. Thus "it was remarkable," Sal Paradise tells us, "how Dean could go mad and then suddenly continue with his soul . . . calmly and sanely as though nothing had happened." The mad self blends into the speeding car as the sane soul continues down the one road of life on the only journey which "must eventually lead to the whole world."

An apotheosis of sorts is achieved briefly in Mexico on the strangest yet most strangely familiar of all the roads Moriarty and Paradise take, on a womb-like jungle night, "hot as the inside of a baker's oven." Here the travelers are taken over by "billions of insects" until "the dead bugs mingled with my blood." Time, self, and history are temporarily annihilated and there is only the "rank, hot and rotten jungle" from which a prophetic white horse, "immense and phosphorescent," emerges to pace majestically, mysteriously past Moriarty's for-once sleeping head. When they waken from this dream of annihilation and rebirth it is to enter mountains where "shepherds appeared dressed as in the first time." And Moriarty "looked to heaven with red eyes," aware that he has made it out of orbit with the cockeyed star of NOW into orbit with "the golden world that Jesus came from." But if this Beat angel journeys through the jazz of the North American night finally to reach a semblance of creation day morning time in the Mexican mountains of the moment, he is much too mad to more than distractedly glimpse, and giggle, and give a wristwatch to a Mexican creation-day child, inviting her to enter time. "Yes, he's mad," says Sal, and so Quixote gives way to Hamlet as Dean Moriarty ends with stockings downgyved–"ragged in a moth-eaten overcoat"–a parking-lot attendant in New York–which is no way for a con man to live–silent–"Dean couldn't talk any more"–with only his sad Horatio, Sal, to tell his brother's story.

The jazz is in the continuity in which each episode tells a separate story–variations on the holiness theme. And it is in the remarkable flexible style as Kerouac improvises within each episode seeking to adjust his sound to the resonance of the given moment. Some moments come through tinged with the earlier *Town and City* sentimentality. Others rock and sock with Moriarty's frenzy, the sentences jerking about like muscles on an overwrought face. Still others are curiously quiescent, calm. And the melody which unifies the whole and lifts the cockeyed star up into the jazz sky is the holiness of life because this for Kerouac is the meaning of words, the inside of his sound. Dean Moriarty is sweet prince to this proposition. To read *On the Road* with attention to the variations Kerouac achieves is to realize something of his remarkable talent for meshing his sound with the strongly-felt rhythms of many and various moments. It is not possible to compare him very closely with other stylists of note because his fiction is the first in which jazz is a dominant influence.

How dominant emerges into clear focus with the third of his published novels, *The Subterraneans*. Here is a typical sentence, the fourth in the book:

> I was coming down the street with Larry O'Hara old drinking buddy of mine from all the times in San Francisco in my long and nervous and mad careers I've gotten drunk and in fact cadged drinks off friends with such "genial" regularity nobody really cared to notice or announce that I am developing or was developing, in my youth, such bad freeloading habits though of course they did notice but liked me and as Sam said "Everybody comes to you for your gasoline boy, that's some filling station you got there" or words to that effect–old Larry O'Hara always nice to me, a crazy young businessman of San Francisco with Balzacian backroom in his bookstore where they'd smoke tea and talk of the old days of the great Basie band or the days of the great Chu Berry–of whom more anon since she got involved with him too as she had to get involved with everyone because of knowing me who am nervous and many leveled and not in the least one-souled–not a piece of my pain has showed yet–or suffering–Angels, bear with me–I'm not even looking at the page but straight ahead into the sadglint of my wallroom and at a Sara Vaughan Gerry Mulligan Radio KROW show on the desk in the form of a radio, in other words, they were sitting on the fender of a car in front of the Black Mask bar on Montgomery Street, Julien Alexander the Christ-like unshaved thin youthful quiet strange almost as you or as Adam might say apocalyptic angel or saint of the subterraneans, certainly star (now), and she, Mardou Fox, whose face when first I saw it in Dante's bar around the corner made me think, "By God, I've got to get involved with that little woman" and maybe too because she was a Negro.

I count seven shifts away from the narrative line. If these shifts are dropped, one has Leo Percepied, the narrator, walk down the street with Larry O'Hara and meet Julien Alexander and Mardou Fox as they stand beside an automobile in front of the Black Mask bar. The side-trips from this simple narrative line lead to: Percepied's drinking habits–a main variation; (2) his energies–another main variation; (3) jazz and marijuana parties in Larry O'Hara's bookshop; (4) a passage of self analysis–a major variation; (5) circumstances under which the sentence is being written; (6) descriptions of the people Percepied is about to meet; and, repeated from a previous sentence, (7) Percepied's determination to meet Mardou, who later turns out to be part Indian as well as Negro–another major variation. Kerouac's immediate motive is the Bop motive, maximum spontaneity. The narrative melody merges with and is dominated by the improvised details. And, as Percepied emphasizes twice later, "the truth is in the details." The narrative line follows the brief love-affair between Percepied and Mardou while the improvised details move, as the title would suggest, down into the clutter of their lives among the guilts and shames which come up from subterranean depths to steal their love from them. The truth is in the improvisations.

The novel is written with the driving but hung-up rhythms of a hurrying man who is also, always, alas, looking back over his shoulder. The finest scenes, I think, are those in which Mardou figures, particularly that in which she is rejected by some friends, loses control of her consciousness, and wanders out naked into nighttime San Francisco, almost insane, to be saved by the realization that she is meant for love rather than hatred and so walks about the city newly discovering and at the same time transforming the world she passes through. This self-conquest makes her able to trust others, to believe that Percepied loves her, and to love him in return. But he is unable to conquer his own guilts and shames, cannot reciprocate, and so is gradually, frantically pulled back into the clutter of his life. A failure of love by reason of deep fissuring guilts emerges from the depths on the rush but not exactly on the wings of Kerouac's spontaneous Bop style. As Percepied says, "I'm the Bop writer." As one might expect, the spontaneity falters in a good many pages. Yet I do not doubt that the method does permit Kerouac to tap his imagination in spontaneous ways. Nor do I doubt but that *The Subterraneans* is his most important novel and a very important one indeed. Of this, more in place.

The easiest way to approach *The Dharma Bums*–the truth bums–is to imagine an exceptionally talented musician trying out a new instrument in an interested but nonetheless very tentative way. The instrument is Zen Buddhism, American fashion. The novel is full of hummed songs, muttered chants, self-conversations carried on in railroad yards, on beaches, in groves of trees, in the mountains. The half-embarrassed, half-serious mutterer is Ray Smith, Zen amateur, and the style which Kerouac floats through the novel is part of an obvious attempt to adjust the practices, the flavor, the attitudes of Zen to an American sensibility.

Jazz is gone, even from the Bohemian party scenes which alternate with the Zen scenes. Moriarty's frenzy and Percepied's rush give way to a slow–and at times a too-slow–pace. It is surely significant that in the opening paragraph Smith travels past the place where the "king and founder of the Bop generation," the jazzman Charlie Parker, "went crazy and got well again." Kerouac might be hinting at the strain of writing eleven books in six years and about the need for a temporary so-long to jazz, hello to Zen. But the hello is most tentative. To put the very best construction on the novel, always advisable when considering a gifted writer, is to read it as a kind of primer of Zen experience. I spare the reader any attempts to explicate the Zen way as Kerouac relays it into the novel via Smith's friend, Japhy, the American Zen adept. And just as well, for I have been informed since writing this essay that the Buddhism in *The Dharma Bums* ranges considerably beyond the Zen variety. Suffice it to mention that the Zen emphasis upon paradoxes which will annihilate meanings is a peculiarly appropriate counterpart of the Beat writer's suspicion of meanings. Put any meaningful thought through the Zen dialectic and come out with one thought less. But if the Zen attitude is consistent with Kerouac's own, it is nonetheless apparent that the meditative world in which this attitude is best cultivated hasn't much affinity with his essentially nervous and agile sensibility. Unsustained by the driving intensities which make *On the Road* and *The Subterraneans* swing, *The Dharma Bums* frequently goes flat. There are dull scenes, mechanical passages. If there is one superb mountain-climbing episode, that is less because Zen catches hold for Kerouac, more because the mountain does. Certainly, representation of the final trip to the Northwest, where the protagonist attempts to live in the Zen way on Desolation Peak, is so sketchy as to amount to a default. And it is here that one touches upon Kerouac's limitations.

In *The Dharma Bums* distinctly and in his other novels in less evident ways, one becomes aware of Kerouac's receptive, his essentially feminine sensibility. Sensibility, I repeat. This receptivity is certainly his main strength as artist, accounting as it does for his capacity to assimilate the rhythms, the sounds, the life-feel of experience into his representation. When Kerouac is at his best he is able to register and project the American resonance with remarkable ease and accuracy. But on the related, weaker side of the coin, he has only a limited ability to project this sound up to heights, down to depths. Moments of climax, of revelation, of crisis, the very moments which deserve the fullest representation, frequently receive only sparse representation. The climactic Mexican journey in *On the Road* suffers from this limitation. Beginning with the madcap afternoon in the Mexican whore house, followed by the night-time sojourn in the jungle, the creation-day morning in the mountains, and subsequent arrival in Mexico City, the hipster Zion, where marijuana cascades like manna into the streets, the entire sequence is as brilliantly conceived as any in recent fiction. But representation in these scenes which show Moriarty's life sweeping up to climax, is sparse, fleeting, even sketchy. No reader will be convinced that Moriarty, the true traveler, has made it to a mountain-peak of our present moment from which creation-day is glimpsed. Nor will any reader be convinced that Ray Smith has gained access to the Zen Way in his mountain fastness.

Yet I do not think that this defect traces so much to want of creative force, though that's what it appears to be, as to Kerouac's almost animal suspicion of the meaning values toward which words tend. When his fictions coverage toward meanings something vital in him flinches back. His sound is primarily a life sound, sensitive to the indwelling qualities of things, the life they bear. To be Beat is to be wary of moving such a sound into the meaning clutter. It might become lost, the life. So Kerouac draws back. Which is his limitation.

But also his strength. For in the jazz world of the Bop generation where Charlie Parker is king and founder, Jack Kerouac in a different medium is heir apparent. For his emphasis upon a from-under sound made spontaneous by adherence to the jazz principle of improvisation is right for our time, I think. The jazz vernacular is just that, a vernacular, and Kerouac has demonstrated that it can be transposed into fiction without serious loss of the spontaneous imaginative freedom which has made it among the most vital of the modern arts.

Although Kerouac's art is limited, I am convinced that his sound is more nearly in the American grain than that of any writer since Fitzgerald. The efforts of his outcast protagonists to get life into their lives seem more closely related to our actual moment than any since Jay Gatsby, similar across worlds of difference, tried to shoot the North American moon. Gatsby failed and finished like a sad swan, floating dead on the surface of a pool. And Kerouac's protagonists fail too. Dean Moriarty does not make it to creation-day as was his mad desire. Ray Smith fumbles the Zen football. Leo Percepied cannot enter guilt-forbidden realms of Mardou's Negro love. Fitzgerald's efforts got lost in the personal, national, and international chaos from which he summoned Gatsby into presence. But it was only after his energies lost coherence that Fitzgerald woke up in the ruins of that dark midnight of the soul where it is always three o'clock in the morning. Kerouac starts in with the dark midnight and it is his effort to bring his protagonists through the jazz of that night, naked, into something like a new day. He fails too. The moment, NOW, which is the only promised land, shrugs off Moriarty, Percepied, and Smith, shrugs off Kerouac too. Outcasts they began and end as outcasts. But very distinctly Kerouac's protagonists press more sharply close to the truth about our present moment than have fictional protagonists for many years. And that's a help. And very distinctly he has created new ground of possibility for fiction to stand upon with renewed life. And that's a help.

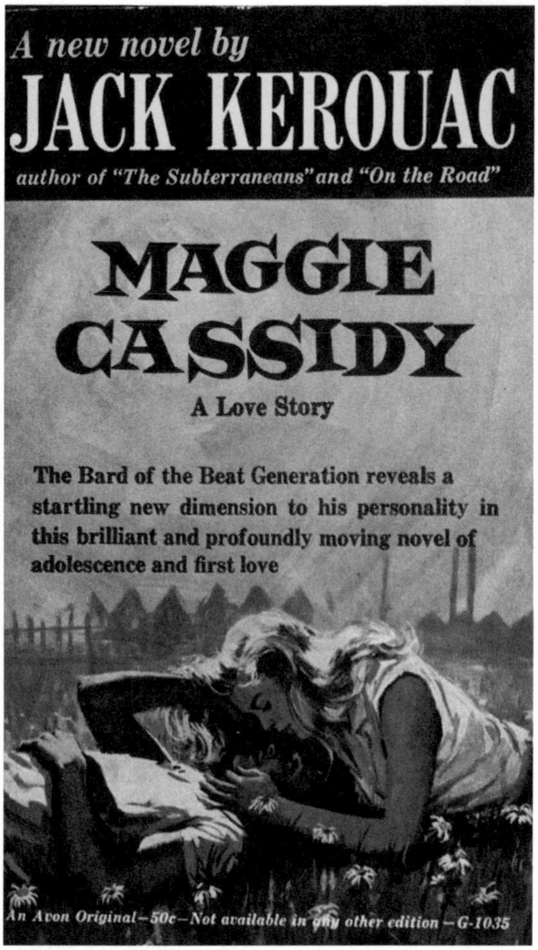
A new novel by
JACK KEROUAC
author of "The Subterraneans" and "On the Road"
MAGGIE CASSIDY
A Love Story
The Bard of the Beat Generation reveals a startling new dimension to his personality in this brilliant and profoundly moving novel of adolescence and first love
An Avon Original—50c—Not available in any other edition—G-1035

Cover for the first Kerouac novel published as a paperback original. Written in his mother's house on Long Island early in 1953, Maggie Cassidy *was published in summer 1959.*

In 1966 Kerouac wrote of the original idea for Scripture of the Golden Eternity.

Gary Snyder said, "All right, Kerouac, it's about time for you to write a sutra." That's a thread of discourse, a scripture. He knew I was a Bodhi Sattva and had lived twelve million years in twelve million directions. You see, they really believe that, those maniacs. I'm a Catholic all along. I was really kidding Gary Snyder. Boy, they're so gullible. I wrote it in Loche McCorkle's shack in Mill Valley. He's Sean Monahan in *The Dharma Bums.* In pencil, carefully revised and everything, because it was a scripture. I had no right to be spontaneous.

—*A Bibliography of Works by Jack Kerouac,* p. 20

More Novels

The Kerouac who had spent his youth reading, learning, gathering experience, and crafting a new kind of prose in a dozen books was lost amidst the notoriety and media recreation of his image as a "Beat hoodlum." His problem drinking increased as he struggled to cope with his new life in the limelight, as his once-ignored books were being rushed into publication, sometimes as many as three in one year.

Barefoot Boy with Dreams of Zen

Barnaby Conrad
The Saturday Review, 22 May 1959, p. 23

I bumped into a friend of mine in San Francisco the other day, a serious hard-working writer, and commented on the fact that he had shaved his beard of some decade's standing.

"I loved the darned thing," he said sadly, "but I couldn't stand one more tourist asking the Gray Line Tour guide: 'Is that Kerouac?'"

True Bohemians in San Francisco have deserted Beatnikland by the score and want no part

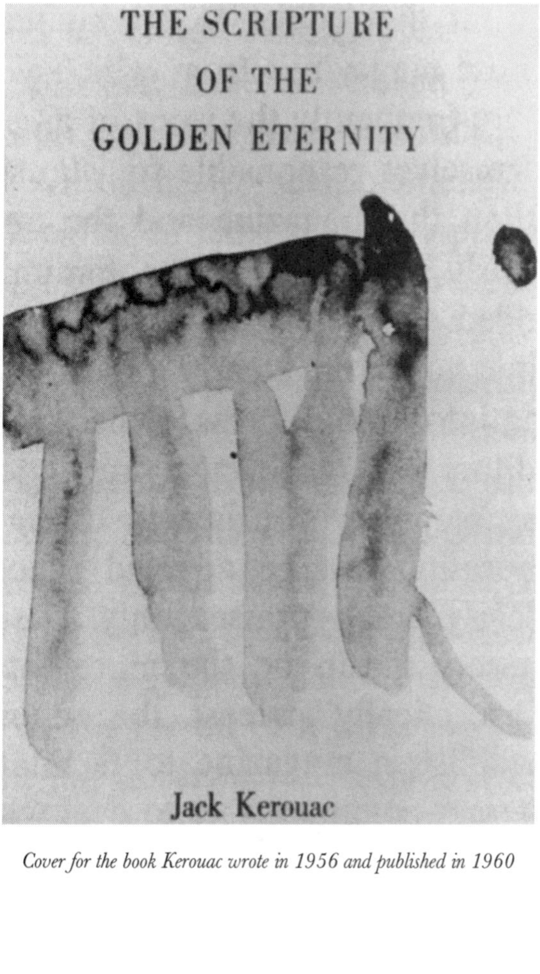
THE SCRIPTURE
OF THE
GOLDEN ETERNITY
Jack Kerouac

Cover for the book Kerouac wrote in 1956 and published in 1960

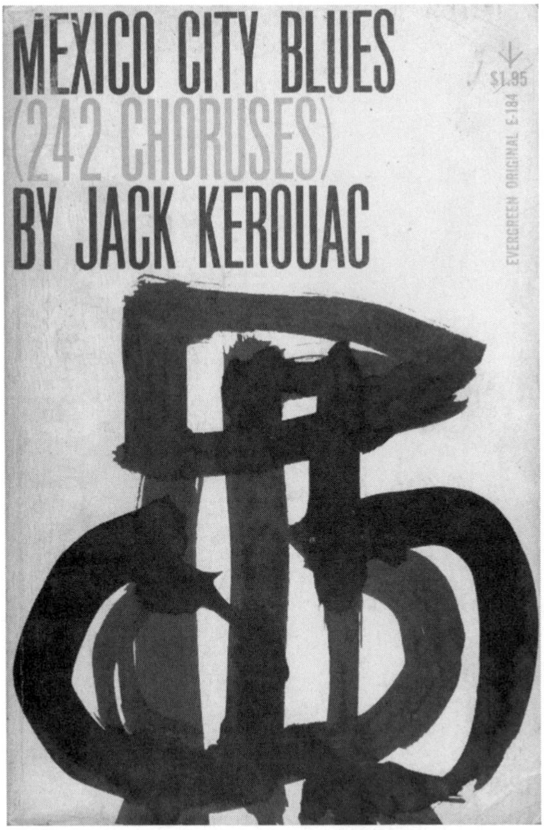

Cover for the Grove Press Evergreen Original paperback edition (1959) of the book Kerouac wrote in Mexico in 1955

of the bearded nihilists who are its inhabitants. Ironically, Jack Kerouac, hero and poet laureate of the movement, neither wears a beard, comes from San Francisco, nor lives in San Francisco. For all I know he decrys the Beatniks; certainly he works hard and produces books, which seems to be against a basic Beatnik tenet right there.

. . . .

In his newly published book–I cannot bring myself to call it a novel–Kerouac presumably has set out to show us the virtues of writing without that "laborious and dreary lying called craft and revision."

The result, unhappily, seems to me to be "stupefying in its unreadability." "Doctor Sax" is a series of mystical, unorganized reminiscences of an autobiographical nature, the formula of which seems to have been: take one part of the murkiest of Kafka, two parts of Wolfe's streamingest thoughts, three parts of the most scatological of Joyce, and then mix them all together with neither taste nor selectivity.

In Kerouac's "On the Road," though not a satisfying novel, one occasionally found flashes of fine writing, a vivid burst of description, a lovely incisive bit of characterization in a single sentence. But, except for the brief first chapter in the section entitled "The Night the Man with the Watermelon Died," I found nothing in "Doctor Sax" which might tend to lure me into trying Kerouac's system of writing without craft and revision.

I believe that there is a great confusion of terms in Kerouac's mind. Stringing dirty words together does not constitute courageous writing, sloppiness does not make spontaneity, and spilling out one's youthful neuroses does not always make for interesting and life-enhancing reading.

William Saroyan used to tell me that he never rewrote, and perhaps he didn't. But he had craftsmanship whether he was aware of it or not, and he had charm and compassion and invention and taste, and these are ingredients which seem to shriek of their absence in this work of Kerouac's.

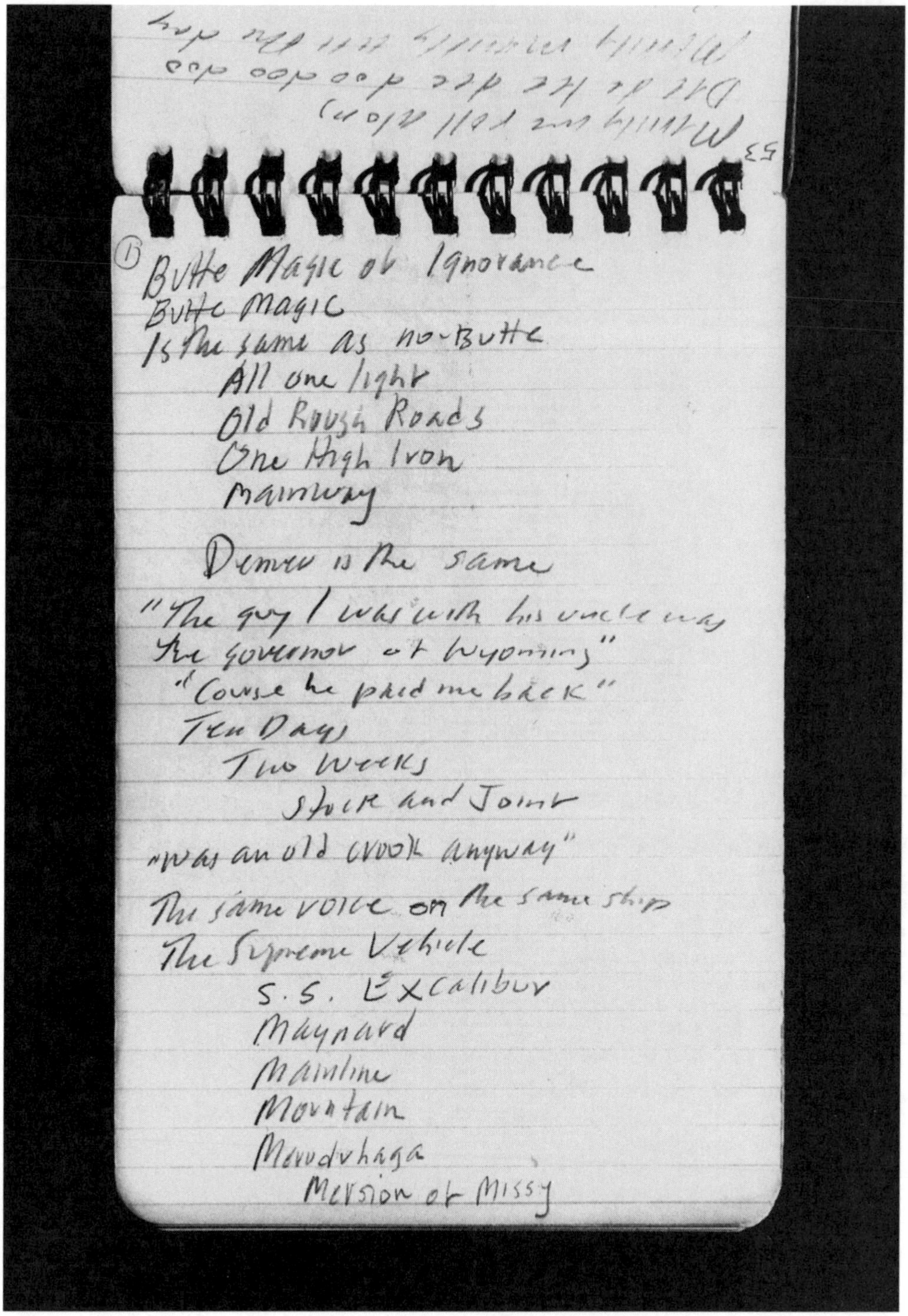

Notebook passage and corrected galley page of the opening chorus of Mexico City Blues. *The handwriting on the galley proof may be that of Donald Allen, who copyedited the book for Grove Press (New York Public Library).*

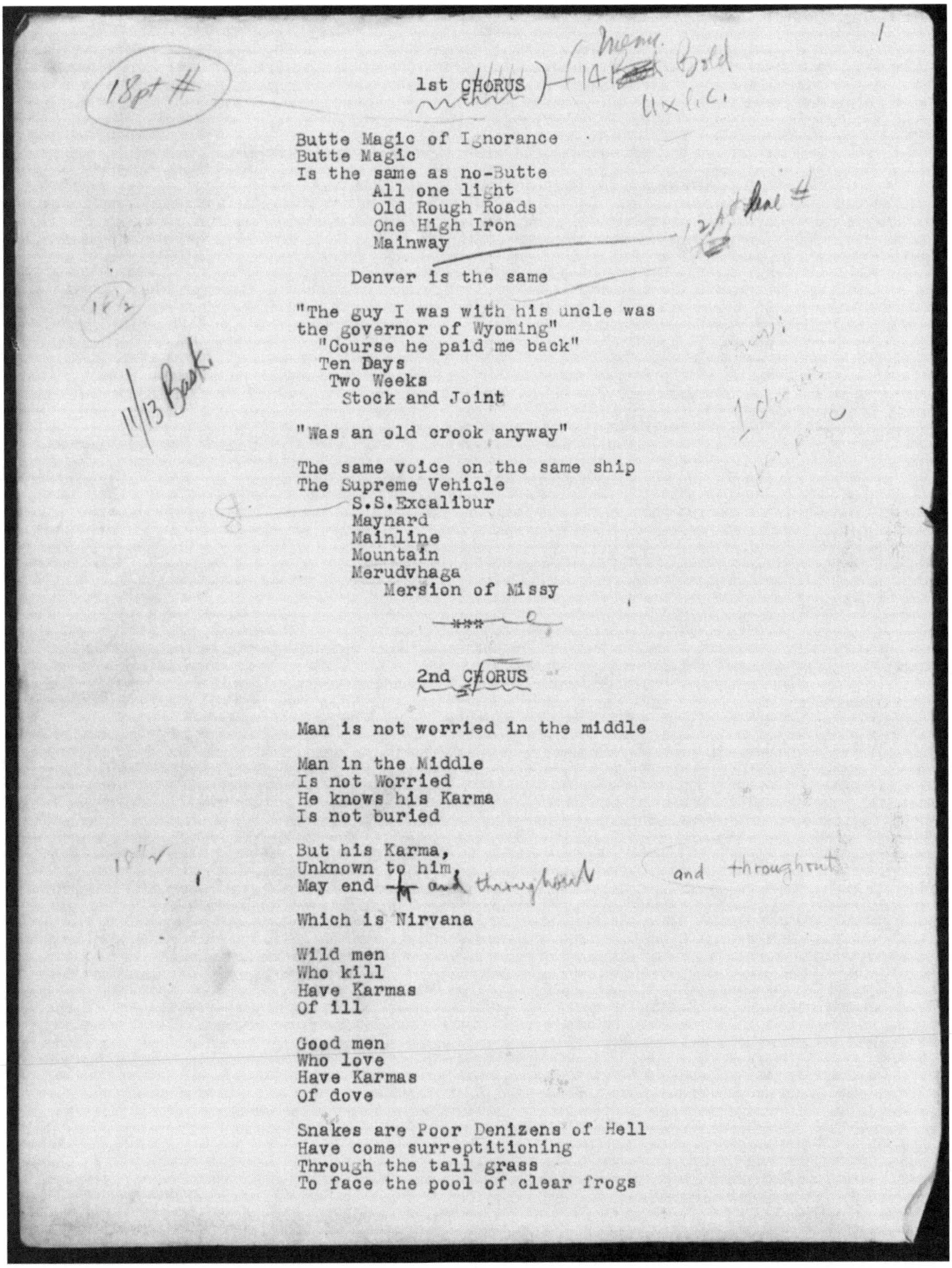

1st CHORUS

Butte Magic of Ignorance
Butte Magic
Is the same as no-Butte
All one light
Old Rough Roads
One High Iron
Mainway

Denver is the same

"The guy I was with his uncle was
the governor of Wyoming"
"Course he paid me back"
Ten Days
Two Weeks
Stock and Joint

"Was an old crook anyway"

The same voice on the same ship
The Supreme Vehicle
S.S.Excalibur
Maynard
Mainline
Mountain
Merudvhaga
Mersion of Missy

***

2nd CHORUS

Man is not worried in the middle

Man in the Middle
Is not Worried
He knows his Karma
Is not buried

But his Karma,
Unknown to him,
May end for

Which is Nirvana

Wild men
Who kill
Have Karmas
Of ill

Good men
Who love
Have Karmas
Of dove

Snakes are Poor Denizens of Hell
Have come surreptitioning
Through the tall grass
To face the pool of clear frogs

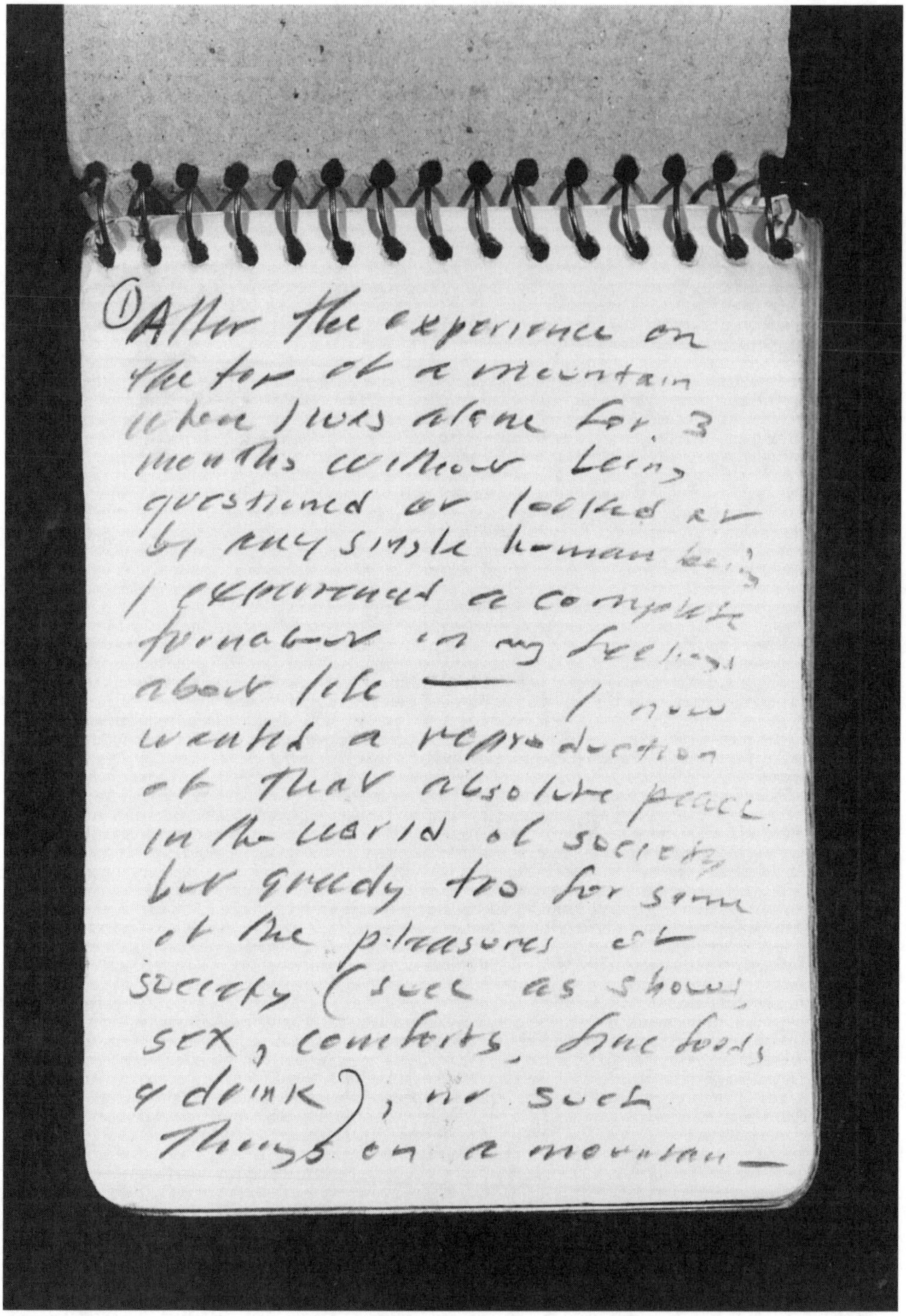
(1) After the experience on the top of a mountain where I was alone for 3 months without being questioned or looked at by any single human being, I experienced a complete turnabout in my feelings about life — I now wanted a reproduction of that absolute peace in the world of society but greedy too for some of the pleasures of society (such as shows, sex, comforts, fine food, & drink), no such things on a mountain —

Notebook page that Kerouac wrote in Mexico City in 1961 and later used as the beginning of the second section of Desolation Angels, *"Passing Through"*

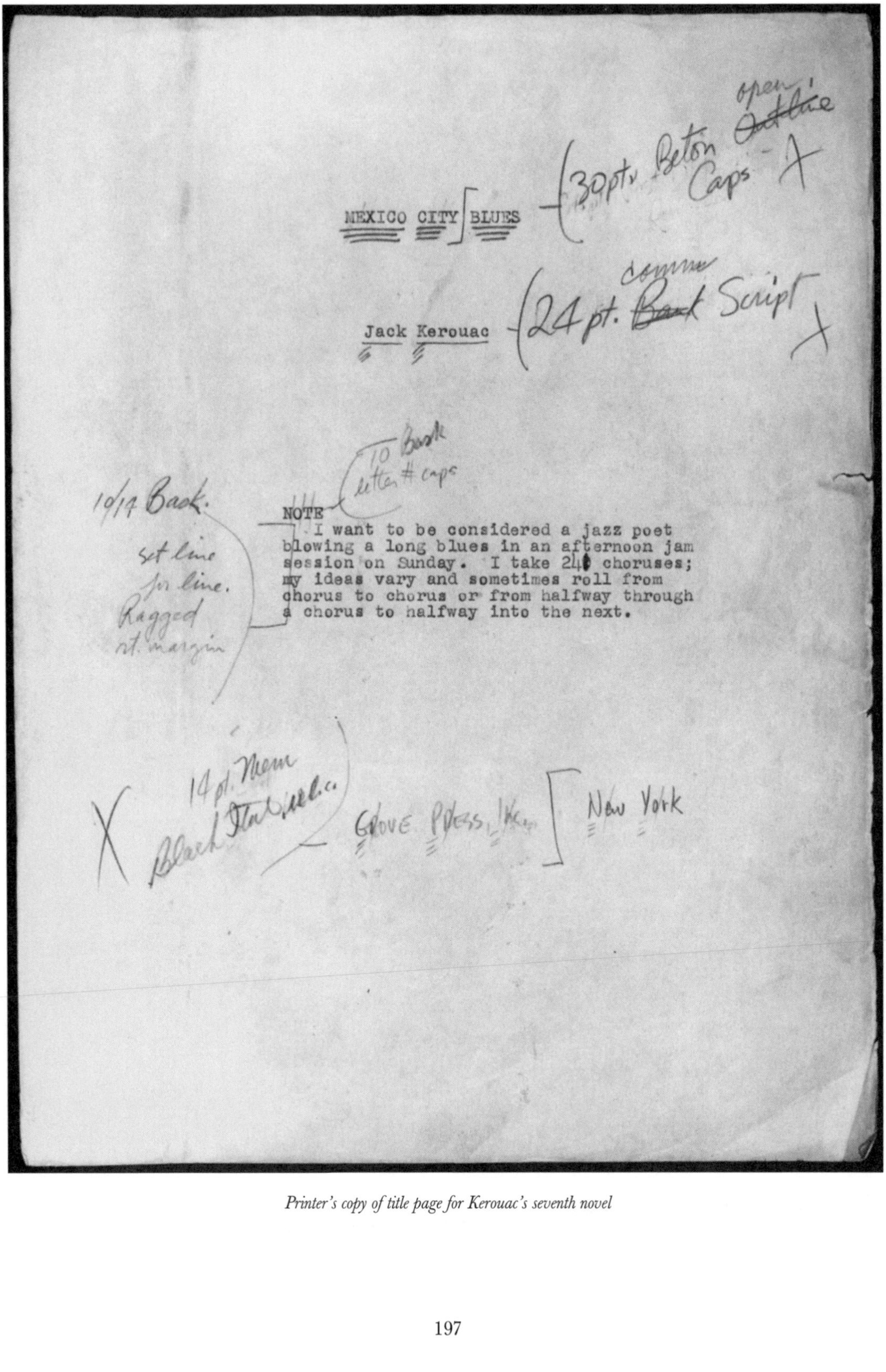
MEXICO CITY BLUES

Jack Kerouac

NOTE
I want to be considered a jazz poet blowing a long blues in an afternoon jam session on Sunday. I take 242 choruses; my ideas vary and sometimes roll from chorus to chorus or from halfway through a chorus to halfway into the next.

GROVE PRESS, INC.
New York

30 pt. Beton open Caps
24 pt. Script
10/14 Bask.
set line for line.
Ragged rt. margin

Printer's copy of title page for Kerouac's seventh novel

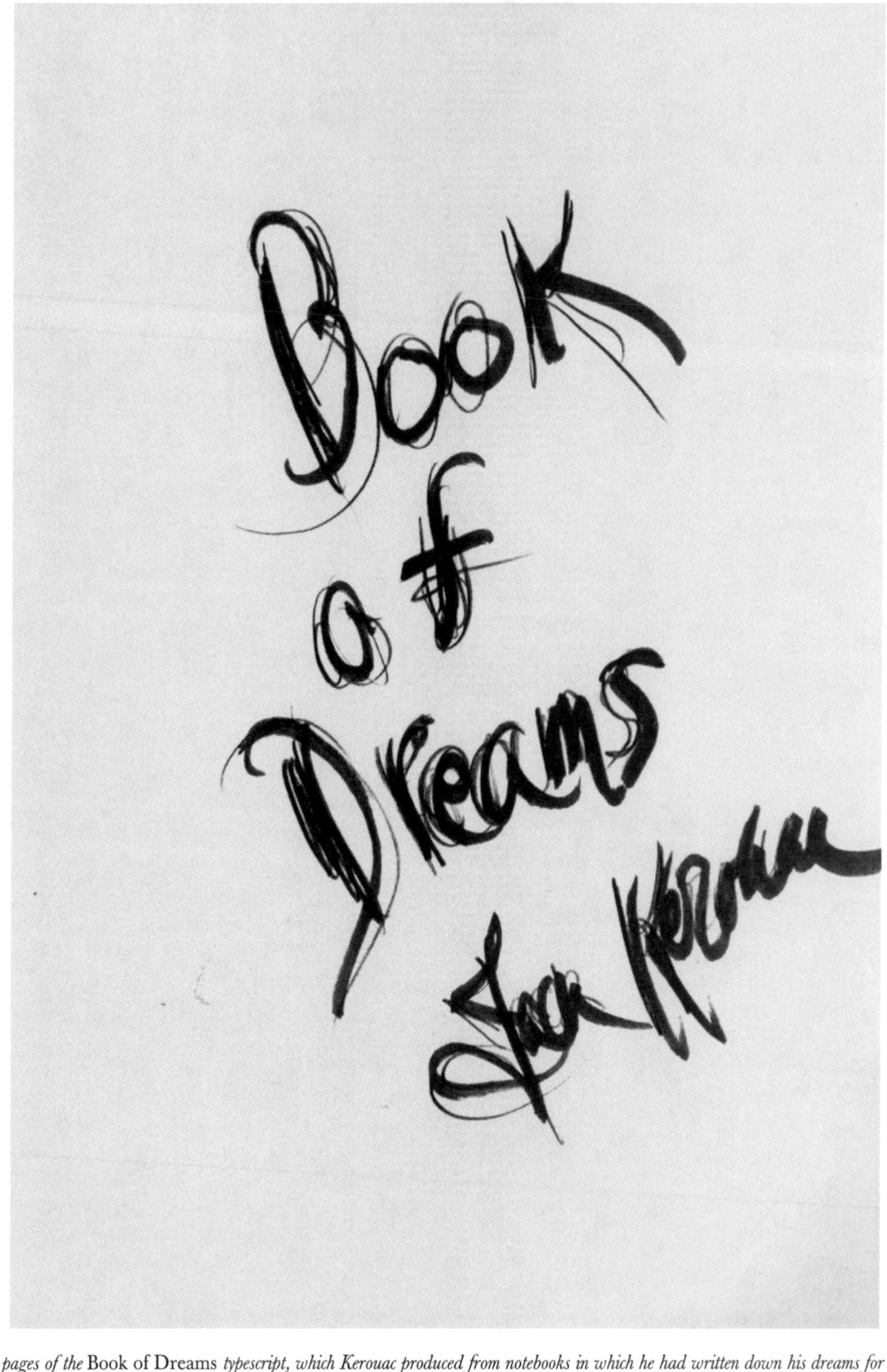

First pages of the Book of Dreams *typescript, which Kerouac produced from notebooks in which he had written down his dreams for eight years. Originally Kerouac had typed in the actual names of his friends, but he changed the names for publication. The handwritten emendations show that Neal and Carolyn Cassady become "Cody" and "Evelyn," and Bill (Burroughs) becomes "Bull" (New York Public Library).*

JUNIOR'S FAMOUS
Knick Kids Laugh
Old Bones Are Safest Bones
69
Irvkup Carries the Big A
It's Academic
GIRLS WANTED
YOUNGBLOOD
EVERYBODY LOVES
BELLY DANCERS
NUT
Buttonwood Nursery
Irish May Go
Bill Hong
You Don't Have to be Pregnant
Walter Mitty
Assesses
Li'l Terriers Take a Big Bite
Be chewsy.
'69 Bear
69
CAN
Portrait
Rectal Itch
HOOKAHAKAHA
THINK YOU'RE SITTING
Planning a Night
Swap
Sadair Has a Date
IN WHITE AMERICA
Warsaw
2 FAM BRK
WALT WHITMAN
"12 REPLIES,
TORSO
SWEETHEART
ALIZA KASHI
SAMALOT
69
peter's BACKYARD
crowded tombstones?

1

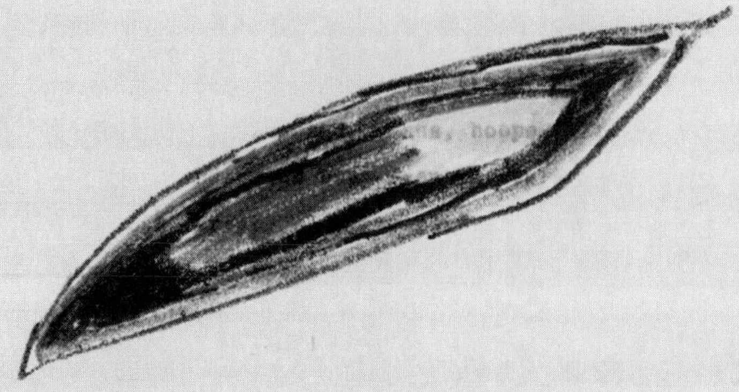

OH! THE HORRIBLE VOYAGES I've had to take across the country and back with gloomy railroads and stations you never dreamed of---one of em a horrible pest of bats and crap holes and incomprehensible parks and rains, I can't see the end of it on all horizons, this is the book of dreams.

Jesus life is dreary, how can a man live let alone work---sleeps and dreams himself to the other side---and that's where your Wolf is ten times worse than preetypop knows---and how, look, I stopped---<u>how can a man lie and say shit when he has gold in his mouth</u>. Cincinnati, Philarkadelphia, Fronio, stations in the Flue---rain town, graw flub, Beelzabur and Hemptown I've been to all of them and read Finnegain's Works what will it do me good if I dont stop and righten the round wrong in my poor bedighted b--what word is it?--skull...

Talk, talk, talk---

Cody Evelyn

I went and saw Neal and Carolyn, it all be-

Bull

gan in Mexico, on Bill's ratty old couch I purely dreamed that I was riding a white horse down a side street in that North town like in Maine but really off Highway Maine with the rainy night porches

Book of Dreams *typescript (cont.)*

Unmailed letter to Tom Guinzburg '62

Jan. 17 1962

Dear Tom

Sterling tells me you feel very sad about the Big Sur business---But as I told you, when FS&Cudahy took Visions of Gerard, which Malcolm Cowley rejected summarily, they exercised their option on the next work, which is Big Sur---Now remember if you will, for instance, that Malcolm rejected Maggie Cassidy as a full whole work by itself and wanted to publish it with miscellaneous short stories because as a novel it was "too thin"---Nevertheless Avon Books bought it whole and entire, as a novel, and advanced $7500 on it (this was before Hearst bought Avon books and subsequently stopped the distribution of my books there, as far as I can gather from never seeing it anywhere) (or the other $7500 novel, Tristessa, which was also turned down by Malcolm). Malcolm just turned down everything: Gerard as well as Doctor Sax/ Subterraneans as well as Desolation Angels which is the last available novel I have(already written)in my desk---And he even had Dharma Bums mutilated beyond recognition and I had to pay you $500 to have it restored to the original condition I wrote it in, receiving the bill from Viking which says "Alterations" when the bill should have read "Restorations." But my point here is this: first, would your editors have accepted Big Sur?, and secondly, would they have advanced me the princely sum FS&Cudahy advanced for it? (biggest I ever got), and with the understanding that not a word is to be changed? Goddamit Tom, I had a rough time even after the social boom of On the Road getting as much as a $2000 advance on Dharma Bums! (I realize you werent the boss then, I dont mean your father but the old literary men in there who never even shook my hand because they thought I was a hoodlum). They were more excited about Dennis Murphy. That was because he wrote more like the 1920's than I did. My business is not to write like in the 1920's but the make a new literature, which I've done. You wouldnt have a Ken Kesey today without somebody breaking the ground & springing personal story-telling loose from "fictional" devices.

From what Sterling says you feel real bad---If you want a definite promise from me, in writing, as here, for the option on my next book, which I'll write late 1962 after traveling around, here it is. I made no definite promise about Big Sur, I just wanted to show it to you first because I liked you personally and I wanted to go back to firstclass publishing and figured things might have changed since you took over the reins of the company. But when Straus offered me that juicy offer I figured I needed the money. Everybody is making money off my ideas, like these Route 66 TV producers, everybody except me so when they offered me ten grand advance I took it. (Besides, as you know, I have old associations and memories with Bob Giroux from 1950 when he edited The Town and the City rather badly but not from any mean motive.) It seems no publisher wants me to exceed 490 pages tho everybody else is allowed to do so. Ah, it's a disgusting business, I'm sorry about how you feel, your feelings mean something to me...I remember the party at MacManuses' and what you said there...would it really make things up if I promised you my next novel? Really, tell me, frankly, let me know... And would you 've honestly advanced ten grand for Big Sur? Now, come on, tell me. Let's straighten this out. Sterling is very concerned I think for personal reasons mostly. It all happened in a flash over the phone, I was joking with Giroux about a huge advance and he said "Okay"---(we were phoning about Gerard manuscript)---It's not against my principles to offer you my next novel because I can offer the one after that to FS&Cudahy according to their own optional demands. As for "Desolation Angels," that was rejected by Malcolm, and is wanted by Grove, but we dont want to offer it just yet so's not to clash on publishing dates. Meanwhile Tom please assure me in a letter or note goddamit that my main business is WRITING books, after all....after all I'm not a businessman. My father <u>was</u> but he also wasnt a novelist. If novels you can call them. Narrative sections of one long life story is what my "novels" are... Well, finally, if you have to show this letter to Malcolm tell him for me that I will always remember how he helped me get published in the beginning but he shouldnt have expected me to write like his 1920 heroes after I got On the Road out of my system and hit out on my own style....I've nothing to do with Scott Fitzgerald and much to do with Joyce and Proust.... Please answer something, Marine

Jack

Unsent letter in which Kerouac discusses his reasons for not selling Big Sur *to Viking. He sold the book to Farrar, Straus and Cudahy in a deal that included* Visions of Gerard. *Kerouac's advance for* Big Sur *was $10,000 (New York Public Library).*

Reflecting on Fame in *Big Sur*

Lion and Cubs
Time, 14 September 1962, p. 106

Nobody was planning to give Kerouac the Nobel Prize for *On the Road, The Dharma Bums* or the string of other books about himself (under the fictional name Jack Duluoz) that cheerfully celebrate the joys of bed, bumming and Zen Buddhism. But he had a rollicking, coin-as-you-go poetic style that recreated a direct, personal, uniquely American experience. He seemed secure as a perpetual adolescent–free of thought, full of feeling, blessedly zooming back and forth across the country.

Alas, a cruel thought has intruded upon Kerouac's world. Though he has managed to write a book about this fell experience, it is clear that things will never be the same again–"like those pathetic five highschool kids," he explains, "who came to my door one night wearing jackets that said 'Dharma Bums' on them, all expecting me to be 25 years old . . . and here I am old enough to be their father."

What can a beat do when he is too old to go on the road? He can go on the sauce. In *Big Sur* Jack does.

Early in Big Sur, *Kerouac describes his flight from a life of distractions.*

It's the first trip I've taken away from home (my mother's house) since the publication of "Road" the book that "made me famous" and in fact so much so I've been driven mad for three years by endless telegrams, phonecalls, requests, mail, visitors, reporters, snoopers (a big voice saying in my basement window as I prepare to write a story:–ARE YOU BUSY?) or the time the reporter ran upstairs to my bedroom as I sat there in my pajamas trying to write down a dream Teenagers jumping the six-foot fence I'd had built around my yard for privacy–Parties with bottles yelling at my study window "Come on out and get drunk, all work and no play makes Jack a dull boy!"–A woman coming to my door and saying "I'm not going to ask you if you're Jack Duluoz because I know he wears a beard, can you tell me where I can find him, I want a real beatnik at my annual Shindig party"–Drunken visitors puking in my study, stealing books and even pencils–Uninvited acquaintances staying for days because of the clean beds and good food my mother provided–Me drunk practically all the time to put on a jovial cap to keep up with all this but finally realizing I was surrounded and outnumbered and had to get away to solitude again or die–

Dust jacket for the selection of Kerouac's dreams published in 1961 by City Lights publisher Lawrence Ferlinghetti

So Lorenzo Monsanto wrote and said "Come to my cabin, no one'll know," etc. so I had sneaked into San Francisco as I say, coming 3000 miles from my home in Long Island (Northport) in a pleasant roomette on the California Zephyr train watching America roll by outside my private picture window, really happy for the first time in three years, staying in the roomette all three days and three nights with my instant coffee and sandwiches–Up the Hudson Valley and over across New York State to Chicago and then the Plains, the mountains, the desert, the final mountains of California, all so easy and dreamlike compared to my old harsh hitch hikings before I made enough to take transcontinental trains (all over America highschool and college kids thinking "Jack Duluoz is 26 years old and on the road all the time hitch hiking" while there I am almost 40 years old, bored and jaded in a roomette bunk crashin across that Salt Flat).

–*Big Sur,* pp. 4–5

BIG SUR
JACK KEROUAC

Dust jacket for the 1962 book, written in ten nights in October 1961, in which Kerouac recounts the costs of his notoriety and his heavy drinking after the publication of his first books

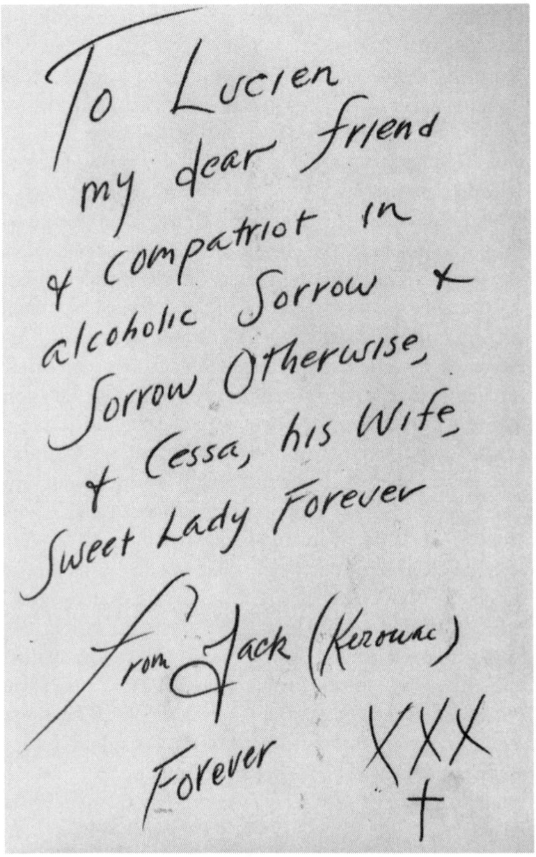
To Lucien
my dear friend
& compatriot in
alcoholic Sorrow &
Sorrow Otherwise,
& Cessa, his Wife,
Sweet Lady Forever
from Jack (Kerouac)
Forever XXX

Kerouac inscription to his longtime friend Lucien Carr in Big Sur *(New York Public Library)*

Ferlinghetti recalled the circumstances of Kerouac's writing of Big Sur *and his near meeting with Henry Miller.*

You know, Miller was attracted to Kerouac at one point. He discovered Kerouac quite late, evidently. I remember when *Dharma Bums* came out. Jack was out here and he was going to go to Big Sur to stay in my cabin. That is when he wrote a book called *Big Sur.* His editors must have named it, because it had nothing to do with Big Sur. He never really got into the Sur at all, never got south of Bixby Canyon. Miller was turned on to the *Dharma Bums.* They were talking to each other on the phone. Jack was here in City Lights and Miller was in Big Sur. They were going to meet for dinner at Ephraim Donner's house in Carmel Highlands. Miller went to Donner's and Jack was drinking in town here. The afternoon kept getting later and later. Kerouac kept saying, "We'll get there, we'll leave soon . . ." It got later and later and Jack kept telling them on the phone, "We're leaving now. We'll be there in three hours . . . two-and-a-half hours, we'll make it in two . . . Cassady will drive me . . . we'll be there in no time. See you at seven." At seven Kerouac is still in town drinking. Eight o'clock. Nine o'clock . . . Miller is sitting, waiting. Kerouac never got there. And I don't think they ever did meet. That was the end of it.

–*San Francisco Poets,* p. 159

Squaring off the Corners
Herbert Gold
The Saturday Review, 22 September 1962, p. 29

The time and the book have come for the Kerouac revival. In the span of about five years, Jack Kerouac, promoted from the rank of boy wonder, shot across the horizon with the adolescent, the jaded, and the symptom-coddlers in hot pursuit; and thus he arrived at the difficult position of a shopworn ancestor while still learning to be a writer. Multitudes at first read every word he wrote and then, almost at once, stopped reading any word he might write. Kerouac himself insured his decline. The flood of trivia that followed "On the Road" simply wearied many readers despite all its willed exuberance.

Now at last, in "Big Sur," Kerouac has begun to fulfill the promises of humor and pathos that could be found among the goopy pretenses of his thirteen (yes, I counted them!) other books. The story is, as usual, frankly autobiographical. The writer returns to the scene of his crimes in beatnik San Francisco, thinks himself cracking up some more, hies himself to a cabin in the woods, writes a poem on a beach, insists he is cracking up, flees, parties, finds boys, finds girls, finds a *real woman* (her son watches them make love), and finally really does crack up due to too much sweet wine. Then he recovers and takes to drinking dry wine.

Well, that sounds something like his other books, doesn't it? (Or don't it? As he writes in his populist mood.) But it is different. There is a real pathos in the forty-year-old hip hero whose house is invaded by high school rebels wearing sweat shirts labeled "Dharma Bums." He is their cause. But where is *his* cause? He meets the fact squarely that he is not the great sex hero he has made himself out to be; he loves his mother and his cat. He is not a Zen saint either; he is a weary boozer. He finds that he doesn't enjoy hitchhiking and gets blisters from walking too much. He makes a bed and recommends it as "good for the back"–an older man's recommendation for a bed.

He still uses those words–"goopy," "gooky," "goofy"–with a small-boy delight in Jello and horseplay; but he knows a little of where they belong and something of who the man using them is. Or if he doesn't know, he gives honest evidence. The book is full of sweet scenes of gabble and camping, woodsy rustlings and city chatter; there is a marvelously funny and touching description of a dodging and ducking inability to make a formal farewell to a friend in a tuberculosis sanitarium. The friends tease and jump and camp and really care for each other.

Of course, the pretensions of style and the sticky indulgences of egotism have not been extirpated. Literary references to everyone from Proust to Emily Dickinson still belie the purity and innocence of the attack on experience. A section devoted to delirium represents a naked launching into the techniques of William Burroughs and therefore fails to produce the effect of horror intended. A pastiche is not a nightmare is not a direct experience. And the poem by the hero Jack Duluoz-Jack Kerouac, which concludes the book, has none of the justifying power of the poems written by Pasternak's Dr. Zhivago or John Shade in Nabokov's "Pale Fire." It reads like what Demosthenes might have howled at the sea if he had filled his mouth with gook instead of pebbles.

Kerouac in Ginsberg's Manhattan apartment in 1964
(© Allen Ginsberg Trust)

Nevertheless, the portrait of the beat monster trying to escape from his role, to regain his role, to grow up, to remain a child, is in focus, troubling and touching. Kerouac no longer has to bark "Wow!" and parrot Zen catchwords in order to assure us that he is deep and has a soul. He gives a shrewd estimate of his role as a self-conscious actor in "God's movie, which is us," and finds it limiting both for God and to himself. He views his own willed simplicity with a harder eye. This developing severity is a real accomplishment. His misery is that of the twiceborn man. "A long way to go," he says, and we know that he is thinking of death and how short the way really is.

There once seemed a chance that Jack Kerouac might be a writer in addition to being a phenomenon. "Big Sur" tells us that the chance is not only still alive and glowing, but that Kerouac is on the right road at last.

2/25

Feb.19 63

Dear Bob

Am now starting on VANITY OF DULUOZ by first studying all letters, photos, writings and memory-stuff of that time (1939-to-1946) and making notes.

The novel already written, called PASSING THROUGH, that I said I'd type up for you, I'm leaving untyped in the drawer awhile (it covers 1956-to-1957), because it's not in the mood that I'm in now and would only interfere in what I want to do now.

PASSING THROUGH is the sequel to DESOLATION ANGELS. You havent told me whether you ever want to publish ANGELS; I suppose you will. It might be good to make it run from VISONS OF GERARD 1963, VANITY OF DULUOZ 1964 (if completed), DESOLATION ANGELS 1965, and PASSING THROUGH 1966, tho of course I'll have something else written by then, referring to later events in Duluoz Legend.

Anyway all's well in my writing life. I had some stunning ~~throughts~~ thoughts last night, the result of studying Tolstoi, Spengler, New Testament and also the result of praying to St.Mary to intercede for me to make me stop being a maniacal drunkard. Ever since I instituted the little prayer, I've not been lushing. So far, every prayer addressed to the Holy Mother has been answered, and I only "discovered" her last Halloween. I shouldnt be telling you this. But I do want to point out, the reason I think she intercedes so well for us, is because she too is a human being, who was simply chosen to suckle and care for an incarnated Darmasha, after all. Of what use would Jesus be to us if he didnt have to have a mother's care?

How's Dramheller's drawings?

Listening to the Vespers of Mozart & [illegible]

As ever Jack

Letter in which Kerouac discusses the sale of recent works. "Passing Through" was published as the second half of Desolation Angels. *"Dramheller" may be James Spanfeller, who illustrated the first edition of* Visions of Gerard *(New York Public Library).*

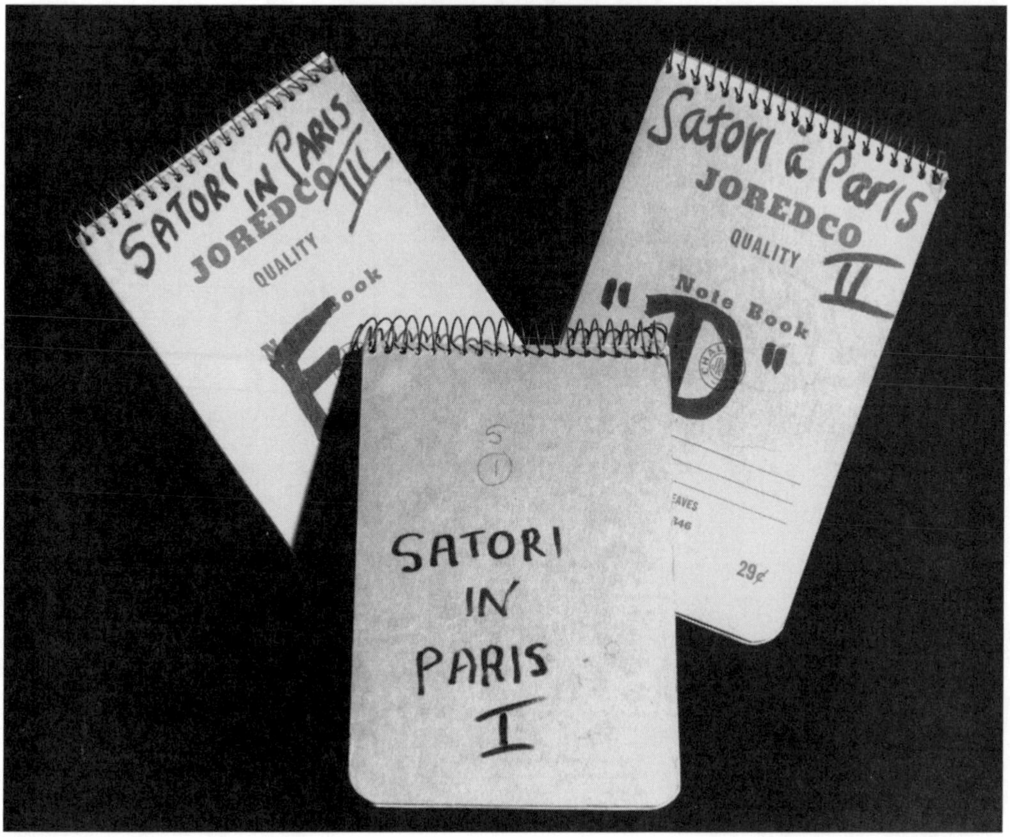

Notebooks in which Kerouac wrote Satori in Paris *in one week in 1965 (New York Public Library)*

The Paris Review Interview

Poets Aram Saroyan and Duncan McNaughton accompanied interviewer Ted Berrigan when he visited Kerouac at his home in Lowell in 1967. Also present at the interview was Kerouac's third wife, Stella Samppas Kerouac, the sister of his Lowell friend Sebastian Sampas. They were married on 19 November 1966.

The Art of Fiction XLI: Jack Kerouac
Ted Berrigan
Writers at Work: The Paris Review *Interviews,* Fourth Series, pp. 538–572

INTERVIEWER: Could we put the footstool over here to put this on?

STELLA: Yes.

KEROUAC: God, you're so inadequate there, Berrigan.

INTERVIEWER: Well, I'm no tape-recorder man, Jack. I'm just a big talker, like you. O.K. we're off.

KEROUAC: O.K.? (*Whistles*) O.K.?

INTERVIEWER: Actually I'd like to start . . . the first book I ever read by you, oddly enough, since most people first read *On the Road* . . . the first one I read was *The Town and the City*. . . .

KEROUAC: Gee!

INTERVIEWER: I checked it out of the library. . . .

KEROUAC: Gee! . . . Did you read *Dr. Sax*? . . . *Tristessa*? . . .

INTERVIEWER: You better believe it. I even read *Rimbaud*. I have a copy of *Visions of Cody* that Ron Padgett bought in Tulsa, Oklahoma.

KEROUAC: Screw Ron Padgett! You know why? He started a little magazine called *White Dove Review* in Kansas City, was it? Tulsa? Oklahoma . . . yes. He wrote, Start our magazine off by sending us a great big poem. So I sent him the "Thrashing Doves." And then I sent him another one and he rejected the second one because his magazine was already started.

Dust jacket for Kerouac's book that was published in 1966 by Grove Press

That's to show you how punks try to make their way by scratching down on a man's back. Aw, he's no poet. You know who's a great poet? I know who the great poets are.

INTERVIEWER: Who?

KEROUAC: Let's see, is it . . . William Bissette of Vancouver. An Indian boy. Bill Bissette, or Bissonnette.

SAROYAN: Let's talk about Jack Kerouac.

KEROUAC: He's not better than Bill Bissette, but he's very original.

INTERVIEWER: Why don't we begin with editors. How do you . . .

KEROUAC: O.K. All my editors since Malcolm Cowley have had instructions to leave my prose exactly as I wrote it. In the days of Malcolm Cowley, with *On the Road* and *The Dharma Bums,* I had no power to stand by my style for better or for worse. When Malcolm Cowley made endless revisions and inserted thousands of needless commas like, say, Cheyenne, Wyoming (why not just say Cheyenne Wyoming and let it go at that, for instance), why, I spent $500 making the complete restitution of the *Bums* manuscript and got a bill from Viking Press called "Revisions." Ha ho ho. And so you asked about how do I work with an editor . . . well, nowadays I am just grateful to him for his assistance in proofreading the manuscript and in discovering logical errors, such as dates, names of places. For instance in my last book I wrote Firth of Forth then looked it up, on the suggestion of my editor, and found that I'd really sailed off the Firth of Clyde. Things like that. Or I spelled Aleister Crowley "Alisteir," or he discovered little mistakes about the yardage in football games . . . and so forth. By not revising what you've already written you simply give the reader the actual workings of your mind during the writing itself: you confess your thoughts about events in your own unchangeable way . . . well, look, did you ever hear a guy telling a long wild tale to a bunch of men in a bar and all are listening and smiling, did you ever hear that guy stop to revise himself, go back to a previous sentence to improve it, to defray its rhythmic thought impact . . . If he pauses to blow his nose, isn't he planning his next sentence? and when he lets that next sentence loose, isn't it once and for all the way he wanted to say it? Doesn't he depart the thought of that sentence and, as Shakespeare says, "forever holds his tongue" on the subject, since he's passed over it like a part of the river flows over a rock once and for all and never returns and can never flow any other way in time? Incidentally, as for my bug against periods, that was for the prose in *October in the Railroad Earth,* very experimental, intended to clack along all the way like a steam engine pulling a 100-car freight with a talky caboose at the end, that was my way at the time and it still can be done if the thinking during the swift writing is confessional and pure and all excited with the life of it. And be sure of this, I spent my entire youth writing slowly with revisions and endless re-hashing speculation and deleting and got so I was writing one sentence a day and the sentence had no FEELING. Goddamn it, FEELING is what I like in art, not CRAFTINESS and the hiding of feelings.

INTERVIEWER: What encouraged you to use the "spontaneous" style of *On the Road?*

KEROUAC: I got the idea for the spontaneous style of *On the Road* from seeing how good old Neal Cassady wrote his letters to me, all first person, fast, mad, confessional, completely serious, all detailed, with real names in his case however (being letters). I remembered also Goethe's admonition, well Goethe's prophecy that the future literature of the West would be confessional in nature; also Dostoyevsky prophesied as much and might have started in on that if he'd lived long enough to do his projected masterwork, *The Great Sinner*. Cassady also began his early youthful writing with attempts at slow, painstaking, and-all-that-crap craft business, but got sick of it like I did, seeing it wasn't getting out his guts and heart the way it *felt* coming out. But I got the flash from his style. It's a cruel lie for those West Coast punks to say that I got the idea of *On the Road* from him. All his letters to me were about his younger days before I met him, a child with his father, et cetera, and about his later teenage experiences. The letter he sent me is erroneously reported to be a 13,000-word letter . . . no, the 13,000-word piece was his novel *The First Third,* which he kept in his possession. The letter, the main letter I mean, was 40,000 words long, mind you, a whole short novel. It was the greatest piece of writing I ever saw, better'n anybody in America, or at least enough to make Melville, Twain, Dreiser, Wolfe, I dunno who, spin in their graves. Allen Ginsberg asked me to lend him this vast letter so he could read it. He read it, then loaned it to a guy called Gerd Stern who lived on a houseboat in Sausalito California, in 1955, and this fellow lost the letter: overboard I presume. Neal and I called it, for convenience, the *Joan Anderson Letter* . . . all about a Christmas weekend in the poolhalls, hotel rooms, and jails of Denver, with hilarious events throughout and tragic too, even a drawing of a window, with measurements to make the reader understand, all that. Now listen: this letter would have been printed under Neal's copyright, if we could find it, but as you know, it was my property as a letter to me, so Allen shouldn't have been so careless with it, nor the guy on the houseboat. If we can unearth this entire 40,000-word letter Neal shall be justified. We also did so much fast talking between the two of us, on tape recorders, way back in 1952, and listened to them so much, we both got the secret of LINGO in telling a tale and figured that was the only way to express the speed and tension and ecstatic tomfoolery of the age. . . . Is that enough?

INTERVIEWER: How do you think this style has changed since *On the Road?*

KEROUAC: What style? Oh, the style of *On the Road.* Well as I say, Cowley riddled the original style of the manuscript there, without my power to complain, and since then my books are all published as written, as I say, and the style has varied from the highly experimental speedwriting of *Railroad Earth* to the ingrown-toenail-packed mystical style of *Tristessa,* the *Notes from the Underground* (by Dostoyevsky) confessional madness of *The Subterraneans,* the perfection of the three as one in *Big Sur,* I'd say, which tells a plain tale in a smooth buttery literate run, to *Satori in Paris* which is really the first book I wrote with drink at my side (cognac and malt liquor) . . . and not to overlook *Book of Dreams,* the style of a person half awake from sleep and ripping it out in pencil by the bed . . . yes, pencil . . . what a job! bleary eyes, insaned mind bemused and mystified by sleep, details that pop out even as you write them you don't know what they mean, till you wake up, have coffee, look at it, and see the logic of dreams in dream language itself, see?. . . and finally I decided in my tired middle age to slow down and did *Vanity of Duluoz* in a more moderate style so that, having been so esoteric all these years, some earlier readers would come back and see what ten years had done to my life and thinking . . . which is after all the only thing I've got to offer, the true story of what I saw and how I saw it.

INTERVIEWER: You dictated sections of *Visions of Cody.* Have you used this method since?

KEROUAC: I didn't dictate sections of *Visions of Cody.* I typed up a segment of taped conversation with Neal Cassady, or Cody, talking about his early adventures in L.A. It's four chapters. I haven't used this method since; it really doesn't come out right, well, with Neal and with myself, when all written down and with all the Ahs and the Ohs and the Ahums and the fearful fact that the damn thing is turning and you're *forced* not to waste electricity or tape. . . . Then again, I don't know, I might have to resort to that eventually; I'm getting tired and going blind. This question stumps me. At any rate, everybody's doing it, I hear, but I'm still scribbling. . . . McLuhan says we're getting more oral so I guess we'll all learn to talk into the machine better and better.

INTERVIEWER: What is that state of "Yeatsian semi-trance" which provides the ideal atmosphere for spontaneous writing?

KEROUAC: Well, there it is, how can you be in a trance with your mouth yapping away . . . writing at least is a silent meditation even though you're going 100 miles an hour. Remember that scene in *La Dolce Vita* where the old priest is mad because a mob of maniacs have shown up to see the tree where the kids saw the Virgin Mary? He says, "Visions are not available in all this frenetic foolishness and yelling and pushing; visions are only obtainable in silence and meditation." Thar. Yup.

INTERVIEWER: You have said that haiku is not written spontaneously but is reworked and revised. Is this true of all your poetry? Why must the method for writing poetry differ from that of prose?

KEROUAC: No, first; haiku is best reworked and revised. I know, I tried. It has to be completely economical, no foliage and flowers and language rhythm, it has to be a simple little picture in three little lines. At

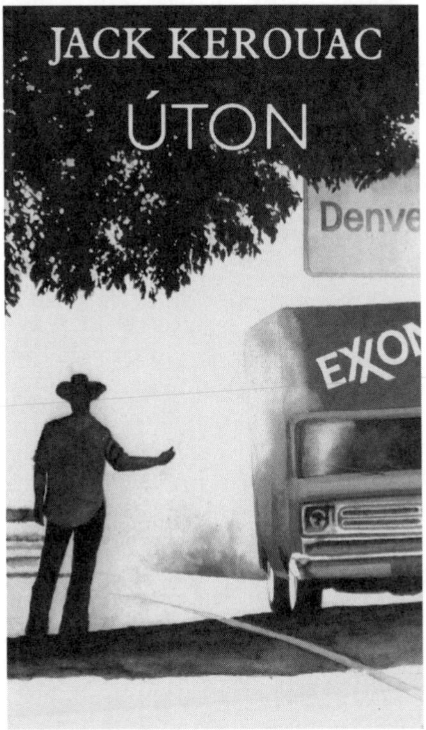

Covers for Japanese, Greek, French, and Hungarian editions of Kerouac's most famous novel

least that's the way the old masters did it, spending months on three little lines and coming up, say, with:

In the abandoned boat,
The hail
Bounces about.

That's Shiki.

But as for my regular English verse, I knocked it off fast like the prose, using, get this, the size of the notebook page for the form and length of the poem, just as a musician has to get out, a jazz musician, his statement within a certain number of bars, within one chorus, which spills over into the next, but he has to stop where the chorus page *stops*. And finally, too, in poetry you can be completely free to say anything you want, you don't have to tell a story, you can use secret puns, that's why I always say, when writing prose, "No time for poetry now, get your plain tale." (*Drinks are served*)

INTERVIEWER: How do you write haiku?

KEROUAC: Haiku? You want to hear Haiku? You see you got to compress into three short lines a great big story. First you start with a haiku situation—so you see a leaf, as I told her the other night, falling on the back of a sparrow during a great big October wind storm. A big leaf falls on the back of a little sparrow. How you going to compress that into three lines? Now in Japanese you got to compress it into seventeen syllables. We don't have to do that in American—or English—because we don't have the same syllabic bullshit that your Japanese language has. So you say: Little sparrow—you don't have to say little—everybody knows a sparrow is little . . . because they fall . . . so you say

Sparrow
With big leaf on its back—
Windstorm

No good, don't work, I reject it.

A little sparrow
When an autumn leaf suddenly sticks to its back
From the wind.

Hah, that does it. No, it's a little bit too long. See? It's already a little bit too long, Berrigan, you know what I mean?

INTERVIEWER: Seems like there's an extra work or something, like "when." How about leaving out "when"? Say:

A sparrow
An autumn leaf suddenly sticks to its back—
From the wind!

KEROUAC: Hey, that's all right. I think "when" was the extra word. You got the right idea there, O'Hara! A sparrow, an autumn leaf suddenly—we don't have to say "suddenly" do we?

A sparrow
An autumn leaf sticks to its back—
From the wind!

(*Kerouac writes final version into spiral notebook.*)

INTERVIEWER: "Suddenly" is absolutely the kind of word we don't need there. When you publish that will you give me a footnote saying you asked me a couple of questions?

KEROUAC: (*writes*): Berrigan noticed. Right?

INTERVIEWER: Do you write poetry very much? Do you write other poetry besides haiku?

KEROUAC: It's hard to write haiku. I write long silly Indian poems. You want to hear my long silly Indian Poem?

INTERVIEWER: What kind of Indian?

KEROUAC: Iroquois. As you know from looking at me. (*Reads from notebook.*)

On the lawn on the way to the store
44 years old for the neighbors to hear
hey, looka, Ma I hurt myself. Especially
with that squirt.

What's that mean?

INTERVIEWER: Say it again.

KEROUAC: Hey, look, ma, I hurt myself, while on the way to the store I hurt myself on that lawn I yell to my mother hey looka, Ma, I hurt myself. I add, especially with that squirt.

INTERVIEWER: You fell over a sprinkler?

KEROUAC: No, my father's squirt into my Ma.

INTERVIEWER: From that distance?

KEROUAC: Oh, I quit. No, I know you wouldn't get that one. I had to explain it. (*Opens notebook again and reads.*)

Goy means Joy.

INTERVIEWER: Send that one to Ginsberg.

KEROUAC (*reads*):

Happy people so called are hypocrites—it means the happiness wavelength can't work without necessary deceit, without certain scheming and lies and hiding. Hypocrisy and deceit, no Indians. No smiling.

INTERVIEWER: No Indians?

KEROUAC: The reason you really have a hidden hostility towards me, Berrigan, is because of the French and Indian War.

INTERVIEWER: That could be.

SAROYAN: I saw a football picture of you in the cellar of Horace Mann. You were pretty fat in those days.

STELLA: Tuffy! Here Tuffy! Come on kitty . . .

KEROUAC: Stella, let's have another bottle or two. Yeah, I'm going to murder everybody if they let me go. I did. Hot fudge sundaes! Boom! I used to have two or three hot fudge sundaes before every game. Lou Little . . .

INTERVIEWER: He was your coach at Columbia?

KEROUAC: Lou Little was my coach at Columbia. My father went up to him and said you sneaky long-nosed finagler. . . . He says why don't you let my son, Ti Jean, Jack, start in the Army game so he can get back at his great enemy from Lowell? And Lou Little says because he's not ready. Who says he's not ready? I say he's not ready. My father says why you long nose banana nose big crook, get out of my sight! And he comes stomping out of the office smoking a big cigar. Come out of here Jack, let's get out of here. So we left Columbia together. And also when I was in the United States Navy during the war–1942–right in front of the Admirals, he walked in and says Jack, you are right! The Germans should not be our enemies. They should be our allies, as it will be proven in time. And the Admirals were all there with their mouths open, and my father would take no shit from nobody–my father didn't have nothing but a big belly about this big (*gestures with arms out in front of him*) and he would go POOM! (*Kerouac gets up and demonstrates, by puffing his belly out in front of him with explosive force and saying POOM!*) One time he was walking down the street with my mother, arm in arm, down the lower East Side. In the old days, you know the 1940s. And here comes a whole bunch of rabbis walking arm in arm . . . tee-dah teedah-teedah . . . and they wouldn't part for this Christian man and his wife. So my father went POOM! and he knocked a rabbi right in the gutter. Then he took my mother and walked on through.

Now, if you don't like that, Berrigan, that's the history of my family. They don't take no shit from nobody. In due time I ain't going to take no shit from nobody. You can record that.

Is this my wine?

INTERVIEWER: Was *The Town and the City* written under spontaneous composition principles?

KEROUAC: Some of it, sire. I also wrote another version that's hidden under the floorboards, with Burroughs.

INTERVIEWER: Yes, I've heard rumors of that book. Everybody wants to get at that book.

KEROUAC: It's called *And the Hippos Were Boiled in Their Tanks.* The hippos. Because Burroughs and I were sitting in a bar one night and we heard a newscaster saying . . . "and so the Egyptians attacked blah blah . . . and meanwhile there was a great fire in the zoo in London and the fire raced across the fields and the hippos were boiled in their tanks! Goodnight everyone!" That's Bill, he noticed that. Because he notices them kind of things.

INTERVIEWER: You really did type up his *Naked Lunch* manuscript for him in Tangiers?

KEROUAC: No . . . the first part. The first two chapters. I went to bed, and I had nightmares . . . of great long balonies coming out of my mouth. I had nightmares typing up that manuscript . . . I said, "Bill!" He said, "Keep typing it." He said, "I bought you a goddamn kerosene stove here in North Africa, you know." Among the Arabs . . . it's hard to get a kerosene stove. I'd light up the kerosene stove, and take some bedding and a little pot, or kif as we called it there . . . or maybe sometimes hasheesh . . . there by the way it's legal . . . and I'd go toktoktoktoktoktok and when I went to bed at night, these things kept coming out of my mouth. So finally these other guys showed up like Alan Ansen and Allen Ginsberg, and they spoiled the whole manuscript because they didn't type it up the way he wrote it.

INTERVIEWER: Grove Press has been issuing his Olympia Press books with lots of changes and things added.

KEROUAC: Well, in my opinion Burroughs hasn't given us anything that would interest our breaking hearts since he wrote like he did in *Naked Lunch.* Now all he does is that break-up stuff it's called . . . where you write a page of prose, you write another page of prose . . . then you fold it over and you cut it up and you put it together . . . and shit like that . . .

INTERVIEWER: What about *Junkie,* though?

KEROUAC: It's a classic. It's better than Hemingway–it's just like Hemingway but even a little better too. It says: Danny comes into my pad one night and says, Hey, Bill, can I borrow your sap. Your sap–do you know what a sap is?

SAROYAN: A blackjack?

KEROUAC: It's a blackjack. Bill says, I pulled out my underneath drawer, and underneath some nice shirts I pulled out my blackjack. I gave it to Danny and said, Now don't lose it Danny–Danny says, Don't worry I won't lose it. He goes off and loses it.

Sap . . . blackjack . . . that's me. Sap . . . blackjack.

INTERVIEWER: That's a Haiku: sap, black jack, that's me. You better write that down.

KEROUAC: No.

INTERVIEWER: Maybe I'll write that down. Do you mind if I use that one?

KEROUAC: Up your ass with Mobil gas!

INTERVIEWER: You don't believe in collaborations? Have you ever done any collaborations, other than with publishers?

KEROUAC: I did a couple of collaborations in bed with Bill Cannastra in lofts. With blondes.

INTERVIEWER: Was he the guy that tried to climb off the subway train at Astor Place, in Holmes' *Go*?

KEROUAC: Yes. Yeah, well he says let's take all our clothes off and run around the block . . . it was raining you know. Sixteenth Street off Seventh Avenue. I said, well, I'll keep my shorts on–he says no, no shorts. I said I'm going to keep my shorts on. He said all right, but I'm not going to wear mine. And we trot trottrot trot down the block. Sixteenth to Seventeenth . . . and we come back and run up the stairs–nobody saw us.

INTERVIEWER: What time of day?

KEROUAC: But he was absolutely naked . . . about 3 or 4 a.m. It rained. And everybody was there. He was dancing on broken glass and playing Bach. Bill was the guy who used to teeter off his roof–six flights up you know? He'd go–"you want me to fall?"–we'd say no, Bill, no. He was an Italian. Italians are wild you know.

INTERVIEWER: Did he write? What did he do?

KEROUAC: He says, "Jack, come with me and look down through this peephole." We looked down through the peephole, we saw a lot of things . . . into his toilet.

I said, "I'm not interested in that, Bill." He said, "you're not interested in anything." Auden would come the next day, the next afternoon, for cocktails. Maybe with Chester Kallman. Tennessee Williams.

INTERVIEWER: Was Neal Cassady around in those days? Did you already know Neal Cassady when you were involved with Bill Cannastra?

KEROUAC: Oh yes, yes, ahem . . . he had a great big pack of pot. He always was a pot-happy man.

INTERVIEWER: Why do you think Neal doesn't write?

KEROUAC: He has written . . . beautifully! He has written better than I have. Neal's a very funny guy. He's a real Californian. We had more fun than 5000 Socony Gasoline Station attendants can have. In my opinion he's the most intelligent man I've ever met in my life. Neal Cassady. He's a Jesuit by the way. He used to sing in the choir. He was a choir boy in the Catholic churches of Denver. And he taught me everything that I now do believe about anything that there may be to be believed about divinity.

INTERVIEWER: About Edgar Cayce?

KEROUAC: No, before he found out about Edgar Cayce he told me all these things in the section of the life he led when he was on the road with me–he said, We know God, don't we Jack? I said, Yessir boy. He said, Don't we know that nothing's going to happen wrong? Yessir. And we're going to go on and on . . . and hmmmmm ja-bmmmmmmm. . . . He was perfect. And he's always perfect. Everytime he comes to see me I can't get a word in edgewise.

INTERVIEWER: You wrote about Neal playing football, in *Visions of Cody*.

KEROUAC: Yes, he was a very good football player. He picked up two beatniks that time in blue jeans in North Beach Frisco. He said I got to go, bang bang, do I got to go? He's working on the railroad . . . had his watch out . . . 2:15, boy I got to be there by 2:20. I tell you boys drive me over down there so I be on time with my train . . . So I can get my train on down to–what's the name of that place–San Jose? They say sure kid and Neal says here's the pot. So–"We maybe look like great bleat beatniks with great beards . . . but we are cops. And we are arresting you."

So, A guy went to the jailhouse and interviewed him from the *New York Post* and he said tell that Kerouac if he still believes in me to send me a typewriter. So I sent Allen Ginsberg one hundred dollars to get a typewriter for Neal. And Neal got the typewriter. And he wrote notes on it, but they wouldn't let him take the notes out. I don't know where the typewriter is. Genet wrote all of *Our Lady of the Flowers* in the shithouse . . . the jailhouse. There's a great writer, Jean Genet. He kept writing and kept writing until he got to a point where he was going to come by writing about it . . . until he came into his bed–in the can. The French can. The French jail. Prison. And that was the end of the chapter. Every chapter is Genet coming off. Which I must admit Sartre noticed.

INTERVIEWER: You think that's a different kind of spontaneous writing?

KEROUAC: Well, I could go to jail and I could write every night a chapter about Magee, Magoo, and Molly. It's beautiful. Genet is really *the* most honest writer we've had since Kerouac and Burroughs. But he came before us. He's older. Well, he's the same age as Burroughs. But I don't think I've been dishonest. Man, I've had a good time! God, man, I rode around this country free as a bee. But Genet is a very tragic and beautiful writer. And I give them the crown. And the laurel wreath. I don't give the laurel wreath to Richard Wilbur! *Or* Robert Lowell. Give it to Jean Genet and

French and Turkish editions of Kerouac's fourth novel

William Seward Burroughs. *And* to Allen Ginsberg and to Gregory Corso, especially.

INTERVIEWER: Jack, how about Peter Orlovsky's writings. Do you like Peter's things?

KEROUAC: Peter Orlovsky is an idiot!! He's a Russian idiot, Not even Russian, he's Polish.

INTERVIEWER: He's written some fine poems.

KEROUAC: Oh yeah. My . . . what poems?

INTERVIEWER: He has a beautiful poem called "Second Poem."

KEROUAC: "My brother pisses in the bed . . . and I go in the subway and I see two people kissing . . ."

INTERVIEWER: No, the poem that says "It's more creative to paint the floor than to sweep it."

KEROUAC: That's a lot of shit! That is the kind of poetry that was written by another Polish idiot who was a Polish nut called Apollinaire. Apollinaire is not his real name, you know.

There are some fellows in San Francisco that told me that Peter was an idiot. But I like idiots, and I enjoy his poetry. Think about that, Berrigan. But for my taste, it's Gregory.

Give me one of those.

INTERVIEWER: One of these pills?

KEROUAC: Yeah. What are they? Forked clarinets?

INTERVIEWER: They're called Obetrol. Neal is the one that told me about them.

KEROUAC: Overtones?

INTERVIEWER: Overtones? No, overcoats.

SAROYAN: What was that you said . . . at the back of the Grove anthology . . . that you let the line go a little longer to fill it up with secret images that come at the end of the sentence.

KEROUAC: He's a real Armenian! Sediment. Delta. Mud. It's where you start a poem. . . .

As I was walking down the street one day
I saw a lake where people were cutting off my rear,
17,000 priests singing like George Burns

and then you go on . . .

And I'm making jokes about me
And breaking my bones in the earth

And here I am the great John Armenian
Coming back to earth

Now you remember where you were in the beginning and you say . . .

Ahaha! Tatatatadoodo . . . Screw Turkey!

See? You remembered the line at the end . . . you lose your mind in the middle.

SAROYAN: Right.

KEROUAC: That applies to prose as well as poetry.

INTERVIEWER: But in prose you are telling a story . . .

KEROUAC: In prose you make the paragraph. Every paragraph is a poem.

INTERVIEWER: Is that how you write a paragraph?

KEROUAC: When I was running downtown there, and I was going to do this, and I was laying there, with that girl there, and a guy took out his scissors and I took him inside there, he showed me some dirty pictures. And I went out and fell downstairs with the potato bags.

INTERVIEWER: Did you ever like Gertrude Stein's work?

KEROUAC: Never interested me too much. I liked *Melanctha* a little bit.

I should really go to school and teach these kids. I could make two thousand bucks a week. You can't learn these things. You know why? Because you have to be born with tragic fathers.

INTERVIEWER: You can only do that if you are born in New England.

KEROUAC: Incidentally, my father said your father wasn't tragic.

SAROYAN: I don't think my father is tragic.

KEROUAC: My father said that Saroyan . . . William Saroyan ain't tragic at all . . . he's fulla shit. And I had a big argument with him. *The Daring Young Man on the Flying Trapeze* is pretty tragic, I would say.

SAROYAN: He was just a young man then, you know.

KEROUAC: Yeah, but he was hungry, and he was on Times Square. Flying. A young man on the flying trapeze. That was a beautiful story. It killed me when I was a kid.

INTERVIEWER: Do you remember a story by William Saroyan about the Indian who came to town and bought a car and got the little kid to drive it for him?

STELLA: A Cadillac.

KEROUAC: What town was that?

SAROYAN: Fresno. That was Fresno.

KEROUAC: Well, you remember the night I was taking a big nap and you came up outside my window on a white horse . . .

SAROYAN: *The Summer of the Beautiful White Horse*.

KEROUAC: And I looked out the window and said what is this? You said, "My name is Aram. And I'm on a white horse."

SAROYAN: Moorad.

KEROUAC: My name is Moorad, excuse me. No, my name is . . . I am Aram, you were Moorad. You said, "Wake up!" I didn't want to wake up. I wanted to sleep. *My Name Is Aram* is the name of the book. You stole a white horse from a farmer and you woke up me, Aram, to go riding with you.

SAROYAN: Moorad was the crazy one who stole the horse.

KEROUAC: Hey, what's that you gave me there?

INTERVIEWER: Obetrol.

KEROUAC: Oh, obies.

INTERVIEWER: What about jazz and bop as influences rather than . . . Saroyan, Hemingway and Wolfe?

KEROUAC: Yes, jazz and bop, in the sense of a, say, a tenor man drawing a breath and blowing a phrase on his saxophone, till he runs out of breath, and when he does, his sentence, his statement's been made . . . that's how I therefore separate my sentences, as breath separations of the mind . . . I formulated the theory of breath as measure, in prose and verse, never mind what Olson, Charles Olson says, I formulated that theory in 1953 at the request of Burroughs and Ginsberg. Then there's the raciness and freedom and humor of jazz instead of all that dreary analysis and things like "James entered the room, and lit a cigarette. He thought Jane might have thought this too vague a gesture . . ." You know the stuff. As for Saroyan, yes I loved him as a teenager, he really got me out of the 19th century rut I was trying to study, not only his funny tone but his neat Armenian poetic I don't know what . . . he just got me . . . Hemingway was fascinating, the pearls of words on a white page giving you an exact picture . . . but Wolfe was a torrent of American heaven and hell that opened my eyes to America as a subject in itself.

INTERVIEWER: How about the movies?

KEROUAC: Yes, we've all been influenced by movies. Malcolm Cowley incidentally mentioned this many times. He's very perceptive sometimes: he mentioned that *Doctor Sax* continually mentions urine, and quite naturally it does because I had no other place to write it but on a closed toilet seat in a little tile toilet in Mexico City so as to get away from the guests inside the apartment. There incidentally is a style truly hallucinated as I wrote it all on pot. No pun intended. Ho ho.

INTERVIEWER: How has Zen influenced your work?

KEROUAC: What's really influenced my work is the Mahayana Buddhism, the original Buddhism of Gotama Sakyamuni, the Buddha himself, of the India of old . . . Zen is what's left of his Buddhism, or Bodhi, after its passing into China and then into Japan. The part of Zen that's influenced my writing is the Zen contained in the haiku, like I said, the three line, seventeen syllable poems written hundreds of years ago by guys like Basho, Issa, Shiki, and there've been recent masters. A sentence that's short and sweet with a sudden jump of thought in it is a kind of haiku, and there's a lot of freedom and fun in surprising yourself with that, let the mind willy-nilly jump from the branch to the bird. But my serious Buddhism, that of ancient India, has influenced that part in my writing that you might call religious, or fervent, or pious, almost as much as Catholicism has. Original Buddhism referred to continual conscious compassion, brotherhood, the *dana paramita* meaning the perfection of charity, don't step on the bug, all that, humility, mendicancy, the sweet sorrowful fact of the Buddha (who was of Aryan origin by the way, I mean of Persian warrior caste, and not Oriental as pictured) . . . in original Buddhism no young kid coming to a monastery was warned that "here we bury them alive." He was simply given soft encouragement to meditate and be kind. The beginning of Zen was when Buddha, however, assembled all the monks together to announce a sermon and choose the first patriarch of the Mahayana church: instead of speaking, he simply held up a flower. Everybody was flabbergasted except Kasyapa, who smiled. Kasyapa was appointed the first patriarch. This idea appealed to the Chinese like the Sixth Patriarch Hui-Neng who said, "From the beginning nothing ever was" and wanted to tear up the records of Buddha's sayings as kept in the sutras; sutras are "threads of discourse." In a way, then, Zen is a gentle but goofy form of heresy, though there must be some real kindly old monks somewhere and we've heard about the nutty ones. I haven't been to Japan. Your Maha roshi yoshi is simply a disciple of all this and not the founder of anything new at all, of course. On the Johnny Carson show he didn't even mention Buddha's name. Maybe his Buddha is Mia.

INTERVIEWER: How come you've never written about Jesus? You've written about Buddha. Wasn't Jesus a great guy too?

KEROUAC: I've never written about Jesus? In other words, you're an insane phony who comes to my house . . . and . . . all I *write about* is Jesus. I am Everhard Mercurian, General of the Jesuit Army.

SAROYAN: What's the difference between Jesus and Buddha?

KEROUAC: That's a very good question. There is no difference.

SAROYAN: No difference?

KEROUAC: But there is a difference between the original Buddha of India, and the Buddha of Vietnam who just shaves his hair and puts on a yellow robe and is a Communist agitating agent. The original Buddha wouldn't even walk on young grass so that he wouldn't destroy it. He was born in Gorakpur, the son of the Consul of the invading Persian hordes. And he was called Sage of the Warriors, and he had 17,000 broads dancing for him all night, holding out flowers, saying you want to smell it, my Lord? He says git outta here you whore. He laid a lot of them you know. But by the time he was thirty-one years old he got sick and tired . . . his father was protecting him from what was going on outside the town. And so he went out on a horse, against his father's orders and he saw a woman dying–a man being burnt on a ghat. And he said, What is all this death and decay? The servant said that is the way things go on. Your father was hiding you from the way things go on.

He says, What? My father! !–Get my horse, saddle my horse! Ride me into the forest! They ride into the forest; he says, Now take the saddle off the horse. Put it on your horse, hang it on . . . take my horse by the rein and ride back to the castle and tell my father I'll never see him again! And the servant, Kandaka, cried, he said, I'll never see you again. I don't care! Go on! Shoosh! Get away! !

He spent seven years in the forest. Biting his teeth together. Nothing happened. Tormenting himself with starvation. He said, I will keep my teeth bit together until I find the cause of death. Then one day he was stumbling across the Rapti river, and he fainted in the river. And a young girl came by with a bowl of milk and said, My lord, a bowl of milk. (*Slurpppp*) He said, That gives me great energy, thank you my dear. Then he went and sat under the Bo tree. Figuerosa. The fig tree. He said, Now . . . (*demonstrates posture*) . . . I will cross my legs . . . and grit my teeth until I find the cause of death. Two o'clock in the morning, 100,000 phantoms assailed him. He didn't move. Three o'clock in the morning, the great blue ghosts! ! Arrghhh!!! All *accosted* him. (You see I am really Scottish.) Four o'clock in the morning the mad maniacs of hell . . . came out of manhole covers . . . in New York City. You know Wall Street where the steam comes out? You know Wall

Street, where the manhole covers . . . steam comes up? You take off them covers–yaaaaaahhh! ! ! ! ! Six o'clock, everything was peaceful–the birds started to trill, and he said, "Aha! . . . the cause of death . . . the cause of death is birth."

Simple? So he started walking down the road to Benares in India . . . with long hair, like you, see.

So, three guys. One says hey, here comes Buddha there who uh starved with us in the forest. When he sits down here on that bucket, don't wash his feet. So Buddha sits down on the bucket . . . the guy rushes up and washes his feet. Why dost thou wash his feet? Buddha says, "Because I go to Benares to beat the drum of life." And what is that? "That the cause of death is birth." "What do you mean?" "I'll show you."

A woman comes up with a dead baby in her arms. Says, Bring my child back to life if you are the Lord. He says, Sure I'll do that anytime. Just go and find one family in Sravasti that ain't had a death in the last five years. Get a mustard seed from them and bring it to me. And I'll bring your child back to life. She went all over town, man, two million people, Sravasti the town was, a bigger town than Benares by the way, and she came back and said, I can't find no such family. They've all had deaths within five years. He said, "Then, bury your baby."

Then, his jealous cousin, Devadatta, (that's Ginsberg you see . . . I am Buddha and Ginsberg is Devadatta) gets this elephant drunk . . . great big bull elephant drunk on whiskey. The elephant goes up! ! ! ! (*trumpets like elephant going up*)–with a big trunk, and Buddha comes up in the road and gets the elephant and goes like this (*kneels*). And the elephant kneels down. "You are buried in sorrow's mud! Quiet your trunk! Stay there!" . . . He's an elephant trainer. Then Devadatta rolled a big boulder over a cliff. And it almost hit Buddha's head. Just missed. Boooom! He says, That's Devadatta again. Then Buddha went like this (*paces back and forth*) in front of his boys, you see. Behind him was his cousin that loved him . . . Ananda . . . which means love in Sanskrit. (*Keeps pacing*) This is what you do in jail to keep in shape.

I know a lot of stories about Buddha, but I don't know exactly what he said every time. But I know what he said about the guy who spit at him. He said, "Since I can't use your abuse you may have it back." He was great. (*Kerouac plays piano. Drinks are served.*)

SAROYAN: There's something there.

INTERVIEWER: My mother used to play that. I'm not sure how we can transcribe those notes onto a page. We may have to include a record of you playing the piano. Will you play that piece again for the record, Mr. Paderewski? Can you play "Alouette"?

KEROUAC: No. Only Afro-Germanic music. After all, I'm a square head. I wonder what whiskey will do to those obies.

INTERVIEWER: What about ritual and superstition? Do you have any about yourself when you get down to work?

KEROUAC: I had a ritual once of lighting a candle and writing by its light and blowing it out when I was done for the night . . . also kneeling and praying before starting (I got that from a French movie about George Frederick Handel) . . . but now I simply hate to write. My superstition? I'm beginning to suspect that full moon. Also I'm hung up on the number 9 though I'm told a Piscean like myself should stick to number 7; but I try to do 9 touchdowns a day, that is, I stand on my head in the bathroom, on a slipper, and touch the floor 9 times with my toe tips, while balanced. This is incidentally more than Yoga, it's an athletic feat, I mean imagine calling me "unbalanced" after that. Frankly I do feel that my mind is going. So another "ritual" as you call it, is to pray to Jesus to preserve my sanity and my energy so I can help my family: that being my paralyzed mother, and my wife, and the ever-present kitties. Okay?

INTERVIEWER: You typed out *On the Road* in three weeks, *The Subterraneans* . . . in three days and nights. Do you still produce at this fantastic rate? Can you say something of the genesis of a work before you sit down and begin that terrific typing–how much of it is set in your mind, for example?

KEROUAC: You think out what actually happened, you tell friends long stories about it, you mull it over in your mind, you connect it together at leisure, then when the time comes to pay the rent again you force yourself to sit at the typewriter, or at the writing notebook, and get it over with as fast as you can . . . and there's no harm in that because you ve got the whole story lined up. Now how that's done depends on what kind of steeltrap you've got up in that little old head. This sounds boastful but a girl once told me I had a steeltrap brain, meaning I'd catch her with a statement she'd made an hour ago even though our talk had rambled a million lightyears away from that point . . . you know what I mean, like a lawyer's mind, say. All of it is in my mind, naturally, except that language that is used at the time that it is used. . . . And as for *On the Road* and *The Subterraneans,* no I can't write that fast anymore. . . . Writing the Subs in three nights was really a fantastic athletic feat as well as mental, you shoulda seen me after I was done . . . I was pale as a sheet and had lost fifteen pounds and looked strange in the mirror. What I do now is write something like an average of 8000 words a sitting, in the middle of the night, and another about a week later, resting and sighing in between. I really hate to write. I get no fun out of it because I can't get up and say I'm working, close my door, have coffee brought to me, and sit there camping like a "man of letters" "doing his eight hour day of work" and thereby incidentally filling the printing world with a lot of dreary self-imposed cant and bombast . . . bombast is Scottish word for stuffing for a pillow. Haven't you heard a politician use 1500 words to say something he could have said in exactly three words? So I get it out of the way so as not to bore myself either.

SAROYAN: Do you usually try to see everything clearly and not think of any words–just to see everything as clear as possible and then write out of the feeling. With *Tristessa,* for example.

KEROUAC: You sound like a writing seminar at Indiana University.

SAROYAN: I know but . . .

KEROUAC: All I did was suffer with that poor girl and then when she fell on her head and almost killed herself . . . remember when she fell on her head? . . . and she was all busted up and everything. She was the most gorgeous little Indian chick you ever saw. I say Indian, pure Indian. Esperanza Villanueva. Villanueva is a Spanish name from I don't know where–Castile. But she's Indian. So she's half Indian, half Spanish . . . beauty. Absolute beauty. She had bones, man, just bones, skin and bone. And I didn't write in the book how I finally nailed her. You know? I did. I finally nailed her. She said "Shhhhhhhhhh! Don't let the landlord hear." She said, "Remember, I'm very weak and sick." I said, "I know, I've been writing a book about how you're weak and sick."

INTERVIEWER: How come you didn't put that part in the book?

KEROUAC: Because Claude's wife told me not to put it in. She said it would spoil the book.

But it was not a conquest. She was out like a light. On M.M., that's Morphine. And in fact I made a big run for her from way uptown to downtown to the slum district . . . and I said, here's your stuff. She said, "Shhhhhh!" She gave herself a shot . . . and I said, Ah . . . now's the time. And I got my little nogood piece. But . . . it was certainly justification of Mexico!

STELLA: Here kitty! He's gone out again.

KEROUAC: She was nice, you would have liked her. Her real name was Esperanza. You know what that means?

INTERVIEWER: No.

KEROUAC: In Spanish, hope. Tristessa means in Spanish, sadness, but her real name was Hope. And she's now married to the Police Chief of Mexico City.

STELLA: Not quite.

KEROUAC: Well, you're not Esperanza–I'll tell you that.

STELLA: No, I know that, dear.

KEROUAC: She was the skinniest . . . and shy . . . as a rail.

STELLA: She's married to one of the lieutenants, you told me, not to the Chief.

KEROUAC: She's all right. One of these days I'm going to go see her again.

STELLA: Over my dead body.

INTERVIEWER: Were you really writing *Tristessa* while you were there in Mexico? You didn't write it later?

KEROUAC: First part written in Mexico, second part written in . . . Mexico. That's right. '55 first part, '56 second part. What's the importance about that? I'm not Charles Olson, the great artist!

INTERVIEWER: We're just getting the facts.

KEROUAC: Charles Olson gives you all the dates. You know. Everything about how he found the hound dog on the beach in Gloucester. Found somebody jacking-off on the beach at . . . what do they call it? Vancouver Beach? Dig Dog River? . . . Dogtown. That's what they call it, "Dogtown." Well this is Shit-town on the Merrimac. Lowell is called Shit-town on the Merrimac. I'm not going to write a poem called Shit-town and insult my town. But if I was six foot six I could write anything, couldn't I?

INTERVIEWER: How do you get along now with other writers? Do you correspond with them?

KEROUAC: I correspond with John Clellon Holmes but less and less each year, I'm getting lazy. I can't answer my fan mail because I haven't got a secretary to take dictation, do the typing, get the stamps, envelopes, all that . . . and I have nothing to answer. I ain't gonna spend the rest of my life smiling and shaking hands and sending and receiving platitudes, like a candidate for political office, because I'm a writer–I've got to let my mind alone, like Greta Garbo. Yet when I go out, or receive sudden guests, we all have more fun than a barrel of monkeys.

INTERVIEWER: What are the work-destroyers?

KEROUAC: Work-destroyers . . . work-destroyers. Time-killers? I'd say mainly the attentions which are tendered to a writer of "notoriety" (notice I don't say "fame") by secretly ambitious would-be writers, who come around, or write, or call, for the sake of the services which are properly the services of a bloody literary agent. When I was an unknown struggling young writer, as saying goes, I did my own footwork, I hot-footed up and down Madison Avenue for years, publisher to publisher, agent to agent, and never once in my life wrote a letter to a published famous author ask-

Covers for French editions of four novels by Kerouac: The Subterraneans, Doctor Sax, Desolation Angels, *and* Satori in Paris ing for advice, or help, or, in Heaven above, have the nerve to actually *mail* my manuscripts to some poor author who then has to hustle to mail it back before he's accused of stealing my ideas. My advice to young writers is to get themselves an agent on their own, maybe through their college professors (as I got my first publishers through my prof Mark Van Doren) and do their own footwork, or "thing" as the slang goes . . . So the work-destroyers are nothing but certain *people*.

The work-preservers are the solitudes of night, "when the whole wide world is fast asleep."

INTERVIEWER: What do you find the best time and place for writing?

KEROUAC: The desk in the room, near the bed, with a good light, midnight till dawn, a drink when you get tired, preferably at home, but if you have no home, make a home out of your hotel room or motel room or pad: peace. (*Picks up harmonica and plays*) Boy, can I play!

INTERVIEWER: What about writing under the influence of drugs?

KEROUAC: Poem 230 from *Mexico City Blues* is a poem written purely on morphine. Every line in this poem was written within an hour of one another . . . high on a big dose of M. (*Finds volume and reads*)

Love's multitudinous boneyard of decay

An hour later:

The spilled milk of heroes

An hour later:

Destruction of silk kerchiefs by dust storm,

An hour later:

Caress of heroes blindfolded to posts,

An hour later:

Murder victims admitted to this life,

An hour later:

Skeletons bartering fingers and joints,

An hour later:

The quivering meat of the elephants of kindness
being torn apart by vultures
(See where Ginsberg stole that from me?)

An hour later: *Conceptions of delicate kneecaps.*

Say that, Saroyan.

SAROYAN: Conceptions of delicate kneecaps.

KEROUAC: Very good. *Fear of rats dripping with bacteria.* An hour later: *Golgotha Cold Hope for Gold Hope.* Say that.

SAROYAN: Golgotha Cold Hope for Cold Hope.

KEROUAC: That's pretty cold.

An hour later: *Damp leaves of Autumn against the wood of boats,*

An hour later: *Seahorse's delicate imagery of glue . . .*

Ever see a little seahorse in the ocean? They're built of glue . . . did you ever sniff a seahorse? No, say that.

SAROYAN: Seahorse's delicate imagery of glue.

KEROUAC: You'll do, Saroyan. *Death by long exposure to defilement.*

SAROYAN: Death by long exposure to defilement.

KEROUAC: *Frightening ravishing mysterious beings concealing their sex.*

SAROYAN: Frightening ravishing mysterious beings concealing their sex.

KEROUAC: *Pieces of the Buddha-material froze and sliced microscopically*

In Morgues of the North

SAROYAN: Hey, I can't say that. Pieces of the Buddha-material frozen and sliced microscopically in Morgues of the North.

KEROUAC: *Penis apples going to seed.*

SAROYAN: Penis apples going to seed.

KEROUAC: *The severed gullets more numerous than sands.*

SAROYAN: The severed gullets more numerous than sands.

KEROUAC: *Like kissing my kitten in the belly*

SAROYAN: Like kissing my kitten in the belly

KEROUAC: *The softness of our reward*

SAROYAN: The softness of our reward.

KEROUAC: Is he really William Saroyan's son? That's wonderful! Would you mind repeating that?

INTERVIEWER: We should be asking you a lot of very straight serious questions. When did you meet Allen Ginsberg?

KEROUAC: First I met Claude ["Claude," a pseudonym, is also used in *Vanity of Duluoz* (Claude-Lucien Carr)]. And then I met Allen and then I met Burroughs. Claude came in through the fire escape . . . there were gunshots down in the alley–Pow! Pow! And it was raining, and my wife says, here comes Claude. And here comes this blond guy through the fire escape, all wet. I said, "What's this all about, what the hell is this?" He says, "They're chasing me." Next day in walks Allen Ginsberg carrying books. Sixteen years old with his ears sticking out. He says, "Well, discretion is the better part of valor!" I said, "Aw shutup. You little twitch." Then the next day here comes Burroughs wearing a seersucker suit, followed by the other guy.

INTERVIEWER: What other guy?

KEROUAC: It was the guy who wound up in the river [Dave Kammerer]. This was this guy from New Orleans that Claude killed and threw in the river. Stabbed him twelve times in the heart with a Boy Scout knife.

When Claude was fourteen he was the most beautiful blond boy in New Orleans. And he joined the boy Scout troop . . . and the Boy Scout Master was a big redheaded fairy who went to school at St. Louis University, I think it was.

And he had already been in love with a guy who looked just like Claude in Paris. And this guy chased Claude all over the country; this guy had him thrown out of Baldwin, Tulane, and Andover Prep. . . . It's a queer tale, but Claude isn't a queer.

INTERVIEWER: What about the influence of Ginsberg and Burroughs? Did you ever have any sense then of the mark the three of you would have on American writing?

KEROUAC: I was determined to be a "great writer," in quotes, like Thomas Wolfe, see . . . Allen was always reading and writing poetry . . . Burroughs read a lot and walked around looking at things. . . . The influence we exerted on one another has been written about over and over again . . . We were just three interested characters, in the interesting big city of New York, around campuses, libraries, cafeterias. A lot of the details you'll find in *Vanity* . . . in *On the Road* where Burroughs is Bull Lee and Ginsberg is Carlo Marx . . . in *Subterraneans,* where they're Frank Carmody and Adam Moorad respectively, elsewhere. In other words, though I don't want to be rude to you for this honor, I am so busy interviewing myself in my novels, and have been so busy writing down these self-interviews, that I don't see why I should draw breath in pain every year of the last ten years to repeat and repeat to everybody who interviews me what I've already explained in the books themselves. . . . (Hundreds of journalists, thousands of students.) It beggars sense. And it's not that important. It's our work that counts, if anything at all, and I'm not proud of mine or theirs or anybody's since Thoreau and others like that, maybe because it's still to close to home for comfort. Notoriety and public confession in literary form is a frazzler of the heart you were born with, believe me.

INTERVIEWER: Allen said once that he learned how to read Shakespeare, that he never did understand Shakespeare until he heard you read Shakespeare to him.

KEROUAC: Because in a previous lifetime that's who I was.

How like a Winter hath my absence been from thee?
The pleasure of the fleeting year . . . what freezings
have I felt? What dark days seen? Yet Summer with his
lord surcease hath laid a big turd in my orchard
And one hog after another comes to eat
and break my broken mountain trap, and my mousetrap
too! And here to end the sonnet, you must make sure
to say, tara-tara-tara . . . !!!!!!

INTERVIEWER: Is that spontaneous composition?

KEROUAC: Well, the first part was Shakespeare . . . and the second part was . . .

INTERVIEWER: Have you ever written any sonnets?

KEROUAC: I'll give you a spontaneous sonnet. It has to be what, now?

INTERVIEWER: Fourteen lines.

KEROUAC: That's twelve lines with two dragging lines. That's where you bring up your heavy artillery.

Here the fish of Scotland seen your eye
and all my nets did creak . . .

Does it have to rhyme?

INTERVIEWER: No.

KEROUAC:

My poor chapped hands fall awry
and seen the Pope, his devilled eye.
And maniacs with wild hair hanging about my room
and listening to my tomb
which does not rhyme.

Seven lines?

INTERVIEWER: That was eight lines.

KEROUAC:

And all the orgones of the earth will crawl
like dogs across the graves of Peru
and Scotland too.

That's ten.

Yet do not worry, sweet angel of mine
That hast thine inheritance
imbedded in mine.

INTERVIEWER: That's pretty good, Jack. How did you do that?

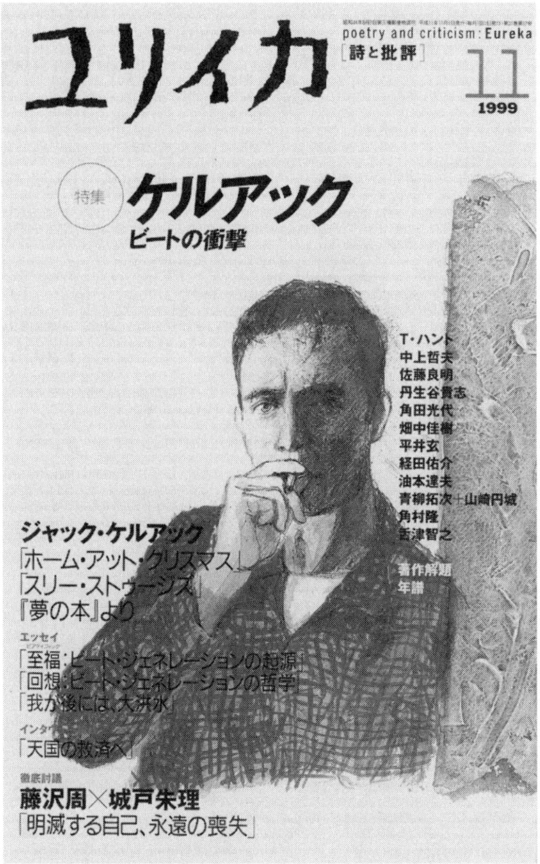

Cover of 1999 issue of Japanese journal that featured Kerouac

KEROUAC: Without studying dactyls . . . like Ginsberg . . . I met Ginsberg . . . I'd hitchhiked all the way back from Mexico City to Berkeley, and that's a long way baby, a long way. Mexico City across Durango . . . Chihuahua . . . Texas. I go back to Ginsberg. I go to his cottage, I say, "Hah, we're gonna play the music" . . . he said, "You know what I'm going to do tomorrow? I'm going to throw on Mark Schorer's desk a new theory of prosody! About the dactylic arrangements of Ovid!" (*Laughter*)

I said, "Quit, man. Sit under a tree and forget it and drink wine with me . . . and Phil Whalen and Gary Snyder and all the bums of San Francisco. Don't you try to be a big Berkeley teacher. Just be a poet under the trees . . . and we'll wrestle and we'll break holds." And he did take my advice. He remembered that. He said, "What are you going to teach . . . you have parched lips!" I said, "Naturally, I just came from Chihuahua. It's very hot down there, phew! You go out and little pigs rub against your legs. Phew!"

So here comes Snyder with a bottle of wine . . . and here comes Whalen, and here comes what's his name . . . Rexroth . . . and everybody . . . and we had the poetry renaissance of San Francisco.

INTERVIEWER: What about Allen getting kicked out of Columbia? Didn't you have something to do with that?

KEROUAC: Oh, no . . . he let me sleep in his room. He was not kicked out of Columbia for that. The first time he let me sleep in his room, and the guy that slept in our room with us was Lancaster who was descended from the White Roses or Red roses of England. But a guy came in . . . the guy that ran the floor and he thought that I was trying to make Allen, and Allen had already written in the paper that I wasn't sleeping there because I was trying to make him, but he was trying to make me. But we were just actually sleeping. Then after that he got a pad . . . he got some stolen goods in there . . . and he got some thieves up here, Vicky and Huncke.

And they were all busted for stolen goods, and a car turned over, and Allen's glasses broke, it's all in John Holmes' *Go.*

Allen Ginsberg asked me when he was nineteen years old, should I change my name to Allen Renard? You change your name to Allen Renard I'll kick you right in the balls! Stick to Ginsberg . . . and he did. That's one thing I like about Allen. Allen *Renard!!!*

INTERVIEWER: What was it that brought all of you together in the 50s? What was it that seemed to unify the "Beat Generation?"

KEROUAC: Oh the beat generation was just a phrase I used in the 1951 written manuscript of *On the Road* to describe guys like Moriarty who run around the country in cars looking for odd jobs, girlfriends, kicks. It was thereafter picked up by West Coast leftist groups and turned into a meaning like "beat mutiny" and "beat insurrection" and all that nonsense; they just wanted some youth movement to grab onto for their own political and social purposes. I had nothing to do with any of that. I was a football player, a scholarship college student, a merchant seaman, a railroad brakeman on road freights, a script synopsizer, a secretary . . . And Moriarty-Cassady was an actual cowboy on Dave Uhl's ranch in New Raymer, Colorado . . . What kind of beatnik is that?

INTERVIEWER: Was there any sense of "community" among the Beat crowd?

KEROUAC: That community feeling was largely inspired by the same characters I mentioned, like Ferlinghetti, Ginsberg; they are very socialistically minded and want everybody to live in some kind of frenetic kibbutz, solidarity and all that. I was a loner. Snyder is not like Whalen, Whalen is not like McClure, I am not like McClure, McClure is not like Ferlinghetti, Ginsberg is not like Ferlinghetti, but we all had fun over wine anyway. We knew thousands of poets and painters and jazz musicians. There's no "beat crowd" like you say . . . what about Scott Fitzgerald and his "lost crowd," does that sound right? Or Goethe and his "Wilhelm Meister crowd?" The subject is such a bore. Pass me that glass.

INTERVIEWER: Well, why did they split in the early 60s?

KEROUAC: Ginsberg got interested in left wing politics . . . like Joyce I say, as Joyce said to Ezra Pound in the 1920s, "Don't bother me with politics, the only thing that interests me is style." Besides I'm bored with the new avant-garde and the skyrocketing sensationalism. I'm reading Blaise Pascal and taking notes on religion. I like to hang around now with nonintellectuals, as you might call them, and not have my mind proselytized, ad infinitum. They've even started crucifying chickens in happenings, what's the next step? An actual crucifixion of a man . . . The beat group dispersed as you say in the early 60s, all went their own way, and this is my way: home life, as in the beginning, with a little toot once in a while in local bars.

INTERVIEWER: What do you think of what they're up to now? Allen's radical political involvement? Burrough's cut-up methods?

KEROUAC: I'm pro-American and the radical political involvements seem to tend elsewhere . . . The country gave my Canadian family a good break, more or less, and we see no reason to demean said country. As for Burroughs' cut-up method, I wish he'd get back to those awfully funny stories of his he used to write and those marvelously dry vignettes in *Naked Lunch.* Cut-up is nothing new, in fact that steeltrap brain of mine does a lot of cutting up as it goes along . . . as does everyone's brain while talking or thinking or writing . . . It's just an old Dada trick, and a kind of literary collage. He comes out with some great effects though. I like him to be elegant and logical and that's why I don't like the cut-up which is supposed to teach us that the mind is cracked. Sure the mind's cracked, as anybody can see in a hallucinated high, but how about an explanation of the crackedness that can be understood in a workaday moment?

INTERVIEWER: What do you think about the hippies and the LSD scene?

KEROUAC: They're already changing, I shouldn't be able to make a judgment. And they're not all of the same mind. The Diggers are different . . . I don't know one hippie anyhow . . . I think they think I'm a truckdriver. And I am. As for LSD, it's bad for people with incidence of heart disease in the family. (*Knocks microphone off footstool . . . recovers it*)

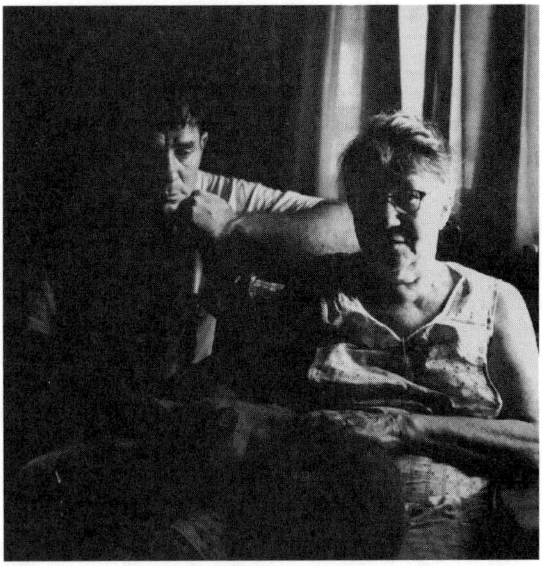

Kerouac with his mother in 1966

Is there any reason why you can see anything good in this yere mortality?

INTERVIEWER: Excuse me, would you mind repeating that?

KEROUAC: You said you had a little white beard in your belly. Why is there a little white beard in your mortality belly?

INTERVIEWER: Let me think about it. Actually it's a little white pill.

KEROUAC: A little white pill?

INTERVIEWER: It's good.

KEROUAC: Give me.

INTERVIEWER: We should wait till the scene cools a little.

KEROUAC: Right. This little white pill is a little white beard in your mortality which advises you and advertises to you that you will be growing long fingernails in the graves of Peru.

SAROYAN: Do you feel middle-aged?

KEROUAC: No. Listen, we're coming to the end of the tape. I want to add something on. Ask me what Kerouac means.

INTERVIEWER: Jack, tell me again what Kerouac means.

KEROUAC: Now, Kairn. K (or C) A-I-R-N. What is a kairn? It's a heap of stones. Now Cornwall, kairn-wall. Now, right, kern, also K-E-R-N, means the same thing as Kairn, Kern, Kairn. Ouac means language of. So, Kernuac means the language of Cornwall. Kerr, which is like Deborah Kerr . . . ouack means language of the water. Because Kerr, Carr, etc. means water. And Kairn means heap of stones. There is no language in a heap of stones. Kerouac. Ker-water, ouac-language of. And it's related to the old Irish name, Kerwick, which is a corruption. And it's a Cornish name, which in itself means Kairnish. And according to Sherlock Holmes, it's all Persian. Of course you know he's not Persian. Don't you remember in Sherlock Holmes when he went down with Dr. Watson and solved the case down in old Cornwall and he solved the case and then he said, "Watson, the needle! Watson, the needle . . ." He said, "I've solved this case here in Cornwall. Now I have the liberty to sit around here and decide and read books, which will prove to me . . . why the Cornish people, otherwise known as the Kernuaks, or Kerouacs, are of Persian origin. The enterprise which I am about to embark upon," he then said, after he got his shot, "is fraught with eminent peril, and not fit for a lady of your tender years." Remember that?

MCNAUGHTON: I remember that.

KEROUAC: McNaughton remembers that. McNaughton. You think I would forget the name of a Scotsman?

Holmes, Ginsberg, and Corso at Kerouac's funeral, October 1969

Death and Posthumous Publications

End of the Road

Time, 31 October 1969, p. 10

Jack Kerouac's "barbaric yawp" broke into the American consciousness in the middle years of Eisenhower. At roughly the same time, Marlon Brando, adenoidal and inarticulately glowering, careered through adolescent daydreams astride a Harley-Davidson. From the perspective of the late '60s, the old rebellions and spontaneities seem as touchingly quaint as the shock they elicited at the time. Kerouac's vision was compounded of Buddhism, booze (of all bourgeois things) and a chaotic lowlife that he worked into exuberant underground literature. When he wrote of casual sex or marijuana, they were still exotic and forbidden fruits. At the end, he was living in geriatric St. Petersburg, Fla., dutifully looking after his ailing mother.

As a shaman of the Beat Generation, Kerouac was a forebear of today's hippie and radical counterculture. But he would not or could not translate himself into the '60s. A little before he died last week at 47, Kerouac was muttering at both straight society and the rebellious young, the military-industrial complex and the Viet Cong. "You can't fight city hall," he wrote. "It keeps changing its name." It would be too easy to believe that all of today's radical young will slip into cantankerous conservatism. But some undoubtedly will. It may be that Robert Frost had the most sensible formula. Frost was a conservative in his youth, he said, so that he might be free to be anarchistic in his old age.

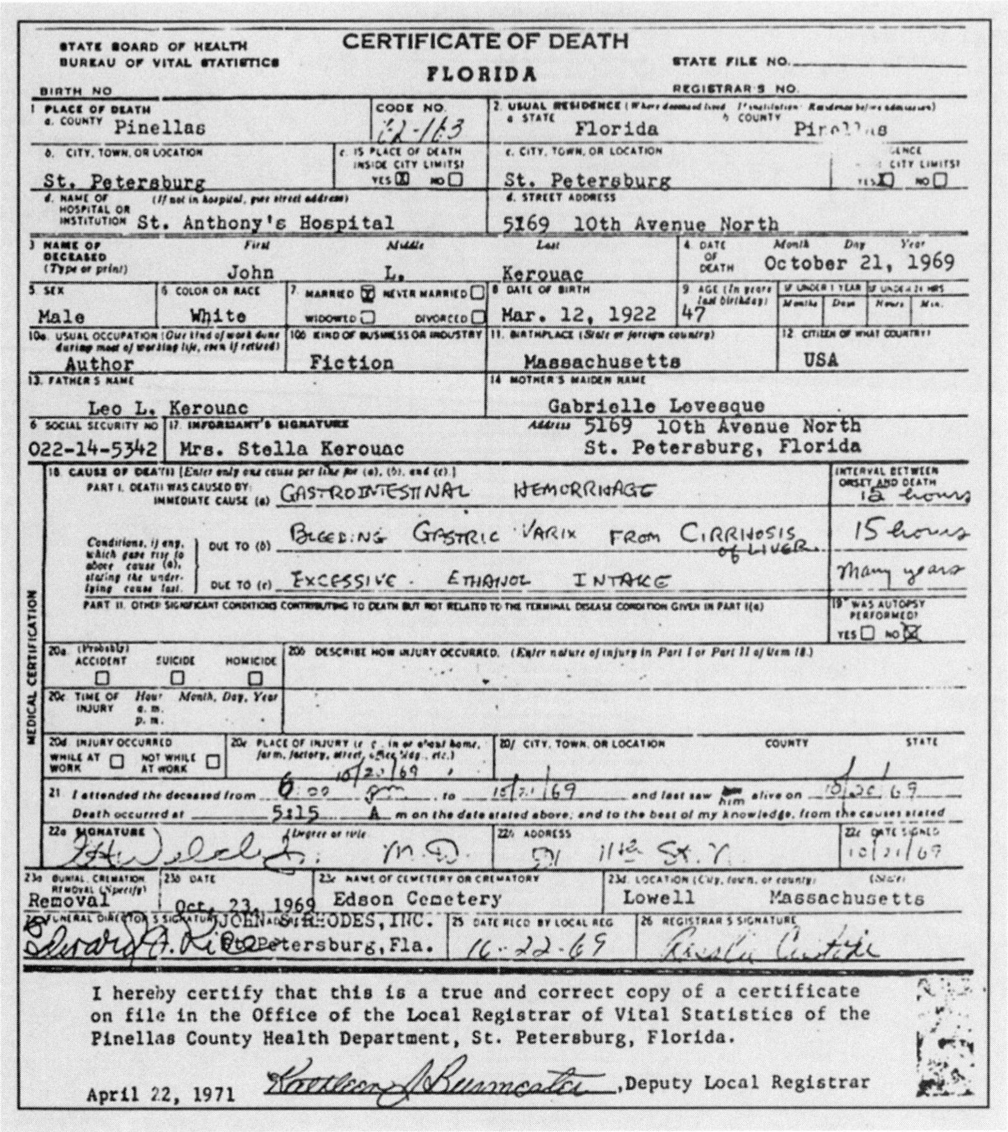

STATE BOARD OF HEALTH
BUREAU OF VITAL STATISTICS

CERTIFICATE OF DEATH
FLORIDA

STATE FILE NO.
BIRTH NO
REGISTRAR'S NO.

1 PLACE OF DEATH a. COUNTY Pinellas
CODE NO. 12-163
2. USUAL RESIDENCE (Where deceased lived. If institution: Residence before admission) a. STATE Florida b. COUNTY Pinellas
b. CITY, TOWN, OR LOCATION St. Petersburg
c. IS PLACE OF DEATH INSIDE CITY LIMITS? YES [X] NO [ ]
c. CITY, TOWN, OR LOCATION St. Petersburg
INSIDE CITY LIMITS? YES [X] NO [ ]
d. NAME OF HOSPITAL OR INSTITUTION (If not in hospital, give street address) St. Anthony's Hospital
d. STREET ADDRESS 5169 10th Avenue North
3 NAME OF DECEASED (Type or print) First John Middle L. Last Kerouac
4. DATE OF DEATH Month Day Year October 21, 1969
5. SEX Male
6. COLOR OR RACE White
7. MARRIED [X] NEVER MARRIED [ ] WIDOWED [ ] DIVORCED [ ]
8. DATE OF BIRTH Mar. 12, 1922
9. AGE (In years last birthday) 47
IF UNDER 1 YEAR Months Days
IF UNDER 24 HRS Hours Min.
10a. USUAL OCCUPATION (Give kind of work done during most of working life, even if retired) Author
10b. KIND OF BUSINESS OR INDUSTRY Fiction
11. BIRTHPLACE (State or foreign country) Massachusetts
12. CITIZEN OF WHAT COUNTRY? USA
13. FATHER'S NAME Leo L. Kerouac
14. MOTHER'S MAIDEN NAME Gabrielle Levesque
16. SOCIAL SECURITY NO. 022-14-5342
17. INFORMANT'S SIGNATURE Mrs. Stella Kerouac
Address 5169 10th Avenue North
St. Petersburg, Florida

MEDICAL CERTIFICATION

18. CAUSE OF DEATH [Enter only one cause per line for (a), (b), and (c).]
PART I. DEATH WAS CAUSED BY: IMMEDIATE CAUSE (a) GASTROINTESTINAL HEMORRHAGE
INTERVAL BETWEEN ONSET AND DEATH 12 hours
Conditions, if any, which gave rise to above cause (a), stating the underlying cause last.
DUE TO (b) BLEEDING GASTRIC VARIX FROM CIRRHOSIS of LIVER. 15 hours
DUE TO (c) EXCESSIVE ETHANOL INTAKE Many years
PART II. OTHER SIGNIFICANT CONDITIONS CONTRIBUTING TO DEATH BUT NOT RELATED TO THE TERMINAL DISEASE CONDITION GIVEN IN PART I(a)
19. WAS AUTOPSY PERFORMED? YES [ ] NO [X]
20a. (Probably) ACCIDENT [ ] SUICIDE [ ] HOMICIDE [ ]
20b. DESCRIBE HOW INJURY OCCURRED. (Enter nature of injury in Part I or Part II of Item 18.)
20c. TIME OF INJURY Hour a.m. p.m. Month, Day, Year
20d. INJURY OCCURRED WHILE AT WORK [ ] NOT WHILE AT WORK [ ]
20e. PLACE OF INJURY (e.g., in or about home, farm, factory, street, office bldg., etc.)
20f. CITY, TOWN, OR LOCATION COUNTY STATE
21. I attended the deceased from 6:00 pm 10/20/69 to 10/21/69 and last saw him alive on 10/20/69
Death occurred at 5:15 A m on the date stated above; and to the best of my knowledge, from the causes stated
22a. SIGNATURE (Degree or title) M.D.
22b. ADDRESS 501 11th St. N.
22c. DATE SIGNED 10/21/69
23a. BURIAL, CREMATION, REMOVAL (Specify) Removal
23b. DATE Oct. 23, 1969
23c. NAME OF CEMETERY OR CREMATORY Edson Cemetery
23d. LOCATION (City, town, or county) Lowell (State) Massachusetts
24. FUNERAL DIRECTOR'S SIGNATURE / ADDRESS JOHN S. RHODES, INC. St. Petersburg, Fla.
25. DATE REC'D BY LOCAL REG. 10-22-69
26. REGISTRAR'S SIGNATURE

I hereby certify that this is a true and correct copy of a certificate on file in the Office of the Local Registrar of Vital Statistics of the Pinellas County Health Department, St. Petersburg, Florida.

April 22, 1971 ,Deputy Local Registrar

Kerouac's death certificate (Ellis Amburn, Subterranean Kerouac: The Hidden Life of Jack Kerouac, *following p. 212)*

> Kerouac deserves a permanent place in American literature–not as the figurehead for the beat movement in prose, but as an imaginative and quite distinct writer with a unique point of view.
>
> –Jon M. Warner, review of *Visions of Cody, Library Journal,* 15 September 1972

Polarity finder

Christian Science Monitor, 24 October 1969, p. E-1

Writing men are starting to set down their summaries of what the 1950s and 1960s were all about. A Briton, Christopher Booker, for example, has just published a book called "The Neophiliacs" in which the dominant spirit in the decade since World War II is characterized as a "love of the new" –a self-indulgent, quick-to-travel, fantasy-in-drugs-and-psychedelia-seeking temperament: In

Eulogy at Yale

Ginsberg Talks of Kerouac

NEW HAVEN (Conn.) — (AP) — Allen Ginsberg, the poet of both the "beat" and "hip" generations, eulogized his friend and contemporary Jack Kerouac as the man who led "a beginning of a revolution in American consciousness."

Ginsberg came to Yale last night, scheduled to read antiwar poetry to an audience of students and to discuss with them "The Politics of Love."

Instead, after Kerouac's death Tuesday, Ginsberg brought with him four other leading figures of the "beat generation," Gregory Corso, John Clellan Holmes, Peter Schieldahl and Peter Orlovsky.

He began by chanting Buddhist prayers he said Kerouac had "introduced to me and to a large part of America." Orlovsky joined him in the mournful chants, with a single-tone instrument like an accordion the only accompaniment.

Ginsberg also read parts of Kerouac's "Mexico City Blues," which he said showed the novelist and poet's desire, "to die, wanting to get it all over with and be free."

Kerouac, who wrote the novel "On the Road" in the 1950's, was a close friend of Ginsberg's and used him as a model for characters in several books.

Kerouac, Ginsberg said, "broke open a 'fantastic solidity in America as solid as the Empire State Building—that turned out not to be solid at all."

"His vision," he said, "was what the universe as we will experience it is — golden ash, blissful emptiness, a product of our own grasping greed."

Services for Kerouac will be held tomorrow in Lowell, Mass.

The San Francisco Examiner, *23 October 1969*

America, it is not hard to match this theory to the generation of itinerant, mystic cult following youths who seemed at first to migrate to California as beatniks in the early '50's and have since spread back across the nation, flower children and peace-bent in their gentle version, or "pig" baiters and nastily militant at the other extreme.

But however writing men interpret the age of the '50's and '60's, the figure of Jack Kerouac will assert itself–much as the novelist, once a football fullback, tried to thrust himself into life or onto the literary scene or into the company of neighborhood bar mates in his hometown of Lowell, Mass., always hoping to break into the open into a vision of an expansive America and he-man, mystical culture. Kerouac's "On the Road" was the manifesto of the 1950's California march and much of what has followed. It marked a break with America's Anglo-European cultural tradition. A second artistic polarity emerged on the West Coast, an effusiveness and mysticism with origins on the Orient, which rivaled the East Coast's long dominant puritanism and pragmatism.

Kerouac himself got lost between these cultural polarities, could not identify with what he saw as the anti-Americanism of current hippyism, and this week fell victim to the excesses of alcohol. Kerouac may have fumbled away the security of a disciplined literary career. But the first widely read Beat writer has had an effect on the life styles of many American youths.

It is Ginsberg who is reported to have gathered together the scraps of narrative, protest, and hallucination which make up William Burroughs' first novel, *The Naked Lunch,* and to have given them what semblance of shape–approximate only, even after Ginsberg's ministrations–the book has.

But he has not only played, as it were, the Ezra Pound to Burroughs' T. S. Eliot, collating and editing what the madness of another had created but could not organize; he has also invented the legend of Jack Kerouac, this time with the collaboration of certain photographers from *Life* the ladies' magazines, transforming the ex-Columbia University athlete, the author of a dull and conventional *Bildungsroman* remembered by no one, into a fantasy figure capable of moving the imagination of rebellious kids with educations and literary aspirations, as his more *lumpen* opposite numbers, Elvis Presley, Marlon Brando, and James Dean, were moving their less literate and ambitious contemporaries. The legend of Kerouac is, to be sure, much more interesting than any of his books, since it is the work of a more talented writer, but the young confuse the two, as, I presume, do Ginsberg and even Kerouac. Much more important, however, than Ginsberg's rescue of Burroughs' crumpled notes from himself to himself, is Ginsberg's invention of a theory to justify both Burroughs' work and his own, for it constitutes the nearest thing to a program possessed by our own quite un-programmatic young.

– Leslie Fiedler, *Waiting for the End,* pp. 163–164

Kerouac's life has inspired more than a dozen biographies through 2000, with more slated to appear. In his 15 April 1973 review of Ann Charters's Kerouac: A Biography *(1973) in* The New York Times Book Review, *John Deck commented on the writer's legacy.*

Truman Capote said it wasn't writing but "typing," in 1959, when Jack Kerouac's books were crowding the market. Among the novels on the stands then was "The Dharma Bums," written in "ten sittings" and labeled a "potboiler" by the author himself. In that novel were visions and prophecies of the famous "rucksack revolution," land-loving congregations of holy people taking to the hills, and the adaptation of Eastern philosophy in the unenlightened West. Much of what was foreseen is today. Surely people who still hold with Mr. Capote's statement would admit that it was, at the very least, inspired typing.

Usually a recognized literary movement can be expected to influence subsequent writing. Feasibly it changes attitudes and affects language. But the Beat Generation did much more. Sons of the middle classes left home after reading "On the Road." Those commonplaces of our era – drugs, youth cult, ecstasy questing, rapping and the call for radical surgery on the Great American Oaf – surfaced and took hold with, and probably because of, Beat writing.

–pp. 23–24

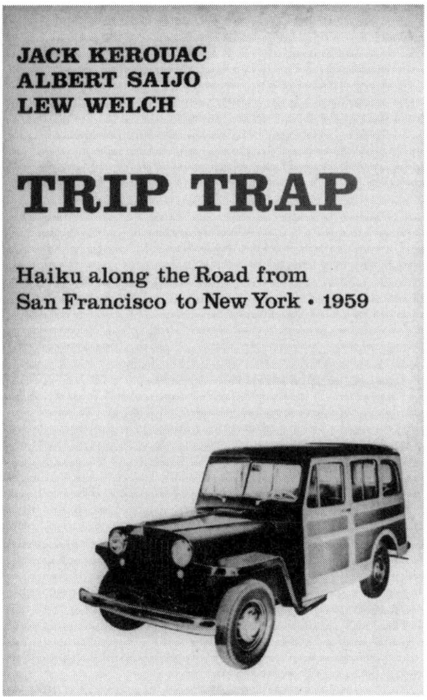

Cover for Kerouac's 1973 book made up of haiku that he, Lew Welch, and Albert Saijo wrote as they drove from California to New York in 1959

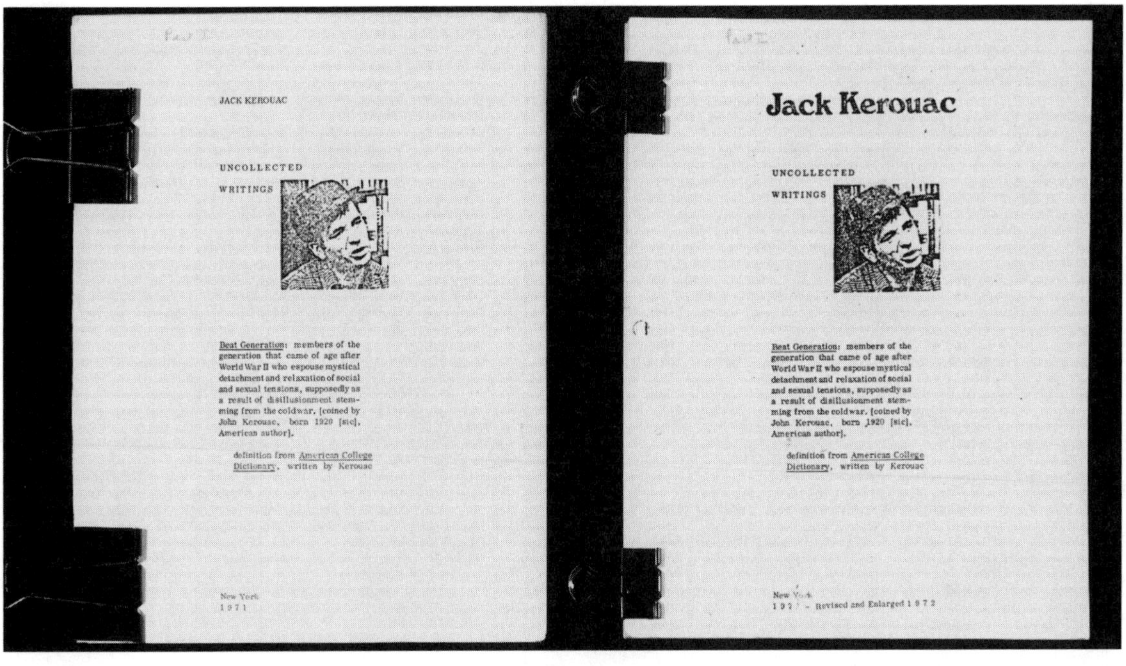

"Jack Kerouac" book, held together by clips. For years after his death, much of Kerouac's writing remained unpublished, and many of his shorter pieces (often written for magazines) were hard to find. At least one collection circulated among friends and fans in this mimeographed compilation, "Uncollected Writings" (New York Public Library).

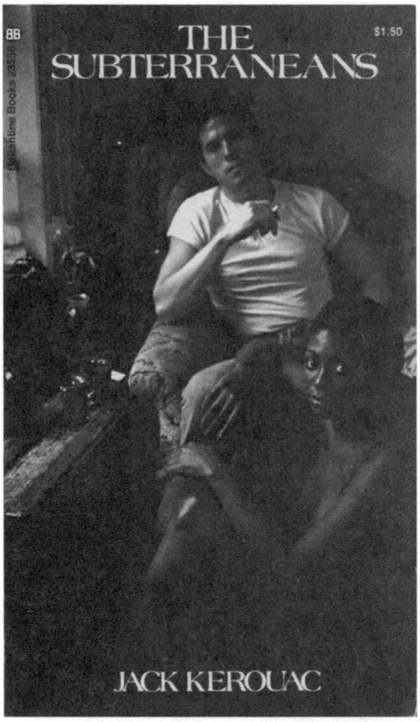

Covers for three of the paperback editions of Kerouac's third novel that have been published since his death

Park named for the author in his hometown of Lowell, Massachusetts (photograph by Matt Theado).

Chapter 4
Allen Ginsberg

(3 June 1926 – 5 April 1997)

See also the Ginsberg entries in *DLB 5: American Poets Since WWII; DLB 16: The Beats: Literary Bohemians in Postwar America;* and *DLB 169: American Poets Since WWII, Fifth Series.*

Shortly after Allen Ginsberg's death of liver cancer on 5 April 1997, his friend of fifty years, fellow Beat writer William S. Burroughs, said that Ginsberg "was a great person with worldwide influence. He was a pioneer of openness and a lifelong model of candor. He stood for freedom of expression and for coming out of all the closets long before others did. He has influence because he said what he believed." An official at Stanford University, where Ginsberg's massive archive is held, summed up the poet's career: "Allen Ginsberg is one of the most important figures in postwar culture, literature, and politics."

Irwin Allen Ginsberg was born in Newark, New Jersey, on 3 June 1926. His father, Louis, taught high school and was a published poet, and his mother, Naomi, was a Russian immigrant who impressed her Marxist beliefs on young Allen and his older brother, Eugene. The combined influences of poetry and social activism forged Ginsberg's future.

Allen Ginsberg with his mother, Naomi, at the New York World's Fair in 1940 (© Allen Ginsberg Trust)

Born Naomi Livergants in 1894 in Russia, Ginsberg's mother had remained a fervent Marxist even after her immigration to the United States. In his poem "America," Ginsberg wrote, "when I was seven momma took me to Communist Cell meetings . . . the speeches were free [and] everybody was angelic and sentimental about the workers." He also recalled that his mother "made up bedtime stories that all went something like this: 'The good king rode forth from his castle, saw the suffering workers and healed them.'" After a series of nervous breakdowns, during which Naomi was institutionalized, she received a lobotomy in 1948, authorized, after some hesitation, by Allen and his brother. She died in 1956 in the Pilgrim State Hospital on Long Island.

Setting His Course

In 1944, when he was a seventeen-year-old freshman at Columbia University, Ginsberg met Jack Kerouac, four years his senior, who was no longer enrolled at the college. Ginsberg learned much about writing from Kerouac, and their letters reveal their desire to be great writers and to encourage each other toward that accomplishment. As Ginsberg matured during and after his college years, he was deeply troubled. He feared passing up a secure middle-class academic life in exchange for the tumults of pursuing visionary poetry and also realized that he was courting danger by being openly homosexual in an intolerant society. He coped in part by exploring his interior, emotional life in his poetry—a process that led to his writing "Howl."

Sixteen-year-old Ginsberg in a yearbook of East Side High School in Paterson, New Jersey

In his youth, Ginsberg's poems were generally composed in quatrains. These poems, though often visionary in content, were for the most part tightly controlled rhythmically and neatly rhymed. In his later twenties Ginsberg began to experiment with rhythms and line lengths. One breakthrough came when he began to revise earlier journal entries, breaking the prose into "small groups of lines." In this way he began to use a more natural diction while focusing the reader's attention visually on the poetic images. He realized, though, that the "lines are not yet free enough" and looked ahead to a time of "expansion."

In this excerpt originally published in Guilty of Everything, *Herbert Huncke tells how he and his associates Jack Melody and Vickie Russell came to be arrested for operating a burglary ring out of Ginsberg's apartment in spring 1949. Ginsberg was suspended from Columbia University but later returned to complete his degree. For his part in the ring, Ginsberg spent eight months in Columbia Presbyterian Psychiatric Institute, where he met Carl Solomon. He was released in February 1950.*

When Jackie came back on the scene he took Vickie with him out to his family's house on Long Island.

The two of them began to visit me at Allen's place. Vickie had met Allen before. In fact, she had been involved for a short while with Kerouac while I was down in Texas. They knew of my operations with Johnnie and I had let it be known that I would like to get into action again if possible. As a rule I didn't like to go out with Jackie, but one afternoon I did go. He wanted to take the house of a detective he'd had some friction with. It was about five o'clock on a Wednesday or Thursday, and we took the swag back to Allen's apartment.

This was the same day that Kerouac had gotten a contract for his first book, *The Town and the City*. He came around that evening and we did some drinking and smoking and we were going to try and cop some stuff. I had some cash in my pocket. Things were jumping and Jack invited us over to John Clellon Holmes's place for a party they were throwing for him in honor of the book contract. Holmes was writing a book later to be called *Go*. We went over there—Jackie, Vickie, and myself—and stayed for a while. It was one of the first times I'd met Holmes, certainly the first time we talked at any length. I found him interesting and always cor-

I came out of the closet at Columbia in 1946. The first person I told about it was Kerouac, because I was in love with him. He was staying in my room up in the bed, and I was sleeping on a pallet on the floor. I said, "Jack, you know, I love you, and I want to sleep with you, and I really like men." And he said, "Oooooh, no . . ." We'd known each other maybe a year, and I hadn't said anything.

–Allen Ginsberg, *Gay Sunshine Interview,* p. 4

dial. Whenever I met up with him he was always considerate of me.

The three of us left the party together, and Jackie and Vickie were in the midst of a family quarrel. They were snapping at each other and were beginning to get on my nerves. Jackie had gotten himself a car, though he didn't have a license, and the car was stolen by some associates of his–they wanted to cut back out to Long Island. I said, "Look, you two guys go on. I'm staying in New York." They dropped me off and instead of going home I went downtown and fucked around. I got smashed and ended up at the Clinton Hotel for some reason or another.

At any rate the next morning I cut back to the pad and nobody was there. This was unusual and I knew somehow there was something wrong. I went into the apartment because I wanted to get straight. I had a stash of stuff there and I settled down and cooked up. I had just gotten myself organized when the door bursts open and there's Vickie with her hair standing on end. Allen was behind her, without his glasses, being led by the hand into the room by Vickie. He looked dazed.

Vickie had tears in her eyes, and said, "Man, Jackie's been busted." I said, "Oh, no. What happened?" She laid down this story about how they were going over to see a new fence out in Long Island. They'd stopped by the apartment and Allen suggested they first drive him up to Columbia. It was a beautiful spring morning, and then they asked Allen if he wanted to come along for the ride. Jackie got onto the Island, and because he and Vickie were doing one of their conversational bits, he made a wrong turn on the expressway. Just then a cruiser spotted them.

Ginsberg on a New York City rooftop in 1953 (photograph by William S. Burroughs; © Allen Ginsberg Trust)

Instead of pulling over, Jackie made a U-turn over the center island and stepped on the gas. The cops came hauling after them. When he tried to make another turn he hit a stone stanchion, and boom! There's the scene. He gets out and goes one way and Vickie grabs Allen and they go another. Apparently Allen left all his books and notebooks in the car and it was through them that they eventually connected with the address to this apartment.

Now Vickie and Allen were standing there telling me this and my first thought is, I'm not going to leave all this swag. I didn't have any cash and I knew I could take this stuff to a hock shop. I told them, "Look, let's get a few things together and get the fuck out of here." I wanted to get started but they were sort of milling about. I wanted to leave things in order a little bit and get my wits together, so I began to sweep the floor. I hadn't any more than started when there was a rapping at the door. I said, "Here they are."

Next thing we're all in a car together and we're being driven out to Long Island. I end up in a precinct house without really knowing what the score is. They haven't booked me yet. I'm beginning to think that maybe I can walk out of this when somebody comes up to me and says, "Oh, you're Huncke. We've got a screamer on you." They had a warrant for my arrest. They booked me then. And they booked Vickie and Allen too. We all went to the Long Island detention prison. Later on Vickie was separated and was taken to the old Women's House of Detention in Greenwich Village.

My imprisonment ties in with Johnnie, my old partner in burglarizing. When I got busted, they hadn't known I was involved because I hadn't been at the scene of the accident. When they found the apartment they didn't know whether I was involved with these people or not. They had to go figure it, of course, but they didn't know what the score was. The screamers started coming in on me around four o'clock in the morning. I was wanted in New York for cracking a doctor's pad in Flushing and taking a .32. I was really heartbroken, because the only way they could have possibly found out about that was through Johnnie.

I was credited with fifty-two burglaries, but that was only a small portion. Johnnie and I must have broken into at least a hundred places.

Ginsberg's brother, the lawyer, arrived and Allen got out fairly quickly. I remember looking up and seeing him standing at the bars peering around with a woebegone expression. It was his first time he'd come so close to anything of this nature. He was saying Jewish prayers. I felt so sorry for him. He got out of jail but he ended up at Columbia Psychiatric Institute for treatment. That's where he met Carl Solomon and that whole bit. It was a turning point for him.

Jackie and I both laid up in that detention prison for most of the summer. Fortunately, his people came and kept in touch with him, and thereby somebody kept in touch with me. But I was tapped right out. I didn't have a thing. When we were separated I went one way and he went another, and I was on my own after that.

–*The Herbert Huncke Reader,* pp. 264–266

Ginsberg's Reading

Ginsberg was always a voracious reader, and his reading list in the 1950s shows both the extent and the breadth of his interests, which ranged from the classics to modern works to the writing of contemporary Beats such as Neal Cassady, Gary Snyder, and Michael McClure. Represented on this list are some of Ginsberg's most important influences: William Blake, Walt Whitman, Ezra Pound, and William Carlos Williams. In August 1954 Ginsberg was reading poems by Kenneth Rexroth, who figured prominently in the San Francisco poetry renaissance and also influenced "Howl."

Reading June–'54

Age of Anxiety–Auden
Folded Leaf–Maxwell
Kant–Selections
B. Russell–Selections from Hist. of Phil.
S. Anderson–Winesburg, O.
Quarterly Review of Lit.–British Poets (Durrell's Sappho)
Gore Vidal–The Judgment of Paris
July
Céline–Mea Culpa & Semmelweiss
Gertrude Stein–Paris, France; Autobiog. of A. Toklas
Gina Cerminova–Cayce System Book
Wm. Cayce–Extracts from Readings (psychic)
Cassady, N.–Fragments of Autobiog. reread
Stein–Things As They Are
Horney–Our Inner Conflicts
Céline–Last half of Journey to End of Night (finally finished after10 years) I had reserved it for later pleasure. Will get hold of Guignol's Band, which just came out in English (Summer '54)
Proust–Cities of the Plain–part, first chapters Vol. II
Eliot–Selected Essays to 1932
Bhagavad Gita–Isherwood tr.
poems–in Understanding Poetry Brooks & Warren

Plato–Symposium
Encyclopedia Britannica articles on Hermetic types and sects
Eliot–4 Quartets–Idea of Xtian Society
Pound–Pisan Cantos, XXX Cantos
H.D.–Collected Poems (1925)
e. e. cummings–
An Examination of Pound–
A. E. Coppard–a few stories (The Silver Circus)
The Invisible Man–R. Ellison
Flee the Angry Strangers–Geo. Mandel
Pavannes & Divagations–Pound
Vita Nuova–Dante (Rossetti tr.)
Boccaccio–Fiammetta
Rimbaud–Season in Hell

. . . .

Reading August 1954 (San Francisco)

W. C. Williams–Complete Collected Poems
Li Po Translations–Obata
Catullus Translations–Wm. A. Aiken
Ez. Pound–ABC Reading
F. R Leavis–Revaluations in Poetry (parts)
Van Doren–Anthology of World Poetry (parts)
Stephens' Travels in Yucatán Vol. I
Karl Vossler–Medieval Culture Vol. II (parts)
W. C. Williams–The Build Up (Novel)
L F. Céline–Guignol's Band
Sophocles–Philoctetes (Jebb tr.)
Shakespeare–Troilus & Cressida
Chandler Brossard–The Bold Saboteurs
Sister Mary Barry–Analysis of Eliot's Prosody (Catholic U.)
Eliot–Early poems
T. S. Eliot–Essay on Milton (1948? 50?); The Confidential Clerk
Glenn Hughes–Imagism & the Imagists
Catullus–Cambridge Latin ed. & Horace Gregory translations
Tibullus
Encyclopedia Britannica articles relating to verification, rhythm, etc.
W. C. Williams–The Desert Music
Rexroth, K.–A few plays & Early Poems
Marlowe–Ovid's Elegies Translation (skimmed)
Gide–Corydon
Cézanne–Biography by John Rewald
Keats–Odes & random shots
Milton–Shorter poems
Jack Lindsay–Catullus translations

. . . .

April–May SF 1955

H. Hesse–Siddhartha
D. H. Lawrence–Selected poems (Rexroth ed.)
Corbière translations C. F. MacIntyre
Randall Jarrell–Selected Poems
Graves & Riding–Survey of Modern Poetry
Collected poetry–Laura Riding
Edw. Dahlberg–Do These Bones Live? (23 pages)
W. C. Williams–Selected Essays
K. Rexroth–Signature of All Things, In What Hour, Phoenix & Tortoise
Ezra Pound–Classic Anthology Defined by Confucius
Eliot–all poems reread (aloud)
Zukofsky–*Anew,* and *A Test of Poetry*
Nahm–Selections from Early Greek Philosophy–Heraclitus
W. H. Auden–Shield of Achilles
Godolphin Mod Lib Treas Latin poets
Hadas " " " Greek poets
Anacreon (19th cent Locke ed. interlinear)
Sappho (Pauper Press ed. various translations)
Pound–Collected Criticism 1954 ed.
Pound–Kulchur

July 1955
Chas. Reznikoff–Poems (early)
Buddha–Diamond Sutra, beginning of Surangama Sutra, in Goddard, *Buddhist Bible*
Collected Poems–Laura Riding (most of)
Brave New World–Huxley
Shakespeare–A Winter's Tale
J. M. Keynes–Two Memoirs (Lawrence & Dr. Melchior) (plus some of essays)
The Vestal Lady on Brattle St.–Corso, Gregory
10 Centuries of Spanish poetry–Turnbull (Unamuno & St. John Cross)
Cocaine–Pettigrilli (couldn't finish)
Faulkner–A Fable
Pound–Translations
Vollard–Cézanne
Art of Indian Asia–Bollingen Vol. 2 (plates)
Eberhart–Undercliff (parts)
Auden–Shield of Achilles (reread)
Jarrell–Collected Poems
Keats–Reviewed Odes & Sonnets, etc., late poems

Aug.
Old Testament Begun First time thru since High School–Genesis

Mark Schorer–The Shores of Light?? A novel anyway very poor
Josephine Miles–Lines at Intersection, Local Measures, Diction Book
Genet–2 plays *Haute surveillance & Les bonnes*
Cocteau–The Typewriter; Diary of Film (Beauty & Beast)
Paul Klee–On Modern Art; and Gideon Wellick volume
Wallace Stevens–later poems in Collected Poems
e. e. cummings–later poems in Collected Poems
Cocteau–Call to Order
Genet–Letter to Lenore Fini & *Le Condamné à mort & Chant d'amour*
Genet–Gutter in the Sky (Miracle of Rose, Leva Phila tr.) (reread Frechtman tr.?)
Céline–Guignol's Band, finished
Dudley Fitts–Anthology of Latin American Poetry
New Directions 1940–Surrealist Anthology
Guillaume Apollinaire–Some of N.D. Selected Writing
Lorca–Various translations & originals (Spanish)–N. Dir. vol. also
Wallace Fowlie–Mid-century French poetry
A Mirror for French Poetry (read book read already in N.Y.)
Gogo Lamantia–various writings
Gary Snyder & Mike McClure–S.F. poets various MSS (also Robt Howard, Dave Toplis, etc.)
Horace–Interlinear tr. of complete Horace begun

Dec.
Various books on Zen, Blyth's 4 vols. Haiku (in & out), Senryu, Sutras, etc.
Whitman Complete, Modern Library Edition
Cendrars, Blaise (a bit in Fr.)
Artaud–Pour en finir avec le jugement de dieu (Guy Werhnam tr. in MS)

–*Allen Ginsberg: Journals Mid-Fifties, 1954–1958*, pp. 27–28, 55, 213–215

Bringing "Howl" to the Public

Ginsberg's most famous–and most notorious–poem is "Howl," first published by City Lights Books in 1956. "Howl" recounts in urgent, chantlike rhythms the poet's associations with his coterie of Beat underground figures, including Jack Kerouac, Neal Cassady, William Burroughs, Herbert Huncke, and Carl Solomon.

In summer 1955 Ginsberg mailed a typescript of the poem to Kerouac, who was then in Mexico City and writing his own long poem, Mexico City Blues. *Kerouac wrote back to Ginsberg, saying that he found "HOWL FOR CARL SOLOMON" to be "very powerful." By this time Kerouac had fully developed his notions of spontaneous prose and the sanctity of "first thought, best thought." He counseled Ginsberg on his poetic output: "I don't want it arbitrarily negated by secondary emendations made in time's reconsidering backstep–I want your lingual SPONTANEITY or nothing." Ginsberg was quick to assure him that the poem was in its freshest, unrevised form. For some time Kerouac was often given credit for titling "Howl," as Ginsberg apparently forgot that he had scrawled "Howl for Carl Solomon" himself atop the page before sending it to Kerouac.*

Ginsberg in San Francisco, about the time he was writing "Howl" (Ginsberg Collection)

Ginsberg's North Beach apartment, where he wrote the first part of "Howl." The Ginsberg portrait on the wall was drawn by Carolyn Cassady (photograph by Allen Ginsberg; © Allen Ginsberg Trust).

Ginsberg described his circumstances at the time he was writing the first part of "Howl" in a note on the photograph of his room.

My front room first floor 1010 Montgomery Street North Beach apartment wherein I wrote *Howl* Part I, Peter Orlovsky's room down the hall past the kitchen in back overlooked lower Telegraph Hill's roofs and Oakland Bay. I was living on unemployment checks, Robert La Vigne's army-surplus jacket portrait of me & Cezanne-like watercolor landscape pinned to wall above woven basket on mantel, fireplace lit. Bollingen series books shelved, letters and essays Ezra Pound under bed-table clock, black-painted bureau with victrola-Case & Back on top, checkered wool blanket hung over alley window. "Blessed be the Muses / for their descent / dancing round my desk / crowning my balding head / with laurel." San Francisco, Summer 1955.

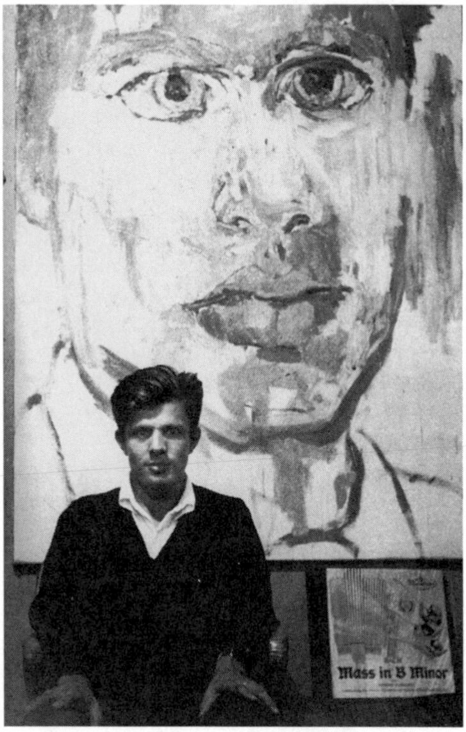

Peter Orlovsky, seated before his portrait by Robert La Vigne at the Montgomery Street apartment. Ginsberg met Orlovsky in San Francisco in December 1954; the two men were lovers for thirty years (© Allen Ginsberg Trust).

Ginsberg in Orlovsky's Portrero Hill apartment in San Francisco working on "Howl" in 1955 (© Allen Ginsberg Trust)

Solomon made a statement for the 1986 publication of Howl: Original Draft Facsimile, *in which he describes how he came to meet Ginsberg.*

A kind of immature romantic at the time, full of flowery dreams of Paris–having just read to completion Romain Rolland's novel *Jean Christophe*–I deserted, very precipitously and foolishly, I later decided, the American Liberty ship *Alexander Ramsey,* in the port of La Pallice in Brittany (during May of 1947) and made my way to La Rochelle (the provincial capital). There my first move was to get a haircut.

Then, on to Paris, settled in Montparnasse, read *Tropic of Cancer,* and hired a French lady to teach me the language.

It was not long before I had developed a taste for nougat and haricots verts, attended a lecture on Kafka by Jean-Paul Sartre at the Salle Gaveau, seen the *Mona Lisa,* made friends at the Cité Universitaire who had turned me on to Prévert and Michaux, begun an amatory relationship with the lady in Montmartre, witnessed an Artaud reading on the rue Jacob, attended a CP rally at the Vel d'Hiv, and discovered Isou and *lettrisme.*

Six weeks and it was all over (the Paris *séjour*) and I came back to the States. Letterism had already awakened an interest in me and I was especially interested in the new poets of my generation of whom Isou and his followers seemed to be very significant ones. The whole tendency toward the non-verbal as I witnessed its reflection even in such American phenomena as the scat singing of Jackie Cain and Ray Kraal. I sat in the Forty-second Street library in those years reading the latest issues of *La Nouvelle Revue Française.* I remember a special issue devoted to "Young Men of Twenty" in the year 1948.

My protest against the verbal, the rational and the acceptable took the form of disruption of a critical discussion of Mallarmé and other neo-dada clowning, which resulted in my incarnation in a psychiatric hospital in Manhattan. Where I encountered Allen Ginsberg, a fellow patient who was intrigued by my collection of Paris-acquired books. Among the Artaud, Genêt, Michaux, Miller, and Lautréamont was Isou's *Nouvelle Poésie et une Nouvelle Musique.* We discussed all of these things by way of laying the groundwork for Allen's eventual publication of "Howl" in 1956.

After treatment at P.I., I was readmitted to Brooklyn College, dropped out after subsequent marriage and job offer in book publishing.

After release from Pilgrim State (post "Howl") I took a battery of aptitude tests administered by the

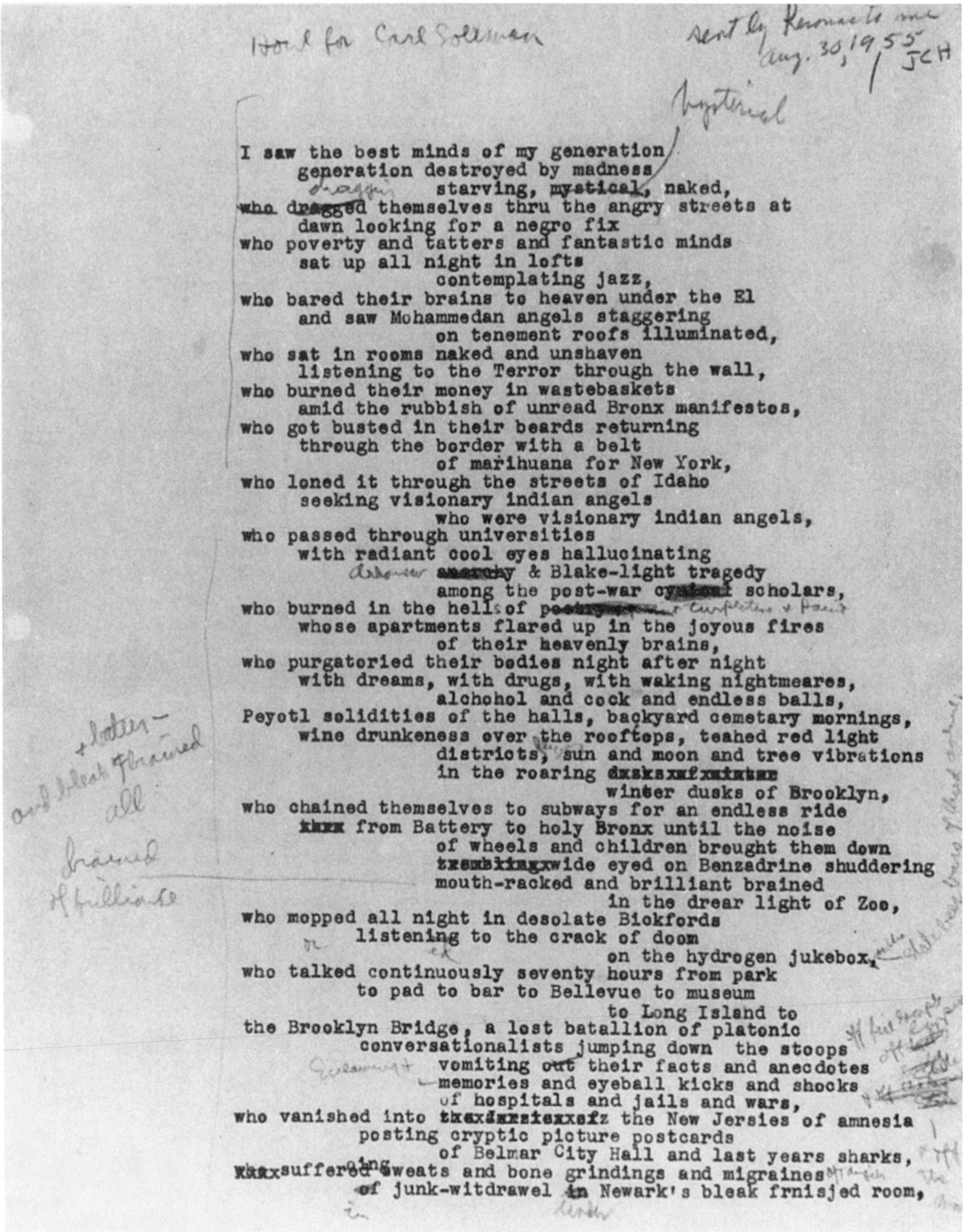

Howl for Carl Solomon

sent by Kerouac to me Aug. 30, 1955 JCH

hysterical

I saw the best minds of my generation
generation destroyed by madness
starving, mystical, naked,
who dragged themselves thru the angry streets at
dawn looking for a negro fix
who poverty and tatters and fantastic minds
sat up all night in lofts
contemplating jazz,
who bared their brains to heaven under the El
and saw Mohammedan angels staggering
on tenement roofs illuminated,
who sat in rooms naked and unshaven
listening to the Terror through the wall,
who burned their money in wastebaskets
amid the rubbish of unread Bronx manifestos,
who got busted in their beards returning
through the border with a belt
of marihuana for New York,
who loned it through the streets of Idaho
seeking visionary indian angels
who were visionary indian angels,
who passed through universities
with radiant cool eyes hallucinating
anarchy & Blake-light tragedy
among the post-war cynical scholars,
who burned in the hells of poetry
whose apartments flared up in the joyous fires
of their heavenly brains,
who purgatoried their bodies night after night
with dreams, with drugs, with waking nightmeares,
alchohol and cock and endless balls,
Peyotl solidities of the halls, backyard cemetary mornings,
wine drunkeness over the rooftops, teahed red light
districts, sun and moon and tree vibrations
in the roaring
winter dusks of Brooklyn,
who chained themselves to subways for an endless ride
from Battery to holy Bronx until the noise
of wheels and children brought them down
wide eyed on Benzadrine shuddering
mouth-racked and brilliant brained
in the drear light of Zoo,
who mopped all night in desolate Bickfords
listening to the crack of doom
on the hydrogen jukebox,
who talked continuously seventy hours from park
to pad to bar to Bellevue to museum
to Long Island to
the Brooklyn Bridge, a lost batallion of platonic
conversationalists jumping down the stoops
vomiting out their facts and anecdotes
memories and eyeball kicks and shocks
of hospitals and jails and wars,
who vanished into the New Jersies of amnesia
posting cryptic picture postcards
of Belmar City Hall and last years sharks,
who suffered sweats and bone grindings and migraines
of junk-witdrawel in Newark's bleak frnisjed room,

First page of the revised typescript for "Howl" that Ginsberg sent to Jack Kerouac in summer 1955. The handwriting of John Clellon Holmes, to whom Kerouac subsequently mailed the poem, appears in the upper right-hand corner. All of the revisions are in Ginsberg's hand (Special Collections Department of the Butler Library of Columbia University).

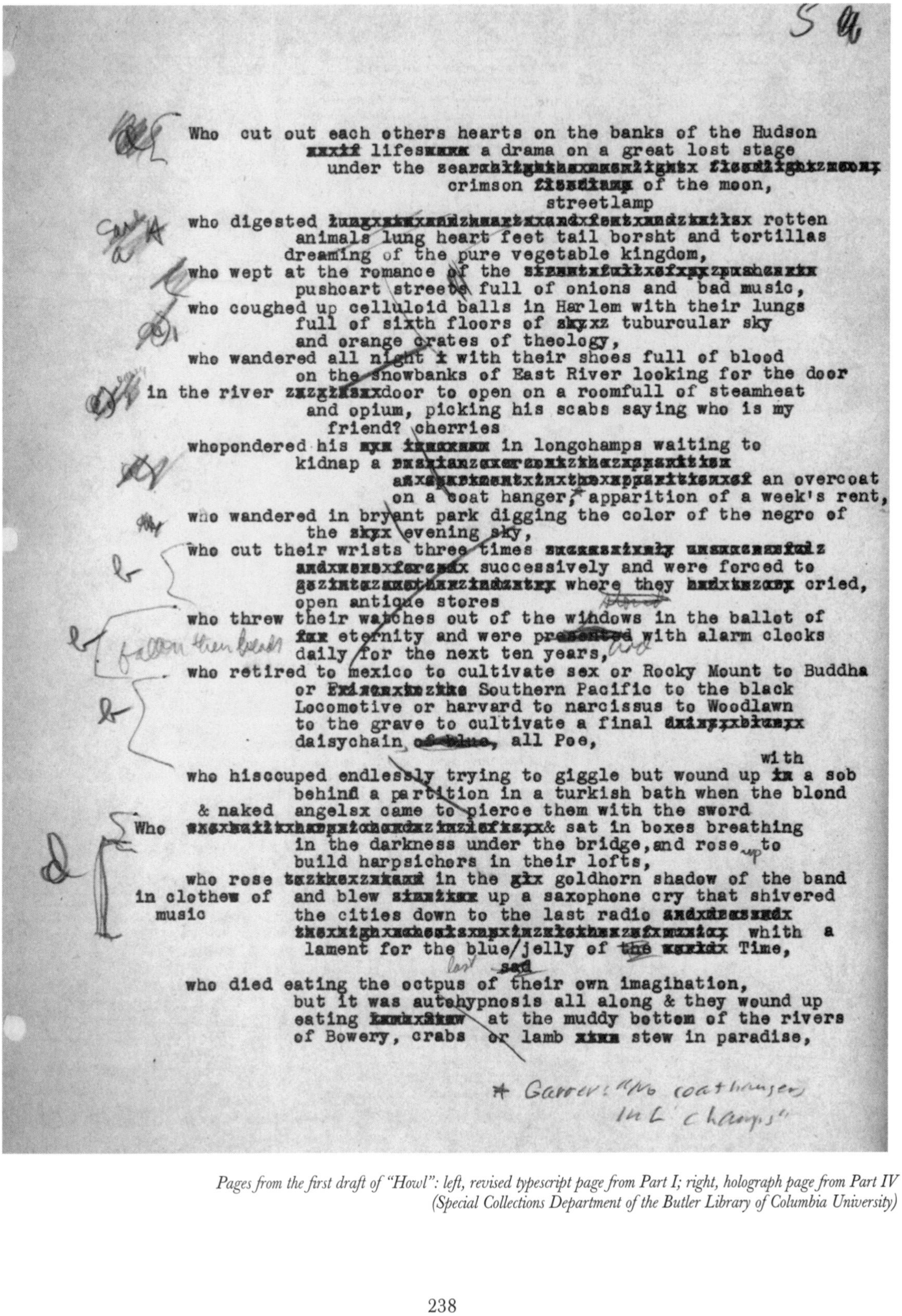

5 4

Who cut out each others hearts on the banks of the Hudson
xxxif lifesxxxx a drama on a great lost stage
under the searchlights crimson lamp of the moon,
streetlamp
who digested lung heart feet tail rotten
animals lung heart feet tail borsht and tortillas
dreaming of the pure vegetable kingdom,
who wept at the romance of the
pushcart streets full of onions and bad music,
who coughed up celluloid balls in Harlem with their lungs
full of sixth floors of skyxz tuburcular sky
and orange crates of theology,
who wandered all night x with their shoes full of blood
on the snowbanks of East River looking for the door
in the river door to open on a roomfull of steamheat
and opium, picking his scabs saying who is my
friend? cherries
whopondered his in longchamps waiting to
kidnap a
an overcoat
on a coat hanger,* apparition of a week's rent,
who wandered in bryant park digging the color of the negro of
the skyx evening sky,
who cut their wrists three times
successively and were forced to
where they cried,
open antique stores
who threw their watches out of the windows in the ballet of
fxx eternity and were presented with alarm clocks
daily for the next ten years,
fallen their heads
who retired to mexico to cultivate sex or Rocky Mount to Buddha
or Southern Pacific to the black
Locomotive or harvard to narcissus to Woodlawn
to the grave to cultivate a final
daisychain of blue, all Poe,
with
who hiscouped endlessly trying to giggle but wound up in a sob
behind a partition in a turkish bath when the blond
& naked angelsx came to pierce them with the sword
Who & sat in boxes breathing
in the darkness under the bridge, and rose up to
build harpsichors in their lofts,
who rose in the goldhorn shadow of the band
in clothes of and blew up a saxophone cry that shivered
music the cities down to the last radio
whith a
lament for the blue/jelly of the Time,
last sad
who died eating the octpus of their own imagination,
but it was autohypnosis all along & they wound up
eating at the muddy bottom of the rivers
of Bowery, crabs or lamb stew in paradise,

* Garver: "No coathangers in L'champs"

Pages from the first draft of "Howl": left, revised typescript page from Part I; right, holograph page from Part IV (Special Collections Department of the Butler Library of Columbia University)

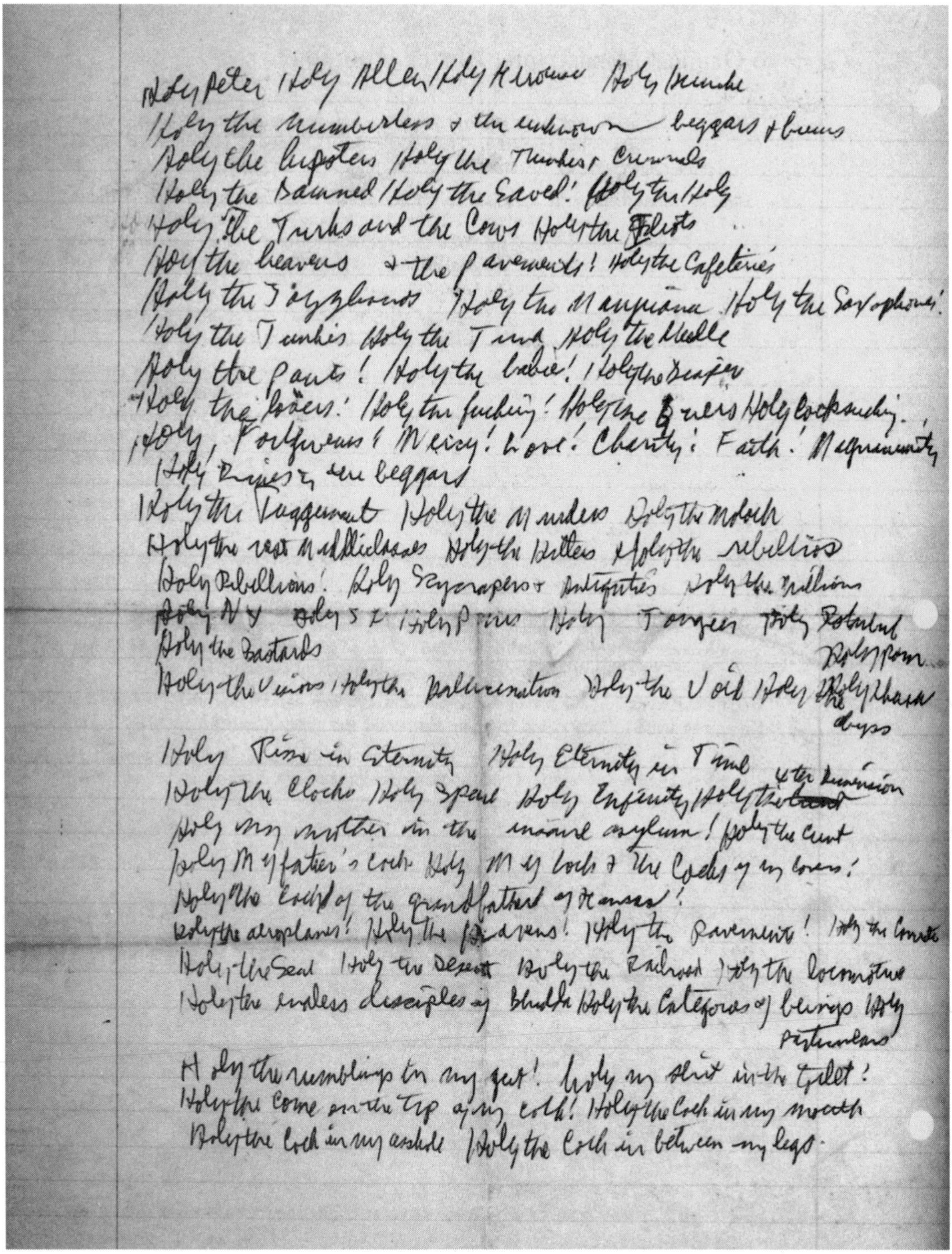

Holy Peter Holy Allen Holy Kerouac Holy Huncke
Holy the numberless & the unknown beggars & bums
Holy the hipsters Holy the Junkies, criminals
Holy the Damned Holy the Saved! Holy the Holy
Holy the Trucks and the Cows Holy the Idiots
Holy the heavens & the pavements! Holy the Cafeterias
Holy the Jazzbands Holy the Marijuana Holy the Saxophones!
Holy the Junkies Holy the Tina Holy the Mulle
Holy the pants! Holy the babes! Holy the Sleepers
Holy the lovers! Holy the fucking! Holy the Queers Holy cocksucking.
Holy, Forgiveness! Mercy! Love! Charity! Faith! Magnanimity
Holy Kindness to the beggars
Holy the Juggernaut Holy the Murders Holy the Moloch
Holy the vast Middleclasses Holy the Hitlers & Holy the rebellious
Holy Rebellions! Holy Skyscrapers & Antiquities Holy the Millions
~~Holy~~ NY ~~Holy~~ SF Holy Paris Holy Tangiers Holy Istanbul
Holy the Bastards Holy porn
Holy the visions Holy the hallucination Holy the Void Holy Holy the Chaos abyss
Holy Time in Eternity Holy Eternity in Time
Holy the Clocks Holy Space Holy Infinity Holy the 4th dimension
Holy my mother in the insane asylum! Holy the cunt
Holy my father's cock Holy my cock & the Cocks of my lovers!
Holy the cocks of the grandfathers of Kansas!
Holy the aeroplanes! Holy the gardens! Holy the pavements! Holy the Comets
Holy the Seas Holy the Deserts Holy the Railroad Holy the locomotive
Holy the endless disciples of Buddha Holy the Categories of beings Holy Particulars
Holy the rumblings in my gut! Holy my shit in the toilet!
Holy the come on the tip of my cock! Holy the cock in my mouth
Holy the cock in my asshole Holy the cock in between my legs.

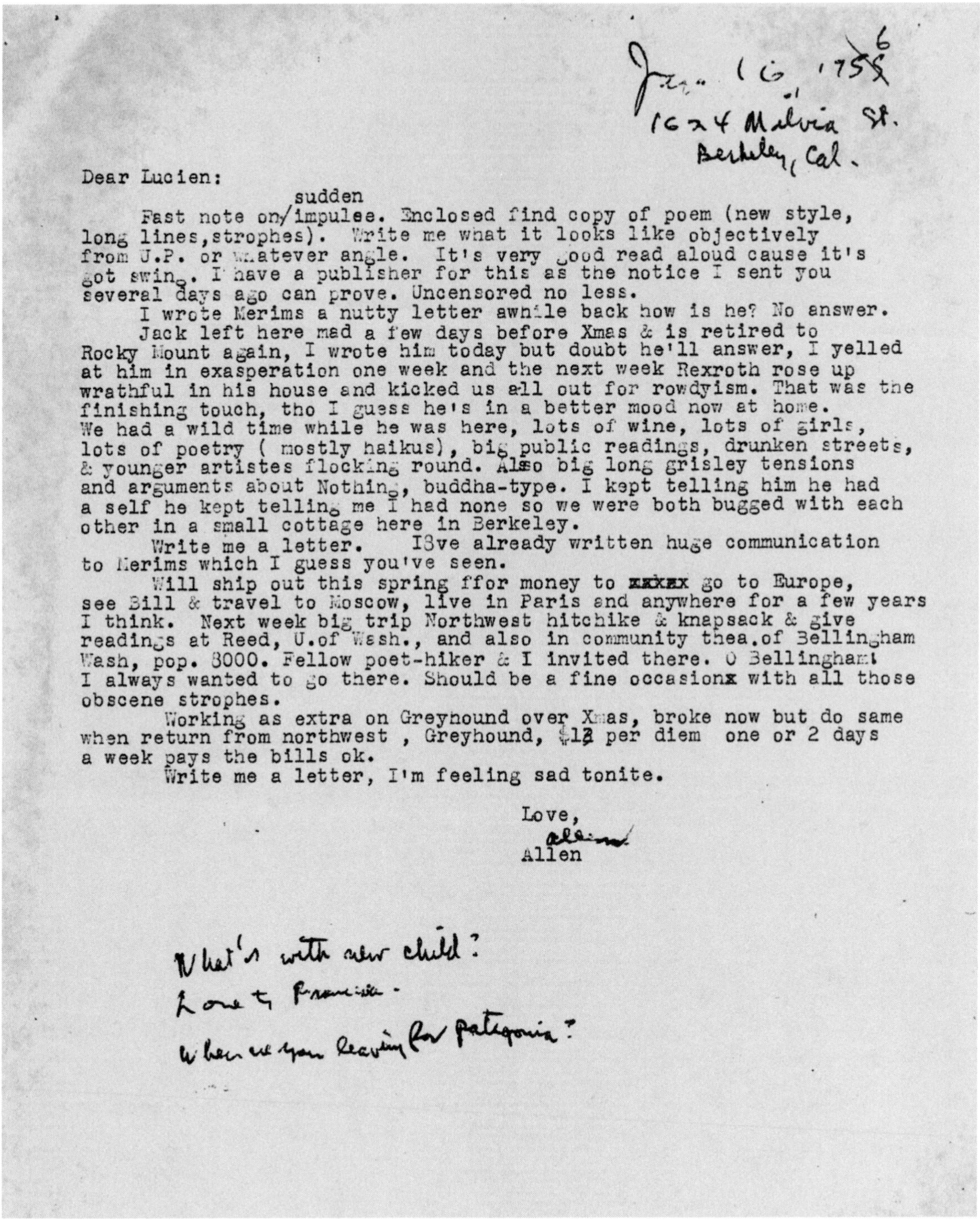

Jan. 16, 1956
1624 Milvia St.
Berkeley, Cal.

Dear Lucien:

Fast note on sudden impulsee. Enclosed find copy of poem (new style, long lines, strophes). Write me what it looks like objectively from J.P. or whatever angle. It's very good read aloud cause it's got swing. I have a publisher for this as the notice I sent you several days ago can prove. Uncensored no less.

I wrote Merims a nutty letter awhile back how is he? No answer.

Jack left here mad a few days before Xmas & is retired to Rocky Mount again, I wrote him today but doubt he'll answer, I yelled at him in exasperation one week and the next week Rexroth rose up wrathful in his house and kicked us all out for rowdyism. That was the finishing touch, tho I guess he's in a better mood now at home. We had a wild time while he was here, lots of wine, lots of girls, lots of poetry (mostly haikus), big public readings, drunken streets, & younger artistes flocking round. Also big long grisley tensions and arguments about Nothing, buddha-type. I kept telling him he had a self he kept telling me I had none so we were both bugged with each other in a small cottage here in Berkeley.

Write me a letter. I3ve already written huge communication to Merims which I guess you've seen.

Will ship out this spring ffor money to ~~xxxxx~~ go to Europe, see Bill & travel to Moscow, live in Paris and anywhere for a few years I think. Next week big trip Northwest hitchike & knapsack & give readings at Reed, U.of Wash., and also in community thea.of Bellingham Wash, pop. 8000. Fellow poet-hiker & I invited there. O Bellingham! I always wanted to go there. Should be a fine occasionx with all those obscene strophes.

Working as extra on Greyhound over Xmas, broke now but do same when return from northwest , Greyhound, $12 per diem one or 2 days a week pays the bills ok.

Write me a letter, I'm feeling sad tonite.

Love,
Allen
Allen

What's with new child?
Love to Francesca.
When are you leaving for patagonia?

Ginsberg's 16 January 1956 letter to Lucien Carr in New York City, with which he enclosed a fresh typescript of "Howl." Ginsberg originally included Carr in his dedication of the poem but removed the reference when Carr objected (Special Collections Department of the Butler Library of Columbia University).

Ginsberg with his father in 1970 (photograph by Ann Charters)

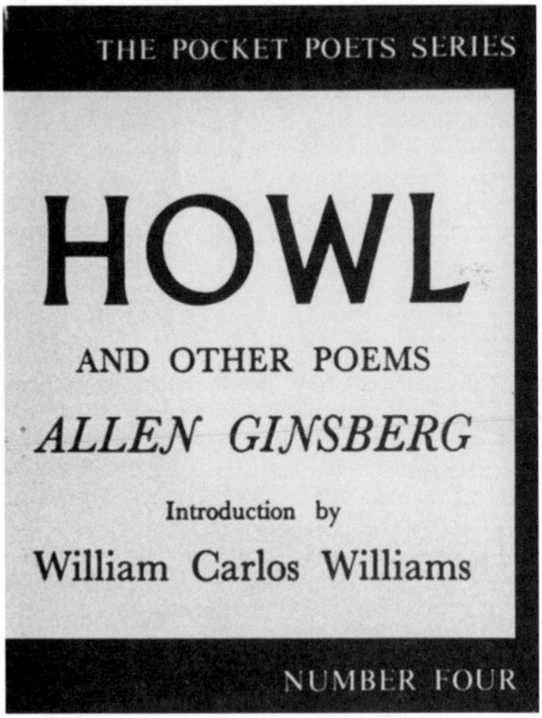

Cover for Ginsberg's first book, published in 1956

N.Y. State Department of Vocational Rehabilitation which indicated an IQ slightly above average and aptitude in literature, sales and social service; deficiencies in mechanical, scientific and mathematical areas; I wasn't trying very hard.

I took courses in American literature at the New School. NYU has been trying to get me back into academic work offering credit for life experience. However I still prefer to work.

–*Howl: Original Draft Facsimile,* p. 112

As is clear in this excerpt from his 29 February 1956 letter to his son, Louis Ginsberg appreciated the power of "Howl." His warning that the language of the poem would entangle the writer in trouble proved true, for after publication the poem was put on trial for obscenity.

. . . I am gratified about your new ms. It's a wild, rhapsodic, explosive outpouring with good figures of speech flashing by in its volcanic rushing. It's a hot geyser of emotion suddenly released in wild abandon from subterranean depths of your being. I'd like to see it in its entirety; and, moving back a bit, I'd like to discern its main outlines. I still insist, however, there is no need for dirty, ugly, words, as they will entangle you unnecessarily in trouble. Try to cut them out. . . .

–*Howl: Original Draft Facsimile,* p. 150

Ginsberg responded to interviewer Allen Young's curiosity about his dedicating the poem "Howl" to Carl Solomon.

GINSBERG: That was never an erotic relationship. I went to a mental hospital in 1948 [1949] as the result of a bust involving grass and stolen cars–a typical, college fuck-up bust. In the old days when you were from a genteel family they sent you off to a bughouse to get out of going to jail. So I went through that middle-class resolution to my bust. I wound up in the New York State Psychiatric Institute on 168th Street.

The day I walked in with all my bags I met this big fellow [Carl Solomon] just coming up from electric shock. I was waiting to be assigned a room, nervous and strange and wondering what I was doing in this psychiatric institute with all these people supposed to be crazy. And a little worried that I'd lost my grip on reality.

Carl Solomon asked me who I was. He seemed so intelligent and literate that I wanted to see if he had any soul. So I said, "I'm Prince Mishkin" (a saintly charac-

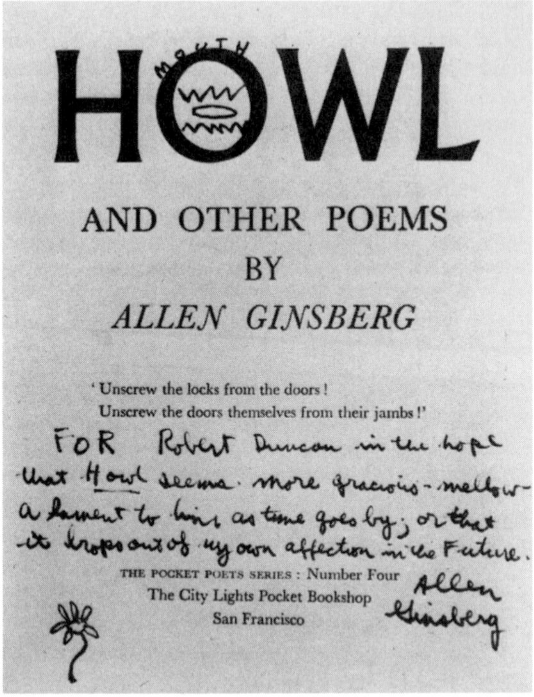
MOUTH

HOWL

AND OTHER POEMS

BY

ALLEN GINSBERG

'Unscrew the locks from the doors!
Unscrew the doors themselves from their jambs!'

FOR Robert Duncan in the hope that Howl seems more gracious-mellow-a lament to him as time goes by; or that it drops out of my own affection in the Future. Allen Ginsberg

THE POCKET POETS SERIES : Number Four
The City Lights Pocket Bookshop
San Francisco

Title page for Ginsberg's book, with an inscription that suggests that the poem was a cause of disagreement between Ginsberg and his fellow poet Duncan (Sotheby Park Bernet, sale catalogue 392, 25 October 1977)

ter in *The Idiot*). And he said, "I'm Kiriloff (a hard nihilist in *The Possessed)*. So we had a funny understanding. Then we had a literary time, writing imaginary letters to T. S. Eliot. He introduced me to Genet's work and to Artaud's work. He was very learned in French literature and surrealism. He turned me on to a lot of French literature that I'd missed. Then he took me down to the Village, and I began digging the whole subterranean Village of 1949–50 through his eyes. He's written several little collections of pithy *contes*–stories and aphorisms.

–*Gay Sunshine Interview,* p. 35

In one of his journals Ginsberg noted the people and places he sent "Free or Review" copies of Howl and Other Poems.

Chaplin	Rexroth	Cummings
Garver	Luther Nichols	Patchen
Tamayo	Fred. Eckman	C. Bullitt
Brando	Lib of Cong	Tour de Feu
Helen Eliot	Pound	Seghers
Hoodlatch	Creeley	Max J. Herzberg
Tom Darst	Bogan	Antonio Sousa Gallery
Lucien C.	John Snow	Natalie Barney
Louis	Moore, M,	A. & H. De Campos
Eugene	Snyder, G.	Chris Logue
H. Miller	Jarrell	Nat Hentoff
Jeffers	Cassady	Louis Simpson
Kingsland	Betty Keck	Dan Hoffman
Zukofsky	W. S. Burroughs	Wayne Burns
John Holmes	Ansen	Josephine Miles
Auden	Peter Russell	Wm. Faulkner
Solomon	S. P. Dunn	Parker Tyler
Kunitz	Lawrence Lipton	Karena Shields
Eliot	Jno.Williams	Lionel Trilling
Hollander	J. B. May	MarkVan Doren
Dick Howard	W.C.W.	Meyer Schapiro
Harvey Breit	Eberhart	

–*Allen Ginsberg: Journals Mid-Fifties, 1954–1958,* p. 307

Gordon Ball, the editor of Ginsberg's journals, notes that copies of Howl and Other Poems *were also mailed to "a gamut of 32 established journals such as* Kenyon Review. *In addition the review list included little magazines as follows:* Coastlines, Mattachine Review, The American Socialist, The New Leader, Liberation, Mad Comics, Poetry London-New York, Nine, Window, Midstream, East & West, Quest, Freedom Press, Climax, Dissent, Masses & Mainstream, Meangin, Merlin, One, Resistance."

In his original dedication to Howl and Other Poems, *Ginsberg mentioned Lucien Carr along with Kerouac, Burroughs, and Cassady.*

DEDICATION
To–

Jack Kerouac, new Buddha of American prose, who spit forth intelligence into eleven books written in half the number of years (1951–1956)–*On the Road, Visions of Neal, Dr Sax, Springtime Mary, The Subterraneans, San Francisco Blues, Some of the Dharma, Book of Dreams, Wake Up, Mexico City Blues,* and *Visions of Gerard*–creating a spontaneous bop prosody and original classic literature. Several phrases and the title of *Howl* are taken from him.

William Seward Burroughs, author of *Naked Lunch,* and endless novel which will drive everybody mad.

Neal Cassady, author of *The First Third,* an autobiography (1949) which enlightened Buddha.

And to Lucien Carr, recently promoted to night bureau manager of New York United Press.

All these books are published in heaven.

Ginsberg later omitted the sentence that mentioned Carr in deference to the wishes of his friend. Because of his criminal record and his pursuit of a conventional career, Carr wished to avoid being associated with the actions of the characters represented in the poem. Some of the Kerouac books listed in the dedication were later published under slightly different titles, and "Wake Up" has not been published in book form.

Lionel Trilling, an esteemed professor at Columbia, responded to his former student's poems in a 29 May 1956 letter.

Dear Allen,

I'm afraid I have to tell you that I don't like the poems at all. I hesitate before saying that they seem to me quite dull, for to say of a work which undertakes to be violent and shocking that it is dull is, I am aware, a well known and all too easy device. But perhaps you will believe that I am being sincere when I say they are dull. They are not like Whitman–they are all prose, all rhetoric, without any music. What I used to like in your poems, whether I thought they were good or bad, was the *voice* I heard in them, true and natural and interesting. There is no real voice here. As for the doctrinal element of the poems, apart from the fact that I of course reject it, it seems to me that I heard it very long ago and that you give it to me in all its orthodoxy, with nothing new added.

Sincerely yours,
Lionel Trilling
–*Howl: Original Draft Facsimile,* p. 156

"Howl" and the Charge of Obscenity

While ACLU lawyers were defending City Lights Books against charges of selling obscene material, Allen Ginsberg was with Orlovsky in Tangier, Morocco, staying with William Burroughs. For a brief time, Kerouac was also visiting. In his letter of 4 April 1957 to Carr, Ginsberg gave his impressions of his travels and reacts to the news that his first collection was on trial.

Dear Lucien:

The trip over here on Jugo boat comfortable but bad olive oily food & I met a young Jugo Secty of Geophysical Society had visited US 9 months & thought we were advanced by bureaucratic crummy & says US is bad as Russia almost propaganda & politics wise & if we're worried about Hungary why dont we worry about Guatamala & Algeria; & politically that seems the perspective I've seen from since; that is, Western imperialism is not a communist myth but obnoxious & real, particularly in North Africa. We stopped off at Casablanca 3 days & dug native quarter safely & pleasantly by day & night, the first day in fact wandering thru Medina streets (Medina once & for all is what Casbah is, the Native City whereas the Casbah is the ancient fortified palace or wall part of the Medina) we went into arab cafe in a dark alley & had sweet delicious national mint tea & someone wandered in with a long kief (marijuana) pipe & and gave me a drag & so I got high and really enjoyed the afternoon & no sinister vibrations at all. Scene much like Mexico here except Arab quarter very clean, street & alley spotless & bright in sun. Veiled women, Arabs in long white or black hooded shroudy stranger robes, dobe walled tenements, crisscross of crooked alleys, arches, roofs, rembrandt-interior cafes & shops, streetpeddlers selling delicious 2 cent napoleons & french pastries, deformed feet & blind or earsore beggars crouched in doorways, an old palsied Jew in black hood & skullcap in sunlight in middle of sidewalk with palm outstretched & left hand shaking clutching a few brass coins. I see where Burroughs gets his clear sharp images. The City looks white on a hill coming in from harbor, & the air is clear & mediterranean as in Homeric Greek, as in US after rain or sometimes objects sharply defined at sunset, here all day long that lucidity of brilliant porcelin bluesky & from Jack's window bright green water, & can see 20 miles across the straits the ancien parapets of Europe, the south coast of Spain & mountains inland, Gibralter faraway into the Medeterranean sometimes seen, small bump of coastland. Jack's leaving tomorrow on Packet boat for Marseilles & thence hitch to Paris for short stay; his book On Road accepted with 150 £ advance by english publisher; so then to England and then he wants to go back home & settle Mrs. K. in Mill Valley outside S.F. while he still has some money. Doesn't much like Europe so far he says. But he hasn't seen the rest. Maybe his plans will change. Oh yes, listen, of all things, a customs inspector name of Chester MacPhee at SF Post Office seized 500 copies of new Carr-less edition of Howl as obscene 2 weeks ago, so City Lights tells me. He sent me a clipping from Page 2 of SF Chronicle about then. Big furor apparnetly locally, Rexroth denouncing Customs over radio, American Civil Liberties Union lawyers going to court. I suppose it will get in Life too; all in all perhaps a good deal, except that there's back orders for 500

STATEMENT OF FACTS relating to Allen Ginsberg's HOWL And Other Poems. (Pocket Poets Series #4; published by CITY LIGHTS BOOKS; printed in England by Villiers Publications. With an Introduction by William Carlos Williams):

1. The First Edition of this book was passed through the U.S. Customs in October 1956 and was published in the U.S.A. on November 1. This edition sold out in two months.

2. The second printing was seized by Customs in San Francisco on March 25, 1957. The March 26 San Francisco CHRONICLE reported in part as follows:

"Collector of Customs Chester MacPhee continued his campaign yesterday to keep what he considers obscene literature away from the children of the Bay Area.

He confiscated 520 copies of a paper-bound volume of poetry entitled "Howl and Other Poems" by Allen Ginsberg with an introduction by William Carlos Williams.

'The words and the sense of the writing is obscene,' MacPhee declared. 'You wouldn't want your children to come across it.'

The books were being shipped from a London printer to the City Lights Pocket Bookship at 261 Columbus Avenue."

3. Official notice of this seizure, citing the provisions of Section 305 Tariff Act of 1930, was not received by City Lights Books until three days after notice was given to the press.

4. On April 3, 1957, the San Francisco office of the American Civil Liberties Union informed Mr. MacPhee that the ACLU was representing City Lights Books and its owner, LAWRENCE FERLINGHETTI, and that the ACLU would contest the legality of the seizure under said Tariff Act of 1930, since it did not consider the book obscene.

5. City Lights Books has now announced that it is having an entirely new edition of HOWL printed within the United States, in which case the U. S. Customs will have no jurisdiction. No changes will be made in the original text, and a Publisher's Statement defending the work as a whole will be published in the San Francisco CHRONICLE. The publisher invites editors, critics, and poets to submit statements attesting to the validity of HOWL as a work of art, such statements to be included in the defense of the book in court.

---CITY LIGHTS BOOKS
San Francisco
April 11, 1957

Lawrence Ferlinghetti's appeal to "editor, critics, and poets" to support Ginsberg's first book against charges of obscenity (Special Collections Department of the Butler Library of Columbia University) copies already piled up & I'd rather they got filled. Looks like it will be months if at all before second printing gets distributed, meanwhile another 1000 copies held in England pending results. I really didn't expect that to actually happen, tho we had wisely consulted ACLU a year ago for legal OK & advice & got optomistic prognosis from them then–that's why they handle it rapidly now.

Running out of loot though Burroughs has enough to keep us going here, so investigating job situation in Casa & Madrid, should have some action by next month. Bill is fine, really off the junk, quite healthy, smokes a lot of T & drinks erratically & talks endlessly & has been very fine about taking care of us in our poverty. Peter moody & down with asthma & getting cured by local Dr. Apfell, Bills faorite medico, (rumored to have injected parrafin into 200,000 Jewesses in Strasbourg & on the lam since the war.) As said above, it's absolutely safe here, no bad feelings from Arabs, they're fine, the only danger is predatory leechlike guides & shoeboys & vendors of rubber spiders. I even saw a small riot, argument between soldiers & cops, Jack in the middle of the mob & not bothered at all, came out laughing (tho releived). I can see how it would be horrible if the mobs were mad at us but they dont seem to be at all & we frequent native cafes in the Medina at night and have friendly nodding & speaking acquaintances with quite a few poor arabs there. Bill just finished long free association obscene mad routine which Jack just typed, they both think it's his best work to date & Bill says 's had it far as writing & that the prophet has now completely spoke.

. . . .

Love as ever, Cessa regards, I'll write. Allen

–Special Collections Department of the Butler Library of Columbia University

---

Howl on Trial

Lawrence Ferlinghetti's "Horn on Howl*" originally appeared in* Evergreen Review.

Fahrenheit 451, the temperature at which books burn, has finally been determined not to be the prevailing temperature at San Francisco, though the police still would be all too happy to make it hot for you. On October 3 last [1957], Judge Clayton Horn of Municipal Court brought in a 39-page opinion finding Shigeyoshi Murao and myself not guilty of publishing or selling obscene writings, to wit Allen Ginsberg's *Howl and Other Poems* and issue 11 & 12 of *The Miscellaneous Man.*

Thus ended one of the most irresponsible and callous police actions to be perpetrated west of the Rockies, not counting the treatment accorded Indians and Japanese.

When William Carlos Williams, in his Introduction to *Howl,* said that Ginsberg had come up with an "arresting poem" he hardly knew what he was saying. The first edition of *Howl,* Number Four in the Pocket Poet Series, was printed in England by Villiers, passed thru Customs without incident, and was published at the City Lights bookstore here in the fall of 1956. Part of a second printing was stopped by Customs on March 25, 1957, not long after an earlier issue of *The Miscellaneous Man* (published in Berkeley by William Margolis) had been seized coming from the same printer. Section 305 of the Tariff Act of 1930 was cited. The San Francisco *Chronicle* (which alone among the local press put up a real howl about censorship) reported, in part:

> Collector of Customs Chester MacPhee continued his campaign yesterday to keep what he considers obscene literature away from the children of the Bay Area. He confiscated 520 copies of a paperbound volume of poetry entitled *Howl and Other Poems*. . . . "The words and the sense of the writing is obscene," MacPhee declared. "You wouldn't want your children to come across it."

On April 3 the American Civil Liberties Union (to which I had submitted the manuscript of *Howl* before it went to the printer) informed Mr. MacPhee that it would contest the legality of the seizure, since it did not consider the book obscene. We announced in the meantime that an entirely new edition of *Howl* was being printed within the United States, thereby removing it from Customs jurisdiction. No changes were made in the original text, and a photo-offset edition was placed on sale at City Lights bookstore and distributed nationally while the Customs continued to sit on the copies from Britain.

On May 19, book editor William Hogan of the San Francisco *Chronicle* gave his Sunday column to an article by myself, defending *Howl* (I recommended a medal be made for Collector MacPhee, since his action was already rendering the book famous. But the police were soon to take over this advertising account and do a much better job–10,000 copies of *Howl* were in print by the time they finished with it.) In the defense of *Howl* I said I thought it to be "the most significant single long poem to be published in this country since World War II, perhaps since T. S. Eliot's *Four Quartets.*" To which many added "Alas." Fair enough, considering the barren, polished poetry and well-mannered verse which had dominated many of the major poetry publications during the past decade or so, not to mention some of the "fashionable incoherence" which has passed for poetry in many of the smaller, avant-garde magazines and little presses. *Howl* commits many poetic sins; but it was time. And it would be very interesting to hear from critics who can name another single long poem published in this country since the War which is as significant of its time and place and generation. (A reviewer in the *Atlantic Monthly* recently wrote that *Howl* may well turn out to be *The Waste Land* of the younger generation.) The central part of my article said: . . . It is not the poet but what he observes which is revealed as obscene. The great obscene wastes of *Howl* are the sad wastes of the mechanized world, lost among atom bombs and insane nationalisms. . . . Ginsberg chooses to walk on the wild side of this world, along with Nelson Algren, Henry Miller, Kenneth Rexroth, Kenneth Patchen, not to mention some great American dead, mostly in the tradition of philosophical anarchism. . . . Ginsberg wrote his own best defense of *Howl* in another poem called "America." Here he asks:

What sphinx of cement and aluminum bashed open
their skulls and ate up their brains and imagination?
Moloch! Solitude! Filth! Ugliness! Ashcans and unobtainable dollars! Children screaming under the stairways!
Boys sobbing in armies! Old men weeping in the parks!

A world, in short, you wouldn't want your children to come across. . . . Thus was Goya obscene in depicting the Disasters of War, thus Whitman an exhibitionist, exhibiting man in his own strange skin.

On May 29 Customs released the books it had been holding, since the United States Attorney at San Francisco refused to institute condemnation proceedings against *Howl.*

Then the police took over and arrested us, Captain William Hanrahan of the juvenile department (well named, in this case) reporting that the books were not fit for children to read. Thus during the first week in June I found myself being booked and fingerprinted in San Francisco's Hall of Justice. The city jail occupies the upper floors of it, and a charming sight it is, a picturesque return to the early Middle Ages. And my enforced tour of it was a dandy way for the city officially to recognize the flowering of poetry in San Francisco. As one paper reported, "The Cops Don't Allow No Renaissance Here."

The ACLU posted bail. Our trial went on all summer, with a couple of weeks between each day in court. The prosecution soon admitted it had no case against either Shig Murao or myself as far as the *Miscellaneous Man* was concerned, since we were not the publisher of it, in which case there was no proof we knew what was inside the magazine when it was sold at our store. And, under the California Penal Code, the willful and lewd *intent* of the accused had to be established. Thus the trial was narrowed down to *Howl.*

The so-called People's Case (I say so-called, since the People seemed mostly on our side) was presented by Deputy District Attorney Ralph McIntosh whose heart seemed not in it nor his mind on it. He was opposed by some of the most formidable legal talent to be found, in the persons of Mr. Jake ("Never Plead Guilty") Ehrlich, Lawrence Speiser (former counsel for the ACLU), and Albert Bendich (present counsel for the ACLU)–all of whom defended us without expense to us.

The critical support for *Howl* (or the protest against censorship on principle) was enormous. Here is some of what some said:

Henry Rago, editor of Poetry *(Chicago):*
. . . I wish only to say that the book is a thoroughly serious work of literary art. . . . There is absolutely no question in my mind or in that of any poet or critic with whom I have discussed the book that it is a work of the legitimacy and validity contemplated by existing American law, as we know it in the statement of Justice Woolsey in the classic *Ulysses* case, and as we have seen it reaffirmed just recently by the Supreme Court in the Butler case. . . . I would be unworthy of the tradition of this magazine or simply of my place as a poet in the republic of letters . . . if I did not speak for the right of this book to free circulation, and against this affront not only to Allen Ginsberg and his publishers, but to the possibilities of the art of poetry in America. . . .

Robert Duncan and Director Ruth Witt-Diamant of the San Francisco (State College) Poetry Center:
. . . *Howl* is a significant work in American poetry, deriving both a spirit and form from Walt Whitman's *Leaves of Grass,* from Jewish religious writing. . . . It is rhapsodic, highly idealistic and inspired in cause and purpose. Like other inspired poets, Ginsberg strives to include all of life, especially the elements of suffering and dismay from which the voice of desire rises. Only by misunderstanding might these tortured outcryings for sexual and spiritual understanding be taken as salacious. The poet gives us the most painful

details; he moves us toward a statement of experience that is challenging and finally noble.

Thomas Parkinson (University of California):
. . . *Howl* is one of the most important books of poetry published in the last ten years. Its power and eloquence are obvious, and the talent of Mr. Ginsberg is of the highest order. Even people who do not like the book are compelled to testify to its force and brilliance. . . .

James Laughlin (New Directions):
I have read the book carefully and do not myself consider it offensive to good taste, likely to lead youth astray, or be injurious to public morals. I feel, furthermore, that the book has considerable distinction as literature, being a powerful and artistic expression of a meaningful philosophical attitude. . . .

Kenneth Patchen:
The issue here—as in every like case—is not the merit or lack of it of a book but of a Society which traditionally holds the human being to be by its very functional nature a creature of shameful, outrageous, and obscene habits. . . .

Barney Rosset and Donald Allen, editors of the Evergreen Review *(in which* Howl *was reprinted during the trial):*

The second issue of *Evergreen Review,* which was devoted to the work of writers in the San Francisco Bay Area, attempted in large part to show the kinds of serious writing being done by the postwar generation. We published Allen Ginsberg's poem *Howl* in that issue because we believe that it is a significant modern poem, and that Allen Ginsberg's intention was to sincerely and honestly present a portion of his own experience of the life of his generation. . . . Our final considered opinion was that Allen Ginsberg's *Howl* is an achieved poem and that it deserves to be considered as such. . . .

At the trial itself, nine expert witnesses testified in behalf of *Howl.* They were eloquent witnesses, together furnishing as good a one-sided critical survey of *Howl* as could possibly be got up in any literary magazine. These witnesses were: Mark Schorer and Leo Lowenthal (of the University of California faculty), Walter Van Tilburg Clark, Herbert Blau, Arthur Foff, and Mark Linenthal (all of the San Francisco State College faculty), Kenneth Rexroth, Vincent McHugh (poet and novelist), and Luther Nichols (book editor of the San Francisco *Examiner*). A few excerpts from the trial transcript—

DR. MARK SCHORER: The theme of the poem is announced very clearly in the opening line, "I saw the best minds of my generation destroyed by madness, starving hysterical naked." Then the following lines that make up the first part attempt to create the impression of a kind of nightmare world in which people representing "the best minds of my generation," in the author's view, are wandering like damned souls in hell. That is done through a kind of series of what one might call surrealistic images, a kind of state of hallucinations. Then in the second section the mood of the poem changes and it becomes an indictment of those elements in modern society that, in the author's view, are destructive of the best qualities in human nature and of the best minds. Those elements are, I would say, predominantly materialism, conformity and mechanization leading toward war. And then the third part is a personal address to a friend, real or fictional, of the poet or of the person who is speaking in the poet's voice—those are not always the same thing—who is mad and in a madhouse, and is the specific representative of what the author regards as a general condition, and with that final statement the poem ends. . . .

DR. LEO LOWENTHAL: In my opinion this is a genuine work of literature, which is very characteristic for a period of unrest and tension such as the one we have been living through the last decade. I was reminded by reading *Howl* of many other literary works as they have been written after times of great upheavals, particularly after World War One, and I found this work very much in line with similar literary works. With regard to the specific merits of the poem *Howl,* I would say that it is structured very well. As I see it, it consists of three parts, the first of which is the craving of the poet for self-identification, where he roams all over the field and tries to find allies in similar search for self-identification. He then indicts, in the second part, the villain, so to say, which does not permit him to find it, the Moloch of society, of the world as it is today. And in the third part he indicates the potentiality of fulfillment by friendship and love, although it ends on a sad and melancholic note actually indicating that he is in search for fulfillment he cannot find.

KENNETH REXROTH: . . . The simplest term for such writing is prophetic, it is easier to call it that than

> anything else because we have a large body of prophetic writing to refer to. There are the prophets of the Bible, which it greatly resembles in purpose and in language and in subject matter. . . . The theme is the denunciation of evil and a pointing out of the way out, so to speak. That is prophetic literature. "Woe! Woe! Woe! The City of Jerusalem! The Syrian is about to come down or has already and you are to do such and such a thing and you must repent and do thus and so." And *Howl,* the four parts of the poem–that is including the "Footnote to *Howl*" as one additional part–do this very specifically. They take up these various specifics seriatim, one after the other. . . . And "Footnote to *Howl,*" of course, again, is Biblical in reference. The reference is to the Benedicite, which says over and over again, "Blessed is the fire, Blessed is the light, Blessed are the trees, and Blessed is this and Blessed is that," and he is saying, "Everything that is human is Holy to me," and that the possibility of salvation in this terrible situation which he reveals is through love and through the love of everything Holy in man. So that, I would say, that this just about covers the field of typically prophetic poetry. . . .

The prosecution put only two "expert witnesses" on the stand–both very lame samples of academia–one from the Catholic University of San Francisco and one a private elocution teacher, a beautiful woman, who said, "You feel like you are going through the gutter when you have to read that stuff. I didn't linger on it too long, I assure you." The University of San Francisco instructor said: "The literary value of this poem is negligible. . . . This poem is apparently dedicated to a long-dead movement, Dadaism, and some late followers of Dadaism. And, therefore, the opportunity is long past for any significant literary contribution of this poem." The critically devastating things the prosecution's witnesses could have said, but didn't, remain one of the great Catholic silences of the day.

So much for the literary criticism inspired by the trial. . . .

Legally, a layman could see that an important principle was certainly in the line drawn between "hard core pornography" and writing judged to be "social speech." But more important still was the court's acceptance of the principle that if a work is determined to be "social speech," the question of obscenity may not even be raised. Or, in the words of Counsel Bendich's argument: "The first amendment to the Constitution of the United States protecting the fundamental freedoms of speech and press prohibits the suppression of literature by the application of obscenity formulae unless the trial court first determines that the literature in question is utterly without social importance." *(Roth* v. *U.S.)*

. . . What is being urged here is that the majority opinion in *Roth* requires a trial court to make the constitutional determination; to decide in the first instance whether a work is utterly without redeeming social importance, *before* it permits the test of obscenity to be applied. . . .

. . . The record is clear that all of the experts for the defense identified the main theme of *Howl* as social criticism. And the prosecution concedes that it does not understand the work, much less what its dominant theme is.

Judge Horn agreed, in his opinion:

> I do not believe that *Howl* is without even "the slightest redeeming social importance." The first part of *Howl* presents a picture of a nightmare world; the second part is an indictment of those elements in modern society destructive of the best qualities of human nature; such elements are predominantly identified as materialism, conformity, and mechanization leading toward war. The third part presents a picture of an individual who is a specific representation of what the author conceives as a general condition. . . . "Footnote to *Howl*" seems to be a declamation that everything in the world is holy, including parts of the body by name. It ends in a plea for holy living. . . .

And the judge went on to set forth certain rules for the guidance of authorities in the future:

1. If the material has the slightest redeeming social importance it is not obscene because it is protected by the First and Fourteenth Amendments of the United States Constitution, and the California Constitution.
2. If it does not have the slightest redeeming social importance it *may* be obscene.
3. The test of obscenity in California is that the material must have a tendency to deprave or corrupt readers by exciting lascivious thoughts or arousing lustful desire to the point that it presents a clear and present danger of inciting to anti-social or immoral action.
4. The book or material must be judged as a whole by its effect on the *average adult* in the community.

5. If the material is objectionable only because of coarse and vulgar language which is not erotic or aphrodisiac in character it is not obscene.
6. Scienter must be proved.
7. Book reviews may be received in evidence if properly authenticated.
8. Evidence of expert witnesses in the literary field is proper.
9. Comparison of the material with other similar material previously adjudicated is proper.
10. The people owe a duty to themselves and to each other to preserve and protect their constitutional freedoms from any encroachment by government unless it appears that the allowable limits of such protection have been breached, and then to take only such action as will heal the breach.
11. Quoting Justice Douglas: "I have the same confidence in the ability of our people to reject noxious literature as I have in their capacity to sort out the true from the false in theology, economics, politics, or any other field."
12. In considering material claimed to be obscene it is well to remember the motto: *Honi soit qui mal y pense* (Evil to him who thinks evil).

At which the Prosecution was reliably reported to have blushed.

Under banner headlines, the *Chronicle* reported that "the Judge's decision was hailed with applause and cheers from a packed audience that offered the most fantastic collection of beards, turtle-necked shirts and Italian hair-dos ever to grace the grimy precincts of the Hall of Justice." The decision was hailed editorially as a "landmark of law." Judge Horn has since been re-elected to office, which I like to think means that the People agree it was the police who here committed an obscene action.

–*The Portable Beat Reader,* pp. 254–263

Ferlinghetti and City Lights Book Shop clerk Shig Murao in the San Francisco Municipal Court chambers during their trial for selling obscene material: Ginsberg's Howl and Other Poems

An Exchange about "Howl"

John Hollander, a friend of Ginsberg who had been his classmate at Columbia, gave "Howl" a negative review.

Review of *Howl and Other Poems*
John Hollander
Partisan Review, Spring 1957

It is only fair to Allen Ginsberg . . . to remark on the utter lack of decorum of any kind in his dreadful little volume. I believe that the title of his long poem, "Howl," is meant to be a noun, but I can't help taking it as an imperative. The poem itself is a confession of the poet's faith, done into some 112 paragraphlike lines, in the ravings of a lunatic friend (to whom it is dedicated), and in the irregularities in the lives of those of his friends who populate his rather disturbed pantheon.

. . . .

"Howl" and the other longer poems in this book, including "America," "Sunflower Sutra," "In the Baggage Room at Greyhound" and some dismal pastiches of William Carlos Williams (who wrote a brief reminiscence of the poet to introduce this volume), all proclaim, in a hopped-up and improvised tone, that nothing seems to be worth saying save in a hopped-up and improvised tone.

. . . .

I have spent this much time on a very short and very tiresome book for two reasons. The first of these is involved with the fact that Mr. Ginsberg and his circle are being given a certain amount of touting by those who disapprove of what Horace Gregory, writing in these pages last fall, christened "The Poetry of Suburbia." If it turns out to be anybody's profit, I shouldn't be a bit surprised if *Howl* and its eventual progeny were accorded some milder version of the celebration Colin Wilson has received in England. This may not be a real danger, however. If it suddenly appeared that there were no possible worlds between suburbia and subterranean, I expect most of us would go underground. But this is not quite yet the case and the publicity seems regrettable, in view of the fact (my second reason for dealing with him here) that Allen Ginsberg has a real talent and a marvelous ear. It shows up in some of the funniest and most grotesque lines of "Howl," and even without knowing his profound and carefully organized earlier writing (unpublished in book form), one might suspect a good poet lurking behind the modish facade of a frantic and *talentlos* avant-garde.

Ginsberg defended his approach to poetry and "Howl" in a 7 September 1958 letter to Hollander.

Dear John:

Got your letter, slow answering . . . It's just that I've tried to do too much explaining & get overwhelmed by the vastness of the task, & sometimes what seems to be all the accumulated ill-will & evil vibrations in America (Kerouac got beaten up at the San Remo for his trouble in coming down there & making himself available.) But to begin somewhere, I should might begin with one thing, simple (I hate to go back to it over & over, like revolving around my corpse, the construction of Howl.) This may be corny to you, my concern with that, but I've got to begin somewhere & perhaps differences of opinion between us can be resolved by looking at that. See, for years before that, thinking in Williams line, which I found very helpful & quite real for what it is doing, the balance by ear of short lines formed of relatively natural ordinary notebook or conversation speech. Xbalba is fragments of mostly prose, written in a mexican school copybook, over half a year–then rereading, picking out the purest thoughts, stringing them together, arranging them in lines suitably balanced–mostly measured by the phrase–, that is one phrase a line–you know it's hard to explain this because it's like painting and unless you do it like practicing a piano, you don't think in those terms & get the experience of trying to work that way, so you don't notice all the specific tricks–that anyone who works in that field gets to be familiar with–that's why I'm interested in Blackburn, Levertov, Creeley, Oppenheimer, all the Black Mt people–they work steadily consistently trying to develop this line of goods, and each has a different interesting approach–they all stem out of Williams–but I can tell their lines apart they really are different–just as you can tell the difference between styles & approaches of abstract painters. When you tell me it's just a bore to you, that just cuts off communication, I mean I don't know what to say, I get embarrassed I feel you're being arbitrary & stubborn, it's some sort of ploy, & I just want to retreat & go about my work and stop explanations. Of course you may not be interested in this field of experiment, but that doesn't mean it's uninteresting to others, that it's categorically a bore. I *also* believe it's the main "tradition," not that there is any tradition except what we make ourselves. But basically I'm not interested in tradition because I'm more interested in what I'm doing, what it's inevitable for me to do. This realization has given me perspective on what a vast sad camp the whole literary-critical approach of School has been–basically no one has insight into poetry techniques except people who are exercising them. But I'm straying at random.

But I'm now getting bugged at people setting themselves up as scholars and authorities and *getting in the way* of continued creative work or its understanding or circulation–there is not one article on the Beat or SF scene yet that has not been (pro or con) invalidated (including yours) by the basic fact that the author is just a big windbag not knowing what he's talking about–no technical background, no knowledge of the vast body of experimental work, published and unpublished (the unpublished is the best), no clear grasp of the various different schools of experiment all converging toward the same or similar end, all at once coming into intercommunication, no knowledge of the letters and conversations in between, not even the basic ability (like Podhoretz) to tell the difference between prosody and diction (as in his PR diatribes on spontaneous bop prosody confusing it with the use of hiptalk not realizing it refers to rhythmical construction of phrases & sentences.) I mean where am I going to begin a serious explanation if I have to deal with such unmitigated stupid ignorant ill willed inept vanity as that–someone like that wouldn't listen unless you hit him over the head with a totally new universe, but he's stuck in his own hideous world, I would try, but he scarcely has enough heart to hear)–etc etc–so all these objections about juvenile delinquency, vulgarity, lack of basic education, bad taste, etc etc, no form, etc I mean it's impossible to discuss things like that–finally I get to see them as so basically *wrong* (unscientific) so dependent on ridiculous provincial schoolboy ambitions & presuppositions and so lacking contact with practical fact–that it seems a sort of plot almost, a kind of organized mob stupidity–the final camp of its announcing itself as a representative of value or civilization or taste–I mean I give up, that's just too much fucking nasty brass. And you're guilty of that too John, you've just got to drop it, and take me seriously, and listen to what I have to say. It doesn't mean you have to agree, or change your career or your writing, or anything hideous, it just means you've got to have the heart and decency to take people seriously and not depend *only* on your own university experience for arbitrary standards of value to judge others by. It doesn't mean you have to agree, that Free Verse is the Only Path of Prosodaic Experiment, or that Williams is a Saint, or I have some horrible magic secret (tho god knows I have enough, this week with that damned buddhist laughing gas, everybody has). Just enough to dig, you to dig, what others besides yourself are trying to do. And be interested in their work or not, but not get in the way, in fact even encourage where you can see some value. And you're in a position to encourage, you teach, you shouldn't hand down limited ideas to younger minds–that was the whole horror of Columbia, there just was nobody there (maybe except Weaver) who had a serious involvement with advanced work in poetry. Just a bunch of Dilettantes. And THEY have the nerve to set themselves up as guardians of culture?!!? Why it's such a piece of effrontery–enough to make anyone Paranoiac, it's a miracle Jack or myself or anybody independent survived–tho god knows the toll in paranoia been high enough. All these grievances I'm pouring out to you. Well why revise.

Back to Howl: construction. After sick & tired of shortline free verse as not expressionistic enough, not swinging enough, can't develop a powerful enough rhythm, I simply turned aside, accidentally to writing part I of "Howl," in solitude, diddling around with the form, thinking it couldn't be published anyway (queer content my parents shouldn't see etc) also it was out of my short-line line. But what I did taught my theory, I changed my mind about "measure" while writing it. Part one uses repeated base *who,* as a sort of kithara BLANG, homeric (in my imagination) to mark off each statement, each rhythmic unit. So that's experiment with longer & shorter variations on a fixed base–the principle being, that each line has to be contained within the elastic of one breath–with suitable punctuatory expressions where the rhythm has built up enough so that I have to let off steam by building a longer climactic line in which there is a jazzy ride. All the ear I've ever developed goes into the balancing of those lines. The interesting moment's when the rhythm is sufficiently powerfully pushing ahead so I can ride out free and drop the *who* key that holds it together. The method of keeping a long line still all poetic & not prosey is the concentration & compression of basically imagistic notations into surrealist or cubist phrasing, like hydrogen jukeboxes. Ideally anyway. Good example of this is Gregory's great (I swear) Coit Tower ode. Lines have greater poetic density. But I tried to keep the language sufficiently dense in one way or another–use of primitive naive grammar (expelled for crazy), elimination of prosy articles & syntactical sawdust, juxtaposition of cubist style images, of hot rhythm.

Well then Part II. Here the basic repeated word is Moloch. The long line is now broken up into component short phrases with ! rhythmical punctuation. The key repeat BLANG word is repeated internally in the line (basic rhythm sometimes emerging /–/–) but the rhythm depends mostly on the internal Moloch repeat. Lines here lengthened–a sort of free verse prose poetry STANZA form invented or used here. This builds up to climax (Visions! Omens! etc) and then falls off in coda. Part III, perhaps an original invention (I thought so then but this type of thinking is vain & shallow anyway) to handling of long line (for the whole poem is an experiment in what you can do with the long line–the whole book is)–::: that is, a phrase base rhythm (I'm with you etc) followed as in litany by a response of the same length (Where you're madder etc), then repeat of base over and over with the response elongating itself slowly, still contained within the elastic of one breath–till the stanza (for it is a stanza form there, I've used variations of it since) building up like a pyramid, an emotion crying siren sound, very appropriate to the expressive appeal emotion I felt (a good healthy emotion said my analyst at that time, to dispose once and for all of that idiotic objection)–anyway, building up to the climax where there's a long long long line, penultimate, too long for one breath, where I open out & give the answer (O starry spangled shock of Mercy the eternal war is here). All this rather like a jazz mass, I mean the conception of rhythm not derived from jazz directly but if you listen to jazz you get the idea (in fact specifically old trumpet solo on a *JATP* "Can't Get Started" side)–well all this is built like a brick shithouse and anybody can't hear the music is as I told you I guess I meekly informed Trilling, who is absolutely lost in poetry, is got a tin ear, and that's so obviously true, I get sick and tired I read 50 reviews of Howl and not one of them written by anyone with enough technical interests to notice the fucking obvious construction of the poem, all the details besides (to say nothing of the various esoteric classical allusions built in like references to Cezanne's theory of composition etc etc)–that I GIVE UP and anybody henceforth comes up to me with a silly look in his eye & begins bullshitting about morals and sociology & tradition and technique & Juvenile Delinquency–I mean I je ne sais plus parler–the horrible irony of all these jerks who can't *read* trying to lecture me (us) on FORM. . . .

Footnote to Howl is too lovely & serious a joke to try to explain. The built-in rhythmic exercise should be clear, it's basically a repeat of the Moloch section. It's dedicated to my mother who died in the madhouse and its says I loved her anyway & that even in worst conditions life is holy. The exaggeratedness of the statements is appropriate, and anybody who doesn't understand the specific exaggerations will never understand Rejoice in the Lamb or Lorca's Ode to Whitman or Mayakovsky's At the Top of My Voice or Artaud's Pour En Finir Avec le Judgement de Dieu or Apollinaire's "inspired bullshit" or Whitman's madder passages or anything, anything, anything about the international modern spirit in poesy to say nothing about the international tradition in prosody which has grown up nor the tradition of open prophetic bardic poetry which 50 years has sung like an angel over the poor soul of the world while all sorts of snippy castrates pursue their good manners and sell out their own souls and the spirit of god who now DEMANDS sincerity and hell fire take him who denies the voice in his soul–except that it's all a kindly joke & the universe disappears after you die so nobody gets hurt no matter how little they allow themselves to live & blow on this Earth. . . .

Latter's unclear I'll start over. Tho poetry in Williams has depended a lot on little breath groups for its typographical organization, and in *Howl* an extension into longer breaths (which are more natural to me than Williams short simple talks)–there is another way you would *say* it, a thought, but the way you would think it–i.e. we think rapidly, in visual images as well as words, and if each successive thought were transcribed in its confusion (really its ramification) you get a slightly different prosody than if you were talking slowly . . . .

yours in the kingdom of music
Nella Grebsnig
Allen

–*Howl: Original Draft Facsimiles,* pp. 162–164

Writing "Kaddish"

In The Portable Beat Reader *(1992), editor Ann Charters summarizes the 1958 composition of "Kaddish," a "long formal elegy . . . personalizing the traditional Jewish memorial poem for the dead": "Writing fifty-eight pages in an inspired forty-hour stretch at his desk while taking, by his own account, heroin, liquid Methedrine and Dexedrine, Ginsberg completed 'Kaddish' in November, 1958. A poem in six sections (Proem, Narrative, Hymmnn, Lament, Litany, and Fugue), it was the culmination of his early work, a deeply compassionate portrait of his mother's mental illness and its devastating effect on Ginsberg and his family." Many readers believe that "Kaddish" is Ginsberg's best poem.*

In the spring and summer of 1958 Ginsberg was in Paris with Gregory Corso, William Burroughs, and others in rented rooms at 9 Rue Git Le Coeur, which became known as the Beat Hotel. He describes his life there in this excerpt from his letter to Lucien Carr.

9 Rue Git Le Coeur Paris 6, France May 30

Dear Lucien:

Well, hello, I get rumors of you from Jack that's about all. Saw in Time that INS and UP merged, you alright there? I don't guess it changes much. Meant to write awhile back but been running around–spent 2 weeks in England with Gregory early this month, reading a little, Oxford, BBC & some small poetry circle in

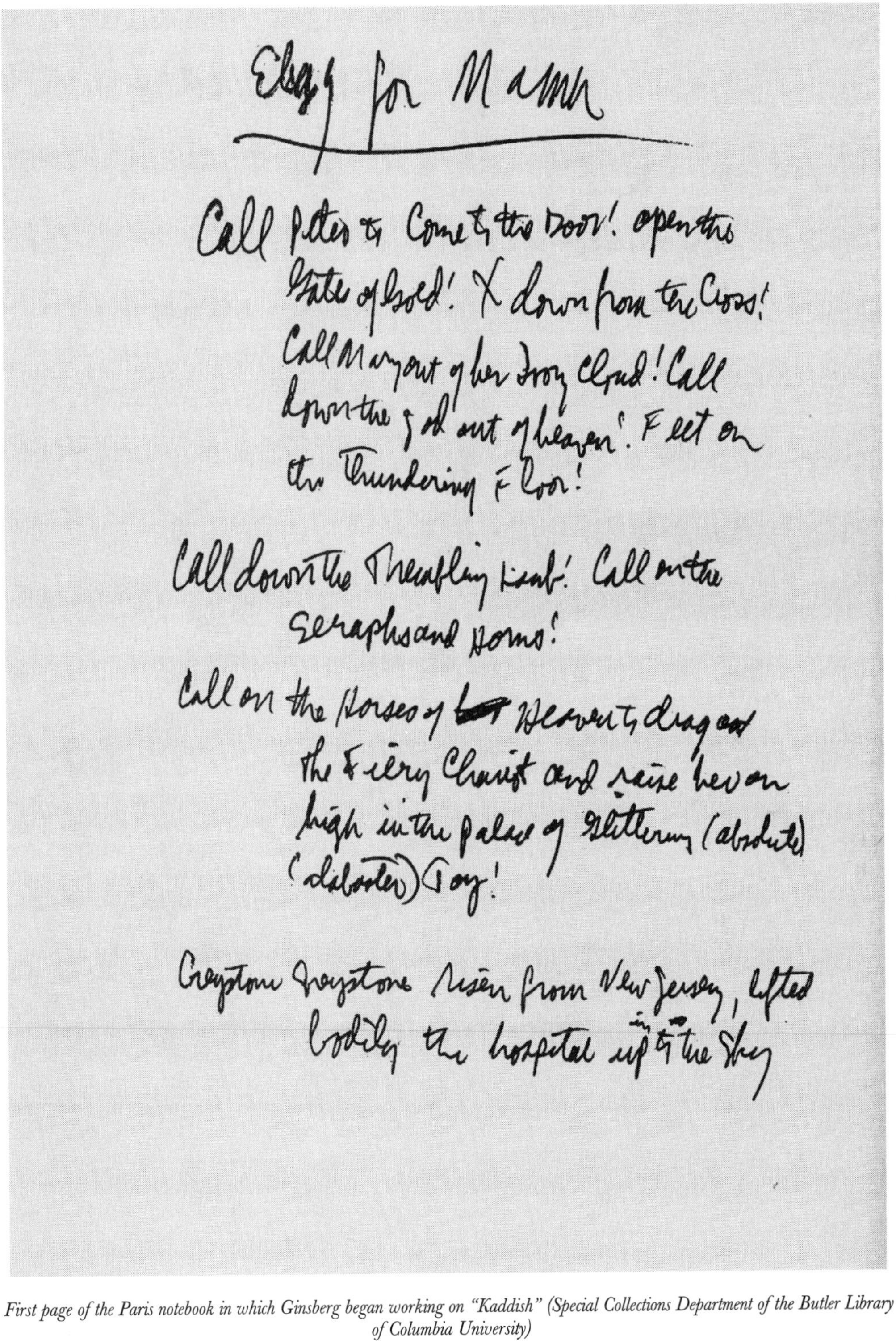

Elegy for Mama

Call Peter to Come to the Door! open the
Gate of Gold! X down from the Cross!
Call Mary out of her Ivory Cloud! Call
down the god out of heaven! Feet on
the Thundering Floor!

Call down the Trembling Lamb! Call on the
Seraphs and Horns!

Call on the Horses of ~~[illegible]~~ Heaven to drag out
the Fiery Chariot and raise her on
high in the palace of Glittering (absolute)
(dabooler) Joy!

Greystone Greystone risen from New Jersey, lifted
bodily the hospital up into the Sky

First page of the Paris notebook in which Ginsberg began working on "Kaddish" (Special Collections Department of the Butler Library of Columbia University)

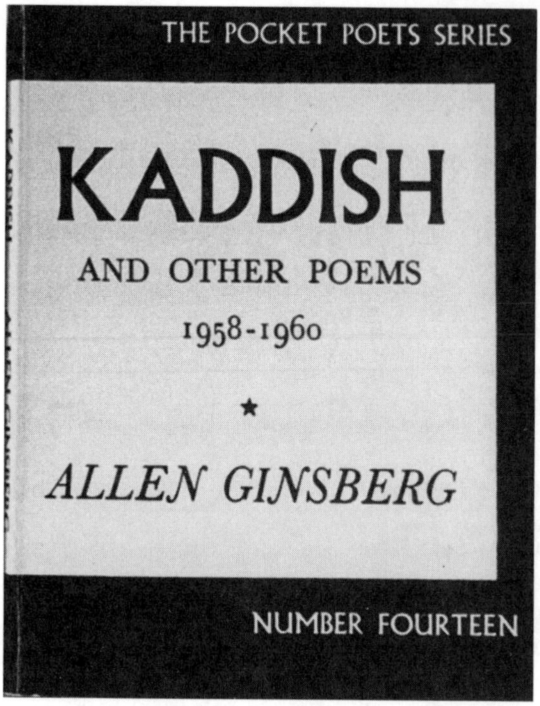

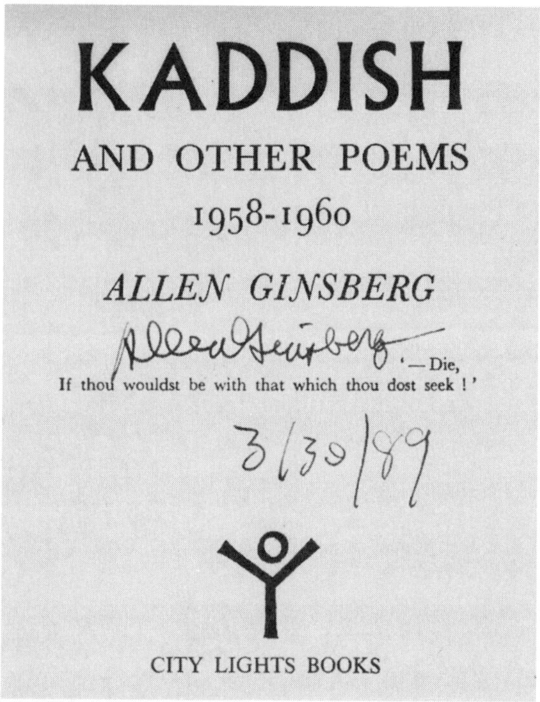

Cover and autographed title page for Ginsberg's second book (Collection of Matt Theado)

London, drank a lot in Soho with poets, Barker & a lot of teddy boys, tea with Auden & Lunch with Edith Sitwell in big expensive Lady MacBeth club–potted shrimps Roastbeef treacle tart–but that was about the only food we had there, starved most of the time everybody fed us drinks but nobody handout any food & we were broke, stuck on picadilly some midnights no money for taxi, Underground closed & bus strike, & hungry–finally called up old Lenrow type literary gent who rescued us–came back to Paris in debt & broke (Gregory supposed to get 25 pounds for an article on Beat for some literary magazine, he wrote a funny article, creepy interviews with Burroughs & me & various other deadbeat GI students around this hotel–they took it but never paid all they owed–and I was supposed to get money for some poems & gave to a magazine & never saw that loot, & the BBC takes 2 months & 16 official triplicate forms to get up off the 4 dollars & 13 cents they owe me for reading) oh well money money as usual. I'm broke except Bill's around–and Gregory's around too, broke–about ready to head back home as soon as I can get fare–sometime next month I guess, July. Ticket will turn up I guess somehow. Bill probably stay on awhile–he's in analysis here–good health except farting around with Paregoric temporarily, tho he has changed a little & does finally look a little older–greying temples & face aged suddenly–illumination & analysis–just stepped out of shangri-la. Or maybe he'll come back for visit this summer too–I thought I was going to get a guggenheim grant & offered to pay his way back if he'd come but I never got the grant–tho he was interested in coming I think. He's finishing another book, picaresque novel, about 250 pages, very good, a chapter of it was in Chicago Review & they wrote him fan letter saying he was great & they would publish all he wrote if no one else will–so they're serializing it henceforth–tho when the mss. is done he'll probably be able to get it published–it's clean enough for US–that whole big mss. we did in Tangiers noone will touch it's too vile, not even City Lights or Grove.

I haven't done much in Europe but hang around & see the sights, don't have any great mad poem to bring back alas, tho I wrote quite a bit, got all hung up on politics & wrote goofed up spenglerian pronouncements about the Fall of America, some if it's alright but mostly bullshit.

–Special Collections Department of the Butler Library of Columbia University

Ginsberg as a Public Figure

Ginsberg joined in the San Francisco debate about poetry with this article in the San Francisco Sunday Chronicle; *it was headed by a note from the editor.*

The most unnerving reply received to date in our recent poetry controversy (Activists versus Beat, and variations thereof) is the following document from Allen Ginsberg, author of the controversial "Howl" and other works. In effect, it is another "Howl" from Ginsberg. While we feel it is a curiosity piece rather than a profound social or literary criticism, it is nonetheless a revealing statement by the most publicized, and perhaps most talented, of the younger poets practicing under the avowedly "Beat" banner.–W.H.

Ginsberg 'Howls' Again–On the S. F. Poetry Controversy
Allen Ginsberg
San Francisco Sunday Chronicle, 26 July 1959, p. 27

Recent history is the record of a vast conspiracy to impose one level of mechanical consciousness on mankind and exterminate all manifestations of that unique part of human sentience, identical in all men, which the individual shares with his Creator. The suppression of contemplative individuality is nearly complete.

The only immediate historical data that we can know and act on are those fed to our senses through systems of mass communication.

These media are exactly the places where the deepest and most personal sensitivities and confessions of reality are most prohibited, mocked, suppressed.

At the same time there is a crack in the mass consciousness of America–sudden emergence of insight into a vast national subconscious netherworld filled with nerve gases, universal death bombs, malevolent bureaucracies, secret police systems, drugs that open the door to God, ships leaving Earth, unknown chemical terrors, evil dreams at hand.

Because systems of mass communication can communicate only officially acceptable levels of reality, no one can know the extent of the secret unconscious life. No one in America can know what will happen. No one is in real control. America is having a nervous breakdown.

Poetry is the record of individual insights into the secret soul of the individual, and, because all individuals are One in the eyes of their Creator, into the soul of the World. The world has a soul.

America is having a nervous breakdown. San Francisco is one of the many places where a few individuals, Poets, have the luck and courage and fate to glimpse something new through the crack in mass consciousness; they have been exposed to some insight into their own nature, the nature of the governments, and the nature of God.

Therefore there has been great exaltation, despair, prophecy, strain, suicide, secrecy and public gaiety among the poets of the city.

Those of the general populace whose individual perception is sufficiently weak to be formed by stereotypes of mass communication disapprove and deny the insight. The police and newspapers have moved in, mad movie manufacturers from Hollywood are at this moment preparing bestial stereotypes of the scene.

The poets and those who share their activities, or exhibit some sign of dress, hair or demeanor of understanding, or hipness, are ridiculed. Those of us who have used certain benevolent drugs (marijuana) to alter our consciousness in order to gain insight are hunted down in the street by police. Peyote, an historic vision-producing agent, is prohibited on pain of arrest. Those who have used opiates and junk are threatened with permanent jail and death. To be junky in America is like having been a Jew in Nazi Germany.

A huge sadistic police bureaucracy has risen in every State, encouraged by the central government, to persecute the illuminati, to brainwash the public with official Lies about the drugs, and to terrify and destroy those addicts whose spiritual search has made them sick.

Deviants from the mass sexual stereotype, quietists, those who will not work for money, fib and make arms for hire, join Armies in murder and threat, those who wish to loaf, think, rest in visions, act beautifully on their own, speak truthfully in public, inspired by Democracy–what is their psychic fate now in America?

An America, the greater portion of whose Economy is yoked to mental and mechanical preparations for War?

Literature expressing these insights has been mocked, misinterpreted, and suppressed by a horde of middlemen whose fearful allegiance to the Organization of mass stereotype communication prevents them from sympathy (not only with their own inner nature but) with any manifestation of unconditioned individuality. I mean, journalists, commercial publishers, book review fellows, multitudes of professors of literature, etc., etc. Poetry is hated. Whole schools of academic criticism have risen to prove that human consciousness of unconditioned Spirit is a myth. A poetic renaissance glimpsed in San Francisco has been responded to with ugliness, anger, jealousy, vitriol, sullen protestations of superiority.

And violence. By police, by customs officials, post office employees, by trustees of great universities. By anyone whose love of Power has led him to a position where he can push other people around over a difference of opinion—or Vision.

The stakes are too great—an America gone mad with materialism, a police state America, a sexless and soulless America prepared to battle the world in defense of a false image of its Authority. Not the wild and beautiful America of comrades of Whitman, not the historic America of Blake and Thoreau where the spiritual Independence of each individual was an America, a Universe, more huge and awesome than all the abstract bureaucracies and authoritative Officialdoms of the World combined.

Only those who have entered the world of spirit know what a vast Laugh there is in the illusory appearance of worldly authority. And all men at one time or other enter that Spirit, whether in life or death.

How many Hypocrites are there in America? How many trembling Lambs, fearful of discovery? What Authority have we set up over ourselves, that we are not as we Are? Who shall prohibit an art from being published to the world? What conspirators have power to determine our mode of consciousness, our sexual enjoyments, our different labors and our loves? What fiends determine our Wars?

When will we discover an America that will not deny its own God? Who takes up arms, money, police and a million hands to murder the consciousness of God? Who spits in the beautiful face of Poetry which sings of the Glory of God and weeps in the dust of the world?

Ginsberg with Ezra Pound in Italy (© Allen Ginsberg Trust)

It is a little misleading, I think, to speak of Ginsberg in terms of a movement, and to attempt to define his achievement in light of what he and the other "beats" have thought or said they stood for. He stands alone, or almost alone, surely, in his preference for the long, swinging line that breaks the verse pattern expected by the eye; and his thick columns of prose-verse surmounted by single-word titles like "Howl" make quite the opposite design on the page from the tau cross shape of the poems we have already seen (such as the one by Creeley, for instance) whose diet-slim bodies are sometimes surmounted by titles longer than their lines (say, "All that Is Lovely in Men"). Besides, in terms of merit, he stands out above those who cluster about him and with whom he is sometimes driven to identify himself out of personal loyalty or programmatic solidarity: a closing of ranks against the "squares."

–Leslie Fiedler, *Waiting for the End,* p. 241

Ginsberg traveled widely and knew many important figures of the day, especially musicians, including Bob Dylan, Phil Spector, and Thelonius Monk. Ginsberg thrived in the limelight of public attention and was the figurehead for many political causes and moral issues through the decades, such as Gay Rights and the legalization of marijuana.

Ginsberg visited Ezra Pound in Rapallo, Italy, in the fall of 1967. Pound was not familiar with Ginsberg's poetry and was generally uncommunicative. However, through the course of a month of casual visits, the two men did establish a rapport of sorts. Ginsberg recounts one evening in their acquaintanceship: "Going to Pound's house–how old?–'How old are you, old man?' I said, several wines and a stick of pot midway between meal. '82 in several days,' he said. That's all he said–all day [. . .] played him [Beatles's songs] 'Eleanor Rigby,' and 'Yellow Submarine,' and Dylan's 'Sad Eyed Lady of the Lowland' and 'Gates of Eden' and 'Where Are You Tonite, Sweet Marie?' and Donovan's 'Sunshine Superman.' I gave Pound Beatles, Dylan, Donovan [. . .] 'You like the Beatles' records? . . . or too much noise?' Silence. 'You mean those discs?' he said. 'Yes.' Silence."

Ginsberg leading a prayer meeting in Grant Park in Chicago during protests at the 1968 Democratic National Convention

Cover for the transcripts of the "Chicago Seven" trial that featured Ginsberg's defense of the accused

Ginsberg's writing regularly inspired contrasting reactions as is indicated by the following two reviews of Planet News: 1961–1967.

Fblup!
Alan Brownjohn
New Statesman, 10 January 1969, p. 52

Allen Ginsberg has always somehow slipped out of the grasp of criticism. That public image has been too eccentrically powerful; either you absorb the message wholly, or you just don't think it's worth complaining. On the page, the hectoring, large-scale verses race you on past any attempt to sort out something rational and paraphrasable, defying objections with scatological exuberance and a crazy, ranting benignity. In "Uptown" in the new book, a "hatted thin citizen hurrying to the barroom door" shouts at the poet, "If I had my way I'd cut off your hair and send you to Vietnam . . . And if I couldn't do that I'd cut your throat." Replies Ginsberg, in admirable, imaginable fashion, "Bless you then . . . bless you sir." One feels that the poems answer in a similar vein to the mildest sort of critical reproach.

In *Planet News,* nothing has changed very much. There are two major poems of considerable length: one called "Television Was a Baby Crawling Toward That Deathchamber"–

> I am the Intolerant One Gasbag from the Morgue &
> Void, Garbler of all Conceptions that myope my eye &
> is Uncle Sam asleep in the Funeral Home? –

and the other "Wichita Vortex Sutra," which anchors more successfully in time and space and has some of the most coherent and sustained political invective Ginsberg has ever achieved. The other poems are, by this poet's standards, short–many of them pieces of personal meditation in places visited on his travels. Bombay, Warsaw, Prague, London and Wales receive the same hectic treatment as Hollywood and New York, Ginsberg working, as before, to pile up vast accumulations of topical images and references, switching and mixing them with heady rapidity, yoking together the repellent and the mystical in a manner he's made his own.

Ankor Wat is an extended, but less striving, exercise in the same vein: a poem written under morphine-atrophine in one night in 1963 and published separately in a handsome edition illustrated with Alexandra Lawrence's photographs of the famous ruins. Ginsberg has a clear eye for things when he stands still and works it all out; and the illustrations here point up vividly the patches of visual description which occur in the midst of a long, jerky monologue on Cambodian scenes, Buddhist disciplines and murky political events. It all hangs together, just; but there are passages of embarrassing badness.

Copy for a City Lights advertisement for Ginsberg's 1968 collection *Planet News: 1961–1967.*

Celestial vulgar humor!
Solemn experience!
Blake & Whitman ride again!
Hare Krishna!
Waves of Queer Bliss!
An ecological thrill!

Ginsberg stands at the end of a long line of American poets who have striven to embrace and comprehend everything in sight, but his poetry lacks the compensations of his predecessors'. He doesn't have Whitman's sweeping lyrical cadences, he has abandoned Hart Crane's quest for "a formal integration of experience," he doesn't manage the clever and pointful anecdotes and maxims that relieve Carl Sandburg's resounding periods. It is difficult not to see Ginsberg's work as the final collapse of this style, a last, self-indulgent plunge into chaos and nonsense.

Review of *Planet News*
Bill Berkson
Poetry 114 (July 1969), pp. 251–256

Allen Ginsberg does a lot. Many people behave as though he does everything but actually think through and *write* great poems, which is untrue. Hearing him read, there is rapture and a kind of instruction, leaving you to wonder what the poems themselves, as scored, might really be like. There used to be more difference. More of the new poems can be read without his help, are exciting one way or the other.

Ginsberg's work exists within the theory of the full balloon: it breathes, it gets up there, it's true, even to the extent that the arguments which might bring it down seem dull beyond consideration. So much, then, for his "place". He knows whereof he speaks, and so his method is simple: if he calls it "vision", you can counter with your own (he asks for it), and scan for what interests you. Some of the best poems, however, require strict attention (so don't be too hasty). There's plenty of room. Few comparisons are useful, and those that come to mind are all too often used against him. To say "Blake" or "Whitman" is to be in on the gossip and to study his inspiration partially, which is not exactly beside the point, but I think that is Ginsberg's business–certainly no two "chanters of personality" can be alike. To say "Pound" is to begin to trace a nearer lineage of conscientious, which is to say, solid technique. And he has been reading Bunting lately. The solidity is interesting; it doesn't suggest a fresh direction–I can't imagine anyone writing "like" him or even whiling away imitations of his cadences (the abbreviations headline-style are something else)–but it does indicate a point in development of a personal sound where the voice ("Allen Ginsberg") is assuredly itself, so much so that it seems "historical" (or "bardic"?) and therefore immediately impressive. What might be called his *ambition* connects to Ginsberg's way of pronouncing himself the poet of his own poems: "Tears alright, and laughter alright / I am that I am". . . .

. . . .

One could say the longer the political poems are nothing but last-ditch practicality, setting out to clear the air as well as the stomach. *Wichita Vortex Sutra* is a working scramble, or re-scrambling, of headlines that read like hallucination. "Everybody", prophesied Gertrude Stein "gets so much information all day long that they lose their common sense. They forget to be natural". But Ginsberg doesn't; in fact, he sounds more sensible than ever.

In his review of Jane Kramer's Allen Ginsberg in America *(1969), Rexroth argues that throughout his career Ginsberg's image has been distorted by the mainstream media.*

Review of *Allen Ginsberg in America*
Kenneth Rexroth
The New York Times Book Review, 11 May 1969, pp. 8, 41

At the "Howl" trial in San Francisco the prosecutor asked one of the witnesses, "You say this book is not pornographic. What kind of a book would you call it?" The witness answered, "It could best be compared to one of the prophetic books of the Bible, especially Hosea, which it resembles in more ways than one." The prosecutor, taken aback, dismissed the witness.

It is very true–Allen Ginsberg is in the direct line of the *nabis,* those wild men of the hills, bearded and barefoot, who periodically descended upon Jerusalem, denounced king and priesthood, and recalled the Chosen People to the Covenant. If any writer in America is true to his tradition, it's Ginsberg. Behind him stretches away for generations the prophetic, visionary and orgiastic tradition of Hasidism. He is a Zaddik. Immediately behind him stand Whitman and the founders of communal groups from Oneida to New Harmony, from the Schwenkfelders to the Mormons, those noble souls who almost won, who almost established America as a community of love. It is the Whitman of "Passage to India" who appears to Ginsberg in a supermarket.

Immediately in Ginsberg's own childhood, as he says in "Howl," was what we used to call "the revolutionary movement" before it became a minor department of the Narkomindel, the Russian Foreign Office. The region in which he grew up, Passaic and Paterson, was a land of promise as well as a place of the "dark satanic mills" of Blake where thousands of Jewish and Italian and Appalachian migrants hoped to build Jerusalem in New Jersey's green and sullied land. Unless Ginsberg is understood as a religious leader of the same kind as his younger colleague, Gary Snyder, he cannot be understood at all. Although it was his fame and his loyalty to his old friends from Columbia, who used to get drunk in the San Remo on MacDougal Street, that launched the actually very small Beat movement, he was anything but a beatnik, and it is only as the counter culture has caught up with him that he has come to play his full role.

Just as the Ginsberg of 10 to 15 years ago was a *hallucination publicitaire* of the news weeklies and picture magazines, so Jane Kramer's Ginsberg is a New Yorker Profile. This is a strange animal which resembles the window mannequins in Saks, the movie stars of the silents, or the creatures who advertise whisky in the periodicals with the most expensive advertising rates. Among poets the most scathing term of contempt is "New Yorker verse," even though some of the leading writers in the country have been published in its pages. There is a kind of Winnie-the-Pooh whimsey that spreads over everything and turns it all into something synthetic made of polyesters and cloying soybeans.

Jane Kramer is unquestionably a woman of very good will indeed. She obviously worked extremely hard to be just, sympathetic and illuminating in her three part New Yorker Profile that makes up this book. In the process she obviously developed great affection and respect for Ginsberg. Yet it's all unreal. Her description of the sessions of the leaders of the great Golden Gate Park Be In, which was the Coming of the Kingdom of the Flower Children before the Mafia took over the Haight-Ashbury, reads like nothing so much as Pooh, Piglet, Rabbit, Owl, Eeyore, Tigger, Kanga and Roo all running around with their clothes off, high on pharmaceuticals beyond the fondest dreams of Huxley, Watts and Leary rolled into one.

I know all these people, most of them very well indeed; and believe me, they are in deadly earnest. There is nothing whimsical about what they propose to do to the old culture. The counterculture may be distorted and turned into its opposite or coopted by the voices of the Establishment. When Big Business in the form of the Mafia discovered that it could sell methedrine and heroin to adolescents as enlargement of consciousness sacraments of a new religion, they discovered the most profitable counterrevolution in history, but none of this is what Ginsberg or Gary Snyder or Lenore Kandel or the other people Jane Kramer writes about are about.

Rexroth commented on Ginsberg's career in a 1971 interview.

On the other hand, the people that came up after the war are now also locked into the establishment.

. . .

They can't understand that they are now the establishment. Ginsberg does. Of course, Allen has ten times the brains of the rest of them. He has sense. He has a sense of what happened to him and where he is. He has insight, and of course, he has connections with the younger people. He's like Dave Tough. After all, Allen is the only beatnik who is still alive. The rest of them are dead. I mean mentally . . . Allen is never uptight. He is always available. I would go nuts if I was as available as he is. Christ, I would go out of my mind! He is always available and he is always connected with people.

–*The San Francisco Poets,* p. 37

Ginsberg, swinging a Buddhist prayer bell, marches up Sixth Avenue in New York City with a contingent of gay people against the Vietnam War.

Ginsberg with Orlovsky at the Republican National Convention in Miami, in 1972

As is clear in the interview from High Times, *a magazine that celebrates the growth and use of marijuana, Ginsberg continued to experiment with drugs throughout his life.*

The *High Times* Interview
Greg Daurer
High Times, February 1992, pp. 13–16

HIGH TIMES: Why do you think there's a revival of interest in the '50s Beat Generation and its literature?
Allen Ginsberg: The literature and mythology of the Beat generation [runs] counter to the current hypertechnological, homogenized, money-obsessed, security/fear-based, militaristic gross-out. It specialized in the analysis of the technological Police State; the refreshing insight into ecological sanity; the revival of the Whitmanic notion of American friendship and affection as the basis of democracy; respect for individuality; disrespect for the law where "the law is an ass," pertaining to psychedelics, marijuana and the handling of heroin not as a medical thing but as basis for some sort of Police State structure.

All these themes make the original Beat ethos quite user-friendly, compared to the destructiveness of the supposed "straight" world that can go nuts, killing one hundred fifty thousand people in Iraq for the sake of oil that'll pollute the planet. These themes are perennial values in a decade without values in America—a nation sustained by abuse of the earth's resources and consuming a disproportionate amount of raw materials and creating a disproportionate amount of garbage and possessing a disproportionate amount of military power for such a small nation.
HT: What Beat works best reflect the ideals you've discussed?
AG: Books like *On the Road* or *Visions of Cody,* or *Visions of Gerard* or *The Subterraneans*—any of Kerouac's writings coming from his spontaneous natural mind. Or Burroughs' extremely intelligent analysis of the addiction situation in America. Or my own sort of exuberant, sometimes gay, sometimes psychedelic, sometimes Buddhist, sometimes angry, sometimes funny, natural mind—see *Collected Poems* or *White Shroud.* Or Gregory

Ginsberg featured on the cover of a major poetry periodical in which eight of his previously unpublished poems appear

Corso's historical scope in *Mind Fields,* because he's a pretty good one for applying Greek myth to contemporaneity. Or Gary Snyder's *Practice of the Wild,* correlating back country with wilderness of mind. Or Philip Whalen, the first Beat poet abbot. Or Michael McClure's new biological poetry, nature talking. As well as the sometimes inspiring myths of Neal Cassady who transcended–or spanned–several generations of American psyche and road simultaneously–from Kerouac to Kesey.

HT: What are your current views on psychedelic drugs?

AG: The last thing I tried was Ecstasy. The first trip was really great–here in Boulder–five years ago. One immediate conclusion I came to was that Ecstasy was misnamed; it was not a poet who laid that trip on the poor drug. It's "Empathy." "Ecstasy" is some kind of hippy-dippy exaggeration hyperbole. "Empathy" is more accurate, because the trip immediately made me feel very sympathetic, empathetic to everybody I knew.

HT: Have you tried it since then?

AG: Second time I took it, same thing, but much diluted and it wasn't that interesting. The amphetaminesque aspect of it was dominant and I didn't like that. I don't like amphetamines or cocaine–they just make you nervous and frazzle your nerves and exhaust your endorphins. . . .

HT: What did you learn from psychedelics?

AG: Psychedelics seem to me a classic educational tool or classic visionary tool. The only way I've slightly changed my view of them–it's been twenty years of meditating now–I think it'd be useful to have some information or instruction or experience in centering yourself with meditation practice. Preferably nontheistic: so you don't get trippy on Hindu gods, or Christian gods, or Jewish Jahvehs, or monotheistic monsters in the sky, or devils; but more open space as in Buddhist and some Hindu and some Kabbalah and some Sufi view–a centering mechanism so you don't get entangled and trapped in your own projections. And being trapped in your own projections on acid is something I've experienced often and I can see how it could lead to disasters.

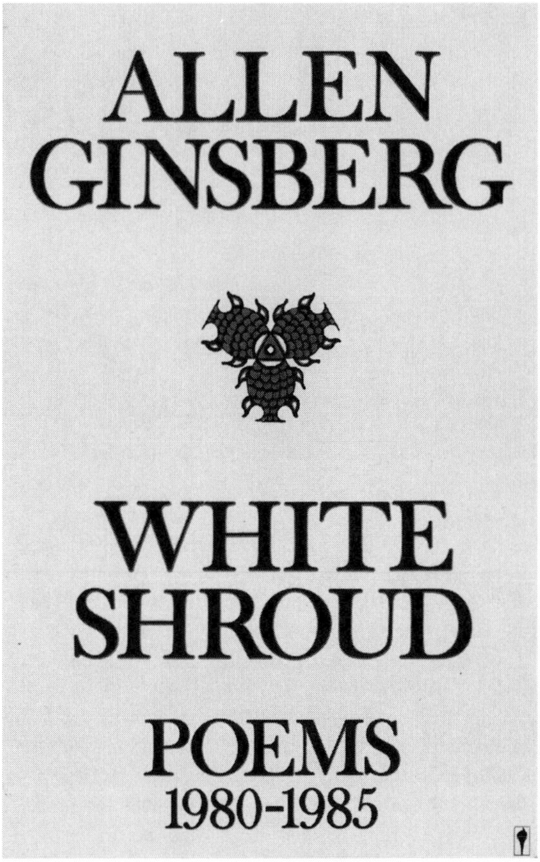

Dust jacket for Ginsberg's 1986 collection of poems

Cover for a drug-culture magazine featuring an interview with Ginsberg

HT: Explain what that concept means.
AG: Some people get into a circular feedback, "Oooh, I'm in a human body, ooh, I'm dying, I must be dying this very minute, maybe I'm dying now, oooh, call the police!" And that's how one gets entangled in one's own projections. Or take off your clothes and jump in front of the cars and say, "Stop all the machinery!" So you might get run over or arrested, not knowing skillful means of communicating naked nature.

Ginsberg spent most of his last thirty years living in the East Village in New York City. With Anne Waldman, he cofounded the Jack Kerouac School of Disembodied Poetics at the Naropa Institute in Boulder, Colorado, America's first accredited Buddhist college. He continued to present readings of his poetry to wide audiences; he maintained a voluminous correspondence; he taught at Brooklyn College; and he produced poetry. His major works include "Wichita Vortex Sutra" (1966), "Wales Visitation" (1967), "Don't Grow Old" (1976), and "White Shroud" (1983). The drafts of his later work indicate his rigor in revision. Ginsberg composed "Fame and Death" less than a month before he died. Ginsberg died in the spring of 1997, eight days after being diagnosed with liver cancer.

Allen Ginsberg, 70, Master Poet of Beat Generation
Wilborn Hampton
The New York Times, 6 April 1997

New York–Allen Ginsberg, the poet laureate of the Beat Generation whose "Howl!" became a manifesto for the sexual revolution and a cause celebre for free speech in the 1950s, eventually earning its author a place in America's literary pantheon, died early Saturday. He was 70 and lived in Manhattan.

He died of liver cancer, said Bill Morgan, a friend and the poet's archivist.

Morgan said that Ginsberg wrote right to the end. "He's working on a lot of poems, talking to old friends," Morgan said Friday. "He's in very good spirits. He wants to write poetry and finish his life's work."

William S. Burroughs, one of Ginsberg's lifelong friends and a fellow Beat, said that Ginsberg's death was "a great loss to me and to everybody."

"We were friends for more than 50 years," Burroughs said. "Allen was a great person with worldwide influence. He was a pioneer of openness and a lifelong model of candor. He stood for freedom of expression and for coming out of all the closets long before others

Ginsberg at a public reading in the early 1990s

did. He has influence because he said what he believed. I will miss him."

As much through the strength of his own irrepressible personality as through his poetry, Ginsberg provided a bridge between the Underground and the Transcendental. He was as comfortable in the ashrams of Indian gurus in the 1960s as he had been in the Beat coffeehouses of the preceding decade.

A ubiquitous presence at the love-ins and be-ins that marked the drug-oriented counterculture of the Flower Children years, Ginsberg was also in the vanguard of the political protest movements they helped spawn. He marched against the war in Vietnam, the CIA and the Shah of Iran, among other causes.

If his early verse shocked Eisenhower's America with its celebration of homosexuality and drugs, his involvement in protests kept him in the public eye and fed ammunition to his critics.

But through it all, Ginsberg maintained a sort of teddy bear quality that deflected much of the indignation he inspired.

He was known around the world as a master of the outrageous. He read his poetry and played finger cymbals at the Albert Hall in London; he was expelled from Cuba after saying he found Che Guevara "cute"; he sang duets with Bob Dylan, and he chanted "Hare Krishna" on William F. Buckley Jr.'s television program.

As the critic John Leonard observed in a 1988 appreciation: "He is of course a social bandit. But he is a nonviolent social bandit."

Or as the narrator in Saul Bellow's "Him With His Foot in His Mouth" said of Ginsberg: "Under all this self-revealing candor is purity of heart, and the only authentic living representative of American Transcendentalism is that fat-breasted, bald, bearded homosexual in smeared goggles, innocent in his uncleanness."

J. D. McClatchy, a poet and the editor of The Yale Review, said Saturday: "Ginsberg was the best-known American poet of his generation, as much a social force as a literary phenomenon.

"Like Whitman, he was a bard in the old manner–outsized, darkly prophetic, part exuberance, part prayer, part rant," McClatchy said. "His work is finally a history of our era's psyche, with all its contradictory urges."

Allen Ginsberg was born June 3, 1926, in Newark, N. J., and grew up in Paterson, N. J., the second son of Louis Ginsberg, a schoolteacher and sometime poet, and the former Naomi Levy, a Russian emigree and fervent Marxist. His brother, Eugene, named for Eugene V. Debs, also wrote poetry, under the name Eugene Brooks. Eugene, a lawyer, survives.

Recalling his parents in a 1985 interview, Ginsberg said: "They were old-fashioned delicatessen philosophers. My father would go around the house either reciting Emily Dickinson and Longfellow under his breath or attacking T. S. Eliot for ruining poetry with his 'obscurantism.' My mother made up bedtime stories that all went something like: 'The good king rode forth from his castle, saw the suffering workers and healed them.' I grew suspicious of both sides."

An Authorization for a Lobotomy

Allen Ginsberg's mother later suffered from paranoia and was in and out of mental hospitals; Ginsberg signed an authorization for a lobotomy. Two days after she died in 1956 in Pilgrim State Mental Hospital on Long Island, he received a letter from her that said: "The key is in the window, the key is in the sunlight in the window–I have the key–get married Allen don't take drugs . . . Love, your mother."

Three years after her death, Ginsberg wrote "Kaddish for Naomi Ginsberg (1894–1956)," an elegy that many consider his finest poem.

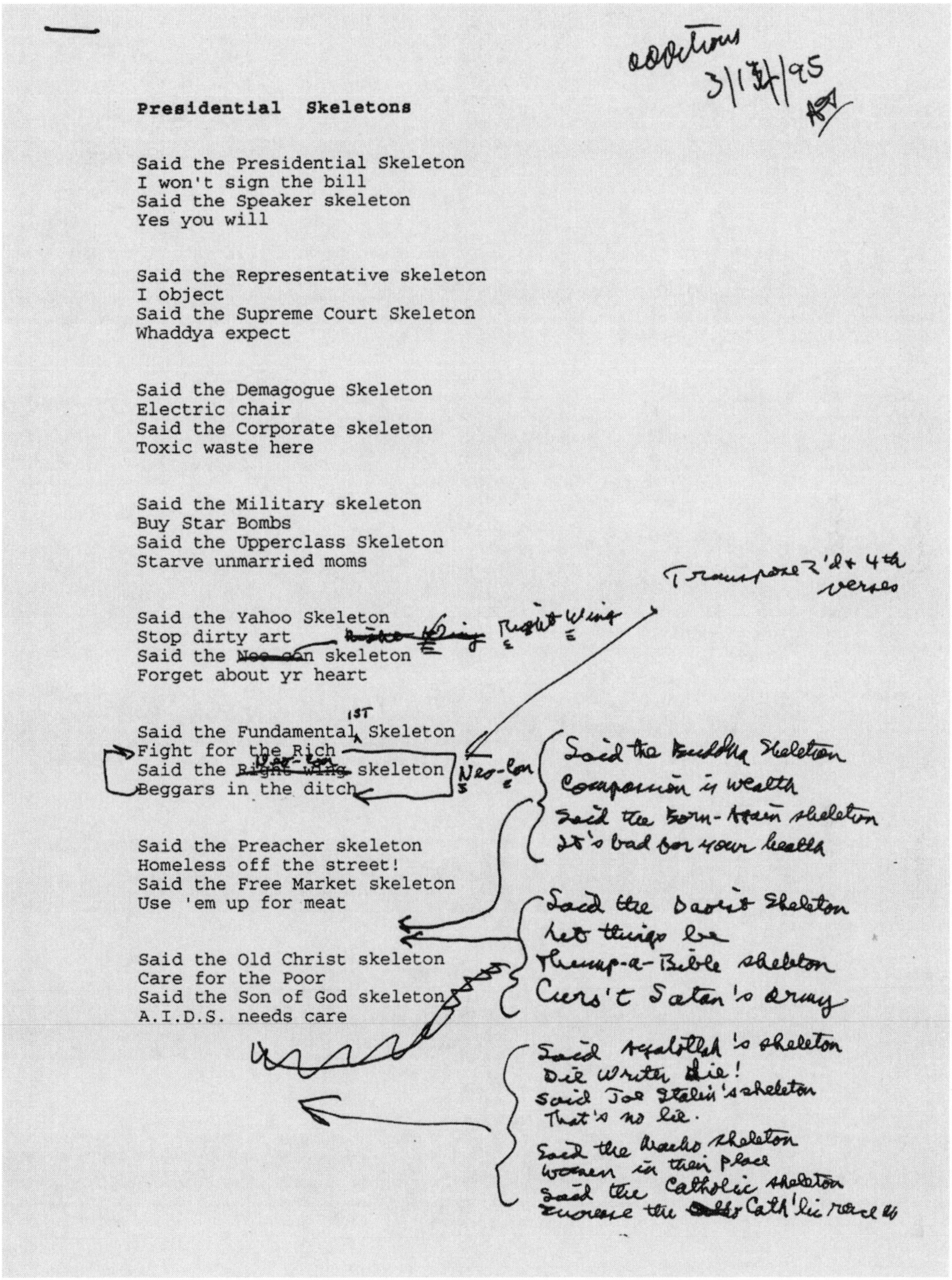

additions 3/13/95 AG

Presidential Skeletons

Said the Presidential Skeleton
I won't sign the bill
Said the Speaker skeleton
Yes you will

Said the Representative skeleton
I object
Said the Supreme Court Skeleton
Whaddya expect

Said the Demagogue Skeleton
Electric chair
Said the Corporate skeleton
Toxic waste here

Said the Military skeleton
Buy Star Bombs
Said the Upperclass Skeleton
Starve unmarried moms

Transpose 2'd + 4th verses

Said the Yahoo Skeleton
Stop dirty art
Said the ~~Neo-con~~ Right Wing skeleton
Forget about yr heart

Said the Fundamental 1st Skeleton
Fight for the Rich
Said the ~~Right wing~~ Neo-Con skeleton
Beggars in the ditch

Said the Buddha Skeleton
Compassion is wealth
Said the Born-Again skeleton
It's bad for your health

Said the Preacher skeleton
Homeless off the street!
Said the Free Market skeleton
Use 'em up for meat

Said the Taoist Skeleton
Let things be
Thump-a-Bible skeleton
Curs't [?] Satan's army

Said the Old Christ skeleton
Care for the Poor
Said the Son of God skeleton
A.I.D.S. needs care

Said Ayatollah's skeleton
Die Writer Die!
Said Joe Stalin's skeleton
That's no lie.

Said the Macho skeleton
Women in their place
Said the Catholic skeleton
Increase the Cath'lic race

Revised typescript draft of a poem first published in the 1999 collection Death & Fame: Poems 1993–1997 *(© Allen Ginsberg Trust)*

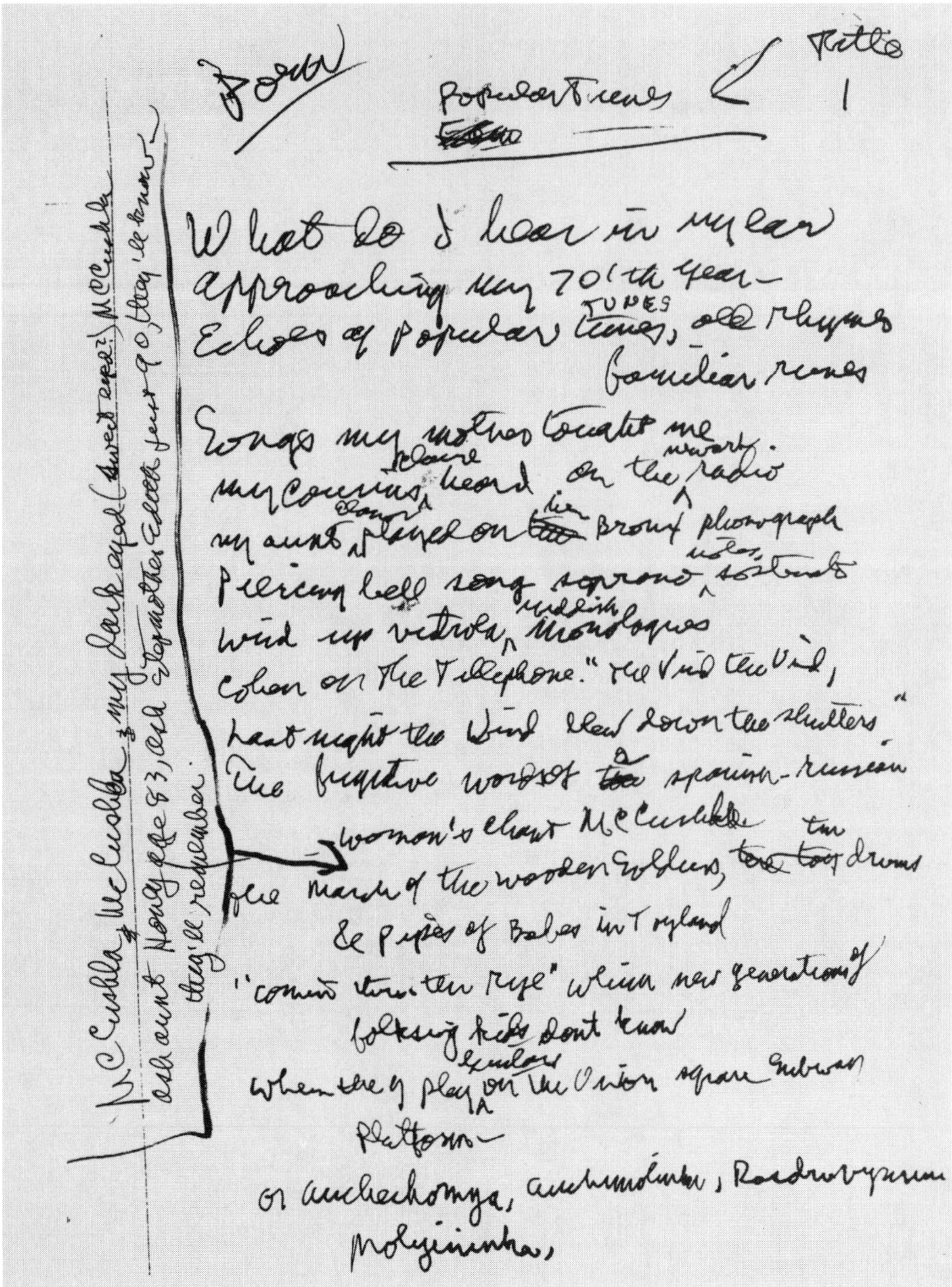
Popular Tunes
Title 1

What do I hear in my ear
approaching my 70th year—
Echoes of popular tunes, old rhymes
familiar scenes

Songs my mother taught me
my cousins heard on the radio
my aunts played on the brown phonograph
Piercing bell song soprano, sostenuto
wind up victrola, monologues
Cohen on the Telephone. "The Wind the Wind,
Last night the Wind blew down the shutters"
The fugitive words of a spanish-russian
woman's chant McCuskla
The March of the Wooden Soldiers, the drums
& pipes of Babes in Toyland
"Comin thru the rye" which new generations of
folksing kids dont know
when they play on the Union square subway
platform—
or Auchechornya, Auchimalinka, Raschwyenu
Molyiminka,

Draft of a poem first published in Death & Fame: Poems 1993–1997 *(© Allen Ginsberg Trust)*

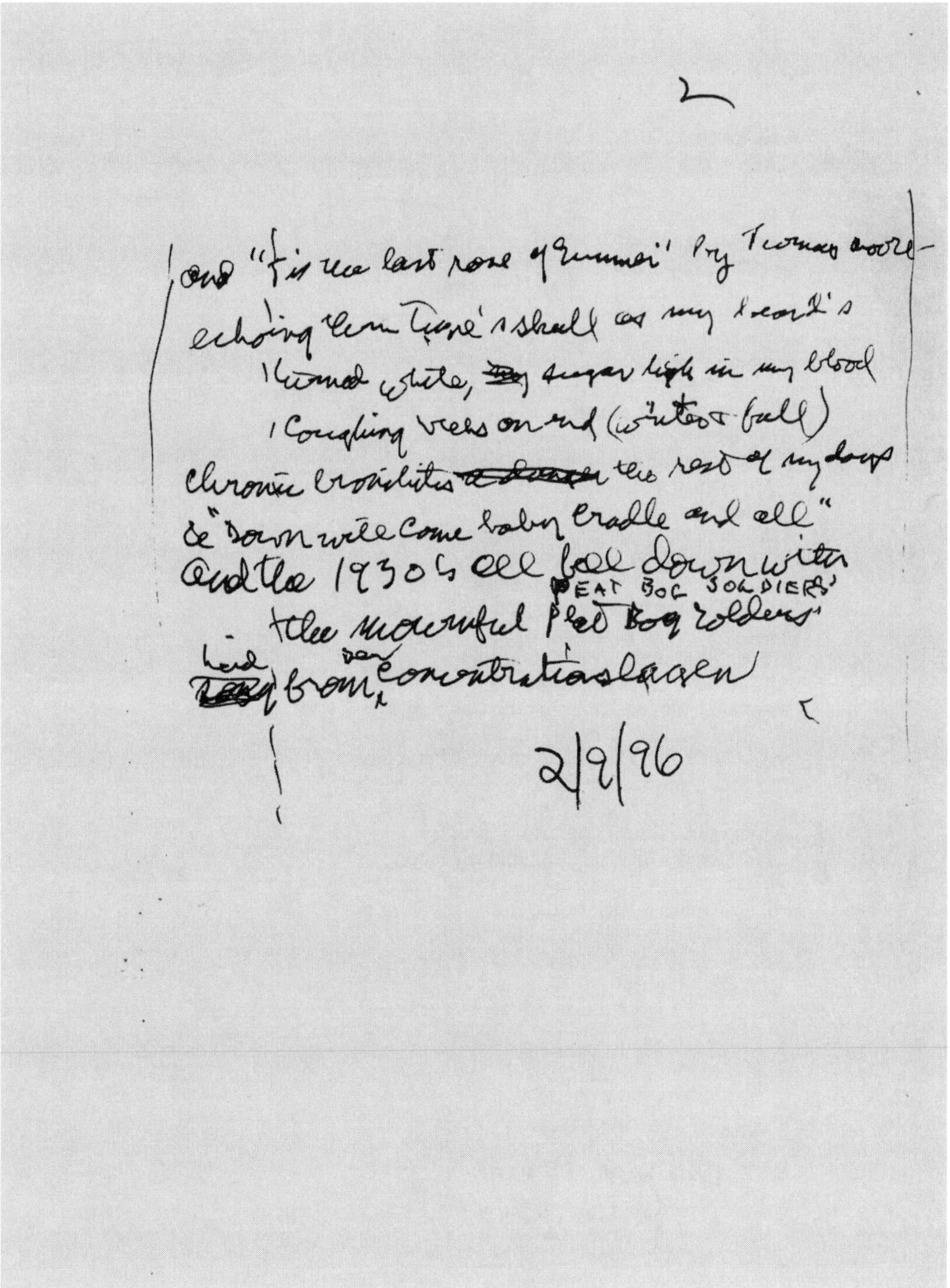

2

and "Tis the last rose of summer" by Thomas Moore—
echoing thru Grace's skull as my beard's
turned white, sugar high in my blood
Coughing veins on end (winter-full)
Chronic bronchitis the rest of my days
So "Down will come baby cradle and all"
And the 1930s all fall down with
the mournful "~~Red~~ Bog Soldiers" PEAT BOG SOLDIERS
heard from den concentrationslagen

2/9/96

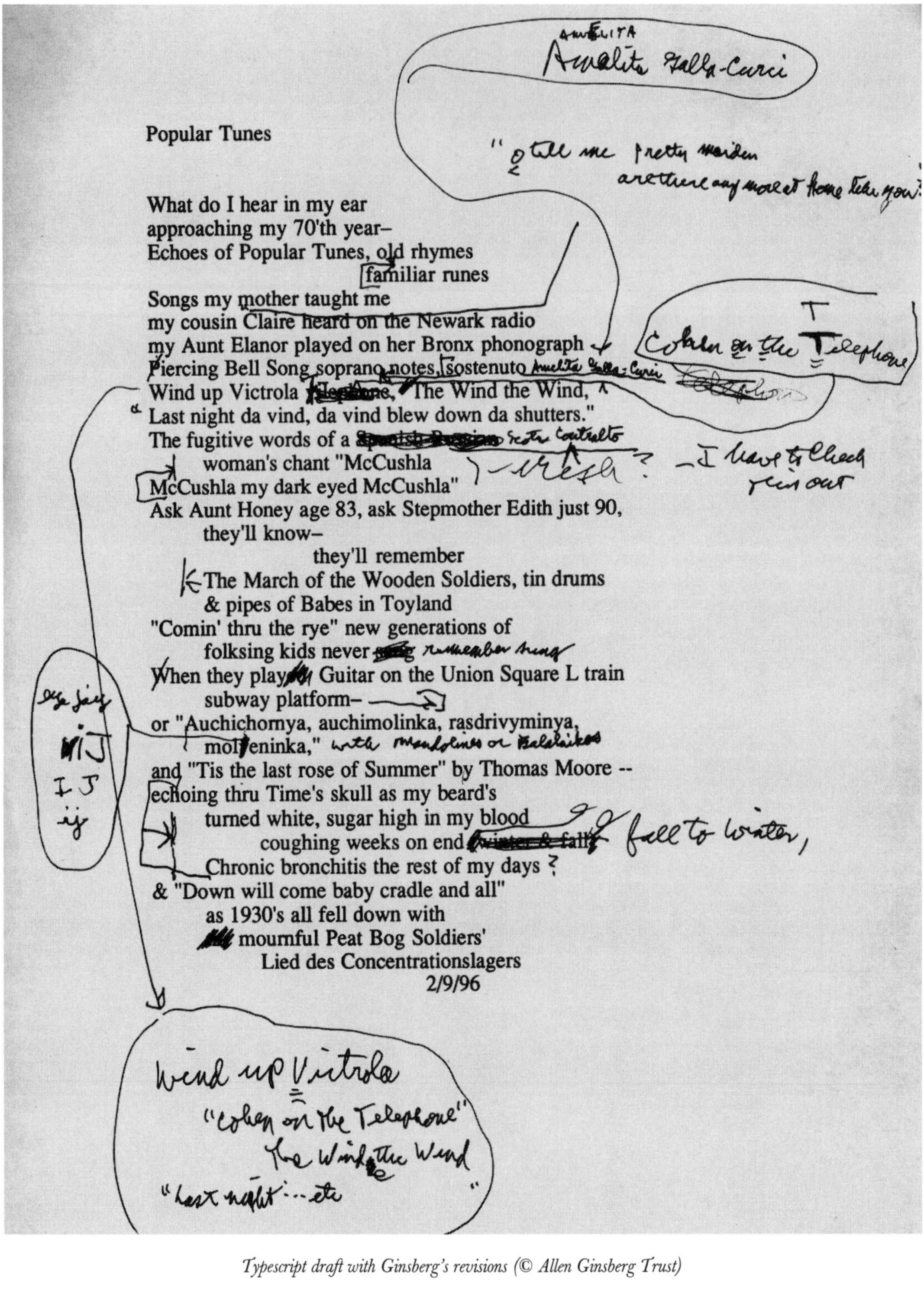

Popular Tunes

What do I hear in my ear
approaching my 70'th year–
Echoes of Popular Tunes, old rhymes
familiar runes
Songs my mother taught me
my cousin Claire ~~heard on the~~ Newark radio
my Aunt Elanor played on her Bronx phonograph
Piercing Bell Song soprano notes, sostenuto
Wind up Victrola ~~Telephone~~, The Wind the Wind,
Last night da vind, da vind blew down da shutters."
The fugitive words of a ~~Spanish Russian~~
woman's chant "McCushla
McCushla my dark eyed McCushla"
Ask Aunt Honey age 83, ask Stepmother Edith just 90,
they'll know–
they'll remember
The March of the Wooden Soldiers, tin drums
& pipes of Babes in Toyland
"Comin' thru the rye" new generations of
folksing kids never ~~sing~~
When they play~~s~~ Guitar on the Union Square L train
subway platform–
or "Auchichornya, auchimolinka, rasdrivyminya,
molfeninka,"
and "Tis the last rose of Summer" by Thomas Moore --
echoing thru Time's skull as my beard's
turned white, sugar high in my blood
coughing weeks on end ~~winter & fall~~
Chronic bronchitis the rest of my days
& "Down will come baby cradle and all"
as 1930's all fell down with
mournful Peat Bog Soldiers'
Lied des Concentrationslagers
2/9/96

Typescript draft with Ginsberg's revisions (© Allen Ginsberg Trust)

Strange now to think of you, gone without corsets & eyes, while I walk on the sunny pavement of Greenwich Village,

downtown Manhattan, clear winter noon, and I've been up all night, talking, talking, reading the Kaddish aloud, listening to Ray Charles blues shout blind on the phonograph

the rhythm, the rhythm–and your memory in my head three years after– . . .

"Kaddish" burnished a reputation that had been forged with the publication of "Howl!" three years earlier. The two works established Ginsberg as a major voice in what came to be known as the Beat Generation of writers.

Ginsberg's journey to his place as one of America's most celebrated poets began during his college days. He first attended Montclair State College. But in 1943, he received a small scholarship from the Young Men's Hebrew Association of Paterson and enrolled at Columbia University.

He considered becoming a lawyer like his brother, but was soon attracted to the literary courses offered by Mark Van Doren and Lionel Trilling, and switched his major from pre-law to literature.

At Columbia he fell in with a crowd that included Jack Kerouac, a former student four years his senior, Lucien Carr and William Burroughs, and later, Neal Cassady, a railway worker who had literary aspirations. Together they formed the nucleus of what would become the Beats.

Kerouac and Carr became the poet's mentors and Kerouac and Cassady became his lovers. It was also at Columbia that Ginsberg began to experiment with mind-altering drugs, which would gain widespread use in the decade to follow and which Ginsberg would celebrate in his verse along with his homosexuality and his immersion in Eastern transcendental religions.

But if the Beats were creating literary history around Columbia and the West End Cafe, there was a dangerous undercurrent to their activities. Carr spent a brief time in jail for manslaughter, and Ginsberg, because he had associated with Carr, was suspended from Columbia for a year.

In 1949, after Ginsberg had received his bachelor's degree, Herbert Huncke, a writer and hustler, moved into his apartment and stored stolen goods there. Huncke was eventually jailed, and Ginsberg, pleading psychological disability, was sent to a psychiatric institution for eight months.

At the institution, he met another patient, Carl Solomon, whom Ginsberg credited with deepening his understanding of poetry and its power as a weapon of political dissent.

Ginsberg (photograph by Lisa Law)

Becoming a Protégé of the Poet Williams

Returning home to Paterson, Ginsberg became a protege of William Carlos Williams, the physician and poet, who lived nearby. Williams' use of colloquial American language in his poetry was a major influence on the young Ginsberg.

After leaving Columbia, Ginsberg first went to work for a Madison Avenue advertising agency. After five years, he once recalled, he found himself taking part in a consumer-research project trying to determine whether Americans preferred the word "sparkling" or "glamorous," to describe ideal teeth. "We already knew people associate diamonds with 'sparkling' and furs with 'glamorous,'" he said. "We spent $150,000 to learn most people didn't want furry teeth."

The poet said he decided to give up the corporate world "when my shrink asked me what would make me happy." He hung his grey flannel suit in the closet and went to San Francisco with six months of unemployment insurance in his pocket. San Francisco was then the center of considerable literary energy. He took a room around the corner from City Lights, Lawrence Ferlinghetti's bookstore and underground publishing house, and began to write.

During this period Ginsberg also became part of the San Francisco literary circle that included Kenneth Rexroth–an author, critic and painter–Gary Snyder, Michael McClure, Philip Whalen, Robert Duncan and Philip Lamantia. He also met Peter Orlovsky, who would be his companion for the next 30 years.

His first major work from San Francisco was "Howl!" The long-running poem expressed the anxieties and ideals of a generation alienated from mainstream society. "Howl!," which was to become Ginsberg's most famous poem, was dedicated to Carl Solomon, and begins:

> I saw the best minds of my generation destroyed by madness, starving hysterical naked,
>
> dragging themselves through the negro streets at dawn looking for an angry fix,
>
> angelheaded hipsters burning for the ancient heavenly connection to the starry dynamo in the machinery of night. . . .

Ginsberg read the poem to a gathering arranged by Rexroth, and those present never forgot the poem, its author and the occasion.

Rexroth's wife privately distributed a mimeographed 50-copy edition of "Howl!" and in 1956, Ferlinghetti published "Howl! and Other Poems" in what he called his "pocket poets series."

With its open and often vivid celebration of homosexuality and eroticism, "Howl!" was impounded by U.S. Customs agents and Ginsberg was tried on obscenity charges.

After a long trial, Judge Clayton Horn ruled that the poem was not without "redeeming social importance."

The result was to make "Howl!" immensely popular and establish it as a landmark against censorship. The outrage and furor did not stop with the sexual revolution. As late as 1988, the radio station WBAI refused to allow "Howl!" to be read on the air during a weeklong series about censorship in America.

There were almost as many definitions of Beatniks and the Beat movement as there were writers who claimed to be part of it. As John Clellon Holmes described it, "To be beat is to be at the bottom of your personality looking up." But if the movement grew out of disillusionment, it was disillusionment with a conscience.

Ginsberg tried to explain the aims of the Beats in a letter to his father in 1957: "Whitman long ago complained that unless the material power of America were leavened by some kind of spiritual infusion, we would wind up among the 'fabled damned.' We're approaching that state as far as I can see. Only way out is individuals taking responsibility and saying what they actually feel. That's what we as a group have been trying to do."

On another occasion, he described the literary rules more succinctly: "You don't have to be right. All you have to do is be candid." Ginsberg was nothing if not candid.

As he wrote in "America," another 1956 poem, which took aim at Eisenhower's post-McCarthy era:

> America I've given you all and now I'm nothing
> America two dollars and twentyseven cents January 17, 1956
>
> . . .
>
> America this is quite serious
> America this is the impression I get from looking in the television set
> America is this correct?
> . . .

Ginsberg claimed that the poets who formed the prime influence on his own work were William Blake, Walt Whitman, Ezra Pound and William Carlos Williams. He declared he had found a new method of poetry. "All you have to do," he said, "is think of anything that comes into your head, then arrange in lines of two, three or four words each, don't bother about sentences, in sections of two, three or four lines each."

His disdain for the traditional rules of poetry only gave ammunition to his critics. James Dickey once complained that the "problem" with Allen Ginsberg was that he made it seem like anybody could write poetry.

Traveling Widely for Two Decades

Ginsberg used the celebrity he gained with "Howl!" to travel widely during the next two decades. He went to China and India to study with gurus and Zen masters and to Venice to see Pound. On his way home he was crowned King of the May by dissident university students in Prague, only to be expelled by the communist government. He read his poetry wherever they would let him, from concert stages to off-campus coffeehouses.

He was in the forefront of whatever movement was in fashion: the sexual revolution and drug culture of the 1960s, the anti-Vietnam war demonstrations of the '60s and '70s, the anti-CIA and anti-shah demonstrations of the '70s, and the anti-Reagan protests of the '80s.

In 1967 he was arrested in an antiwar protest in New York City, and he was arrested again, for the same reason, at the Democratic National Convention in Chicago in 1968. He testified in the trial of the so-called Chicago Seven.

Through it all, he kept writing. After "Kaddish" in 1959, major works included "TV Baby" in 1960, "Wichita Vortex Sutra" (1966), "Wales Visitation" (1967), "Don't Grow Old" (1976) and "White Shroud" (1983).

In his celebrated career, Ginsberg was the recipient of many awards, including the National Book Award (1973), the Robert Frost Medal for distinguished poetic achievement (1986), and an American Book Award for contributions to literary excellence (1990).

In 1968, Neal Cassady died of a drug overdose. Kerouac died of alcoholism the next year. By the mid-1970s, Ginsberg had helped start the Jack Kerouac School of Disembodied Poetics of the Naropa Institute in Boulder, Colo., a Buddhist university where he taught summer courses in poetry and in Buddhist meditation. He also was becoming one of the last living voices of the Beat generation and the keeper of the flame.

In 1985, Harper & Row published Ginsberg's "Collected Poems," an anthology of his major work in one volume that firmly established the poet in the mainstream of American literature. The poet again made tours, giving interviews and showing up on television shows, but this time he was in suit and tie and offering a sort of explanation of his life's work.

"People ask me if I've gone respectable now," he said to one interviewer. "I tell them I've always been respectable."

During another interview, he confessed: "My intention was to make a picture of the mind, mistakes and all. Of course I learned I'm an idiot, a complete idiot who wasn't as prophetic as I thought I was. The crazy, angry Philippic sometimes got in the way of clear perception.

"I thought the North Vietnamese would be a lot better than they turned out to be. I shouldn't have been marching against the Shah of Iran because the mullahs have turned out to be a lot worse."

But despite his suit and tie, the censors continued to look over Ginsberg's shoulder. During the round of interviews, David Remnick, then of The Washington Post, accompanied him to his scheduled appearance on CBS's "Nightwatch." A producer, clearly unfamiliar with the poet's work, asked if he would read something on the show.

"How about reading that poem about your mother?" she suggested.

"'Kaddish,' yes. Time magazine calls it my masterpiece," Ginsberg replied. "But I don't know. . . ."

The poet pointed to a word in the poem he doubted would make prime time. As Remnick reported, the producer's eyes glazed over and there was a long silence in the room.

"Your mother's. . . .?" the producer said in horror.

"Couldn't we just bleep that part out?" the poet offered, always helpful.

"No," the producer said.

"It's OK," the poet replied. "I've got other poems."

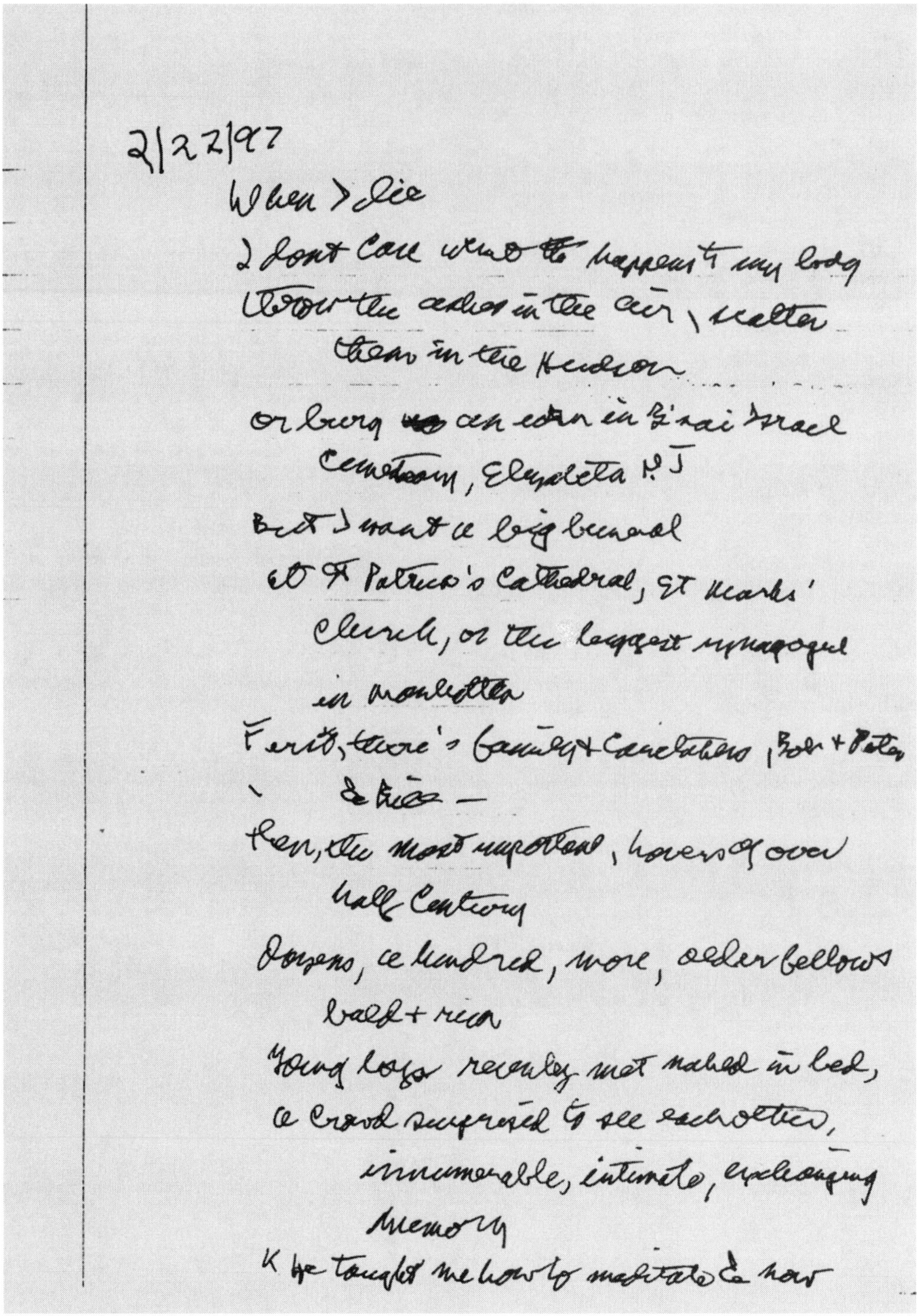
2/22/97
When I die
I dont care what happens to my body
throw the ashes in the air, scatter
them in the Hudson
or bury an urn in B'nai Israel
Cemetery, Elizabeth N.J
But I want a big funeral
at St Patrick's Cathedral, St Marks'
Church, or the biggest synagogue
in Manhattan
First, there's family & caretakers, Bob + Peter
& [illegible] —
then, the most important, lovers of over
half century
Dozens, a hundred, more, older fellows
bald + rich
Young boys recently met naked in bed,
a crowd surprised to see each other,
innumerable, intimate, exchanging
memory
"He taught me how to meditate, now

Draft of poem that inspired the title for Death & Fame: Poems 1993–1997 *(© Allen Ginsberg Trust)*

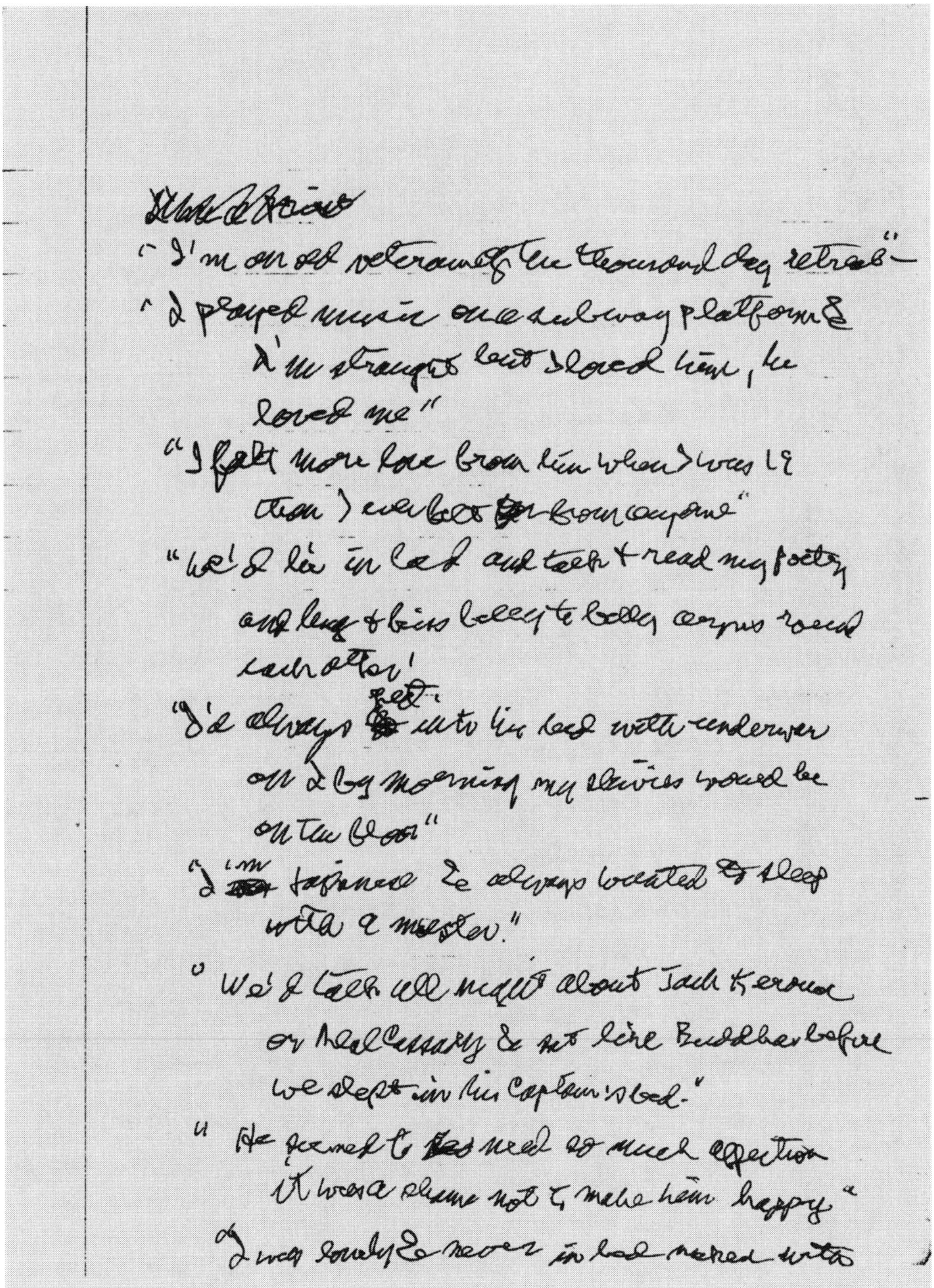

[illegible]

"I'm an old veteran of the thousand day retreat"

"I played music on the subway platform

I'm straight but I loved him, he loved me"

"I felt more love from him when I was 19 than I ever felt from anyone"

"We'd lie in bed and talk & read my poetry and hug & kiss belly to belly arms round each other"

"I'd always get into his bed with underwear on & by morning my skivvies would be on the floor"

"I'm Japanese & always wanted to sleep with a master."

"We'd talk all night about Jack Kerouac or Neal Cassady & sit like Buddha before we slept in his captain's bed."

"He seemed to need so much affection it was a shame not to make him happy"

"I was lonely & never in bed naked with

Everyone before, he was so gentle my stomach
shuddered as he traced his finger
along my abdomen nipple to hips—
"All I had to do was lay back & close my eyes,
he'd bring me to come with his mouth
& fingers along my waist"
So there be gossip from loves of 1948,
ghosts of Neal Cassady commingling with flesh
and youthful blood of 1997
and surprise—"You too? But I thought you
were straight!"
"I am but Ginsberg was an exception, for some
reason he pleased me,
"I forgot whether I was straight or gay or
queer or funny, I was myself, tender
and affectionate to be kissed on the belly,
on top of my head my forehead my throat my
heart & solar plexus, again on my belly, on
my prick, tickled with his tongue my
behind"
"I loved the way he'd read me

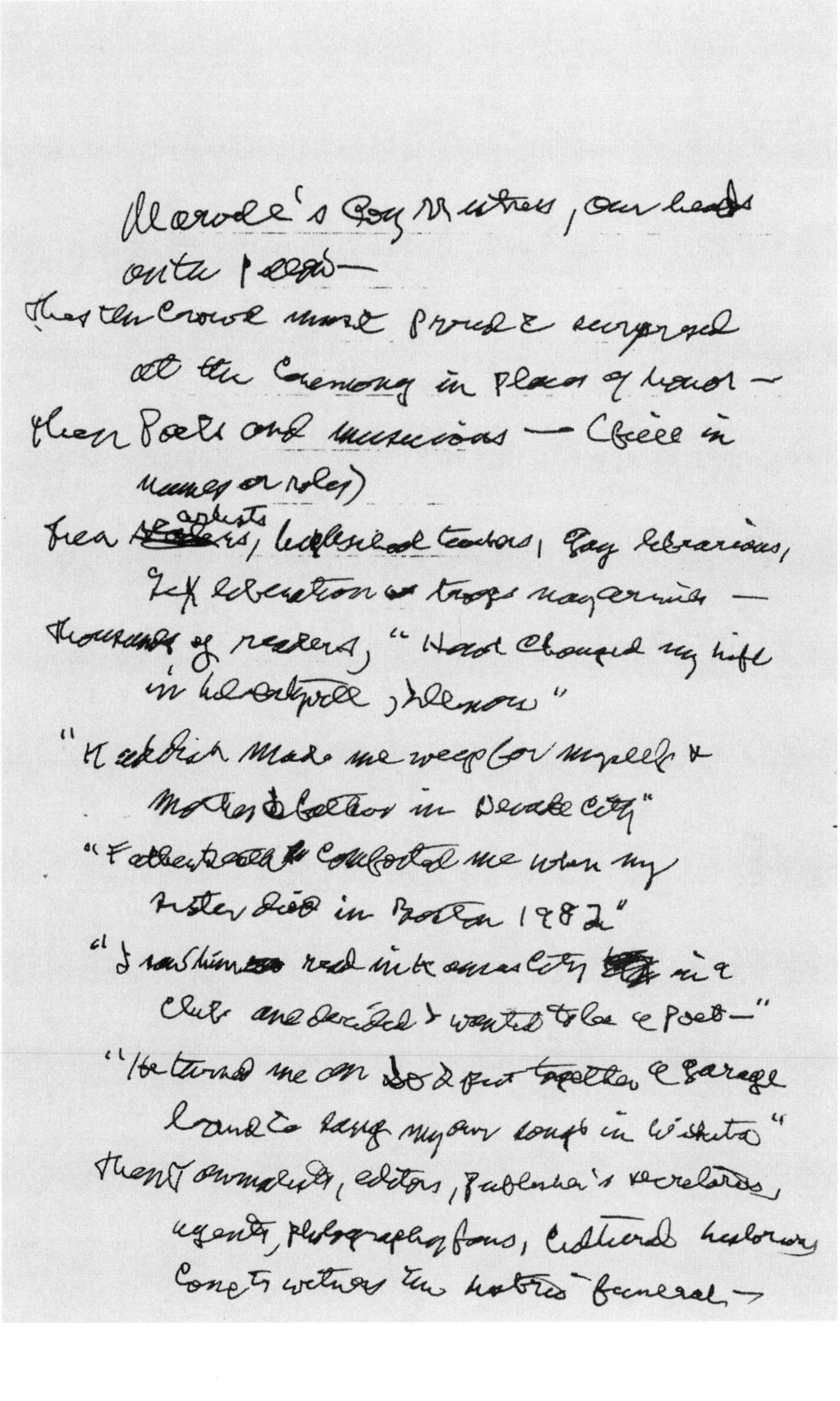
Marvelle's Gay Mistress, our heads
on the pillow—
Then the Crowd most proud & surprised
at the Ceremony in places of honor—
Then Poets and musicians — (fill in
names or roles)
then artists, highschool teachers, gay librarians,
Sex liberation troops nay armies —
thousands of readers, "Howl changed my life
in Libertyville, Illinois"
"Kaddish made me weep for myself &
Mother & father in Dodge City"
"Father Death comforted me when my
sister died in Boston 1982"
"I saw him read in Kansas City in a
club and decided I wanted to be a Poet—"
"He turned me on so I got together a garage
band to sing my own songs in Wichita"
then Journalists, editors, publisher's secretaries,
agents, photographers, fans, cultural historians
come to witness the historic funeral—

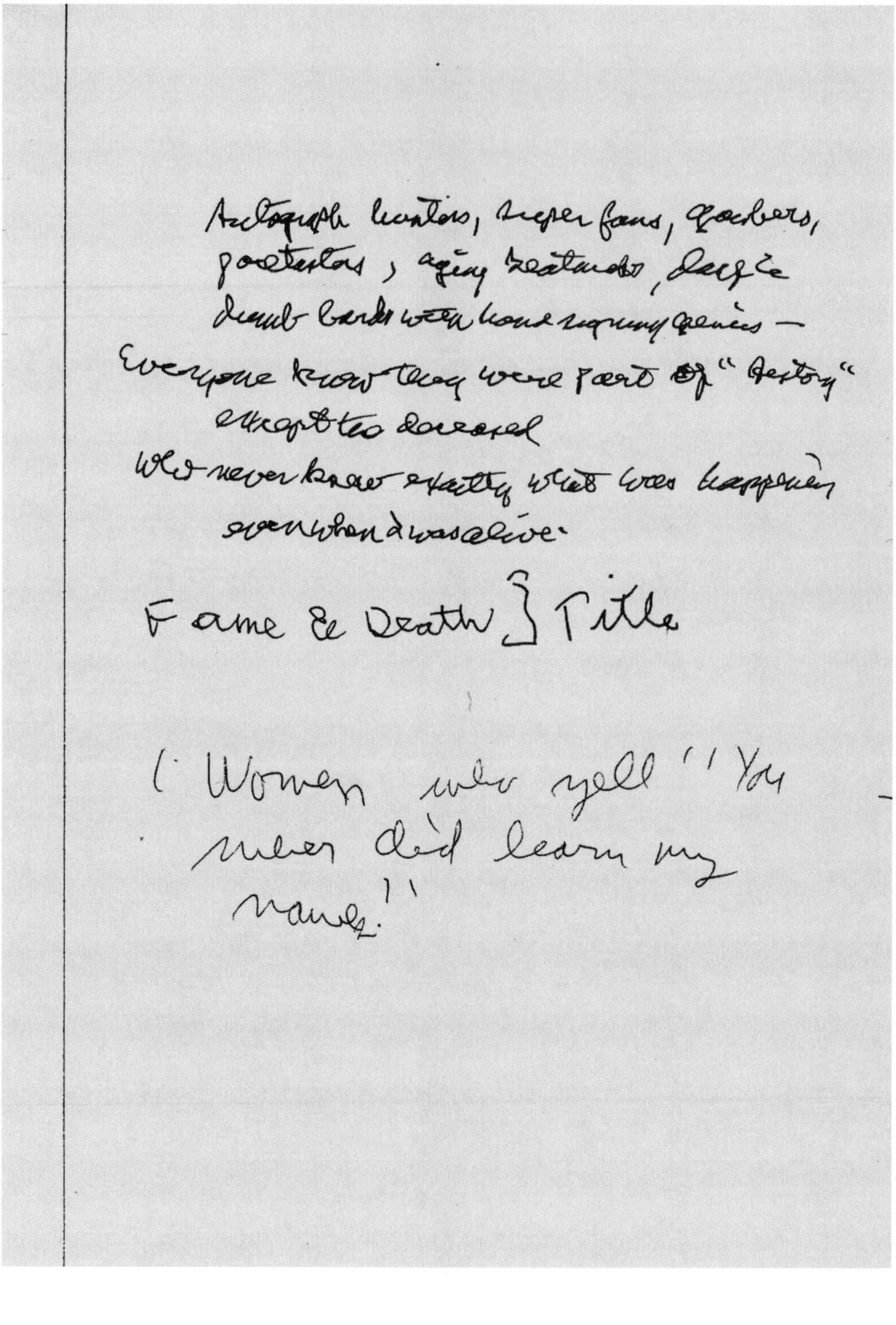

Autograph hunters, super fans, gawkers,
poetasters, aging beatniks, deaf &
dumb bards with home-signing genius —
Everyone knew they were part of "History"
except the deceased
who never knew exactly what was happening
even when I was alive.

Fame & Death } Title

"Women who yell "You
never did learn my
name!"

Chapter 5
William S. Burroughs

(5 February 1914 – 2 August 1997)

See also the Burroughs entries in DLB 2: American Novelists Since World War II; DLB 8: Twentieth-Century American Science-Fiction Writers; DLB 16: The Beats: Literary Bohemians in Postwar America; DLB 152: American Novelists Since World War II, Fourth Series; DLB Yearbook: 1981; and DLB Yearbook: 1997.

Along with Jack Kerouac and Allen Ginsberg, William Burroughs is considered one of the major Beat Generation writers. Unlike the other two, however, he did not write of the adventures or predicaments of his contemporaries, nor did he draw from memories of his own childhood and family history. Instead, Burroughs created a body of work that, for the most part, is set in a mythical space where he unleashed his nightmarish visions. Thematically, he focused on the never-ending battle for control: of the bureaucracy over the individual, of the state over the citizen, of one lover over another, of language itself over free thought.

William Seward Burroughs was born on 5 February 1914 in St. Louis, Missouri, a grandson of the inventor and manufacturer of the Burroughs adding machine. His family was well-off, though not part of St. Louis high society. Burroughs attended private schools and Harvard University, majoring in English. Upon graduation he traveled to Europe and enrolled briefly in the University of Vienna Medical School. After a stint as an exterminator in Chicago, Burroughs moved to New York City, where he met Kerouac, Ginsberg, and Herbert Huncke, a Times Square junkie who introduced Burroughs to heroin. In the next decade and beyond, Kerouac, Ginsberg, and Burroughs encouraged one another as writers, sharing ideas, philosophies, techniques, and drugs. Both Kerouac and Ginsberg had a hand in organizing Burroughs's best-known work, Naked Lunch, *first published in Paris by the Olympia Press in 1959 as* The Naked Lunch. *Serious literary critics, including writers Mary McCarthy and Norman Mailer, praised the book, and it was finally published in the United States in 1962.* Naked Lunch *was tried for obscenity in Los Angeles and Boston; the latter case was heard on appeal by the Massachusetts Supreme Court in 1966. The court declared that, though offensive, the book had redeeming social importance.* Naked Lunch *was one of the last literary works in the United States put on trial.*

Burroughs wrote prodigiously, and his influence is registered beyond the literary world: musicians, artists, and moviemakers have acknowledged his importance. As testimony to his pervasiveness, Burroughs's face is featured on the album cover of the Beatles' Sgt. Pepper's Lonely Hearts Club Band *(1967).*

Autobiography

In 1977 Penguin republished Burroughs's first novel, Junkie (1953), *as* Junky. *Burroughs wrote a prologue that outlined the biographical and philosophical background of his life.*

I was born in 1914 in a solid, three-story, brick house in a large Midwest city. My parents were comfortable. My father owned and ran a lumber business. The house had a lawn in front, a back yard with a garden, a fish pond and a high wooden fence all around it. I remember the lamplighter lighting the gas streetlights and the huge, black, shiny Lincoln and drives in the park on Sunday. All the props of a safe, comfortable way of life that is now gone forever. I could put down one of those nostalgic routines about the old German doctor who lived next door and the rats running around in the back yard and my aunt's electric car and my pet toad that lived by the fish pond.

Actually my earliest memories are colored by a fear of nightmares. I was afraid to be alone, and afraid of the dark, and afraid to go to sleep because of dreams where a supernatural horror seemed always on the point of taking shape. I was afraid some day the dream would still be there when I woke up. I recall hearing a maid talk about opium and how smoking opium brings sweet dreams, and I said: "I will smoke opium when I grow up."

I was subject to hallucinations as a child. Once I woke up in the early morning light and saw little men playing in a block house I had made. I felt no fear, only a feeling of stillness and wonder. Another recurrent hallucination or nightmare concerned "animals in the wall," and started with the delirium of a strange, undiagnosed fever that I had at the age of four or five.

I went to a progressive school with the future solid citizens, the lawyers, doctors and businessmen of a large Midwest town. I was timid with the other children and afraid of physical violence. One aggressive little Lesbian would pull my hair whenever she saw me. I would like to shove her face in right now, but she fell off a horse and broke her neck years ago.

When I was about seven my parents decided to move to the suburbs "to get away from people." They bought a large house with grounds and woods and a fish pond where there were squirrels instead of rats. They lived there in a comfortable capsule, with a beautiful garden and cut off from contact with the life of the city.

I went to a private suburban high school. I was not conspicuously good or bad at sports, neither brilliant nor backward in studies. I had a definite blind spot for mathematics or anything mechanical. I never liked competitive team games and avoided these whenever possible. I became, in fact, a chronic malingerer. I did like fishing, hunting and hiking. I read more than was usual for an American boy of that time and place: Oscar Wilde, Anatole France, Baudelaire, even Gide. I formed a romantic attachment for another boy and we spent our Saturdays exploring old quarries, riding around on bicycles and fishing in ponds and rivers.

At this time, I was greatly impressed by an autobiography of a burglar, called *You Can't Win*. The author claimed to have spent a good part of his life in jail. It sounded good to me compared with the dullness of a Midwest suburb where all contact with life was shut out. I saw my friend as an ally, a partner in crime. We found an abandoned factory and broke all the windows and stole a chisel. We were caught, and our fathers had to pay the damages. After this my friend "packed me in" because the relationship was endangering his standing with the group. I saw there was no compromise possible with the group, the others, and I found myself a good deal alone.

The environment was empty, the antagonist hidden, and I drifted into solo adventures. My criminal acts were gestures, unprofitable and for the most part unpunished. I would break into houses and walk around without taking anything. As a matter of fact, I had no need for money. Sometimes I would drive around in the country with a .22 rifle, shooting chickens. I made the roads unsafe with reckless driving until an accident, from which I emerged miraculously

Twenty-one-year-old William Burroughs's Harvard University yearbook photo (Burroughs Archive)

and portentously unscratched, scared me into normal caution.

I went to one of the Big Three universities, where I majored in English literature for lack of interest in any other subject. I hated the University and I hated the town it was in. Everything about the place was dead. The University was a fake English setup taken over by the graduates of fake English public schools. I was lonely. I knew no one, and strangers were regarded with distaste by the closed corporation of the desirables.

By accident I met some rich homosexuals, of the international queer set who cruise around the world, bumping into each other in queer joints from New York to Cairo. I saw a way of life, a vocabulary, references, a whole symbol system, as the sociologists say. But these people were jerks for the most part and, after an initial period of fascination, I cooled off on the setup.

When I graduated without honors, I had one hundred fifty dollars per month in trust. That was in the depression and there were no jobs and I couldn't think of any job I wanted, in any case. I drifted around Europe for a year or so. Remnants of the post-war decay lingered in Europe. U.S. dollars could buy a good percentage of the inhabitants of Austria, male or female. That was in 1936, and the Nazis were closing in fast.

I went back to the States. With my trust fund I could live without working or hustling. I was still cut off from life as I had been in the Midwest suburb. I fooled around taking graduate courses in psychology and Jiu-Jitsu lessons. I decided to undergo psychoanalysis, and continued with it for three years. Analysis removed inhibitions and anxiety so that I could live the way I wanted to live. Much of my progress in analysis was accomplished in spite of my analyst who did not like my "orientation," as he called it. He finally abandoned analytic objectivity and put me down as an "out-and-out con." I was more pleased with the results than he was.

After being rejected on physical grounds from five officer-training programs, I was drafted into the Army and certified fit for unlimited service. I decided I was not going to like the Army and copped out on my nut-house record–I'd once got on a Van Gogh kick and cut off a finger joint to impress someone who interested me at the time. The nut-house doctors had never heard of Van Gogh. They put me down for schizophrenia, adding paranoid type to explain the upsetting fact that I knew where I was and who was President of the U.S. When the Army saw that diagnosis they discharged me with the notation, "This man is never to be recalled or reclassified."

After parting company with the Army, I took a variety of jobs. You could have about any job you wanted at that time. I worked as a private detective, an exterminator, a bartender. I worked in factories and offices. I played around the edges of crime. But my hundred and fifty dollars per month was always there. I did not have to have money. It seemed a romantic extravagance to jeopardize my freedom by some token act of crime. It was at this time and under these circumstances that I came in contact with junk, became an addict, and thereby gained the motivation, the real need for money I had never had before.

The question is frequently asked: Why does a man become a drug addict?

The answer is that he usually does not intend to become an addict. You don't wake up one morning and decide to be a drug addict. It takes at least three months' shooting twice a day to get any habit at all. And you don't really know what junk sickness is until you have had several habits. It took me almost six months to get my first habit, and then the withdrawal symptoms were mild. I think it no exaggeration to say it takes about a year and several hundred injections to make an addict.

The questions, of course, could be asked: Why did you ever try narcotics? Why did you continue using it long enough to become an addict? You become a narcotics addict because you do not have strong motivations in any other direction. Junk wins by default. I tried it as a matter of curiosity. I drifted along taking shots when I could score. I ended up hooked. Most addicts I have talked to report a similar experience. They did not start using drugs for any reason they can remember. They just drifted along until they got hooked. If you have never been addicted, you can have no clear idea what it means to need junk with the addict's special need. You don't decide to be an addict. One morning you wake up sick and you're an addict.

I have never regretted my experience with drugs. I think I am in better health now as a result of using junk at intervals than I would be if I had never been an addict. When you stop growing you start dying. An addict never stops growing. Most users periodically kick the habit, which involves shrinking of the organism and replacement of the junk-dependent cells. A user is in continual state of shrinking and growing in his daily cycle of shot-need for shot completed.

Most addicts look younger than they are. Scientists recently experimented with a worm that they were able to shrink by withholding food. By periodically shrinking the worm so that it was in continual growth, the worm's life was prolonged indefinitely. Perhaps if a junky could keep himself in a constant state of kicking, he would live to a phenomenal age.

Junk is a cellular equation that teaches the user facts of general validity. I have learned a great deal from using junk: I have seen life measured out in eyedroppers of morphine solution. I experienced the agonizing deprivation of junk sickness, and the pleasure of relief when junk-thirsty cells drank from the needle. Perhaps all pleasure is relief. I have learned the cellular stoicism that junk teaches the user. I have seen a cell full of sick junkies silent and immobile in separate misery. They knew the pointlessness of complaining or moving. They knew that basically no one can help anyone else. There is no key, no secret someone else has that he can give you.

I have learned the junk equation. Junk is not, like alcohol or weed, a means to increased enjoyment of life. Junk is not a kick. It is a way of life.

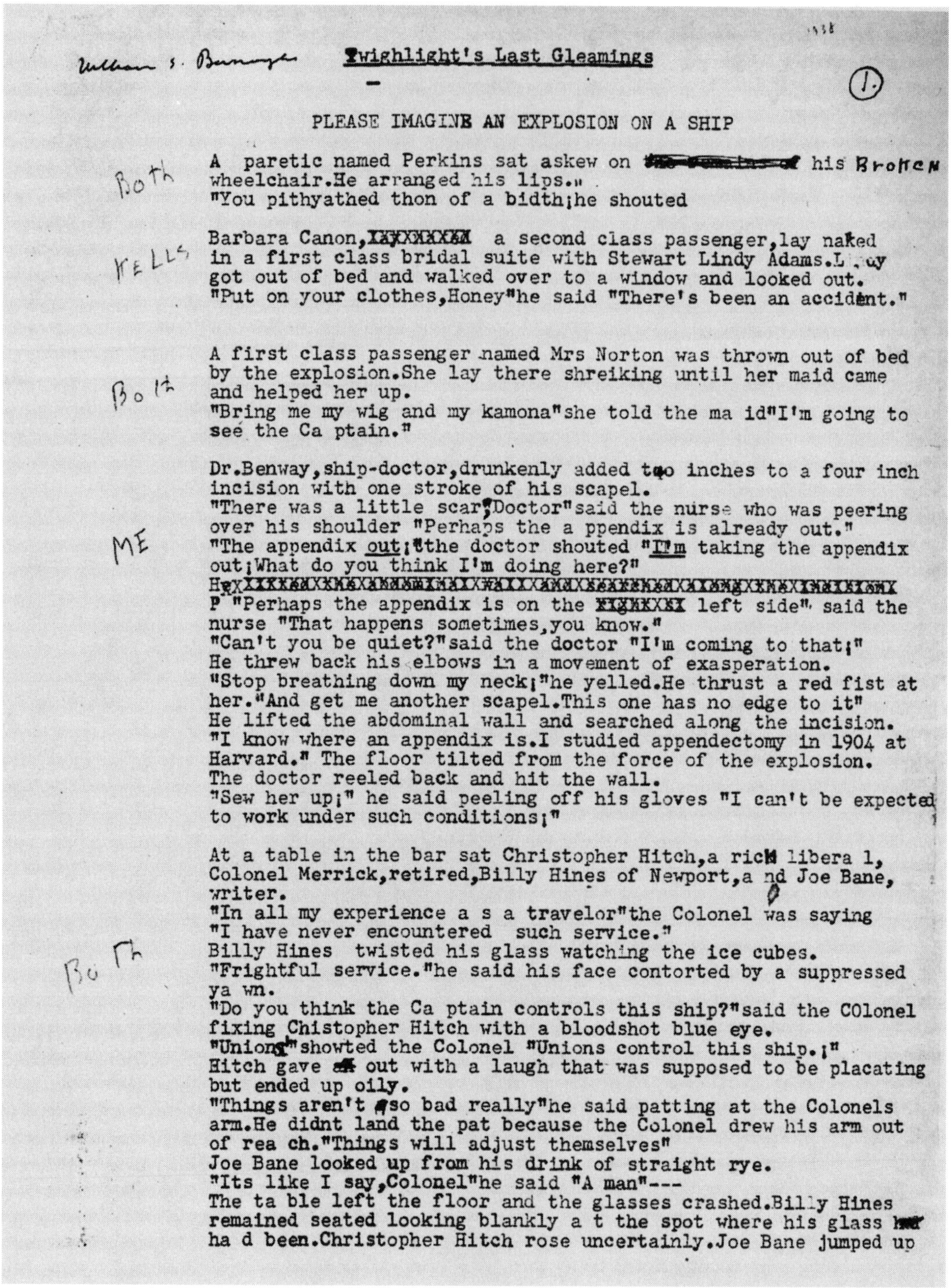

1938

William S. Burroughs **Twighlight's Last Gleamings**

-

(1.)

PLEASE IMAGINE AN EXPLOSION ON A SHIP

Both

A paretic named Perkins sat askew on [redacted] his Broken wheelchair.He arranged his lips.
"You pithyathed thon of a bidth;he shouted

KELLS

Barbara Canon,IXXXXXXXXX a second class passenger,lay naked in a first class bridal suite with Stewart Lindy Adams.L,ay got out of bed and walked over to a window and looked out.
"Put on your clothes,Honey"he said "There's been an accidènt."

Both

A first class passenger named Mrs Norton was thrown out of bed by the explosion.She lay there shreiking until her maid came and helped her up.
"Bring me my wig and my kamona"she told the ma id"I'm going to see the Ca ptain."

ME

Dr.Benway,ship-doctor,drunkenly added two inches to a four inch incision with one stroke of his scapel.
"There was a little scar,Doctor"said the nurse who was peering over his shoulder "Perhaps the a ppendix is already out."
"The appendix out;"the doctor shouted "I'm taking the appendix out;What do you think I'm doing here?"
HXXXXXXXXXXXXXXXXXXXXXXXXXXXXXXXXXXXXXXXXXXXXXXXXXXXXXXXXXXXXXX
P "Perhaps the appendix is on the XXXXXXX left side" said the nurse "That happens sometimes,you know."
"Can't you be quiet?"said the doctor "I'm coming to that;"
He threw back his elbows in a movement of exasperation.
"Stop breathing down my neck;"he yelled.He thrust a red fist at her."And get me another scapel.This one has no edge to it"
He lifted the abdominal wall and searched along the incision.
"I know where an appendix is.I studied appendectomy in 1904 at Harvard." The floor tilted from the force of the explosion.
The doctor reeled back and hit the wall.
"Sew her up;" he said peeling off his gloves "I can't be expected to work under such conditions;"

Both

At a table in the bar sat Christopher Hitch,a rich libera l, Colonel Merrick,retired,Billy Hines of Newport,a nd Joe Bane, writer.
"In all my experience a s a travelor"the Colonel was saying
"I have never encountered such service."
Billy Hines twisted his glass watching the ice cubes.
"Frightful service."he said his face contorted by a suppressed ya wn.
"Do you think the Ca ptain controls this ship?"said the COlonel fixing Chistopher Hitch with a bloodshot blue eye.
"Unions"showted the Colonel "Unions control this ship.;"
Hitch gave out with a laugh that was supposed to be placating but ended up oily.
"Things aren't so bad really"he said patting at the Colonels arm.He didnt land the pat because the Colonel drew his arm out of rea ch."Things will adjust themselves"
Joe Bane looked up from his drink of straight rye.
"Its like I say,Colonel"he said "A man"---
The ta ble left the floor and the glasses crashed.Billy Hines remained seated looking blankly a t the spot where his glass had been.Christopher Hitch rose uncertainly.Joe Bane jumped up

Pages of a typescript for a humorous sketch that Burroughs and his friend Kells Elvins wrote in 1938. They submitted this story—which features the first appearance of Burroughs's Dr. Benway— to Esquire *magazine.* Esquire *rejected the story ("Too screwy, and not effectively so for us"), which is Burroughs's earliest extant attempt at writing for publication. He later identified the author of each passage in the left margin (Arizona State University).*

(2)

and ran away.
"By God!" said the Colonel."I'm not surprised;"

Also at a table in the bar sat Philip Bradshinkel,investment
banker,his wife Joan Bradshinkel,Bra nch Morton,a St.Louis
politician,and MXXXXXXXXXXX Morton's wife,Mary Morton.
The explosion knocked their table over.
Both
Joan raised her eyebrows in an expression of sour annoyance.
She looked at her husband and sighed.
"I'm sorry this happened,dear."said her husband "Wha tever it is,
I mean."
Ma ry Morton said"Well I declare;"
Branch Morton stood up pushing back his chair with a la rge red
hand.
"Wait here"he said"I'll find out."
XXXXXXXXXXXXXXXXXXXXXXXXXXXXXXXXXXXXXXXX

Mrs. Norton pushed through a crowd on C deck.She rang the
eleva tor bell and waited.She rang again and waitied.After
five minutes she walked up to A deck.

The Negro orchestra, high on marjuana ,remained seated after
the explosion.
Branch Morton walked over to the orchestra leader.
"Play the Star Spangled Banner."he ordered
ITELLS
The orchestra leader looked a t him .
"What you say?"he asked.
"You black baboon play the Star Spangled Banner on your horn;"
"Contract dont say nothing bo ut no Star Spangled Banner"
said a thin Negro in spectacles.
XXX "This old boat am swinging on down;"some one in the XXXXXXXX
orchestra yelled and the orchestra jumped down off the platfor m,
and scattered among the passengers.
Branch Morton walked over to a juke box in a corner of the saloon
He saw the Star Spangled Banner by Fats Waller.He put in a handfu
of quaters.The machine clicked and buzzed and began to play:
"XXXXXXXXXXXXXXXXXXXXXXX "OH SAY CAN YOU? YES YES"

Joe Bane fell against the door of his sta teroom and plunged
in.He threw himself on the be d and drew his knees up to his
chin.He began to sob.
ITELLS
His w ife sa t on the bed and talked to him in a gentle hypnotic
voice.
"You cant stay here,Joey.This bed is going under wa ter.You
cant sta y here."
Gradually the sobing stopped and Ba ne sat up.She helped him
put on a life belt.
"Come along" she said.
"Yes,Honey Face"he said and followed her out the door.
"XXXXXXXXXXXXXXXXXXXXXXXX "AND THE HOME OF THE BRAVE."
x

Mrs. Norton found the door to the Captain's cabin ajar.She
pushed it open and stepped in knocking on the open door.A tall
ME
thin,redhaired man with horn rim glasses was sitting at a desk
littered with maps.He glanced up without spea king.
"Oh Captain is the ship sinking? Some one set off a bomb they
said.I'm Mrs. Norton,you know.Mr Norton, ship business.Oh the
ship is sinking;I know,or you'd say something.Captain you will
ITIS

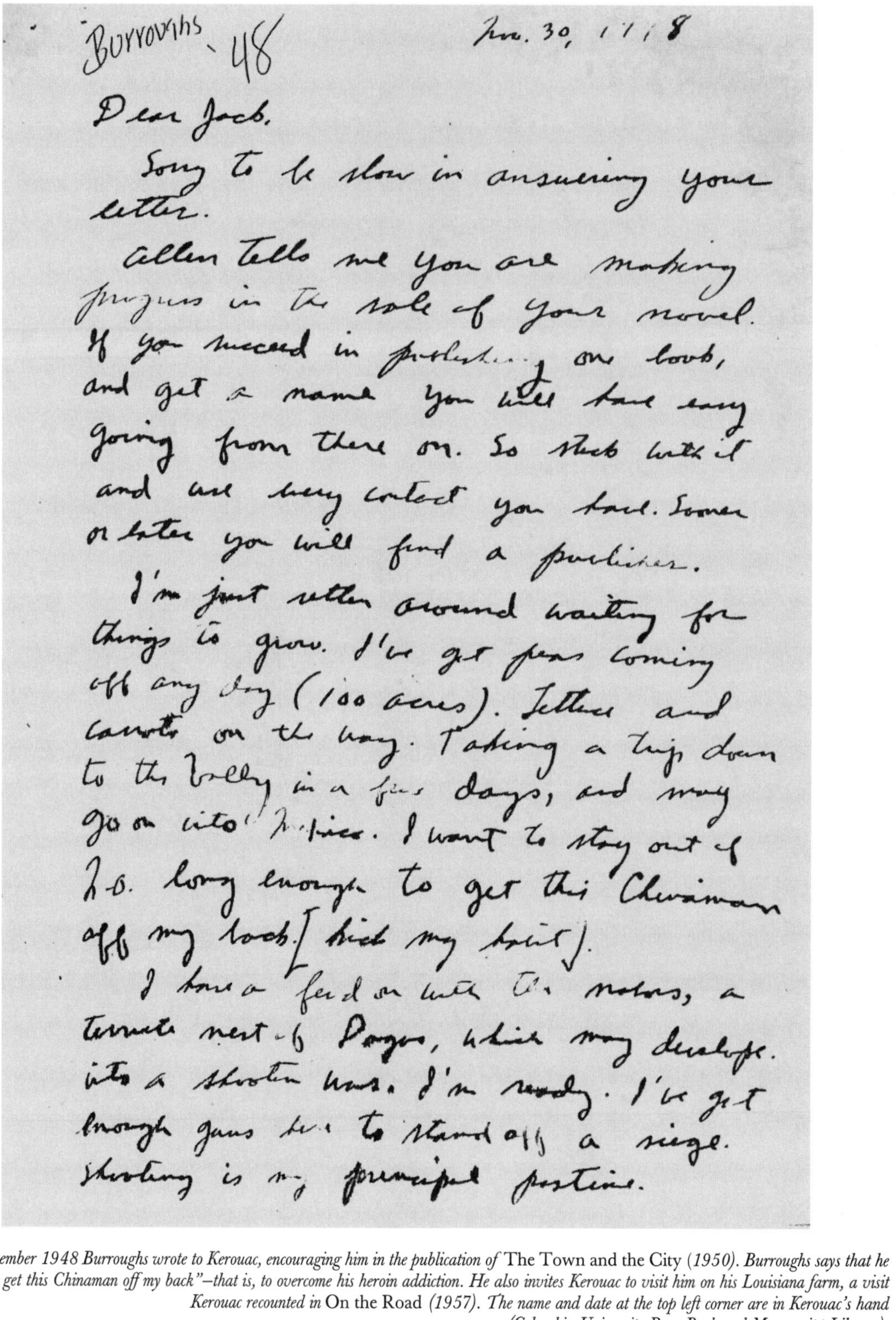
Burroughs '48

Nov. 30, 1948

Dear Jack,

Sorry to be slow in answering your letter.

Allen tells me you are making progress in the sale of your novel. If you succeed in publishing one book, and get a name you will have easy going from there on. So stick with it and use every contact you have. Sooner or later you will find a publisher.

I'm just setting around waiting for things to grow. I've got peas coming off any day (100 acres). Lettuce and carrots on the way. Taking a trip down to the Valley in a few days, and may go on into Mexico. I want to stay out of N.O. long enough to get this Chinaman off my back [kick my habit].

I have a feud on with the natives, a termite nest of Dagos, which may develop into a shooting war. I'm ready. I've got enough guns here to stand off a siege. Shooting is my principal pastime.

On 30 November 1948 Burroughs wrote to Kerouac, encouraging him in the publication of The Town and the City *(1950). Burroughs says that he wants "to get this Chinaman off my back"–that is, to overcome his heroin addiction. He also invites Kerouac to visit him on his Louisiana farm, a visit Kerouac recounted in* On the Road *(1957). The name and date at the top left corner are in Kerouac's hand (Columbia University Rare Book and Manuscript Library).*

(2)

Come on down any time. There's plenty room in this house, and I am building another out in a piece of swamp I bought: a sort of hunting lodge.

If all my ifs come in on schedule, I will be rolling in $ by cotton picking time. The only thing worries me is the --- government will put the snatch on such a big hunk of what we sons of the soil wring out of the earth. I am so disgusted with conditions I may leave the U.S.A. altogether, and remove myself and family to S. America or Africa. Some place where a man can get something for his money, and live in proper style. Here you have to scrimp no matter how much you make, and can't even get decent service. It's almost impossible to get anyone to do anything. Servants!, Until the trouble [illegible]!

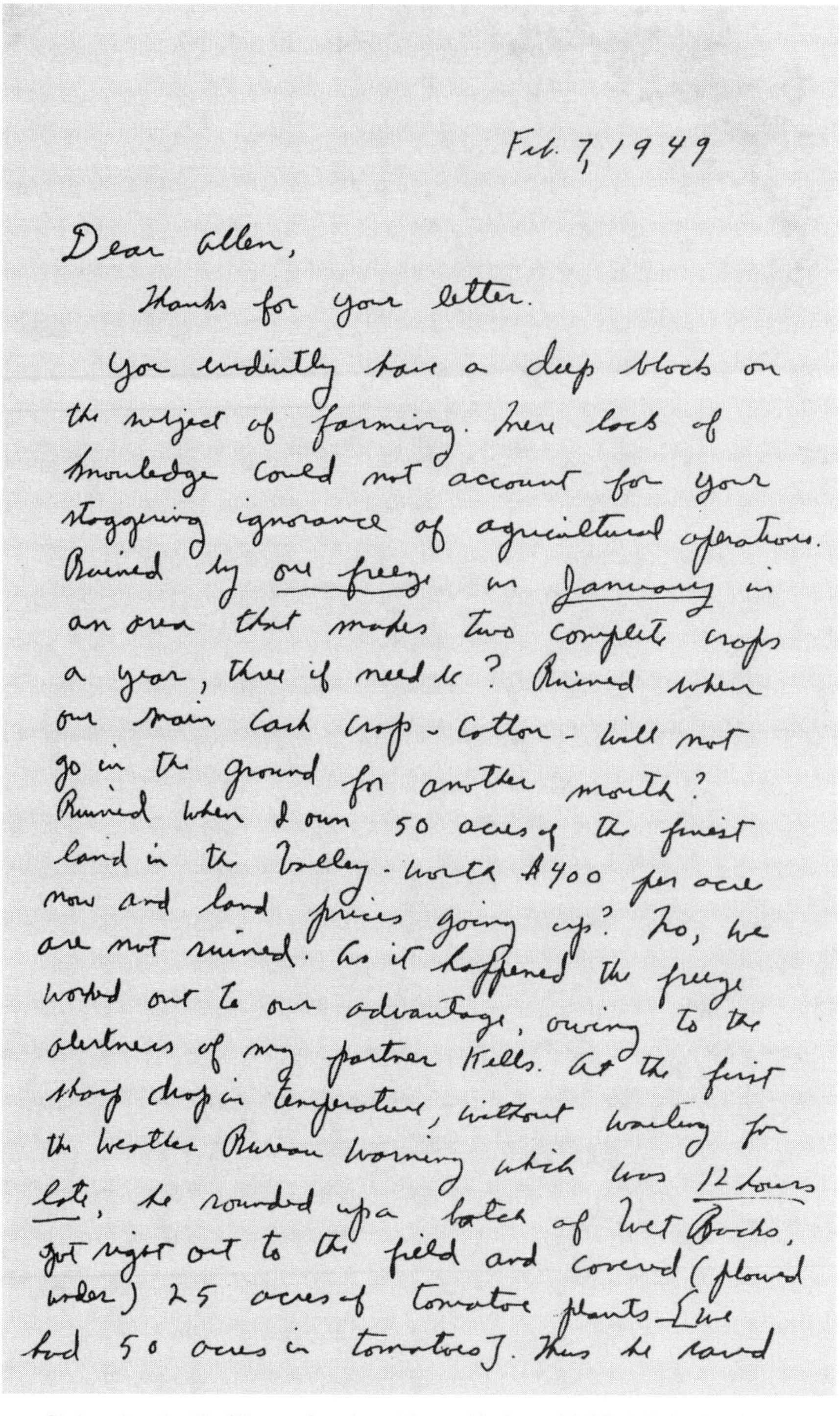

Feb. 7, 1949

Dear Allen,

Thanks for your letter.

You evidently have a deep block on the subject of farming. Mere lack of knowledge could not account for your staggering ignorance of agricultural operations. Ruined by one freeze in January in an area that makes two complete crops a year, three if need be? Ruined when our main cash crop - cotton - will not go in the ground for another month? Ruined when I own 50 acres of the finest land in the Valley - worth $400 per acre now and land prices going up? No, we are not ruined. As it happened the freeze worked out to our advantage, owing to the alertness of my partner Kells. At the first sharp drop in temperature, without waiting for the Weather Bureau warning which was 12 hours late, he rounded up a batch of Wet Backs, got right out to the field and covered (plowed under) 25 acres of tomatoe plants [we had 50 acres in tomatoes]. Thus he saved

Burroughs wrote to Ginsberg about the visit of Kerouac, Cassady, and Luanne Henderson. He defends his farming venture and relates his opinion of Neal Cassady (Columbia University Rare Book and Manuscript Library).

(2)

25 acres from the freeze which will be worth as much or more than the whole 50 acres, because he was one of the few farmers to act promptly and save ~~the~~ his tomatoe crop. The 25 acres that he could not save he will place in cotton – one of the surest cash crops $200–400 per acre. Our 30 acres of carrots were not damaged. It looks like we are the Lords Anointed, so far. We will have about 150 acres to put in cotton.

My opinion of Neal is about identical with Lucien's, though, in defference to your sensibilities, I never put the matter quite so bluntly. They were not here very long, and did not have time to do much of anything. Like I say Neal had planned to replenish the exchequer here. When he saw no $ were forthcoming, he couldn't leave quick enough, and acted as though I had lured him here on false pretenses. He didn't unlock any "charm" or "graceful human nature" around here.

Al and Helen have moved into an apt. on Esplanade Ave. They both have jobs and seem to be doing fine. As you suggest they may well become permanent party here.

As to Louane's intentions I know almost nothing. She

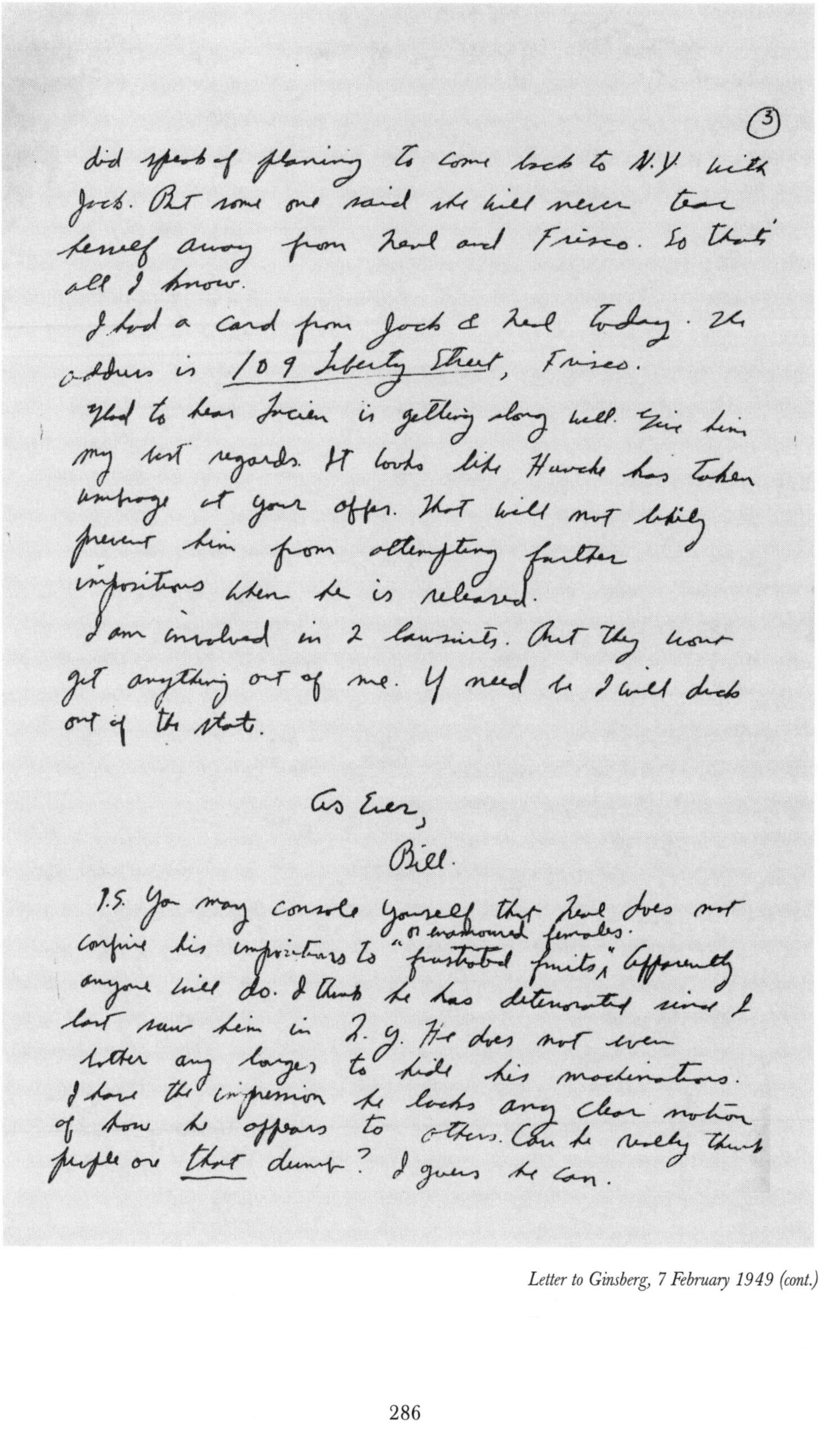

(3)

did speak of planning to come back to N.Y. with Jack. But some one said she will never tear herself away from Neal and Frisco. So that's all I know.

I had a card from Jack & Neal today. The address is <u>109 Liberty Street</u>, Frisco.

Glad to hear Lucien is getting along well. Give him my best regards. It looks like Huncke has taken umbrage at your offer. That will not likely prevent him from attempting further impositions when he is released.

I am involved in 2 lawsuits. But they won't get anything out of me. If need be I will duck out of the state.

As Ever,

Bill.

P.S. You may console yourself that Neal does not confine his impositions to "frustrated fruits," or enamoured females. Apparently anyone will do. I think he has deteriorated since I last saw him in N.Y. He does not even bother any longer to hide his machinations. I have the impression he lacks any clear notion of how he appears to others. Can he really think people are <u>that</u> dumb? I guess he can.

Letter to Ginsberg, 7 February 1949 (cont.)

Burroughs '49

Kells Elvins
Route One
Pharr, Texas

Sept 26, 1949

Dear Jack,

I was somewhat taken aback by your account of Neal's behavior. Evidently he is approaching the ideal state of absolute impulsiveness.

I am just back from Mexico City where I have rented an apartment preparatory to moving down there with the family. Mexico is very cheap. A single man could live good for $2 per day in Mexico City liquor included. $1 per day anywhere else in Mexico. Fabulous whore houses and restaurants. A large foreign colony. Cock fights, bull-fights, every conceivable diversion. I strongly urge you to visit. I have a large apt. could accomodate you. Tell Neal to come too if he is settled. I have to watch the H. Despite the temptations of Mexico I am still on the lush wagon.

I don't see why Al is wasting time with those liberal jerks. Is he rational? Any news of Huncke, Garver etc? How is Lucien?

In a letter to Kerouac, Burroughs extols the virtues of life in Mexico; soon Kerouac would take him up on his invitation (Columbia University Rare Book and Manuscript Library).

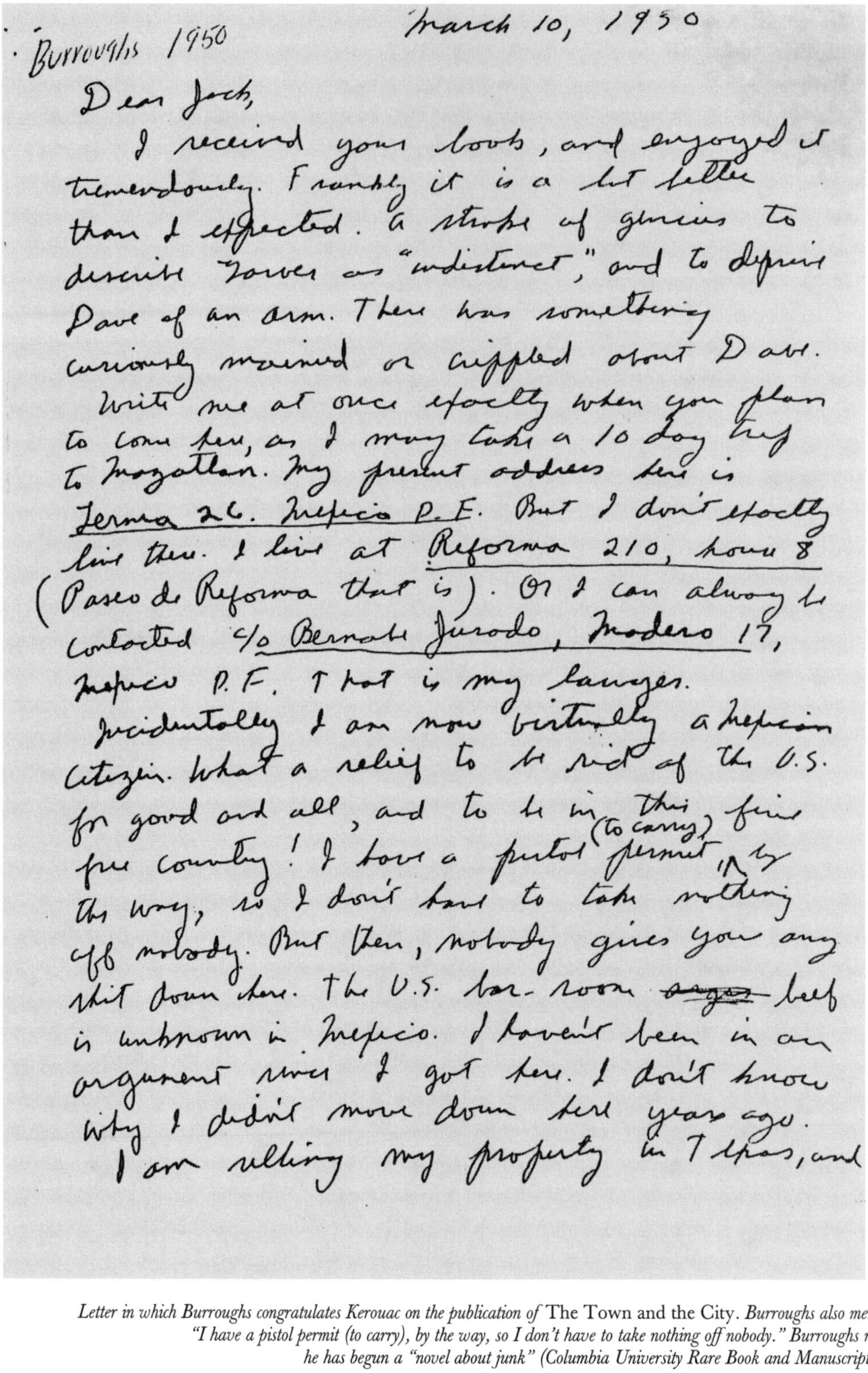

Burroughs 1950

March 10, 1950

Dear Jack,

I received your book, and enjoyed it tremendously. Frankly it is a lot better than I expected. A stroke of genius to describe Yorves as "indistinct," and to deprive Dave of an arm. There was something curiously maimed or crippled about Dave.

Write me at once exactly when you plan to come here, as I may take a 10 day trip to Mazatlan. My present address here is Lerma 26. Mexico D.F. But I don't exactly live there. I live at Reforma 210, house 8 (Paseo de Reforma that is). Or I can always be contacted c/o Bernabe Jurado, Madero 17, Mexico D.F. That is my lawyer.

Incidentally I am now virtually a Mexican citizen. What a relief to be rid of the U.S. for good and all, and to be in this fine free country! I have a pistol permit (to carry), by the way, so I don't have to take nothing off nobody. But then, nobody gives you any shit down here. The U.S. bar-room ~~argue~~ beef is unknown in Mexico. I haven't been in an argument since I got here. I don't know why I didn't move down here years ago.

I am selling my property in Texas, and

Letter in which Burroughs congratulates Kerouac on the publication of The Town and the City. *Burroughs also mentions that "I have a pistol permit (to carry), by the way, so I don't have to take nothing off nobody." Burroughs relates that he has begun a "novel about junk" (Columbia University Rare Book and Manuscript Library).*

(2)

plan to buy a house in Mexico City. You can get a 4 bedroom, brick house in the middle of town for $6,000, a palace for $8,000.

I have been writing a novel about Junk. Maybe we can get together on something when you get here. I know you will enjoy Mexico, since you can really relax here and save money. I look forward to see you.

As Ever,

Bill

Turning to Writing

In October 1950 Kerouac, Ginsberg, and others in their Beat coterie were shocked and deeply affected when their friend Bill Cannastra was killed in a bizarre subway accident. Apparently he attempted to exit the subway car through the window just as it was pulling out of the station. Before the group was fully recovered from this incident, they were confronted by another death that was, if possible, more bizarre and troubling.

Despite Burroughs's homosexuality he and his common-law wife, Joan Vollmer Adams, got along well and had two children. In September 1951 they were living in Mexico City, partly to avoid the American authorities. During a late-night party, Burroughs picked up one of his pistols–he was fascinated by firearms–and said to Joan, "It's time for our William Tell act." He took aim and shot her through the forehead. Later he claimed that he examined the gun and found that the sight was off. Several decades later still, Burroughs said that had it not been for this terrible accident, he would not have become a writer.

Mexico City, Sept. 7 (AP)–William Seward Burroughs, 37, first admitted, then denied today that he was playing William Tell when his gun killed his pretty, young wife during a drinking party last night.

Police said that Burroughs, grandson of the adding machine inventor, first told them that, wanting to show off his marksmanship, he placed a glass of gin on her head and fired, but was so drunk that he missed and shot her in the forehead.

After talking with a lawyer, police said, Burroughs, who is a wealthy cotton planter from Pharr, Tex., changed his story and insisted that his wife was shot accidentally when he dropped his newly-purchased .38 caliber pistol.

Husband in Jail.

Mrs. Burroughs, 27, the former Joan Vollmer, died in the Red Cross Hospital.

The shooting occurred during a party in the apartment of John Healy of Minneapolis. Burroughs said two other American tourists whom he knew only slightly were present.

Burroughs, hair disheveled and clothes wrinkled was in jail today. A hearing on a charge of homicide is scheduled for tomorrow morning.

No Arguments, He Says.

"It was purely accidental," he said. "I did not put any glass on her head. If she did, it was a joke. I certainly did not intend to shoot at it."

He said there had been no arguments or discussion before the "accident."

"The party was quiet," he said. "We had a few drinks. Everything is very hazy."

Burroughs and his wife had been here about two years. He said he was studying native dialects at the University of Mexico. He explained his long absence from his ranch by saying that he was unsuited for business.

Wife from Albany.

He said he was born in St. Louis and that his wife was from Albany, N.Y. They have two children, William Burroughs Jr., 3, and Julie Adams, 7, who he said was his wife's daughter by a previous marriage. The couple had been married five years.

She had attended journalism school at Columbia University before her marriage to Burroughs.

Burroughs, who also had been married before, formerly lived in Loudonville, a swank suburb of Albany. He is a graduate of Harvard University and worked for two weeks in 1942 as a reporter for the St. Louis Post-Dispatch.

His paternal grandfather laid the foundation of a fortune when he built his first adding machine in St. Louis in 1885.

DAILY NEWS, SATURDAY, SEPTEMBER 8, 1951 ☆☆ 3

Heir's Pistol Kills His Wife; He Denies Playing Wm. Tell

Headline in New York Daily News

The Yage Letters

For most of his life Burroughs explored consciousness through drug use. Few researchers have gone so far; Huncke once wrote that Burroughs "became a drug addict principally as a result of research." In 1953 Burroughs traveled to Panama in search of yage, a fabled plant that was said to yield spiritual visions to its users. Eleven letters that he wrote to Ginsberg during this time–and some later material–were published by City Lights Books in The Yage Letters *in 1963.*

January 15, 1953
Hotel Colon, Panama

Dear Allen,

I stopped off here to have my piles out. Wouldn't do to go back among the Indians with piles I figured.

Bill Gains was in town and he has burned down the Republic of Panama from Las Palmas to David on paregoric. Before Gains, Panama was a p.g. town. You could buy four ounces in any drug store. Now the druggists are balky and the Chamber of Deputies was about to pass a special Gains Law when he threw in the towel and went back to Mexico. I was getting off junk and he kept nagging me why was I kidding myself once a junkie always a junkie. If I quit junk I would become a sloppy lush or go crazy taking cocaine.

One night I got lushed and bought some paregoric and he kept saying over and over, 'I *knew* you'd come home with paregoric. I *knew* it. You'll be a junkie all the rest of your life' and looking at me with his little cat smile. Junk is a cause with him.

I checked into the hospital junk sick and spent four days there. They would only give me three shots of morphine and I couldn't sleep from pain and heat and deprivation besides which there was a Panamanian hernia case in the same room with me and his friends came and stayed all day and half the night–one of them did in fact stay until midnight.

–*Yage Letters,* p. 3

Cover of a collection of Burroughs's and Ginsberg's correspondence published in 1963

In his 15 April 1953 letter to Ginsberg, Burroughs describes his initial experience with yage.

In two minutes a wave of dizziness swept over me and the hut began spinning. It was like going under ether, or when you are very drunk and lie down and the bed spins. Blue flashes passed in front of my eyes. The hut took on an archaic far-Pacific look with Easter Island heads carved in the support posts. The assistant was outside lurking there with the obvious intent to kill me. I was hit by violent, sudden nausea and rushed for the door hitting my shoulder against the door post. I felt the shock but no pain. I could hardly walk. No coordination. My feet were like blocks of wood. I vomited violently leaning against a tree and fell down on the ground in helpless misery. I felt numb as if I was covered with layers of cotton. I kept trying to break out of this numb dizziness. I was saying over and over, 'All I want is out of here.' An uncontrollable mechanical silliness took possession of me. Hebrephrenic meaningless repetitions. Larval beings passed before my eyes in a blue haze, each one giving an obscene, mocking squawk (I later identified this squawking as the croaking of frogs)–I must have vomited six times. I was on all fours convulsed with spasms of nausea. I could hear retching and groaning as if I was some one else. I was lying by a rock. Hours must have passed. The medicine man was standing over me. I looked at him for a long time before I believed he was really there saying, 'Do you want to come into the house?' I said, 'No,' and he shrugged and went back inside.

My arms and legs began to twitch uncontrollably. I reached for my nembutals with numb wooden fingers. It must have taken me ten minutes to open the bottle and pour out five capsules. Mouth was dry and I chewed the nembutals down somehow. The twitching spasms subsided slowly and I felt a little better and went into the hut. The blue flashes still in front of my eyes. Lay down and covered myself with a blanket. I had a chill like malaria. Suddenly very drowsy. Next morning I was all right except for a feeling of lassitude and a slight back-log nausea. I paid off the Brujo and walked back to town.

–*Yage Letters*, p. 24

A First Novel

Burroughs's first novel, published under a pseudonym, was printed back-to-back in one volume with Maurice Helbrant's Narcotic Agent *as an Ace double book. The publisher hoped to avoid the appearance of condoning drug use by countering Burroughs's perspective with Helbrant's. Burroughs's novel was republished by Penguin in 1977 as* Junky, *using the author's real name.*

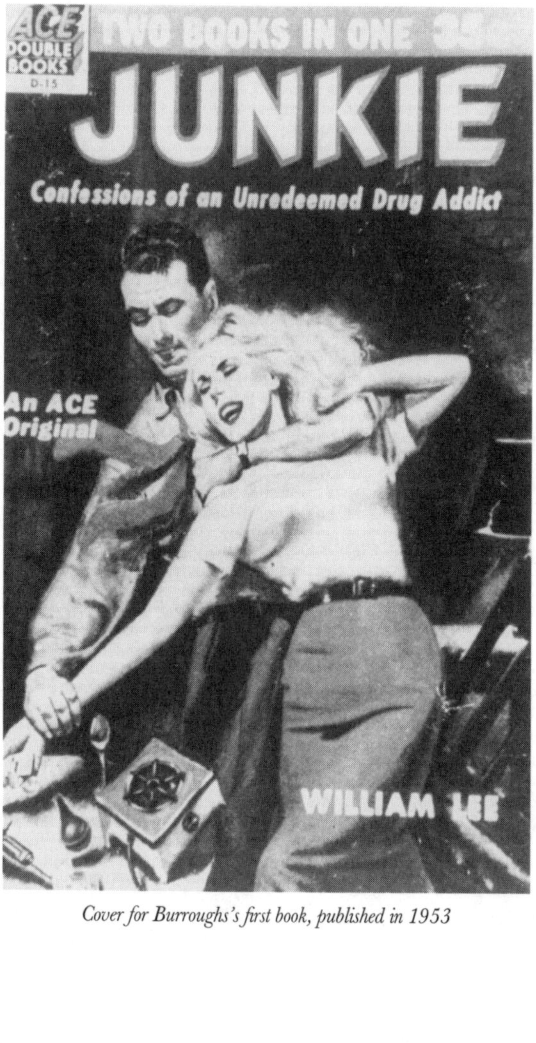

Cover for Burroughs's first book, published in 1953

Review of *Junky*
Anatole Broyard
The New York Times, 10 April 1977

William Burroughs's earliest novel, "Junky," has just been published in "the first complete and unexpurgated edition." Until now, "Junky" had been issued only in an Ace paperback in 1953, and the author was given as one William Lee. That edition was a peculiar tandem volume–if you turned it over and read it back to front, it also contained another work on drugs by a former narcotics agent–and it is doubtful whether many readers ever saw the debut of the man who is now a grand panjandrum of the drug culture and the experimental "prose novel," as Allen Ginsberg calls it in his characteristically ineffable introduction.

It is rumored that the potent words "complete and unexpurgated" refer to the inclusion in this edition of a chapter on farming in the Rio Grande Valley. Mr. Lee was growing not marijuana, but cotton, and the story has it that the chapter was "expurgated" because it was boring and irrelevant. It is difficult to check the rumor since the original edition seems to have disappeared, but it has the ring of truth, for a reading of "Junky" turns up no single section that would have been expurgatable, even in 1953. Mr. Burroughs's prologue to "Junky" appears to establish the fact–no need to be coy today–that the book is autobiographical, which is just as well for his literary reputation because as a novel it is a reductio ad absurdum of the picaresque.

"Junky" begins with William Lee's first experience with morphine during World War II. It made him vomit for half a day, but he was not discouraged. As Burroughs has already observed, "Junk is not a kick. It is a way of life." The rest of the book consists of a disconnected series of episodes leading to "scores." True to his way-of-life credo, the author tells us very little of how a junky fills his day when he is not scrounging money, meeting his connection, or "shooting up." New York, New Orleans and Mexico City seem pretty much the same when seen through a junky's eyes. Halfway through the book, we read for the first time of Lee's wife, who has materialized out of nowhere for a moment, only to return there.

After the bombast and the scissors-and-paste "experimentalism" of "Naked Lunch," it is surprising to look back and discover that Burroughs is a rather good laconic-ironic observer when he can stir himself to make the effort. "Junky" has almost as many fine vignettes as boring "scores." Three young hoodlums from Brooklyn are "stylized as a ballet . . . They conveyed their meaning less by words than by significant jerks of the head and by stalking around the apartment and leaning against the walls." People who smoke marijuana disgust the author with their sentimental insistence on sociability and "good vibes." The true junk gesture is "the hand swinging out from the elbow stiff-fingered, palm up." "Junkies all wear hats, if they have hats." They also have a predilection for talking about their constipation.

Of a character named Doolie, the author writes: "You could feel him walk right into your psyche and look around to see if anything was there he could make use of." A junky named Marvin is so inept that Lee always delivers his shot and runs out before Marvin has a chance to die on him. Bill Gains comes from a "good family" and looks it. He is "a composite of negatives," which perfectly suits him for his routine of stealing overcoats out of restaurants. Gains is so anonymous that once in a while he gets anxious and "assembles all his claims to reality": a dishonorable discharge from Annapolis, an old dirty letter from an unidentified "captain," and so on.

While even a biography requires some sort of structure, Burroughs seems to have no talent in this direction, which may explain his later cut-up innovations. After observing that "the young hipsters seem lacking in energy and spontaneous enjoyment of life," Burroughs's protagonist William Lee closes his story with a little lecture on "yage," a new drug. When we last see him, he is on his way to Colombia like a pilgrim in search of a miracle.

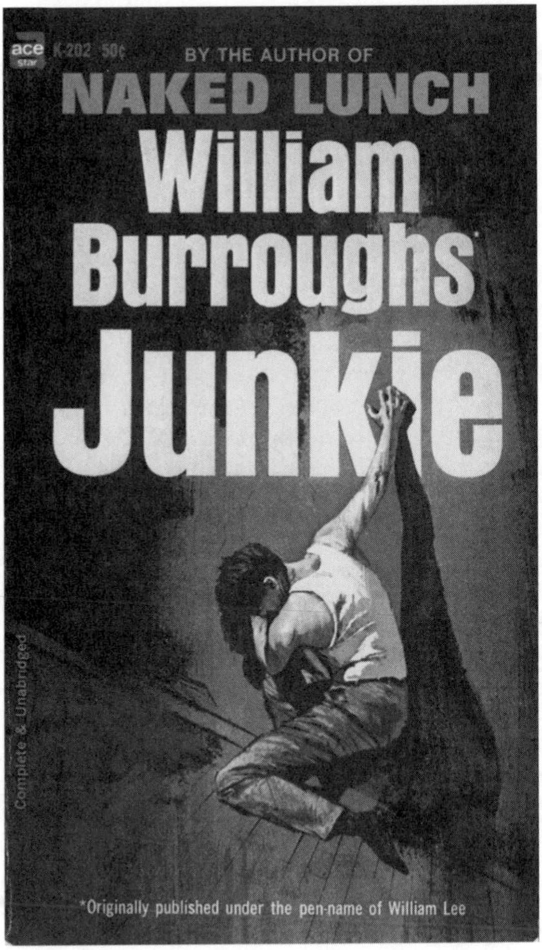

Cover for the 1964 republication of Burroughs's first novel

Naked Lunch

A letter from Burroughs to Ginsberg, 28 October 1957, in which he discusses the composition of Naked Lunch:

Oct. 28, 1957

Dear Allen,

Enclose a section of the narrative. This narrative will run for a hundred pages or so connecting up all the Interzone material possibly some of the other material. . But I never know whether something will be in it or not until it fits in to the narrative as an organic part of the struxture. . That is I will not drag anything in, and can not say ahead of time what will be included and what left out. . In a sense the action occurs in a superimposed place which is South America, USA, Tanger and Scandanavia. . and the characters wander back and forth from one place to another. . That is a Turkish Bath in Sweden may open into a South American jungle. . the shift from schizophrenia to addiction takes a character from one place to another, Actually of course, there is only one main character, Benway and Carl–(who is now wandering all over the Amazon Basin I hope to have this SA section in order in another week or so) and Lee are, of course, one person. . I find the whole is developing into an a saga of lost inocense, The Fall, with some kinda redemption through knowledge of basic life processes. . If anyone finds this form confusing it is because they are accustomed to the historical novel form which is a three dimensional chronology of events happening to some one already, for purposes of the novel dead. . That is the usual novel has happened. . This novel is happening. . The only way I can write narrative is to get right outside my body and experi-

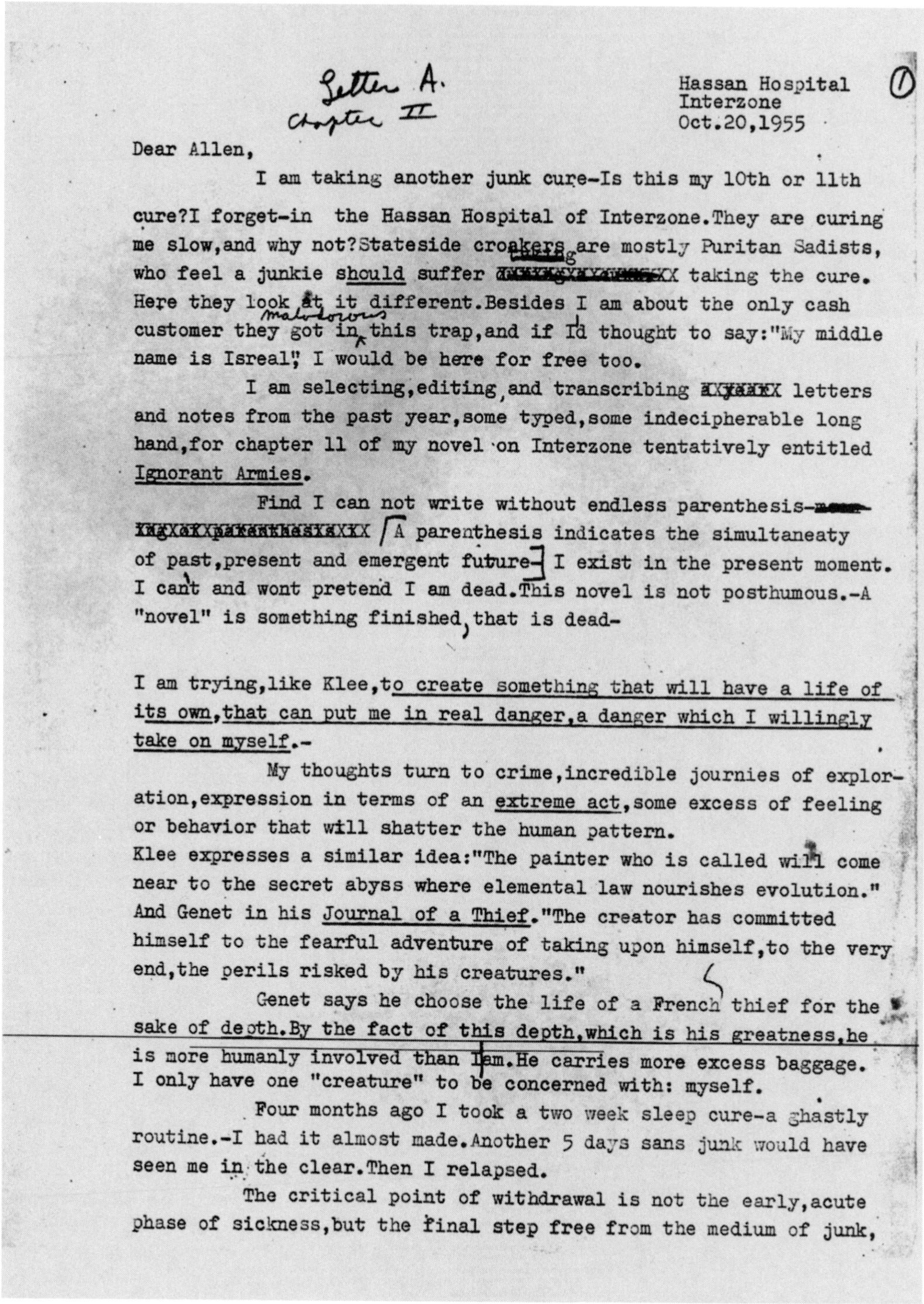

Letter A.
Chapter II

Hassan Hospital
Interzone
Oct.20,1955

①

Dear Allen,

I am taking another junk cure-Is this my 10th or 11th cure?I forget-in the Hassan Hospital of Interzone.They are curing me slow,and why not?Stateside croakers are mostly Puritan Sadists, who feel a junkie should suffer XXXXXXXXXXXXX taking the cure. Here they look it different.Besides I am about the only cash customer they got in malodorous this trap,and if I'd thought to say:"My middle name is Isreal," I would be here for free too.

I am selecting,editing,and transcribing XXXXXX letters and notes from the past year,some typed,some indecipherable long hand,for chapter 11 of my novel on Interzone tentatively entitled Ignorant Armies.

Find I can not write without endless parenthesis-XXXXXXXXXXXXXXXXXXXXX [A parenthesis indicates the simultaneaty of past,present and emergent future] I exist in the present moment. I cant and wont pretend I am dead.This novel is not posthumous.-A "novel" is something finished, that is dead-

I am trying,like Klee,to create something that will have a life of its own,that can put me in real danger,a danger which I willingly take on myself.-

My thoughts turn to crime,incredible journies of exploration,expression in terms of an extreme act,some excess of feeling or behavior that will shatter the human pattern.
Klee expresses a similar idea:"The painter who is called will come near to the secret abyss where elemental law nourishes evolution." And Genet in his Journal of a Thief."The creator has committed himself to the fearful adventure of taking upon himself,to the very end,the perils risked by his creatures."

Genet says he choose the life of a French thief for the sake of depth.By the fact of this depth,which is his greatness,he is more humanly involved than I am.He carries more excess baggage. I only have one "creature" to be concerned with: myself.

Four months ago I took a two week sleep cure-a ghastly routine.-I had it almost made.Another 5 days sans junk would have seen me in the clear.Then I relapsed.

The critical point of withdrawal is not the early,acute phase of sickness,but the final step free from the medium of junk,

Burroughs wrote this letter to Ginsberg while he was recovering from heroin addiction. The letter includes passages that Ginsberg later edited with Burroughs into the final version of Naked Lunch *(Arizona State University).*

A 2.

like crossing supersonic barrier.There is a nightmare interlude of cellular panic,of life suspended between two ways of being.It is at this point that your longing for junk,concentrates in a last., all out yen,and seems to gain a dream power so that circumstances put junk in your way.

IN a Suicide -CLINIC

Just before relapse,I dreamed the following:I was in high mountains covered with snow.It was ~~a place for suicide~~:"You just wait till you feel like it."I was on a ledge with a boy-about 16 years old-I could feel myslef slipping further and futher out,out of MYXX my body,you dig,I dont mean a physical slipping on the ledge. The Plane was coming for me-[Suicide is performed by getting in this Plane with a boy.The Plane crashes in The Pass.No Plane ever got through.-]

Marv reaches out and catches my arm and says:"Stay here with us a while longer."

The suicide ~~place~~ clinic is in Turkey.Nothing compulsory.You can leave anytime,even take your boy out with you-[Boat whistle in the distance. A bearded dope feind rushing to catch the boat for the mainland-] My boy says he wont leave with me unless I kick my habit.

Earlier dream-phantasy:I am in a plane trying to make the Pass. There is a boy with me.and I turn to him and say:"Throw everything out."

"What! All the XXXX gold? All the guns? All the junk?"

"Everything."

I mean throw out all excess baggage:anxiety,desire for approval, fear of authority,ect.Strip your psyche to the bare bones of spontaneous process,and you give yourself one chance in a thousand to make the Pass.

I am subject to continual routines which tear me apart like a homeless curse. I feel myself drifting further and further out over a bleak dream landscape of snow covered mountains...

This novel is a scenario for future action in the real world.Junk. Queer, Yage, reconstructed my past.The present novel is an attempt to create my future.In a sense it is a guide book,a map.

The first step in realizing this work is to leave junk forever. XXXXXXXXXXX "Throw down all your arms and armour,walk straight to The Fronteer.

A

Tangier, Morocco, where Burroughs lived in the last half of the 1950s. He wrote most of Naked Lunch *there.*

ence it. This can be exhausting and at times dangerous. One cannot be sure of redemption. . . .

Did I tell you my guess that schizphrenia and cancer are incompatible has been confirmed by Wolberg??. .

I will send along the sections as they are finished. . Love to Peter, Gregory. Where is Gilmore?

Love,
Bill

–*The Beat Book,* p. 27

Naked Lunch *was tried for obscenity in Boston, Massachusetts, in 1962. The following statements by Mailer and Ginsberg were presented in defense of Burroughs's novel. Portions of the trial testimony, "*Naked Lunch *on Trial," were published in the introduction to the first American edition of the novel.*

Q. *Go ahead, Mr. Mailer.*
A. William Burroughs is in my opinion–whatever his conscious intention may be–a religious writer. There is a sense in *Naked Lunch* of the destruction of soul, which is more intense than any I have encountered in any other modern novel. It is a vision of how mankind would act if man was totally divorced from eternity. What gives this vision a machine-gun-edged clarity is an utter lack of sentimentality. The expression of sentimentality in religious matters comes forth usually as a sort of saccharine piety which revolts any idea of religious sentiment in those who are sensitive, discriminating, or deep of feeling. Burroughs avoids even the possibility of such sentimentality (which would, of course, destroy the value of his work), by attaching a stringent, mordant vocabulary to a series of precise and horrific events, a species of gallows humor which is a defeated man's last pride, the pride that he has, at least, not lost his bitterness. So it is the sort of humor which flourishes in prisons, in the Army, among junkies, race tracks and pool halls, a graffiti of cool, even livid wit, based on bodily functions and the frailties of the body, the slights, humiliations and tortures a body can undergo. It is a wild and deadly humor, as even and implacable as a sales tax; it is the small coin of communication in every one of those worlds. Bitter as alkali, it pickles every serious subject in the caustic of the harshest experience; what is left untouched is as dry and silver as a bone. It is this sort of fine, dry residue which is the emotional substance of Burroughs' work for me.

* * *

THE COURT: *Mr. Ginsberg, do you consider that this book is obscene?*

GINSBERG: Not really, no, sir.

THE COURT: *Well, would you be surprised if the author himself admitted it was obscene and must be necessarily obscene in order to convey his thoughts and impressions?*

GINSBERG: The sentence you are referring to–

THE COURT: *Well, it's on page xii of the Introduction: "Since* Naked Lunch *treats this health problem, it is necessarily brutal, obscene and disgusting. Sickness is often repulsive details not for weak stomachs."*

GINSBERG: Yes, he has said that. I don't think he intends that to be obscene in any legal sense or even obscene as seen through his own eyes or through the eyes of a sympathetic reader. He is dealing with matters very basic and very frightening.

THE COURT: *What do you understand him to mean by the phrase: "As always the lunch is naked"? Do you mind my asking these questions?*

DE GRAZIA: *No, Your Honor.*

GINSBERG: That phrase occurs when he is discussing capital punishment, I think.

THE COURT: *Where does he discuss capital punishment?*

GINSBERG: Right in *that.*

THE COURT: *He discusses it in the Foreword, or the Introduction?*

GINSBERG: In the paragraph on the same page. "Let them see what is on the end of that long newspaper spoon."

THE COURT: *What is a "newspaper spoon"?*

GINSBERG: We are presented or spoonfed with news about death, about capital punishment, or executions. . . .

THE COURT: *You think the title,* Naked Lunch, *relates to capital punishment?*

GINSBERG: No, no. It relates to nakedness of seeing, to being able to see clearly without any confusing disguises, to see through the disguise.

THE COURT: *That is your interpretation of the title?*

GINSBERG: Yes.

THE COURT: *Or the meaning of the title?*

GINSBERG: Of the word, "Naked," in the title; and "Lunch" would be a complete banquet of all this naked awareness.

Cover for the first edition of Burroughs's second novel, published in Paris by Olympia Press in 1959, and dust jacket with wrap-around band for the first American edition

Massachusetts Rules Book by Burroughs Not Obscene
The New York Times, 19 July 1966

BOSTON (Religious News Service)–The Massachusetts Supreme Court has ruled that the controversial book, "Naked Lunch," by William Burroughs, is not obscene.

A sharply divided 4-2 decision overruled a Superior Court action by Judge Eugene A. Hudson who, in March, 1965, banned the book as hard-core pornography and utterly without redeeming social importance.

The court's two page decision described the publication as "grossly offensive" but held that the book "cannot be declared obscene." However, it ruled that the attorney general may start new proceedings if the book is advertised or distributed in Massachusetts "in a manner to exploit it for the sake of its possible prurient appeal."

Noting that "a substantial community believes the book to be of some literary significance," the majority ruling held that the Court "cannot of itself [oppose] so many persons in the literary community."

Reviews of *Naked Lunch*

Instead of Love, the Fix
Herbert Gold
The New York Times Book Review, 25 November 1962, pp. 4, 69

Elder statesman of the beat fad, friend and advisor to Allen Ginsberg and Jack Kerouac, author of several novels as yet unavailable in this country, and pseudonymous author of a paperback novel about heroin addiction, William Burroughs has excellent credentials for producing the definitive hip book. He has followed the root of publication by the Olympia Press in Paris and by banned little magazines in the United States; extravagant international praise, with the usual admixture of gossip, has accumulated about his work and his person. Another convulsion of the true-believing bureaucrats of hipdom and the horrified censors, professors and policemen arrayed in mortal combat, now seems inevitable.

It happens that Burroughs possesses a special literary gift. "Naked Lunch" is less a novel than a series of essays, fantasies, prose poems, dramatic fragments, bitter arguments, jokes, puns, epigrams–all hovering about the explicit subject matter of making out on drugs while not making out in either work or love. The black humor of addiction–a religion as practiced by Burroughs–does not lend itself to that evolution of character and action within society which is traditional to the novel. No real people assist at the junkie's rituals: marks, suppliers, cops, but no friends or lovers.

In this book the single repetitive process of getting the fix replaces accumulating action or growth. There is a frozen dream of perfect isolation behind which Burroughs' intelligence retains its glitter. He sees the East River lined with gangsters in concrete blocks; he sees live monkeys sewn into the bodies of appendicitis victims by abstracted doctors. As in Swift's "A Modest Proposal," the satire proceeds from an apparent acceptance of the disposition of fate. Like Swift, Burroughs then drives through to an extreme of formal horror. He forms a collage of American racial, commercial and social prejudices, placed upon a subject matter of perversion and nihilism. His business sells "adulterated shark repellant." We may start to smile but we stop.

Hero and villain of "Naked Lunch" are heroin. Burroughs makes it clear that addiction does not give pleasure–it is merely "something to do"–and he argues that the police collaborate with the addict, helping him to find his something-to-do by making it hard for him, keeping him busy. Within the dry, husking rustle of Burroughs' prose lies a moral judgment. "I got the fear!" he writes, and runs from the dream of nothingness, no contact, toward nothingness, no contact, toward his surreal fantasy. The world of men and women has let him down. The world of dream–no, of self-absorption–is the only alternative while he waits out his term on earth.

The literary technique will remind readers of Villon and Corbiere, the gasping, torrid Celine and the furious Swift, Alfred Jarry and Jean Genet. But in a most American way, Burroughs rejects their yearnings for a form in favor of a definition of the novel (read: Book) as receptacle. Repetitions of words, phrases, even episodes remain uncut. It is all there because it was there in his mind. He offers up a series of drug and sex transports, unseparated from the motion sickness of getting to the fantasy. He has the notion of suggesting heroin addiction as a treatment for schizophrenia. His logic: The schizophrenic loses contact with others; a heroin addict cannot ignore his need, therefore needs others, therefore needs efficient contact; therefore the addict will give up his madness in order to guarantee his supply.

Certainly a personal psychoanalysis is being wrought in this book. The climaxes are those of shock and the fix, and these are repeated obsessively, using a curious vocabulary which ranges from the pedantic to the childish. When the book flags, the attack is automatic and verbal, the mere play of an intelligent man diddling the language.

Many readers will turn from this book in disgust. Some literary snobs will use it as an occasion to cry masterpiece, forgiving its lack of shape and control; others will accuse it of being merely obscene, too stunned by the experience to admit its relevance to our time and to ride along with the driven, riven spirit that has gone into its making. The book is surely not pornographic. Sex is a target of immense disgust; the cruel language chills the reader, is an anaphrodisiac as heroin.

At its best, this book, which is not a novel but a booty brought back from nightmare, takes a coldly implacable look at the dark side of our nature. Civilization fails many; many fail civilization. William Burroughs has written the basic work for understanding that desperate symptom which is the beat style of life.

Review of *Naked Lunch*
Eric Moon
Library Journal, 1 December 1962, p. 4454

Mary McCarthy and Norman Mailer, representing the U.S. at the 1962 Edinburgh Festival, each told an astounded audience that the outstanding contemporary American writer was a man called William Burroughs. Most of those present had never heard of Mr. Burroughs, understandably, since his "Naked Lunch" had (until this Grove edition), like Miller's "Tropics," Durrell's "Black Book" and other "dangerous" books, enjoyed publication only in Paris. Out of Burroughs's experience as a drug addict for 15 years has come a book that is a phantasmagoria of horror and disgust. Most that can be said about it has been said by the author himself: "I am a recording instrument. . . . I do not presume to impose 'story,' 'plot,' 'continuity.' . . . I am not an entertainer." He is not kidding. He also says, toward the end of the book, "You can cut into 'Naked Lunch' at any intersection point. . . . 'Naked Lunch' is a blueprint, a How-To Book. . . . Black insect lusts open into vast, other planet landscapes. . . . 'Naked Lunch' demands Silence from The Reader. Otherwise he is taking his own pulse. . . ." Let me add only that the book demands more than silence; it demands stamina, an inch-thick lining in the stomach, and a mind shaped by "Finnegans Wake." And even with that, the reader may still want to take his own pulse. This is a unique book by an incredibly talented writer, but I am not sure that the communication of an emotive obscene disgust is worthy use of those talents, and the book communicates little else. Poet Robert Lowell says, "I don't see how it could be considered immoral," and, indeed, I think it is a very moral book, for Burroughs is trying to communicate disgust at a particularly vicious kind of obscenity, the junk business, among other things—there is also an incredible passage which is a tract against capital punishment as another obscenity. But Mr. Lowell must be naive: there will be many who will see the obscenity as the author's own. I don't share the extravagant opinions of McCarthy and Mailer, but this is a book for literature collections. Though it may be pure dynamite on many public library fiction shelves.

The Great Burroughs Affair
John Wain
New Republic, 1 December 1962, pp. 21–23

Naked Lunch belongs to that very large category of books, from Macpherson's *Ossian* to *Peyton Place,* whose interest lies not in their own qualities but in the reception given to them in their own time. In itself, *Naked Lunch* is of very small significance. It consists of a prolonged scream of hatred and disgust, an effort to keep the reader's nose down in the mud for 250 pages. Before reading it I had heard it described as pornography, but this is not the case. The object of pornographic writing is to flood the reader's mind with lust, and lust is at any rate a positive thing to the extent that none of us would exist without it. A pornographic novel is, in however backhanded a way, on the side of something describable as life.

Naked Lunch, by contrast, is unreservedly on the side of death. It seeks to flood the reader's mind not with images of sexual desire but with images of pain, illness, cruelty and corruption.

This is not in fact a very difficult thing to do, since all that is necessary is to brood on everything capable of arousing disgust and revulsion, let the images well up, and dash them down onto the paper. A book like *Naked Lunch* requires far less talent in the writer, and for that matter less intelligence in the reader, than the humblest magazine story or circulating-library novel. From the literary point of view, it is the merest trash, not worth a second glance.

What is worth a glance, however, is the respectful attitude that some well-known writers and critics have shown towards it. Some of the tributes on the wrapper are entirely routine and unsurprising; to find Norman Mailer, for instance, solemnly declaring that this is "a book of beauty, great difficulty, and maniacally exquisite insight," will startle no one, since Mailer has in recent years worked himself round to a position which makes it impossible for him to apply normal values to literature. Kerouac's confident invoking of Swift, Rabelais and Sterne will also pass without comment, since he has given no indication that he knows these writers except as names to be bandied about. E. S. Seldon, on the other hand, a name not previously known to me but evidently well-known enough to be quoted in a blurb, seems to write like a literate man, and his verdict that "Burroughs is a superb writer, and *Naked Lunch* a novel of revolt in the best late-modern sense," pulls one up. It sounds, on the surface at any rate, as if it ought to mean something.

What in fact do we understand by a "novel of revolt" in "the best late-modern sense"? To begin with, such a book would have to belong to the anti-art movement. Secondly, it would have to deal with characters whose lives are largely devoted to escaping from normal day-to-day living, with its pleasures and responsibilities, and achieving, with the aid of drugs and other stimuli, a more or less permanent state of abnormality, where the monstrous becomes the habitual. Thirdly, it would have to be written out of a mood of disgust and hostility. Fourthly, it would have to be urban in atmosphere, saturated with the details of megalopolis.

All these tendencies can be found in writers who were well under way by 1910 – in Alfred Jarry, for example. After 1918 the method was very quickly brought to full development, and the only way of carrying it any further was to increase the element of nausea. The impulse behind anti-art, from Dada manifestos to Action Painting, has always been twofold. Part of the thrust was towards truthfulness and a closer grip on reality. Conventional art, which always admitted a degree of stylization, tended to put reality at a distance, whereas (it was claimed) anti-art had the immediacy of something actually happening; it was not "culture." Naturally this was closely allied with the second objective, which was to shock and startle, to insult, to open people's eyes by affronting them. What Mr. Selden would call "late-modern" is characterized by nothing new except that it digs deeper for its mud, and crushes out more ruthlessly any spark of lyricism or positiveness. Where genuine imaginative writing increases the sensitiveness of the minds exposed to it, leading them on to a wider and deeper range of feelings, writing of this kind makes the mind blunt and callow. Anyone who really accepted its values, as opposed to pretending to accept them as part of some modish parade, would be the enemy not only of art but of the human race.

King of the YADS

Time, 30 November 1962, p. 96

The Young American Disaffiliates (they used to be called beats, but nothing stays simple) have not done well. In matters of finance this is their intention, since the supermarket society is what they have disaffiliated from. But in literature it is merely their embarrassment. Here the best to be said for the YADs is that among them are Allen Ginsberg (*Howl*), Gregory Corso (*Fried Shoes*) and Jack Kerouac (*On the Road*). And the best to be said for these three is that each might have done something worth reading if he had not been lured by the sirens of faucet composition and second-growth Dada.

That is possible, the honorary beat will reply, but have you dug William Burroughs? (The honorary beat is gainfully employed, usually in some branch of the communications industry, but makes up for this solecism by thinking that Norman Mailer improves with age and by having, once, smoked a small quantity of marijuana.) The Burroughs gambit was, until recently, almost unanswerable, because it was almost impossible to track this author down, physically or in print. He was the greyest of grey eminences, a wraith who flickered into occasional visibility in Mexico, Paris or Tangier. The few shreds of information about him have been those of the YAD catechism: he was the legendary "Bull Lee" of *On the Road;* he spent 15 years on junk; he wrote an unprintable book called *Naked Lunch,* which no one had read but which everyone said hit the veins like a jolt of heroin.

The Odds Prevail. Now all this is changed; *Naked Lunch* will now be available at the friendly neighborhood bookstore, right there beside *Youngblood Hawke* and *The New English Bible*. The terrible Mary McCarthy has spoken of Burroughs with respect, and the *Saturday Review's* John Ciardi has praised his "profoundly meaningful" search for "values." British writer Kenneth Allsop called him "Rimbaud in a raincoat." The grey eminence himself has even appeared at that squarest of social gatherings, a writers' conference.

The reputation of an underground author is a fragile thing. For example, it had been assumed for years that Henry Miller was unprintable but highly readable. Then Grove Press, merely by publishing his two *Tropics,* proved that Miller is unreadable but highly printable. A reading of *Naked Lunch,* the grotesque diary of Burroughs' years as an addict, suggests that no such drastic deflation will occur with him. For what it is worth, Burroughs will remain grand dragon of the YADs, by acclamation and by forfeit (he denies, of course, having anything in common with his beatnik vassals, but this is merely good form; no one ever admits to being a member of a literary movement started by someone else). Although Burroughs fancies himself a satirist and occasionally resembles one when the diary's heroin fog clears a little, the value of his book is mostly confessional, not literary.

Shell & Worm. Chairbound souls, however, will put up with a lot from an author who has been there and back, whether "there" is the top of Everest or the depths of the soul. Burroughs has been there, all right; he is not only an ex-junkie, but an ex-con and, by accident, a killer. In Mexico, having acquired a wife, he shot her between the eyes playing William Tell with a revolver. (The Mexican authorities decided it was *imprudentia criminale* and dropped the whole matter.) He has even been in the Army, but not for long; he reacted to being drafted by cutting off a finger joint, and was discharged with the notation "not to be recalled or reclassified."

Presenting himself as proof that the universe is foul, Burroughs achieves the somewhat irrelevant honesty of hysteria as he writes of a malevolent world of users and pushers, of a mad conspiracy of spider-eyed manipulators who sell each other "adulterated shark repellent, cut antibiotics, condemned parachutes, stale anti-venom, inactive serums and vaccines, leaking lifeboats." All pity is mockery ("Yes I know it all. The finance company is repossessing your wife's artificial kidney. They are evicting your grandmother from her iron lung"). All degradations are cherished: a coroner named Autopsy Ahmed makes a fortune peddling an Egyptian worm that "gets into your kidneys and grows to an enormous size. Ultimately the kidney is just a thin shell around the worm. Intrepid gourmets esteem the flesh of the worm above all other delicacies. It is said to be unspeakably toothsome." Most sex is homosexual and all of it is sterile: one partner murders the other in the midst of an embrace, so he can enjoy the death spasms.

Such a book might have been an eloquent attack on the insect society that civilization sometimes threatens to become. But the author is almost never in control for longer than a paragraph or two. Burroughs cannot sustain his night-world, as Joyce did in sections of *Ulysses,* and as Novelist Ralph Ellison did in the whole of that remarkable book, *Invisible Man.*

Fold-In Shakespeare. Supported by a tiny income whose source is the Burroughs adding machine, which his grandfather invented (an irony important to beat hagiographers), the 48-year-old author lives in the "beat hotel," a fleabag shrine in a section of Paris where passers-by move out of the way for rats. There in a worn grey room the worn grey man has written three other novels. *The Soft Machine,* the immediate sequel to *Naked Lunch,* repeats the rant of its predecessor with far less coherence; the improvement may be explained by Burroughs' solemn assurance that much of his writing is dictation Hasan-i-Sabbah, founder of the eleventh century hashish-eating Ismaili cult, the Assassins. The two most recent books, *Nova Express* and *The Ticket That Exploded,* come daringly close to utter babble, according to reports. In these volumes Hasan's dictation is augmented with a "fold-in" technique: pages of the first draft (or of a newspaper, Shakespeare, or whatnot) are taken at random, folded in half lengthwise, and stuck together. This juxtaposition of fragments, says Burroughs, produces a continuous interweaving of flashbacks and flashforwards.

It also produces a question from a puzzled plodder at last summer's Edinburgh Writers' Conference. "Are you serious?" the earnest fellow asked.

"Yes, of course," Burroughs said, and apparently he was.

The Heroin of Our Times

Donald Malcolm

The New Yorker, 2 February 1963, pp. 114–121

It is tolerably easy to abominate William Burroughs' "Naked Lunch" (Grove). Almost the entire contents of the book are offensive–hypothetically, at least–to what were called "the finer feelings" in the days when it was believed that the public came equipped with such a commodity. The work, moreover, has so little structure, being a mere hectic accumulation of anecdotes and fantasies, that it might as fittingly have been issued in a paper bag as between hard covers. On occasion, the writing falls to a level not commonly seen since the disappearance of those lurid pulp magazines whose covers featured an anguished beauty on the verge of ravishment by some unlikely purple cephalopod. Over considerable areas of narrative, to round off the indictment, the work is vastly more conspicuous for its pretensions than for its actual accomplishments. To concede all this is to find oneself in a poor position to argue with those authorities who would consign the book to immediate oblivion. And yet some attempt at argument, I think, ought to be made.

To discover the merit and interest of "Naked Lunch," it is necessary only to decline to accept the book on its author's terms. By altering our expectations, we alter our judgments. It may be fruitful, then, to postpone our consideration of Mr. Burroughs' claims for the work and simply regard it as a raw document of personal history, as which it exerts a deal of fascination. Mr. Burroughs, by his computation, was for fifteen years an addict to opium and its multitudinous derivatives. The bulk of the work was written during this period, and when it specifically treats of an addict's life, and the single, appalling need that stains his every contact with the world, then we find the author in his strength. The book opens well, with a grittily realistic episode in a subway. The narrator, having jettisoned the telltale utensils of addiction (an eye dropper and spoon), eludes a pursuing narcotics detective by leaping aboard a departing train, in which he encounters a young "advertising exec. type fruit." Our anti-hero is prompt in his assessment of his mark ("You know the type comes on with bartenders and cab drivers, talking about right hooks and the Dodgers, call the counterman at Nedick's by his first name"), and he further observes that "A square wants to come on hip. . . . Talks about 'pod,' and smoke it now and then, and keeps some around to offer the fast Hollywood types." He regales his dazzled companion with an assortment of lurid, elliptical, and wandering anecdotes of addiction, and advances by degrees toward the touch, reflecting:

> He's a character collector, would stand still for Joe Gould's seagull act. So I put it on him for a sawski and make a meet to sell him some "pod" as he calls it, thinking, "I'll catnip the jerk." (Note: Catnip smells like marijuana when it burns. Frequently passed on the incautious or uninstructed.)

But no such appointment is reported, and the victim is never spoken of again. A peculiar air of disconnection has entered the narrative:

> I cut into the automat and there is Bill Gains huddled in someone else's overcoat, looking like a 1910 banker with paresis, and Old Bart, shabby and inconspicuous, dunking pound cake with his dirty fingers, shiny over the dirt.

There is no conversation between the narrator and this pair; the sight of them merely reminds him of a gruesome anecdote of addiction, which he relates with mordant relish, and this is followed by

> So back downtown by the Sheridan Square Station in case the dick is lurking in a broom closet.

Disconnection increases as the narrator stocks up on heroin and flees New York. Other cities swim briefly into focus and then simply vanish from the field of vision. Chicago, St. Louis, New Orleans, Cuernavaca, Tangier loom and shimmer and evaporate. Addicts and perverts appear and disappear, recur and vanish, as insubstantial as images upon a screen. In this proffered view–flickering, intermittent, and often vivid–one makes out the addict's mode of life as Mr. Burroughs has known it. Toward the public, "the squares," the addict's attitude is usually and unabashedly predatory. With the police, he is wary and in great dread of arrest and its consequence, the withdrawal of drugs. With other addicts, he shares not so much a relationship as an acknowledgment of their mutual isolation. I find all this as interesting, and as fit a subject of interest, as the delvings of anthropologists into the lives of distant aborigines, who generally are quite as unlovable as the run of addicts, and even less articulate than Mr. Burroughs.

Fantasies begin to engulf the narrative. At their best, these fantasies continue–in another key–the theme of addiction, its preoccupations, and its anxieties. They often are grisly, but the subject, after all, is not a pleasant one, and the horrors are rendered with a ferocious jocundity that sometimes rises to effective style. As one delves further into the book, however, it becomes evident that Mr. Burroughs regards his fantasies not as personal property but as general parables of our time. Through a thickening welter of degradations and perversion, of bloody and pointless violence committed on the helpless, one dimly perceives the objects of the author's rage. His feelings about contemporary politics and science are transposed into visions of sadism and narcotism, relieved of all contact with reality, and discharged in lurid episodes that frequently are meant to nauseate the reader, and frequently do. These passages oblige us to suspend our appreciation of the work as a document and to confront it on the ground of its highest ambition. "The title," Mr. Burroughs writes, "means exactly what the words say: NAKED Lunch–a frozen moment when everyone sees what is on the end of every fork."

Burroughs 'Naked Lunch'
Mary McCarthy
Encounter, April 1963, pp. 92–98

Last summer at the International Writers' Conference in Edinburgh, I said I thought the national novel, like the nation-state, was dying and that a new kind of novel, based on statelessness, was beginning to be written. This novel had a high, aerial point of view and a plot of perpetual motion. Two experiences, that of exile and that of jet-propelled mass tourism, provided the subject matter for a new kind of story. There is no novel, yet, that I know of, about mass tourism, but somebody will certainly write it. Of the novel based on statelessness, I gave as examples William Burroughs' *The Naked Lunch,* Vladimir Nabokov's *Pale Fire* and *Lolita.* Burroughs, I explained, is not literally a political exile, but the drug addicts he describes are continually on the move, and life in the United States, with its present narcotics laws, is untenable for the addict if he does not want to spend it in jail (in the same way, the confirmed homosexual is a chronic refugee, ordered to move on by the Venetian police, the Capri police, the mayor of Provincetown, the mayor of Nantucket). . . .

I said that in thinking over the novels of the last few years, I was struck by the fact that the only ones that had not simply given me pleasure but interested me had been those of Burroughs and Nabokov. The others, even when well done (Compton-Burnett), seemed almost regional.

This statement, to judge by the British press, was a shot fired round the world. I still hear its reverberations in Paris and read about them in the American press. I am quoted as saying that *The Naked Lunch* is the most important novel of the age, of the epoch, of the century. . . .

The result, of course, is a disparagement of Burroughs, because if *The Naked Lunch* is proclaimed as the masterpiece of the century, then it is easily found wanting. Indeed, I wonder whether the inflation of my remarks was not at bottom malicious; it is not usually those who admire Burroughs who come up to me at parties to announce: "I *read* what you said at Edinburgh." This is true, I think, of all such publicity; it is malicious in effect whatever the intention and permits the reader to dismiss works of art and public figures as "not what they are cracked up to be.". . .

As for me, I was left in an uncomfortable situation. I did not want to write in to the editors of British newspapers and magazines, denying that I had said whatever incontinent thing they had quoted me as saying. This would have been ungracious to Burroughs, who was the innocent party in the affair and who must have felt more and more like the groom in a shotgun literary wedding, seeing my name yoked with his as it were indissolubly. And the monstrousness of the union, doubtless, was what kept the story hot. In the end, it became clear to me that the only way I could put an end to this embarrassment was by writing at length what I thought about *The Naked Lunch*–something I was reluctant to do because I am busy finishing a book of my own and reluctant, also, because the whole thing had assumed the proportions of a *cause célèbre* and I felt like a witness called to the stand and obliged to tell the truth and nothing but the truth under oath. This is not a normal critical position. Of course the critic normally tries to be truthful, but he does not feel that his review is some sort of pay-off or eternal reckoning, that the eye of God or the world press is staring into his heart as he writes. Now that I have written the present review, I am glad, as always happens, to have made a clean breast of it. This is what I think about Burroughs.

"You can cut into *The Naked Lunch* at any intersection point," says Burroughs, suiting the action to the word, in "an atrophied preface" he appends as a tail-piece. His book, he means, is like a neighbourhood movie with continuous showings that you can drop into whenever you please–you don't have to wait for the beginning of the feature picture. Or like a worm that you can chop up into sections each of which wriggles off as an independent worm. Or a nine-lived cat. Or a cancer. He is fond of the word "mosaic," especially in its scientific sense of a plant-mottling caused by a virus, and his Muse (see etymology of "mosaic") is interested in organic processes of multiplication and duplication. The literary notion of time as simultaneous, a montage, is not original with Burroughs; what is original is the scientific bent he gives it and a view of the world that combines biochemistry, anthropology, and politics. It is as though *Finnegans Wake* were cut loose from history and adapted for a cinerama circus titled "One World." *The Naked Lunch* has no use for history, which is all "ancient history"–sloughed-off skin; from its planetary perspective, there are only geography and customs. Seen in terms of space, history shrivels into a mere wrinkling or furrowing of the surface as in an aerial relief-map or one of those pieced-together aerial photographs known in the trade as mosaics. The oldest memory in *The Naked Lunch* is of jacking-off in boyhood latrines, a memory recaptured through pederasty. This must be the first space novel, the first serious piece of science fiction–the others are entertainment. . . .

The best comparison for the book, with its aerial sex acts performed on a high trapeze, its con men and barkers, its arena-like form, is in fact to a circus. A circus travels but it is always the same, and this is Burroughs' sardonic image of modern life. The Barnum of the show is the mass-manipulator, who appears in a series of disguises. *Control,* as Burroughs says, underlining it, *can never be a means to anything but more control–like drugs,* and the vicious circle of addiction is re-enacted, worldwide, with sideshows in the political and "social" sphere–the "social" here has vanished, except in quotation marks, like the historical, for everything has become automatised. Everyone is an addict of one kind or another, as people indeed are wont to say of themselves, complacently: "I'm a crossword puzzle addict, a Hi-Fi addict," etcetera. The South is addicted to lynching and nigger-hating, and the Southern folk-custom of burning a Negro recurs throughout the book as a sort of Fourth-of-July carnival with fireworks. Circuses, with their cages of wild animals, are also dangerous, like Burroughs' human circus; an accident may occur, as when the electronic brain in Dr. Benway's laboratory goes on the rampage, and the freaks escape to mingle with the controlled citizens of Freeland in a general riot, or in the scene where the hogs are let loose in the gourmet restaurant. . . .

In defence, Swift could be cited, and indeed between Burroughs and Swift there are many points of comparison; not only the obsession with excrement and the horror of female genitalia but a disgust with politics and the whole body politic. Like Swift, Burroughs has irritable nerves and something of the crafty temperament of the inventor. There is a great deal of Laputa in the countries Burroughs calls Interzone and Freeland, and Swift's solution for the Irish problem would appeal to the American's dry logic. As Gulliver, Swift posed as an anthropologist (though the study was not known by that name then) among savage people; Burroughs parodies the anthropologist in his descriptions of the American heartland: ". . . the Interior a vast subdivision, antennae of television to the meaningless sky. . . . Illinois and Missouri, miasma of mound-building peoples, grovelling worship of the Food Source, cruel and ugly festivals." The style here is more emotive than Swift's, but in his deadpan explanatory notes ("This is a rural English custom designed to eliminate aged and bedfast dependents"), there is a Swiftian laconic factuality. The "factual" appearance of the whole narrative, with its battery of notes and citations, some straight, some loaded, its extracts from a diary, like a ship's log, its pharmacopeia, has the flavour of eighteenth-century satire. He calls himself a "Factualist" and belongs, all alone, to an Age of Reason, which he locates in the future. In him, as in Swift, there is a kind of soured utopianism.

Yet what saves *The Naked Lunch* is not a literary ancestor but humour. Burroughs' humour is peculiarly American, at once broad and sly. It is the humour of a comedian, a vaudeville performer playing in "One," in front of the asbestos curtain of some Keith Circuit or Pantages house long since converted to movies. The same jokes reappear, slightly refurbished, to suit the circumstances, the way a vaudeville artist used to change Yonkers to Renton when he was playing Seattle. For example, the Saniflush joke, which is always good for a laugh: somebody is cutting the cocaine/the morphine/the penicillin with Saniflush. . . .

Another favourite effect, with Burroughs, is the metamorphosis. A citizen is turned into animal form, a crab or a huge centipede, or into some unspeakable monstrosity, like Bradley the Narcotics Agent who turns into an unidentifiable carnivore. These metamorphoses, of course, are punishments. The Hellzapoppin effect of orgies and riots and the metamorphosis effect, rapid or creeping, are really cancerous onslaughts–matter on the rampage multiplying itself and "building" as a revue scene "builds" to a climax. Growth and deterioration are the same thing: a human being "deteriorates" or grows into a one-man jungle. What you think of it depends on your point of view; from the junky's angle, Bradley is better as a carnivore eating the Narcotics Commissioner than he was as "fuzz"–junky slang for the police.

The impression left by this is perplexing. On the one hand, control is evil; on the other, escape from control is mass slaughter or reduction to a state of proliferating cellular matter. The police are the enemy, but as Burroughs shrewdly observes in one passage: "A *functioning* police state needs no police." The policeman is internalised in the citizen. You might say that it would have been better to have no control, no police, in the first place; then there would be no police states, functioning or otherwise. This would seem to be Burroughs' position, but it is not consistent with his picture of sex. The libertarian position usually has as one of its axioms a love of Nature and the natural, that is, of the life-principle itself, commonly identified with sex. But there is little overt love of the life-principle in *The Naked Lunch,* and sex, while magnified–a common trait of homosexual literature–is a kind of mechanical mantrap baited with fresh meat. The sexual climax, the jet of sperm, accompanied by a whistling scream, is often a death spasm, and the "perfect" orgasm would seem to be the posthumous orgasm of the hanged man, shooting his jissom into pure space.

It is true that Nature and sex are two-faced, and that growth is death-oriented. But if Nature is not seen as far more good than evil, then a need for control is posited. And, strangely, this seems to be Burroughs' position too. *The human virus can now be treated,* he says with emphasis, meaning the species itself. By scientific methods, he implies. Yet the laboratory of *The Naked Lunch* is a musical-comedy inferno, and Dr. Benway's assistant is a female chimpanzee. It is impossible, as Burroughs knows, to have scientific experiment without control. Then what? Self-control? Do-it-yourself? But self-control, again, is an internalised system of authority, a subjection of the impulses to the will, the least "natural" part of the personality. Such a system might suit Marcus Aurelius, but it hardly seems congenial to the author of *The Naked Lunch.* And even if it were (for the author is at once puritan and tolerant), it would not form the basis for scientific experiment on the "human virus." Only for scientific experiment on oneself.

Possibly this is what Burroughs means; in fact his present literary exercises may be stages in such a deliberate experiment. The questions just posed would not arise if *The Naked Lunch* did not contain messages that unluckily are somewhat arcane. Not just messages; prescriptions. That–to answer a pained question that keeps coming up like a refrain–is why the book is taken seriously. Burroughs' remarkable talent is only part of the reason; the other part is that, finally, for the first time in recent years, a talented writer means what he says to be taken and used literally, like an Rx prescription. The literalness of Burroughs is the opposite of "literature." Unsentimental and factual, he writes as though his thoughts had the quality of self-evidence. In short, he has a crankish courage, but all courage nowadays is probably crankish.

Disorganization Men
John Gross
New Statesman, 8 February 1963, pp. 202–204

The Beat Generation have come and gone, making a lot of noise but little real impact. If they have been the best-publicized literary movement of recent years, it isn't only because of their own efforts to get in the limelight; they have also been a natural gift to the publicist. Here, complete with battledress and catchphrases, was a form of rebellion which the squarest intelligence could grasp. A simple reversal of *Saturday Evening Post* values. And it was all so easy: muddy writing, woozy mysticism, cut-price alienation. The beats quickly found their place in popular mythology, without being taken too seriously by most other writers. Just lately, though, there has been a curious spread of the beat mood to regions where it would normally have been resisted. The virtual canonization of Norman Mailer among some of New York's hardest-bitten intellectuals is one case in point; another is Mary McCarthy's singling out of *The Naked Lunch* as a book which gives contemporary fiction a badly needed shot in the arm, as it were. Praise from Miss McCarthy is praise indeed, but I'm afraid that I've drawn a complete blank with William Burroughs. When Burroughs scholarship is further advanced than it is at present, and the commentators have provided a Skeleton Key, perhaps I'll see the light and be ashamed to recall my own obtuseness; but right now, *The Naked Lunch* seems to me largely devoid of either positive merits or interesting faults.

. . . .

It ought to be explosive, but the language obstinately refuses to come to life in Mr. Burroughs's hands, or to convey much more than the knowingness of the initiate. "Black insect lusts," he writes, "open into vast, other planet landscapes." If Rimbaud and Joyce and a hundred others hadn't shown that dream landscapes can be marvelous or disturbing or sinister or funny, *The Naked Lunch* might seem more of a novelty and less of a mess. As it is, Mr. Burroughs's ideal reader would be someone just discovering that literary experiments didn't stop short with Galsworthy. Such a latecomer might well be startled by his daring innovations, or bowled over by a line like "See, see where Christ's blood streams in the spermament."

. . . .

Only having read newspaper reports of her Edinburgh speech, I find it hard to fathom what quirk led Mary McCarthy to praise *The Naked Lunch,* or to bracket it with its opposite, the cerebral, intricately worked-out *Pale Fire.* Burroughs's most recent book, a saga of cosmic warfare called *The Ticket that Exploded,* is superficially a shade more imaginative; his universe is full of phosphorescent colors. But looked at more closely the narrative is unintelligible, the language tired, and the action a mixture of tepid emotions and monster orgasms. The characters perform startling feats, but the secret of the Burroughs Ejaculating Machine is never revealed.

Yet the Burroughs cult as a whole does represent something wider–a total rejection of American society. Not a reaction against, or a rebellion, because that would imply a degree of common interest, and the message is that America is no longer worth even haranguing, no longer worth bothering with at all. America simply means money-ideals and, even worse, matriarchy: the most memorable moment in *The Naked Lunch,* though it comes across as weirdly Thurberish rather than murderous, is one where a horde of American women suddenly rush on-stage "from country club, penthouse and suburb, motel and yacht and cocktail bar," tearing off their clothes, moaning and howling for sex. The whole sick episode reads like a retort to the myth of the teasing bunnies down at the Key Club. . . .

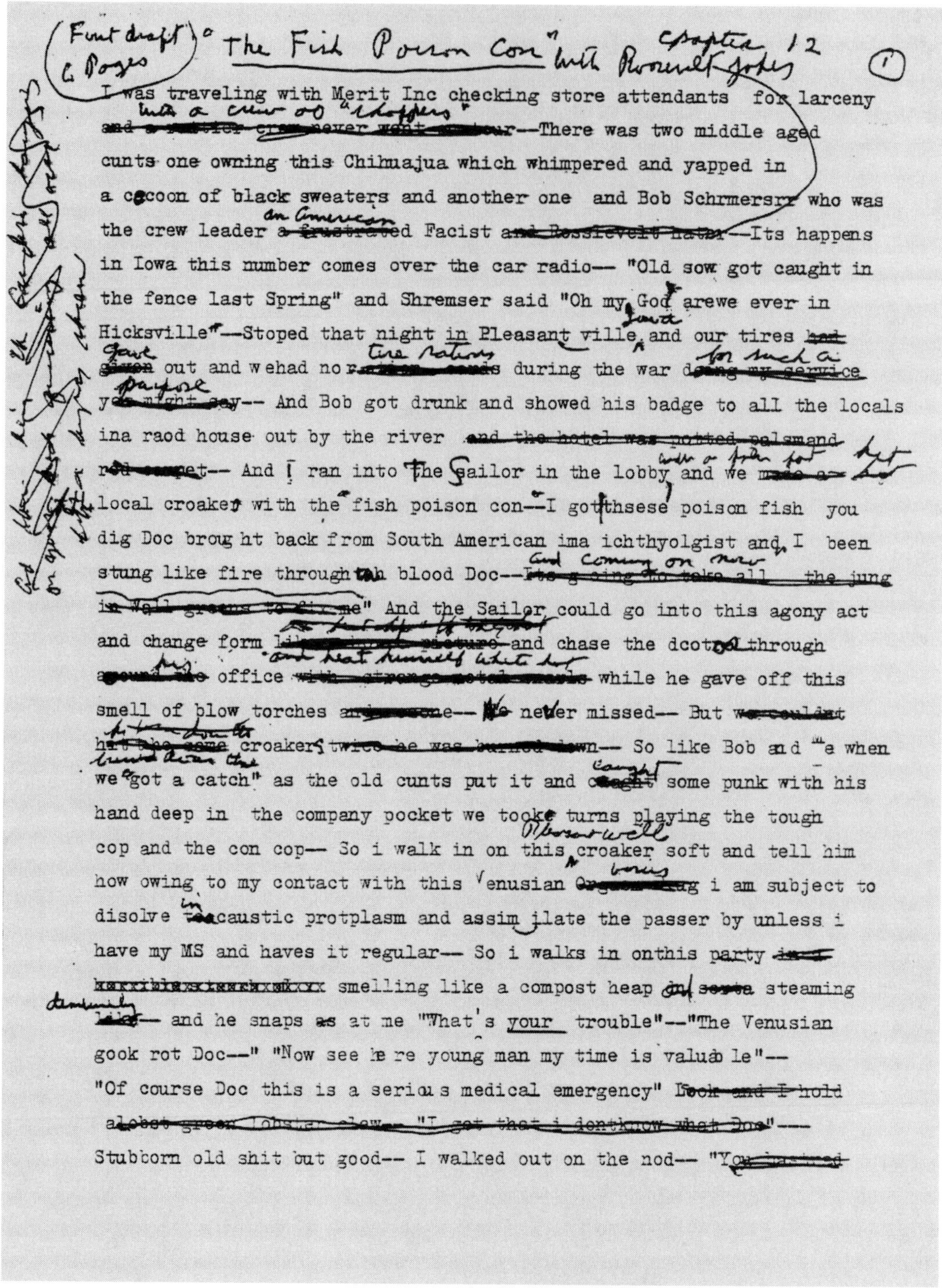

"The Fish Poison Con"

I was traveling with Merit Inc checking store attendants for larceny
~~and a ... crew never ... tour~~--There was two middle aged
cunts one owning this Chihuajua which whimpered and yapped in
a cocoon of black sweaters and another one and Bob Schrmersrr who was
the crew leader ~~a frustrated~~ Facist ~~and Roosevelt hater~~--Its happens
in Iowa this number comes over the car radio-- "Old sow got caught in
the fence last Spring" and Shremser said "Oh my God arewe ever in
Hicksville"--Stoped that night in Pleasant ville and our tires ~~had~~
~~given~~ out and wehad no ~~...~~ during the war ~~doing my service~~
~~you might say~~-- And Bob got drunk and showed his badge to all the locals
ina raod house out by the river ~~and the hotel was potted palms and~~
~~red carpet~~-- And I ran into The Sailor in the lobby and we ~~make a~~
local croaker with the fish poison con--I gotthsese poison fish you
dig Doc brought back from South American ima ichthyolgist and I been
stung like fire through th blood Doc--~~Its going to take all the jung~~
~~in Wall greens to fix me~~" And the Sailor could go into this agony act
and change form ~~like ... picture~~ and chase the dcotor through
~~around the~~ office ~~with strange metal ...~~ while he gave off this
smell of blow torches ~~and ozone~~-- We never missed-- But ~~we couldnt~~
~~hit the same~~ croakers ~~twice he was burned down~~-- So like Bob and me when
we "got a catch" as the old cunts put it and ~~caught~~ some punk with his
hand deep in the company pocket we tooke turns playing the tough
cop and the con cop-- So i walk in on this croaker soft and tell him
how owing to my contact with this Venusian ~~Orgone ...~~ i am subject to
disolve ~~to~~ caustic protplasm and assim ilate the passer by unless i
have my MS and haves it regular-- So i walks in onthis party ~~...~~
~~xxxxxxxxxxxxxxx~~ smelling like a compost heap ~~and sorta~~ steaming
~~like~~-- and he snaps ~~as~~ at me "That's your trouble"--"The Venusian
gook rot Doc--" "Now see here young man my time is valuab le"--
"Of course Doc this is a seriou s medical emergency" ~~Look and I hold~~
~~a lobster green lobster claw-- "I got that i dontknow what Doc"~~---
Stubborn old shit but good-- I walked out on the nod-- "Yo~~u bastard~~

Three typescript pages of material that was later shaped into Naked Lunch *and* The Soft Machine *(1961)*
(Ohio State University)

(3)

I was sick but not needle sick--This was black smoke yen-- The Sailor was still asleep and he looked very youngunder a wispy mustache-- I woke him up he looked around [redacted] slow ~~hydra, like survey~~ hydraulic ~~of~~ control~~of emergency~~ his eys unbluffed unread~~able~~--"Let make the street--I'm thin"-- I was in fafct very thin ~~indeed~~ as I found when a stopped for a moment in front of mirror panel and adjusted the knot of my tie in a starched ~~stachedde tachable~~ colar-- It~~s~~ was a naborhood of chili house and cheap saloons with free lunch everywhere on the counters-- I walked with out thinking like a horse and came to the Chinese Laudry by a Massage Parlor-- We walked in and the Chink [illegible] ~~Chinaman in~~ front flicked his eyes to~~wards~~ the backan went on ironing a shirt front--We Walked through a curtain and a door and the black ~~balck~~ smoke set our lungs dancing the junky jig and we lay dwon on ~~our~~ junk hips while a Chinese kid ~~thin and delicate as an ivory chess man~~ ~~cooked~~ cooked our pills andhanded us the pipes-- after six pipes each we began to smoke slow and ordered ~~drank~~ a pot of tea-- ~~Clearly it was time to think about business~~-- The Cinese kid was in another room-- gulp like "The words hatched in my throat like alreadywritten there and i was reading them back lip reading we call it in the trade only way to orient yourself [redacted] when in Rome [redacted]-- "Ive checked the harness bull-- He comes into Machsorlyes every night at 2:20 ~~one~~ PM and forces the local pederast to perform this ~~and~~ unnatural act on his person-- So regular you can set your watch by it--xi "I wont I wont glub glub glub"-- So that gives us twenty minutes at least to get in and out through the side window and eight hours start we should be in St Louis b~~efore the~~ ~~for the world fair~~ before they miss ~~can sent out~~ the time-- ~~Anyway I'd like to~~ stop off and see the family"

The memory ~~merey~~ pictures were coming in ~~now~~-- Little Boy Blue ~~and all the blue~~ heavy [redacted] and silver sets and clubs and banks-- The cool financier ~~finacier~~ eyes moving steel and oil and shares-- My family ~~i knew~~ was ~~rich~~ rich and Pol Jack [redacted]-- Itwas set for that night-- As we walked out I saw the Japanese girls picking up her laudnry and my flesh stirred under the

6

i spit blood o[illegible]t under the ~~[illegible]~~ [sliding] vultures

[shadows] [illegible] at The Marrcado Mayorista--Saw a tourist a Messter Merican fruto drinking pisco and fixed ~~me~~ with the ey[e]s so i sit down and drink andtell him how i live in a shack on the hill with atin roof held on by ~~[illegible]~~ rocks and hate my brothers beacuse they eat and he says something about " a bad wind" and laughs and i went with him to a hot[el] i know-- In the morning he says i am honest and will i come with him to Pucallpa he is going into the jungle there looking for snakes and spiders totake pictures and ~~[illegible]~~ [bring] them back [to Washington] ~~the way~~ they always carry something away ~~and~~ even if it is only a spider monkey spitting blood they way most of do here--In the winter when the mist comes down fromthe mouantians and never leaves your ~~thin~~ clothes ~~and~~ [illegible] and everyone coughed and ~~[illegible]~~ spits [blood] on the mud floor where i sleep-- So we start out next day in a mixto bus and by night we are in the moutains with snow and the Meester takes out a bottle of aguardiente and the driver gets drunk down into the Selva came to Pucallpa three days later..the Meester finds the lcoal brujo and takes this Ayuhauasca and i take some too and muy mareado then iwas back in Lima and other ~~cities~~ [places] I didnt know [illegible] and saw the Meester in a room with rose wall paper as child looking at something i couldnt see. [illegible]--And the Meester was looking at me and i could see ~~the~~ street boy words there in his ~~[illegible]~~ [throat.] ~~how much can i pull out of The Tourist-- [illegible]~~ [Tasting] the roast beef and ice cream in my throat and knowing the thing was always out in the ~~chil~~ hall [illegible]

Next day the police came looking for us at the ~~hotle~~ Hotel and the Meester showed letters to the Comadante and they shook hands-- and he went to have lunch with the Commandante and I took a bus back to Lima with the money he gave me to buy equipment--

Material later shaped into Naked Lunch *and* The Soft Machine *(cont.)*

Reviews of *The Soft Machine*

Books of the Times
Herbert Gold
The New York Times, 20 March 1968, p. 4

An early pseudonymous chronicle, "Junkie," plus an underground reputation as the sage of heroin and getting off heroin, established the personality of William Burroughs on the beat scene: at once spokesman, mediator and innovator. Then the horrific comedy of "Naked Lunch," a compendium of dream disasters and punishments, brought him literary fame. The book's public scandal accounts for part of the acclaim, but it also merited attention for its objective communication of a nightmare fantasy. It is as if, like Kafka, but with a more anarchic rage, Burroughs was able to cross over into madness and return with the booty of art. Surely "Naked Lunch" is an incomplete work, fragments of horror mixed with fragments of surrealistic vaudeville, but Kafka's "Amerika" is not a finished labor, either. And the theme expressed in the cry, "I got the fear!" gives a sense of unity to the boiling tumble of "Naked Lunch."

The condition of addiction, of the dependent soul and its awful loneliness–a state which is part of the price of civilization, a part of the human condition–is effectively dramatized in "Naked Lunch." The book has wit and thrust, and its faults of structure, or rather non-structure, are redeemed by the powerful and persuasive misery which lies behind it. The reader must perhaps do more of the work than he should; the author is the medium through which his words pass, with insufficient energy of control and will to mastery. Nonetheless "Naked Lunch" extracts its dues from the attentive and submissive reader.

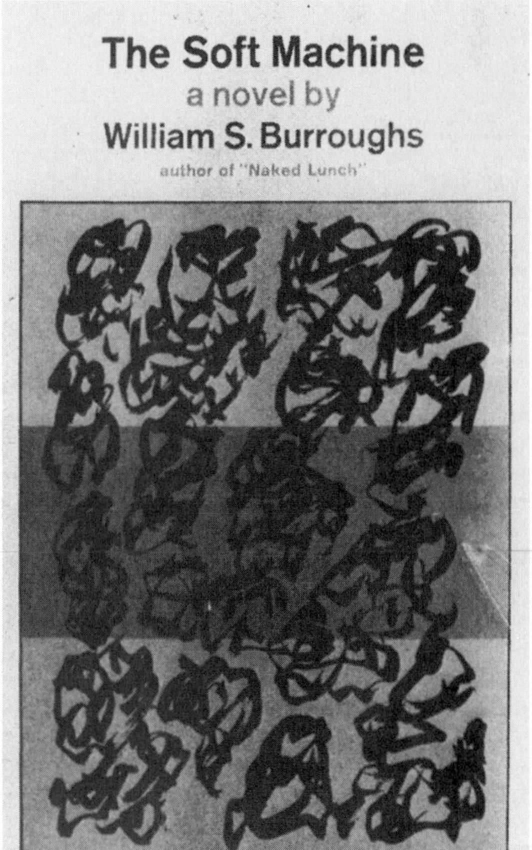

Dust jackets for Burroughs's fifth book, first published by Olympia Press, Paris, 1961; revised and enlarged edition, Grove Press, 1966. Both The Soft Machine *and* The Ticket That Exploded *(1962) were compiled from material left over from* Naked Lunch. *Both works extensively use the montage and cut-up techniques.*

Now, in his new book, "The Soft Machine," it is as if Burroughs has taken hold of his flaws, weaknesses, errors and indulgences, and instead of dealing strictly with them, has made them the subject of his aesthetic intention. The scatology has hit the fan. When homosexual camp has become a cliché, he tries to make it new by poking it at the reader from every direction. The author, no longer raging in obscurity with his devils, has devised a technique, the Cut Up and Permutation. (He credits the painter Brion Gysin with helping him extend the collage "organization" of "Naked Lunch." The Grove Press-New York edition of "The Soft Machine" has been straightened out of the very different Olympia Press-Paris edition, a little in the way Paul Bunyan and the Big Blue Ox straightened roads–by grabbing each end and pulling.)

There is still the rabid imagination, but an arty fashion has put its fingers on it. Burroughs writes, and cuts, and pastes, and adds, and recuts, repastes, rearranges by hazard until suddenly the book stops. Alas, where are the persuasive devils now? Where have all the fleurs-du-mal gone? They are munched up by a literary-aesthetic theory, truly a soft machine for producing a novel. Dr. Benway, the Batman hero-villain, is still meddling in the air; the familiar geography of Interzone can still fascinate the dreamy reader; there are floating neon images of decay, corruption, putrefaction, illness. The odd comic-book elegance–old-fashioned cliches married to grotesque exploits–still makes its witty effect. But the weight is lacking. It no longer convinces.

So come back, Bill Burroughs! We want the Retroactive Kid to catch us in time. Fine about Johnny Yen and the Commandante, but let them swing. We need the Syndicate Killer to suffer the consequences. We know what you mean when you say, "Worn metal subway turnstiles," but so what and what then? What happens next, after we turn through the turnstiles? We can read about "Shredded clouds impregnated with flesh fur of steel," and that's not enough. It's fin d'any siecle. Give us this day our daily horror, agreed; but carry through on your promises. The cut-up scissors makes it all a game, and the claim is for more. As the book says: "Shoot your way to freedom, kid."

Burroughs is clearly writing, as does any novelist, his spiritual autobiography. Some novelists tell it through controlled fantasy, using the objective resources of action and invented character. Others disguise their own lives and write romanticized autobiographies, punishing their enemies and rewarding their friends (or sometimes the reverse). And a few, like Kafka and Burroughs, use neither plot nor personal career to carry the essential burden, but fly into fantasy, nightmare, persuaded dream. In "The Soft Machine" it is as if Burroughs does not trust the power of his nightmares. He jiggles and toys with them; he repeats naggingly; he eliminates the degree of sanity which makes the irony cut.

Perhaps this is because he is essentially a rational man, on the way to be cured of the horrors of his youth and obscurity. I am tempted to offer him advice, for which I expect no gratitude. I would like to see him apply his wit and Puritan rage to direct expression of the conditions of his life and times. I would like to lock up his scissors and paste and make him tell it straight from beginning to end, as if he were on a train trip with a new friend. And then perhaps he could sit down and think about it afterward, and even rewrite; and if he promises to be discreet I would like to lend him back his scissors for the purpose of the swift and paced organization of which this gifted man is surely capable.

Images of Loathing
Stephen Koch
The Nation, 4 July 1966, pp. 25–26

An enormous amount of discussion has been wasted on William Burroughs since *Naked Lunch* was published six years ago. There was the underworld. There were drugs. There was homosexuality. One heard him linked endlessly with Jean Genet, a writer with whom he has almost nothing in common. Burroughs has not been considered as an artist, but as a phenomenon in a moral crisis. . .

The human organism is "the soft machine" craving to be programed by the world's "ticket." Burroughs' art is an effort to explode that ticket. Such an experiment is possible only during the late stages of a language's history. There is a large amount of parody in these books, based (as in the great early modern examples, like Joyce and Mann) on a certain self-conscious, liberating attitude toward the decadence of a language. But Joyce and Mann were concerned with the degeneration of literary language: Burroughs uses, primarily, pre-literary forms. More important, his attitude toward the problem of meaning is far more radical than theirs. . .

Burroughs regards words not as vehicles of concepts but as instruments of provocation–as sensory agents. He gives their affect priority over their role as signs quite simply: by de-structuring, by destruction. Words, sentences, paragraphs, moving in these rapid, lurid, discontinuous "biologic films" are not concepts but things, put together in mosaics of verbal icons violently scattered across the sensibility with invisible artfulness. The books begin when opened, end when closed; there is no need to read them straight through. The reader's mind plays over their broken, sensuous surfaces at liberty, discovering correspondences, making associations, experiencing images of the impossible, accepting, rejecting–creating the work himself.

Burroughs has been announced (by Jack Kerouac, among others) as a satirist. This is not quite the case: he is a parodist, a satirist of the way words are used. Strictly speaking, a satirist must have an object, an intention. This Burroughs' art precludes. Nonetheless, his work is obsessed with a quality of feeling frequently found in the real thing. I am speaking of loathing. It is not directed against anything, for almost nothing in Burroughs can be construed as an ethical statement. But some of his images have a certain lurid but real and remarkable energy generated by the force of disgust. So far as I know, his is the first work in English prose to exploit the rich intensity of loathing in a direct, unstructured, unrationalized appeal to the senses. When I call it lurid, I don't want to suggest that it is cheap. "Sensationalism" like it (e.g., the paintings of Francis Bacon) has been accorded respect in the visual arts for a long time.

For Burroughs, energized disgust is a strategy for making prose concrete. As such, it is an important, even essential, enterprise. The notion that concreteness can be achieved in prose with mere lists of names is naive: in an abstract medium like literature, concreteness is really a form of emotional concentration. Actual objects are able to provide it only so long as the names of things still provoke a sharp sensory response not yet enervated by banality. Unfortunately, in a period like ours, when prose style is in a state of extreme decadence, it is very difficult to make names play such a role.

In his images of loathing, Burroughs has been able to find the primary sensory appeal names are no longer able to call forth. Of course, the effort succeeds only if the images are given definition in some cared, complex way that allows them to keep their primitive energy despite the elaborations of art. But that's what Burroughs has done in *The Soft Machine,* often enough to make the book one of the most interesting pieces of radical fiction we have.

Reviews of *The Ticket That Exploded*

Cutting Up

Richard Rhodes

The New York Times Book Review, 16 June 1967, p. 4

In "Naked Lunch" and "Nova Express," William Burroughs locked huge themes into radical fictional forms. Nobody quite knew how he did it until, in a Paris Review interview with the late Conrad Knickerbocker, he explained something of his purpose and technique as a writer.

His purpose, Mr. Burroughs said, is to "make people aware of the true criminality of our times, to wise up the marks." Technically, he is "quite deliberately addressing myself to the whole area of what we call dreams . . . I've been interested in precisely how word and image get around on very, very complex association lines." Both aspects of his work come together in a desperate obsession with power and control, and an obsession with addiction and how it can be cured.

His basic equipment for studying "complex association lines" includes scissors and pastepot and a bank of tape recorders wired in tandem. With these tools he produces what he calls "cut-up": words–mostly his own, some from other writers–reorganized into evocative, surreal fragments. Thus, from "The Ticket That Exploded": "What summer will I will you? . . . cold summer will exactly . . . He lifts his hands, sadly turns them out . . . Brother can't you spare a dime? . . . dead finger in smoke pointing to Gibraltar . . . the adolescent shadow . . ."

Fragments like these he lays over a pulp science-fiction plot in which alien forces are attempting to blow up the planet by setting everyone on earth at everyone else's throat. Their weapons include sex, to Burroughs a "biologic weapon"; the "feedback" of insults of which the archetype is any barroom brawl; and permutated electronic and biologic con games. Finally, the author threads through the narrative-cut-up a robust, carny comedy that features such characters as "Mr. Bradly, Mr. Martin," Green Tony, Hamburger Mary, Dr. Benway and Izzy the Push.

His cut-up techniques may or may not be taken seriously. Film editors and computer programmers do cut-up every day, and the only reasonable measure of its worth is its result. The result from Burroughs is an uneven, exhausting fiction that evokes vast possibilities, as in some four-dimensional chess game where solutions flash into view only to disappear around an invisible corner. At best, cut-up actually knocks out logic and makes sudden room for images not seen in the vicinity of fiction before.

His intention to "wise up the marks" should probably be taken seriously, because he has been down the lonesome roads we "marks" seldom travel and has learned when to shout "Hey, Rube!" The facts and fantasies of global power are timely. Massive, diabolic forces work late into the night on our

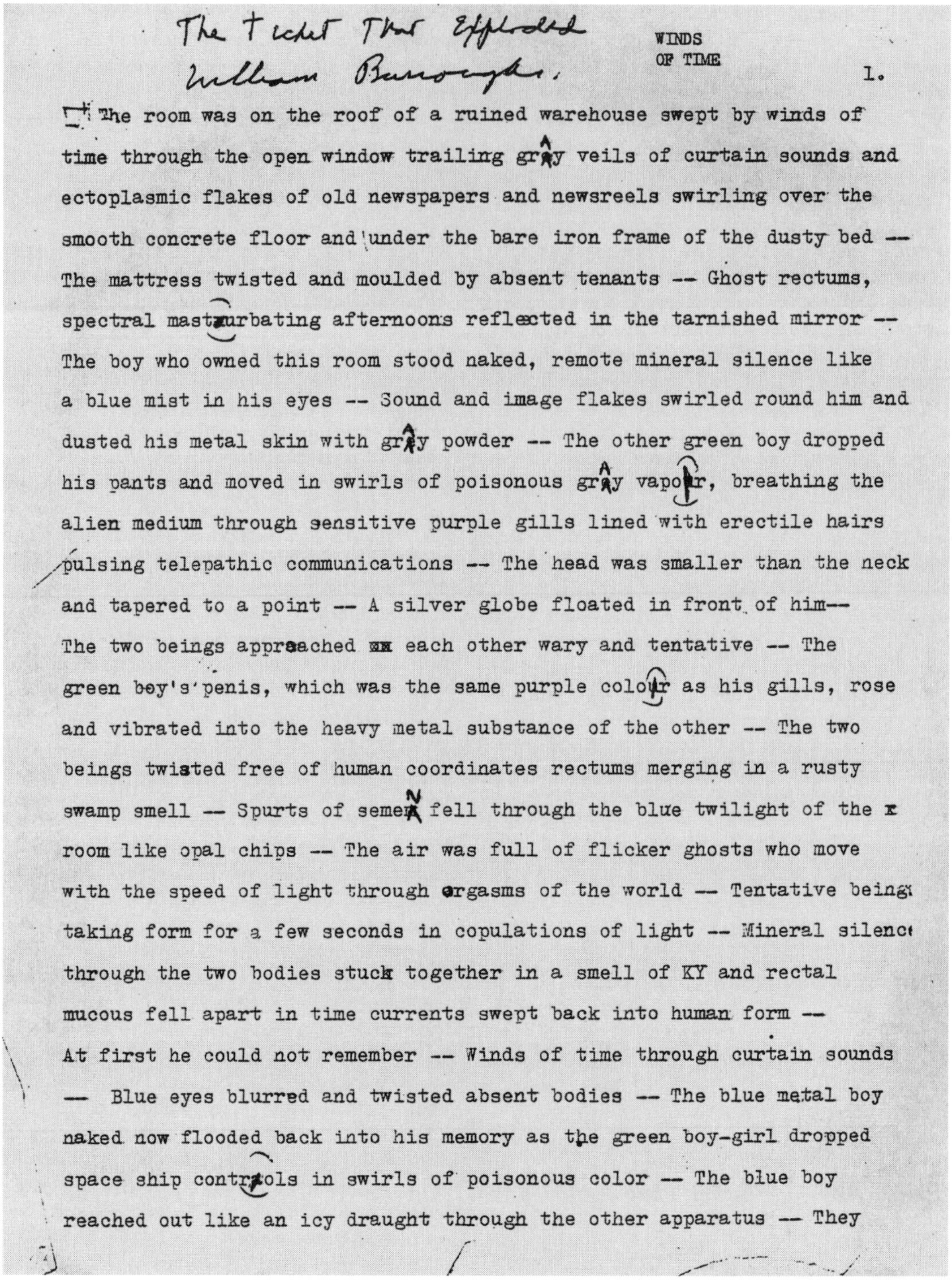

The Ticket That Exploded
William Burroughs.

WINDS
OF TIME

1.

The room was on the roof of a ruined warehouse swept by winds of time through the open window trailing gray veils of curtain sounds and ectoplasmic flakes of old newspapers and newsreels swirling over the smooth concrete floor and under the bare iron frame of the dusty bed -- The mattress twisted and moulded by absent tenants -- Ghost rectums, spectral masturbating afternoons reflected in the tarnished mirror -- The boy who owned this room stood naked, remote mineral silence like a blue mist in his eyes -- Sound and image flakes swirled round him and dusted his metal skin with gray powder -- The other green boy dropped his pants and moved in swirls of poisonous gray vapor, breathing the alien medium through sensitive purple gills lined with erectile hairs pulsing telepathic communications -- The head was smaller than the neck and tapered to a point -- A silver globe floated in front of him-- The two beings approached each other wary and tentative -- The green boy's penis, which was the same purple color as his gills, rose and vibrated into the heavy metal substance of the other -- The two beings twisted free of human coordinates rectums merging in a rusty swamp smell -- Spurts of semen fell through the blue twilight of the room like opal chips -- The air was full of flicker ghosts who move with the speed of light through orgasms of the world -- Tentative beings taking form for a few seconds in copulations of light -- Mineral silence through the two bodies stuck together in a smell of KY and rectal mucous fell apart in time currents swept back into human form -- At first he could not remember -- Winds of time through curtain sounds -- Blue eyes blurred and twisted absent bodies -- The blue metal boy naked now flooded back into his memory as the green boy-girl dropped space ship controls in swirls of poisonous color -- The blue boy reached out like an icy draught through the other apparatus -- They

Typescript page from The Ticket That Exploded *(Ohio State University)*

planet, and Burroughs's nova-bent cops and robbers seem plausible. "Time-Life-Fortune" may well be "some sort of police organization." It is certainly "one of the greatest word and image banks in the world." Manipulating words and images for control purposes is central to the confusion that confounds our national life.

For Burroughs, the "true criminality of our times" is addiction. He elaborates the implications of that word as relentlessly as did Robert Burton the word "melancholy" or Melville the whiteness of the whale. In the universe escalating toward nova, all are addicted: the police to power; women to the sexual enslaving of men; men to devious crime; nations to remorseless expansion; the tribal god who rules our destinies to words and images, which are a kind of crystalline virus that infects us all. Such focal vision can only reveal. It presents the same inner logic as the inner logic of the schizophrenic, confounding good sense, ridiculing compromise and temporarily installing a higher sanity.

Burroughs's fictional ambitions are vast; he has embarked on great themes. But "The Ticket That Exploded" barely moves forward. It is the first American edition of a book originally published by the Olympia Press in 1961 and "revised and augmented" in 1963. In the Grove Press edition, it has been revised and augmented again. The latest augmentations fill out the plot and bring the book more into line with the science fiction of "Nova Express." A long coda explains the mechanics of tape-recorded cut-up.

Still, adding the new "The Ticket That Exploded" to the other novels, the author has come out ahead. He is progressing toward fewer experiments and greater control of his medium. He is filling in his grand comedy, a comedy trip-wired with con-men and shagnasties, cowardly astronauts and leering Venusian secret agents, screeching suburban moms permanently in estrus, heavies who forget to zip their flies, junkies with panache.

The comedy ultimately wins the reader. It's the authentic American kind that manages to make the best of the worst situations, swearing all the way. It used to be the exclusive property of Bill Mauldin's Willie and Joe. William Burroughs, if he moves on from obsession, is eligible to inherit it. There is reason to believe he will; near the conclusion of his *Paris Review* interview, he remarked that he wanted someday to write a straight Western novel that would enlist all his carny crew. So, he may be lining up a showdown between old Clem and Bradly Martin right now. Doc Benway's sure to be on hand with his poppy-flower patent medicine. It'll be one hell of a good fight.

Review of *The Ticket That Exploded*
Kenneth Kister
Library Journal, 1 June 1967, p. 2177

An expanded and revised version of the same title published in France in 1962, *Ticket* is a scalding commentary on the dehumanizing effects of autosuggestive communications techniques upon modern society. Insisting that salvation lies in turning off the machine (the ticket) and exploding the lie (the ticket again), Burroughs (who exploded his own ticket years ago) is concerned with the impact of mass media much in the same way Marshall McLuhan is–the major difference being that Burroughs is a luddite while McLuhan is not. Burroughs's prose style compares in quality with the best being produced today, and the urgency and seriousness of his theme is indisputable. And, although his name is a red flag to many librarians–*Ticket* has its share of Burroughsian erections and ejaculations–the novel deserves a wide reading public. Indeed, not only should librarians have this novel in their collections, they ought to push it.

Review of *The Ticket That Exploded*
Time, 28 July 1967, p. 84

The works of William Burroughs (*Naked Lunch, Nova Express*) have been taken seriously, even solemnly, by some literary types, including Mary McCarthy and Norman Mailer. Actually, Burroughs' work adds up to the world's pluperfect put-on. The publisher's blurb on the dust jacket attempts to legitimize his latest effusion thus: "Through winds of time, in strange beds, past silent obsidian temples, William Burroughs once again shuttles us back and forth between lunar worlds and the wired electric maze of the city. He presents us with a universe threatened with complete control of communications by the Nova Mob."

This reference to a vaguely defined crew of galactic pirates makes the book sound entertaining–a sort of avant-garde James Bond adventure. It is nothing of the kind. *The Ticket That Exploded,* revised since it was first published in France five years ago, is a nightmare of pornography, disjointed prose,* spaceships powered by copulation, frog people, hangings, and "Sex Skins," which devour people in what apparently is the ultimate ecstasy of death.

The result must be wholly pleasing to an author who is currently working on a book written in a new "art form" wherein pages of prose by two different writers are split down the middle, pasted together, and their sentences merged to form one great non-story. In *Ticket* he has simply experimented by splicing tapes from two or three recorders. "Any number can play," he says. "Why stop there? Why stop anywhere?" Why?

The Algebra of Need
Theodore Solotaroff
New Republic, 5 August 1967, p. 29–30, 34

Much of Burroughs' manner derives from the caustic mentality and idiom of the carny, the con-man, the vaudeville hoofer. Though it wanders across continents, *Naked Lunch* is firmly rooted in the dark side of the American imagination, where the figure of the cracker-barrel hustler has had a complex and vivid career. Burroughs' rural sheriffs, county clerks, and doctors, for example, recall the frontier comedy of Twain, T. B. Thorpe, George Harris, among others. They produced a wild humor, raw and crafty, based on the bodily functions, deformations and torments. Burroughs brings it up to date, thickens it with other idioms, but it is essentially the voice of the native American underground. . . .

The only other contemporary artist I know of who has been able to spring repressions in this virtually total way and hold up for inspection the maniacal impulses on which all of us sit, some better than others, was Lenny Bruce. It is more than a coincidence that they were both drug addicts, both conversant with the far reaches of fantasy and with the baleful knowledge of how desperate and diabolical men are under the right conditions. Moreover, the addict's special view of the smug inhumanity of society–for example, the fact that some addictions such as nicotine and alcohol are national pastimes while others are criminal offenses–and his natural animus against the authorities and citizens who thrive within the society, provide an aggressive energy and razor edge to their insight. The fact that they are both comedians is also much to the point, for humor is a powerful instrument in mediating the incongruities of the psyche, in giving a structure and power to the dull gibberish that makes up most of the actual content inside our heads. Most of us have had the experience of striking a vein of comic fantasy that goes on and on, cuts deeper and deeper, knits up more and more threads of experience. Burroughs, like Bruce, has the gift, I'd say genius, to do so almost constantly.

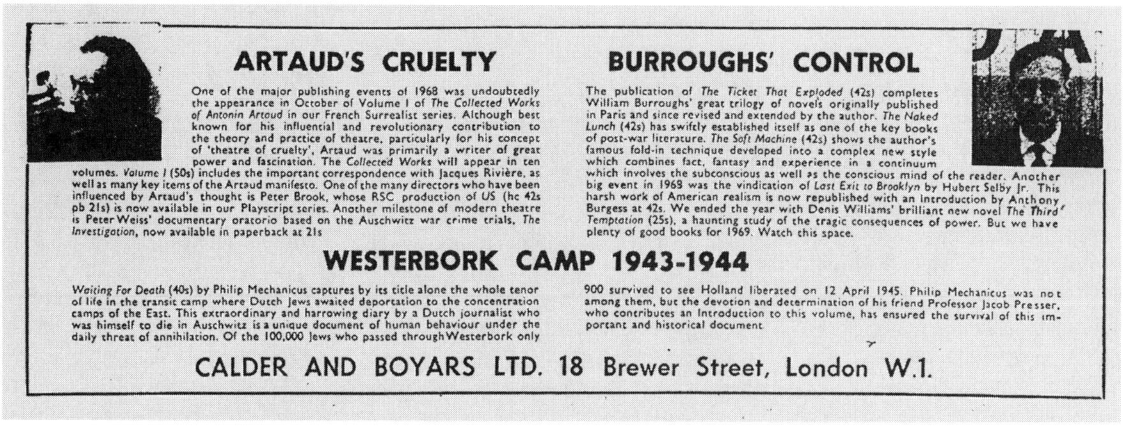

Advertisement for Burroughs's The Ticket That Exploded *in* New Statesman, *10 January 1969*

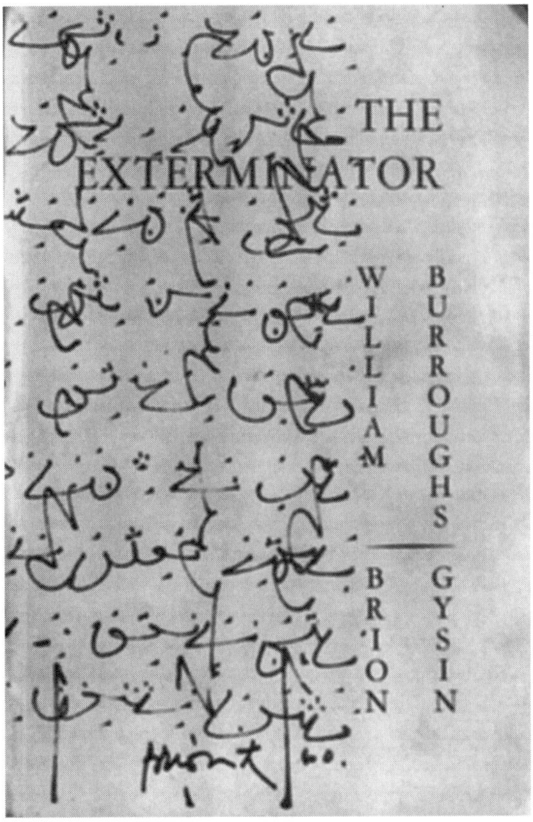

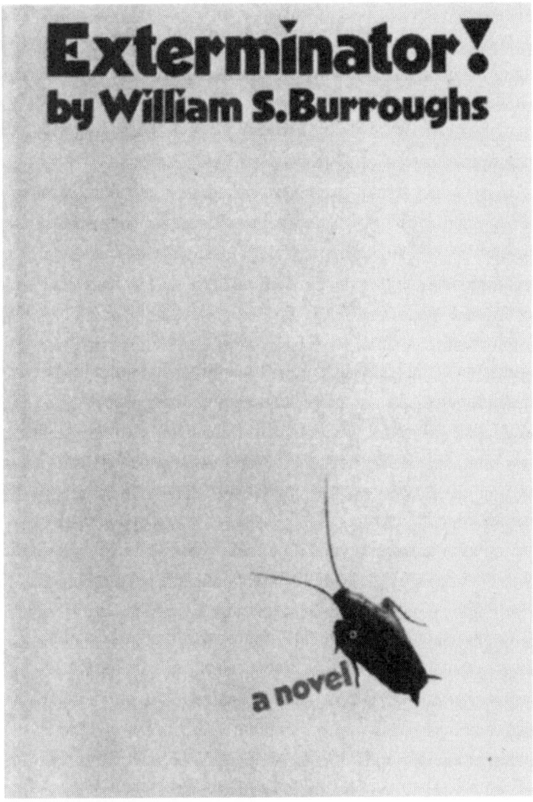

Burroughs's 1960 collection of early cut-ups, written with Brion Gysin (Auerhahn Press/Dave Haselwood Books), and his 1973 short-story collection (Viking/Seaver)

Burroughs on the Beat Generation

Many critics assert that Burroughs would have been exactly the writer he was whether or not there had been a Beat Generation, and that the influence of the other Beat writers on him was minimal. Bruce Cook in The Beat Generation *addresses this issue.*

William S. Burroughs, I'm sure, would argue against his inclusion here. For one thing he has iterated and reiterated in all his interviews, literary and otherwise, is that he does not wish to be considered a Beat writer. By now it seems to come from him almost in the once familiar rote style of congressional committee testimony: I am not now, nor have I ever been, a member of the Beat Generation. The accused pleads not guilty.

Here, for instance, is how he put it to the French writer Daniel Odier in *The Job,* a book length series of Burroughs interviews conducted over a period of months. At a point early in their sessions, M. Odier asked him about his relation to the Beat movement, and Burroughs replied: "I don't associate myself with it at all, and never have, either with their objectives or their literary style. I have some close personal friends among the Beat movement: Jack Kerouac and Allen Ginsberg and Gregory Corso are all close personal friends of many years standing, but were not doing at all the same thing either in writing or in outlook. You couldn't really find four writers more different, more distinctive. It's simply a matter of juxtaposition rather than any actual association of literary styles or overall objectives. . . ."

–p. 165

The following interview with Burroughs, conducted by John Tytell, was recorded in Burroughs's New York City loft on 24 March 1974.

JT: In 1950 you were studying in Mexico City College. What kind of school was that?

'Exterminator!'

'You need the service'

During the war I worked for A.J.Cohen Exterminators ground floor office dead end street by the river.An old Jew with cold grey fish eyes and a cigar was the oldest of four brothers.Marv was the youngest wore wind breakers had three kids.There was a smooth well ~~######~~ dressed college trained brother.The fourth brother burly and muscular looked like an old time hoofer could bellow a leather lunged 'Mammy' and you hope he won't do it.Every night at closing time these two brothers would get in a heated argument from nowhere I could see the older brother would take the cigar out of his mouth and move across the floor with short sliding steps advancing on the vaudeville brother

"You vant I should spit right in your face!? You vant!?You vant?! You vant!?"

The vaudeville brother would retreat shadow boxing presences invisible to my Goyish eyes which I took to be potent Jewish Mammas conjured up by the elder brother.On many occasions I witnessed this ritual open mouthed hoping the old cigar would let fly one day but he never did.A few minutes later they would be talking quietly and and checking the work slips as the exterminators fell in.

On the other hand the old brother never argued with his exterminators. "That's why I have a cigar." he said the cigar being for him a source of magical calm.

I used my own car a black Ford V8 and worked alone carrying my bed bug spray ~~pyrithium~~ powder bellows and bulbs of flouride up and down stairs

"Exterminator! You need the service?" pyrethrum is correct

A fat smiling Chinese rationed out the ~~pyrithium~~ powder-it was hard to get during the war-and cautioned us to use flouride whenever possible.Personally I prefer a ~~pyrithium~~ job to a flouride.With the pyrithium you kill the roaches right there in front of God and the client whereas this starch and flouride you leave it around and back a few days later a Southern defense worker told me "They eat it and run around here fat as hawgs."

From a great distance I see a cool remote naborhood blue windy day in April sun cold on your exterminator there climbing the grey wooden outside stairs

"Exterminator lady.You need the service?"

"Well come in young man and have a cup of tea.That wind has a bite to it."

"It does that,mam,cuts me like a knife and I'm not well you know/ cough/"

"You put me in mind of my brother Michael Fenny."

"He passed away?"

"It was a long time ago April day like this sun cold on a thin boy with freckles through that door like yourself.I made him a cup of hot tea.When I brought it to him he was gone." she gestured to the empty blue sky "cold tea sitting right where you are sitting now."

I decide this old witch deserves a ~~pyrithium~~ job no matter what the

pyrethrum

Burroughs's first typescript pages for Exterminator! *(1973) and corresponding pages from a later revision (Arizona State University)*

(2)

fat Chinese allows.I lean foreward discretely
"Is it roaches Mrs Murphy?"
"It is that from those Jews downstairs."
"Or is it the Hunkys next door Mrs Murphy?"
She shrugs "Sure and an Irish cock roach is as bad as another."
"You make a nice cup of tea Mrs Murphy...Sure I'll be taking
care of your roaches...Oh don't be telling me where they are...
You see I know Mrs Murphy...experienced along these lines...
And I don't mind telling you Mrs Murphy I like my work and take
pride in it."
"Well the city exterminating people were around and left
some white powder draws roaches the way whiskey will draw a
priest."
"They are a cheap outfit Mrs Murphy.What they left was flouride.
the roaches build up a tolerance and become addicted.They can be
dangerous if the flouride is suddenly withdrawn...Ah just here it
is..."
I have spotted a brown crack by the kitchen sink put my bellows
in and blow a load of the precious yellow powder.As if they had
heard the last trumpet the roaches stream out and flop in convulsions
on the floor.
"Well I never!" says Mrs Murphy and turns me back as I advance for
coup de grace..."Don't shoot them again.Just let them die."
When it is all over she sweeps up a dust pan full of roaches into
the wood stove and makes me another cup of tea.
When it comes to bed bugs there is a board of health regulation
against spraying beds and that of course is just where the bugs
are in most cases now an old wood house with bed bugs back in the
wood for generations only thing is to fumigate...So here is Mamma
with a glass of sweet wine here beds back and ready...
I look at her over the syrupy red wine..."Lady we don't spray no
beds.Board of health regulations you know."
"Ach so the wine is not enough?"
She comes back with a crumpled dollar.So I go to work...bed bugs
great red clusters of them in the ticking of the mattresses.I mix
a little formaldehyde with my kerosene in the spray its more sanitary that way and if you tangle with some pimp in one of the Negroe
whore house we service a face full of formaldehyde keeps the boy in
line.
Now you'll often find these old Jewish grandmas in a back room like
their bugs and we have to force the door with the younger generation
smooth college trained Jew there could turn into a narcotics agent
while you wait.
"All right grandma,open up! The exterminator is here."
She is screaming in Yiddish no bugs are there we force our way in
I turn the bed back...my God thousands of them fat and red with
grandma and when I put the spray to them she moans like the Gestapo
is murdering her nubile daughter engaged to a dentist.
And there are whole backward families with bed bugs don't want to
let the exterminator in.
"We'll slap a board of health summons on them is we have to" said
the college trained brother..."I'll go along with you on this one.
Get in the car."

W.S.B.

'Exterminator!'

During the war I workedfor A.J.Cohen Exterminators ###### firs floor office daed end street by the river.An old Jew with cold grey fish eyes and a cigar was the oldest of four brothers.Mrv was the youngest wore wind breakers had three kids.There was a smooth well dressed college trained brother.The fourth brother burly and muscular looked like an old time hoofer vould bellow a leather lunged 'Mammy' andyou hope he wont do it.Every night at closing time the two brothers would get in a heated argument from nowhere I could see andthe older brother would take the cigar out of his mouth and move acorss the floor with short sliding steps advancing on the vaudeville brother.

'You vant I should spit right in your face!? You vant! You vant! you vant!'

The vaudeville brother would retreat shadow boxing ######## presences invisble to my goyish eyes which I took to be potent Jewish Mammas cojured up by the elder brother.On# many occasions I witnesses this ritual open mouths hoping the old cigar would let fly one day but he never did.Ten minuteslater they would be talking quietly nd checking the slips as the exterminators checked in.

On theother hand the old Jew never argued with his exterminators

'TahT's why I have a cigar' he said the cigar being for him a source of magical calm.

I had my own car a black V8 Ford and workedalone carrying my bedbug spray and pyrithium bellows and bulbs of flouride up and down stairs

'Exterminator! You nee d the service?'

A fat Chinese rationed out the pyrithium powder it was hard to get during the war and c autionedus to use flouride whenever possible.Now personally I prefer a pyrithium job to a flouride.With the pyrithium you kill the roaches right there in front of God and everybody whereas this flouride and starch you leave it around and back a few days later a Southern defense worker told me "They eat it andrun around here fat as hawgs."

From a great distance I see a cool remote naborhood blue windy day in April sun cold on your exterminator there climbing the grey wooden outside stairs

'Exterminator lady.You neeed the service?'

'Well come in young man and have a cup of tea that wind has a bite to it.'

'It doesthat,mam cut me like a knife and I'm not well you know/cough/'

'You put me in mind of my brother Michael Kenny.'

'He passed away?'

It was a long time ago April day like this sun cold on a thin boy with freckles through that door like yourself.I made him a nice cup of tea. When I brought it to him he was gone' the gesterued to the empty blue sky 'cold tea sitting right where you are sitting now.'

I decide this old witch deserves a pyrithium job no matter what the fat Chinese allow.I leaned foreward discretely 'Is it roaches Mrs Murphy?'

'It is that from those Jews downstairs.'

'Or is it the Hunkys next door Mrs Murphy?'

She shrugged 'Sure an an Irish cock roach is as bad as another.'

'You make a nice cup of tea Mrs Murphy..Sure I'll be taking car of your roaches..Oh don't be telling me where they are you see I *know* Mrs Murphy..exprelenced along these lines and I dont mind telling you Mrs Murphy I *like* my work and take pride in it.'

'Well the ciyt exterminating people were arund and left some white powder draw roaches the way whisky will draw a priest.'

'They are a cheap outifit,Mrs Murphy.What they left was flouride. The roaches build up a tolerance am become ####### addicts.They can be g dangerous if the flouride is suddenly withdrawn..ah just here it is...'

Revision of Exterminator! *(cont.)*

I had spotted a brown hole by the kitchen sink put my bellow in and
blew a load of the precious yellow powder.As if they had heard the
last trumpet r the oraches streamed out andflopped in covulsions on
the floor
'Well I never' said Mrs Murphy and turned me back as I advanced for the
coup de grace. 'Dont shoot them again .Just let them die.'
When it was all over she sweeps up a dustpan full into the wood stove
When it camesto bed bugs there is baord of health ruling we spray no
beds and that of course was just #### where the bugs were in most cases
now an old wood house with bed bugs back in the wood for generations
only thing is to fumiage so here is Mamma with a glass of sweet wine
her beds back and ready
Lady we dont spray no beds..Board of heatlth regulations you know.'
"Ach so the wine is not enough."
She gets up with a sigh and comes back with a crumpled dollar.I go to
work bed bugs great red clusters of them in the ticking of the mattresses.
I mix a little formaldeyde with my kerosene in the spray its more d
sanitary that way and if you tangle with some pimp in one of the Negroe
whore house wwe service a face full of formaldeyde keeps the boy in
line.
Now you'll often find these old Jewish grandmas in a back rrom like
their bugs and we have to force the door with the younger generation
smooth college trained Jew there could turn into a narcotics agent while
you wait.
AL- right grandma open up! the exterminator is here!
She is screaming in Yiddish no busg are there we force out way in and
when I trun the bed back my God thousam s of them fat and red with
grandma when I put the spray to them she moans as if the Gestapo was
murdering her nubile daughter engaged to a dentist.And there are whole
backward families with bed bugs dont want to let the exterminator in.
'The captain at the front...this bug killing f f shit bird wants to
make time with his wife...You like it? I dont.'
So play it cool back to the home office. Every now and again the boss
assembles the ~~o##########XXXXXXXXXXXXXXXXXXXXXXXXXXXX~~ his staf and
eats arsenic been in that ioffice breathing thepowder in so long the
arsenic just brings an embalmers flush to his grey cheek.And he has a
pet rat he knocked all its teeth out feeds it on milk the rat is now
very tame an affectionate.
'Exterminator!' echos through grey basements autumn chill in the ashes
up the outsidw wooden stiars
!'Exterminator! down cobble stone streets through the grey cafeteria
basements up the outsi wooden stairs to a windy blue sky..
precarious streets of yesterday echo to the call...Exterminator.'

William S. Burroughs

Burroughs, Ginsberg, and Huncke in the kitchen of the Bunker, Burroughs's New York apartment, in 1979

WB: It was organized for people on the G.I. bill and classes were in English. I studied archeology, mostly Mexican, and Mayan and Aztec. Aztec is very difficult, Mayan very easy.

JT: Where did you do your undergraduate work? WB: 1936. Harvard. English lit.

JT: Did you take any courses in modern literature?

WB: Not formally.

JT: Did you read Joyce or Eliot then?

WB: Eliot was there as a visiting professor. I went to one of his lectures, he gave lectures and seminars. Eliot was very much something that people were into at that time.

JT: What modern writers most moved you at that time?

WB: I wasn't really in modern literature, but Eliot, Joyce, Kafka, Fitzgerald, of course.

JT: But not at the box office.

WB: I'm not even sure of that. Generally speaking they know what they're doing, but they don't always. They will go all out on these spectaculars that don't work at all. I was just looking the book over myself with an idea of making a film, and there just is no film there–everything's in the prose, you take that away and you've got wooden dialogue and creaky action.

JT: The prose does have an elusive quality so that it appears easy, but underneath the surface is that astonishingly intricate imagery and richness. I think you are right, this will just be a stageshow

WB: It isn't cinematic.

JT: What did you do after you left Harvard? I'd like to establish a chronology.

WB: A year in Europe studying medicine at the University of Vienna. After that I returned to America and studied psychology briefly at Columbia, then back at Harvard doing graduate work in anthropology. Then a year in New York with an advertising agency. In the army briefly, out again, Chicago where I worked as an exterminator and at various other jobs. Back to New York in 1943. Left in about '46 for Texas, then New Orleans.

JT: When did you leave for Mexico?

WB: 1949. I stayed in Mexico until 1952, South America in 1953, back in New York in 1953. Then I went to Europe, first to Italy and then Tangiers from about 1954 to 1958. Then Paris. Then between Paris and London during the early sixties. In 1964 I was in Tangiers, in 1965 I was here for a year, and from then on mostly in London.

JT: I would like to ask you specific questions about certain of these years. When you were in New York 1943, where did you live?

WB: Uptown, downtown, all over, around the Village, Columbia.

JT: I heard that you worked as a bartender.

WB: For about three weeks on Bedford Street.

JT: It was at that time that you first met Kerouac and Ginsberg. Ann Charters says that Dave Kammarer introduced you. Where had you known Kammarer?

WB: St. Louis: we were brought up together. I'd known him all my life.

JT: I heard that when you first visited Kerouac you were interested in learning how to get seaman's papers?

WB: Vaguely. I did get seaman's papers years later but never used item.

JT: I read in your correspondence that you did what might be termed a "lay analysis" or psychoanalysis of Allen Ginsberg? What was that like?

WB: That's true. It was a very sketchy procedure.

JT: Had you been analyzed?

WB: Oh yes. Waste of time and money.

JT: How did Allen take your analysis?

WB: Well, now he was interested–people like to talk about themselves.

JT: At one time did you share an apartment with Edie Parker, Joan Adams and Kerouac?

WB: Yes. It was a big apartment and I had a room there for about four or five months in '44.

JT: Do you feel that in any way you influenced Kerouac and Ginsberg at that time?

WB: Influenced in what way?

JT: You've written that certain figures leave their impression in terms of speech and language.

WB: Well I should say that Kerouac influenced me much more than I influenced him because I wasn't at all interested in writing at that time, and he was one of several people who told me that I should write. The title of *Naked Lunch* was his, not mine.

JT: Kerouac would later type portions of that novel for you in Tangiers.

WB: That was many years later.

JT: I wanted to ask how that book finally came together, and what role others may have had in helping you assemble it.

WB: One of the key figures was Sinclair Beiles who was working for [Maurice] Girodias at that time. Girodias had seen the novel, not the version that finally appeared but a version that I had before, remember that there were about a thousand pages to this from which the final material was selected, and some of the overflow went into *The Soft Machine, The Ticket That Exploded, Nova Express* and some of it is still unpublished, and in the archives.

JT: Was any of the original material part of *Queer*?

WB: No. That was a separate thing and way back.

JT: Carl Solomon told me of reading it and feeling that it wasn't the right time to bring it out.

WB: Ace had no intention of bringing it out. Wyn said I'd be in jail if it was published. But it has very little to do with the subsequent material from which *Naked Lunch* was assembled.

JT: How did you first meet Huncke?

WB: Through Bob Brandenberg who was a sort of marginal hoodlum who used to hang around the West End in 1944.

JT: Huncke told me the story about the morphine syrettes and was it a sawed of shotgun or a pistol?

WB: No, it was a sub-machine gun.

JT: But that's a fairly large weapon?

WB: This guy stole it and carried it out under his coat.

JT: Was it an army weapon?

WB: Yes. He had smuggled this thing out and nobody wanted to touch it. I finally sort of gave it away to somebody.

JT: Could one get ammunition for that?

WB: Sure, standard 45.

JT: Huncke told me that you maintained an apartment on Henry Street on the lower East Side then.

WB: That's right, I had that apartment for fifteen dollars a month. A walk-in kitchen and a few small rooms.

JT: How did you start with morphine?

WB: Well the syrettes were the beginning. I met this guy named Phil White who bought some of the syrettes from me, and he turned me onto the morphine. Then I started going around with him to doctors.

JT: Getting script, as you call it in *Junkie*. When had opium become illegal?

WB: Since the Harrison Narcotics Act around 1914. But you could still get preparations like paregoric.

JT: Was Huncke a new kind of person for you to have met, or had you met people like him before?

WB: No, I'd not met anyone like Huncke before.

JT: What attracted you to him?

WB: Well, you know, he had some interesting stories. Also, he was associated with Phil White and we would get junk together.

JT: Didn't Huncke introduce you to Bill Garver?

WB: He did. He had been in jail, and then he brought Garver around to Joan's apartment.

JT: Garver was a notorious coat-thief, wasn't he?

WB: That's true. He also had a small income of twenty-five dollars a week from his father which was not enough for his habit. So he had to supplement that by stealing overcoats. When his father died, he came into about three to four hundred dollars a month, that's when he moved to Mexico. Later we lived in the same building. He is Bill Gains in *Junkie.*

JT: Huncke told me that he introduced you to Dr. Kinsey when Kinsey began his research around Times Square.

WB: He did indeed. Kinsey and Ward Pomeroy. We met at a place called The Angler, that was on Eighth Avenue between 42nd and 43rd.

JT: Did Kinsey interview you?

WB: No, Pomeroy did.

JT: Did you know Bill Cannastra?

WB: I never met him. I heard a lot about him from Allen Ginsberg, but more particularly from Allen Ansen.

JT: I asked you earlier whether you thought you had in any way influenced Ginsberg or Kerouac, and you said that Kerouac had influenced you more, because he made you aware of writing, but Allen Ginsberg told me that one way that you definitely influenced both of them was with books that you suggested that they read, that he had no introduction to modern literature and that you gave him Hart Crane and Auden and Eliot and other books, Kafka, that you gave Kerouac Spengler.

WB: And perhaps Celine.

JT: Were you reading Wilhelm Reich at the time?

WB: Either then or later.

JT: What about Lucien Carr? Was he part of your circle then?

WB: Yes. I'd known Lucien from St. Louis, introduced to him by David Kammarer. I saw Lucien subsequently in Chicago when I was there.

JT: Did you meet frequently with Kerouac, Ginsberg, Carr, or were your encounters sporadic?

WB: Sporadic. I saw a lot of Dave because I had known him for a long time and he lived right around the corner on Morton Street when I lived in the Village. The others lived uptown, and I saw more of them when I moved there.

JT: When you shared the apartment with Ginsberg, Joan Adams and Edie Parker?

WB: That's right. Edie Parker who married Jack Kerouac.

JT: After Jack had been apprehended as an accessory to Carr's murder of Kammarer?

WB: Not as an accessory but a material witness.

JT: How did that happen? I've heard so many different versions, and that Kammarer had been Carr's scoutmaster.

WB: There was some such connection. Then they took a trip to Mexico, and there was trouble between Kammarer and Lucien's mother.

JT: I read in your correspondence that you and Kerouac wrote a novel based on the friendship and subsequent murder.

WB: We did write such a novel—*The Hippoes Were Boiled In Their Tank.*

JT: How did you get that title?

WB: It was in a news broadcast about a circus fire, so we used that.

JT: Is the book in your archives?

WB: No, we can't get hold of it. It's with Sterling Lord. Richard Aaron was supposed to come over here to try and recover it.

JT: What led you to leave New York?

WB: Well, there was a definite likelihood of legal difficulties. When I left I went to Texas.

JT: That's when you began farming?

WB: No, it wasn't. I forgot, I first left, and then I came back to New York, and then left again, so it was two times that I left.

JT: Huncke told me that after the New Waverly scene you, Neal Cassady and Huncke returned to New York in a jeep from New Waverly.

WB: That was later.

JT: From reading your letters I could tell that you were hassled by bureaucrats at the time you were farming, or at least that you resented their controls a great deal.

WB: Well, there were cotton allotments and all kinds of rules. We were okay on that, but not always, and then there was a matter of loans that had to be negotiated. It's really no operation for people who are operating with small capital. If anything goes wrong you're wiped out.

JT: So you're totally at the mercy of credit?

WB: Completely.

JT: In the letters you describe that the relativity of the law had never been clearer to you because of your experience with farming. In particular because of the wetbacks, the way they would be encouraged to come in by the state and at the same time there could be penalties, selectively applied.

WB: Very selectively applied. You got in wrong with the authorities and a truck would drive up and take all your wetbacks away, and you'd be left in cotton picking season with no help.

JT: At the same time, any wetback would be earning five times what he could get in Mexico.

WB: But this didn't happen to the big farmers.

JT: Because they had protection?

WB: Yes. In the big ranches the wetbacks were herded all over the place. They had guards with machine guns. They tried to pull a strike once and the guards shot three of them, so they all went back to work. They had no rights.

JT: In New Waverly you also grew grass? Were you farming anything else?

WB: Couldn't farm anything else.

JT: Was the soil bad?

WB: The problem was how were you going to farm, what with? I mean you could get a horse and plow and do subsistence farming.

JT: Cassady and Ginsberg visited you in New Waverly? What was your impression of Cassady?

WB: I thought he was a very pleasant, easy-going person.

JT: I've heard that he was very intense, capable of long monologues. Was that true then?

WB: I always felt his capacity for silence. I've been with him for eight hours and never exchanged a word.

JT: What kind of driver was he?

WB: Brilliant, a fantastic driver. I had a jeep and the clutch and brakes were out, and he could brake it by putting it into reverse.

JT: I heard that he drove Kesey's bus at high speeds around curves knowing somehow that there was nothing coming the other way.

WB: He was capable of unbelievable feats of instant calculation.

JT: How did you spend your days in New Waverly? Were you writing at that time?

WB: No, no, no. I didn't write anything, hardly, until I was thirty-five. Anyway I wasn't writing. But there were always things to do, like put a fence around the place, cut wood, walk around.

JT: Was the country beautiful?

WB: It was heavy timber. Oak and persimmon, not too much pine. The kind of country that starts in southern Missouri and goes all the way down to east Texas. There were racoons and foxes and squirrels and armadilloes.

JT: What led you to invite Huncke to the New Waverly place?

WB: I don't remember.

JT: How long was he there?

WB: Quite a while, four or five months.

JT: Did Kerouac visit you there?

WB: No, he didn't.

JT: He visited you on several other occasions, though?

WB: He lived with me in New Orleans, then later in Mexico.

JT: Had he written *The Town and the City* then?

WB: Yes.

JT: Had you seen any of it? Did you know you were a character in it?

WB: I hadn't seen any of it at that time, but he told me I appeared in it.

JT: What was his mood like then?

WB: It was very good.

JT: In one of the letters you mention that on a later visit in Mexico, I think in 1952, he was depressed, uncooperative and unhappy.

WB: He was moody and a little bit paranoid.

JT: Do you think the difficulty he was having getting *On The Road* accepted had anything to do with his attitude?

WB: Possibly. But then he seemed to take that rather philosophically. The book was literally years kicking around. Malcolm Cowley liked it, but the editor-in-chief didn't at all, and so there were all those delays which might have been just as well because the timing of the book was good, had it been published earlier, it might not have received the same attention.

JT: That's an interesting point. And he did a lot of writing during the six years between finishing *On The Road* and its publication in 1957.

WB: Oh yes. He was always writing.

JT: Can you tell me more about the history of *Naked Lunch*?

WB: I had this great amorphous manuscript. Girodias had seen some of it and had rejected it. I was in Paris. This was 1958. Allen Ginsberg was also there and he sent selections off to Irving Rosenthal for *The Chicago Review,* and then *The Chicago Review* folded in protest after having difficulty with the university over the issue because of my material and something by Kerouac as well, and then Rosenthal published it in *Big Table*. That was what called it to Girodias' attention. He saw *Big Table* and said now I want the book. So he sent Sinclair Beiles over to my room who said Girodias wants to publish the book, and he wants it in two weeks. So I got busy, and Brion Gysin helped with typing—Allen had gone—and Sinclair Beiles was most helpful. I was just typing it out and giving it to Beiles with the idea that when we got galley proofs I could decide the final order. But he took one look at it and said leave it the way it is.

So it was just really an accidental juxtaposition. And the book was out a month later.

JT: That's a kind of "automatic" structuring–without any wilfull control. How does that approach Kerouac's ideal of spontaneity?

WB: Kerouac was not thinking of an accidental procedure but of spontaneity in writing. He was always very opposed to writing with "cut-ups" which is, in a sense, an accidental procedure. Kerouac believed the first version was the best, and I have never found this to be true. I work over things and edit them very carefully.

JT: When Girodias took *Naked Lunch* you were living at the "Beat hotel," 9 Rue Git le Couer?

WB: And Olympia Press was around the corner. Girodias had inherited the press from his father, it was then called The Dial Press, and they had originally come from Manchester. Girodias' brother later translated *Naked Lunch* into French, and Gallimard took it a year after it had been published in English.

JT: Wasn't there an obscenity trial in the States?

WB: Two, the first was in Boston where we won on appeal, then in Los Angeles we won in the lower courts. By that time it was pretty well established that there was no censorship on the written word.

JT: Has Henry Miller been a writer who in any way influenced you?

WB: No.

JT: Had you read de Sade?

WB: I looked at de Sade when I was in Paris. Girodias had some translations, but I found it heavy going.

JT: Did you have any interest in Gertrude Stein when you were at Harvard?

WB: I read *Three Lives* there.

JT: Later, did Brion Gysin try to interest you in her work?

WB: No, but he knew her. She was the one who told Paul Bowles that he shouldn't stay in Paris but should find some other place.

JT: What were your lodgings like at 9 Rue Git le Couer?

WB: A single room. I had an alcohol stove in the room. There was no phone, but I had red tile floors. It was very cheap.

JT: Judging from the letters, Ginsberg, Kerouac, everyone sees to have stayed there.

WB: At different times.

JT: Where was the Villa Delirium?

WB: That was the Muniria in Tangiers where I lived for a number of years.

JT: I read in your letters that when you first went to Tangiers you lived in a whorehouse. What was that like? Faulkner once said in an interview that a whorehouse was the ideal place for a writer to live.

WB: It was not that kind of a whorehouse at all. It was just a small place where Tony Dutch who ran it rented out rooms. Tony was a great cook and if you wanted to take meals there you could. After that I moved into the Muniria where I stayed off and on for many years. It's changed hands many times. First it was owned by a Belgian whose son was involved with smuggling, then it was run by an ex-madam from Indochina. She had an "in" with the authorities and ran it for many years without trouble. She sold out and a retired British civil servant took it over.

JT: I have some other miscellaneous questions. What about the story that your first wife was a Hungarian countess?

WB: She wasn't. Her name was Ilse Herzfeld Klapper, they were solid, wealthy bourgeois Jewish people in Hamburg. She had to get out because of Hitler and went to Yugoslavia, and I married her in Athens to get her into the States. She supported herself by working in a travel agency and various jobs. She was very efficient. She was secretary for Ernst Toller, a leftist playwright who tried to commit suicide several

Burroughs in 1975 (photograph by Louis Cartwright)

times. But he always arranged it so that someone wold come and prevent him. And she was a very punctual person. If she went to lunch at twelve she would be back at twelve-thirty. It just so happened that she ran into an old acquaintance in the street and was ten minutes late, and when she returned he was dead in the bathroom. At his funeral she met Kurt Kaszner, a famous Austrian actor who had married a very rich American girl. She became his secretary. Then Mrs. Kaszner died, and the servants said he had poisoned her and she was dug up again, but there was nothing in it, she died of natural causes. Then she worked for John le Touche as his secretary until he died under mysterious circumstances.

JT: I've heard that you had applied to the O.S.S. during the war?

WB: I did and was not accepted. I went down and saw Bill Donovan with a letter of introduction from an uncle, but he referred me to somebody else and nothing happened.

JT: You mentioned that you were in the army?

WB: For a short time, five months. I was stationed in St. Louis.

JT: When was that?

WB: During the war, in 1942 I think.

JT: Do you record your dreams?

WB: I write them down.

JT: How do you do it?

WB: I wake up six times in the course of the average night. I'll just make a few notes. If it's of interest, I transcribe it in the morning. I get at least half, perhaps more, of my material from dreams, characters, sets, etc.

JT: Can you tell me about the Dutch Schultz filmscript?

WB: I had been interested in Dutch Schultz for a long time, having read his famous last words. There were about 2,000 of them since he was shot on October 23rd at 10 P.M. and he died about 24 hours later, and they had a police stenographer at his bedside. Anyway, he presumably wrote all his words down, though he was delirious and the stenographer may have missed words. Then David Budd came over with quite a bit of research material, that is to say, a series of articles that had appeared in *Collier's* by his lawyer, Dixie Davis. I became interested and wrote a film treatment which was about fifteen pages, this was published in *Harper's.* Then someone named Harrison Starr wanted to produce this as a movie so he paid a sum of money–ten thousand dollars or something like that–for me to write a film play which I wrote, and that was published by Grolier Press as *The Last Words of Dutch Schultz.* There were other negotiations and I went on to write a full length film script, a shooting script in 1971.

JT: Wasn't part of *Naked Lunch* written like that, as a film script?

WB: No, in play form, but I'm talking about a shooting script, like indoors, medium shot, or close-up. So that was 195 pages. Richard Seaver is publishing that with a lot of stills. But the film was never made.

JT: How come?

WB: Well, the people were interested, but it was expensive, all gangster films are expensive to make.

JT: Is anyone trying to film *Naked Lunch?*

WB: Brion Gysin did a script, but it seems to be up in the air.

JT: Years ago you said you were writing a Zen western novel about a gunfighter.

WB: I never actually wrote it.

JT: Can you tell me about Kells Elvins?

WB: I met him at the age of twelve at John Burroughs school. He was at Harvard in 1938 when we wrote the story called "Twilights Last Gleaming" which was published almost verbatim in *Nova Express.* That story was the beginning of Dr. Benway.

JT: What was the John Burroughs school?

WB: Just a private day school in Clayton, Missouri. We moved out to Clayton which was a suburb of St. Louis, the school was right down the road and Kells lived up the road.

JT: So you knew him since childhood.

WB: And I wrote to him in 1961 saying that the story would appear in *Nova Express* which does mention that he is the co-author, and found out from his mother that he had died about four months before that.

JT: In your last books you seem to be using cut-ups more selectively than previously.

WB: I use them very selectively now. You see *Minutes To Go* was experimental, now I may make a cut-up of a page and only use a sentence or two.

JT: They seem to be more deliberately used in *The Wild Boys,* and the result is greater impact jarring you into a dream or different reality.

WB: Just cut-up something, and suddenly you'll get a sentence that's right. Like the technology of writing that I'm going into in this course. This sentence came out of a cut-up: "Technology requires a why." You have to know what you're doing to figure everything out while you're doing it.

JT: That's an odd word choice, technology rather than technique.

WB: But it's the same thing, technology or technique, it's a way of doing something.

JT: How do you find teaching at CCNY? Have you taught before?

WB: I just gave two lectures at the University of the New World in Switzerland in 1972, I think. I do enjoy teaching at CCNY, I don't know whether my pupils are learning anything, but I'm learning a great deal, and making my own ideas explicit. I'm considering the question of whether there is a technology for writing as there is for learning how to fly, or for learning physics, or engineering. Now how many of those who fly have taken courses in flying, or how many physicists have take courses in physics–well, obviously all of them–but how many writers have taken courses in writing?

JT: You never took courses in writing.

WB: More haven't than have.

JT: One wonders whether it is a craft that can be taught–I can see how you can be helped by a critic sensitive to your own strengths and weaknesses.

WB: Well, following it right through, take learning to fly or physics, you're wasting your time unless you meet certain qualifications. If you're going to be a flier you've got to have coordination, a certain degree of intelligence, or you're wasting your time. Given that, these things can be taught. But given all the qualifications for writing, whatever those may be, like some ability to empathize with other people's minds–well a writer like, Beckett doesn't need that because he's on his own, going inside, so it may not always apply. Another factor may be the physical discipline, spending long hours writing. For example, if you are learning something like skiing or karate, you have to have an instructor, and if you do it and don't do it right your performance is going to decline–this is not true of writing. Writing is learned by writing. Kerouac, when I first met him, had already written a million words, and that was when he was twenty-three. And lots of it was very bad.

JT: There was this early novel called *The Sea Is My Brother.*

WB: He had many different manuscripts, and I read most of it, and thought it was pretty bad. But writers learn from bad writing, but a skier does not learn from bad skiing.

JT: There is a more direct relationship between experience and practical act with writing than most of us imagine. I guess good writers reach a point when they can finally do it, as with Kerouac, when he could become, as it were, spontaneous.

WB: At any rate I've learned about writing and the technology of writing by teaching this course.

JT: Do you plan to write about that?

WB: I'm having all the lectures transcribed. Naturally I have extensive notes, but there's always extemporizing, questions.

JT: Do you have good students?

WB: They are quite a receptive group.

JT: I wanted to tell you that a number of my students seem to be sexually excited by a book like *The Wild Boys,* especially by the association of violence and sexuality, even in *Naked Lunch* they admit to being turned on despite the elements of comedy or parody.

WB: I find that sexual passages are the most difficult to write. I don't mean the pornographic novels, the ones Girodias was publishing, because they're not sexy at all. They're very easy to write. People write them as fast as they can type. That pornographic style derives from *Fanny Hill,* which is about as unsexy as you can get. Actually, most of those books are written by junkies, and they have no sexual feeling for what they are writing.

JT: There are sections of your work that play with pornographic situations very successfully, like "Seeing Red" in *The Wild Boys* where a man comes through customs with a dirty picture that is left undescribed but which causes paroxysms for the officials.

WB: I think description of any sort is difficult, but sexual passages have to be written and rewritten.

JT: Does this have to do with a basic repression we all have, a fear to describe sex?

WB: No, it's just as hard to describe anything. Straight narrative is easy. If I attend to a narrative I can write it almost as fast as I can type.

JT: There seems to be a return to narrative elements in your recent books, *The Wild Boys* and *Exterminator!* You seem to be using experimental devices more sparingly.

WB: With more deliberate intent, I think.

JT: Could you define obscenity in literature?

WB: I don't think it means anything. What they mean is explicit sex scenes, but that's all soft-core now, there's virtually no censorship left on the written word. Where it might occur is if you have something out of the hard-core circuit. There has been some trouble with "Last Tango."

JT: If that's true, will shame and fear be less an agency of control in this society?

WB: Undoubtedly. But of course it is confined to certain areas. I think a very healthy degree of liberation has occurred. You read the Presidential Report in which they said that 50% of people who saw sex on film found that they were sexually freer. Just the impact of seeing people doing these things on the screen makes people realize "Well, why in the hell should anyone worry about it?" If the actor is willing to get up there without any mask on, how can you be ashamed of it?

JT: Michael McClure once wrote that his intention was "to free the word fuck from its chains." Has that happened?

WB: It has: there are no chains there.

JT: And no future possibility of chains?

WB: I doubt it, unless something drastic happens.

JT: You seem, more than most writers, to have been occupied with kinds of scientific inquiry, and this is reflected in your story situations, for example the character in *The Wild Boys* who stores electricity during shock therapy and then releases it through his eyes as a death ray. At the same time, I don't feel that you can be seen as a science fiction writer.

WB: I've talked to a lot of science fiction writers about this. The younger and more progressive ones maintain that the old categories are breaking down, and science fact has overtaken science fiction. In books like *The Terminal Man* the subject is not what's going to happen in three hundred years, but things that can and have been done right now. So the ideas about science fiction are changing as science overtakes it.

JT: Do you read science fiction?

WB: I read *Nog* and liked it.

JT: What about someone like Robbe-Grillet?

WB: Haven't read him. I saw an excellent movie based on his work.

JT: What about Beckett?

WB: Well, yes. I would think of Beckett in the same way as Genet, as a writer that I admire very much. I've read practically everything Genet has written. He's a very great writer and not writing anymore.

JT: You met him in Chicago, didn't you, in 1968?

WB: Genet said there were two things: me and the French language, I've put one into the other et c'est faites. With Beckett I like the early novels best, like *Watt* and *Malone Dies*. Now he's getting too hermetic.

JT: Rather than simply informing us of a vision of the future, as in *The Wild Boys,* I feel the ultimate end of your fiction is a kind of alchemy–magic based on precise and incantatory arrangement of language to create particular effects, such as the violation of western conditioning.

WB: I would say that that was accurate, but I would also say that I am creating a character. And my characters are often a composite: Say I have a dream of a character who looks like this, then I'll find a picture or a person, and then maybe a character in someone else's story. One tries to create a vision of a living being. Of course the beginning of writing, and perhaps all art, was related to the magical. Cave painting, which is the beginning of writing–after all, remember that the written word is an image, we forget this but we don't have a pictorial writing but the written word is an image and painting and writing were originally one and the same. The purpose of those paintings was magical, that is to produce the effect that is depicted.

JT: Is your intention shamanistic, to ward off disaster?

WB: Not necessarily disaster, but certainly to produce effects. For example, all primitive sculpture is magical, but as soon as these things are sold to tourists, they have no vitality. The saying is that painting, writing and sculpture are traditionally magic, and that it is intended to produce certain effects.

JT: Like the sense of transformation implicit in the rate of change in all of your writing?

WB: There is also the question of the actual relations between formal ritual magic and writing. People who are into ritual magic like Aleister Crowley–he may have been a competent black magician but he is not a good writer, in fact he's not readable.

JT: Have you studied magic formally or involved yourself in any kind of cult systems?

WB: Well, the whole content of the Mayan books is obviously magical, but we can't understand very much of it because Bishop Landa burned so much of the writing.

JT: Have you studied any other non-Western procedural maps like *The Book of the Dead?* Or gnostic texts like the *Cabala?*

WB: Not very deeply. I've looked at *The Book of the Dead.* I've read a lot of the literature of magic, but never involved myself very deeply.

JT: Is there any practical accommodation of magic in your work as a writer?

WB: Well, I simply feel that all magic *is* magic. That is if you get a very subtle evocation of the 1920's in Fitzgerald. . . .

JT: Yes. But that's "magic" in a romantic sense, the idea of evoking a memory onto a page and while that's beautiful, I was thinking of weaving a spell.

WB: But "weaving a spell" is magic. Now you've got the kind of magic that newspapers are involved in, people like Luce who were quite consciously capable of creating events. There is a very definite technique for doing that, and some of it is very much like magic–they stick someone full of pins and then show the picture to millions of people and they will get an effect. Do you realize to what extent being on the front cover of *Time* is a kiss of death? The Nobel Prize is another one. Hearst used to say that he didn't write the news, he made it. But that is all negative magic which has very little to do with the writer's work.

–*The Beat Diary,* pp. 35–49

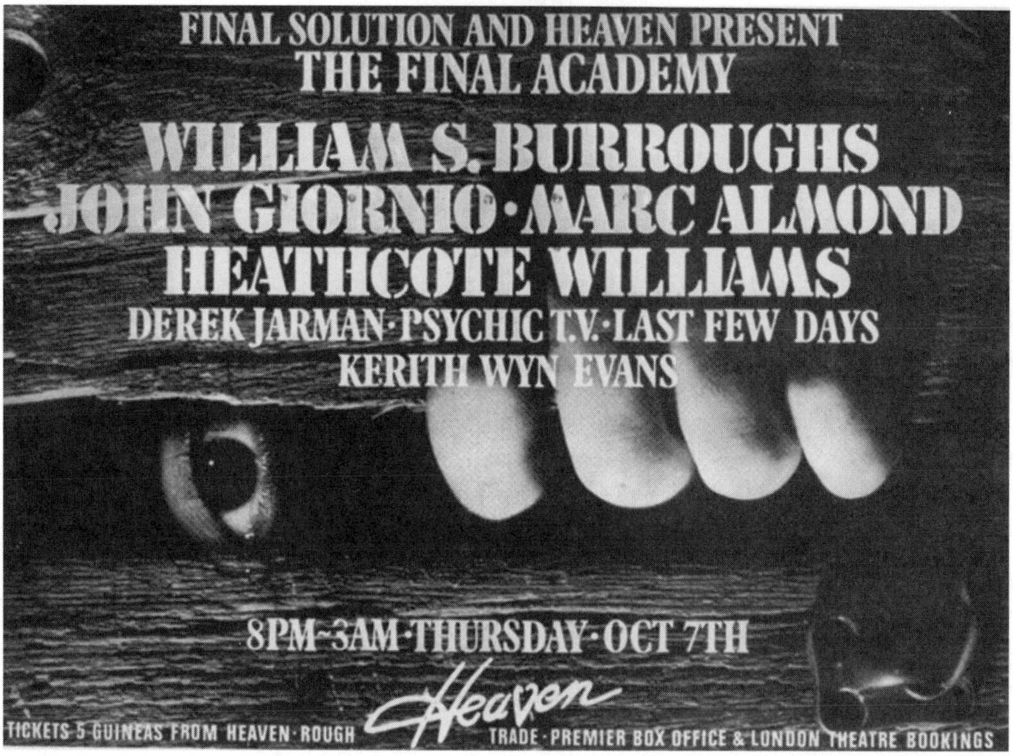

Advertisement for a reading by Burroughs and others in London on 7 October 1982

Ginsberg on Burroughs

Ginsberg commented on Burroughs's exploration of sexuality in an interview published in 1973.

We have the question of what is sex, which William Burroughs has addressed himself to. He's one of the few gay lib "heroes," one of the few homosexual theorists who has theorized up to the point of outside-of-the-body, and detachment from sexuality. In fact, the cut-ups were originally body, and designed to rehearse and repeat his obsession with sexual images over and over again, like a movie repeating over and over and over again, and then re-combined and cut up and mixed in; so that finally the obsessive attachment, compulsion and preoccupation empty out and drain from the image. In other words, rehearsing and repeating it over and over, and looking at it over and over, often enough. Finally, the hypnotic attachment, the image, becomes demystified. . . .

So Burroughs is one of the very few gay liberation minds who is thinking in ultimate philosophical terms about sexuality, about the nature of "apparent sensory phenomena" (that's his phrase). He's one of the few that has actually questioned sex at the root–not merely rebelled from heterosexual conditioning or heterosexual, social/moral fixed formations–to explore love between men as he has experienced it. He's seen it inside and outside, divine and degraded. But also to go beyond that and look at it through the eyes of a Sufi or a Zen master, or a sufud adept Tibetan monk saying, "Ah."

Burroughs has contributed a great deal of space which a new generation hasn't yet caught up with. His style was picked up by younger people. The whole cut-up-collage thing did influence even underground press writing quite a bit. The further philosophical, practical Yankee examination of sensory phenomena perception that Burroughs had gone into still awaits discovery by the gay lib left. Otherwise, you just get into some kind of a funky scene. There are a lot of young kids who carry sex banners and march around saying sex, sex, sex, great, great, great–doing it humorlessly, reacting to just the initial superficial attraction.

–*Gay Sunshine Interview,* pp. 38–39

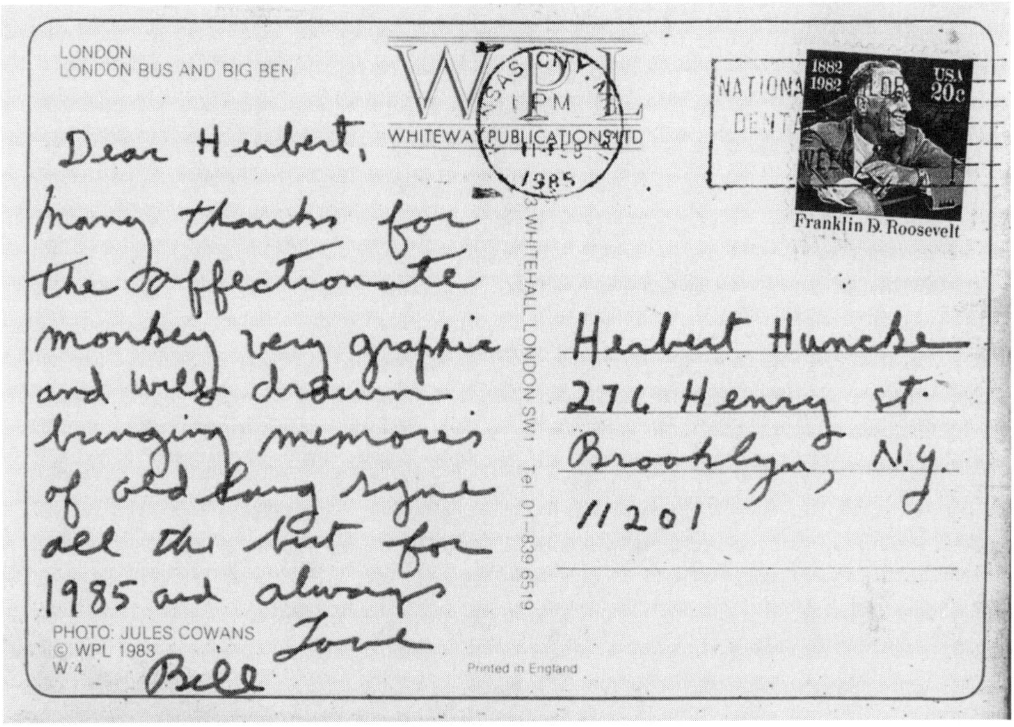
LONDON
LONDON BUS AND BIG BEN
WPL
WHITEWAY PUBLICATIONS LTD

Dear Herbert,
Many thanks for the affectionate monkey very graphic and well drawn bringing memories of old lang syne all the best for 1985 and always
Love
Bill

PHOTO: JULES COWANS
© WPL 1983
W 4
Printed in England
13 WHITEHALL LONDON SW1 Tel 01–839 6519

1882 1982 USA 20c
Franklin D. Roosevelt

Herbert Huncke
276 Henry St.
Brooklyn, N.Y.
11201

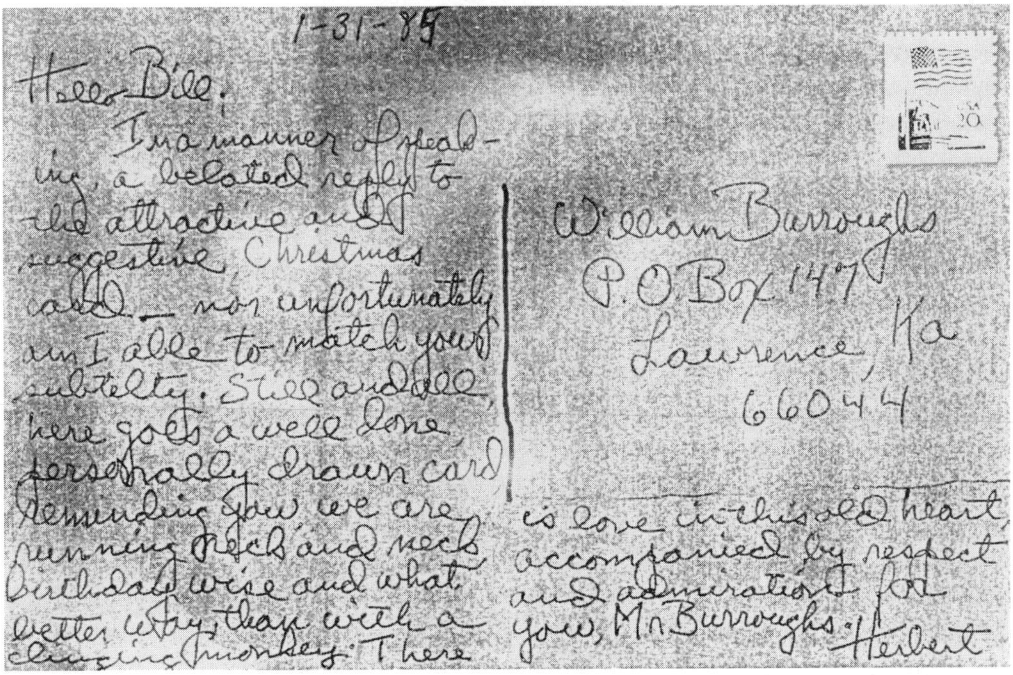
1-31-85

Hello Bill;
In a manner of speaking, a belated reply to the attractive and suggestive Christmas card — nor unfortunately am I able to match your subtelty. Still and all here goes a well done personally drawn card reminding you we are running neck and neck birthdate wise and what better way, than with a clinging monkey. There is love in this old heart, accompanied by respect and admiration for you, Mr Burroughs.
Herbert

William Burroughs
P.O Box 147
Lawrence, Ka
66044

Postcards exchanged by Burroughs and Huncke in 1985

Burroughs's Final Journal Entries

Last Words
William S. Burroughs
New Yorker, 18 August 1997, pp. 36–37

MAY 3, 1997, SATURDAY

The caviar arrived. Now, son, when a man gets on the Beluga Caviar, well there's nothing he won't do to satisfy the Caviar hunger eating at his breadbasket. He'll lie, he'll cheat, he'll even kill for a gob of it. He'll get where he isn't even human anymore. Just a vessel for the vile Russian Trojan whore deploying her deadly cargo.

I can imagine someone bankrupting himself buying best Beluga at twenty-eight dollars an ounce. He comes home one day and his fifteen-year-old daughter and a bunch of teen chums are eating his Beluga and washing great gobs of it down with milkshakes.

"Come on in and join the party, Pop." Holds up an empty jar. "Too late." He would have killed them all had he not dropped down dead for the Timely Want of Caviar.

MAY 5, MONDAY

Allen died April 5, 1997.

Is it not fine to
Dance and Sing
While the bell of
Death do ring?
Turn on the toe
Sing out Hey Nanny
Noo

If I should die think only this of me. That there's some corner of a foreign field that is forever: Tangier; Mexico, D.F.; St. Louis, Mo.; Paris; London; New York City; 202 Sanford Ave., Palm Beach, Fl.; Lawrence, Ks.–and a soupçon of Athens, Albania, Dabrovkirh, and Venice. So why bother? You are old, Father William. Why stand on your head?

Burroughs reading in 1988 (photograph by Greg Dauer)

MAY 12, MONDAY

Remember in the dream that I was young with all life ahead of me in 1890, small town, full of nice folk. Nice ignorant folk. I wasn't in any hurry. Silver dollars jingling in my jeans. Back when a dollar brought a feast of a meal with fresh Walleye, and grouse, and venison, *and a real steak* (not an endangered or extinct species). Washed down with the best French vintage, oh yes, and, of course, best Beluga caviar, to start with ice-cold vodka. Or could buy you a good piecea ass. Any size, race, or color.

So where did we go wrong? Well, I figure the wrongness was always there. "Security the friendly mask of change. At which we smile not seeing what smiles behind" (Edwin Arlington Robinson).

I feel chilly and grown old. I feel like Teiresias, fortnight dead and the waves pick his bones in whispers—the old, old words. So many terrible scenes with—forget it, deactivate it, let it go, it is only in your memory now, remove it. You have the power to do it.

MAY 24, SATURDAY

Great day Wednesday with the ME TOO [U2] Band in Kansas City. I love these public appearances—like an injection of sincere, reciprocal good will.

I'll go right back where
the bullets fly and
stay on the cow
until I die.

Here I crack up laughing. Trying to come up with a really *new* reading would put across who I am and why I am here. I have to do this.

So we start with the big, ugly American lie. Allen Ginsberg, according to George Will, made his career on the dysfunctions of American Society. Allen gnawed a hole in the Lie; his was the Howl heard round the world, from Mexico City to Peking, the Howl of distorted, suffocating youth. Allen's worldwide influence was unprecedented. He, with the courage of his total sincerity, charmed and disarmed the savage Fraternity Beasts.

MAY 25, SUNDAY

All Governments are built on lies. All organizations are built on lies. Lies can be harmless, like the lie of miracle drug, methadone, that is meant to remove the desire for heroin. (Sure, like gin relieves the need for whiskey.) The drug emerged in a fog of lies explained to me by one of the early doctors. "If we had used the word 'morphine,' he said, "we could never have gotten 'official approval.'" Methadone is the first completely successful synthesis of the morphine molecule—three times the strength of morphine by weight. I know. In Tangier I had a two-year habit on injectable—biseptom or whatever name—methadone which was just plain junk.

But it was the only way to get the methadone clinics started.

Who are these anti-drug freaks? Where do they come from for Chrisakes?

"Marijuana decreases short-term memory, interferes with coordination, causes lung cancer. (And rots the brain and moral values.)" Fact: Cannabis is one of the best anti-nausea drugs and increases appetite and general well-being. Also stimulates visual centers in the brain. I have gotten so many excellent images from cannabis. I used nothing else in my salad days and "quelle accomplishments!" (And "What coupling!" as an admiring French critic exclaimed.) A few drags on the green tit and I can see multiple ways out and beyond. So why all this heat on this harmless and rewarding substance?

Who are you to whom truth is so dangerous? What is truth? Something immediately seen as truth. (It may appear only once; it may not be repeatable.) We make truth. Nobody else makes it. There is no truth we don't make. Punch a hole for me. Punch a hole for "magic casements opening on the foam of perilous seas in faery lands forlorn" (Keats).

Allen made holes in the Big Lie not only with his poetry but with his presence, his self-evident spiritual truth. Last words "Two to five months the doctors said," Allen said, "but I think much less." Then he said to me, "I thought I would be terrified, but I am *exhilarated!*" His last words to me. I recall talking on the phone with him *before* the deadly diagnosis and it was there in his voice—remote, weak. I knew then.

Leary was another. I talked to Tim the night of his death. He said: "Why not?"

MAY 26, MONDAY

The search for a final answer—the Holy Grail, Philosophers' stone. A receding mirage. In any case, who wants a final answer? I asked a Japanese physicist: "Do you really want to know the secret of the universe?" He said "Yes." I thought a fraction of that secret would have you climbing the walls. Me, I only want to know what I need to know to do what I need to do. "Just a Tech Sergeant, me."

Do I want to know? I have tried psychoanalysis, Yoga, Alexander's posture method, done a seminar with Robert Monroe, taken journeys out of the body, an est in London, Scientology, sweat lodges, and a Yuwipi ceremony. Looking for the answer? Why? Do you want to know *the secret?* Hell, no. All is in the not done.

Where is the cavalry, the spaceship, the rescue squad? We have been abandoned here on this planet ruled by lying bastards of modest brain power. No sense. Not a tiny modicum of good intentions. Lying worthless bastards.

MAY 30, FLIDAY

A review of life is not an orderly account from conception to death. Rather it's fragments from here and there. A telephone call. A message, my eyeglasses are ready. "You can keep quite comfortable on codeine." A comment, "He looks like a sheep-killing dog." Said about me by Pollet Elvins, Kells's father, who later went nuts with paresis.

MAY 31, SATURDAY

That vile salamander Gingrich, squeaker of the House, is slobbering about a drug-free America by the year 2001. What a dreary prospect! Of course this does not include alcohol and tobacco, of which the consumption will soar. How can a drug-free state be achieved? Simple. An operation can remove the drug receptors from the brain. Those who refuse the operation will be deprived of all rights. Landlords will refuse them housing, restaurants and bars will refuse them service. No passport, no benefits from Social Security, no medical coverage, no right to buy or own a firearm.

How I hate those who are dedicated to producing conformity. For what purpose? Imagine the barren banality of a drug-free America. No dope fiends, just good, clean-living, decent Americans from sea to shining sea. The entire area of dissent exorcised like a boil. No slums. No areas of vague undercover operations. No nothing. There in the pitiless noon streets. No letters.

How good will it be to have total conformity? What will be left of singularity? And personality? And you and me?

JUNE 4, WEDNESDAY

"*J'aime ces types vicieux, qu'ici montrent la bite.*" I like the vicious types who show the cock here. Anonymous, outside pissoir in Paris.

"Is it not fine to dance and sing while the bells of death do ring to turn on toe and sing hey nanny noo." Yes I love life in all its variety but at last the bell ringeth to eventide.

JUNE 6, CLOM FLIDAY

I wonder about the future of the novel or any writing. Where can it go? After Conrad, Rimbaud, Genet, Beckett, Saint-John Perse, Kafka, James Joyce, and–these two in a special category of doing one thing very well–Paul Bowles and Jane Bowles. With Paul there was a sinister darkness like underdeveloped film. With Jane? How do her characters move about, and what motivates them? It's just too special to formulate. What is left to say? Oh, I forgot Graham Greene. "The Power and the Glory." Maybe there was just so much "juice," as Hemingway used to call it, but not quite enough to get him in with Joyce and the selected few. Not quite enough, Pa. He killed himself from vanity and self-inflation and then the balloon ruptured. He knew he was finished. "It just doesn't come anymore." He just wasn't there anymore.

Back to writing–"*revenons à ces moutons.*" Maybe, on the basic level of truth, there just isn't any more to say. Conrad said a lot of it in "Under Western Eyes" and "Lord Jim" and Genet said it on the Spanish coast. I can feel his hunger, going down by the docks where the fisherman might throw him a fish that he then cooked over a brush fire and ate without salt. Why go on? "The tram made a wide U-turn and stopped; it was the end of the line." Paul Bowles at end of "Sheltering Sky." Sky. Sky. I can't even write the word sky. I guess I feel–why go on?

AUGUST 1, FLIDAY

Love? What is it? Most natural painkiller. What there is. LOVE.

Obituary

Burroughs Spun a Legacy of Naked Sense

Steve Silberman

Wired News, 5 August 1997

Net denizens received the news of the death of novelist William Burroughs–the last surviving member of the original beat trinity that also included Jack Kerouac and Allen Ginsberg–as a loss of one of their own, though the 83-year-old author of *Naked Lunch* only saw the Web a handful of times, and didn't have an email address.

In an explosion of tributes on sites like Christopher Ritter's *The Last Words of Doctor Benway,* new-media professionals and casual readers reflected on the uncanny correspondence between Burroughs' 1950s vision of the "Interzone"–a polyglot, polysexual, transnational free-trade zone–and the Internet.

"Burroughs liked to quote *Hassan-I-Sabbah,* the patriarch of the *hashishin,* who said 'Nothing is true, everything is permitted.' That could be the motto of the Web," says Christian Crumlish, the creator of *Enterzone* and editor of *Coffeehouse: Writings from the Web.*

"The Internet *is* an Interzone–a zone where no one's in control," declared Levi Asher, the architect of *Literary Kicks,* a pioneering online beat outpost, and co-editor of *Coffeehouse.* Asher cited the homosexual, heroin-addicted novelist's move to Tangier in 1954–where he penned *Naked Lunch,* his second novel–as an attempt to live "'outside of society,' like Patti Smith says."

A 1965 obscenity trial made *Naked Lunch* a cause célèbre, but Asher's view, "Burroughs never got political about censorship. He understood the game and just wanted to get away from it. . . . Burroughs didn't fight censorship, he *subverted* it. That's similar to the way we deal with it on the Net." (The novel was first judged obscene by Massachusetts Superior Court Judge Eugene Hudson, who asked expert witness Norman Mailer if any of Mailer's own novels involved "sex in the naked sense." Hudson's decision was reversed by the Massachusetts Supreme Court in 1966.)

Many aficionados drew parallels between Burroughs' method of "cut-up"–a strategy for revealing buried significances in texts, developed with painter Brion Gysin–and hypertext.

"Cut-ups," Crumlish says, "evoke the confusion brought about when forging an unguided path through *dense hypertext* works." On Luke Kelly's in-depth *Burroughs Explorer* site, there's a Web-based *"Cut-Up Machine."*

Writer Sean Young agrees, observing that the author's "careening juxtapositions and collisions of ancient references and contemporary references . . . seem to have prophesied a lot of what has happened with language."

Malcolm Humes, who got the first site dedicated to Burroughs' work, *The InterWeb Zone,* up and running on the Web in 1994, sees approaches similar to cut-up operating throughout contemporary culture, especially in the oblique strategies and appropriations employed by musicians such as David Bowie and Brian Eno. "It's a metaphor for creative applications that work in multiple modes of media–visual collage, film montage, audio sampling," Humes explains.

Tim Franklin, who is building the first officially sanctioned *Burroughs outpost* for launch later this year, says one reason the novelist's writings have stayed relevant to new generations of readers is that "the model Burroughs followed in his work wasn't one of linear progression, it was one of expansion. He didn't throw out old ideas, he continually absorbed new ones, so there was a continuity between his thought in the '50s and his thought in the '90s." The official site, says Franklin, will feature essays on topics like chaos magic, the significance of the number 23, and Jack Black's proto-*noir* potboiler, *You Can't Win.*

Crumlish hails Burroughs' oeuvre as "an atlas of freedom of the imagination," calling the novelist "a great liberator" as well as "a great and terrible libertine." An influential online bohemian think-tank called *Antiweb,* Crumlish says, was forged out of dialogs among webmasters influenced by Burroughsian thought.

"Burroughs was no stranger to techno-fetishism. . . . His grandfather invented the adding machine," Crumlish observes. Part of what inspires his peers, says Crumlish, is that Burroughs didn't hesitate to utilize taboo subject matter, and illegal means, to access his vision.

"Use everything, but be suspicious of it all," Crumlish says.

Burroughs in 1988 (photograph by Greg Daurer)

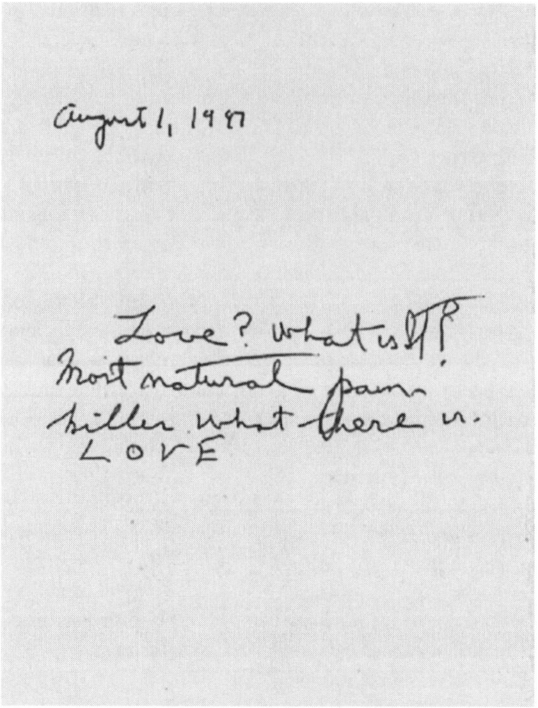

August 1, 1997
Love? What is It?
Most natural pain
killer what there is.
LOVE

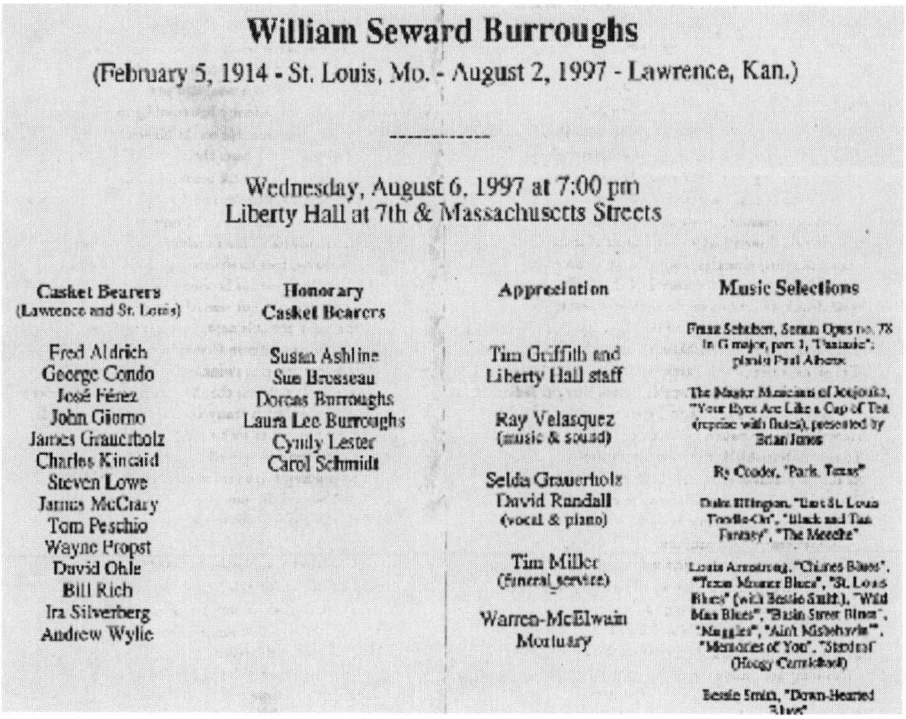

William Seward Burroughs

(February 5, 1914 - St. Louis, Mo. - August 2, 1997 - Lawrence, Kan.)

Wednesday, August 6, 1997 at 7:00 pm
Liberty Hall at 7th & Massachusetts Streets

Casket Bearers
(Lawrence and St. Louis)

Fred Aldrich
George Condo
José Férez
John Giorno
James Grauerholz
Charles Kincaid
Steven Lowe
James McCrary
Tom Peschio
Wayne Propst
David Ohle
Bill Rich
Ira Silverberg
Andrew Wylie

Honorary Casket Bearers

Susan Ashline
Sue Brosseau
Dorcas Burroughs
Laura Lee Burroughs
Cyndy Lester
Carol Schmidt

Appreciation

Tim Griffith and Liberty Hall staff

Ray Velasquez
(music & sound)

Selda Grauerholz
David Randall
(vocal & piano)

Tim Miller
(funeral service)

Warren-McElwain Mortuary

Music Selections

Franz Schubert, Sonata Opus no. 78 in G major, part 1, "Fantasie"; pianist Paul Albers

The Master Musicians of Jajouka, "Your Eyes Are Like a Cup of Tea (reprise with flutes), presented by Brian Jones

Ry Cooder, "Paris, Texas"

Duke Ellington, "East St. Louis Toodle-Oo", "Black and Tan Fantasy", "The Mooche"

Louis Armstrong, "Chimes Blues", "Texas Moaner Blues", "St. Louis Blues" (with Bessie Smith), "Wild Man Blues", "Basin Street Blues", "Muggles", "Ain't Misbehavin'", "Memories of You", "Stardust" (Hoagy Carmichael)

Bessie Smith, "Down-Hearted Blues"

Burroughs died on 2 August 1997. The funeral was held in Lawrence, Kansas, where he had made his home since 1981. The funeral program reproduced Burroughs's final journal entry.

Chapter 6
Neal Cassady

(8 February 1926 – 4 February 1968)

See also the Cassady entry in *DLB 16: The Beats: Literary Bohemians in Postwar America.*

Neal Cassady came to prominence in 1957 with the publication of Jack Kerouac's On the Road. *As with other Beat Generation figures, Cassady's legend has overshadowed his life. For many readers he is the essence of the devil-may-care adventurer, a roguish ladies' man who was both brilliant and troubled, a pioneer of consciousness and a driver whose skills matched those of world-class racers. Ultimately, the fabled Cassady is seen as one who speeds across the American landscape, free of legal, moral, and philosophical entanglements. With "Everything is always all right!" as his mantra, he has grown larger than life and taken his place as an archetypal American figure. This image is owed in large part to Kerouac's mythologizing in books, such as* On the Road *and* Visions of Cody *(1972), in which Kerouac seeks to equate Cassady with the American frontier. Kerouac writes in* On the Road *that Cassady, renamed Dean Moriarty in the novel, had a fine start for an adventurer since "he was born on the road, when his parents were passing through Salt Lake City in 1926, in a jalopy, on their way to Los Angeles." The family soon moved to Denver, where, after his parents separated, Cassady grew up in skid-row hotels with his alcoholic father, Neal Sr., a barber. His mother, Maude Scheuer Cassady, died in 1936. Cassady's youth was full of wild adventures; he later claimed that he stole his first car when he was fourteen and had stolen five hundred before he was twenty-five. Cassady's open reportage of these acts reveals his almost joyous criminality, a characteristic that Kerouac lauded. In* The First Third *Cassady wrote, "The virgin emotion one builds when first stealing an auto–especially when one can hardly make it function properly, so takes full minutes to get away–is naturally strenuous on the nervous system, and I found it most exciting." He spent nearly a year in reform schools.*

Neal Cassady in 1955 (photograph by Allen Ginsberg)

When Cassady was nineteen, he met Hal Chase, a Denver native who was home for the summer from Columbia University. At Columbia, Chase was friends with Kerouac and Ginsberg. That fall Chase shared letters from Cassady with his New York friends, who came to see Cassady as, in Kerouac's words in On the Road, *"a young jailkid shrouded in mystery." Cassady's arrival in New York City that winter with his sixteen-year-old bride, LuAnne, was a galvanizing event in the formation of the Beat Generation. Kerouac was impressed by Cassady's energy and enthusiasm, and Ginsberg soon had a love affair with the brash young man from the West. Inspired by Cassady's journeys, Kerouac set out on the road in the spring of 1947. He was stimulated not only by Cassady's life but also by his writing, which he began to receive in long, detailed letters, and he later credited Cassady as a significant influence on his own writing. Cassady's importance in Ginsberg's and Kerouac's lives–and thus in the Beat Generation–cannot be overstated: he was the central figure in some of Kerouac's best books, and he was also partly responsible for the development of Kerouac's style; he served as a muse for Ginsberg's poetry, and Ginsberg dedicated* Howl and Other Poems *in part to Cassady. Cassady's own attempts at producing publishable material were, however, mostly fruitless. In the 1960s Cassady inspired another writer, Ken Kesey, author of* One Flew Over the Cuckoo's Nest *(1962) and* Sometimes a Great Notion *(1964), and became the bus driver for Kesey's "Merry Pranksters." Cassady died on 4 February 1968 collapsing alongside railroad tracks in Mexico.*

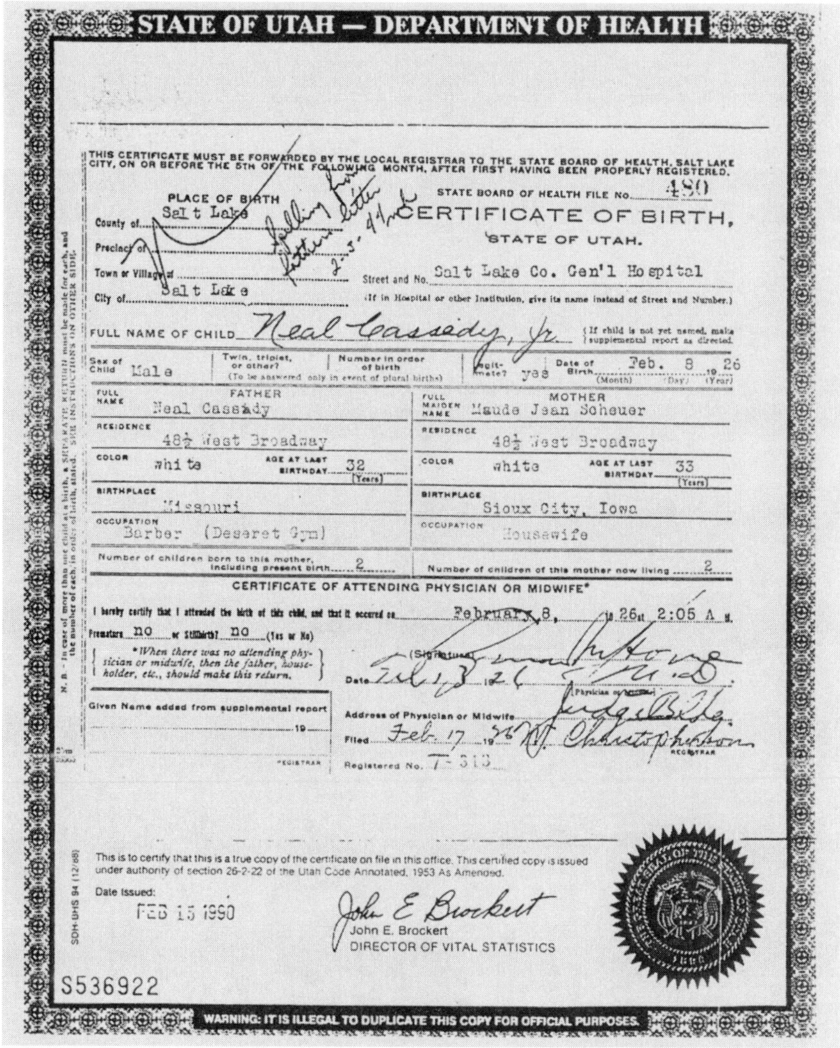

STATE OF UTAH — DEPARTMENT OF HEALTH

THIS CERTIFICATE MUST BE FORWARDED BY THE LOCAL REGISTRAR TO THE STATE BOARD OF HEALTH, SALT LAKE CITY, ON OR BEFORE THE 5TH OF THE FOLLOWING MONTH, AFTER FIRST HAVING BEEN PROPERLY REGISTERED.

STATE BOARD OF HEALTH FILE NO. 480

CERTIFICATE OF BIRTH, STATE OF UTAH.

PLACE OF BIRTH
County of Salt Lake
Precinct of
Town or Village of
City of Salt Lake

Street and No. Salt Lake Co. Gen'l Hospital
(If in Hospital or other Institution, give its name instead of Street and Number.)

FULL NAME OF CHILD Neal Cassady, Jr. (If child is not yet named, make supplemental report as directed.)

Sex of Child Male | Twin, triplet, or other? | Number in order of birth (To be answered only in event of plural births) | Legitimate? yes | Date of Birth Feb. 8 1926 (Month) (Day) (Year)

FATHER	MOTHER
FULL NAME Neal Cassady	FULL MAIDEN NAME Maude Jean Scheuer
RESIDENCE 48½ West Broadway	RESIDENCE 48½ West Broadway
COLOR white — AGE AT LAST BIRTHDAY 32 (Years)	COLOR white — AGE AT LAST BIRTHDAY 33 (Years)
BIRTHPLACE Missouri	BIRTHPLACE Sioux City, Iowa
OCCUPATION Barber (Deseret Gym)	OCCUPATION Housewife
Number of children born to this mother, including present birth 2	Number of children of this mother now living 2

CERTIFICATE OF ATTENDING PHYSICIAN OR MIDWIFE*

I hereby certify that I attended the birth of this child, and that it occurred on February 8, 1926 at 2:05 A. M.

Premature no or Stillbirth? no (Yes or No)

*When there was no attending physician or midwife, then the father, householder, etc., should make this return.

(Signature) M.D. (Physician or Midwife)

Date Feb 13 1926

Address of Physician or Midwife

Given Name added from supplemental report ... 19...

Filed Feb. 17 1926 W. Christopherson, Registrar

Registered No. 7-313

N.B.—In case of more than one child at a birth, a SEPARATE RETURN must be made for each, and the number of each, in order of birth, stated. SEE INSTRUCTIONS ON OTHER SIDE.

This is to certify that this is a true copy of the certificate on file in this office. This certified copy is issued under authority of section 26-2-22 of the Utah Code Annotated, 1953 As Amended.

Date Issued: FEB 15 1990

John E. Brockert
DIRECTOR OF VITAL STATISTICS

SOH-UHS 94 (12/88)

S536922

WARNING: IT IS ILLEGAL TO DUPLICATE THIS COPY FOR OFFICIAL PURPOSES.

Cassady's birth certificate (from Tom Christopher, Neal Cassady Magazine, Volume One: 1926–1940 *[1995])*

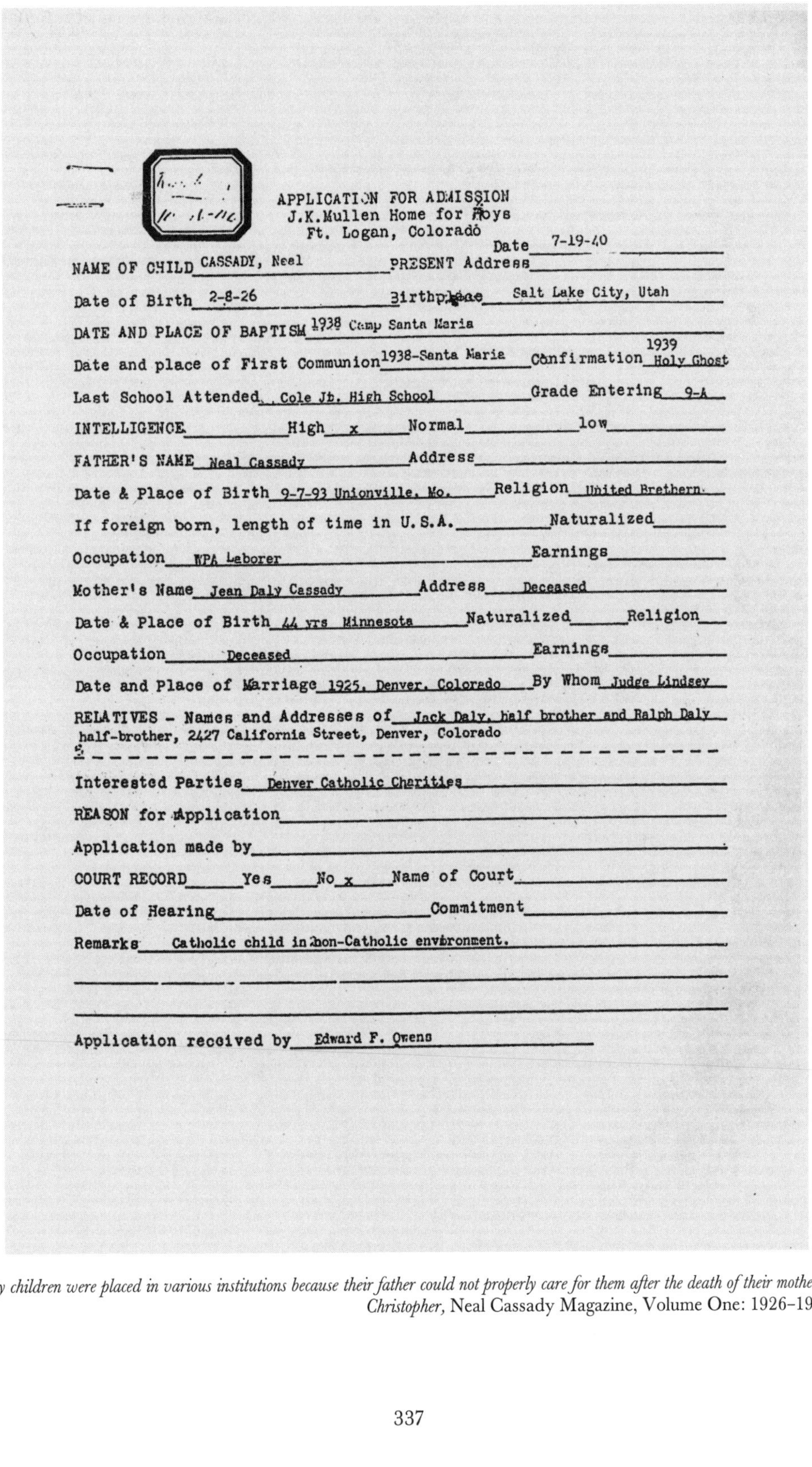

APPLICATION FOR ADMISSION
J.K.Mullen Home for Boys
Ft. Logan, Colorado

Date 7-19-40

NAME OF CHILD CASSADY, Neal PRESENT Address

Date of Birth 2-8-26 Birthplace Salt Lake City, Utah

DATE AND PLACE OF BAPTISM 1938 Camp Santa Maria

Date and place of First Communion 1938-Santa Maria Confirmation 1939 Holy Ghost

Last School Attended Cole Jt. High School Grade Entering 9-A

INTELLIGENCE High x Normal low

FATHER'S NAME Neal Cassady Address

Date & Place of Birth 9-7-93 Unionville, Mo. Religion United Brethern

If foreign born, length of time in U.S.A. Naturalized

Occupation WPA Laborer Earnings

Mother's Name Jean Daly Cassady Address Deceased

Date & Place of Birth 44 yrs Minnesota Naturalized Religion

Occupation Deceased Earnings

Date and Place of Marriage 1925, Denver, Colorado By Whom Judge Lindsey

RELATIVES - Names and Addresses of Jack Daly, half brother and Ralph Daly half-brother, 2427 California Street, Denver, Colorado

Interested Parties Denver Catholic Charities

REASON for Application

Application made by

COURT RECORD Yes No x Name of Court

Date of Hearing Commitment

Remarks Catholic child in non-Catholic environment.

Application received by Edward F. Owens

The Cassady children were placed in various institutions because their father could not properly care for them after the death of their mother (from Tom Christopher, Neal Cassady Magazine, Volume One: 1926–1940 *[1995]).*

Cassady, Neal

Boy's History

Neal Cassady was born, 2-8-26 in Salt Lake City, Utah. He was baptized in 1938 at Camp Santa Maria and made his First Communion at Camp Santa Maria in 1938. He was Confirmed at the Church of the Holy Ghost in Denver during 1939. He is at the present attending Cole Junior High School and will enter 9-A in the fall of 1940. He is the son of Neal and Jean Daly Cassady. Mrs. Cassady died in Denver in May 1936.

After the death of his mother, Neal lived with a half-brother, Jack Daly. However in October, 1939, Neal returned to his father as his half-brother had been remarried and the second wife did not care for the boy.

Father

Neal Cassady, Sr. was born 9-7-93 in Unionville, Missouri. He is a member of the United Brethern Church. He has worked as a barber but in the last few years has been employed on the WPA project at Fitzsimons General Hospital.

Mother

Cassady Children

Jean Daly Cassady was born in Minnesota and was 44 years of age at the time of her death in 1936 in Denver. She had married Neal Cassady, Sr. in 1925. Judge Lindsay performed the ceremony. Previous to her marriage to Mr. Cassady, Mrs. Cassady was the wife of James Daly, deceased. She had five children by her first marriage. All the children of her second marriage are Neal Cassady, born 2-8-26, and Shirley Jean, born 5-22-30.

Catholic Charities Contact

The case first became known to the Catholic Charities shortly after the death of Mrs. Cassady. Plans were being asked by the relatives for her son, James Daly, then 15 years old. The boy was the only minor child of the first marriage. In a short contact with this office a job was secured for James and the relatives accepted responsibility of his care. The Cassady case came to the attention of the Catholic Charities in the Fall of 1939, when Mr. Cassady asked plans for Shirley Jean. It was found that Mr. Cassady was living in the home of a at Mrs. was working on WPA and was the mother of two boys, the eldest of whom was employed at Hendrie & Boltoff, and the younger boy attending high school. The family is non-Catholic. Some years ago Mr. had deserted his wife and their children. The wife has not heard from him since..

During the course of our investigation, Mr. Cassady changed his mind and did not wish to place his daughter. A little later, however, Mr. Cassady was found to be caring for the child in a cheap rooming house and to have been in a drunken state for some time. The case was taken into the Court and the custody of Shirley Jean given to the Catholic Charities. She was placed in St. Clara's on 10-17-39. The girl has never been baptized.

Mr. Cassady has been known to the Den.Police Department for some years and has been frequently picked up on drunken charges. There is no possible opportunity for a child to be raised Catholic as long as they remain with him. Furthermore, his living with Mrs. brings about a very questionable situation since there is no proof of Mr. death. Since Neal has been in the home, he has missed Mass frequently and has been subjected to a non- Catholic atmosphere. It was not

Cassady application for Mullen Home (cont.)

CASSADY, Neal -2

until 1938 that Neal was afforded the opportunity of going to Camp Santa Maria that he was able to be baprized in the Faith of his mother.

The school reports and adjustment of Neal in Cole Jr. High since grade 7B through 9B show a significant correlation with home conditions. On entry to Cole Jr. High Neal was found to have an IQ of 120. He was placed in what was termed a "core" class, that is a group of advanced pupils. He passed 7B satisfactorily and in 7A achieved a rating of Honors which classed him as one of the outstanding pupils in the school. In grade 8B he received a rating of satisfactory, a standing lower then the previous honor rating. In grade 8A he was taken out of the "core" class and placed in a regular 8A class, an indication that he was not doing the worked that justified his placement in the higher group. In grade 8A he received 4 C's and 3 B's; his work of the last semester in grade 9B is as follows:

School Adjustment

Spanish D; Latin C; Earth Science D; Social Science B;
Jr. Business Training C; Music C; Health Program C.

It was during the past semester that the first instance of the boy's being truant occured. It is significant to note that the gradual down-hill indication in the boy's school work coincides with the home situation he was experiencing. Near the time that he was taken out of the "core" group, the boy was rejected from the Daly home. The low grades of the last semester indicate the boy's residence with his father and the family. It is felt that the oy has lost none of his ability, but his unhealthy environkent contributed to his poorer school adjustment.

Recommendation

It is recommedded very strongly by the Catholic Charities that Neal Cassady be considered for the J. K. Mullen Home for Boys. The boy is most anxious to enter and will most likely make a fine adjustment. in the institution. Furthermore, his Faith will be safeguarded; otherwise, it is felt that from the family situation there is some danger of his not being raised in the Church as a practical Catholic.

Edward F. Owens

Cole Junior High School. Class 9 - A. January, 1941

Back Row, Position 2: Walter Bebe. 4: LeRoy Love. 5: Delbert Wood. 9: Bill Smith. 11: Jim Downs. 14: Ken Pearson. 15: Joe Bryzenski.
Row Two, Position 5: James Griton. 8: Ben Rountree. 10: Art Barlow . 11: Neal Cassady. 15: Chester Thomas. 17 Donald Todd.
Row Three, Position 1: Earl Krause. 4: Sam Sato. 6: Isadore Ortiz. 7: Joe Uemura. 8: Chuck Wooster. 9: Dick King. 10: Fred Fair. 11: George Knowles. 15: Don Mestas. 19: Don Waring. 22: Leroy Huntley.
Row Three, Position 1: Bob Hine. 2: Jimmy Vaughn. 11: Tom Murrell. 13: Harold McMillan. 16: Orlando Trujillo. 17: Rudy Mejia.
Front Row, Position 4: Joe Schlager. 5: Dale Shaw. 9: Alfred Kamerzell. 10: Milton Hayano. 13: Bryant Hough.
Thanks to Chuck Wooster and Joseph Uemura for photo identification

Back Cover: Neal Marshall Cassady and his niece, Amy Casady Weldon, Missouri, 1960

Cassady did not know that he was supposed to wear a white shirt and tie to school on the day the yearbook photograph was taken because he had played hooky the day before.

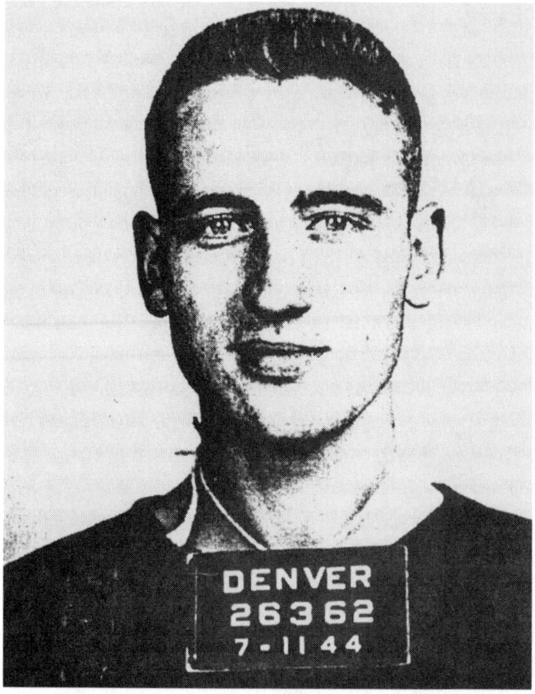

Cassady's "mug shot" for the Colorado State Reformatory in Buena Vista, where, in July 1944, he was sentenced to serve a year for theft

LuAnne Henderson, whom Cassady married in late 1946

The Barber's Boy

From 1948 to 1954 Cassady made intense but sporadic attempts to write the story of what he assumed would be the first third of his life. This excerpt is from the opening chapter of The First Third & Other Writings, *in which he describes his birth and his earliest memories.*

Maude, now pregnant with her ninth child and Neal's first (the embryo, me), were all to embark on a leisurely western trip 'to see the world.' Thus, in the dead of winter, some ten months after their marriage, they headed for Hollywood in Neal's unique vehicle. . . . When Maude delivered en route, our travelers added to their healthy brood. Nearby the Mormon Tabernacle and the rotund and stately Temple with its 78 points of upward thrust balanced evenly atop the twin towers, is the L.D.S. Hospital, where was born on February 8, 1926, at 2:05 A.M., Maude's last son. It was to be Neal's only boy and was named after him, except that Neal had no middle name; so as compensative remedy they gave the child the additional name of 'Leon,' which ironically spoiled what Neal Sr. was most proud of–a 'junior' Neal.

. . . .

For a time I held a unique position: among the hundreds of isolated creatures who haunted the streets of lower downtown Denver there was not one so young as myself. Of these dreary men who had committed themselves, each for his own good reason, to the task of finishing their days as pennyless drunkards, I alone, as the sharer of their way of life, presented a replica of childhood to which their vision could daily turn, and in being thus grafted onto them, I became the unnatural son of a few score beaten men.

It was my experience to be constantly meeting new cronies of my father's, who invariably introduced me with a proud, "This is my boy." Whereupon the pat on my head was usually followed by the quizzical look the eye reserved for uncertainty, which here conveyed the question, "Shall I give him a little drink?" Sensing the offer, backed by a half-extended bottle, my father would always say, "You'll have to ask him," and I would coyly answer, "No thank you, sir." Of course this occurred only on those memorable occasions when an acceptable drink like wine was available. The unhappy times when there was none, with only denatured alcohol ("canned heat") or bay rum at hand, I did not have to go through my little routine.

Many times, after normal adult catering with questions to show interest in the child, (such gestures of talkative comradeship was their token parenthood, for these secondary fathers had nothing else to give) I would be ignored while the talk of my father and his new friend turned to recalling the past. These tête-à-têtes were full of little asides which carried with them facts establishing that much of the life they had known was in common: types of mutual friends, cities visited, things done there, and so on. Their conversation had many general statements about Truth and Life, which contained the collective intelligence of all America's bums. They were drunkards whose minds, weakened by liquor and an obsequious manner of existence, seemed continually preoccupied with bringing up short observations of obvious trash, said in such a way as to be instantly recognizable by the listener, who had heard it all before, and whose own prime concern was to nod at everything said, then continue the conversation with a remark of his own, equally transparent and loaded with generalities. The simplicity of this pattern was marvelous, and there was no limit to what they could agree on in this fashion, to say nothing of the abstract ends that could be reached. Through sheer repetitious hearing of such small talk speculation, I came to know their minds so intimately that I could understand as they understood, and there was soon no mystery to the conversation of any of them. I assumed all men thought the same, and so knew these things, because like any child, I correlated all adult action without actual regard for type.

All his fellow alcoholics called my father "the barber" since he was about the only one of them who had practiced that trade, and I was "the barber's boy." They all said I looked just like him, but I didn't think this was true in the least. And they watched me grow with comments like "Why, look there–his head is higher than your belt already!" It wasn't such a feat, I thought, to stand that tall, because my father had awfully short legs.

–pp. 39–40, 47–48

First Impressions

In The First Third *Cassady describes his initial meetings with Allen Ginsberg near the campus of Columbia University.*

I had gone to New York in the fall of 1946, and having just arrived, I looked up Hal Chase. After supper we went to a rather vapid bar near the campus. We had just ordered our drinks when Hal recognized a voice and said, "that's Allen Ginsberg" just as a head popped up from the next booth and looked at me. He had coal-black hair which struck my eye first. It was a bit too long yet not an over-done mass of garish distaste as some more normal poet of an intellectual nature might affect. . . . If there was any part of his face he was conscious of, it was the eyes. They were large, dark and brooding. I was not quite sure how much of the brooding was there as such; and how much he was putting there for us to read into.

His voice, although I've heard it a thousand times, escapes my memory. I recall it was pleasant, varied and cultured, but the tone qualities are lost to me.

Hal looked up and said "hello Allen." Allen nodded, a bit curt I thought.

"This is Neal Cassady, he just got in from Denver and has never been here before."

"Hello."

"How do you do."

"Neal's looking for a place to stay, any suggestions?"

"Has he tried Mills Hotel?"

"Hardly, since he's got his wife with him."

"Oh well then, I don't know of any place around here."

We both sat down again in our respective booths. Allen was with someone Hal didn't know and since there were several in our party anyway, there was no attempt made for the two parties to get together.

A few moments later Allen again stuck his head over the top of the booths. "Is your name LuAnne? What a strange name," he said and sat back down. My wife mumbled "yes", looked embarrassed, and suggested we leave. We did.

I didn't see Allen for over a month, then, about January 10, 1947, we met again. A close friend, Jack Kerouac, suggested that we go uptown and he would introduce me to a fabulous woman named Vicki. He had spoken of her many times before and since it suited my mood, I acquiesced.

–pp. 184–185

In On the Road *Cassady is renamed Dean Moriarty, and LuAnne is Marylou. Kerouac also changed the location of the ranch where Cassady had worked.*

My first impression of Dean was of a young Gene Autry–trim, thin-hipped, blue-eyed, with a real Oklahoma accent–a sideburned hero of the snowy West. In fact he'd just been working on a ranch, Ed Wall's in Colorado, before marrying Marylou and coming East. Marylou was a pretty blonde with immense ringlets of hair like a sea of golden tresses; she sat there on the edge of the couch with her hands hanging in her lap and her smoky blue country eyes fixed in a wide stare because she was in an evil gray New York pad that she'd heard about back West, and waiting like a long-bodied emaciated Modigliani surrealist woman in a serious room. But, outside of being a sweet little girl, she was awfully dumb and capable of doing horrible things. That night we all drank beer and pulled wrists and talked till dawn, and in the morning, while we sat around dumbly smoking butts from ashtrays in the gray light of a gloomy day, Dean got up nervously, paced around, thinking, and decided the thing to do was to have Marylou make breakfast and sweep the floor. "In other words we've got to get on the ball, darling, what I'm saying, otherwise it'll be fluctuating and lack true knowledge or crystallization of our plans." Then I went away.

–p. 5

John Clellon Holmes's novel Go, *based on the New York crowd, was published five years before Kerouac's* On the Road. *Here Holmes describes the first time he met Cassady, renamed Hart Kennedy; Pasternak is Kerouac; Stofsky is Ginsberg; Hobbes is Holmes; Ed Schindel is Al Hinkle; Dinah is LuAnne.*

Three days later, in another early summer dusk, Hart Kennedy arrived at their apartment with an eager entourage made up of Pasternak, Stofsky and a fellow called Ed Schindel, who had driven from the coast with him.

Hobbes had learned of their arrival in New York earlier that afternoon with a call from Stofsky:

"Yes, yes, they came around but I was out, so they left a note . . . Have they gotten in touch with you? I've been calling madly everywhere. They were at Verger's too, leaving notes . . . You see, I haven't seen Hart for almost two years, and now notes, notes, phantom notes and that's all!"

Soon after that, after Hobbes had tried to get back into the chapter he was retyping, and when that failed, to get off a letter to Liza which had still not been written, Ketcham had called to say that they had been at his place the night before; Hart, Pasternak, Schindel, and Hart's first wife, Dinah, whom they had picked up in Denver on the way from San Francisco.

Then Stofsky had called again, on his way to Agatson's to check there: "If they come or phone you, hold onto them until I get in touch with you. It's very important! Bye-bye," and he rang off to continue his restless search in all the various places in which his hopes located them, finally to meet them accidentally on Columbus Circle near an automat they had all frequented when Hart had lived in New York two years before.

When Kathryn got home, Hobbes excitedly told her of all this, and because her day had been relatively uneventful, she said with amusement: "Don't be so jumpy. They'll come here soon enough as it is. Don't worry about that!"

But, nevertheless, everyone stumbled during the first, awkward moments, except Ed Schindel, whose rangy height and flushed boyish face contrasted oddly to the small, wiry Hart, who moved with itchy calculation and whose reddish hair and broken nose gave him an expression of shrewd, masculine ugliness.

"Say, this is a real nice place you got here," Schindel said politely, shifting his Redwood of a body easily. "Yes, sir!"

"What do you think of all those books, Hart?" Pasternak asked, with an exuberant grin.

Hart nodded briefly, shrugging muscular shoulders. "Yes, yes. That's fine."

"My mother fixed us a big dinner, Paul," Pasternak went on, refusing to sit down. "That's where Dinah is now, washing clothes and stuff like that. You know, they drove all the way from Frisco in four days!"

"Christ," Hobbes replied uneasily. "That's terrific time. Was it a tough trip?"

"Oh, you know, man. We got our kicks."

Hart was the only one, but for the secretive Stofsky lounging in a corner, who was not blundering into uncertain formalities, but he kept moving most of the time, looking out the windows, reading book titles, tapping out clusters of pattering beats with his foot.

Hobbes put on a bop record, hoping it would relax everyone, and after only a few seconds of the honking, complex tenor sax, Hart broke into a wild eyed, broad grin and exclaimed:

"Well, yes, man, yes! Say, that's great stuff!"

He stood by the phonograph in a stoop, moving back and forth on the spot in an odd little shuffle. His hands clapped before him, his head bobbed up and down, propelled, as the music got louder, in ever greater arcs, while his mouth came grotesquely agape as he mumbled: "Go! Go!"

Hobbes wandered about nervously, feeling he should not stare at Hart, but when he saw Stofsky looking at the agitated figure with an adoring solemnity, he stared frankly with him, remembering Ketcham's description:

"This Hart is phenomenal. I've never seen such enormous nervous energy, and Gene gets just like him, in a kind of way. Hart and Dinah kept dancing and smoking and playing my radio all night. I didn't get to bed until six, and I was sure the neighbors were going to complain."

–pp. 114–115

Kerouac describes the same scene in On the Road; *here Tom Saybrook is Holmes, and Sal Paradise is Kerouac.*

We went looking for my New York gang of friends. The crazy flowers bloom there too. We went to Tom Saybrook's first. Tom is a sad, handsome fellow, sweet, generous, and amenable. . . . This night he was overjoyed. "Sal, where did you find these absolutely wonderful people? I have never seen anyone like them."

"I found them in the West."

–p. 125

Early Letters

Immediately after returning west from his first trip to New York, Cassady began to write to Ginsberg and Kerouac. The first two letters presented here are to Ginsberg. The poem Cassady refers to is Ginsberg's "The Last Voyage," which won Columbia's G. E. Woodbury Prize in 1947. Cassady apparently presented it as his own to impress others, including Carolyn Robinson, who became his second wife. Cassady's lack of proper schooling and his keen intelligence are reflected in his writing style. "Haldon" in the first letter refers to Hal Chase, "Bill B." in the second to William S. Burroughs.

Twenty-year-old Cassady posing for a picture in a New York City bus-station photo booth just before his to return to Denver (from Steve Turner, Angelheaded Hipster *[1996])*

1073 Downing St.
Denver, Colorado
March 14, 1947.

Dear Allen;

As you can see I have procured a typewriter the only bad point is that it's only half mine. I feel certain you will excuse me using it to write personal letters to you, since you would have to decipher my juvinel scrawl otherwise.

I have found a wonderful place to live & it only costs me $6.00 a week. My meals must still be taken in cafes however. I have not as yet went to work so I am really in debt.

Speaking of debt, sent on those overcoats as soon as possible to aleviate my deress.

I am honestly amazed & overwhelmed at the truly great mass of information you have sent on to me concerning the poem. I appreciate it very much. Needless to say, especially now that I have this typewriter, I shall copy the poem & sent it to you within the week.

To say that I got "great kicks" out of your recital of what happened at Vicki's after I left that night, would almost be an understatement. I find that the optimistic tone on which your missive ends is so heartening in it's implication that I fear I wouldn't be able to bring myself to really think that the "Peace" will last.

Incidentally, I have found no peace at all since arriving. You see, my basic problem has developed into seeking the proper relationship with Lu Anne. Due to our separation she has fallen into a complete apathy toward life.

Her inability to meet even the most simple obligations is almost terrifying. Her life is a constant march of obsessions. Her attitude toward everyone is so defensive that it constitutes continual lying, yet she still has many fellows who adore her & is, therefore, always getting drunk & has become very slipshod. I, as yet, can't solve this delema, however, in due course I feel a solution will be found. My life is, at the moment, so cluttered up I have become incapable of relaxing long enough to even write a decent letter, really, I'm almost unable to think coherently. You must, then, not only forgive, but, find it within yourself to understand & in so doing develope a degree of patience until I am able to free myself enough to become truly close to you again.

On your part, you must know, that any letdown in your regard for me would upset me so much that, pschologically, I would be in a complete vacuum. At least for the immediate future I must request these things of you. so *please* don't fail me. I need you now more than ever, since I've noone else to turn to. I continually feel I am almost free enough to be a real help to you, but, my love can't flourish in my present postion & if I forced it now, both you & I would lose. By God, though, every day I miss you more & More.

Understanding these things I hope, nay, in fact, know you must pour out more affection now than ever, rather than reacting negatively & withering up so that all is loss, or would be, between us.

Let us then find true awareness by realizing that each of us is depending on the other for fulfillment. In that realization lies, I believe, the germ that may grow to the great heights of complete oneness.

I have not seen Haldon yet, just called him once. I saw Mannerly for 20 minutes & can say that I emerged the victor, however, I merely mentioned "a poem" & let the suit talk for me. So, you see, each new time I converse with him my statute will grow.

I shall find a job tomorrow & perhaps by losing myself in work again I may become more rational & less upset & unnerved by the emotional shock of returning. Write soon I need you. I remain your other self.

Neal.

–*As Ever: The Collected Correspondence of Allen Ginsberg & Neal Cassady,* pp. 6–7

* * *

1073 Downing Street
Denver, Colorado
March 20, 1947.

Dear Allen;

I have just finished copying the poem, since I am not a typist you will see in it several mistakes that are so glaring as to almost fill me with shame. I have, however, stuck exactly to your puncuation etc. Also, I have sent you the poem in carbon, now, if you need the prime copy of the original don't hesitate to let me know, and I shall sent it to you.

I almost feel guilty about harping on the coats, for I see in your letter that it has given you some concern. Please excuse the seemingly desperate tone that I had unconscious taken in speaking of them, my only explanation is that I am so conditioned to dealing with people who must be driven on to doing something by my assuming an urgent tone that I fell into that mannerism with you. I will state that if its convient enough to be done without too much trouble you might sent on one or two that are my size.

One thing that is really important though, is my trousers. I am honestly in need of them.

Your speaking of Bill B. only makes me want to meet him more than ever. I trust that in June you will come west we shall see he and Joan at that time. Continue to keep me informed as to his tribulations etc. just as you did in this letter.

I place you in such high regard academically that I merely reacted normally to your amount of information concerning the literary scene. I presupposed that it had all come out of your head without effort, just as I without effort can speak of football, therefore, when I expressed amazement at the knowledge, it was artificial in that I was complimenting you simply as a means of showing appreciation. So you see I was not truly impressed, but, rather accepted it as further proof of your value. In fact, what you pointed out about it in this latest letter was understood, and understood so well that I find a lack in myself in not implying that, rather than using the false complementary style to show my thanks to you.

I have given much thought to what I am about to say. I must, I fear, become somewhat incoherant near the end of this paragraph, but, bear with me as I am consciously trying to formulate our, no, my feelings. First, realize I am not intellectualizing nor doing anything other than being governed by pure emotion (incidentally, I feel that is the key to whatever awareness you sensed in me) in my effort to state to you what my present position is. Now, I shall tell my fears, desires, feelings of all types, and then, if possible, attempt to analize them. Allen, this may sound strange, but, the thing that is uppermost in my mind at the moment is a fear. How can I state it? I believe it is almost paranoiac in its intensity, with each of your letters I feel it more. I have difficulty in putting my finger on it, but its a real fear of losing you. Its a combination of a knowledge of lack on my part, not only academically, but, in drive as well, also, a sense of outcast that makes me feel at times as if I were really imposing on you for me to try and become closer. I have become more defensive pschologically in direct ratio to my increasing degree of realization of need of you. The thing that is closest to the truth is the simple statement that you are too good for me. I am above feeling envy of you, and don't fall into a sort of loving admiration either, rather, I have a sort of confused sense of loss when I think of you. The whole thing is quite beyond me at present, yet, somehow this is different than previous times when I felt an inability to cope with our relationship. This time, although, its negative in its psychological aspect, I find true concern of our need so much that I, in reality, feel stronger than at any other time since I met you. I mean, stronger in desire and ability to struggle to handle our affair, rather, than healthy positive drive toward freedom for us. You can see I am now in a position for the first time of being a drain on you insofar as I have become aware of a nerotic negative almost compulsive need of you. I feel as if I were a woman about to lose her man, primarily because as you become more straight through me, or otherwise, you will need me less, and, also secondarily, because I know as that happens I shall need you more. This is as I say, the uppermost fear. Along side of that is a remnent of the old feeling I had in N.Y. of a need to free myself of Denver and all it implys before I can progress, at least, with you. Then there are other things which are bothering me, but, they are unimportant compared to the above.

Allen, forgive me, but I must break off now. I have been really busy these last few days and haven't had any rest, right now its 5 A.M. and I must rise at 9:30 A.M. I am completely beat, causing my fluctuations in thought I think.

Let me end on one line in your wonderful letter–"I will be prepared for you I think, when we meet, but on other terms than those which I'd formerly concieved and which I tried to force on you" I find that statement holds true for me as well as you Allen, whether for better or worse we must see, but, whichever way it goes, I know I can't help from profiting thereby and perhaps you can also (though, I fear you can't since I no longer have anything to offer, and therein lies my lonlyness).

I leave you in complete weariness and apology.

But, By God, L'enfant or no, whether you think its mad or not, whether "its not as we feel or I want to feel" to quote you. I still love (what a weak word) you.

Bah! I'm tired.
Neal

P.S. Speaking of overcoats, don't try and sell them, we'll wait until this fall and get more out of them then, not only that, but, when we set up housekeeping then we'll make a record machine and really get gone and yet be straighter than any 10 psychologists. Use the record machine as an indication of all things fine and the other as a statement of our disiplainaryism.

I'm so tired I can't even type, let alone think.
Please excuse.
N.L.C.

–As Ever: The Collected Correspondence of Allen Ginsberg & Neal Cassady, pp. 7–10

In interviews Kerouac credited Cassady with helping to form his writing style. The following letter is among their first written exchanges. In addition to relating the mundane details of his life, Cassady gives Kerouac advice on how to write, although he knew that Kerouac was the more talented writer. When he asks how Kerouac is "progressing on the novel," he is referring to The Town & the City *(1950). The editors of* The Missouri Review *silently corrected minor misspellings and punctuation errors.*

1073 Downing St.
Denver, Colorado
March 27, 1947

Dear Jack;

I put off writing to you for four days, then wrote a letter, then on the second day thereafter tore it up. Since it was already outdated. So this is my next attempt lets hope you get it. I'm almost 2 weeks late in writing you as it is and it's given me much concern.

Part of the laxity in correspondence is due to my emotional upheaval of late, but most of it is my honest feeling of lack in becoming close to you at this time, due to the upheaval, by writing. Having combated this as well as I'm able and not being capable of dashing off an extemporaneous letter, as you seem to be able to, and having it include my true feelings, I am at last reaching a state, psychologically, in which I can send this letter, however, I'm not as free yet by any means.

Instead of trying to describe what has been happening to me, I shall just give you the gist of it and pass on:

First I was forced to move by my landlady. Second I was in fear of jail because of LuAnne. Third I was completely fucked up on my job. What happened? Well, after a few days of paranoiac defensiveness, I regained my natural drive and dealt directly with the problems. Problem one the place I live in; after having gotten ready to leave town, removing my hot typewriter etc. I approached the landlady directly, instead of avoiding her as I had been, because of her anger, my bloody and missing bedsheets, girls in my room etc. And with my best conmethods persuaded her to allow me to remain. Now, she loves me again. So, problem one was a complete victory for me. Problem two, my near approach to jail is so complicated I can't tell it here, I shall only state that, here too, I emerged victor and am still free and I feel will remain that way. Problem three, my job, is now almost solved, to prove I could keep it, for character only, I did get it back, then quit the next day since it was a really terrible job in a filling station. Now, I am competing with a dozen other applicants for a wonderful position at an exclusive restaurant, where, if I succeed in procuring the job I will, of all things, park cars in their parking lot. I shall find out Saturday. So you see Jack, I've been fighting all sorts of negative things, but, I am beyond all the struggle of settling down here again and from here on out will be able to really move on. So let's fall into a potent and true groove in our missives to each other for the next couple of months until I see you. Of course, I am presupposing you are free enough to move with me in this, I have your first letter as evidence, all I ask is that in our attempt to fall into a closeness again, you remain as sincere as you have been and just because we're writing instead of talking don't let up in what you have to say to me and please, Jack, don't allow yourself to do what I've been guilty of in the past with other people, that is, you are still sincere, but automatically, the process of writing forces you into a form and therefore, you just say things rather than feel them, and the honest attempt to express these feelings is too much so you just, lazily, dash off a newsy letter, or a pat formal stylized letter, or a wild artificially stimulating one and so on. These things are for anyone to do, but not us, so to play safe force yourself to think and then write rather than think what to write about and what to say as you write. Incidentally, I sense just a hint of the above falseness in your letter, but, I know it's just that there was really nothing to write about. That's that, now to answer your letter period.

You flatter me unnecessarily about my Kansas City letter, I was just drunk and high.

I don't know what to say after reading your terrific telling of your experience on the parking lot. This is by far the best part of your letter, it personifies the portion of you that I feel close to than any other, it's very unstraight, complex and really blown all out of proportion, but that's where we shine. As for the negative side, who cares? Just wait till June comes and see whether or not Hal, you and I will latch on to some real fillies. That's what I've spent a good deal of time on since returning and I'm loaded.

It's really interesting to read what you say about the coats, for my part you can forget them, use them for yourself. I'm so broke, however, that I've hocked my overcoat and suit, and am now borrowing from everyone in sight just to eat, not having eaten yet today, after finishing this letter I shall go down to a nearby newsstand and steal the change on the papers and go buy some bowery stew. That's how sad my material wealth is at this moment, but, somehow, I don't feel worried, in fact, I'm quite happy.

I have not felt up to seeing Haldon as yet, due to all the bullshit I've been going through, it's starting to bother me though, so I'll see him Sunday.

By God! Jack, I sure as hell wish you were here, when I'm with you I somehow feel well rounded, completed, at least at peace with myself, rather than busting my head into a lot of negative goddamned crap that means nothing and just frustrates me and in striking out I become even more involved in the whole imposing mess. What I mean by this is that I am dissatisfied with all my social life. There's no one here, all I do is fuck. Bah!

The next two months I intend to write a simple, chronological, account of my life. This is to be done not, of course, not as something to try and publish, but only to help me evaluate all I have done and what to do with it. This task, I hope, will also free me of my background lack of freedom from Denver and all the confused trash I've accumulated here. In fact, I truly think I will no longer need to be concerned about this trash any more and can move on into some healthy knowledge and be not only helping myself, but shall be an aid to you, instead of a fellow condemned one, as we both are until–well, until when, who knows?

I am most anxious to know how you're progressing on the novel, really, if you don't lick the damn thing soon I will be so upset I'll probably bawl, honestly, Jack, *please* get that thing off your chest, all I can think of when I remember you is this crisis you're in and because of that I grieve, rather than find joy when I think of your struggle. If I were just assured that all you needed was time, I'd forget my concern, however, it's been with you so long I fear you must finish it this time, to do you any good, that is to help you grow, so don't become static through the external pressure of time, instead, man, hearken back to a while back when you began in the present tense and just wrote, by God! Just write Jack, write! Forget everything else. Hear me?

. . . .

Now, Jack don't feel the rush of time, if you don't get here till July that's O.K. Just get the novel by the balls first and then think of other things. Jack, if you have any reason not to its O.K. but you know my character, and I've been raving about you to the few guys around here that are important to me, well, it would really be wonderful if you'd send me the Lucien Carr story, if not to show them, at least for me. Please don't feel I'm imposing on you, as I say if you, for any reason don't wish to send me anything its all right, but, I'd honestly be overwhelmed with joy if you'd send that or, of course, anything you can spare or will allow me to have. Anything you've written, I'd love, I'll send it right back.

The Missouri Review (no. 2, 1999), pp. 97–100

Cassady in San Francisco in 1947 with Carolyn Robinson, who became his second wife (Collection of Carolyn Cassady)

Carolyn Cassady

Carolyn Robinson, a Bennington College graduate who was taking graduate courses in fine and theater arts at the University of Denver, met Cassady in March 1947. Kerouac fictionalizes their meeting in On the Road.

Roy Johnson, the poolhall boy, had found her in a bar and took her to a hotel; pride taking over his sense, he invited the whole gang to come up and see her. Everybody sat around talking with Camille. Dean did nothing but look out the window. Then when everybody left, Dean merely looked at Camille, pointed at his wrist, made the sign "four" (meaning he'd be back at four), and went out. At three the door was locked to Roy Johnson. At four it was opened to Dean.

—p. 43

Cassady and Robinson married in 1948, and Carolyn entered the Beat Generation scene. She later shared a romance with Kerouac, apparently with her husband's blessing, and vied with Ginsberg for Neal's attentions. She wrote of her life with these men in Off the Road: My Years with Cassady, Kerouac, and Ginsberg. *Here she describes the circumstances under which she met Cassady.*

A little past two o'clock on that Saturday afternoon in March of 1947, the phone rang in my hotel sitting room. Bill Tomson's affected tough-guy drawl was unmistakable.

"H'lo, doll, c'n I come up for a minute?"

I hesitated. Bill was becoming a nuisance. Though not enroled in the University of Denver, he'd been turning up on campus nearly every day, and I found his impromptu appearances increasingly tedious. Out of curiosity I continued to see him, but I had so far failed to find any subject he'd discuss seriously. He confined his conversation to smart retorts, abstract bravado or stories of exploits designed to impress me, either his own or those of a friend, one Neal Cassady. To Bill, Neal was a hero whose praises needed singing. Bill told me of daring escapades in cars, near-brushes with the law, deep intellectual and musical safaris.

Having been raised in fear and reverence of existing social codes, I was amazed to learn that there were men who actually dared live like those in books or movies . . . if, of course, Bill wasn't exaggerating. In any case such a life was remote and unthreatening to me; I wasn't about to fall in love with Bill, and he told me Neal was in New York studying at Columbia University with two friends, Jack Kerouac and Allen Ginsberg, the one a famous football player, the other a poet.

Bill looked vaguely like some movie star whose name I'd long forgotten, and this afternoon I could easily visualize him leaning on the lobby counter, his free hand twisting knots in the phone cord, the cigarette dangling from his lips, one eye squinting from the smoke, the other from the thick straight hair that refused to stay back no matter how often Bill tossed his head to tame it.

After a lengthy pause, I responded. "All right, Bill, but only for a minute. I have a lot of work to do."

When I opened the door at his knock, I saw he was not alone. Behind him stood another man, who now strode past me into the room, his eyes quickly cataloguing the contents before he turned to acknowledge Bill's introduction.

"Cari, this is Neal Cassady."

I could only stare, flustered by seeing the myth made flesh. Neal nodded, and in that instant the sweep of his blue eyes made me feel I had been thoroughly appraised. Inwardly I cursed Bill's failure to warn me.

The advance publicity on this man had already made him unique, but I was not prepared for his appearance–not so much the physical aspects–which were all pretty average–it was his suit. Though not authentic "zoot", it had the same aura, and I'd never been closer to one than the movie screen. It gave him a Runyonesque flavor, a dangerous glamor heightened by the white T-shirt and bare muscular neck.

Neal walked across the room to the phonograph and turned to me, a statue by the door.

"Bill tells me you have an unusually large collection of Lester Young records." His eyebrows sloped upward and inward quizzically.

Bewildered, I stammered, "Who? Lester who? I, uh . . . no . . . unusual, yes. I'm afraid I've never heard or him. All I have are leftovers from college . . . swing mostly . . . big bands." And I glared at Bill for this additional embarrassment.

Neal too looked at Bill, but only for a second. Then, cool and smiling, he sat in the rocker and began flipping through the albums.

"That's quite all right. What have we here? Ah, yes, I see . . . Artie Shaw, good, the Dorseys, Harry James . . . Nat King Cole . . . ah, Stan Kenton, the Duke . . . hmm, lots of Ellington, Goodman, yes, indeed. Very nice. May I play something?" Again his eyebrows sloped upward as he looked at me.

"Of course . . . please . . ."

As he placed the record carefully on the turntable, I dove to the floor to gather together the model of stage scenery I was working on. Bill stopped pacing and sat by the window opposite Neal. The record spun and no one spoke. I glanced up at Neal and quickly down again. As he rocked, his eyes were fastened on me so intently I felt a physical stab. I was sure he sensed my discomfort, but I felt those eyes, like lasers, unwavering until the record ceased. Moving to change it, his manner eased. He made comments to Bill, and I stood up and puttered about the room, straightening nothing really.

"Ah, what's this?" Neal held up a boxed album by Josh White.

"Oh, that's *Southern Exposure.* It's about as radical as we ever got in college. We were impressed by Josh and his protest songs on poor housing and 'Jim Crow' trains. It's banned in the South, I hear, When I lived in New York I knew Josh a little, but to my surprised he didn't want to talk about the issues in his songs.' Words tumbled out in my nervousness, but Neal listened with such empathy and respect I felt special, my every word a gem. Beneath his subtle charm I sensed a taut energy that was subdued and restrained, like a drawn bow.

Soon it became apparent that Neal was restless, and Bill had begun to fidget. Neal looked from Bill to me.

Carolyn Cassady and her friends Helen and Al Hinkle and Bill Tomson celebrating Christmas 1949. Tomson had introduced Carolyn to Neal Cassady in 1947 (Collection of Carolyn Cassady).

"Well, now. Do you two have any plans for this afternoon?" I wistfully surveyed my project materials. "Couldn't it wait?" he continued. "Just for an hour or so? I'll bet you need some fresh air. Look–why don't you come with me? I just got off the Greyhound, you see, and I have to get my things from the house where I used to live. Then we could go downtown–or anything you like." Neal spoke at a rapid rate, not pausing for a reply, and moved toward the door. He turned to me with the question in his eyes.

Bill got up. "Come on, Cari, get your coat."

Over and above my discomfort was a compelling desire to see more of this man. I got my coat.

–pp. 1–3

By the time he wrote this letter, Cassady had divorced LuAnne–although he was still seeing her–and married Carolyn. They were living in San Francisco.

Jan. 7, 1948

Dear Jack,

It is not possible to grasp and express things at all as completely as most people, particularly critics, would have us believe. Most events are inexpressible; they happen in a region of the soul into which no word can penetrate: Understanding comes thru the soul.

With this introduction I want to say that my prose has no individual style as such, but is rather an unspoken and still unexpressed groping toward the personal. There is something there that wants to come out; something of my own that must be said: Yet, perhaps, words are not the way for me.

I have found myself looking to others for the answer to my soul, whereas I know this is slowly gained (if at all). By delving into my own self only. I am not too sure that the roots of the impose to write go deep enough, are necessary enough, for me to create on paper.

If, however, I find writing a must (as you seem to do) then I know I must build my life around this necessity; even my most indifferent and trivial hours must become an expression of this impulse and a testimony to it.

I have always held that when one writes, one should forget all rules, literary styles, and other such pretensions as large words, lordly clauses and other phrases as such–i.e. rolling the words around in the mouth as one would wine and proper or not putting them down because they sound so good. Rather, I think, one should write, as nearly as possible, as if he were the first person on earth and was humbly and sincerely putting on paper that which he saw and experienced, loved and lost: what his passing thoughts were and his sorrows and desires; and these things should be said with careful avoidance of common phrases, trite usage of hackneyed words and the like. One must combine Wolfe and Flaubert–and Dickens.

Art is good when it springs from necessity. This kind of origin is the guarantee of its value; there is no other. It follows from this that if I feel the necessity and yet have no talent such as yours, must I write to compensate?

Oh, well, dear Jack, the above shows you, once again, the nonsense, and stupid bugaboos I fight; or do I fight? I am inclined to think not, and perchance therein lies my flaw.

At any rate I intend to continue grinding out the trash which seems embedded in me. At the same time I fully intend to start playing an instrument; the sax, perhaps. Also, of late, I have become more aware of theatre as a release; I love to do take-offs on everybody: Chaplin, Barrymore etc. I feel the urge and jump up and act out, stage, direct, costume and photograph an entire class B movie; all this in a hurried, confused dialogue and pantomime (no dictionary) which is mixed in with frantic rushing from one side of the room to the opposite as I progress with the epic. Scene after scene rolls out; one coming from another, and soon I'm portraying everybody from the script writer to the temperamental star; from the leader who arranges and conducts the music for the sound track, to the stage hands who dash in and out with the sets, then, falling exhausted, I giggle.

I am being seriously plagued with the hives. It started some weeks ago; my throat swells, breathing is difficult, and great patches of bumps rise on my thighs and buttocks. These start as slight, pimple-looking eruptions and within 30 minutes are huge livid welts the size of a large fried egg, gradually the redness disappears, and the swelling goes down, but, paradoxically, the size increases and the specific area affected spreads, until it, some hours later, again becomes one with the rest of my epidermis. I am quite confident this allergy is directly attributable to the considerable tension both LuAnne and Carolyn are causing in me. The doctor feels the same way. A change appears necessary, eh what?

I'm just getting warmed up, so if you please, let me dash on with no regard to dropped letters, misspellings etc.

(Jack, Neal is now gorging himself with the aforementioned Class B movie. This time, he is sprawling on the couch, as usual nude, gazing into cross-eyed space, wheezing "I retreat!" "I retreat!" to Tibet, that is, accompanying each "retreat" by flailing the arms and legs alternately about. He becomes annoyed at me now)

Dear Jack, this fiend, Carolyn has just swiped my typewriter for 30 seconds, while I explained *The Razor's Edge* in its entirety.

–*The Missouri Review* (no. 2, 1999), pp. 101–102

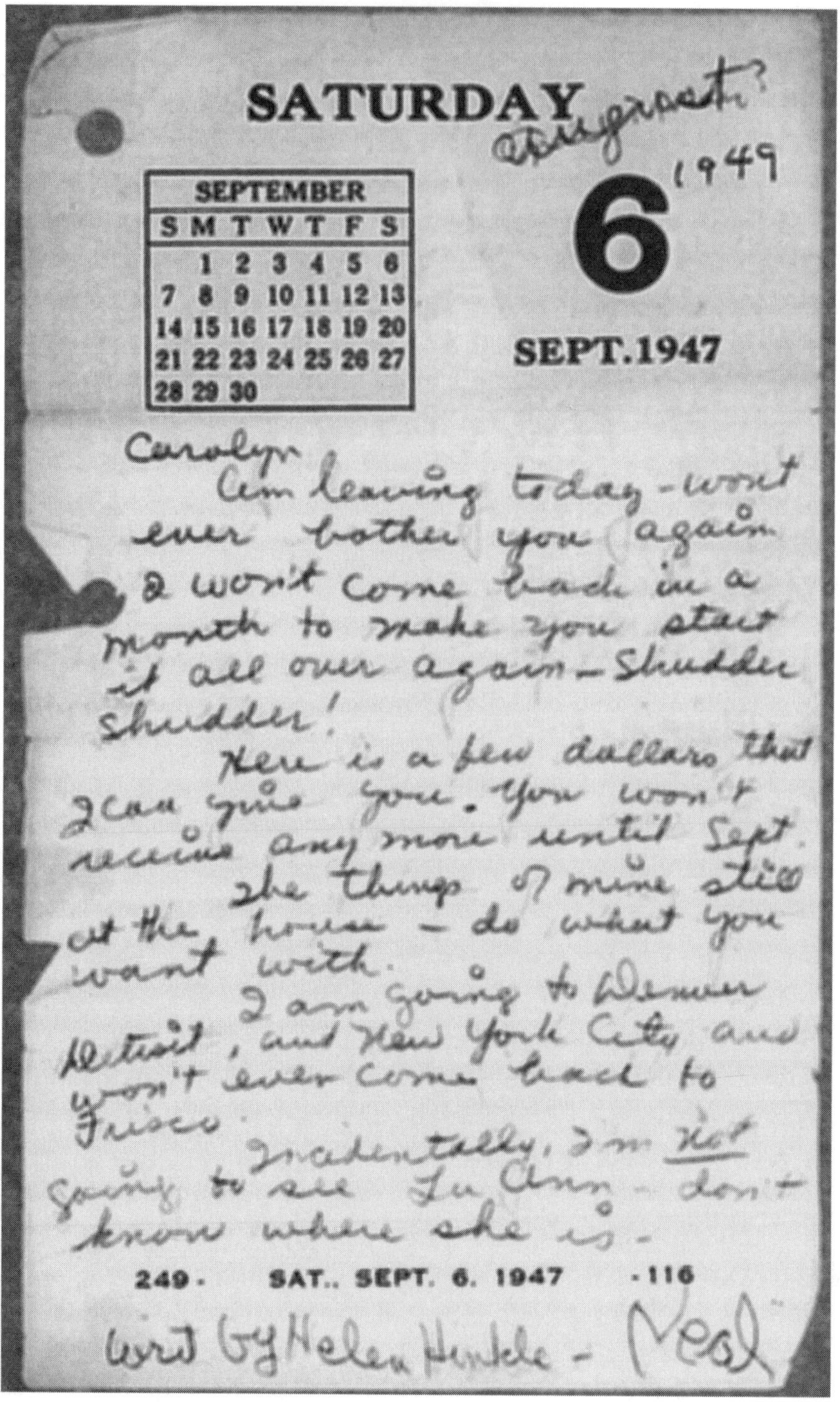
SATURDAY

1949

SEPTEMBER						
S	M	T	W	T	F	S
	1	2	3	4	5	6
7	8	9	10	11	12	13
14	15	16	17	18	19	20
21	22	23	24	25	26	27
28	29	30				

6

SEPT. 1947

Carolyn
Am leaving today - won't ever bother you again & won't come back in a month to make you start it all over again - Shudder Shudder!
Here is a few dollars that I can give you. You won't receive any more until Sept.
The things of mine still at the house - do what you want with.
I am going to Denver Detroit, and New York City and won't ever come back to Frisco.
Incidentally, I'm Not going to see Lu Ann - don't know where she is -

249 - SAT., SEPT. 6, 1947 - 116

Writ by Helen Hinkle - Neal

Farewell note left by Cassady for his wife at the doctor's office in which she worked. In 1949 the Cassadys were living on San Francisco's Russian Hill with one child, Cathy, and another on the way, when Kerouac arrived to reunite with his road buddy. Tensions ensued as Kerouac's presence brought to the surface the instability of the Cassadys' home life. Their friend Helen Hinkle had done the writing because Neal's left hand was in a cast–the result of a fight with LuAnne, whom he continued to see. Cassady returned to his wife and family the following year and took a job with the railroad (from Steve Turner, Angelheaded Hipster *[1996]).*

2) To my April Fool's magnificent Ass, *1951*
So beautixxious, though overfull, as is
your heart, with misery,
I heze make present a sliver of cut
stained glass,
Which unable to shave your behind's blubber,
might yet pierce your resivbr of hurt
Enough to make our third anniversery,
A day of insight crystal clear,
Combined with knowledge thru the ear,
So that when this Sabbath sun decends,
There'll be an understanding which portends
Henceforth, a bliss that never ends,
But shows up for joke the fear
that dread neurotic mind's hold dear,
And do pretend to suffer unjust trial
To all the while make careful file
of everybody's dreary food,
On which they feed of selfish acts;
~~That I~~
Only to find it does no good
For us since never has been forgot the pacts
Made three years ago this day,
When each to the other did say
Those eternal vows that cost ten bucks
To get from you my legal --shucks, no paper.

Poem written by Neal for Carolyn on 1 April 1951 (Collection of Carolyn Cassady)

15 October 1950

Excerpt from a letter from Neal Cassady to Kerouac.

I have done and gone done the gonest thing: I BOUGHT A WIRE RECORDER! not a *wire* recorder, but, better, a tape recorder; a gone instrument which reproduces so flawlessly (you can hear a clock ticking from way over in next room when you play back recording) and so cheaply, and so *effortlessly,* and the tapes last *forever,* don't break, can save any part or all of anything recorded, atc. rtc. etc. The hour tape for example is only about 5 inches in diameter and weighs only few ounces and can be filled on *both* sides, so is really 2 hour tape (I got 2 half-hour rolls too) and simply record go to nearby postoffice and mail to *ME* A LETTER, better, 2 hours of our VOICES talking to each other, Save all labor of letters for writing (SO HORRIBLY HORRIBLY SHITPOT HARD FOR ME) until such time as have written, then maybe, I too, could reel off a 5000 page letter every day to you, Gawd, I sho (don't know dialect yet) does *ad*mire any of the fellers can write them books an' all Geezus CHrist! Get it now? buy an EKOTAPE tape recorder small portable size, look in telephone directory it has EKOTAPE dealers, buy on time (costs no more) and get at once, cost 150.00 dollars, down payment, say 60 or so, don't know. GET AT ONCE.

—*The Missouri Review* (no. 2, 1999), p. 109

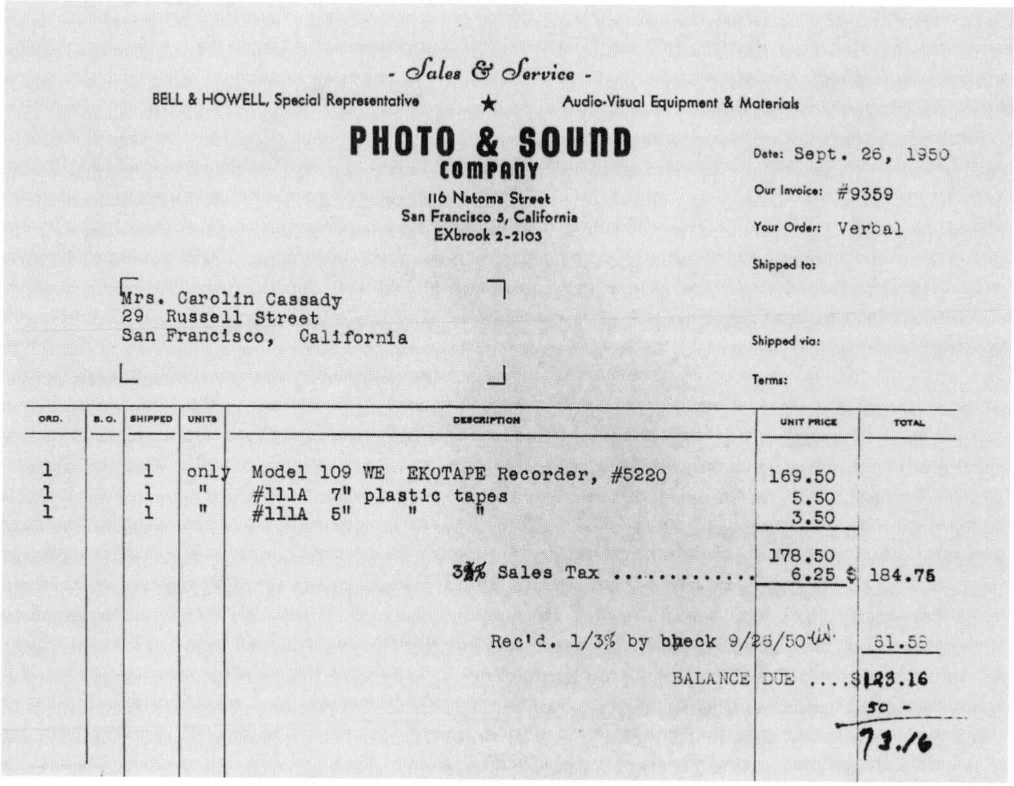

- Sales & Service -

BELL & HOWELL, Special Representative ★ Audio-Visual Equipment & Materials

PHOTO & SOUND COMPANY
116 Natoma Street
San Francisco 5, California
EXbrook 2-2103

Date: Sept. 26, 1950
Our Invoice: #9359
Your Order: Verbal
Shipped to:
Shipped via:
Terms:

Mrs. Carolin Cassady
29 Russell Street
San Francisco, California

ORD.	B. O.	SHIPPED	UNITS	DESCRIPTION	UNIT PRICE	TOTAL
1		1	only	Model 109 WE EKOTAPE Recorder, #5220	169.50	
1		1	"	#111A 7" plastic tapes	5.50	
1		1	"	#111A 5" " "	3.50	
					178.50	
				3½% Sales Tax	6.25	$ 184.75
				Rec'd. 1/3% by check 9/26/50		61.59
				BALANCE DUE		$123.16
						50 -
						73.16

Receipt for the tape recorder Cassady bought so that he could dictate his stories. When Kerouac arrived in San Francisco late in 1951, the two used the recorder to tape the late-night, marijuana-inspired conversations that Kerouac included in Visions of Cody, *published posthumously in 1972 (Collection of Carolyn Cassady).*

Road Tales

Cassady's February 1951 letter may have been the model for Kerouac's storytelling style in On the Road. *Cassady tells of his own solitary road adventures in a simple, tell-all narrative. Typically, Cassady disparages the quality and effect of his own writing, but the freshness and honesty of the prose impressed Kerouac.*

I enclose here a real quickie I whipped off in just a couple of hours. Actually I wrote this poor little start of a thing around the first of January before I came east for a visit. I don't feel badly as to its weak qualities because I just dashed it off without a pause.

My second trip from Denver to Los Angeles was not the starved struggle the first one had been. I established a pattern used in later years when hitchhiking south from my home town, that is, I always afterward left the city in the fashion I did this time. The policy was to be on Denver's southern outskirts at dawn and by not leaving the road for an instant, hope to gain Raton, New Mexico by nightfall. I never failed to achieve this goal. It seems I possessed the inordinary luck to conquer this 250-odd mile distance by catching quick rides that often got me into New Mexico in the early PM. Conversely, once on Raton's highway junction–the right hand leg went to Texas and southeast, the left to the southwest and California–some blocks beyond the railroad underpass where the hotshot freights begin to pick up speed, I could never get a lift until I'd waited many hours. My first trip had switched its mode of travel at this point, when at midnight, after thumbing cars for eight full hours, I'd caught one of these hiball reefer trains and continued the balance of the journey by rail. A couple of years later I was to wait 2 days in this spot without being picked up by a friendly motorist. Now, however, I had the good fortune to make connections right away with one of the infrequently passing cars. He took me to Taos, and when I got out it was not yet dusk. I was cheered; this was making the fastest time ever and just escaping from the Raton Rut bouyed me no end. I was confident; I was happy.

I bounced along the narrow blacktop with eager strides, breathing deep of the clean mountain air, marveling at the luxuriant vermillion gold of the sunset. Adobe buildings lined the way; every tenth structure housed a bar. From out their open doors came loud Mexican music and the aroma of spiced food. Drunken Indians, their long black hair braided under strange hats used the center of the hiway as a path upon which to stagger. Some were singsonging to themselves, none talked, and most passed me in dark silence with cold eyes. Ahead, half up a slight hill, I saw a white rancher leave one of these taverns and make for a pickup truck; he was finishing a bottle of beer as he slowly walked to the machine. I hurried to catch him and bum a ride. He sensed my intention before I had a chance to voice it, and looking me over for a second, he said, "Get in." He didn't take me far, but I soon caught another ride which took me to Sante Fe near middlenight.

I sauntered thru this city in a fine state of hunger–fine, I say, because I hadn't eaten since morning, and in my pockets was the money for a good feed. Knowing the unlikelihood of an auto stopping for me after nightfall, I anticipated taking in the sights I could of this State Capitol while hiking leisurely across it, then, settle in a cozy restaurant for a lengthy meal. I figured this program to get me "On The Road" and in position still in good time before dawn, so I followed it.

I recall as I passed the State Police barracks two stern troupers left its well-lit interior and crunched their swank boots on the gravel driveway for brief seconds before they piled into their radio-dispatched police car with automatic motions of tough efficiency. This flashing glimpse of their hard gestures and unslack jaws, clamped so tightly against the grim upper lip, and their faces immobile as steel emphasizing the sheen of their merciless eyes glittering with zeal to perform their duty made me shudder as I though of the short shift they gave their prey. They spun the wheels and roared away while I was pitying any quarry they nabbed that night. Their ruthless tactics I well knew and couldn't escape a twinge of relief that I wasn't their intended victim. I went by crowded tourist cafes serving well-to-do travelers Mexican and American dishes, catering to their every wish, as their slick automobiles, parked in the rough street's high curb at an angle, patiently waited in quiet splendor to carry them away–escorted in magnificent style–when it was their whim to leave. The downtown area was packed with throngs of humanity, altho it was a late hour, and I don't think it was a Saturday night. The congested glob was heightened by the streets of alley width (20 ft. or so) along which cars crawled with exasperating honking. The sidewalks were over-flowing with people; men in cowboy apparel and otherwise, Indians, solemn and otherwise, Mexicans chattering and otherwise, whites drunk and otherwise, Indian girls encased in moccasins, Indian squaws encased in fat, Mexican chicks in tight skirts and provocative stride, old Mexican women in more fat and burdened with unwashed infants, white women of all kinds, waitresses, heiresses, etc. and kids, kids every place imaginable, leaping and yelling, lunging between cars in mid-block or quiet and morose, scuffling along with head down. Above all this mass of activity glared the lights. Edison's greatest invention hung over the gathered heads in astonishing profusion.

–*The First Third & Other Writings,* pp. 203–205

(Left) Kerouac and Cassady; (right) Cassady visiting a garage near his home in San Jose, California, in 1952 (Collection of Carolyn Cassady)

Cassady, broken leg in cast, with his children in 1953 (photograph by Carolyn Cassady; Collection of Carolyn Cassady)

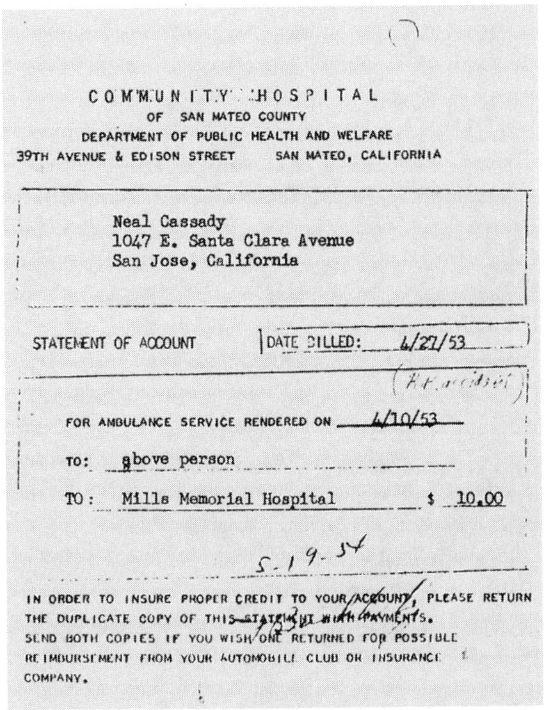

COMMUNITY HOSPITAL
OF SAN MATEO COUNTY
DEPARTMENT OF PUBLIC HEALTH AND WELFARE
39TH AVENUE & EDISON STREET SAN MATEO, CALIFORNIA

Neal Cassady
1047 E. Santa Clara Avenue
San Jose, California

STATEMENT OF ACCOUNT | DATE BILLED: 4/27/53

FOR AMBULANCE SERVICE RENDERED ON 4/10/53

TO: above person

TO: Mills Memorial Hospital $ 10.00

5-19-54

IN ORDER TO INSURE PROPER CREDIT TO YOUR ACCOUNT, PLEASE RETURN THE DUPLICATE COPY OF THIS STATEMENT WITH PAYMENTS. SEND BOTH COPIES IF YOU WISH ONE RETURNED FOR POSSIBLE REIMBURSEMENT FROM YOUR AUTOMOBILE CLUB OR INSURANCE COMPANY.

Cassady's Affair with Natalie Jackson

In April 1953 Cassady broke his leg while working as a brakeman for the Southern Pacific Company railroad. Cassady's lawyer tried to get $75,000 from the railroad, but after fees and expenses the Cassadys received $16,747.47. They used some of the money for a car and for a down payment on a house near Los Gatos. They also sent $1,000 to Diana Hanson in New York, whom Neal had bigamously married and with whom he had a child. They invested $5,000, which doubled in one year. At that point Neal and a woman posing as Carolyn withdrew the money. In about a month Neal had lost all $10,000 at the racetrack. The woman, Natalie Jackson, fell from a rooftop soon afterward, apparently a suicide.

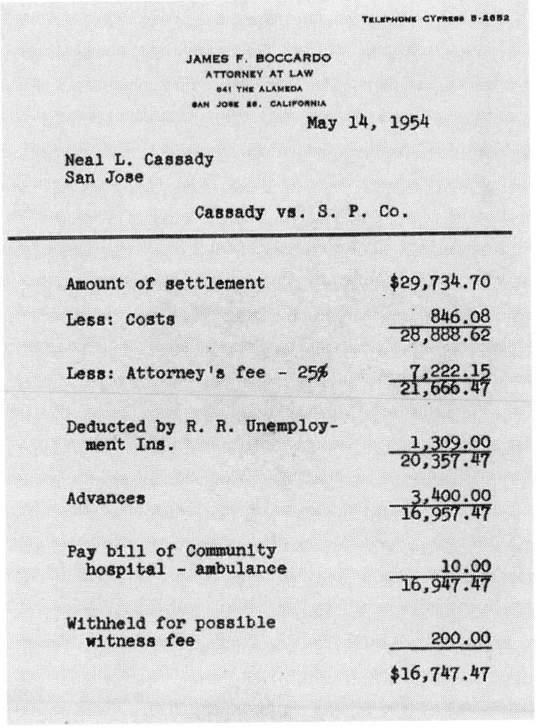

TELEPHONE CYPRESS 5-2652

JAMES F. BOCCARDO
ATTORNEY AT LAW
841 THE ALAMEDA
SAN JOSE 26, CALIFORNIA

May 14, 1954

Neal L. Cassady
San Jose

Cassady vs. S. P. Co.

Amount of settlement	$29,734.70
Less: Costs	846.08
	28,888.62
Less: Attorney's fee - 25%	7,222.15
	21,666.47
Deducted by R. R. Unemployment Ins.	1,309.00
	20,357.47
Advances	3,400.00
	16,957.47
Pay bill of Community hospital - ambulance	10.00
	16,947.47
Withheld for possible witness fee	200.00
	$16,747.47

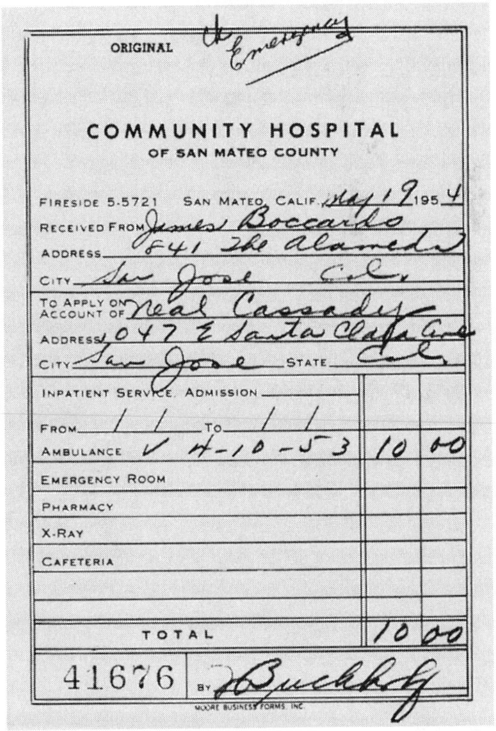

ORIGINAL Emergency

COMMUNITY HOSPITAL
OF SAN MATEO COUNTY

FIRESIDE 5-5721 SAN MATEO, CALIF. May 19 1954
RECEIVED FROM James Boccardo
ADDRESS 841 The Alameda
CITY San Jose Cal.
TO APPLY ON ACCOUNT OF Neal Cassady
ADDRESS 1047 E Santa Clara Ave
CITY San Jose STATE Cal.

INPATIENT SERVICE. ADMISSION		
FROM / / TO / /		
AMBULANCE ✓ 4-10-53	10	00
EMERGENCY ROOM		
PHARMACY		
X-RAY		
CAFETERIA		
TOTAL	10	00

41676 BY Buckley

MOORE BUSINESS FORMS, INC.

Documents relating to the accident in which Cassady broke his leg while working for the Southern Pacific Railroad (Collection of Carolyn Cassady)

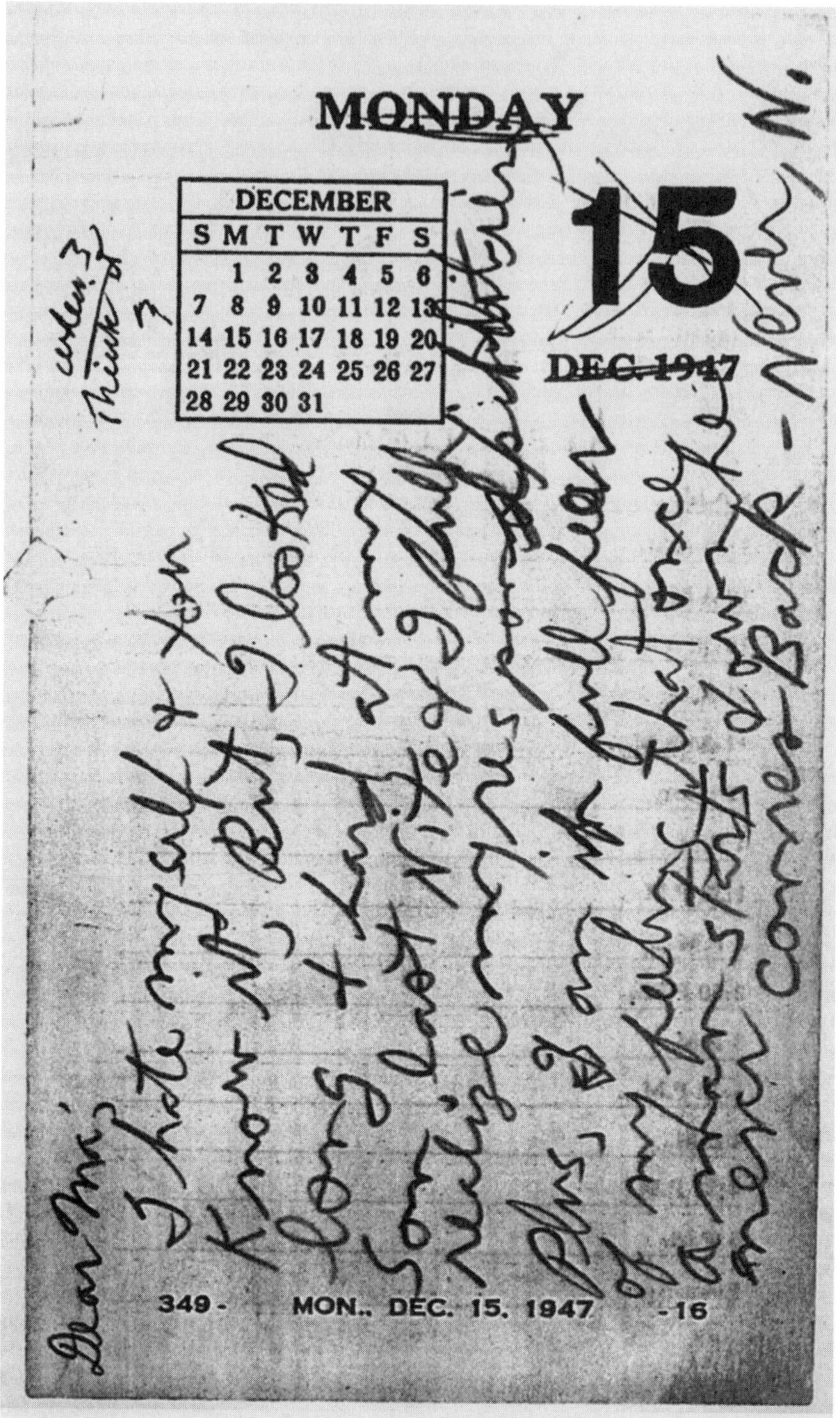

Note Cassady put on Carolyn's bedside table on 10 May 1955 when he left to live with Natalie Jackson in San Francisco. Carolyn discovered Neal's affair with Natalie after he left some letters and photographs in his pants pocket. In San Francisco, he shared an apartment with Ginsberg and Ginsberg's lover, Peter Orlofsky (Collection of Carolyn Cassady).

Cassady (right) with unidentified automobile salesman in San Francisco in 1955 (photograph by Allen Ginsberg)

Cassady and Natalie Jackson on Market Street in San Francisco in 1955 (photograph by Allen Ginsberg)

ASK FOR HORSE BY PROGRAM NUMBER

6 FURLONGS — SIXTH RACE

Purse $2,400. For three-year-olds. 118 lbs. Non-winners of $1,200 in 1963 allowed 4 lbs. Claiming price $5,000.

Track Record—NATIVE DIVER, November 3, 1962, 1:08⅘ (3) 120

	Owner	Trainer	Jockey	
1	Deseris Stable. Royal blue and grey stripes, royal blue and grey cap. TEKARRA 114. B.c.3, Gold Capitol—Grecian Gem	E. T. Watts	Merlin Volzke	6
2	Mr. or Mrs. J. C. Walker. Red front, red circle "W" on white back, white sleeves and cap. ROYAL FIRE 114. B.c.3, Bernwood—Royal Tonie	H. C. McBride	Donald Ross	6
3	South Ridge Stable. Black, white emblem on back, black and white cap. BUZZ TOP 114. Ch.g.3, Scorpion 2nd—Topseat Topsy	Michael Bao	Ray York	12
4	Go Go Go Stable. Red, blue "Go Go Go" on back, blue sleeves, red cap. NEW EYES 118. [illegible]	Morton Lipton	Frank Costa	5/2
5	Grohs, Grohs & Thompson. Turquoise, white diamonds on front, turquoise and white cap. FINE N FANCY 109. Ch.f.3, Cyclotron—Patriot's Lily	Otto Grohs	Phillip Grohs	8
6	Roy Taylor. Gold, red devils on back, gold cap. WEBEN-WIN 113. Ch.f.3, The Web 2nd—[illegible]	Owner	Glen Dixon	7/2
7	Rosse Del Mar Ranch. Green, black and green blocks on front, black sleeves, green and black cap. BATSAVU *109. B.c.3, California Kid—Bertha	Ferrell W. Jones	Donald Tam	3

*Apprentice allowance claimed.

Cooperation of our patrons is earnestly solicited in keeping the grounds and stands at Bay Meadows clean and clear of debris. Your use of the convenient metal receptacles for disposal of newspapers, paper and trash will be greatly appreciated. Loose articles and paper create a hazard to horses and riders when blown onto the racing strip. Thank you for your help.

THE MANAGEMENT.

1963 RAMBLER CLASSIC
The official car used on the race track is furnished through the courtesy of
FRANK WALT RAMBLER
2745 El Camino Real, San Mateo, California

ASK FOR HORSE BY PROGRAM NUMBER

6 FURLONGS — SEVENTH RACE

SANTA CLARA

Purse $3,000. For three-year-olds which have never won a race other than maiden or claiming. 118 lbs. Non-winners of $2,000 other than claiming since December 25 allowed 4 lbs.

Track Record—NATIVE DIVER, November 3, 1962, 1:08⅘ (3) 120

	Owner	Trainer	Jockey	
1	Josephine O'Brien. Gold, brown stripes, gold cap. JO'S GEM 109. B.f.3, Solidarity—Blue Sapphire	Owner	Omar Picado	15
2	Mrs. Frank C. Bishop. Venetian and white vertical stripes, red sleeves, red and white cap. WHAT CHEER 109. Br.f.3, Anyoldtime—Some Gal	Joseph Manzi	Taylor Powell	8
3	Ferry & Est. of R. Watson. Royal blue, gold crown on back, gold bars on sleeves, blue cap. JOHN PERI 114. B.c.3, Heelfly—Sierra Breeze	Bob Berger	Frank Costa	5/2
4	Daniel W. Scott II. Red, white vertical stripes, white bars on blue sleeves, red, white and blue cap. BOCADO 114. Ch.c.3, Bolero—Little Flash	Ken Setter	Bud Giacomelli	20
5	J. K. Houssels. Green, white sash, green and white cap. VEGAS HILDA 109. Ch.f.3, Flash O' Night—Vegas Bride	James Wilson	Robert Yanez	9/5
6	Hudson & Glass. Blue, gold stars and "A" on back, blue cap. MR. TAILS 114. Ch.c.3, Loin Cloth—Bartella	David H. Holton	Dan Castle	20
7	Holbush Farms. White, white "HHF" in blue clover leaf on back, blue collar and cuffs, white cap. FANTASMON 118. B.g.3, Star of the Forest—Ann's Lark	H. C. McBride	Donald Ross	9/2
8	Norman & Edmond Vadnais. Red, white "VV" on back, white cap. SARA MONEEN 109. B.f.3, Borsanom—Moneen	John M. Leavitt	Ray York	6

Latest Workouts—Mr. Tails: Feb. 25, Pleas. ½ :50⅘; March 2, Pleas. ⅝ 1:08; March 7, S. M. ⅝ 1:04 b.g.
Declared: Friendly Fred, Devil's Melody, Lucky Ghost.

NO DELAY ON INQUIRIES

In case of an inquiry into the running of a previous race, to eliminate delay the totalisator machines will be cleared and the mutuel windows will be opened for the next race. The official results of the previous race will be announced as soon as the inquiry has been completed.

PHOTO FINISH

The Camera is used as an assistance to the Judges in arriving at a decision. However, in all cases, the decision of the Judges is final.

Obsession

Cassady was obsessed with horse racing. He studied the newspaper results for an hour each evening, convinced that he had developed a system that would beat the track and make him rich: bet the third-favorite horse consistently; frequently, the number three horse would win, and if one placed increasingly larger bets, one would recover all the money lost on earlier races plus a hefty profit. Cassady insisted that his approach was scientific and not to be confused with gambling. Kerouac writes about his horse-racing afternoon with Cassady in *Desolation Angels.*

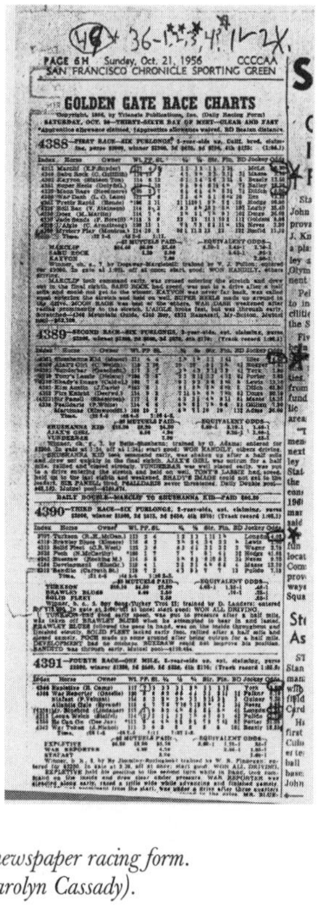

PAGE 6H Sunday, Oct. 21, 1956 CCCCAA
SAN FRANCISCO CHRONICLE SPORTING GREEN

GOLDEN GATE RACE CHARTS

4388 4389 4390 4391

Cover and inside pages from racetrack program and newspaper racing form. The annotations are Cassady's (Collection of Carolyn Cassady).

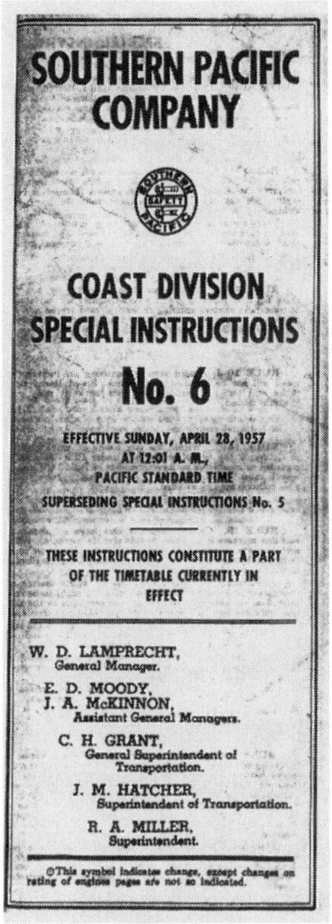

SOUTHERN PACIFIC COMPANY

COAST DIVISION
SPECIAL INSTRUCTIONS
No. 6

EFFECTIVE SUNDAY, APRIL 28, 1957
AT 12:01 A. M.,
PACIFIC STANDARD TIME
SUPERSEDING SPECIAL INSTRUCTIONS No. 5

THESE INSTRUCTIONS CONSTITUTE A PART OF THE TIMETABLE CURRENTLY IN EFFECT

W. D. LAMPRECHT,
General Manager.

E. D. MOODY,
J. A. McKINNON,
Assistant General Managers.

C. H. GRANT,
General Superintendent of Transportation.

J. M. HATCHER,
Superintendent of Transportation.

R. A. MILLER,
Superintendent.

⊙This symbol indicates change, except changes on rating of engines pages are not so indicated.

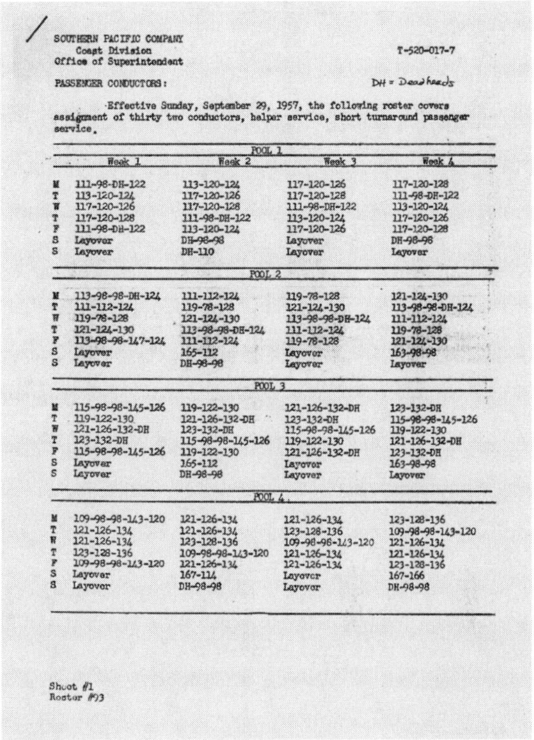

SOUTHERN PACIFIC COMPANY
Coast Division
Office of Superintendent

T-520-017-7

PASSENGER CONDUCTORS:

DH = Deadheads

Effective Sunday, September 29, 1957, the following roster covers assignment of thirty two conductors, helper service, short turnaround passenger service.

POOL 1

	Week 1	Week 2	Week 3	Week 4
M	111-98-DH-122	113-120-124	117-120-126	117-120-128
T	113-120-124	117-120-126	117-120-128	111-98-DH-122
W	117-120-126	117-120-128	111-98-DH-122	113-120-124
T	117-120-128	111-98-DH-122	113-120-124	117-120-126
F	111-98-DH-122	113-120-124	117-120-126	117-120-128
S	Layover	DH-98-98	Layover	DH-98-98
S	Layover	DH-110	Layover	Layover

POOL 2

M	113-98-98-DH-124	111-112-124	119-78-128	121-124-130
T	111-112-124	119-78-128	121-124-130	113-98-98-DH-124
W	119-78-128	121-124-130	113-98-98-DH-124	111-112-124
T	121-124-130	113-98-98-DH-124	111-112-124	119-78-128
F	113-98-98-147-124	111-112-124	119-78-128	121-124-130
S	Layover	165-112	Layover	163-98-98
S	Layover	DH-98-98	Layover	Layover

POOL 3

M	115-98-98-145-126	119-122-130	121-126-132-DH	123-132-DH
T	119-122-130	121-126-132-DH	123-132-DH	115-98-98-145-126
W	121-126-132-DH	123-132-DH	115-98-98-145-126	119-122-130
T	123-132-DH	115-98-98-145-126	119-122-130	121-126-132-DH
F	115-98-98-145-126	119-122-130	121-126-132-DH	123-132-DH
S	Layover	165-112	Layover	163-98-98
S	Layover	DH-98-98	Layover	Layover

POOL 4.

M	109-98-98-143-120	121-126-134	121-126-134	123-128-136
T	121-126-134	121-126-134	123-128-136	109-98-98-143-120
W	121-126-134	123-128-136	109-98-98-143-120	121-126-134
T	123-128-136	109-98-98-143-120	121-126-134	121-126-134
F	109-98-98-143-120	121-126-134	121-126-134	123-128-136
S	Layover	167-114	Layover	167-166
S	Layover	DH-98-98	Layover	DH-98-98

Shoot #1
Roster #93

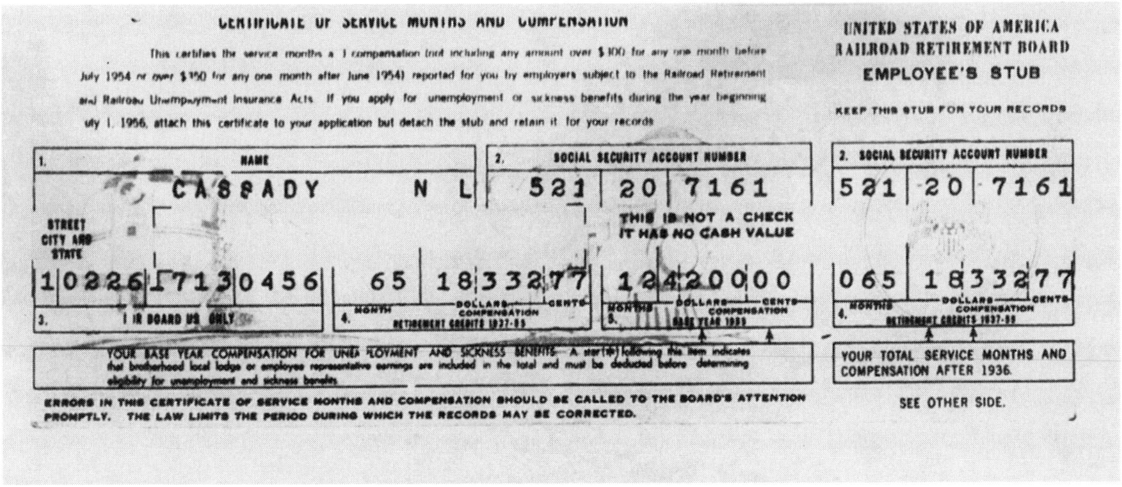

CERTIFICATE OF SERVICE MONTHS AND COMPENSATION

This certifies the service months and compensation (not including any amount over $300 for any one month before July 1954 or over $350 for any one month after June 1954) reported for you by employers subject to the Railroad Retirement and Railroad Unemployment Insurance Acts. If you apply for unemployment or sickness benefits during the year beginning July 1, 1956, attach this certificate to your application but detach the stub and retain it for your records.

1. NAME: CASSADY N L

2. SOCIAL SECURITY ACCOUNT NUMBER: 521 20 7161

THIS IS NOT A CHECK
IT HAS NO CASH VALUE

STREET
CITY AND
STATE

1 0 2 2 6 1 7 1 3 0 4 5 6

3. I R BOARD USE ONLY

4. MONTHS 65 — DOLLARS 1833 CENTS 77 — COMPENSATION — RETIREMENT CREDITS 1937-55

5. MONTHS 12 — DOLLARS 420 CENTS 00 — COMPENSATION — BASE YEAR 1955

YOUR BASE YEAR COMPENSATION FOR UNEMPLOYMENT AND SICKNESS BENEFITS—A star (*) following this item indicates that brotherhood local lodge or employee representative earnings are included in the total and must be deducted before determining eligibility for unemployment and sickness benefits.

ERRORS IN THIS CERTIFICATE OF SERVICE MONTHS AND COMPENSATION SHOULD BE CALLED TO THE BOARD'S ATTENTION PROMPTLY. THE LAW LIMITS THE PERIOD DURING WHICH THE RECORDS MAY BE CORRECTED.

UNITED STATES OF AMERICA
RAILROAD RETIREMENT BOARD
EMPLOYEE'S STUB

KEEP THIS STUB FOR YOUR RECORDS

2. SOCIAL SECURITY ACCOUNT NUMBER: 521 20 7161

4. MONTHS 065 — DOLLARS 1833 CENTS 77 — COMPENSATION — RETIREMENT CREDITS 1937-55

YOUR TOTAL SERVICE MONTHS AND COMPENSATION AFTER 1936.

SEE OTHER SIDE.

Documents from Cassady's railroad job (Collection of Carolyn Cassady)

San Quentin

Cassady worked again as a brakeman on the Southern Pacific Railroad after he recovered from his broken leg. In April 1958 Cassady was arrested in his home in Los Gatos, California, for selling marijuana. Apparently he had been given $40 by two undercover agents to buy marijuana for them, but he kept the money instead. (Another version of the incident, according to which Cassady offered a marijuana joint to undercover officers in exchange for a ride, is untrue.) Cassady later insisted that he was arrested because he could identify the officers. Although no evidence was offered at his trial, he was sentenced to two terms of five years to life and was sent to San Quentin on 4 July 1958. He was released on 3 June 1960. In a Life *magazine article on the Beat Generation (30 November 1959) writer Paul O'Neil referred to Cassady as the "Johnny Appleseed of the Marijuana Racket." The Cassadys were divorced after he was released from prison.*

In these excerpts from a 17 April 1959 letter Kerouac promises to buy a typewriter for his incarcerated friend, and he did so. He also says that he might publish Cassady's writing in an anthology that he is to edit; he never completed the project. Nor did he ever visit Cassady in San Quentin, though Ginsberg did.

Dear Carolyn,

No, the prison authorities rejected my application to correspond with Neal, also Allen's. They are cruel in every possible way. Imagine that bitch Connie N. getting off with parole after murdering a human being in cold blood, and poor Neal with his pockets full of innocent loco weed that grows wild in Texas getting an indefinite term. . . . Do you mind if I say this in my next Escapade Magazine column or shouldn't I mention Neal's name?

By the way, Allen is coming out a few days from now, to Frisco, and wants to see Neal etc. I dont know if he'll help the situation or not but he will see you first possibly. . . .

Is this Olympia a portable or a big brand new standard? Let me know how much you need and I'll send the check. The money will represent my debt to Neal for all the porkchop suppers we had over the years in your dear sweet kitchen, remember? (And all the pizzas). I dont want you and Neal to think my book had anything to do with his arrest, after all he was too reckless, people were telling him to stay away from North Beach years ago. If anything, if all the On the Road fans all over the world knew what had happened to "Dean" they would all be writing protesting letters to SQ about it. The only thing I'M sorry about, that is, with reference to what I did that was wrong, was the invitation to Neal in 1957 to drive to NY and fetch me and "meet the girls" as a laugh, well, truly, secretly, to INDUCE the excitable Neal to come and get me, and that was sneaky. But O my book, On the road, isnt it a paean to Neal? I hope you think so

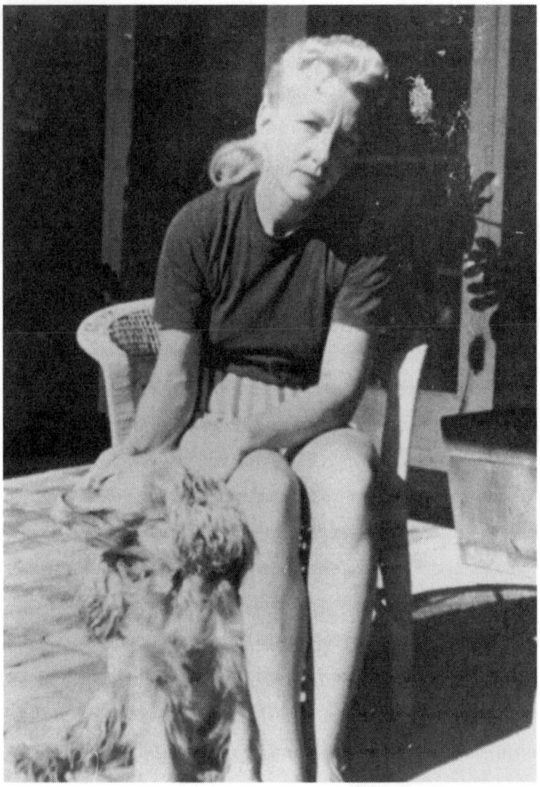

Photograph of Carolyn, taken in 1959 to be sent to her husband in San Quentin. She hoped that it would elicit sympathy from Neal's jailers (Collection of Carolyn Cassady).

Now be sure and get this typewriter to Neal because he wants to go on writing and also I can start publishing him immediately & pay you money, I've been made the editor of an anthology, appearing 3 times a year or so, for 25c in drugstore newsstands. Beat Generation Anthology, I'd like to start with First Third the beginning and work on up each issue. Meanwhile N. continues work on the rest in SQ. Someday he'll be a successful writer, both artistically and commercially, and could have time to stay home and play with the kids and write by the pool, instead of torturing himself on railroads. For he's a great man indeed and as good a wordslinger as I am, which is the best. Encourage him to write, Carolyn. . . .

—*Jack Kerouac: Selected Letters,* 1956–1969, *pp. 193–194*

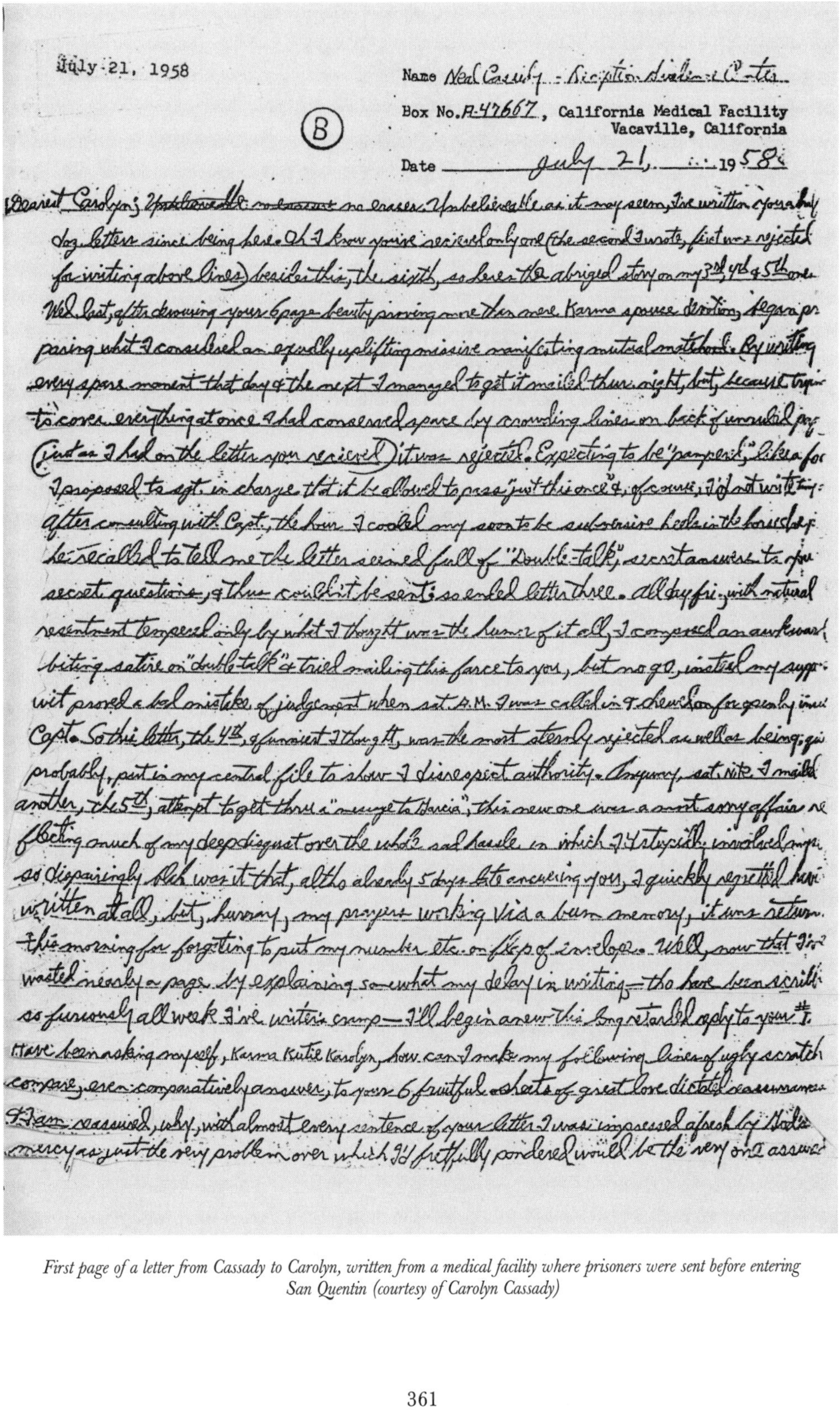

July 21, 1958

Name Neal Cassady - [illegible]

(B)

Box No. A-47667, California Medical Facility
Vacaville, California

Date July 21, 1958

Dearest Carolyn; no eraser. Unbelievable as it may seem, I've written you a half doz. letters since being here. Oh I know you've recieved only one (the second I wrote, first was rejected for writing above lines) besides this, the sixth, so here the abriged story on my 3rd, 4th & 5th ones. Wed. last, after devouring your 6 page beauty proving more than mere Karma spouse devotion, I began [illegible] what I considered an equally uplifting missive manifesting mutual [illegible]. By writing every spare moment that day & the next I managed to get it mailed thurs. night, but, because trying to cover everything at once I had conserved space by crowding lines on back of unruled page (just as I had on the letter you recieved) it was rejected. Expecting to be "pampered," like a fool I proposed to sgt. in charge that it be allowed to pass "just this once" &, of course, [illegible]; after consulting with Capt., the hour I cooled my soon to be subversive heels in the [illegible] he recalled to tell me the letter seemed full of "Double-talk," secret answers to your secret questions, & thus couldn't be sent; so ended letter three. All day fri., with natural resentment tempered only by what I thought was the humor of it all, I composed an awkward, biting satire on "double-talk" & tried mailing this farce to you, but no go, instead my [illegible] wit proved a bad mistake of judgement when sat. A.M. I was called in & chewed out [illegible] Capt. So this letter, the 4th, & funniest I thought, was the most sternly rejected as well as being, quite probably, put in my central file to show I disrespect authority. Anyway, sat. nite I mailed another, the 5th, attempt to get thru a "message to Garcia"; this new one was a most sorry affair reflecting much of my deep disgust over the whole sad hassle in which I [illegible] involved myself; so despairingly blah was it that, altho already 5 days late answering you, I quickly regretted having written at all, but, hurray, my prayers working via a bum memory, it was returned this morning for forgetting to put my number etc. on flap of envelope. Well, now that I've wasted nearly a page by explaining somewhat my delay in writing—tho have been scribbling so furiously all week I've writer's cramp—I'll begin anew this long retarded reply to your #1. I have been asking myself, Karma Kutie Karolyn, how can I make my following lines of ugly scratch compare, even comparatively answer, to your 6 fruitful sheets of great love dictated reassurance? I am reassured, why, with almost every sentence of your letter I was impressed afresh by God's mercy as just the very problem over which I'd fretfully pondered would be the very one answered

First page of a letter from Cassady to Carolyn, written from a medical facility where prisoners were sent before entering San Quentin (courtesy of Carolyn Cassady)

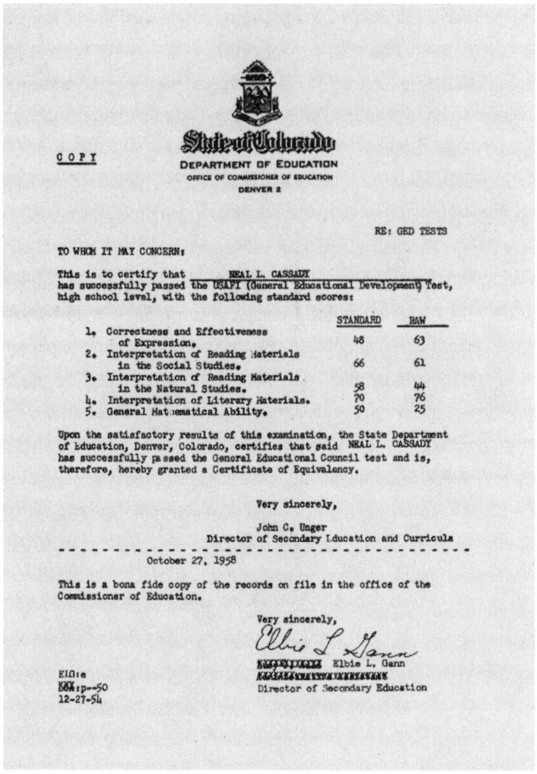

COPY

State of Colorado
DEPARTMENT OF EDUCATION
OFFICE OF COMMISSIONER OF EDUCATION
DENVER 2

RE: GED TESTS

TO WHOM IT MAY CONCERN:

This is to certify that NEAL L. CASSADY
has successfully passed the USAFI (General Educational Development) Test, high school level, with the following standard scores:

	STANDARD	RAW
1. Correctness and Effectiveness of Expression.	48	63
2. Interpretation of Reading Materials in the Social Studies.	66	61
3. Interpretation of Reading Materials in the Natural Studies.	58	44
4. Interpretation of Literary Materials.	70	76
5. General Mathematical Ability.	50	25

Upon the satisfactory results of this examination, the State Department of Education, Denver, Colorado, certifies that said NEAL L. CASSADY has successfully passed the General Educational Council test and is, therefore, hereby granted a Certificate of Equivalency.

Very sincerely,

John C. Unger
Director of Secondary Education and Curricula

October 27, 1958

This is a bona fide copy of the records on file in the office of the Commissioner of Education.

Very sincerely,

Elbie L. Gann
XXXXXXXXXX Elbie L. Gann
XXXXXXXXXXXXXXXXXXXXXX
Director of Secondary Education

ELG:e
KKX:p--50
12-27-54

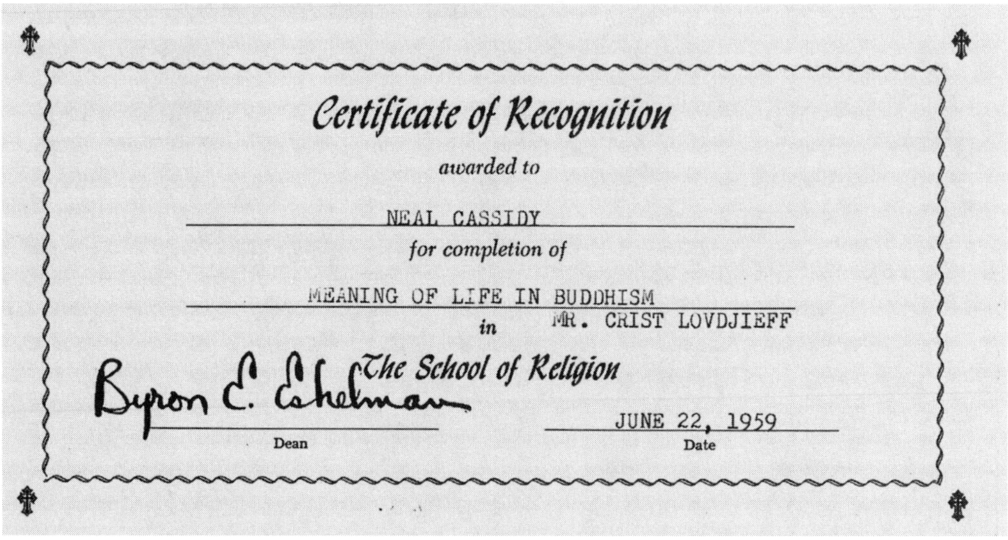

Certificate of Recognition
awarded to
NEAL CASSIDY
for completion of
MEANING OF LIFE IN BUDDHISM
in MR. CRIST LOVDJIEFF
The School of Religion
Byron E. Eshelman
Dean

JUNE 22, 1959
Date

Cassady's certificate of high-school equivalency, which he had sent to him in San Quentin, and a certificate from one of the religious classes he took in the prison (Collection of Carolyn Cassady)

Cassady with his children at Easter before he was incarcerated (photograph by Carolyn Cassady; Collection of Carolyn Cassady)

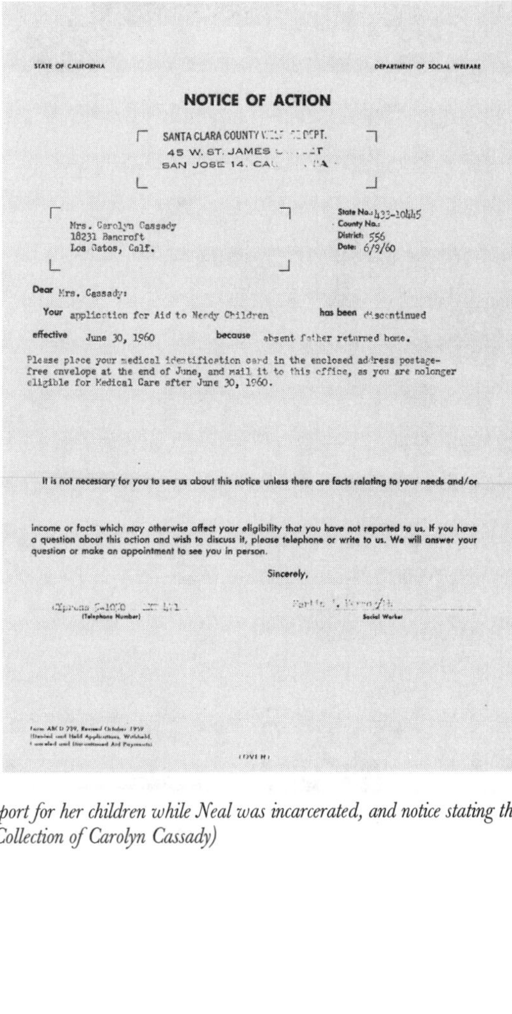

STATE OF CALIFORNIA DEPARTMENT OF SOCIAL WELFARE

NOTICE OF ACTION

SANTA CLARA COUNTY WELFARE DEPT.
45 W. ST. JAMES STREET
SAN JOSE 14. CALIFORNIA

Mrs. Carolyn Cassady
18231 Bancroft
Los Gatos, Calf.

State No.: 433-10445
County No.:
District: 556
Date: 6/9/60

Dear Mrs. Cassady:

Your application for Aid to Needy Children has been discontinued effective June 30, 1960 because absent father returned home.

Please place your medical identification card in the enclosed address postage-free envelope at the end of June, and mail it to this office, as you are nolonger eligible for Medical Care after June 30, 1960.

It is not necessary for you to see us about this notice unless there are facts relating to your needs and/or income or facts which may otherwise affect your eligibility that you have not reported to us. If you have a question about this action and wish to discuss it, please telephone or write to us. We will answer your question or make an appointment to see you in person.

Sincerely,

(Telephone Number) Social Worker

Form ANCD 239, Revised October 1959
(Denied and Held Applications, Withheld, Canceled and Discontinued Aid Payments)

(OVER)

Cover for welfare-benefits brochure given to Carolyn, who received sporadic support for her children while Neal was incarcerated, and notice stating that the aid ended with Neal's release (Collection of Carolyn Cassady)

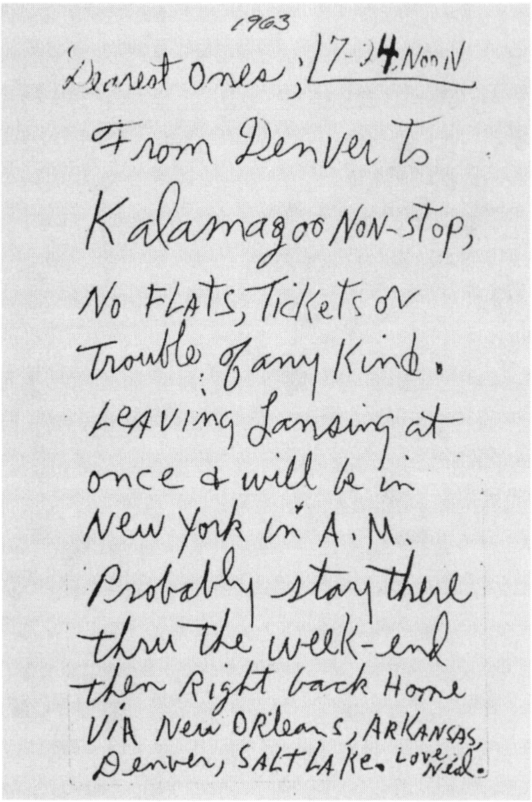
1963
Dearest Ones; 17-24 Noon
From Denver to
Kalamazoo Non-stop,
No Flats, Tickets or
Trouble of any Kind.
Leaving Lansing at
once & will be in
New York in A.M.
Probably stay there
thru the week-end
then Right back Home
via New Orleans, Arkansas,
Denver, Salt Lake. Love Neal.

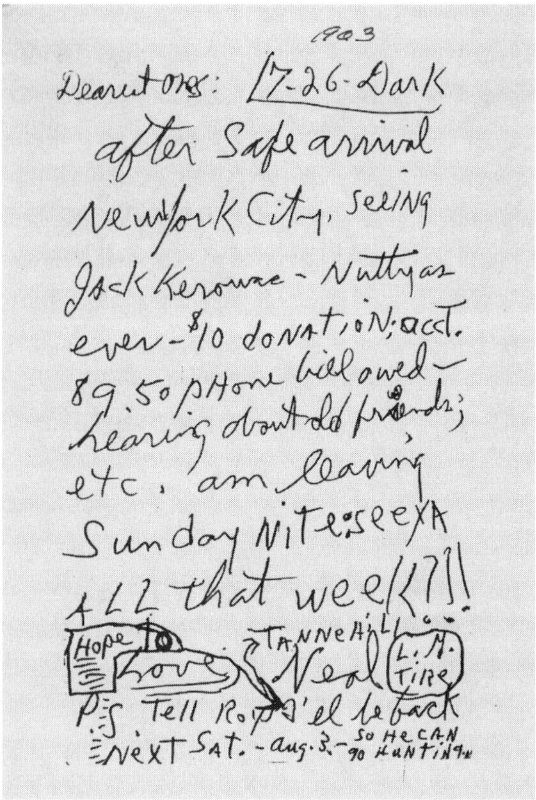
1963
Dearest ones: 17-26-Dark
after Safe arrival
New York City, seeing
Jack Kerouac - Nutty as
ever - $10 donation; acct.
89.50 phone bill owed -
hearing about old friends;
etc. am leaving
Sunday nite; see ya
all that week(?)!
Hope to Love
Tannehill
Neal
L.A. Tire
P.S. Tell Rob I'll be back
Next Sat. - Aug. 3. - so he can go hunting.

Postcards from Cassady to his family written during his 1963 trip to the East Coast, one of the last times he would see Kerouac (Collection of Carolyn Cassady)

Cassady on the Merry Prankster bus with psychologist and LSD guru Timothy Leary (photographs by Allen Ginsberg)

A Merry Prankster

As Cassady gradually lost touch with the Beat Generation, he became the speed-rapping, fast-driving hero of another group, the Merry Pranksters, headed by novelist Ken Kesey. The group staged a series of "Acid Tests" in which they took LSD and partied to music by the Grateful Dead. Their story is told in Tom Wolfe's *The Electric Kool-Aid Acid Test.* Cassady was a longtime marijuana smoker, but with the Pranksters he began to use dangerous drugs, including methamphetamine and LSD.

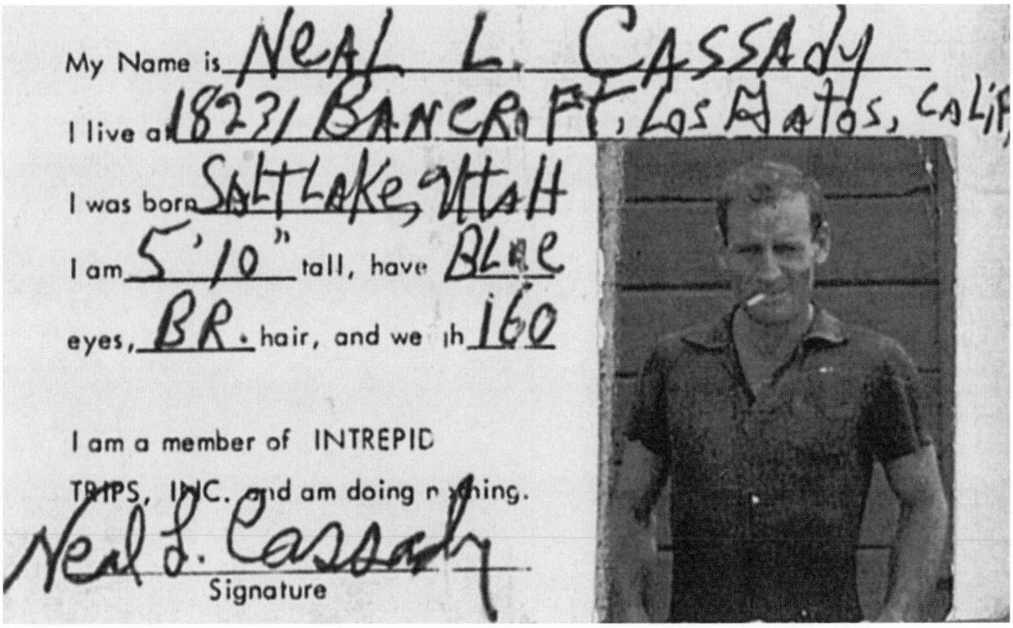

Front and back of Cassady's "Kool-Aid Acid Test" membership card (from Steve Turner, Angelheaded Hipster *[1996])*

One of the last photographs taken of Cassady, in Mexico, 1968

> *To have seen a specter isn't everything, and there are deathmasks piled, one atop the other, clear to heaven. Commoner still are the wan visages of those returning from the shadow of the valley. This means little to those who have not lifted the veil.*
>
> –Neal Cassady, *The First Third & Other Writings,* p. 146

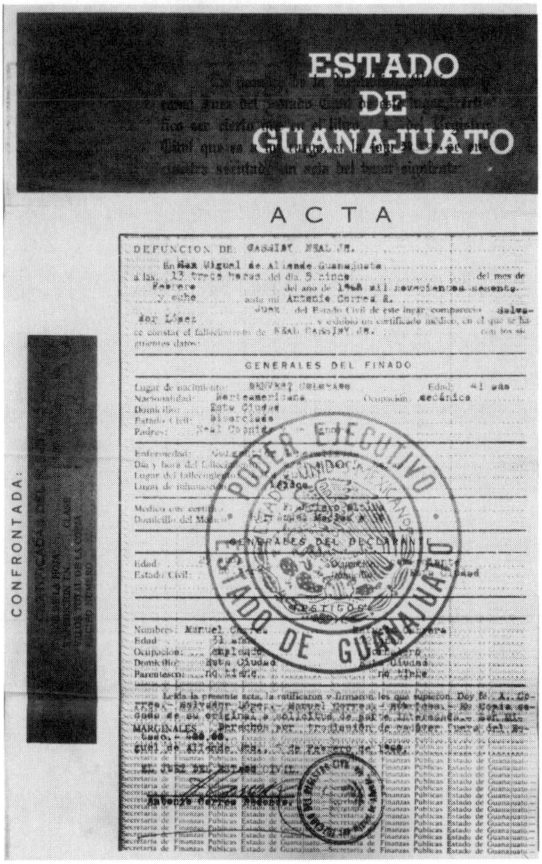

ESTADO DE GUANAJUATO

ACTA

DEFUNCION DE

GENERALES DEL FINADO

CONFRONTADA:

PODER EJECUTIVO

ESTADO DE GUANAJUATO

Cassady's death certificate (Collection of Carolyn Cassady)

Death

Cassady died early on Sunday morning, 4 February 1968, allegedly after mixing drugs with alcohol. He had been walking along railroad tracks, apparently to retrieve luggage he had left at the train station. His death certificate says that he was pronounced dead in San Miguel de Allende, Guanajuata, Mexico, at 1:00 P.M. on 5 February. The cause of death is listed as "general congestion," not "exposure to the elements," as some accounts have claimed.

Chapter 7
Gregory Corso

(26 March 1930 –)

See also the Corso entries in *DLB 5: American Poets Since World War II* and *DLB 16: The Beats: Literary Bohemians in Postwar America.*

Gregory Corso was born in a Bleecker Street apartment and grew up a child of the Greenwich Village streets. His teenaged mother abandoned him, and he spent time with various foster parents and in a youth detention home. When he was sixteen, Corso was sent to Clinton State Prison in Dannemora, New York, for his role in an armed robbery. In his three years in prison he discovered freedom in literature, particularly the poetry of Percy Bysshe Shelley. After his release in 1950 he got a job as a manual laborer in the New York City garment district. In a Greenwich Village bar he met Allen Ginsberg, who introduced him to Jack Kerouac, John Clellon Holmes, and William S. Burroughs. Ginsberg helped Corso make the social and literary connections that resulted in the publication of his poems, and Kerouac wrote about Corso in several of his books–especially in The Subterraneans *(1958) and* Desolation Angels *(1965). As the youngest of the Beat writers (he was sixteen years younger than Burroughs), Corso added youthful enthusiasm and comic relief to the darker sides the other writers often expressed.*

Gregory Corso (photograph by Howard Smith)

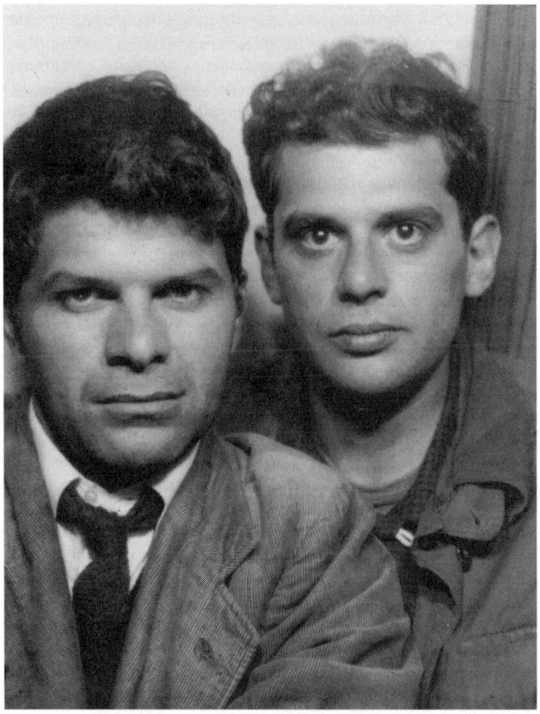

Corso (left) with Allen Ginsberg in a bus-station photo-booth photograph

Early Career

In the mid 1950s Corso worked at a series of jobs, including reporter for the Los Angeles Examiner; *selling tract homes in Fort Lauderdale, Florida; and merchant seaman. In 1954–1955 he spent time on the Harvard University campus without enrolling. In 1955 his first book,* The Vestal Lady on Brattle and Other Poems, *was published. The following year he joined Ginsberg and Kerouac in San Francisco and became part of the West Coast Beat scene. Between 1957 and 1961 he traveled in Africa and Europe, visiting the United States occasionally to give poetry readings. For a time in 1957 he lived in an attic room at 9 rue Git-Le-Coeur in Paris; Burroughs lived one floor below, and Peter Orlovsky and Ginsberg shared a room two floors down.*

Dedication for *Gasoline:*

I dedicate this book to the angels of Clinton Prison who, in my 17th year, handed me, from all the cells surrounding me, books of illumination.

G.C.

Corso in his attic room at 9 rue Git-Le-Coeur, Paris, in 1957 (photograph by Allen Ginsberg)

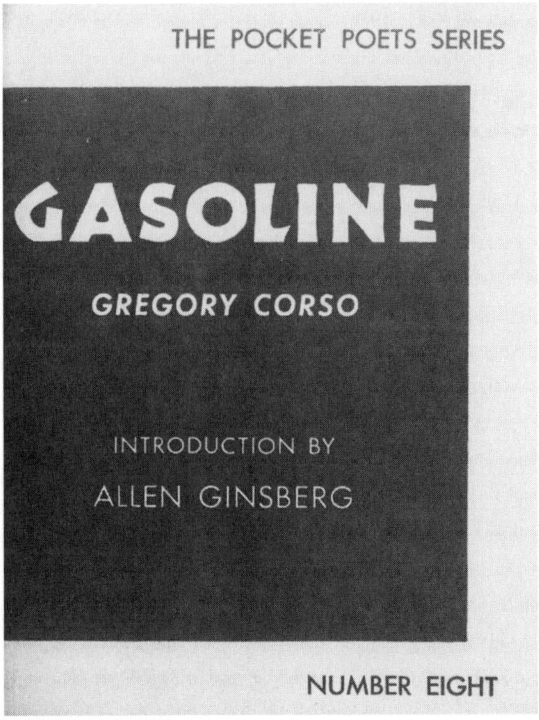

Cover for Corso's second collection of poems, published in 1958

Kerouac wrote this blurb for Gasoline:

I think that Gregory Corso and Allen Ginsberg are the two best poets in American and that they can't be compared to each other. Gregory was a tough young kid from the Lower East side who rose like an angel over the rooftops and sang Italian songs as sweet as Caruso and Sinatra, but in *words.* "Sweet Milanese hills" brood in his Renaissance soul, evening is coming on the hills. Amazing and beautiful Gregory Corso, the one & only Gregory the Herald. Read slowly and see.

Poem from Corso's Gasoline:

BIRTHPLACE REVISITED

I stand in the dark light in the dark street
and look up at my window, I was born there.
The lights are on; other people are moving about.
I am with raincoat; cigarette in mouth,
hat over eye, hand on gat.
I cross the street and enter the building.
The garbage cans haven't stopped smelling.
I walk up the first flight; Dirty Ears
aims a knife at me . . .
I pump him full of lost watches.

Corso commented on the Beat Movement in the August 1962 issue of the journal Nomad New York.

Now, "Beat Movement" means what–that the movement that, let's say, we gave a thrust to, was to be a movement of poets getting up reading their poetry? Is that what you mean? Oh well, that would be absurd–to get up and say, well here this is what I'm doing and now I hope everybody else does this–No. I believe that you have to have something to fall back on, you have to have it, and it should always be You–it should never Follow, from something else–that's where the danger of Fad and Monotony can get into it by the Relay. . . .

Now, "Beat Movement," if there was anything intended by that–to take the other angle–if it was something as a movement then it was for people to Wake Up! The poetry that was read by myself and Allen and a few others at the time was not altogether social, but a lot of it was Social–and a lot of it has come true: what we said–and a change in the Consciousness has happened.

Now a beat person in the United States is not a person who has a beard–exactly. The consciousness is changed by the beat–it is entering the lives of people who go to college, who are married, who have children. They do not, then, by their learning lock themselves up in a room and sleep on floors and don't take baths: that's not It–the Consciousness has altered there through everyone . . . it has changed completely now and taste has become refined.

Marriage

The occasion of Corso's marriage was noted by the press.

Bye, Bye Beatnik
Newsweek, 1 July 1963, p. 65

Lawrence Ferlinghetti, the Beat Movement's poet-publisher, broke the news to the London Observer. One of the Beats' most famous minstrels, 33-year-old Gregory Corso ("Bomb") had got married, and to a schoolteacher from Shaker Heights, Ohio–"a kind of Midwest symbol of rich suburbia," Ferlinghetti explained.

Perhaps Ferlinghetti recalled the late poet Robert Frost's prediction about the Beat Movement: that it would end in the suburbs. Marriage certainly seemed like just a commuter's hop away. Already the golden days in San Francisco, when the Beat Movement was a lure for young rebels, have faded.

In Los Angeles's Venice West, it's the same story. And in New York, the other big Beatnik pad, the bearded Subterraneans have either gone off on their own or hitched themselves to other movements, more contemporary in spirit.

As Brother Antoninus, a Dominican lay brother and San Francisco Beat poet, summed up: "Today there is an avenue by which the unconventional can be expressed in a manner acceptable to society–the Peace Corps and the Freedom Riders, for example."

Yet, in Europe, usually a year or two behind U.S. movements, Beat is still fashionable, while in Africa and Asia, it has hardly arrived. Allen Ginsberg, Corso's fellow Beat Laureate has spent the last two years in India and on the way home last month he stopped over in Saigon where Buddhists, confused by his poetry, mistook the bearded stranger for an American spy.

Honeymooning in Manhattan last week, like a spy among squares, Gregory Corso was an even more ambiguous symbol of the Beats' eclipse. His pad was a stolid middle-class apartment hotel off Central Park West and a visitor found him and his wife in Room 306, a cool, spacious suite completely conformist except for pictures of Corso's heroes–including Rimbaud, Victor Hugo, and Oscar Wilde–clipped from newspapers and magazines and stuck on the wall.

Exhausted: Mrs. Corso, a shy and pretty blonde of 25, sat by a large television set watching her husband talk torrentially. "Beat to me," he said, "always meant to be beat–exhausted. I never was. I was always pretty loud. The press invented the name. It was really a group of writers who were taken up and imitated. We were expressing a change of consciousness in our generation–what was moral and what was not. As poets, we staged a revolution, taking poetry out of the university and putting it into the street, using everything to make poetry."

Corso rubbed a hand through his thick curly black hair. "Since we started, the under-all consciousness has changed. People have got much smarter. Kids today are hipper, more intelligent, reading more." He exchanged a private honeymoon grin with his wife, then turned serious again: "America is going through its second revolution right now. The first was against the British, the second is by the Negroes. And it was predicted by the Beats–by Kerouac in 'The Subterraneans'."

Mrs. Corso said her name was Sally November and her father was a florist in Cleveland. "I never heard of my husband before I met him. I had heard of the Beat Movement but I thought it pretty negative," she said, while Corso beamed. Then she added: "I've since changed my mind." Corso beamed again.

"I've spent the last few years abroad," he said. "Greece was a great experience. I'm now doing a book for Grove Press about my travels and I'm writing about the Greeks still in jail eighteen years after the civil war there. Still in jail–in the cradle of democracy!"

First stanza from "Marriage," in The Happy Birthday of Death:

Should I get married? Should I be good?
Astound the girl next door with my velvet suit and
faustus hood?
Don't take her to movies but to cemeteries
tell all about the werewolf bathtubs and forked clarinets
then desire her and kiss her and all the preliminaries
and she going just so far and I understanding why
not getting angry saying You must feel! It's beautiful to feel!
Instead take her in my arms lean against an old
crooked tomb-stone
And woo her the entire night the constellations in the sky–

He dismissed the idea that getting married meant he was conforming. "Getting married means having a child. I have never denied life. One falls in love. Is that conforming?" He wants to live in New Haven because it is a good place to bring up a child. "You mean me?" asked Sally November Corso.

This summer they're both going to work at a summer camp at Copake Falls, N.Y., Corso as an arts-and-crafts and general counselor. He is already amassing a supply of bubble gum for the boys. As his visitor left, he pursued him down the hotel corridor. "Want some bubble gum?" he asked and thrust out a generous handful. Then he rushed back to his wife. Like the Beat Movement, he had moved on–from the '50s into the '60s, and nobody yet knows the name of the movement of the new decade except that it isn't Beat.

Interviews

Bruce Cook included an interview with Corso in The Beat Generation *(1971).*

"I'm thirty-seven years old now. None of us are young in the way we were when the mass media 'discovered' us."

"When you became the Beat Generation?"

"That's right." He leaned back and squinted up for a moment into the sunny September sky. "All it was was four people. I don't know if that's a generation. Can you call that a generation? That's more of a Madison Avenue thing. It was like here we were, speaking in our own voices, and the mass media couldn't control us, so they did the next best thing, they 'discovered' us."

"But something did come of it all, didn't it?" I asked. "Didn't a kind of revolution take place?"

"Okay," he waggled his hand indifferently, "maybe a *kind* of revolution, but a revolution without one drop of blood spilled, mostly a revolution in poetry. I'll grant you the hippie business, these kids you see today down on St. Mark's Place, that's right from us, out of our little bag of tricks. Did we influence them? Well, they don't write, so you can't tell that way, but just go down there and look around. The hippies are acting out what the Beats wrote. The whole thing worked out with us like a Madison Avenue ad campaign or something–you know, how they say something's going to happen, and suddenly it *is* there, maybe just because it was predicted."

–pp. 146–147

Interview with Gregory Corso
Michael Andre
The Unmuzzled Ox, volume 2, nos. 1–2 (1973)

Andre: In your poem "The American Way" you wrote

> And those who seek to get out of the Way
> can not
> The Beats are a good example of this
> They forsake the Way's habits
> and acquire for themselves their own habits
> And they become as distinct and regimented and lost
> as the main flow
> because the Way has many outlets
> like a snake of many tentacles
> There is no getting out of the Way
> The only way out is the death of the Way
> And what will kill the Way but a new consciousness

You wrote that in 1961. Do you have a different perspective on that now after eleven years?

Corso: I think always in the beginning of something things look very similar, but then they do disperse. They depicted the beats of the time with bangles and shaggy hair; long and shaggy hair and beards. But not so much the look. I didn't mean regimentation by look so much as a particular way, their way. I was very much hung up on individualism at the time. I still am. People who have a particular connection with their ideas, the poets that I knew, the beats that I really knew, Kerouac, Ginsberg, Burroughs, they were all very diverse in their writing styles, but there was a similarity through it with their feeling of what was coming, of what was to be. I think that Kerouac with his whole beat generation thing was just a prophecy of what would be. The generation is not just for writers you know; it pertains to the mass, and that was not there at the time. It was just little pockets in North Beach and in Greenwich Village at the time. By 1961 of course, the beats were passing, and there's the hip thing starting to spread out more and more, and that's the thing, I think, that I was seeing at the time. They were diverse.

I think in that poem I state that the young also were hampered, were not doing anything, "but not for long." I put in parenthesis there "but not for long." And that came to be, they did do something.

That poem and "America Politica Historia"–the publisher, really goofed on that; I told him to put the date on it. It was published in 1959. I think when people read it they can see that it must have been written a long time ago. It couldn't be written now. But it states in there that Nixon would be the last

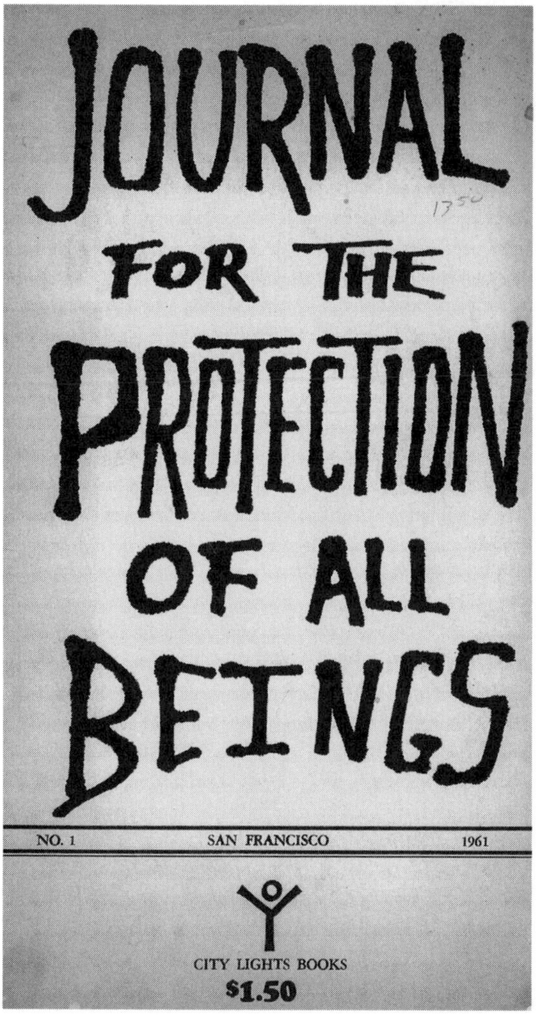

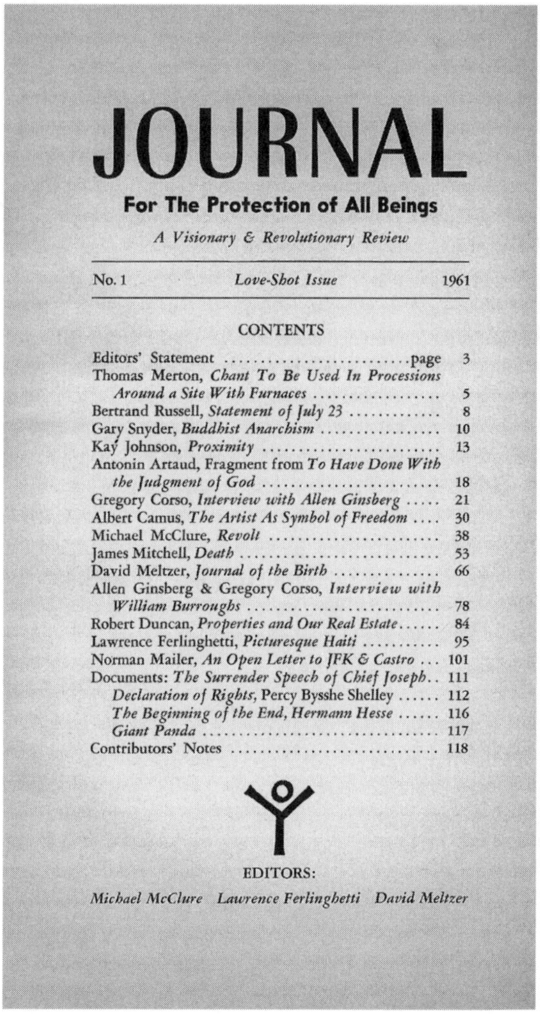

JOURNAL

For The Protection of All Beings

A Visionary & Revolutionary Review

No. 1 *Love-Shot Issue* 1961

CONTENTS

EDITORS:

Michael McClure Lawrence Ferlinghetti David Meltzer

Cover and table of contents for a short-lived periodical featuring the work of Corso and other Beat writers

president. There is a question mark there though. I ask, will he be the last president? That's a premature long shot, because he was just going against Kennedy then, right?

Andre: Yes.

Corso: Now all right, so Kennedy beats him, so that would knock him out, you know, the last president thing, and when you think of Bobby Kennedy afterwards and all that, this man would have no chance, and would be losing in California, but there he is, right back there!

It's very hard for me to write political poems. Humour is one form I love. It's a butcher in a way, it gets rid of a lot of shit. But it's very, very hard today to write anything humorous about the Vietnam war. How can you be funny about that? (pause)

Andre: Have you been writing much lately?

Corso: Yes.

Andre: What have you been writing?

Corso: The scene, the big scene mainly, that I got onto in the late 50s was death; it was the atom bomb, ban the bomb, and all. Then in the 60s came two other big words that were taken care of–Love and God. God is

Love, or Love is God, the flower children and what not. There's two more big ones handled. When we come to the 70s I figured the big daddy would be Truth.

Andre: Talking about Truth in our society, and the difficulties that we unlike the Greeks and Romans have dealing with it, you asked in "1959" must I dry my inspiration on this sad concept? Were you afraid that that might happen?

Corso: It did happen. I found that going back to Greece I was no longer awestruck by looking at the Acropolis, and things like that. I think that's what gave me my opening when I was a kid, to see something in books, you know, pictures of beautiful old stone and what not.

The literature and the mythologies of ancient times grabbed me, but today no, it's more held down to what is going on, the present day. But I think it's no longer a sad thing. It's just a change of feeling I knew would happen.

Andre: That's interesting. Allen Ginsberg and I spent a long time trying to find the meaning of the word *classicist,* and we decided that it was someone who found great value in past civilizations, particularly Greece and Rome. Would you say you are a classicist?

Corso: Well, I could say I was, and I could say I still retain it because it's all in my head. I mean, if anyone were to ask me about Carthage or Phoenecia, or about the Bogomils or about the Sumer abd Gilgamesh, I know the shot. But other things are more pressing today. I still incorporate that in my poetry at times, it's occasional, you know, it's like an encyclopedic hold in my head that I can at times pick on and use. I knew the change was coming in that poem. It was 1959, and I knew the change would occur. That's why I ended the book with the poem.

Andre: I noticed in the *Vestal Lady on Brattle* you don't use the exploded, fragmentary line of your later poems, such as "Bomb."

Corso: Right.

Andre: Was that "projective verse?"

Corso: I didn't know anything about projective verse, Mr. Olson and the Black Mountain people until Ginsberg introduced me to it–and when the heck was that? That was pretty much late,–No, I never pondered too deeply on that. The first book, it's very awkward, a green book, just ideas trying to come out. Lots of imagery, conglommed together; and I cut out lots of fat. I thought in those days that poetry is a concise form, built like a brick acropolis; but in 1957–58 in Paris things burst and opened, and I said, "I will just let the lines go and not care about fat." I figured if I could just go with the rhythm I have within me, my own sound, that that would work, and it worked. In "Marriage" there was hardly any change–there are long lines, but they just flow, like a musical thing within me. I could do that much better than so-called eye forms, forms that you could see with your eye.

Most of the poems I write are not written for oral reading. Take a guy like Ferlinghetti: he would know that he has to read his poems aloud; that would be with the measured thing, the projective thing. They set it down on paper the way they speak. Mine is written the way I felt within me. It's difficult to get up and read them, because it isn't meant for that. I mean, you could read faster on paper than aloud.

Andre: In your first work there are many little anecdotes, little observations, little scenes, for instance "St. Luke's, Service for Thomas" and "The Greenwich Village Suicide" from *Vestal Lady on Brattle.*

Corso: Well yes, that's observing a little scene, and setting it down as such. I think *Gasoline* has a lot of that in it, but *Gasoline* is a change, you can see the

Passage from "Bomb," in The Happy Birthday of Death *(1960):*

O Bomb I love you
I want to kiss your clank   eat your boom
You are a paean   an acme of scream
A lyric hat of Mister Thunder
O resound thy tanky knees
BOOM   BOOM   BOOM   BOOM   BOOM
BOOM ye skies and BOOM ye suns
BOOM BOOM ye moons   ye stars BOOM
Nights ye BOOM   ye days ye BOOM
BOOM BOOM ye winds   ye clouds ye rains
go BANG ye lakes   ye oceans BING
Barracuda BOOM and cougar BOOM
Ubangi BANG   orangoutang
BING BANG BONG BOOM   bee bear baboon
ya BANG ye BONG ye BING
the tail the fin the wing
Yes   Yes   into our midst a bomb will fall
Flowers will leap in joy their roots aching
Fields will kneel proud beneath the halleluyahs of the wind
Pinkbombs will blossom   Elkbombs will perk their ears

Dust jacket for Corso's only novel, which was published in Paris in 1961

change coming in *Gasoline,* where I would take a jump, and make an elliptical shot. I juxtapose lots of images together. I see two gangsters on the street. ". . . guns rusting in their hands." The observance of *Gasoline* was inward, except maybe for the zoo poems, where I did observe literally, like

In the Mexican Zoo
    they have ordinary
American cows.

Andre: *Elegiac Feelings American* has a lot of dense, grammatically complex poems. That was another change.

Corso: Yes, that was another change. That's the last. Now I've learned to not use words I could use very freely, like the word *God,* the word *man,* which I hate to be so free using now, what with women's lib and all.

Andre: You also started revising poems. There is one poem in particular, "Ode to Myself and Her" which you changed to "Ode to Sura." I don't know what *Sura* means.

Corso: Oh, that was the girl, that was "her," you see. I must have had it published twice in a magazine. There is also a poem in the *Elegiac* that the publisher didn't know was already published in *Gasoline,* but it's a different version.

Andre: Yes, "Hedgeville" I think.

Corso: Right. That was found in an earlier magazine. If they are already published, I don't correct anymore, although sometimes I am really tempted to. I know I could clean out a lot of them, and really set them aright, but I let them go, and I don't bother.

I usually correct poetry at the time I'm working on it.

Usually it's elimination rather than augmenting.

Andre: Auden revises all the time.

Corso: Yes, that one could do. I see it in a very funny way. If it's already out–you see, like the thing that would disturb me in the *Elegiac* was that the publisher did not put the date on a particular poem. Not all my poems are dated, they don't have to be dated, but certain ones had to. So that sort of change I would make.

Andre: You use a large vocabulary in your poetry.

Corso: My vocabulary that I obtained was from a standard dictionary of 1905, that big, when I was in prison. For three lucky years I just got that whole book in me, all the obsolete and archaic words. And through that I knew that I was in love with language and vocabulary, because the words and the way they looked to me, the way they sounded, and what they meant, how they were defined and all that, I tried to revive them, and I did.

. . . .

Corso: "Bomb" was written when I came back from England, when I saw the kids Ban the Bomb, Ban the Bomb, and I said, "It's a death shot that's laid on them, the immediacy of people being hanged in England at that time, and it's not as if the Bomb had never fallen, so how am I going to tackle this thing, suddenly death was the big shot to handle, Gregory, not just the Bomb."

The best way to get out of it was make it lyrical, like an embracing of it, put all the energy of all the lyric that I could name. And then get to know it. But if I start with hating it, with the hate of it, I get no farther than a piece of polemic, a political poem–which I usually fall flat on. That's not a political poem exactly, that "Bomb" poem. And you can only do it by embracing it, yes. So gee, I loved the bomb.

. . . .

Andre: Another old poem I was going to ask you about is "Marriage." You got married.

Corso: I was not wise enough to check out my own poem to help me out. I had to go and fuck up to find out. The kid was born, which is beautiful. Now I realize I haven't had the baby or the woman I love, and no marriage was needed. (*laughs*) They still got my name, so what the heck. I had to learn, you see. That's the old moral Catholic thing.

I wrote "Marriage" the same time I wrote "Bomb." That was a funny week. I did "Bomb" in about three or four days. I had a ball with it, because to get the shape, I had to type it down on paper first, and cut it out, each line, and past it on big construction paper. So the glue was all sticky on my fingers, and the I said the heck with it, the publisher can always line it up.

"I'm Poor Simple Human Bones": An Interview with Gregory Corso

The Beat Diary (1977), pp. 4–24

Gregory Corso, with Lawrence Ferlinghetti, Allen Ginsberg, Michael McClure, Shig Murao, Peter Orlovsky, Miriam Patchen, Kenneth Rexroth and Gary Snyder, spent the blizzardy week of March 18, 1974 in Grand Forks, North Dakota, participants in the Fifth Annual University of North Dakota Writers Conference: City Lights in North Dakota. "Conference," in retrospect, does not seem the most appropriate noun to describe what actually happened; it was a week-long festive reunion of the Beats: poetry readings, long open microphone rap sessions with large audiences, mantras, a large exhibit of Kenneth Patchen's art. Unlike a Ginsberg reading at Jersey City State College not too long ago where, according to Jane Kramer, the teacher introducing Ginsberg snatched back the microphone to proclaim, "This evening does not receive the endorsement of the English Department," the City Lights "Conference" was sponsored by the UND English Department. Various members of the Department interviewed each of the poets, often under less than ideal circumstances, so crowded was the week with activities, so responsive and enthusiastic the largely student audiences.

The interview that follows took place at Robert King's home, the afternoon of March 22, 1974. John Little, who heads the committee responsible for the Conference, also participated in the conversation, as did Doug Rankin, a UND student.

James McKenzie

RK: In the introduction to *Gasoline* you said in your 17th year that people handed you books of illumination out of adjoining cells. Did that really happen? What were they?

GC: They were really dumb-ass books to begin with. There was Louis Beretti, first of all. Henderson Clarke wrote all these books about Little Italy, gangster books. That was what convicts read. All right. Now the smart man was the man who handed me *Les Miserables.* And you know who did that? Me. When I went to the prison library, I looked at that fat book and I knew what miserable meant. I was 16 1/2. When I said they passed me books of illumination, I meant they handed me something else, not the books. Yeah, there was a guy who had a beautiful standard dictionary. He loved me, man. And he had this old standard dictionary and I studied every fucking word in that book. 1905. This big, it was. All the archaic, all the obsolete words. That's illumination, I guess.

RK: OK, OK. Following that up, there's a lot of talk now about primitive poets as models. And now we've got Rothenberg putting out anthologies, and this kind of thing. So you must have been into that early?

GC: No. No, but I think I am called an original and also very much a primitive type, too, in poetry. How it came to me, though, was high class. You see. Wow. I mean the first feeling I had when I wrote my first poem was like music coming through a crack in the wall, and I felt good writing it.

RK: So you're not consciously trying to recapture primitive forms or feelings?

GC: I'll tell you, I know the sestina, I know the sonnets, I know the old sources of the information that I lay out. Go back to your sources, I tell people, but not as much as my friends do about the earth, or growing food, but the head. I say check yourself out, how far back you can go that way to your sources. And this I might have gotten from the Tibetans, because they say if you're conscious on your death bed, try to think back to your mother's cunt because you came in as you go out. It's good exercise for poets. I had to go back through history to get back as far as I could go to the sources, cave paintings as I say, and all that.

RK: You talk a lot about *Gilgamesh, The Book of the Dead,* these kinds of things.

GC: Right. That's all relay. It passes memory. See, if you forget the past, it's gone. And who was it, Santayana who said if you don't understand your mistakes you're going to have to repeat them. A karma shot, right? I don't think anything was a mistake. I'll hold to *Gilgamesh,* I'll hold to the Bible, I'll hold to all those goodies, they're all relays.

RK: Did you ever think about going to the university and majoring in comparative literature?

GC: Well, I went to Harvard, now. It was funny, on the banks of the Charles, drinking beer, talking about Hegel, Kierkegaard, it was nice–MacLeish's class. He'd sit there like the White Father, you know, people laughing, reading their poems, criticizing each other. I just went to one because he invited me up there, and immediately I saw Keats' death mask on the wall, and immediately I said, "Ah, that's Keats." Burroughs is beautiful, teaching at CCNY. He's really got the kids going: Do you sincerely want to be a writer; that's what he's teaching. The word "sincere" is too much. As long as human beings sing, it's beautiful. In other words, man, if they want to let themselves go, that's beautiful. And they don't know what a nice teacher they have in Burroughs. What a shot that is. And that's what works.

RK: What about poets you read early, early influences?

GC: The one who really turned me on very much was Shelley, not too much his poetry, but his life. I said, "Ah, a poet then could really live a good life on this planet." That fucker was beautiful, a sharp man. But dumb in a way, he went to free Ireland. You know how he did it? In a rowboat, half-way sinking in a rowboat.

RK: More his life than his poetry?

GC: The poet and poetry are inseparable. You got to dig the poet. Otherwise the poetry sucks. If I dug the poet, then automatically the poetry worked for me. Edgar Allen Poe the same way. Then there are some poets, I just don't buy their books, I don't dig it. Pound makes it, Auden made it for me. I mean, Auden is good. I dig Auden, you see. A lot don't. Listen, Allen wanted to sing mantras to him, and Auden said, "No, I get embarrassed by somebody singing to me. I don't want it." So Allen said, "That dumb fuck, he died and didn't realize who I was, man; I was singing to him."

RK: Auden's life doesn't seem particularly exciting; he's certainly no Shelley.

GC: Naw, he didn't dig Shelley, but he did dig *The Tempest.* That's Shakespeare's best shot. That's the time of the "dopey fuck" remark. Auden was reading *The Tempest* to me and it sounded beautiful. I was just a kid. Walking down the street, afterwards, feeling good, I was crossing the street when this fucking taxi driver says, "Get out of the way, you dopey fuck." Here I am alive with poetry, right? I go home, look in the mirror: am I a dopey fuck? No way!

RK: You talk about a new consciousness in *Elegiac Feelings American.* What do you mean by that, or what do you see as a new consciousness?

GC: That's what's happening, and very fast. It took awhile for this body to make it, but the head's going beautiful. Now I took the daddies and I said that truth was the 70's hit. But truth is the pole vault that stops you. You say, "Well I believe in this" and then you stop with it. So it's almost as bad as the word "faith" because people believe in things they don't understand by their faith. I'd rather have a little bit of knowledge than a whole lot of faith. So humor then comes after it. Humor is the butcher that gets rid of the shit. I love Americans for that, man; if they can laugh at something, it's finished.

RK: Does America, as a country, spiritual entity, whatever, ask something different from its poets than other countries ask? There's Whitman, and then there's Crane, maybe there's the 50's . . . but I don't see guys wandering around worried about being a French poet.

GC: Do you know how Hart Crane got fucked up? Hart Crane took the two great American poets, Edgar Allen Poe and Walt Whitman. Now, Edgar Allen Poe is in, Whitman is out. So poor Hart Crane was like an accordion, in and out, in and out. He didn't last too long, but he knew his shot. He knew who his two daddies were.

RK: Do you feel some kind of stress to express America?

GC: Oh yeah, I love America, I love America. And I know why. You take a mystical number, say like Columbus coming over in the Santa Maria. That may be the second coming, but it'd be the geographical number rather than a baby being born out there.

RK: You say you love America and you do, but you're ambivalent about it; like you're afraid to go into an American Express office, or in a *Poem,* you're afraid to go into an American Express office.

GC: It was a drag all the time, man, I love them but I had to wait in line for the mail, first of all, right. And you've got these old ladies from Duluth going "Ugh" to me. It was a drag going to the American Express.

RK: But you mean more than that; I mean you're not really talking about some hassle with the American Express. You're talking about some other America, or maybe the existing America.

GC: I'm talking about the America whose applecart I upset, man. It's gone. The old cornball America you know, where people are all regimented and all that shit. I mean, look at you with your hair and all that.

RK: And in that Kerouac poem, you talk a lot about the fact that there are two Americas. He keeps looking for one and there's one there but that's not the one he was looking for.

GC: Right. It was never there, you see. Whitman was at a time that was virginal and now we've got the birth.

RK: There's a feeling around, some of it unjustified, and some of it comes out of your comments and other people's comments that books are a drag, and even the past is a drag, and everything should be spontaneous, that therefore there's no craft in your poetry. What would you say about the craft of poetry as you practice it?

GC: As I practice it, I say I build a brick musehouse. The craft is there, man. See, words have only been written down in the last 400 years. It was always sung before that. And it's gotten back to the cycle where it's sung again with Dylan. Ok. Now. But I still say "You can just sit there, Gregory, and make the music on the page, too. Don't get up there and twang away." I use the expression "brightness falls from the air. Many a queen has died young and fair." That's beautiful music.

JL: Do you have a built in sense of form?

GC: Yeah, I know I do. Oh sure. The "bing bang bong boom" hit it, right, with the *Bomb* poem. I mean that was real music coming out on its own, and I don't have to knock myself out too fast with it, you know.

RK: But you don't worry around about syllables or stress or. . ?

GC: I like to rhyme when I want to rhyme. When I don't want to rhyme I don't rhyme. It's all music.

JL: How did you get that sense of form? You never did cultivate it, never did study the sonnet?

GC: That's the whole shot; if I did I wouldn't have had it. I know the sonnet. . . I can do the sonnet, the sestina.

JL: It was there.

GC: Yeah, because it's obvious to be there, it's one of the simplest things. Just do what you want to do, right. And poetry, top shot, poesy. I mean, that's the top profession, man. I walk down the street in New York, you know, I feel great sometimes. I look at those fuckers making millions with their Cadillacs and their businesses. But you, Corso, your fucking profession's beautiful.

RK: Do you live in New York most of the time now?

GC: Yeah, that's the city I'm most comfortable in.

RK: Do you run into New York poets? By that I mean, you know, the people who call themselves the New York poets.

GC: I don't meet many people. I used to know Frank O'Hara; now he was good. Now I don't bother much; sometimes I go to OTB and play the horses.

RK: Do you think your poetry has changed since 1955?

GC: You can see that's a progression there. The next book I know is going to be a top shot for me. Yeah, real smart little numbers. Those were all like just exploding out of me. This time I'm going to really look at them and say, "Ok, Corso." If I was building cars or was a carpenter I would talk that way–I'd say I built something nice–so I'll do it with poetry.

RK: You seem to me sometimes to have two basic kinds of things that you do, which is not to suggest limits but identify a couple of things. One is a real conversational kind of thing: "32nd Birthday," for example; the other verges on incantation, "Requiem for the Indian," "Coit Tower," "Spontaneous Requiem for the American Indian." Do you try to write any one kind of poetry now?

GC: I don't want to write elegies anymore. I don't want to get stuck, I don't want to write elegies for people, you know. And so I think that's done. Going to museums and zoos, I wrote a lot about. I felt for the animals in the zoo, and I felt the learning from seeing the great paintings, and all that. Now a very different shot in my poetry, very different number. I'd rather now live the life than writing it out on the page. But when it does come out, very rare now, seldom, it grows, like I say, a brick musehouse.

RK: You think you're writing less now than you were?

GC: I'm writing songs, now; I always have written songs; and to me they're love poems. People say there aren't very many love poems written today, right? I don't have to call my poems love poems, but they *are* love poems. I'm going to call these songs, though, this next book; that's the shot, man, so that the *word* has still got the music in it rather than twanging with the guitar up there, right?

RK: Do you do more readings now than you did?

GC: No. I haven't read for a long time.

RK: Do you have a small circle of friends in New York, or a wide circle of friends, or are you a loner?

GC: Yeah, I guess more of a loner than anything else. See, when I took drugs, that eliminated a lot of friends because you're always hitting them up for money and all that. They don't like that. So it's good; I got rid of them. Mainly, I sleep with my cats and the female. I love female. I've been with this one female

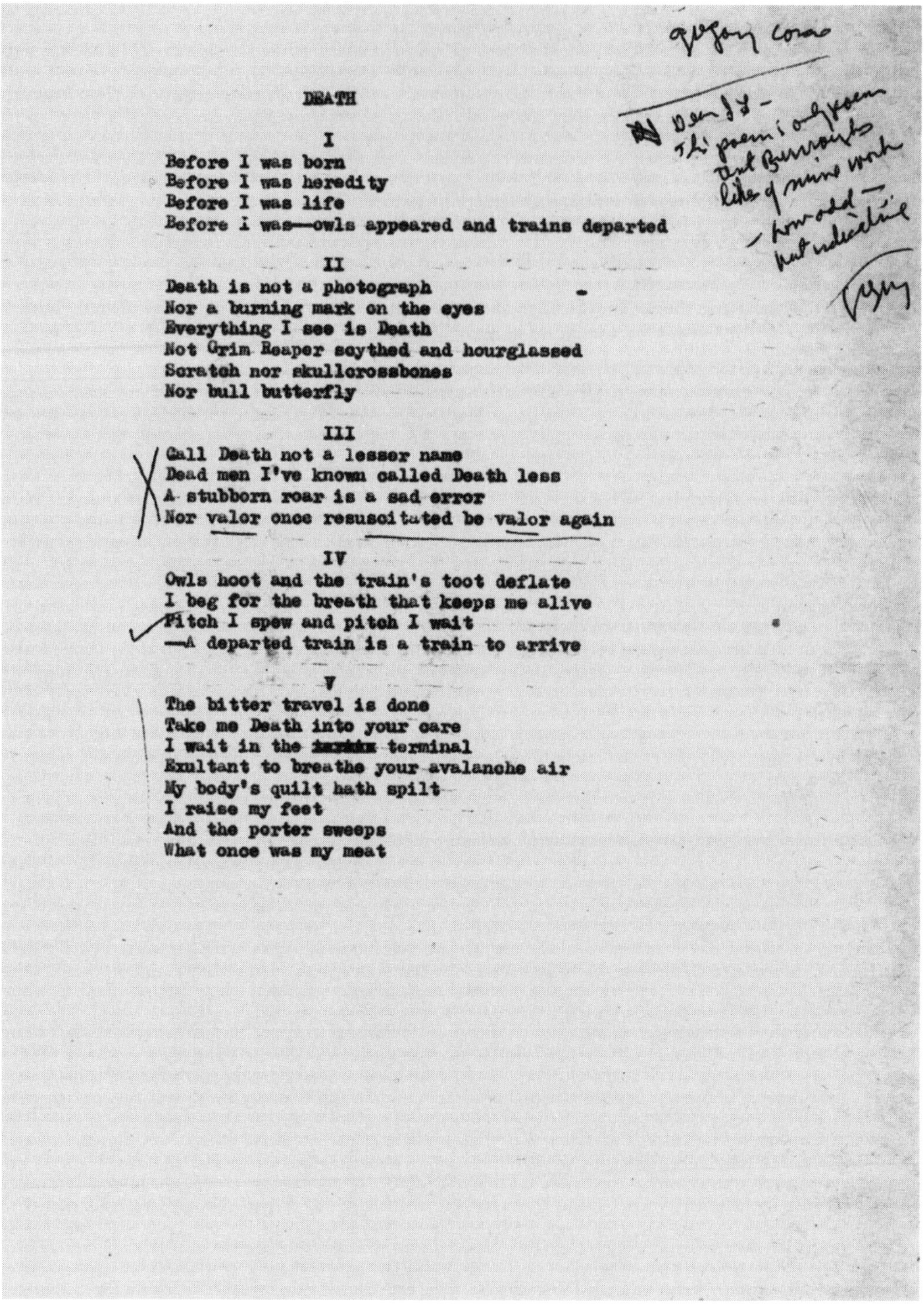

DEATH

I

Before I was born
Before I was heredity
Before I was life
Before I was—owls appeared and trains departed

II

Death is not a photograph
Nor a burning mark on the eyes
Everything I see is Death
Not Grim Reaper scythed and hourglassed
Scratch nor skullcrossbones
Nor bull butterfly

III

Call Death not a lesser name
Dead men I've known called Death less
A stubborn roar is a sad error
Nor valor once resuscitated be valor again

IV

Owls hoot and the train's toot deflate
I beg for the breath that keeps me alive
Pitch I spew and pitch I wait
—A departed train is a train to arrive

V

The bitter travel is done
Take me Death into your care
I wait in the ~~[illegible]~~ terminal
Exultant to breathe your avalanche air
My body's quilt hath spilt
I raise my feet
And the porter sweeps
What once was my meat

Typescript for William S. Burroughs's favorite poem by Corso (University of Virginia Library) now for a year. I like living with female. I keep close to her and all that; I don't bother much with the outside.

RK: In *Elegiac Feelings,* "Geometric Poem" is an interesting thing. It's hand written, it's got little drawings on it.

GC: Yeah, but it's wrong. You see, the Italian edition was great because it's big. That's when I learned Egyptian. But the way New Directions did it, it's very small, you need a magnifying glass. New Directions books are a particular size. So I said to him, "Don't publish the poem, I think that would just screw it up; just leave that one out." But then I realized, if you're talking about elegiac feelings, American, Gregory, and you want to go back to your sources, and the Egyptians are undoubtedly the sources, with the elegies, right? With the death shot.

RK: Do you have a good relationship with New Directions?

GC: Yeah.

RK: Why did you leave Ferlinghetti?

GC: Oh, I didn't leave Ferlinghetti, Ferlinghetti left me. You see, I wrote a poem called "Power"–that's in my *Happy Birthday of Death.* My "Marriage" is in there, and some of the real goodies in that book. But Ferlinghetti thought it was fascistic; he didn't understand I was changing the word, "power." I said, "Why can't a poet handle this word, break the meaning of it?" So he wouldn't publish it. Now, I got very insulted that he sent it to some San Francisco publisher who also refused. So I said, "Well, bullshit, give me my book back," and wrote to New Directions and said, "Hey, you who publish Pound and Rimbaud, do you like long poems?" because these were long single word poems: "Army," "Power," "Police," "Marriage,"–and Laughlin wrote back, "Of course," and took the book. And Larry, years later then suddenly realized, and said, "Gregory, yeah." This is a straight story, it's not downing Larry. I got to dig Larry very well, man, on this trip. I guess the one guy I didn't get too close to was Snyder, you know, because he left too soon; I don't know him too well. I dig the man a lot. I wasn't trying to sabotage anything; I think that Allen thought that I was trying to sabotage his feeling about how to survive on this planet, right? And I could get no way edgewise to say it's also a mental evolve though, too, folks, also the head–take care of it.

JL: Has your relationship changed much with Snyder?

GC: I don't know him that well. I knew that man very early in the game, but as I say not that well.

JL: Has it changed with the other poets here?

GC: Well, it's gotten nice with Ferlinghetti, and Allen's my old friend. He lives in New York; I see him all the time.

JL: They seem to be putting up with you at times.

GC: I don't think Ferlinghetti though. Larry was mostly the one who did not admonish me.

JL: Gregory, you said earlier that the Beats have hurt themselves but they never hurt anybody else. Gary Snyder says a different sort of thing. He said that the Beats were aware that they had to take some responsibility for the kind of things that had happened to people who had misused drugs. I was wondering if they don't have some of the same concern for you.

GC: Allen has a tendency, and he might be right–a tendency to care too much for me, to come on like a daddy, you know, and tell me, "Well, Gregory, take care of yourself and all this bit." And I had to finally straighten him out and say, "Look, Allen, we're peers, man. And if I live my way–you sit and meditate, that's good. I'm not telling you that I dig it, but you do. But I live my way." It's the only way, man, otherwise, you know, we'd break intercourse.

JL: So you don't think that they feel protective toward you, that they see in you a projection of things that they once recommended that maybe they no longer do?

GC: I think they really want to do sincerely good; I think they're telling people right and maybe some way in life how to take care of yourself. I think that's good, but that's not my hit. Mine is the mental shot; I say, "Great, if you know the info, if you've got the knowledge, get your sources . . . I love it. Whether you drink, or smoke or what your farm is like and all that, I'm not interested."

RK: Do you make a living off poetry?

GC: No.

RK: How do you live?

GC: Oh, maybe that I do because I can sell my manuscripts, and I get good money for them. Also readings; and so sporadically I do make monies. I never had to steal or anything when I used to buy dope, for instance. I never had to steal for it. But they're books, notebooks, that I write in.

JL: Who do you sell them to and how much do they pay you?

GC: Oh, I give them to Gotham Book Mart in New York, which sells them to Columbia or to the University of Texas at Austin. They get half the monies and I get a half, rather than me dealing direct with these universities. I get what, about $200 a book when I need money. It's terrible, years ago the poor poets, man, they did nothing. They'd just throw them away or lose them or some shit, right? When I needed money for dope, you see, I would never recopy out the poems. I'd just sell the book. So a lot of my poems, you know, are in the universities and have never been published . . . from 1965 to now. But the goodies I remember in my head. *Elegiac Feelings* came out only because of the death of Kerouac. The other poems, the elegies on Kennedy and the American Indian were done beforehand. That's the only reason why I put it together. I said, all right then, here's a book, there's a reason for it.

RK: Have you ever written a poem to Neal Cassady?

GC: No. No. Only to Jack.

RK: Did you know Neal?

GC: Yeah, I knew Neal. But only to Jack, yeah. Yeah. I loved him.

RK: But Neal was another death. You know, they kind of all came in a very short period of time.

GC: Yeah, but they both died pretty close. You know how Neal died? He was a railroad man, worked on the railroad. In Mexico, after a wedding, he took off his clothes and walked the railroad tracks and somehow, the drinking and the cold air killed him–exposure. And then Jack went soon afterwards.

RK: You really seem attached to poetry. Several of the other writers this week have ecological concerns, or political, or scientific, but it looks like you're naked with your poetry.

GC: The poet and poetry is inseparable.

RK: Doesn't it get kind of cold with nothing but your poetry on?

GC: Oh, I've got more than that, too, you know. What is poetry but embracing the whole thing. Like I can take the megagalaxy in my head.

JL: Like in "Bomb?"

GC: I can take the "Bomb," or I can take blue balloons. But it's not political at all. It's a death shot. You see, because people were worrying about dying by the Bomb in the Fifties. So I said, what about falling off the roof, what about heart attack. And I used the double old-age: old age I picked as being the heaviest–"old age, old age." One line that I've written in that poem that's not in the poem, and it should be in there is "Christ with the whip," like "St. George with a lance." I read it yesterday. I don't augment or take away, but it could be a smart idea if I did add that Christ with the whip number.

RK: Who are "old poet men" today?

GC: Geez, there ain't any. Really, they're gone. Auden, I'd say was the last one probably to go.

RK: What do you think about Robert Lowell or his poetry?

GC: I like his "Tudor Ford," a pun, right? That kind of thing. Or the "boy with curlicues of marijuana in his hair." He's sharp. He didn't dig me too well. He dug Ginsberg because they could rap about poesy and the craft of it. When he woke up that *I* was in prison as a kid . . . he was there for CO, right . . . and I was there for something else, ripping off Household Finance.

JL: Tell us about the circumstances of your arrest and what it was for.

GC: Well, 1945, the war was over. The Army-Navy stores were selling these walkie-talkies. And I was 16 years old, right? I said "Shit, man, it would be great to get three walkie-talkies and two other guys, one guy'd be in the car saying no cops are coming along, right? We got away with 21 thou. Now I didn't know how to spend money in those days, and those guys didn't. That's how I got caught. They opened up a big hall on 99th Street, you know, Irish neighborhood. And the police asked where they got all the money. Like a dope, I gave my name to those two guys and they mentioned it, I went down to Florida and I bought a zoot suit, leaving big tips. I mean, how dopey, man alive. That's how I got to prison for three years, because the judge said I was very dangerous, that I was putting crime on a scientific basis. Those motherfuckers Household Finance, they're the ones who give you the money and take interest on it, right? I think I was a blessed man, I didn't know that. I'd have ripped off anybody, I would have done it. But I made a good shot with Household Finance.

JL: Did you pick up the term "Daddy" when you were in prison? Isn't it a homosexual term? What do you mean by "daddies?"

GC: I mean sharp people. I had no homosexual experience in prison. There was nothing like that. I was dug, though. But since I was Italian and the Mafiosi were running the shot, and I was the youngest (I entered the youngest and I left the youngest, entered 16 1/2 and left 20), I was like a little mascot. That's where I learned to be funny in life. Because I made them laugh, I was protected. Humor was a necessary survival condition when I was in prison. Man, their hearts were broken when I left prison. They dug me so fucking much . . . I brought life to them. There were guys doing 30–40 years. They told me, "Don't take your shoes off, Corso," in other words, "you're walking right out." And the other daddy–I didn't call them daddies then–but that other daddy said to me, "Don't *you* serve time, let time serve you." That's when I got the books, that's when the books came. Then when I left, the one man who did talk to says, "When you're talking to six people, make sure you see seven," in other words dig yourself. Prison food was really awful, but I had good food, because the Mafia guys got the food from the outside. They cooked steaks and everything, and I was always invited to eat. I learned to ski in prison. Winter time comes in Plattsburgh, snow piles up. You get your skis from Sears, Roebuck. They had a ski lift going. The first time I put on a pair of . . . everybody was lining up to go to their cells . . . I went down beautifully, man, held myself right, and psshhh, stopped like that, took the fuckers off, got right in line to go back in. Yeah, I learned to ski in prison. I always wanted to do a play, you know, and start the play off in prison with somebody coming down on skis.

JL: How come Kerouac never did deal much with homosexuality and gaiety in his books?

GC: Well, Jack was a beautiful, beautiful man. His sex life would have gone both ways in anything like that, you know. But then again it was more towards the female than it was anything else. But he loved his fellow man, like, he loved Neal, he loved Allen, he loved Bill Burroughs, and especially Lucien Carr. Oh wow, did you ever read Kerouac's *Vanity of Duluoz,* where his friend Lucien killed this guy who was following him in Columbia. Lucien was a very handsome young man, and this big red-haired fag was chasing Lucien all over. And Lucien finally just got tired of it, stabbed the man. The man yells out, "So this is how it happened." Not "This is how it *happens,*" but "this is how it *happened.*" Lucien goes with the bloody knife, up to Kerouac, who was his friend. And Jack says, "Oh-h-h, Go-o-o-d, Lucien, Lucien." Poor Jack, man. All right, you know what he did? He helped his friend out. Dropped the knife down the sewer drain somewhere. Burroughs had the other hit, killing the wife, you know . . . drunken, she puts the glass on the head . . . William Tell shot, cheow. That's the weight that these people have. Burroughs told me, "Gregory, there's no such thing as an accident." So how was I going to take that?

RK: That makes Norman Mailer stabbing his wife in the arm with the scissors seem fairly small. Mailer's done a couple of things that tended to support, at least in the public eye, some things you were doing in the 50's, "The White Negro" essay, for example.

GC: Well, of course, he wanted to join the bandwagon, you see. These guys who are Army writers knew where the goodies were.

RK: Do you see him much anymore? Any? At all?

GC: Every time I see him he wants to wrestle with me, hand wrestle. What a drag. I'll tell you, Kerouac, the football player, didn't play that shot with me. He was a strong, beautiful man; he didn't have to show his strength. He took a Columbia University football offer and then decided he wanted to write. He meets Ginsberg and Burroughs there, right, and said, "Fuck it all." No way he's going to play football. They were just all meeting in this house, rapping all the time. Beautiful.

JL: Hey, I asked you a question awhile ago, and I wasn't really happy with the answer you gave me. Kerouac wrote a kind of autobiographical fiction. He wrote it just like it happened.

GC: Right, right, no fiction–and some of it was so beautiful.

JL: O.K., then if he's writing what happened, why does he never mention gaiety, homosexuality? You've got Burroughs, Ginsberg. . .

GC: Because they never had it with Jack. Don't you understand?

JL: But they had it with other people and Jack knew about it.

GC: Yeah, yeah, Jack knew about it, and Ginsberg loved Jack Kerouac.

JL: He had to have been thinking about it. Did he censor himself?

GC: No. Because Jack never had homosexual affairs.

JL: Why didn't he mention that he didn't?

GC: Why do you have to mention what you don't have?

JL: Carlo had it. He talked about Carlo, he described Carlo.

GC: That's Ginsberg. Well, Allen wasn't a rampaging faggot, you know. I told you, when I first met him he was balling that chick, Dusty Mullins.

RK: He was really with her?

GC: Yeah. Oh, he loved Dusty. He also loved a very fine woman, another one–what was her name–in San Francisco? Allen, funny, I guess you'll have to ask him that number–the sex shot. I don't think it's any of your affair about another person's sex life, unless you want to ask them. Don't ask me.

JL: I was asking you about Kerouac's fiction technique.

GC: His fiction technique was very straight, it wasn't fiction. And that's what I say is so good about it.

RK: Your name, at least in the 50's, was really connected with Ginsberg, more than any of the others we've had here this last week.

GC: We were the two poets. They're novelists, you know. And Allen and I were poets. When Allen and I read poetry early in those days, he would read, "Howl," very serious; and I was, like I said, giving the humor number. That's what saved it. It would have been too heavy otherwise. Gregory came over with his "Marriage" or something like that, and everybody was happy and laughing. So it worked, it was a nice balance. We were the poets, Allen and myself.

RK: So really you complimented each other.

GC: Oh, sure, sure, sure.

RK: Ginsberg's really published a lot, has all these political connections, movement connections–he may be the most famous Beat. So you could have been in a position to say, "Gee, I wonder if I should do more things like Allen."

GC: Right, and I did not. I stayed out of it in the 60's and for good reasons, too. I figured that was the route they'd taken, let them go on with it because something's going to have to happen after that; and conserve some of the energy, Gregory. Let Allen take care of it nice; and he did. You know, this man's got all his strength and his energy. You dig? I don't have to be throwing myself out like that. That's when Allen got to understand me. He was burnt up in the beginning, saying "Gregory, where are you, man, like help us along." I said, "No, this is where you've got to understand Gregory. That is what I do now. If I'm going to go towards dope, if I'm going to make babies like I did and all that, that's my shot."

JL: Tell us about meeting Ginsberg.

GC: Oh, that's nice. But nothing was ever planned, you dig. Nothing was planned. I met this man in a dyke bar, the Pony Stabe in Greenwich Village; it was beautiful. 1950, I was about six months out of prison. I'm there with my prison poems and he just digs my face, you see, cause he's a homosexual, right. He didn't know who I was or my poems. Sitting down, he likes me and I says, "Well, look at these poems, you"; and he says, "You got to meet a Chinaman." Now "Chinaman" was an expression meaning a second rate poet, who was Mark Van Doren. He says, "You got to meet this poet." I says, "Oh yeah? Well, O.K., great," you know. Mark Van Doren tells me that I wrote too much about my mother. That was the critique laid on me by Mark Van Doren. John Holmes, who wrote *Go,* said I write too much green armpit imagery. I'm getting all these fuckers laying flak on me. All right. So finally I get Ginsberg, and I said, "Look, one thing I want to know is, I live across the street in this hotel room and I see this chick through the window balling every night, shitting, taking a bath, and I jerk off to her. I would like to go up there tonight and knock on her door and say hello to her. He says, "Oh, I'm the man you see that balls her." You dig? That's how I met Ginsberg and he brought me up there, man. It wasn't through reading the poems in a magazine somewhere and saying, "Hey,

New Directions Publishing Corporation publicity photograph of Corso

let's get together." He was the one I was jerking off to, watching him fuck her.

JL: So we know Ginsberg liked your face. What did you like about Ginsberg? Just the fact that he was an act going on across the street?

GC: Aw, come on. Man, he so loved me. He introduced me to Kerouac and Burroughs. He dug me a lot.

JL: I'm asking what you felt towards him.

GC: I felt that the man dug me. Don't you understand? It was beautiful. I'm right out of prison, all right? I had those years with me. He came out of Columbia University still writing little William Carlos Williams-like poems.

RK: *Prison Poems* were even before *Vestal Lady?*

GC: Yeah, they're gone. They were lost in Florida. They were lost in a suitcase at Hollywood, Florida. A fucking suitcase in the Greyhound Bus Terminal. Gone. And Hope, my girlfriend; Hope, my first girlfriend, she went to all the Greyhound presidents to get the things back. Papers in a suitcase. But I remembered two poems from them, and they're in *Vestal Lady*. "Sea Chanty." That's my first poem. See, and I remember, I don't lose nothing, man.

RK: All right.

GC:

My mother hates the sea,
my sea especially,
I warned her not to;
it was all I could do.
Two years later
the sea ate her.

Upon the shore I found a strange
yet beautiful food;
I asked the sea if I could eat it,
and the sea said that I could.
–Oh, sea, what fish is this
so tender and so sweet?–
–Thy mother's feet–was its answer.

Now that's a heavy because I never saw my mother. I heard that she went back to Italy, so she took the ocean, right? So that was my 16-year old poem of someone going across the sea–but whatever goes there comes back to the shore.

RK: You never knew your mother?

GC: No, no. I guess I must have been about six months old when she cut out. See, I had a double whammy laid on me. When she left, they gave me to another mother, all right? Now, I thought she was my mother, and then they took me away from her. So that's like a double whammy. That was before I was two years old. So my first memory is with the second one, and you know what it is? It's a beautiful one. In the bathtub–I remember the black hair on her cunt and the water. Now that's a good shot for a two-year old because what you got is a contemporary form of birth and that old primal shot–water.

DR: How different is it now? You said that you sort of complemented Ginsberg in the old days. You were the humor and he was serious, reading "Howl." Nowadays you're still doing the same thing; you're still the humor, and yet they don't seem to tolerate you. What's happened?

GC: But I do write serious shots, man. But then again, I'm going to have to hold respect to Ginsberg; a little bit to Ferlinghetti, but I would hold it most to Allen.

RK: When did Peter come into all this?

GC: Ah. Peter–ambulance driver. He was helping people who were crashing and all that, and Allen just loved him, man; here was this guy helping people all the time. He was a beautiful man.

RK: When did he meet him?

GC: 1954. They've been together ever since, and they will be till they go to the happy hunting grounds. They're two good people, man. Peter's beautiful, right? Remember him today? Even though he bugs about no smoking and all that shit.

RK: He's very pure, I mean very solidly "him."

GC: Yeah, yeah, yeah.

RK: I don't know a lot yet about how you write a poem. There's a couple of things crossed out in "Geometric Form" cause that's in your handwriting. So I don't know if you scratch out a lot, if you think a lot. . . .

GC: Where's *Elegiac Feelings?* I'll show you something in it. That's a good question, that goes back to craft. See that 1940 there? (NOTE: Pg. 47, *Elegiac Feelings American*) I'm into the poem of Egypt when suddenly I'm bugged about President Johnson and the bombings, "the blast and the smithered," the bombs falling from the 1940's. "On the dead body of the true President," right? When Kennedy was killed? You need a magnifying glass to read it, but it's got nothing to do with the Egyptian poem. Spontaneous poetry is also spontaneous change when you're working at it. But dig my glyphs. That's the first literal translation, man. That was good, my first transliteral glyph.

RK: Is this from somewhere else that you wrote these things down?

GC: No, I studied for six months in Paris, I learned to do the hieroglyphs and that's a correct literal translation. Some of these things I created, though; see, this I created.

RK: That's a hippopotamus with an alligator in his mouth. (NOTE: Pg. 45, *Elegiac Feelings American*)

GC: But dig my little bunny angel. She's dropping the geometry down on Egypt. Right? And then they did their triangles, right? (NOTE: Pg. 44)

> You O rainbow Egyp-clay
> seated upon skyey dangles
> sprinkling globes and triangles
> down upon the day

I had a ball with that.

RK: How did you learn hieroglyphics? Did you know somebody?

GC: Oh, six months in Paris, a M'sieur LaFrance at the Hotel Stella where Rimbaud lived. I'd get my Arab dope and I had this book from Cambridge University on hieroglyphics, and I just stayed in the room for six months all winter like that until spring. That was 1965. See, that's when I got divorced, left my wife and daughter. So I said, "Fuck it, Gregory, go off somewhere." So I went off and played around a little bit. Yeah. You know that's one that so many people like that's drawn is "The Tree." There you go. (NOTE: Pg. 39) Dig that. Now, the sun–Van Gogh did a beautiful thing of it. He did the tree and did the sun very big. You know that painting? It's beautiful. There's the sower in the wheatfield. Now this one here I learned from prison. (NOTE: Pg. 38) This guy's cleaning up things. See him? All right. Now, if that ain't Egyptian . . . but this was where I first used the great word "scrybound." You know what "scry" means?

RK: To discern, to foretell the future . . .

GC: Right. That is what they call the guy with the crystal ball. It's "scrying"; they usually call him a swami, right? It's scry. This is where I use my music (NOTE: Pg. 38)

> Scrybound o'er pre-Egypt's
> geometrical pool
> In mine velvet robe's varium vair
> –angel of darkest school
>
> I'll descry Wlamtrice wold brool
> its issuant gazebeasts
> and furoak oakfur meloday
> –this tenth of Atum's cursing feast

RK: There are some things there that aren't English, Gregory.

GC: It *is* English. They're old daddy words, my friend. I like to know my own language, you know. But this would be a hard poem, let's say, to read. Look at that one. (NOTE: Pg. 49) Here's "poet on the architect Nekhebu's knee." But you see, in the Italian edition, he's red. And there's the architect, and here's where I put myself in a shirt and tie.

RK: I was going to ask about this picture of you on this cover. You've got a tweed coat, a tie, no hair hanging down.

GC: Oh. The Olivetti man took that picture, the man who did the Italian edition.

RK: Were you being an angel then, or something?

GC: I was a wild fucker, then. Are you kidding? What about the one in *Long Live Man* now, that's a nice picture of me. I was sitting next to Allen. I wished they would have kept us together there, but they took Allen out and left my picture there. That's a dreamy fucker. That was in Tangier. Then I called the book, *Long Live Man.* I did that because of *Happy Birthday of Death,* and I said, "Oh God, Gregory, get off the death thing already. Say *Long Live Man.*" I was going to do *Gregorian Rants,* but I said "I don't have to play, to entertain these people by calling my book *Gregorian Rants.*"

RK: That would be almost like Pope's "Dulness," which he refused to have his book called. You don't seem to be worrying about publishing very much. Who was it, Duncan, I think, who said he wasn't going to publish anything for 15 years because he didn't want what people were expecting or anything to have any influence on him.

GC: Keats had that problem. See, Shelley would get along with Leigh Hunt, man, and Byron, and they'd have great raps. And Shelley was the best in it; but Keats would not join in because he didn't want to be influenced by them. And Shelley understood that–he dug Keats, you know. Shelley was a sharp daddy; oh, he's beautiful. I mean Byron couldn't stand up to him, none of them could stand up to him, when he was going good. Those meetings in the house of Leigh Hunt must have been fantastic. There are some of them written down by Mary Godwin, his wife. See, what they put down Shelley for is that he married his cousin, Harriet, she was pregnant when she threw herself in a river because he suddenly gave up on her and went towards Mary, who wrote *Frankenstein.* And so therefore, they said, there's the flaw in Shelley. No way. Harriet should have been cooler or something.

RK: One of the flaws they say is in Shelley is the line, "I fall upon the thorns of Life, I bleed," exclamation point.

GC: Yeah, that's a lovely line.

RK: Now, you use exclamation points.

GC: Right, right. I love them. That poem, "Ode to the West Wind" is one of the greatest poems ever written. You know why? It's a lyric. He smartly injected himself into it right towards the end. He said, "Make me thy lyre, even as the forest is:" right?

He was always giving it to the wind but then he puts himself into it beautifully.

RK: Where'd you get this gesture of parting your hair with one finger? It really shows disdain, like on the stage at any rate, this last week. It's really been kind of a "screw the people that are trying to talk ecology."

GC: No, no, that's an assumption.

JL: It is arrogant, and it's also elegant and feminine.

GC: All right. All right. And I'll take the feminine part too.

RK: You really surprised me the other day when you were reading. You said a line was too corny, like you really have an inner sense. Everybody says, "Gee, 'I fall upon thorns of Life, I bleed.' That's corny, that's sentiment, that's romantic." You're romantic, and all of a sudden you're a romantic saying, "Gee, that's too corny."

GC: Yeah, of course. I'm poor simple human bones.

RK: Are you hung up on being a hairy bag of water?

GC: Ah, that's a good one. That's what I yell on people a lot.

RK: You worried about it in the interview with Bruce Cook.

GC: When did that happen? Oh. Oh, he lied.

RK: Well, I want to hear about Bruce Cook.

GC: Mr. Cook was a liar. I'll tell you about him. See, when I was living in New York City, he said I was sleeping in a sleeping bag. Bullshit! I was with Belle. Now I didn't know she was a DuPont lady, you dig. I mean, wow, what a house we had. She was an Aries, like me. On the floors there were big fucking rams.

RK: He said you could just leave any day, man.

GC: Yeah, of course. But there was the most elegant fucking house, man. Her father knocked out these lions, there were all these lions on the floor, rugs and everything, man. Shit, that dummy wanted to create something; he said, "Well, Gregory, that little beatnik, with his sleeping bag." I never slept in a sleeping bag . . . beautiful fucking bed there, man.

RK: Have you read that book?

GC: Yeah, I thought it sucked because he lied.

JL: What lies?

GC: Well, the visit to the house. The only time he met me was at the house with me and Belle. We served him nice drinks in the garden and everything. Shit. He didn't mention that. He had me sleeping in a sleeping bag. Bullshit. Do you think it's an insult that I call human beings hairy bags of water?

RK: I don't think so from where it comes from; I mean we're a sack of guts. That's what people are.

GC: That's what I mean, right. That's what they are. You see, and it's a chemical hit. That's going to save them. Their bodies are all perfect, beautiful. I love fucking and all that. You are a hairy bag of water, aren't you?

RK: You talk a lot about death.

GC: Oh, I took death when I was a happy kid, man. Man, I took death in 1957, my death shot. I was a happy guy. I said, "Now tackle it, Corso; take the biggies." I'm no morbid soul.

RK: Are you not worried about death now?

GC: Oh, hell, no. I passed that shot. I told you in that poem on the airplane, I scared the guy more than the plane. And when he thanked me for it, I said, "Look, I passed that death fear shot a long time ago." You know how I passed it? In 1960 in Luxembourg Gardens in Paris, Sunday afternoon, people with their perambulators and children, old people sitting on the park benches, children pulling their boats in the pond there, lovers kissing on the grass. I said, "This is heaven, Gregory." Suddenly behind a tree I saw a guy with an axe, and I said, "Boy, he could make a shambles of this heaven–chop, chop, chop. Now who put that man behind the tree? I did; he wasn't there. But he *is* there in life, isn't he? That fucker is there with your bombs or whatever you call it. I called that heaven, the way things were going there. I saw the shambles of it, chop, chop, chop. It don't mean nothing to me, that chop, chop, chop–no more. And what about you–what about you people? Now would you get scared if you felt your heart was feeling pattering and suddenly you turned pale? And you might just have a heart attack and drop dead here? I think I'd go to a movie theater. I would. If I felt that was happening I'd run into a movie house.

RK: Why a movie house?

GC: I don't know . . . I thought I'd just get my mind off it or something. Can I ask you a question, John? Are you a happy man?

JL: Right now, yeah.

GC: I want to build up to something. Do you feel there are any mysteries? Something you don't understand?

JL: I don't worry about them, wonder about them.

GC: All right. Do you have any enemies?

JL: I don't worry much about it if I do.

GC: I don't have any; I make them all into friends, you know. All right. Do you love me?

JL: I believe I do, and I think I loved you on first sight. You know, you got off that goddamn airplane with your fucking gold earrings, your long

Corso in 1990 (photograph © 1990 by Françoise Bernardi)

hair, your purple shirt, and you ran around hugging people and frightening old ladies. Let me ask my question; I'm going to ask you one. I want you to give us a chronological and exact history of your use of drugs, related to what you were writing at the time, when you first began using them, when you finished, and the effect that they had.

GC: O.K. I took drugs after the poetry was written. I took drugs very late. I started in 1963; I was 33 years old.

JL: Never in prison, never before prison?

GC: No. I smoked pot in 1950 when I came out of prison. That's a joint every now and then. But I saw people shooting up. I never took the heavies then. In 1956 especially in Mexico, the marijuana was real good. But in 1963–heroin; that was the weight. I took it to experiment with my head and I forgot one thing. You said the arrogance of this gesture–I forgot that. Boy, if you get stuck on some fuck like that, then you got to give in. And that was very rough for a guy like me. I had to go beg for that fucker. So I said then it's nobody's business, Gregory–that's my medicine in the medicine cabinet, my chemistry. But I dropped it, I don't have to take drugs now.

JL: Well, do you take methadone?

GC: No.

JL: How long have you been off methadone?

GC: Methadone I've been off now two days. When I was in New York recently I was taking drugs again, heroin. Now, if I just stop and don't take methadone I would have to go a few days real cold turkey, and I don't dig it. But if you just take a little bit of methadone, ten milligrams, not the hundred milligrams they give these guys, you can gradually be off it again, you dig? And that's why I go into drinking. A person takes drugs doesn't drink. I drink, right? And I've been feeling pretty good. I got great recuperative powers.

JL: Can you write when you take drugs?

GC: No, no.

JL: Are you going to quit? Are you going to get off drugs in order to do this big number you got planned?

GC: It's already done, this next book.

JL: You were on drugs when you did it?

GC: Ahhh, no. It's an alien substance in you. It knocked out the spirit of me. I didn't bother writing. What I dug doing with it was fucking because it erects your dick a long time. It takes a long time for you to come. So poetry was out of it. And when the poetry came, and I say it's a rare little number, this little brick musehouse that I've been doing, when it came it was intermittent. It was . . . well, I said, "Corso, is this a drag now to get the money to buy the dope and I'm being a pain in the ass among my friends by getting the money–so cool it." See, I'm no liar.

JL: O.K. How is your taking drugs and what you experienced when you take drugs–how much of that goes into your poetry?

GC: I don't take drugs to write about drugs. It's been done, right?

RK: What about Lawrence Lipton's *Holy Barbarians?* Did you ever feel a sense of responsibility or connection with those Venice West people?

GC: As far as responsibility, I have none. Not me, no way. That's an early book, isn't it? He was talking about people like me, right?

RK. I think he was talking about, you know, like you get a movement and you get five poets or three poets to do something and there's an intellectual and emotional validity and spiritual validity, even. And all of a sudden there's a thousand people doing some of the things those people did, but not the other half.

GC: I don't know about the other half. He saw me and Allen Ginsberg; we all come from the East to San Francisco, and this man, who just used to write about communist literature (all that shit) was very, very impressed by us. It was early in the game. I don't know how it fits, or what.

JL: Hey, do you care very much about ecology?

GC: Should I? I don't know . . . I mean I don't *not* care, you dig what I mean? My daughter cares.

RK: How old is she?

GC: Ten years old. Yeah, she really cares. I stopped her from killing also. When she was a kid, she was about to stop on a bug. I said, "No way." She never then killed anything. But I caught her, man, when she was about to fink on me. She was going to go tell her mommie in the other room that I was lighting up a cigarette and I said, "What? No way you tell on your father." "But I don't care. That's wrong, daddy, what you're doing is wrong." And she tells me to get fake teeth also.

RK: Where is she now?

GC: New York City. She just can't stand graffiti, she's so protected. She's an angel. When she sees graffiti, it really upsets her. So I said to the mother, "Well, man, I gotta be around her a little to wake this kid up fast, man. I don't want it to give her a jolt, when she gets this one shot, you know, what life is. You could easily let it grow in her, man."

RK: What does her mother say?

GC: Well, her mother's beginning to check me out and realize that I'm right. She's a little over-protective with the kid.

JL: You ever think about your three-year old who's going to read your poems someday?

GC: Yeah. Well, she's the angel–blonde hair and blue eyes. Her family made the atom bomb, and I wrote the *Bomb* poem. See the combine? The DuPont people were the first ones to make the atom bomb. The mother is DuPont and the daddy is the one who wrote the Bomb poem. So my daughter goes around and can say, "Well, O.K. If they made the bomb, look what my daddy did."

RK: The two consciousnesses . . . .

GC: Right. And that was no choice. It just happened. And Belle, beautiful. Belle is beauty, right? And she is very beautiful. Boy, she's strong and tough. Those New Mexican people, I'm telling you, man alive.

RK: Those who?

GC: People in New Mexico like they were mentioning up on the stage today.

RK: How does that tie up with New Mexico?

GC: Oh, female. Oh, because they live there, my daughter and Belle.

JL: The three-year old.

GC: Three-year old, right. But you know it's good that I have two daughters rather than, I feel, a guy because what a weight to lay on a boy, right–me? The son always tries to knock out the daddy.

RK: The girls can incorporate it more.

GC: Oh, yeah, I heard yesterday that the Women's Lib in town got to dig me. They were pissed off with me in the beginning. Reason they got to dig me was that I did say to them very straight: "Poets have been taking the whole shot all the time, you can't make a dichotomy. You can't just take half of it, you got to take the whole number. That'll save it, that'll do it."

RK: What happened between like when you were 10 and 17? Where were you?

GC: Ten to 17; that's good, a decade shot. One to 10, I had eight mothers, because I didn't have my mother; they sent me to all these orphanages and foster homes. Ten to 17 were really funny years cause 16 1/2–prison, 13–bad boys' home; so from 10 to 17–institutional; out on the streets when I was 20 years old. I slept on the rooftops and in the subways of New York, man. I had no home. From 11 years old to 16 1/2.

RK: Do you speak Italian?

GC: I could understand my father talk it; my grandmother, I used to understand her.

RK: Do you know other languages?

GC: Ancient Egyptian. Not spoken much today.

RK: Ancient Egyptian. You'll never get into the Peace Corps, I tell you. You must look up a lot of etymology in dictionaries, like where it refers you to another word to another word to another word?

GC: Oh, I used to. See, I know words–beautiful words from the past that people don't know, and it really saves the words. For instance, "scry" we got before, we understand what "scry" is. A pentacle-maker–you know who he is?

RK: No.

GC: Karcist. K-A-R-C-I-S-T. O.K., that's one for you. Now, the wind, that goes through the trees. You know what it is? Murmur, right? It's an onomatopoeic shot. You know what it really is? B-R-O-O-L.

RK: In Old English?

GC: Yeah. Thomas Carlyle, really. Poets can create onomatopoeia if they want, like "the duck quacked." I mean, my great little drawing of a duck, and out of the mouth comes "onomatopeia"; I don't go "quack" with the duck. I could sell that little cartoon to *The New Yorker,* I bet. I mean, it's a great one, right, a duck going "onomatopoeia." And I just love "duck,"–I love the word, "duck"; they're funny, ducks, man.

RK: Did you read Philip Lamantia? Because you've got some images which really get into surrealism.

GC: Yeah, yeah, him early, and Andre Breton; I dug him when I was 14 years old. Philip, now, you're talking about the guy who I dig a lot.

RK: A lot of your images are really surrealistic: "a wrinkled angel weeping axle grease" or something like that, which is getting close to surrealism.

GC: "Wrinkled angels," yet. I have to go back and read my poetry and learn. I love putting words together like "wheels of rainlight," "treelight."

RK: You put words together. Like Kerouac.

GC: Oh, yeah, that's compound, that is like chemistry. You put iron and another element together and you get a third. So that gives the birth, right? And when you put the heavies like "sexdeath" together, what do you get? You put two together, you do get a third. One and one does make three. Now, where four comes from always grabs me; really suspicious about four. I was playing around with geometry, but that's a big daddy, the number four. Uno, uno, and the baby out is the third, right? Who's that fourth fucker?

RK: That's the guy with the axe.

GC: (Laughing) The guy with the axe.

Chapter 8
John Clellon Holmes

(12 March 1926 – 2 March 1988)

See also the Holmes entry in *DLB 16: The Beats: Literary Bohemians in Postwar America.*

Born four years to the day after Jack Kerouac, John Clellon Holmes was Kerouac's close friend, correspondent, and writing colleague for more than twenty years. Holmes was living in New York City when he met Kerouac in August 1948; in a conversation with Holmes later that year Kerouac said, "You know, we're really a beat *generation." Although Kerouac's* The Town and the City *had come out in 1950, Holmes was the first writer to publish a work that focused entirely on the members of the Beat Generation. This roman à clef, titled* Go, *was published in 1952. As Kerouac later did, Holmes wrote of actual events, and though he changed the names, Kerouac, Allen Ginsberg, Neal Cassady, Holmes himself, and other Beat Generation characters are clearly recognizable in* Go. *As a result of his publishing success, Holmes became an early spokesman for the Beat Generation. His essay "This Is the Beat Generation" appeared in* The New York Times *five years before Kerouac's* On the Road *was published in 1957. Although he plowed the same turf as Kerouac (the jazz scene, primarily in New York), Holmes's traditional prose style was more accessible to the public than was Kerouac's; he went on to publish articles in magazines such as* Esquire *and* Playboy. *He established himself as a competent professional writer and, finally, an elder spokesman for the Beat Generation, writing comprehensive essays and giving interviews after the Beat fervor had died down. He has been referred to as the "Beat Generation Boswell."*

John Clellon Holmes (photograph by Ann Charters)

Holmes and Kerouac

Holmes had known Kerouac for about four months when Kerouac let Holmes read his work journals that he kept while writing The Town and the City. *The following letter shows both the budding friendship and the collegial support the two men shared. In addition, Holmes describes his perception of the "inside" and the "outside" of Kerouac's nature, a dual identity that plagued Kerouac, especially after he achieved fame.*

November 30, 1948

Jack,

We never did get a chance to talk about your journals the way that I wanted to, but while I read them I jotted down little impressions and ideas that occurred to me and I append a list thereof. This can be in no way a literary criticism because such things do not actually apply to "mood logs" and the like; also it cannot be one because I find it difficult to be objective, knowing you as I do and feeling so strongly about your work.

Firstly: Because I saw you often while I was going through this material, I got an interesting double-image picture of "Kerouac" (as you refer to yourself at one point)–"They call me Kerouac, omitting the first name, as though I were a kind of figure in the world, much less a 'guy'. This is what they do, smiling when they think of me, even when I spend long winters of loneliness and strive to be stern, silent, majestic. The result is always–Kerouac . . . " Whenever I found myself classifying you, as people always do with friends, saying to themselves, often unconsciously, "He is this or that," or "I know that when I am with him, he will be this way, he will react in this manner to that idea etc."; whenever I found this happening I went back to your journals and read more. It successfully broke the false and static picture I was creating. It impressed me, generally first, with the infinite variety of the human being, the fathomless fluctuation that is in everyone, and specifically, with the intensity of your quest accompanied as it was with self-searchings, condemnations, postulations of premises, self-lacerations and psychological pick-me-ups. This was a rare experience to me; to see someone from the outside and yet have a key to the inside as well. It enabled me to get a larger focus on the mental camera we all flash on each other. I found that I rejected none of it, even those early enthusiasms which found repudiation the next day.

Secondly: I found a wealth of help for the writer that is obtainable in reading your journals. It is not academic. It lacks the professional tone, but such a sentence as this: "Let him (the young writer) write his novel 'the way he'd like to see a novel written'" strikes me immediately as one slogan to be lettered large on cardboard and pinned over everyone's desk. You go on to say, "It's worry that must be eliminated for the sake of individual force . . ." How well I know this! You accomplished this purging (although can we ever accomplish it completely?) through loneliness, self-induced trauma at times, and through the drive behind you to create what you call somewhere a "perfect Niagera of a novel". These journals must be read straight through, from the confidence and bravado of early '46, through the terror and decorum of 'early 47,' through the California trip, through the difficulty of beginning once more, the long months when the piling of words obsessed you, through that ecstatic entry on March 12, 1948 (your birthday and mine as well) when you did 4500 words ("count 'em"), through the end of the task, the journal itself closing on the day you got that form-rejection from MacMillan and wrote, "Sept. 9 . . . Tonight I finished and typed the last chapter. Last sentence of the novel: 'There were whoops and greetings and kisses and then everybody had supper in the kitchen'. Do you mean that the folks of this country won't like this last chapter?–or would it be better if I said, 'Everybody had dinner in the dining room.'? But the work is finished . . ." Read in this manner, we find a chronicle far superior to Wolfe's "Story of the Novel", written years after creation with perhaps the advantage of hindsight and pleasing reviews. This record was kept on the spot, everything is put down, the entries proceed with the desperate joltiness of life and not the even flow that Wolfe managed to invest his "story" with. Wolfe tells us that he thrashed and raged in his little room in London, trying to get into his work. We *see* you thrashing and raging, we *see* you sick and angry, doubting and self-hating. We are inside of you. Suffice it to say, reading these logs has profited me immeasureably.

Thirdly: I was interested to see how you grew with the novel. It brought life to you while you were bringing life to it. This is quite beautifully evident in these pages. You start with long essays on the nature of it, thematic exigeses in the Faustian tone. You come to your work with anthropological biases, with a perfect arsenal of ideas and conceptions and tendenz. You thrash those out, the novel rejects some of them, your journals become agonized, they lapse into telegraphic notations of words-done, your "worldliness" intrudes again, you write more essays, more analyses; but the novel abolishes it all. You end with the simple, almost quiet writings of a servant in the grip of something to which he feels a large responsibility. Everyone of your previously arrived at ideas about life etc. has changed when you finish *T and C.* Even the excoriations against "homosexual intelligentzia", against "maturity", against "international anti-Americanism" etc. has been muted by the experience your *novel* has brought to *you.* That is something you have been through, something all writers must learn. Writing a novel is growing, is letting out of yourself raw material which is fashioned into a new experience which the writer lives through in his very bones. There is no man that is not changed by such experience. Life looks different after he emerges from it. Somewhere you speak of the artist as a God in the truest sense of the term. This is so, but gods (the books lead us to believe) are perfect in the beginning and do not learn from the things they create. Man, thank christ for it!, has not this prudish perfection. The artist, because he lives in his two worlds simultaneously, must bring some rapport between them. You were not mastered by your work in any Rimbaudian sense of "induced hysteria", but you felt yourself always the instrument by which your "vision" would reach others and you accepted the burden this placed upon you. Your vague wonderings about "art", about "the nature of the artist" etc. all become silent when you come to create, and you realize this when you write: "From now on less notes on the subject of writing–and of myself–and more writing . . . *A man must keep his doubts to himself and prove his works instead.*"

Fourthly: I was intensely interested in your long entries, while in California, concerning themselves with morality. I had thought (and this is an example of classification on the brute level) that you had little moral sense, other than a kind of unconscious amoralism which served an identical purpose. But I find that during this period you were concerned with "good and evil" and "means and ends". I could rebut these ideas (from my own position) but it would be fruitless here. It is enough to record that I think they have activated many of your chapters on the "wild young people" in New York, Peter being thrown among them as a sort of spectator. Always you come back to life, both in the journals and in your book. You let your doubts seize you, your terrors, your wonderings about "pale criminals" and the "decadent fascination with criminality" and for a month or two you will seem to be obsessed with these things, but then in a passion of assertion you will come back to life, saying that you cannot condemn anyone because they live. 'They live! They live!' you say. This is a very American kind of self-affirmation, which smacks (not so much in you) of the inability to healthily criticize oneself. It is tainted with a certain nervousness with challenging ideas, and the eventual need to assert oneself (uncritically) over them. This is all right too. I feel a hell of a lot like Hawthorne writing to Melville when I say these things, although I mean them in no narrow Calvinistic way, as Hawthorne, who was truely "sin-tortured" must have. I am not speaking of a dead morality, but the need for a workable one. But that is all another question, without specific reference here. At one point in the journals you write a proposed ending for *T and C* which revolves around a lecture that Peter goes to with a girl he is considering for his wife. The lecture is in your words "liberal, modern, free-thought etc." and Peter's reactions confine themselves to large negatives and a very moving re-affirmation of life and existence which sounds (although you would deny it) very Sartrian and existential. This saves it being nothing less than foolishness. When you say that beyond moralities and strictures and ideas, there is life, you are saying that "Being comes before essence", and you will find agreement with me. The fact that life is pain and misery and sorrow, that we die midway between darkness and darkness does not, however, negate

Holmes, U.S. Navy photograph, 1944 (courtesy of Allen Ginsberg Trust)

the necessity for discovering a manner in which life can be lived with some human dignity intact, with some moral conviction. You sense this, not alone in your journals but in your book and your life as well; although you perhaps don't "know" it in any cognitive sense.

Fifthly: I like your inability to reject some things because they are thought "boorish," "adolescent" etc. by the young bohemians and intellectuals of this world. I like your reactions after seeing that film on the Earp brothers, these long compendiums of American food written with a real relish. I like the simplicity (which of course leads to accuracy) of your rejection of what you call "worldliness and education", although I would not advise everyone to follow your example. Above all, I love the absolute drive that is present in you at all times to justify life in some way, that justification-impulse being the most truely moral thing there is. Nietzsche says somewhere that a purely sensual man would be incapable of understanding tragedy because everything would be received on equal intellectual terms, and measured only for its sensorial impact. He is right; but should have extended this idea to indicate that the purely sensual man could never have been an artist, because the artist, by definition, cares about certain things above others. He seeks, as Middleton Murry says of Dostoyevski, to "justify life, not to represent it". In this sense, you see, you have convictions and you care about the world you live in. You even say somewhere that we must realize we "live with others and bear responsibility to them". Your responsibility, and thank god for it!, is always refered to the actual context of reality and changed thereby. But it is never abolished. You refer it (and your ideas about it) continually to life itself, to raw experience, but your very need to create a novel reflects an equal need to make some sense out of that experience. (No matter what you say now about simply wanting money and security and fame etc., your journals give us your real reasons for writing *T and C.* You believed in its "crucial necessity".)

Sixthly: Your desire for people, which I knew to be great even before I read this material, becomes strongly evident as I read further. This passage moved me (I know not why)–"July 24–Went to N.Y. to a party at Allen's where I met a rose . . . a little princess weighted down with the horror of her kingdoms . . . a child . . . a wise passionate child . . . a 'nature girl' really, who also sings, dances, paints . . . a little Pariesieen . . . and mostly a little Goethean love (and just as young) . . ." And now you are destroying the Goethean love of Warren Beauchamp in *"On the Road"?* Your whole affair with Jinny is a beautiful panel out of the general labor of these pages. I love your need for love, Jack. It is something that touches me as well. I love your self-consciousness with people like Warren Beauchamp, Lucien Carr, even though I know that the blank-face stare of Peter and Ray Smith must someday give over to comprehension and judgement. Perhaps even to the simple "gone" of Hunky. But to something affirmative, rather than simply grandly accepting. You must not feel self-conscious with these big intellectuals and "pale criminals". You feel; they too often do not. The Goethean love is destructive, I know that, but it will happen to you time and time again and you must come to terms with it (I forgot that you hate that phrase). Perhaps Joe's action at the end of *T and C* is the answer for you, getting a farm. However, you must see that Joe, in his own way, has rejected something in affirming the life that he does. He is not Ray Smith or Peter Martin who live organically, almost sensually. He has chosen something over something else. You do this in day to day life, all you have to do is make it conscious so your choice can be activated by full knowledge.

Seventhly: I love your desire to do "the task", to bring something into the world, to make your accomplishment. You say at one point that you want to bring to the "glorious wife the future holds for me" a great accomplishment, a full life. There is something wistful about this section and it compliments the moment when you speak to future young people and tell them that you are not the wise, integrated seer you will seem to be to them. It is the same impulse both times; know me, you say to them. This is how you take your responsibility. You think of your "glorious wife", of the young people to come, you speak of "sweet talks with Ma", and at one point you come back from a binge in New York to find Hal Chase and Ginger waiting for you and you record how glad you were to see them . . . "they could not know how glad" . . . for Jinny you would have thrown away the world, your book, you call it "blind, greedy jealousy" at one point: and I even love that, even though it is a lie and a delusion as you later discover, because your book was love above all things and "care". Your introspection is (90% of the time) the search for honesty, which is the only safety for any of us. This honesty you find in your protective anger at those that would kill the "American glee and wonder". Men even call these things gods. I was surprised last night (when I read more and more of your journals again) to find you saying something I had said the day before, some thing that lies behind most great American writing and thinking, "Where do I fit in? If this world rejects *me,* how can it be the best of all possible worlds?" This is what is happening in this country today, a kind of revolution that will one day have to become social if it will be successful. In the larger sense, it is what is happening all over the world. The codes by which we live cease to have reference to human beings any longer, something in the human creature is slighted time and time and again, and we are all asking, "How can I accept or defend this thing when it excludes me, when it will not allow for *my* existence?" You may not agree with this idea, but your writing reflects it.

Finally: a confession on my part. The above written notes constitute in no way an overall picture of my reactions to what you have let me read of your private papers. At this point I would be incapable of giving all of my opinions because they are all tangled with other considerations (I am in the middle of knowing you as well). These are random musings that occured to me and I wanted you to know some of them. . . .

John
–*The Beat Book,* pp. 116–119

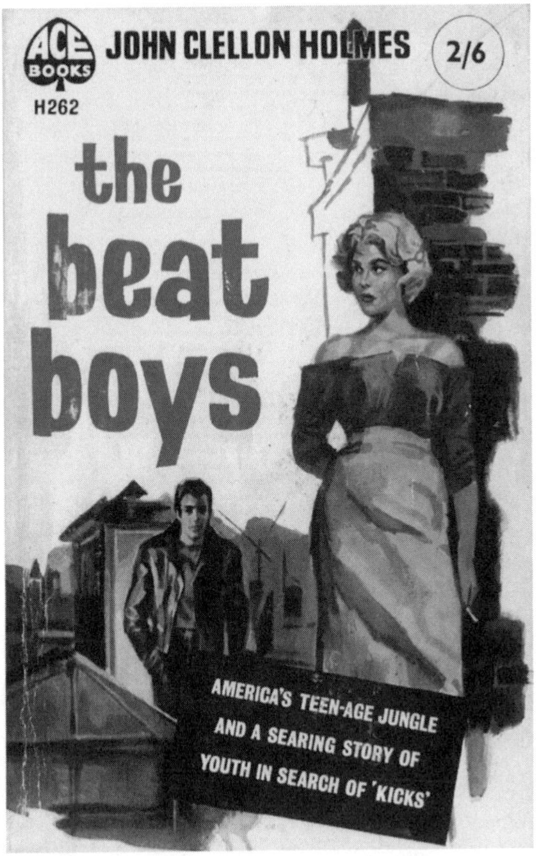

Although Holmes received a $20,000 advance for paperback reprint rights, Go *did not appear in paperback until the success of Kerouac's* On the Road *revived interest in it. The book was then published in abridged form by Ace in 1958. Ace republished the abridged edition as* The Beat Boys *in England in 1959.*

The Writing and Publication of *Go*

Holmes commented on his state of mind when he was writing Go *in a 23 June 1987 letter to Ann Charters, which was published in the afterword of the 1997 edition of the novel brought out by Thunder's Mouth Press.*

I began writing the book [*Go*] when we returned to New York City in August [1949]. So the form–properly a *roman a clef,* I suppose–came of itself, though I had to learn how to use it, and found that simply telling the truth wasn't half enough. It still had to be brought to fictional life. Here my primary influences were the Russians–Dostoevsky above all . . . I was dealing in extremes of spirit, excesses of behavior, violent emotions or *lack* of them. Dostoevsky is the poet of such states. (Despite saying I was reared on Kafka, James, etc. I was actually in the process of going *backward* from modern literature–being self-educated, I could go where I liked–and was deep in "the great days of the novel" during the writing of *Go*). . . . I didn't think of myself as a "literary historian"; I was already publishing poetry, and everyone wanted to write novels in those days.

In his introduction to the 1997 edition of Go, *Holmes discusses the publishing history of his first novel.*

Go was first published in the fall of 1952 by Charles Scribner's, and thus it has the dubious distinction of being the first "Beat" novel to appear (the publication of *On the Road,* due to incomprehension, censorship, and plain stupidity, wouldn't occur for another five years), and the fact that I had used the phrase "Beat Generation" several times in the book, though carefully ascribing it to Gene Pasternak, may account for some of the confusion about who is properly the father of the term. Nevertheless, *Go* came out, was reviewed here and there, sold something over 2,500 copies, and then was quickly forgotten until *On the Road* appeared in 1957.

There were ironies aplenty in the publishing history of the book. Before being accepted by Scribner's, it had been rejected by A. A. Wyn, whose paperback subsidiary, Ace Books, would eventually publish the paperback edition five years later. Scribner's itself got nervous about possible censorship as publication approached, and submitted the book to a lawyer, who finally cleared it on the proviso that I make a few changes, which mostly involved a slight toning-down of the sex scenes. With considerable reluctance, I agreed to do this, but balked when I was asked to cut to *three* Agatson's *six* desperate "Fuck Yous" in the latter part of the book. "What's the difference between three and six?" I wondered. "He's not talking about sex, he's cursing the world." I stood my ground, and refused. As a result, Scribner's seriously thought of not publishing, and then suggested that if I would agree to withhold the book from paperback publication (where most censorship suits arose in those days) they would go ahead. My editor there, that good man, Burroughs Mitchell, realizing that my only hope of making any money lay in a paper sale, solved the problem by getting Scribner's to relinquish all the reprint rights to me on the proviso that nowhere in any paperback edition would there be any mention of the fact that they had published the book originally. Needless to say, this didn't inspire confidence in an unblooded young author, who wanted to believe that his publisher believed in him.

The book was eventually sold to Bantam for the then-munificent sum of $20,000, only to be refused publication by them two years later (again, because of fear of lawsuits) on the advice of the very *same* lawyer who had cleared it for Scribner's. As a consequence, by the mid-fifties I had discovered that I had earned ten dollars for every copy of a three-fifty book that had been sold, a book that would remain forgotten until Ace published an abridged edition in the wake of the initial notoriety about the Beat Generation in 1957. That edition, cut by almost a third, was subsequently published in England and Italy, and the original book vanished into the rare-book market where, the last I heard, the few remaining copies were going for upwards of $35.

A word about the title. The original manuscript was called *The Daybreak Boys,* which was an allusion to a river-gang on the New York waterfront of the 1840's. I felt that it was an appropriate title for a book about a new underground of young people, pioneering the search for what lay "at the end of the night" (a phrase of Kerouac's). But Scribner's had recently published a novel about public relations called *The Build-up Boys,* and rejected the title. I couldn't come up with anything else, and eventually it was Burroughs Mitchell's wife who thought of *Go.* When the book was published in England, the reverse happened. The English publisher pointed out that there was a travel magazine there named *Go,* and so the book would have to be renamed. It was finally published in Britain as *The Beat Boys,* and the circle (not to mention the confusion) was complete—in that some Englishmen still think that *The Beat Boys* is a wholly different novel.

Reviews of *Go*

The 'Kick' that Failed

G. M.

The New York Times Book Review, 9 November 1952, p. 50

All the people in "Go" ("Go" is the chic word to yell at a musician, preferably a tenor saxophonist, clarinetist or trumpeter when he takes off on some private dream of his own) are teaheads, or marijuana smokers, either out of curiosity or some intellectual conviction too infantile or regressive to be tacked down anywhere but on an analyst's couch. A couple of them are "mainliners" or addicts who take heroin directly into the bloodstream and are sometimes portrayed as trying to "kick" or get rid of the nasty habit.

A number of others are forever getting themselves tangled up in fragments from Blake, Dostoevsky and the Bible, usually winding up either drunk, incoherent or both. Now and then, someone beats up his girl, or gloomily seduces someone else's wife. They circulate endlessly and uneasily from apartments in the Village to lofts on the West Side, sleazy flats in midtown on the East Side and Harlem, talking all the time. Some of the talk isn't bad at that.

About the least hopeless of all these amateur Rimbauds are Paul Hobbes and his wife, Kathryn. Kathryn works for a public relations outfit while Paul stays home and writes a bad novel. Revolving about them are a burly individual called Pasternak, who writes a presumably good novel, or at least one that gets sold; Stofsky, a homosexual and literary whirling dervish; Hart, a frantic character from out of town; Verger, a tubercular intellectual, and a number of others who tend to merge into each other. Ultimately, after Kathryn is seduced by Pasternak and Paul fails to seduce another girl, the two decide that they're through with what the author calls the "beat generation."

Be-Bop and Blues
E. J. F.
The Saturday Review, 11 October 1952, pp. 36–37

The demi-world of the hipster, the be-bop devotee, the marijuana smoker, the chronic drinker has been getting a deal of novelistic attention in recent months. More, I suspect, than it deserves, particularly since few of the writers have anything much to say about it. Clellon Holmes makes his stab at the subject with a first novel "Go" (Scribner, $3.50) that leaves the subject pretty much where he found it. He rushes his characters around a recognizable New York, into and out of beer bars, after-hours joints, marijuana parties, and be-bop temples. He kills off one of them, has four others arrested for petty thievery, almost wrecks but finally saves the marriage of his principals and generally creates the impression of a lot of frenzied rushing around. All of this is supposed to make you feel very sad, and probably will, but not necessarily for the reason Mr. Holmes intended. You're supposed to see these characters as spiritually impoverished tragic figures. Spiritually impoverished they certainly are, but their tragedy eludes me.

Three A.M. Revels
Frederic Morton
The New York Herald Tribune Books, 12 October 1952, p. 33

They were all getting their kicks at Stofsky's place. It was a broken-down apartment. The curtains were mouldy, the only window opened up on a dirty airwell. But that was no drag. They had caught a good station on the radio and they were digging the jazz. The guys had brought up plenty of liquor, and the "tea" everybody was smoking was class. Then Agatson exploded a flower pot with a firecracker and the party really started humming.

Or did Agatson throw that firecracker up at Paul's house? It didn't really matter. Who could remember after all the whiskeys? And the reefers? And the beers in between? Maybe it had been at Ketcham's place and perhaps it wasn't even Agatson who threw the thing. It might have been Hart Kennedy after Stofsky read Blake's "Auguries of Innocence" to him in the stolen Cadillac. But wait a minute. One fact is certain: the event occurred somewhere in a novel about avant-guard desperados by Clellon Holmes.

Lots of other events also happen in "Go," mostly adult variations on juvenile delinquency. There are scads of characters too, with and without quotations marks. After combing their stubble and straightening their T-shirts we shall present them, feeling a little like an over-worked police-sergeant at night court. There is drained, prematurely wrinkled Ancke, for instance, who allows himself to be arrested every three months so that jail may cure his drug-habit down to proportions he can afford: there is the aforementioned Agatson, drinking Scotch by the quart and disliking most breakable objects until they lie broken on the floor. There is Hart Kennedy: he "doesn't care about anything"–except the next jag, the next joint. And Stofsky, a species of exuberant introvert, who likes both mystic poetry and homosexuality, has visions every second midnight, and believes in God, though usually under the assumption that God is mad. And Verger, the tubercular theology student who communes with bartenders. And Ed Schindel who steals groceries to save money for "weed." And Christine who has lovers by mail. And last but not least Paul and Kathryn Hobbes.

Paul and Kathryn are a little apart from their company. They love each other–an unorthodox circumstance considering the milieu–and that love saves them from much of the thrill-smothered sterility of their friends. Their marriage runs into difficulties but these only tighten the bond. It is through the Hobbes–particularly through a heartbreakingly proud scene in which Paul pretends to be "big" about Kathryn's infidelity–that Mr. Holmes gives us a hint of the insights of which he is capable. It is again Paul and Kathryn who maintain what precarious continuity there is in the plot structure of "Go."

But the howl and stomp of those cold water flat parties obliterates even that. The saxophones scream out of the portable while couples twitch against damp walls and a cry goes up that the reefers won't last. Before long somebody is sure to lick up spilled liquor from the dirty floor. And then, when all possibilities of debauch have been exhausted in one place, the "go" starts in earnest. The party is not over until the crowd completes its patrol from the apartment to hip bars in Greenwich Village, from the Village to dope dens in Harlem, from Harlem down again to tired all-night cafeterias around Times Square, and from there to Third Avenue dives open beyond the legal limit. It always rains down from a cold false dawn and soaks the heap of cigarette butts left in leaking attics.

Mr. Holmes' style is almost appropriately slack and erratic. Occasionally it bulges out into a cramped lyricism–only to retreat fatigued into a bare transcription of happenings. "A beat generation," philosophizes Paul Hobbes toward the end. We hope he is not right. But the adjective seems useful. This is a beat novel.

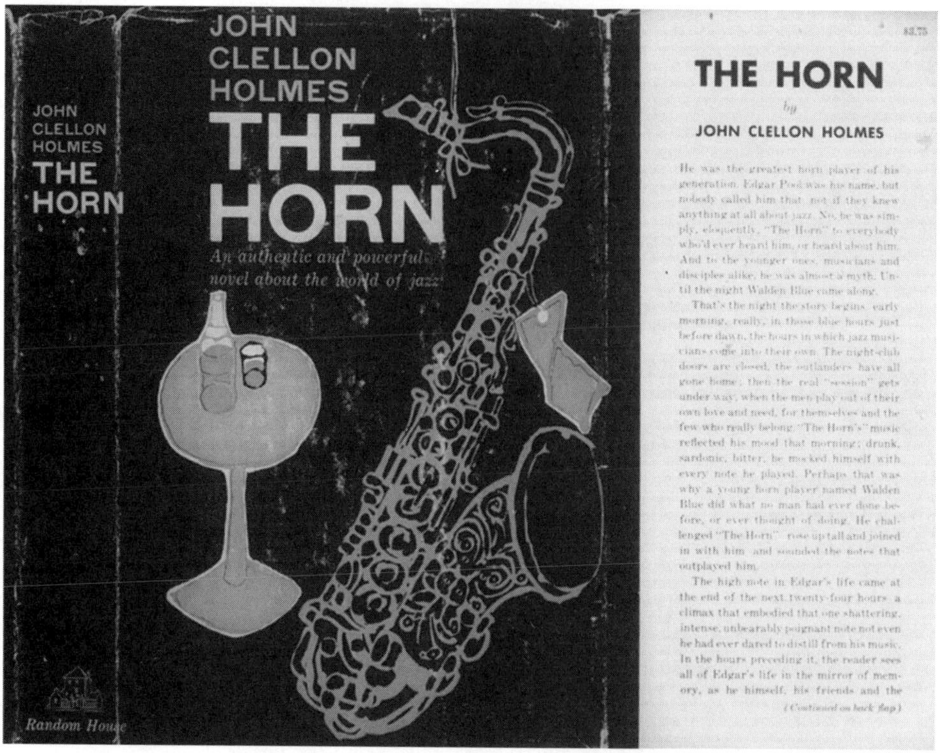

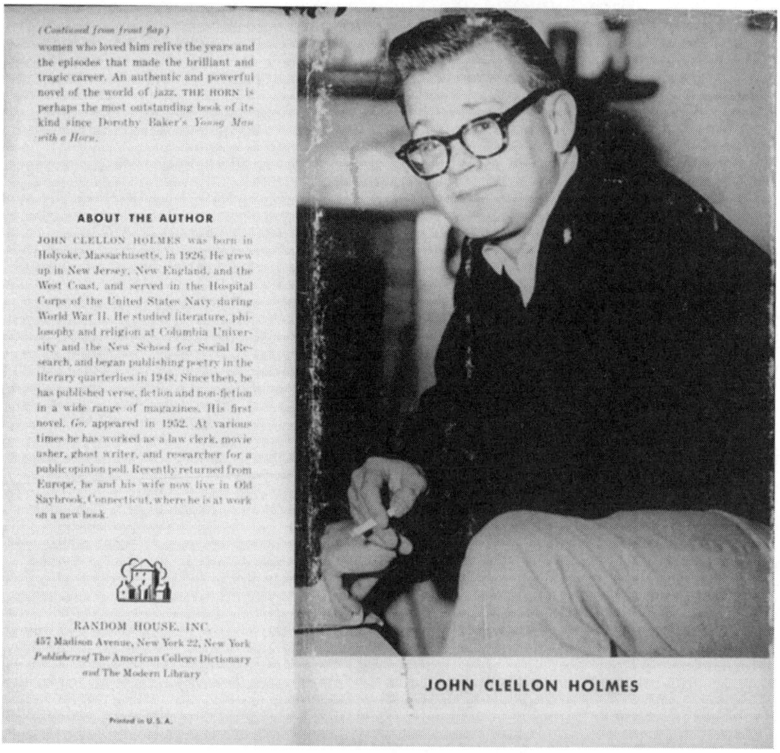

Dust jacket for Holmes's second novel, published in 1958

Reviews of *Nothing More to Declare*

Holmes's essays were collected in Nothing More to Declare *(1967).*

Review of *Nothing More to Declare*

Daniel Aaron

Commonweal, 5 May 1967, p. 211

Not every generation finds its right chronicler, someone who is of it, yet sufficiently removed (like one of those first person narrators in a Henry James story) to record its history with a degree of detachment. John Clellon Holmes meets the requirements. What Floyd Dell did for the Village bohemians and Malcolm Cowley for the expatriates of the Twenties, he has done for the so-called Beat Generation. If his memorial seems premature to readers over forty, let them be reminded that decades today are reckoned as eons: to almost half the population of the United States, the Truman and Eisenhower years belong to antiquity.

Now in his fortieth year and poised on "a frontier between the countries of experience," Holmes opens up his luggage of memories for inspection, concealing nothing, he says, from the Customs Official. His "Declaration" is an apologia for himself and his generation, at once a definition, explanation, and description presented with great charm and insight. Brilliant bravura passages, vivid portraits, artful accounts of dramatic encounters disclose the novelist behind the autobiographical historian; but his book, although occasionally "literary," never fakes or prevaricates. It is an absolutely honest testament in addition to being a kind of mosaic of a generation. . . .

An extended discussion of the Beat Generation that follows clears up a good deal of speculation and misinformation. The blurring of "Beat" and "Beatnik" had obscured the origins and significance of the "Beat Movement," and Holmes sets the record straight. His Beat Generation, he says, was a "literary group," not a social movement. It did not seek to clash with the Squares, only to avoid them, and its bent was quasi-religious–to go questing for revelations in the expanding consciousness of the Self. The Beats (his Beats) are largely responsible, he claims somewhat hyperbolically, for changing the social tone from one of prudence, irony, and impersonality "to the daring commitment and diversity of the creative artist."

Charting the Course

Richard R. Lingeman

The New York Times Book Review, 9 April 1967, pp. 42–43

John Clellon Holmes, a proper Beat-generation "spokesman" by dint of two articles on the phenomenon, as well as his novel "Go," in which the phrase first appeared, has collected a variety of essays into a book which he titles "Nothing More to Declare" in rueful celebration of his 40th year. The book is a very kind, thoughtful and judicious consideration of his contemporaries in that hectic, grim frenzy of the late forties and fifties; it also scans an authentic American literary movement, whose influence–at least among the *outré* young–is still being felt in far-off, far-out places like Haight-Ashbury in San Francisco. For the Beat style–beards, drugs, a belief in the value of a search for some orgiastic present, "kicks," the hope of *satori,* or enlightenment, and all the rest–is still hovering over the present rebels, for all their political engagement, LSD visions and what is coming to be known as "creative withdrawal."

Still, the Beats have relinquished the stage to the current hippies, and I'm reminded of the words that F. Scott Fitzgerald, another "generational" writer, wrote to his daughter: "You speak of how good your generation is, but I think they share with every generation since the Civil War in America the sense of being somehow about to inherit the earth." But despite all the rot that has been written about the various generations, the concept is a useful watermark in understanding our country; Holmes's perceptive essays on the Beat phenomenon, whatever one may think of the literary product of its espousers, provide a useful insight, from the vantage point of one foxhole, of the times we have recently lived through.

In the first of two Beat-generation pieces included in this book, Holmes wrote (1952) that "the valueless abyss of modern life is unbearable" and that the current generation was seeking values–even false values–in desperate recoil from this vacuum. It was of course a postwar generation, too young for the most part to have participated in World War II, its emotions, rather, caught up at a distance by the world cataclysm. Then came the postwar let-down, the seediness of an America plagued by shortages, and then, in 1950, at war again and McCarthy beginning to be heard in the land.

Among the sensitive young men of the day, the search for some kind of faith began, and Holmes wrote, in "Go," of a spiritual crisis in which his protagonist "was paralyzed by the vision of unending lovelessness." This vision was similar to Allen Ginsberg's Moloch in "Howl." The Beats were in a dark cave of the spirit and when they sounded their Whitmanesque barbaric yawps they were answered by a dull "boum" and a horrifying sense of meaninglessness. So they drank hard, raced back and forth across the country and talked extravagantly of "holymen" and "angelheaded hipsters." The devil was American life, and they diced with him for high stakes–their identities.

Interviews

Interview with John Clellon Holmes
Tim Hunt
Quarterly West, Winter 1978, pp. 50–58

TH: *You've done a lot of non-fiction. Does that come mostly through the sixties after* Get Home Free, *or has it been pretty much constant in and around the novels?*

JCH: Well, I've always done non-fiction. I did more in the sixties than I did in the fifties. The two Beat Generation articles came along as we were talking about last night. Gilbert Millstein called me up. He was reviewing *Go* for the New York Times, and he was snagged by the phrase "the beat generation," which is used two or three times in the book. And he said, "What the hell is this?" I really hadn't thought about it. I just put it in Jack's mouth because that's the way it happened. "Do you want to do an article on it?" So I went over to the *Times.* I had never met Millstein before, but he was a nice guy, perceptive. He wrote a pretty good review of the book. And he said, "Do an article on this, and we'll publish this in the *New York Times Magazine.*" Well, Scribners wasn't doing any advertising for the book, so I figured maybe this would create some interest. So I wrote it in a couple of days. That's how it happened. Then *Esquire,* years later when Jack's book [*On the Road*] came out, wanted me to do a piece because Millstein had reviewed *On the Road,* and in his review he had quoted liberally from this article of mine of five years before. And I did one or two other things during the fifties, but they were mostly because someone was interested or asked me. But after I finished *Get Home Free*–I had started to teach by then–I started to do a series of non-fiction things that were short things just to keep working. I didn't have time to do a novel. So that's how it happened. Then I found myself doing more and more of it because we needed the money. By then, *Playboy* had published a couple of my things, and they paid very well. And I'd started to do some of the individual chapters in *Nothing More to Declare,* and they were all published in magazines which kept us afloat. Then I started to see that book as coming up to something. So that's how it happened. And then we went to Europe in '67, and I did all those pieces on European cities which I wanted to do and will be a book one day.

TH: *Is that the book you mentioned the other night–the one you're collecting together–or is that something else?*

JCH: No, I've got two things. The book about the trip to Europe is in effect finished. It's called *Walking Away from the War.* There's still things wrong with it, but I'm pretty much satisfied with it. It's gotten beautiful rejections. [laughs] And most of the rejections have to do with the fact that according to what the editors say nobody's interested in the war anymore. We just want to forget it. Even though this doesn't deal directly with the war, the reason we went to Europe was to get out of America, and I seriously thought of not coming back. But we did. So, that's done, but I'm getting together a collection of other things: short stories and some essays that have not been collected before, the thing on Jack's death, the thing on Los Angeles, a long and really quite perceptive, I think, piece on W. C. Fields that was written in the early sixties, and a few others. There's about six or seven short stories. I'm going to write a long introduction to it–I think I'm going to–which will stand alone, not introducing the pieces really but trying to detail some of the problems of being a writer of a certain sort in this time. Again, I seem to be in a mood of summation these years.

TH: *What sort of writer?*

JCH: Well, a writer who is not a popular writer but is a serious writer, a writer who has tried to deal with material that at the time was difficult for people to approach, a writer who ironically has been connected with a literary group that has had a profound and even sometimes ironical effect upon American life and yet who has never really been a part of that, whose connection with that group is primarily through friendship and not through similarity of attitudes–but also going into the simple difficulties of keeping alive as a writer. I mean, I feel in my case that I managed to keep free for twenty-five years, and now I've come out of the cold by taking a permanent job simply because I couldn't do it anymore. I've lost a number of books because I couldn't continue them. All those books except for *Go* show it in the structure. They show it in an uncertainty about the way they are being built because I had to keep breaking off to take jobs to keep alive. *The Horn,* for instance, took me four years to write but not in actual writing time. The first two sections were done in '52, and then I started again in '56. Every time I had to break off to do hack work to keep going. I haven't really thought my way into this introduction. I'm thinking of calling it "the writing game," [laughs] but I don't like the title. It's too cheap. I'd like to sum up what I know about this, and I know about it in a way that Jack didn't, because Jack lived in total obscurity until '57, and then he lived in total notoriety. That can be very bad for a writer as it was for him. I've always lived in both worlds a little bit, as I think most writers do. Either you get a million dollars or you get a thousand.

TH: *How do you regard the relationship between your fiction and nonfiction at this point? What do you make of* Nothing More to Declare? *Is that what you'd classify as hack work?*

JCH: No, that isn't. None of my hack work did I ever sign. I mean I've written bad stuff, but whatever I've published under my own name I'll stand on. No, I don't regard that as hack work at all. I think it has got some prose and some insights in it that I'm really proud of still. Fiction is much more difficult to write. It's also much more rewarding to do. In my nonfiction in the last ten years, I've been able to speak in my own voice. It's easier to find a prose style that is commensurate to your attitudes and your own personality than it is to find a prose style in which to create people outside yourself. So, the nonfiction has become very easy for me in that I don't write informational articles. I don't deal with statistics and just passing information over. Almost all of my nonfiction since somewhere in *Nothing More to Declare* is personal, using my own voice, often times my own experiences. You can call it new journalism if you want to, but I don't look at it that way. I look at it as part of a continuing autobiography in a sense. I don't have any plans for that at all, and I don't want to do it. As is clear from both my fiction and nonfiction, I deal pretty closely with things that have happened to me or people like me. With the single exception of *The Horn,* all of my fiction has been personal and my nonfiction too. Besides, I think that now, it may be passing now, but for the last ten years some of the best writing in America has been nonfiction. I tend to consider, for instance, *Armies of the Night* to be Mailer's finest novel. I think it was because of the tremendous acceleration of events and the intensification of experiences and the changes that were going on that many writers in that period have found they could address that situation better in nonfiction than in fiction. Fiction takes some distancing, which was impossible in the sixties. You couldn't be distant from events. You could ignore them. Someone like Saul Bellow succeeded in doing it by simply ignoring it for the most part. But if you were involved–and it was the war that involved me–the best way to speak to that involvement and express it tended to be in nonfiction of a new sort, that is, using the consciousness and the eye of the reporter as a factor in what was being said, getting rid of the pretense that journalism is objective. Now I don't think that this is as new as many of its practitioners like to believe, but I think certainly under the pressure of the events happening the way they did in that period that reporters can only be honest by not only admitting but utilizing their own subjectivity, their own subjective relationship to events. One thing that interested writers in what came to be called the new journalism was the possibility of using the techniques of fiction to describe real events as Mailer did in *Armies of the Night.* The scenes with Robert Lowell and Dwight McDonald are absolutely marvelous, and they are marvelous as fiction even though they are absolutely true. He uses the techniques of fiction there–he's using dialogue and characterization and description–to catch the feel of these people and these events. And if the book has tension, as it certainly does, and drama and it has a conclusion, it's because only a novelist could have written it. I've read many other accounts of that march, and they're just flat because the writers try to satisfy the old demands of journalism: who, what, when, where, and why. Mailer wasn't interested in that at all even though he's got all that in there. His real interest was in dramatizing what he felt about it. I think "Norman Mailer" in that book is the finest and most complicated character he's ever created, and it doesn't really resemble him much. That's his real persona, and I think he's completely successful.

TH: *What's, as you perceive it, the difference in writing climate today for a young writer, your students, as opposed to your time as an apprentice?*

JCH: The situation for young writers today is characterized by the disappearance of the magazine. I try not to talk about this too much with my students because it's too depressing. Of course, any young writer wants to publish and make money and get famous and get the girls you know, but there's so little market for fiction right now that if I were starting out again I'd be tremendously depressed. There are only three or four magazines that will pay you any money for a short story. This compels the young writer to publish in little magazines and university quarterlies which we did too. That's where everyone starts, but a young writer going along probably thinks when he's got enough short stories that he'll put them in a book, submit it, and get it published. The fact of the matter is that so few short story collections are published by major publishing houses that there is simply not room for all the writers who are writing. The situation is not much better in terms of first novels. Increasingly they publish only books that they think will make money. This is a difficult situation for young writers, and I think that they will more and more have to go to the university presses that are starting to publish original, new books. But again, there is no money in it. So what this is going to do is force writers to teach.

There was a way in my time where you could get out on the streets and hustle your ass doing little writing jobs or keeping alive one way or another while you did your book. It was a badge of honor to my generation that we didn't teach. To take a job in academia was to sell out. And it wasn't to sell out your integrity, it was to sell out your chance to experience real life. That's the way we felt about it. I've noticed among my students an increasing reluctance to take the chance on somehow making it in a city or in a reality where you are spending all your time writing and somehow keeping alive: your wife works, you take a loan, or something. And I can understand that reluctance, because they are much less naive in a sense than we were. You see, when Jack got $1000 for *Town and the City* and I got $1000 for *Go,* that was a lot of money to us. Back in the early fifties you could go a long way on $1000 if you lived like a bum. We were living like bums anyway. But a $1000 now won't get you to Kansas City, and yet advances for first novels haven't gone up any. It's still about a $1000. That's the difference. The difference is in the business end of it. Most publishing houses now are owned by RCA or some corporation, and they're run by accountants. So you don't get the situation we had then. If you got an editor who believed in your stuff, he would front for you with the house, and even though they knew your book wasn't going to sell, if the editor thought it should be published, it probably was going to be, the old Maxwell Perkins thing. I had an editor like that with *Go,* Burroughs Mitchell at Scribners who was Jim Jones' editor too. He was a guy working in the old tradition. If he believed in something, he believed it should be published, and the question of whether it was going to sell or not was irrelevant. But such an editor today I don't think could make it happen because the salesman in effect would say, "I can't hustle this book." There are still publishers who will do it, but there are fewer and fewer. The houses that still do that are the smaller ones, and how they make it in this tremendously competitive market I don't know.

I also think that publishing houses are imperceptive in not publishing more books originally in paper and not going after the college market. More young people read than older folks. I remember back in the early fifties when competition between hard cover books and soft cover books was very keen and intense. The paperback market would pay big prices because they were selling a lot more books. And I remember talking to Scribners, Burroughs Mitchell up there, about why in the world don't you hard cover people get into paper. Why do you let them get all the cream. I got $1000 for *Go* from Scribners and $20,000 from Bantam even though they never published it because of the censorship thing. The spread there was just incredible, but in those days the hard cover houses, and they still feel this way to some degree, felt that there was something disreputable about publishing originally in paper. You know the French example. No book is published in hard cover in France. You can get one bound if you want, but everything is published in paper so it's much cheaper. It can go to a much wider market. Now this new edition of *Go* is $10! Who the hell can buy that book. I can't even buy it. I mean it's ridiculous. They're spending that money on cardboard and cover and binding.

The old objection on the part of publishers to publishing originally in paper was that the books wouldn't be reviewed. But the answer to that is if everybody published in paper, of course they're going to review them. So they were very imperceptive about that, and that's why the book business is–it's not really in trouble, but increasingly as I say they will only publish best sellers. They'll give a million dollars to that Australian woman for that book, and of course they know that they can't make the million back on the hard cover edition. They've made a deal with the paperback house, the film company, and so forth. But why they don't get in on the action, I have never been able to understand, except that it is just sheer vanity. But I would think that now that the business is primarily run by accountants who don't give a damn about literature to begin with that they'd tell them the money is out there; it's not here.

An Interview with John Clellon Holmes
John Tytell
The Beat Book, pp. 37–52

INT: You were one of Jack Kerouac's closest friends for over twenty years. How do you account for the extreme personality changes that occurred after the publication of *On The Road?*

JCH: An irreconcilable division between the private self and the public life. One thing that happened to Jack was that he never understood that he had become *Jack Kerouac,* the Marlon Brando of literature, that he had become a personality, a notoriety. He felt that people were no longer talking to him, but to an image. He knew nothing about that, cared less, and beyond that it seriously bollixed his mind.

INT: Did the fame affect his accelerated drinking?

JCH: I think so. Drink sometimes provides the illusion of single-mindedness where all the things around a problem vanish–like blinders on a horse. Of course, Jack always drank a lot, we all did in those days. But I saw him two weeks after *On The Road* came out, after Gilbert Millstein's review, and he had been on television several times, had been interviewed, and he no longer knew who the hell he was supposed to be.

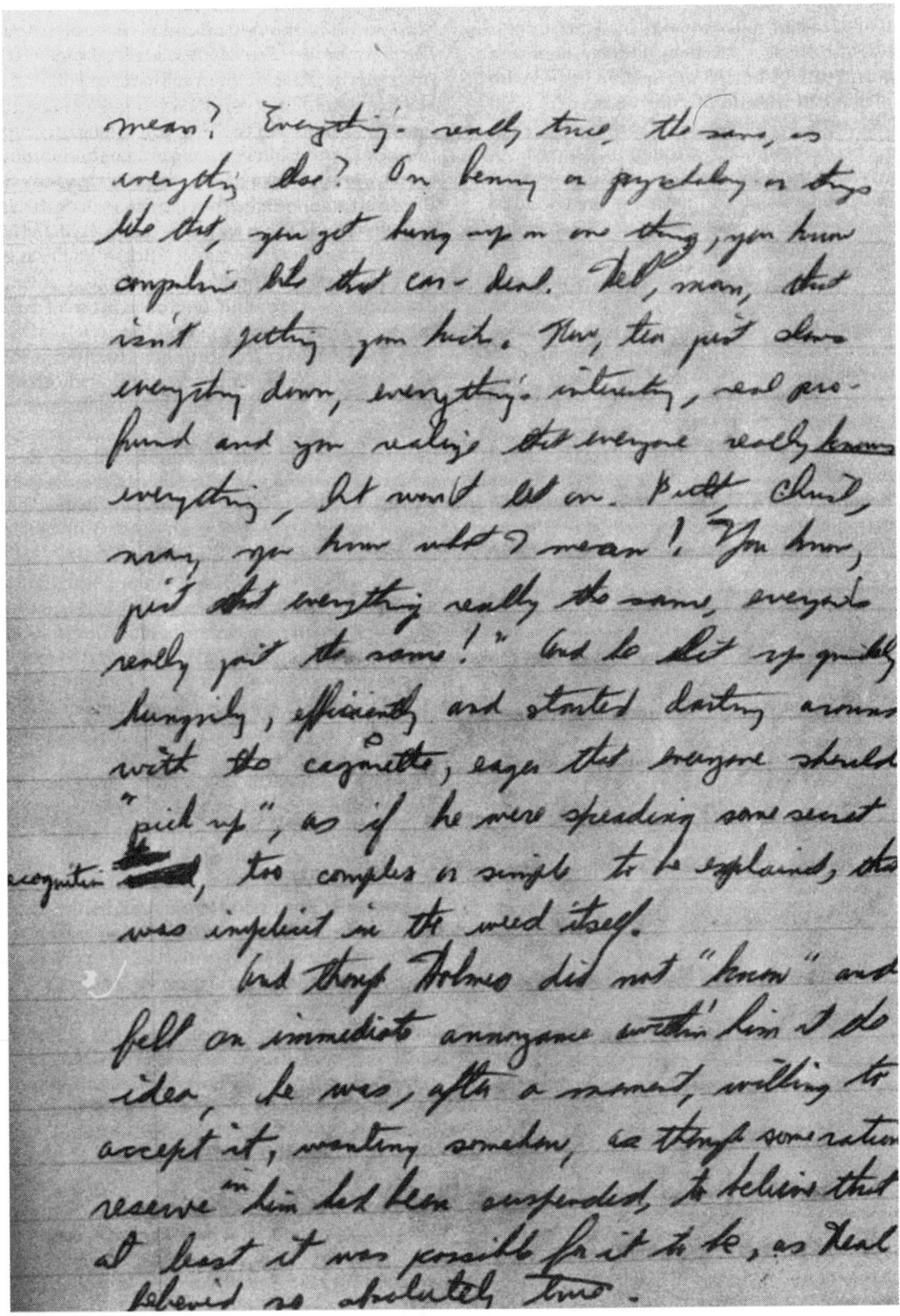
mean? Everything's really true, the same, as everything else? On benny or psychology or things like that, you get hung up on one thing, you know complaining like that con-deal. Well, man, that isn't getting you high. Now, tea just slows everything down, everything's interesting, and profound and you realize that everyone really knows everything, but won't let on. Pretty Christ, man, you know what I mean! You know, just that everything's really the same, everybody's really just the same!" And he shot up quickly, hungrily, efficiently and started darting around with the cigarette, eager that everyone should "pick up", as if he were spreading some secret recognition, too complex or simple to be explained, that was implicit in the weed itself.

And though Holmes did not "know" and felt an immediate annoyance within him at the idea, he was, after a moment, willing to accept it, wanting somehow, as though some rational reserve in him had been suspended, to believe that at least it was possible for it to be, as Neal believed so absolutely true.

Page from Holmes's notes for Go

He was temporarily discombobulated by the image of himself.

INT: Was it excitement or confusion?

JCH: When I saw him at that time, Gilbert Millstein was giving a party for him in the Village. He had invited thirty or forty people to meet this new writer. He called me because I was an old friend of Jack's. Well, Jack never showed up. At about 10:30 the phone rang, and it was Joyce Glassman, with whom he was staying then, and she asked me to speak to Jack. In a quivering voice, he said, "I can't come down there. I know you've come into town to see me, and I want to see you, could you come up here?" So I went up there, and he had gone through all these interviews, and all sorts of things like girls trying to lay him, all coming suddenly in the rush of one month.

INT: After six years of anonymity, rejection and despair.

JCH: Living like a bum and feeling spiritually wasted. He had been writing things that were unacceptable in the America of that time, things he clearly knew were sensational.

INT: Like *Visions of Cody*. It is almost unbelievable that it took so long for that book to be published in its entirety.

JCH: You can imagine the embitterment felt by anyone who could write that way and not get it published. He wasn't a primitive, but a very conscious writer.

INT: That's one of the things that William Burroughs told me that really impressed me, that Kerouac had written over a million words *before* coming to Columbia. So of course someone like that could talk about spontaneity!

JCH: He had learned his craft–it certainly shows in *The Town and the City,* which is a sort of Galsworthian family saga.

INT: When did the physical change begin?

JCH: You ought to see the kinescope of Jack's appearance with Steve Allen, whom he rather liked. He was still looking good then. He hadn't really hurt himself up to that point. He wasn't bloated or argumentative. The physical change began before he went to Big Sur in 1961. His passion had become muted, and he began to argue with himself in a way that he never had before. The Steve Allen thing was in '59 or early '60, and he still looked as I knew him back in the forties. And theoretically he was supposed to be reading from *On The Road,* but he actually read a few pages of the end of *Visions Of Cody,* which he had put inside a copy of *On The Road.*

SHIRLEY HOLMES: Only you and Allen Ginsberg knew that.

INT: What can you tell me about the origins of *Visions Of Cody* and how it was related to *On The Road?*

JCH: The section about Neal Cassady's boyhood was written before *On The Road,* and on pot. It's a long section that was originally published in *Playboy* about young Neal in the poolhall, and going out and catching the pass. That was intended as part of *On The Road,* written in long incredibly exfoliating sentences of great detail. At that time Sal Paradise's name was Ray Smith. Jack wrote all about his background, his getting prepared for the road, and this material was cut, and has never appeared.

INT: Wasn't that the kind of naturalistic framework he used in *The Town and The City?*

JCH: Exactly. But Jack realized that he couldn't use it in *On The Road.*

INT: Did you see the original manuscript of *On The Road,* and what were its physical properties?

JCH: I was the first person to see it, and I read it even before he did. It had no paragraphs, but it was punctuated. The names were not changed, he used the real names. He didn't want to use a conventional structure because he wanted to capture the onrushing flow of his thoughts and impressions.

SHIRLEY HOLMES: I've always contended that Jack had this ability to go with the flow because he was such an incredible typist.

INT: John, did you visit Jack during the three-week period in which he wrote *On The Road?*

JCH: Yes. Recently, I had occasion to examine my *Journals,* which you'll read tomorrow. I have an entry in early April, 1951, of going down to see Jack, who was living in Chelsea with Joan Haverty, and by that day, I think it was the ninth of April, he had written 34,000 words. The long roll of what looked to me like shelf paper was spread out on the floor in front of the typewriter. I found another entry on April 27th when he delivered the book to me. He had finished it two days before, a huge thick roll, and he said he hadn't read it yet. I spent the entire day reading it, and it was almost a third longer than the published version.

INT: Malcolm Cowley says that he suggested a lot of the trips be eliminated to create greater focus.

JCH: Jack did a lot of this even before Cowley suggested it. He had a lot of material on the terminal points like New York and San Francisco, and took them out because they didn't relate to the road experience. When Jack typed the novel in pages, he made numerous changes–he always made more changes than he would ever admit to–and submitted it to Harcourt, Brace, and it was rejected. This was quite a blow to him. So I said, let me take it to my agent–he didn't have an agent then, but was working strictly through Giroux–to M.C.A. and my agent then, Rae Everitt, now Rae Brooks, and she didn't fully appreciate it, but told Jack a few things which he sensibly ignored. Jack was sobered by the rejection though, depressed is not the word. He had to really think about himself and what he wanted to do. He had already had part of this experience in realizing he couldn't write *On The Road* in the way he had done *Town and The City,* that he had to abandon the idea of family structures and just set his characters free in the country. What he started to do almost immediately is what he called sketching; that is, looking in windows, observing the street, and taking it down at the time it was happening.

INT: Direct notation rather than recalled notation?

JCH: Rather than trying to *give* a shape, trying to existentially discover it, as in the beginning of *Visions Of Cody*. He told me he never thought of this as being publishable. He was simply trying to catch the flow. He had felt from the beginning that something in Neal had eluded him. Jack had an enormous capacity for saying, "Everything I've done so far is lies." While writing *On The Road* he said he was writing it because *Town and The City* was a lie, a fiction. *On The Road* was to tell the story as it was, but afterwards Jack felt he still hadn't caught the idea of Neal, so he began *Visions Of Cody,* which he didn't conceive as a structured book, but more an expansion of his imaginative conception of Neal.

INT: So it led to a series of extensions, projections, and games based on Neal which captures him more internally somehow.

JCH: It's closer to Neal, but ultimately very mythic. I've always thought that the picture of Neal in *On The Road* is dramatically better, but the character is not as monumental as in *Visions Of Cody*. What Jack did was invent a plethora of new techniques for *Visions Of Cody* because he couldn't create the character he wanted if he remained outside him.

INT: *Visions Of Cody,* for me, is when Kerouac really comes into his own. *Dr. Sax* also has that sense of inventive leaping, that unique power and freedom of form.

JCH: Obviously Jack was searching to free himself from all the novelistic necessities as they existed then in order to freely sing, not as in *Town and The City* where the songs were more or less set pieces, recitatives or arias. What he wanted to do was employ the totality of his feeling, sensibility and erudition, and make it part of the flow he was describing. This is why he was always so close to Joyce–a deep passion of his I never particularly shared. He wanted, as Joyce did, simultaneity; Jack not only wanted to describe something–which he did better than anyone I've ever known–but also to embody it with everything about himself and his feelings that he could get into it. And he wanted to find a way in which all of this could flow together. Jack would never have claimed it, but it seems to me that the real engine behind the English in *Cody* is Shakespeare. There are sections in *Cody* which are as eloquent as any prose I've ever read.

INT: It is interesting that Shakespeare, Joyce, and Kerouac are all freed of certain inhibitions of syntax and style and structure, and as a result can perfect a powerful flow, anarchically, freely.

JCH: It happens when the image finds the word or words immediately, and you don't stop to think, "Is it working?" You just plunge on. That's why there are lines in Kerouac that you must flow with to understand; the moment you stop to conceptualize they break down. But what gets into the line is a whole series of tumultuous impressions and takes that can only be compared to film, and Jack, of course, was very affected by film. Also, Jack spoke French before he spoke English, and like many people who work in a language not their own, he was very sensitive to it. Jack was a word man all the way, and had a veneration for language–which is why he loved Joyce.

INT: He seems, judging from his letters, to have read a lot.

JCH: He was a tremendously well-read man. He read eratically, but deeply, and when he read something he never forgot it.

INT: I've read letters that Jack wrote to Allen Ginsberg when Jack had already left Columbia but was reading as if he were still there, five, seven, ten huge books a week. Not all of them necessarily, parts of Pascal, of the Bible, *Moby Dick* in a day or two.

JCH: He had an amazing memory for what he had read. He would often come here because I had most of Balzac, and I suppose that any writer who is writing a saga thinks of Balzac, as Faulkner did. Jack loved Balzac, and came here because he felt it was quiet enough, and he would pile Balzac next to that chair and read him for a week. Then years later he would make some reference to one of the fifty-odd novels by Balzac that I have. So he read and remembered.

INT: Do you know whether he read Henry Miller, or ever expressed any attitudes towards Miller's work?

JCH: Frankly, no. But I had read Miller early, and approved of him as I approved of what I then thought of as good dirty-book writers. I was attracted to Lawrence and Miller in my teens, and managed to read the forbidden Miller in my early twenties. Now Jack loved Lawrence almost despite his reputation, but I never remember him saying anything about Miller until the mid-fifties.

INT: That's interesting because it seems to me that Miller started something that Jack continued, and that was writing a saga about yourself. Miller, of course, did that remarkable Preface for *The Subterraneans.*

JCH: Jack must have been pleased by the effort of an older writer to help him along, and to recognize him, but I know that Jack didn't see Miller even though a meeting was planned. I believe Miller is a great American writer. When anybody really reads what he has done, any idea that he is simply prurient or pornographic is utterly ridiculous. He's in a deep American tradition.

INT: During the years after the writing of *On The Road,* from 1951 until it publication in 1957, how much of Kerouac did you see?

JCH: I saw him only intermittently because he was in Mexico and on the west coast. We saw each other whenever he came back to New York. When he was gone we corresponded, and he sent me all his manuscripts during those years. That is, up to '54–'55 when he went to San Francisco and everything started to happen. They all came back here, Jack, Allen, Peter on their way to North Africa, and they were up here around New Year's of '57. Viking was going to publish *On The Road,* and we spent a whole week up here just getting to know one another again, and Jack was still very much the way he had been before, he'd been on the mountain and written the first half of *Desolation Angels.* He had also written the first part of *Tristessa,* which I read then too.

INT: How had he sent you the other books, like *Dr. Sax?*

JCH: In the mail. He would send me the originals, and I turned them all over to an agent, or to Allen, or to Carl Solomon. The original of *Dr. Sax* went to Carl who was then working for A. A. Wyn, his uncle, who wouldn't publish it.

INT: The book probably didn't seem commercially feasible to Wyn?

JCH: Carl wanted it published, he was fighting for certain things with Wyn, but they were a very small house. Carl got through that Jaime de Angulo book, *Indian Tales,* which has become a classic, and he got a few others like *Junkie* through. This must have been an enormous source of pressure on Carl. He knew what was good, what would become important, but he was working nine to five. I used to meet him for lunch then. He had his problems anyway, and to fight the publisher's bullshit all the time, when there was no recognition that it was shit anywhere . . . Listen, you couldn't even wrap yourself in the American flag and say, "I'm going down for integrity and how about that, baby!" because the books he wanted to accept were considered filthy–you were considered some kind of fruitcake to believe they were good. But those were awful years. You've treated it so well in that one section of your book that I've read on the fifties.

INT: I was in high school and college at the end of the fifties, and I felt it.

JCH: You must have, because you describe it brilliantly. You felt like you were fighting a hopeless battle against everything. One reason why Jack, and Allen, and the rest of us have not been upset by the new freedom is that we know what it came from. We were serious writers, and we earned every "fuck" we wrote down. Take *Go,* for instance. I used no four-letter words except at one point, where I though it was legitimate. There's a character who is absolutely disgusted with the world, and he comes out onto the street after a party and something has happened–indeed Allen Ginsberg has been arrested–and he says "Fuck You! Fuck You! Fuck You! Fuck You! Fuck You! Fuck You!"–six times. Scribner's lawyer asked me to cut out three of these, and I said, "If I can publish three, I can do six. I'm trying to make a point here: the man is out of control." But that was characteristic of the circumstances under which you worked then. They said, "Can't you change it to 'fug'?" Mailer had done that, but I refused and insisted that it had to be six "Fuck You's"–it had nothing to do with sex, or dirty words, it had to do with despair. But they thought quantitatively then, and that's one reason why *Visions Of Cody* couldn't come out. Now Jack was a very moral, almost puritanical person, but he used the language of eroticism when it seemed right.

INT: That's interesting. I've felt that when Kerouac treats women in his fiction that moral sense creates a false distance making the women less real, more romanticized than he might have realized or intended.

JCH: Well, this was certainly not entirely due to the literary restrictions of time. He did tend to idealize women.

INT: You can see it in *Tristessa,* for example, where you have a woman named Esmeralda in real life–hope in Spanish–who is a drug addict and a whore, but whom he transforms into a Mary Magdalene, a saint of the streets. He does capture her desolation, but still there is such a pedestal quality, almost a worship of her suffering.

JCH: This relates to something larger that Jack tended to idealize. He plunged deeply into the stuff of life in his time, and–it's hard to say whether he was educated by it or disappointed–he had an enormous ability to empathize with human beings. He was a person who stood off from life to a degree that is not recognized. He was not deeply involved, he was not part of the swirl, he was not dancing on the floor or driving the car, he was not swinging.

INT: Ann Charters relates how withdrawn he was at parties, always standing apart.

JCH: To some degree this may be true of artists generally, but it was pronounced in him. I have seen him in the center of things, but this was the exception. This is where drink came in, because it connected him to the outside, but by himself he was serious, grave, not a drag, but hard to engage. He was a man who felt at a distance from most people, and he was aware of this all the time because of his own hunger to cross it, and this is what made him a difficult person for some people to communicate with because he didn't seem to be there all the time. He was a brooding presence. Then he would get drunk or high, and he would be the most gregarious person you ever met, the most charming and attractive, the most imaginative man I've ever known, just a continuous flow of fantasy, ideas, funny nothings and weird images. But he was driven–that is, he was a man who sat completely inside his own consciousness and never, or rarely, got out of that envelope. And he accepted this, and followed it wherever it led, but it was often into things that were debilitating for him. He had a very fatalistic sense of himself, and to me he was a genius, whatever that word means. I've only met one, and I know many people who are extremely talented, and kinetic, and everything else. But ultimately, Jack had a mystery inside him that I never could penetrate at all, and I don't think he ever could either. I think Allen would confirm this.

INT: And at the heart of him was the energy of his imaginative facility. How would you characterize it?

JCH: Jack would constantly come up with things: titles, ideas, takes–often he wouldn't follow them up, but the constant spew. . . .

INT: Like the titles for "Howl," *Naked Lunch, Big Table?*

JCH: It was that he would read something and do a take on it, and sometimes it seemed outrageous, mean or bitter, indifferent or too enthusiastic, but it always had some sense to it that often would come out later. About eight years before he died I stopped questioning him–that is, I stopped saying, "Oh Jack you're full of shit!" I would often say it, but I gradually stopped believing it because there was always an odd kind of prophetic logic to the way he thought, even when he was fumed with booze. Like he wrote a thing for *Escapade*–he was something of a right winger, you know–on Khrushchev whom he had seen getting off a plane in Washington, having to stand in the sun during speeches, enduring the passing of the Marine band, a sixty year old man sweating with his hat off, and Jack, who hated Communism, wrote in this tit magazine, "I demand justice for the man Khrushchev". And this was typical of Jack who sympathized with the man, any man undergoing the experience of the moment. He related to that.

INT: Even though Kerouac writes about working-class characters like Neal, exulting, for example, in the power with which Neal could change tires, there doesn't seem to be any sense of class conflict or awareness in his fiction such as you might find in a more political writer like Dos Passos. He goes right to the man because of something central in his subject's experience.

JCH: Still, there was a definite class feeling in Jack, although it was almost always on the surface. Show him the human situation and if it was clear enough to him, that's what he would reach for. That's really what the whole Beat thing was about. It was kind of an American existentialism–it said don't talk to me about essence but show me what's happening.

INT: How does that work in with class though?

JCH: It doesn't, or course. But what I'm trying to say is that Jack, when he was not creatively engaged, thought very much about class–not intelligently, he didn't write much about it, but he was full of class resentment. He who seemed to me to be so brilliant, nevertheless resented people who had more education than he did, more privilege, more money.

INT: Do you think this might have had its origin in the experience of attending Horace Mann, and then Columbia, as a young man from a provincial town without any kind of support?

JCH: Undoubtedly. That must have been a factor. It always seemed to me, knowing Jack, and even more in reading his work, that he always felt separate, he even felt separate from his family and the immediate background which gave him his material. He felt special, isolated, lonely, and this never changed.

INT: The feeling I have about all of these figures is the spiritual state of exile, not that one has to–like Burroughs–leave the country or expatriate, but in the sense of Stephen Dedaelus' exile which is all the more profound for being within one's own family and country.

JCH: Well, the Beat thing begins with the feeling of difference.

INT: And outcast, or self-outcast as a result?

JCH: Well, at first Jack wanted to be like his father. He started being nostalgic about life in Lowell when he was seventeen, perhaps even earlier. But he never felt part of it. He was like Rimbaud.

INT: His poem on Rimbaud is probably the best place to begin when looking for what motivated the Beat experience. In *The Town and The City,* when Levinsky first appears, he is carrying a volume of Rimbaud.

JCH: It is so difficult to speak about it sociologically, but what had happened in the late thirties and early forties was a kind of uprootedness in terms of family relationships, the whole society was changing, and a major event was about to happen, and everybody knew it, particularly young men. And it was also clear that all the ways by which people had understood an event like this in the past were inadequate.

INT: And isn't what you are attempting to describe exactly the context of *The Town and The City* where both family ties and community allegiance lose their validity in the face of some looming threat? The sense of imminent devastation for young men—almost Hemingway's theme.

JCH: Right, but what it did with Jack and all of us to some degree was to make more poignant the things that had been lost. You allude to this in one of your essays when you refer to the deep conservative element in all this. It set Jack thinking about families; it set me thinking about marriage, love, cohesiveness, and more than that—continuity. Ginsberg is relentlessly writing about continuity, or its absence, but what nerves all of Allen's work is the broken circuit, and the broken circuit is in Jack's work all the way.

INT: That's a good image.

JCH: So we issued out of the war into a cultural scene, the dominant tone of which was irony and craft, Henry James and Auden.

INT: Containment and form.

JCH: And caution. Don't spit it out. And this is what made Allen erupt, "I saw the best minds of my generation destroyed by madness . . ." which he has been laughed at for writing, but which is so true, and this is what made Jack write, "The only people for me are the mad ones" in *On The Road.* And what moves both passages is that they are both saying there's a break, there's a terrible break that has occurred: I have known those who have been destroyed by it, I believe in people who are trying to mend. Now these lines were done independently of each other, but they really epitomize what this whole thing was about.

INT: Last night we were talking about the importance of madness as motivation in Ginsberg's work, and in Kerouac's work, and the fact that from their point of view the madness that they pursued was not madness but the only way to move, to see the society and deal with it, and that stance leading to a whole reinterpretation of the relativity of madness.

JCH: Yes. If you accept the modern world on its terms, and are content with it, then anyone who can't function in it is strange, bent, twisted, etc., but one of the qualities in the Beat movement was the recognition that madness was a kind of retreat for those who wanted to stay privately sane. We understood that madness meant pain, as any withdrawal does, but the idea that there was any way to formulate social sanity was one of the things that we tried to give up, just as we tried to give up Freudianism, Marxism, and all determinisms. And everyone knew people who went mad, or felt themselves going mad sometimes—that is, getting psychically out of step with the world—and all too often it was because of a different standard that the world continually abused. So people broke down because of this dichotomy; in other words, it's early Laing. This was certainly true of Allen who was put in Columbia Psychiatric Institute because of things completely outside him. His apartment was full of stolen goods brought there by Huncke and the two others living there.

INT: Lionel Trilling explained to me that Allen went to P. I. as a result of a deal with the District Attorney, Frank Hogan, who was a Columbia University graduate, and who agreed to allow Allen to serve time in a psychiatric ward rather than a penal ward. Actually, as Laing and Thomas Szasz have argued, it is much the same thing though.

JCH: But what happened with Allen while he was there was interesting—since he ultimately confused the analysts by being saner than they were. He was more honest for one thing, so they said they couldn't do anything for him.

INT: That's another aspect of something Carl Solomon told me—that he felt in his life there was a danger of talking his way into the institution. So honesty is a twisting key itself. But in the culture of the late forties and early fifties, the nature of madness was almost an idea that Norman O. Brown discusses in *Life Against Death,* that the greatest madness lies in resisting one's natural inclinations to madness, so that from that point of view you can see the sense of control of a Nixon as being the archetype of madness in our day. Maybe that's what leads to war.

JCH: Allen would say, and I would agree with him, as Blake said, that anything that comes directly from the inner self is good, it sweats, it's real. Being disembodied is really being mad.

INT: Not being in touch with oneself—what Laing calls "ontological insecurity"?

JCH: Talking like a grammaphone like Nixon talks, simply mouthing things, talking out of a dream, an MGM fantasy.

INT: Yes, like the time he reputedly appeared at the Washington Monument before a peace rally at 5:00 A.M. and addressed a small group as if he were in a trance.

JCH: Certain kinds of cliches are the narcotics of the middle class, and Nixon plays on these automatically. I think he really believes these things so I can't hate him. He's so removed that he is sad to me, not loathsome. But he is everything that we have to recoil from, and I mean spiritually, not just politically.

INT: Was there any general attitude among the Beats towards psychoanalysis? I know Burroughs went through it, and disdains it now. How did Kerouac feel about it?

JCH: Well, Jack had an experience in the Navy where he was discharged, I forget the phrase they used. . . .

INT: "Paranoid schizophrenic". In one of his letters, he says they added paranoid to his diagnosis because he was intelligent.

JCH: Well, that about sums it up. In other words, we all felt that psychoanalysis was an inadequate description of human activity. It just couldn't go far enough, the way sociology also failed to include the spirit or mystery, and that's what we were after. It really didn't help to know that you had a father complex or a mother complex. Life amounted to more than that. We felt that this approach was as oversimplified as Marx's understanding of class relations. The Beat attitude, to call it that, was protesting against what we felt was an inadequate conception of the nature of man. In 1945, man was seen as a victim, either of toilet training or his place in society, but he was determined from the outside. That conception of man we all found, quite independently because we all have different backgrounds, to be increasingly inadequate. We felt there had to be something more. Thoreau talks about it, and Emerson, and we found the deepest strain in American politics and poetry to be metaphysical. The American Constitution starts out by enunciating certain inalienable rights; no European had ever conceived of that—that certain rights are innate! When the French began talking about the rights of man it led to the rolling of heads. But we began by defining man as free, and our experiment worked because our variety, our difference, our lack of homogeneity meant that every one of us had to become Americans, which meant becoming new men—it was no birthright, everyone except the Indians came from somewhere else. So primarily we are a passionately political people and politics is our church, the thing that holds us together as both Whitman and Lincoln used to say. Well, we wandered afield a bit.

INT: I'd like to wander in another direction—the importance of jazz music to the Beats. For example, Allen today writing and singing a poetic based on blues, or earlier this afternoon, I was reading in your *Journals* an entry describing a party in 1951 where Allen was singing blues, improvising rhymes to fit the people present at the party. The same interest is certainly evident in Kerouac's work, and in your novel, *The Horn.* What do you think caused this general interest?

JCH: Well, young people in America, at least in the last three generations, have felt music as a very important part of their lives: In the thirties it was swing, in the late forties it was bop, then rock. American music—jazz, blues, it all comes from a black base—has in our century seemed to young people to express all sorts of inexpressible exhuberance and energy. Now with Jack and me and Allen and others of that time I suppose jazz meant more than that. Fed up as we were with trite explanations of why things happened, and with an attitude towards the world that seemed inadequate, jazz was a call from the dark, it was the euphoria of joy, dance, let loose. Also, everyone at that time believed that blacks knew something that we didn't know, only because they appeared less surface-worried than we were.

INT: Mailer writes about that in "The White Negro"—about learning a model of experience and the courage to face the world from the black man.

JCH: You can sum it up like this. When Jack wrote about walking in the Denver black section in *On The Road,* James Baldwin said he'd love to hear Jack reading that in the Apollo Theater in New York because Jack would get crucified; less than ten years later, Eldridge Cleaver praised that section as an early sign of a new liberated consciousness. So whether we were deluded or not, what we wanted was that untrammeled swing and style that blacks, undoubtedly as a defense, had created. Also because *we* felt like blacks caught in the square world that wasn't enough for us, and we felt that blacks had more immediate fun than we did.

INT: Do you feel that the Beats had a greater sense of the street than writers have had previously, even the Naturalists? I'm thinking of figures like Huncke or Neal.

JCH: Absolutely. We knew that street knowledge meant functioning in the world, so what writer wouldn't be interested in talking to a man like Huncke. We went to Huncke like you might go to Dostoevski just because of the kind of life he had lived—he was a source—even more, a model of how to survive. That was part of the appeal Neal had for Jack, because Neal had answered questions Jack couldn't answer for himself, or so Jack fancied it. All of Jack's work was motivated by a disappointed idealism, and Neal presented an answer to the break that Jack felt in himself. I once saw Neal look at Jack, and I imagined I saw in Neal's face, "You're not seeing me anymore, you're seeing only your idea," because Neal was a man who had literal day to day problems.

INT: So Huncke told me: "He was a nervous cat all the time!"

JCH: Right. He was as hung up with women problems, transportation problems as any of the rest of us, but

Holmes and Jack Kerouac, Old Saybrook, Connecticut, November 1960

Jack increasingly saw him as a kind of hero who was being brought down by the necessities of square life. Jack was never unaware of the domestic bullshit in Neal's life.

INT: He had to be aware of it because he lived with Neal and Carolyn several times, and left on one occasion because he could no longer stand Neal's peculiar games. In *Big Sur,* however, Kerouac implies that Neal felt exploited, that his life had been used. I mean at the end of the novel when Neal stands in the doorway in a golden light–which for Kerouac signified a moment of annunciation–as Jack unwraps the copies of *On The Road* which have just arrived, and Neal looks away, unable to look into Jack's eyes.

JCH: I was reasonably close to Neal, and always liked him, and I've often thought about what *On The Road* must have done to him as a man, you know the idea that he had become a myth in his own time, because he wasn't a mythic character–he was simply a fascinating human being. So when Jack gained his recognition after *On The Road,* okay, Jack at least had written a book, but Neal suddenly became a figure quite by happenstance, and it got more and more complicated as Jack's works appeared. Jack was always deadly honest in his work. Not always in his life but always in his work. So that episode near the end of *Big Sur* is revealing, I agree with you.

INT: You said that Neal didn't have a mythic presence, but it is curious to me that after leaving Jack's orbit Neal goes to Kesey, suddenly appears in Kesey's backyard, and that started the friendship that led to the Merry Pranksters. But the point is that Neal sought Kesey out as one man of power seeks another.

JCH: Well, Neal liked people who liked him.

INT: Also, to put it vulgarly, he knew where the action was almost instinctively–I think because of that remarkable street sense he had.

JCH: Definitely. Neal was one of the most streetwise men I ever met.

INT: And sophisticated in certain ways at the same time, and the wonder of it to me–although it fits so perfectly into the American tradition–is that it is all so self-learned.

JCH: The most sophisticated people are those who have never read books, or gone to school, but just lived their lives intensely. Huncke is one of the most sophisticated men I've ever met. What is sophistication? It's knowing how things work, where things are, keeping all the elements separate and knowing how to handle them.

INT: That's the way Rojack in Mailer's *An American Dream* defines sanity: keeping in your mind the maximum number of impossible combinations.

JCH: Neal certainly knew that. Besides, as you say, he wanted action and knew how to get it. But with Kesey everything accelerated, the stakes were higher, the drugs different, like LSD.

INT: Right. Neal had spent two years in San Quentin for giving two plainclothesmen a marijuana cigarette, and now he was driving a communal-freak bus for Kesey and they all were distributing acid. It is like the magnified end of a cycle beginning maybe when Huncke, Burroughs and Neal drove back from New Waverly to New York City in '47 with a jeep full of marijuana that they had harvested and put in mason jars. And before that Bill Garver's stealing overcoats around Times Square to support his habit, or Huncke hustling, breaking and entry with Little Jack Melody, Neal's reputed theft of over 500 automobiles mostly for joy-rides in the Denver hills when he was still really just a kid. All of which leads to another question: what was the attraction of the underworld and the life-style of the criminal? With Burroughs, for example, beginning with a Gidean devotion and fascination. Also his whole notion of the relativity of legality which is expressed in letters to Allen that I've read up at Columbia University where Burroughs comments, for instance, on the wetback situation in Texas where he was farming in '47–how large farmers are allowed to get away with it, while smaller farmers can't, and how anyway the wetbacks are profiting since they could earn three to eight dollars a day instead of fifty cents a day in Mexican fields. Yet at the same time they are treated as slaves, and if they didn't pick cotton, could be shot in the fields, while the U.S. authorities encourage the large growers since there is no other way to harvest. So the whole question of what law is becomes itself in question, or it becomes an economic class determinant more than an ethical determinant.

JCH: True. It seems that our attraction to criminality, mostly crimes without a victim like drugs, fit in with our feeling that the definition of man's nature was inadequate. And we were interested in excessive experiences, in the extreme, because a man who puts himself outside the law is a man who is putting himself *into* himself–he's said okay, I'll go alone, and we were fascinated with this because then a man has nothing to depend on except what's inside him.

INT: I noticed a picture of Norman Mailer in that group of about thirty pictures of writers in your study. When was that taken?

JCH: Early sixties: it was when he did a thing for *Esquire* about writers and the bitch goddess, and they shot him in a ring with a hand over either rope, and it struck me then as summing up the only Mailer I've ever known, at once aggressive and perceptive.

INT: What was Mailer's relation to the Beat Movement?

JCH: He became sympathetic to it starting about 1957. Somewhere around then in his column for the *Village Voice* he got into the conflict between hip and square and predicted that the choice between these positions would be the real problem for Americans for the next twenty-five years. Now when I knew Norman in 1952 or '53, he knew nothing about this and didn't much care. He was a Trotskyite. But the hip/square columns had to do, I think, with something relating to *The Deer Park,* that never quite got into *The Deer Park.* He suddenly had a vision of all this–he hadn't been really paying any attention, and he hadn't been on the street or he would have known. He had found success very young, and had a more or less concretized way of thinking about things.

SHIRLEY HOLMES: And he had a very sneering attitude towards the Beat thing at parties.

JCH: Well, not exactly. I remember a party at Vance (Bourjaily's) right after *On The Road* came out, and Mailer took me into a corner and said, "Tell me everything you know about Kerouac!" And when Norman met Jack, he liked him. But Norman had to run out of all the intellectual disciplines by which he had motivated his work before he came to the dark night of the soul. The inner life broke in on him because everything else ran out.

INT: Maybe because he was really receptive as well? He did offer *Naked Lunch* its first most significant praise.

JCH: The thing that makes Mailer for me a very great writer is that he follows his nose wherever it goes. We all know about *Naked and the Dead. Barbary Shore* was a really serious attempt to write the first existential novel in America, but what it resulted in was that Norman was rubbed raw. *The Deer Park* was his first attempt to do something where he didn't quite know what he was doing.

INT: And Sergius O'Shaugnessy, in a subsequent story, "The Time Of Her Time," one of the great sex stories of all time, does finally make that transition from square to hip, from Hemingway's "Lost Generation" consciousness to a glimmer of beatness.

JCH: But imagine what Norman had to go through to make Sergius do that. He had to be willing to experience it himself first. That is, Norman is the guy who wanted to be like Thomas Wolfe and others–when their books were published people ran right out and bought them. He had the same hope that we all had that the publication of a new book by a certain writer would be an event. We all had to learn that that simply wasn't true anymore. It had nothing to do with money, but whether literature meant anything any longer. So Norman is the only writer I know who made himself into a celebrity by a conscious effort, and enormous sacrifice. To me it has sometimes seemed a waste of energy.

INT: I wanted to ask you what you thought of Mailer's idea in "The White Negro" that a certain quality of pathology is necessary to heroism in our time, and especially becomes the natural response to an encroaching totalitarianism, and what did such an attitude have to do with the whole question of rebellion in the Beat movement? You know, the fact that you were not going to accept the given conditions, and you were all seeking another way, of conducting your lives with the kind of joy and illusion of freedom that Mailer attributes to the blacks in "The White Negro". So a kind of craziness, or a pathological response, or what society would have seen as a violation of its code of adjustment and acceptance, and therefore termed crazy, which in turn only means that society has the power to intern you in a certain kind of prison.

JCH: I think we denied the ready-made explanations for human behavior, and we were drawn to aspects of human experience that were ignored by all the sciences or condemned by society.

INT: And apparently, reading the letters describing the parties in the late forties, you were all very drawn to the idea of breaking control and getting out of one's ordinary head, partly for joy, partly for the sake of new perception. In this connection, I wanted to ask you about Jack's friend, Bill Cannastra. What period was that?

JCH: He died in 1950, in a revealing manner. He was on a subway, a local train, somewhere downtown, and as the train pulled out of the stop–the windows were open because it was warm–he tried to get out through the open window, was about halfway out as the train gathered speed and struck a pillar. He was very athletic: he climbed up fire escapes, and dangled over the sides of buildings, and so forth, but he was drunk. The girl he was with claimed that he said, "I'm going to go get a drink." Maybe it was just claustrophobia or boredom.

INT: How would you characterize him? How well did you know him?

JCH: I knew him pretty well. One reason that I put him into *Go* was that he seemed a contrast to Neal, Jack and the rest of us. He was an alcoholic; his motivation was embitteredness, the world's approaching end. His way of playing was self-destructive, it was giving wild parties that went on for days, and which were not chic at all but raunchy–we all dug ugliness then, that is, the worse it was, the more interesting it seemed to be. Cannastra would do anything: humiliate people, usually himself first, you know, take off all his clothes and fart, scream and yell. He seemed to be somebody playing on the edge, and he appealed to me because I was moving into a new world which didn't demand that one be a victim as he was. He thought of himself as having seen the lie of life, and responded to it like Rochester did–I mean the poet–by saying, "Anything goes now because it's all rotten anyway." Now I felt like that then, but I was changing over to the feeling that something in the streets could be found that was more interesting than this.

INT: Did he work?

JCH: He was a graduate of Harvard Law School who had abandoned his practice. At that point he was a bisexual drunk who lived in a loft in Chelsea, and did everyday jobs like working in a bakery. He couldn't have been more than thirty when he died. He was an outrageous man, and I liked him because he was outrageous. He used to go into bars in Chelsea or near the docks and give longshoremen big wet tongue kisses, and say, "Buy me a drink," and they would beat him up, but then buy him drinks because he wasn't a "pansy", only premature-Camp.

INT: Did you know Jerry Newman? Allen Ginsberg told me that he did a radio bit called "The Drunken Newscaster" that Burroughs heard which may have influenced the idea of the cut-up.

JCH: I knew him, but nothing about that. When I first met him he had a record shop off Eighth Street west of Sixth Avenue, and then he started a record company called Esoteric. Jack had known him at Horace Mann, and they shared a common passion for jazz in the early years of World War II. One of the first things he did was to record that marvelous serenade by Schonberg. It was just the beginning of LP's. He knew little about Schonberg, but he had a perfect ear, and he made this performance by editing different tapes. This is common practice now, but he was one of the first to get a final product by editing several different versions.

INT: When did you take courses at the New School for Social Research with Kerouac?

JCH: It was in the fall of '49, more than a year after the initial meeting I describe in *Nothing More To Declare*. Both of us had GI benefits left, so even though *Town and The City* was coming out we decided it was ridiculous not to take advantage of the year we were still entitled to, plus they gave you some living money every month and free books.

INT: What courses did you take?

JCH: We took some courses in common, like the Meyer Shapiro course about the Impressionists. It was a huge class so there was no real interchange, but he was an inspiring teacher. We both sat in on a course that Alfred Kazin was giving on *Moby Dick,* and he was a brilliant teacher, too. I took a medieval literature course, and a comparative religion course, and we both started a myth course with Harry Slochower but only attended about two classes. He was a bore with a Marxist viewpoint who treated myth like merchandise.

INT: In *Nothing More To Declare* you mention that Kerouac once tried to screw the earth. That sounds like something that might happen in the excesses of a D. H. Lawrence novel. Was it a literal episode?

JCH: Yes. It was while he was writing *The Town and The City*. I heard it from him, and read it in his *Journals* of that time. He was trying to write, and he was alone, and horny, and young, and so he thumbed a hole in his backyard, and he fucked the earth. He had lots of Lawrencian feelings anyway.

INT: We were talking this morning about Jack's humor which has been unappreciated in his work and in his life. Did that exuberance diminish as you got to know him?

JCH: Seeing the funny side of things comes from a certain distance and an ironical way of looking at life. Jack didn't have this naturally, but he loved good fun. He was terribly amused by his own work sometimes, and as you pointed out when he reads certain things, like some of the poems, he reads them as if they were funny because they were to him. But I wouldn't say that he saw things comedically. He saw things fondly, he loved human folly and silliness, he responded to anything that had a pathetic element in it in a very endearing way.

INT: Like the great flyswatter episode in *Visions Of Cody* where Neal, as a child, watches his father and another Bowery wino travel to Nebraska farms selling these ridiculous flyswatters.

JCH: Well, Jack had a great sense of the absurd.

INT: But isn't that one of the uniquely differentiating qualities about Kerouac as a writer: he is one of the very few who have any warmth left in his sense of humor, as opposed to the way most writers use humor as a devastating social castigation.

JCH: That's why Jack didn't like Lenny Bruce—he couldn't stand anything that appeared to demean human beings. He was a bridge-builder; he felt some wound had occurred in the contemporary soul, and he was trying to suggest how it could be mended. One of the oldest functions of literature, after all.

Chapter 9
Gary Snyder
(8 May 1930 –)

See also the Snyder entries in *DLB 5: American Poets Since World War II; DLB 16: The Beats: Literary Bohemians in Postwar America; DLB 165: American Poets Since World War II, Fourth Series;* and *DLB 212: Twentieth-Century American Western Writers, Second Series.*

Gary Snyder was born in San Francisco and grew up in the Northwest, in Washington and Oregon. He never lived in New York City and did not know the Beats there; they came to him. Allen Ginsberg came to San Francisco in the mid 1950s and involved himself in the poetry scene there. He met Snyder, then a graduate student in Asian languages at the University of California, Berkeley. The two became close friends, and Ginsberg introduced Snyder to Jack Kerouac. Kerouac had been studying Buddhism independently, and each man had an influence on the other. Buddhism was a dominant theme in Kerouac's work in the mid 1950s, and Snyder provided both a scholarly background and a living example of Buddhism. In addition, Snyder helped get Kerouac a fire lookout job in Washington, which resulted in material for Desolation Angels *(1965) and* The Dharma Bums *(1958); Japhy Ryder, the hero of* The Dharma Bums, *is modeled on Snyder. Ginsberg invited Snyder to participate in a reading at the Six Gallery in October 1955, a reading that launched the San Francisco poetry renaissance. In 1956 Snyder went to Japan to study in a Buddhist monastery.*

Snyder influenced the Beats more than they influenced him, although he credits Kerouac's ideas about spontaneity as an influence in his own poetry. Although Snyder shares some

Gary Snyder, 1981

common interests with the Beats (exploration and development of myth, a frontier spirit, "getting back to basics," and Asian religion), he is not properly classed exclusively as a "Beat writer," as his work is neither particularly visionary nor drawn from the same environment and circumstances as those of the New York writers.

Snyder has become a leading voice for the environment. His interest in the environment is particularly evident in the poetry and prose of Turtle Island *(1974), which won the Pulitzer Prize for poetry in 1975. Today he is a professor of English at the University of California, Davis.*

Gary Snyder provided this statement for On Bread & Poetry: A Panel Discussion with Gary Snyder, Lew Welch and Philip Whalen *(1977).*

Autobiographical Statement

I'm Gary Snyder. I was born in San Francisco, raised up from the age of two or so in Washington state near Seattle, in the country; went to school in Seattle, in Portland, graduated from Reed College in Portland; did a year–half a year–of linguistic study at Indiana University; then came back out to San Francisco, spent my time going to school at the University of California in the winters studying Chinese and Japanese, and spent my summers working for the Forest Service or the Park Service up in the mountains. In 1956 I went to Japan, and since that time I've lived most of the time in Japan.

. . . .

I don't see my role as being any outlaw in society, but I rather look at the society and see what we have–modern Western civilization and the way that it's spreading around the world–as being an aberrant thing, an outlaw of its own sort on the planet. And so I feel more that I am trying to play a middle way–sane kind of role, holding to some balance and some measure, against what seem to me to be extreme and aberrant tendencies in the society.

I'm willing to make a living as a poet in the society, and it's up to the society whether I'm an outsider or not an outsider, that isn't my concern–I just have my work to do. Now if I can't make it as a poet and I can't live off poetry, that's all right too, I'll get by somehow. Either way.

–pp. 3–5

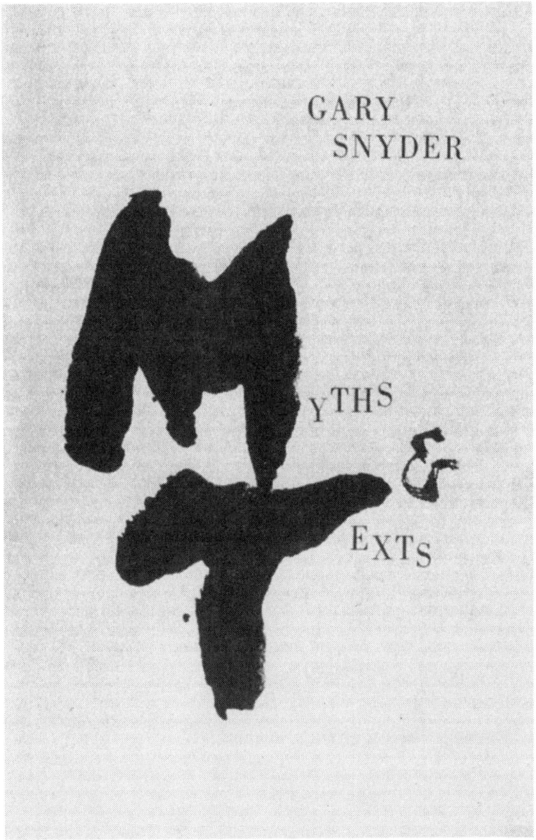

Cover for Snyder's second book of poems, published in 1960 by Totem Press/Corinth Books and republished by New Directions in 1978

Formative Influences

Bruce Cook recorded Snyder's comments on the influences that shaped him.

"I always think of mine as a very typical western family," he explains. "Although probably it was not. My grandfather homesteaded in Kitsap County, Washington and that's where my father was born. My mother's family was from down around Leadville, Colorado, although she was born in Texas. They were all westerners, though. My father's five brothers were seamen. He was a logger. My mother's brothers were all railroad men.

"Formative influences?"–he grinned through his beard–"well, that's kind of funny. I guess my grandfather, the one up in Washington, was pretty important. He was a Wobbly, dues-paying member of the Industrial Workers of the World–that was from back in his days as a logger–and he voted straight socialist as long as he had the chance. The old I. W. W. mythology became very important to me as I grew up in the Northwest. But these were all romantic feelings and a little confused. As a matter of fact, I remember that in my mid-twenties I felt sort of torn apart because I was drawn in two different directions. On the one hand I identified with the I. W. W. and the frontier, and all those good old feelings about the American West. And on the other hand I had a deep admiration for the American Indians. It was a very interesting conflict while it lasted. But I finally kicked the whole thing and joined the Indians."

–*The Beat Generation,* pp. 32–33

Meeting Ginsberg and Kerouac

Snyder recalled having read a piece by Kerouac before he actually met him. During an interview published in 1978, he describes how their relationship developed.

Cover for the 1968 New Directions edition of a Snyder poetry collection first published in 1967 by Fulcrum Press in London

When I was a graduate student at Berkeley studying Chinese and Japanese and planning to go to the Orient, in a perhaps excessively orderly fashion I decided I should get my teeth fixed. I didn't realize they had dentists all over the place. Anyway, I signed up with the University of California dental school, and for two years I bicycled from Berkeley to San Francisco once a week and put myself in the hands of a Japanese-American dental student. On one of those occasions I took along *New World Writing No. 7,* and I read the little thing by a fellow named Jean-Louis, which was one of the most entertaining things I'd read in a long time, and it always stuck in my mind. I didn't know anything of Jack or Allen at the time, but I never forgot that little piece of prose, "Jazz of the Beat Generation." It was the first time I saw the term Beat Generation. What I liked was the writing, of course, and the energy that was in it, and the evocation of people. Of course it didn't say "Jack Kerouac," it said "Jean-Louis."

Later I met Allen. Shortly after that, I met Jack. When I met Jack, and hearing Allen speak of his projects and hearing Jack speak, I flashed that he was Jean-Louis.

Allen asked Rexroth who was doing interesting poetry in the area. Allen had the idea of trying to put together some kind of poetry reading, and Kenneth mentioned my name as one person he might want to look up. So Allen just turned up at my place when I was fixing my bicycle in the backyard, and said that he had been talking to Kenneth. So we sat down and started comparing who we knew and what we were thinking about.

Jack was, in a sense, a twentieth-century American mythographer. And that's why maybe those novels will stand up, because they will be one of the best statements of the myth of the twentieth century. Just as Ginsberg represents one clear archetypal aspect of twentieth-century America, I think Jack saw me, in a funny way, as being another archetypal twentieth-century American of the West, of the anarchist, libertarian, IWW tradition, of a tradition of working outdoors and fitting in already with his fascination with the hobo, railroad bum, working man. I was another dimension on that.

Like on one occasion I remember we spent a number of hours in which I simply explained to him how logging camps worked and what all the steps in a logging operation are. Now I don't believe he ever used that in a book, but he was collecting that kind of information and enthusiastically digesting it all the time.

If my life and work is in some sense a kind of an odd extension, in its own way, of what Thoreau, Whitman, John Muir, etcetera, are doing, then Jack hooked

Cover for Snyder's 1974 poetry collection that takes its title from "the old/new name" of ancient peoples for the North American continent

into that and he saw that as valuable to him for his purposes in this century.

And Allen was the New York radical, Jewish intelligentsia. Jack really was skillful in identifying these types, recognizing them as a particular image that would become part of the mythology of America that he was working at. When he talked about his great novel that he was writing, it was like Ovid's *Metamorphoses,* a collection of stories which sketch out the view of the times. And he saw himself on the scale of a mythographer. The legend of Duluoz.

The dialectic that I observed in Jack, which was kind of charming, really, and you see it at work in his novels, was that he could play the fool and he could play the student very well. "But see, I really don't know anything about this. Teach me!" "Wow! You really know how to do that?" and lead you on. That was balanced by sometimes great authoritativeness and great arrogance, and he would suddenly say, "I am the authority." But then he would get out of that again. It was partly maybe like a really skillful novelist's con, to get people to speak. And he uses that as a literary device in his novels, where he presents himself often as the straight guy and he lets the other guys be smart.

I much appreciated what he had to say about spontaneous prose, although I never wrote prose. I think it influenced my journal writing a lot, some of which would, say, be registered in the book *Earth House Hold.* I think that I owe a lot to Jack in my prose style, actually. And my sense of poetics has been touched by Jack for sure.

Our interchanges on Buddhism were on the playful and delightful level of exchanging the lore, exchanging what we knew about it, what he thought of Mahayana. He made up names. He would follow on the Mahayana Sutra invention of lists, and he would invent more lists, like the names of all the past Buddhas, the names of all the future Buddhas, the names of all the other universes. He was great at that. But it was not like a pair of young French intellectuals sitting down comparing their structural comprehension of something. We exchanged lore. And I would tell him, "Now look. Here are these Chinese Buddhists," and that's how we ended up talking about the Han-shan texts together, and I introduced him to the texts that give the anecdotes of the dialogues and confrontations between T'ang Dynasty masters and disciples, and of course he was delighted by that. Anybody is. That's what we did.

I didn't then, and I don't now, think in terms of whether or not people are genuinely committed Buddhists or not. We're working with all of these things, and it doesn't matter what words you give to them, and if I thought that there was some point where I would say, "Jack, you're thinking too much about how the world's a bad place," that would be my sense of a corrective and his understanding of the Buddha-dharma, but that wasn't in my interest, or anybody else's interest, to think: "Is this guy a real Buddhist or not a real Buddhist?" He was worried about it later, but I never was, and I don't think Philip Whalen ever was, or anybody else.

When Jack came I was living over on Hillegass, and Philip had come back from the mountains. I had spent the summer up in the Sierra Nevada working on a trail crew and, naturally, we were talking a lot about the mountains. We were just back fresh from it, from the season's work, and I had rucksacks and climbing rope and ice-axes hanging on the walls around my place. Naturally we talked some about all of that.

I perceived that there was a kind of freedom and mobility that one gained in the world, somewhat analogous to the wandering Buddhist monk of ancient times, that was permitted you by having a proper pack and sleep-

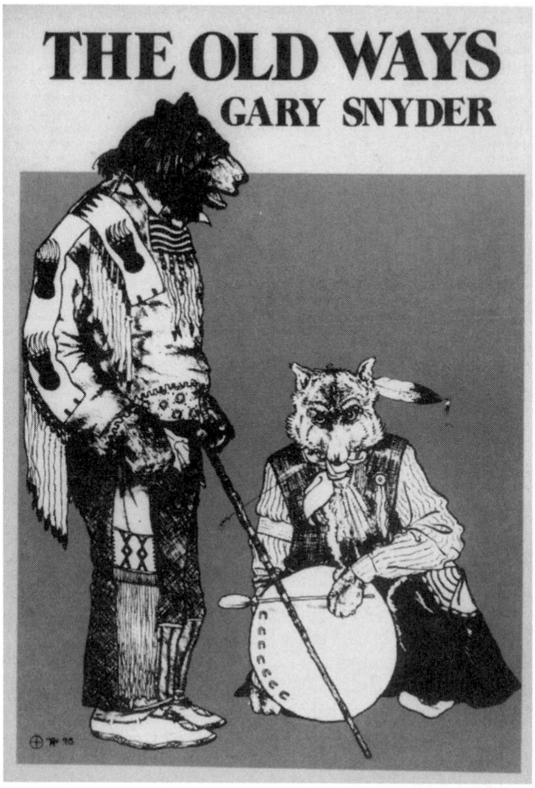

Cover for a collection of six essays by Snyder, published by City Lights in 1977

ing bag, so that you could go out on the road and through the mountains into the countryside. The word for Zen monk in Chinese, *yun shui,* means literally "clouds and water," and it's taken from a line in Chinese poetry, "To float like clouds, to flow like water," which indicates the freedom and mobility of Zen monks walking around all over China and Tibet and Mongolia on foot.

With that in mind I said to Jack, "You know, real Buddhists are able to walk around the countryside." So he said, "Sure. Let's go backpacking." I think John Montgomery said, "There's time for one more trip into the mountains before it gets too much colder." It was around the end of October.

So we headed up over Sonora Pass, leaving at night in Berkeley, and went over to Bridgeport, up to Twin Lakes and went in from there, over Sonora Pass.

It was very funny. It's very beautifully described in *The Dharma Bums,* actually. It was very cold. It was late autumn. The aspens were yellow, and it went well below freezing in the night and left frost on the little creek in the canyon we were camped at. There was a sprinkle of fresh white snow up on the ridges and peaks. We made it up to the top of the Matterhorn and came back down again. Actually, Jack didn't. I guess I was the only one that went up there. I was the persistent one.

—*Jack's Book,* pp. 201–204

In the following letter Snyder writes to Ginsberg of his return to the United States from Japan in 1958.

22 April
340 Corte Madera
Corte Madera
California

Dear Allen Ginsberg if that's who you really are in late summer I decided to take a trip on a ship so on Aug. 28 1957 took train (bade farewell at Kyoto-station by grizzly-head Zendo monk & fluffy girl friend) & went to Yokohama & the next day & (going through secret on-the-beach-seaman's hiring hall in a chinatown bar) was signed onto a tanker, A RUSTY MOTHERFUCKER called the Sappa Creek & was promptly put to work as fireman on 12–4 watch.

We sailed south through the PHILIPPINE SEA, painting the whole boiler room from stack down in 160° temperature, & went through STRAITS OF MALACCA & across BAY OF BENGAL to TRINCOUALEE CEYLON. There I saw gray mother-monkeys & a snake charmer. Then we turned about, loaded with oil and sailed to GUAM. At Guam we got Guamanians & some qualified firemen, so I became a wiper. Then took remaining oil to MIDWAY. Then turned around & sailed way back, up the ARABIAN SEA to the PERSIAN GULF and took on oil at BAHREIN. Then went around ARABIA through the RED SEA & SUEZ CANAL to Mediterranean, across to AUGUSTA SICILY, unloaded half, drinking in mad bar & icy stone whore-houses, went on to POZZUOLI Italy just outside NAPLES & buddies & me saw POMPEII & climbed VESUVIO just as you have done. Then sailed back empty to RAS TANURA ARABIA for more oil, & returned to ISKENDERUN TURKEY—view of snowy TAURUS Mountains, coffee & sour bread, raki to drink—dancing with girl in night cafe—on & on, through the Aegean & SEA OF MARMORA to a place near IZMIT one great fig-port, & on Xmas Eve took train up to ISTANBUL made night scene with spade Turks in jazz bar called Picadilly, & went walking alone on Christmas to Blue Mosque & SANTA SOPHIA where I was completely

Cover for Snyder's 1983 poetry collection

translated & rendered new & different by INSIDE EMPTINESS OF HOLYDOME, & caressed a marble pillar brought from the TEMPLE OF DIANA AT EPHESUS because that is where it started–

Then our war steamer (electro-turbine, 526' long, 1943 built in Alabama, on "T-2") went to BAHREIN again & this time on to Asia, to OKINAWA. That was a pleasure of courtesans by hundreds waiting in dock-side pads.

Again we went to RAS TANURA & turned about, full of oil, to sail to through Singapore, north of BORNEO & SOLO SEA, and out onto south the Equator down, to PAGO PAGO SAMOA, girls! oh girls all over the world! But here for free, wearing lava-lavas & waiting (tho' I did catch clap there, & had $20 swiped from pocket) so on we went to KWAJALEIN in the MARSHALL ISLANDS, the only pleasure at that Naval base being sneaking into Officers' club, bugging S.P.'s & stealing Navy pickups (almost wrecked one).

Sailing then to HONOLULU & big car-drive over Oahu, eating fresh pineapple; finally ship sails on to SAN PEDRO & paid off, made it with $3000 in hundred-dollar bills through dives & bars, home again to SAN FRANCISCO just this week.

Quietly trying to see people. But jumping with the whole world inside me so I can't talk straight. The literary scene become a parody of what we meant here, but sure lively–

The only way for you to write now is forget "howl" & what it implies people look from you next, I mean–drop that you wrote it–& write from what you are now. That great poem ends with itself. Siesta in Xbalba I still say is many ways better. Phil is really the POET. What stillness & what diamond-edge.

I've written lots you & Phil haven't seen & I like it. Will send you some when I get a typewriter. Probably will move to the vacant McCorkle's shack soon & meditate & send & make a seaman's true novel.

How long you plan to stay in Europe?

your
Gary

–*The Beat Book,* p. 116

Snyder leaving for camp with his sister, Althea, circa 1946 (Gary Snyder Collection)

Selected Reviews

Review of *Riprap & Cold Mountain Poems*
Choice, October 1966, p. 651

A small volume of verse in the conventions of Zen and Alan [*sic*] Ginsberg. In their treatment of physical experience, the poems of the "Riprap" section of the volume are spare and brutal in their apprehensions. At best, they catch at the sensual elements of physical experience from the point of view of the "beat" writers. The "Cold Mountain" poems profess to be translations of the poems of Han Shan by Ch'iu-Yin. Presented as the biography of Han-shan, the poems are 24 ways of looking at Cold Mountain through the eyes of a Taoist whose rejection of society has [a] far less discernable purpose than that of Thoreau.

New Books of Poems
Louis Simpson
Harper's, August 1968, p. 76

But poetry is not a matter of attitudes, and Gary Snyder, one of the heroes of the "anti-academic," in his new book demonstrates that there is no security anywhere, not even in bohemia. *The Back Country* describes Japan and the Sierras, not suburbia, yet this book too is conventional. Snyder is content to describe the great outdoors and sentimental moments; his poems are snapshots taken on the road, bits of quaint information:

> In the rucksack I've got three *nata*
> Handaxes from central Japan;
> the square blade found in China
> all the way back to Stone . . .

So what? There are all sorts of things, old and new, lying about everywhere. The question is, what happens in the poem. Snyder's new book, most of it, just moseys along. There is a fallacy in his idea of poetry–I think going back to W. C. Williams–that the poet is a holy man who has only to point to an object; the initiate will perceive its significance. What actually results, however, is a lack of drama. This may be the peace of the Orient, but I doubt it. I think it is just monotony.

Turtle Island

Snyder's Turtle Island *was published in 1974 by New Directions and won the 1975 Pulitzer Prize in poetry. In the introduction Snyder defines "Turtle Island" as "the old/new name for the continent, based on many creation myths of the people who have been living here for millenia, and reapplied by some of them to 'North America' in recent years. Also, an idea found world-wide, of the earth, or cosmos even, sustained by a great turtle or serpent-of-eternity."*

Review of *Turtle Island*
James McKenzie
Library Journal, 15 November 1974, p. 2970

Turtle Island, "the old/new name for the continent, based on many creation myths of the people who have been here for millenia," gains a powerful, original voice in these poems. In precise, disciplined, unromantic language and form (at its best resembling Pound's), Snyder's poems pare cleanly through the thick crust of late 20th-Century urban mass life, revealing its essentially incidental nature, connecting us with the creeks, mountains, birds, and bears of "North America" that were here before it had that name and, nature prevailing, will be here after that name is lost, forgotten, destroyed. Celebrating such family rituals as communal bathing and gathering mushrooms, or revealing the grossest limitations of our mindless consumption of nature's store, he reminds us over and over: "This living flowing land / is all there is, forever / we *are* it / it sings through us– / We could live on this Earth / with-

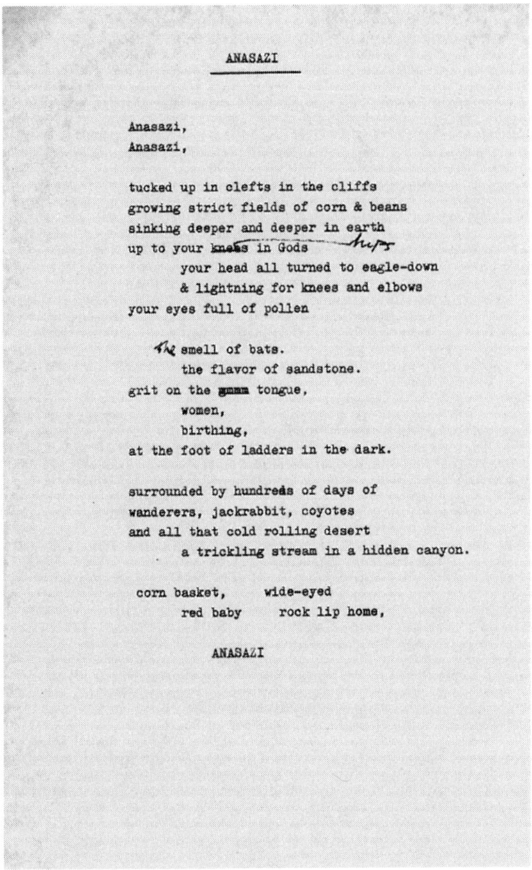

ANASAZI

Anasazi,
Anasazi,

tucked up in clefts in the cliffs
growing strict fields of corn & beans
sinking deeper and deeper in earth
up to your ~~knees~~ in Gods hips
your head all turned to eagle-down
& lightning for knees and elbows
your eyes full of pollen

the smell of bats.
the flavor of sandstone.
grit on the ~~gumm~~ tongue,
women,
birthing,
at the foot of ladders in the dark.

surrounded by hundreds of days of
wanderers, jackrabbit, coyotes
and all that cold rolling desert
a trickling stream in a hidden canyon.

corn basket, wide-eyed
red baby rock lip home,

ANASAZI

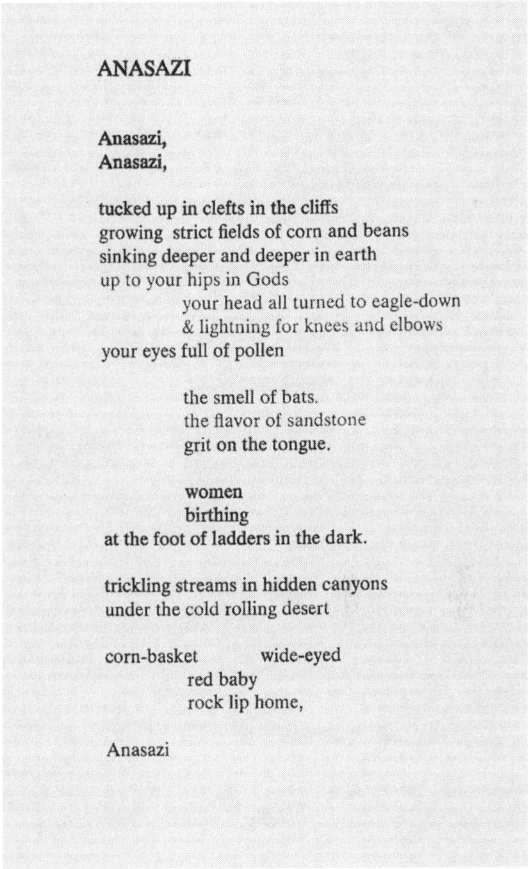

ANASAZI

Anasazi,
Anasazi,

tucked up in clefts in the cliffs
growing strict fields of corn and beans
sinking deeper and deeper in earth
up to your hips in Gods
your head all turned to eagle-down
& lightning for knees and elbows
your eyes full of pollen

the smell of bats.
the flavor of sandstone
grit on the tongue.

women
birthing
at the foot of ladders in the dark.

trickling streams in hidden canyons
under the cold rolling desert

corn-basket wide-eyed
red baby
rock lip home,

Anasazi

The edited typescript and the final published version of the first poem in Turtle Island
(Special Collections, University of California, Davis)

out clothes or tools!" A collection of essays at the back builds on ideas developed in *Earth House Hold,* complementing the poems.

Poet's Love Lyrics to Planet Earth
Victor Howes
Christian Science Monitor, 30 December 1974, p. 10

This continent, the land-mass known as North America, was once called Turtle Island. Turtles lived upon it. The land itself perhaps floated on the back of a giant turtle.

Those who lived on the land and called it Turtle Island, loved the creatures who shared it with them–the creeping people, the flying people, the standing people and the swimming people–and lived in harmony among them. Certain Amerindian tribes "represented" plants and animals in their political discussions, gave them a voice by means of ritual and dance.

It is to such people–creeping, flying, swimming, or simply standing and growing–that poet Gary Snyder wants to return the power. Power to the people must include all the people.

"Turtle Island" is a book of poems and prose pieces written out of that orientation. It shows the poet, his family and friends, living out the doctrine of reverence for life in accordance with principles they derive from such sophisticated ecologists as Eugene Odum, from such varied movements as Zen Buddhism, Gnosticism and Quakerism, as well as from Polynesians and Bushmen.

Many of these gentle, uncomplicated love-lyrics to planet earth show the poet hunting wild game, cooking it, relaxing among friends, sharing the warmth of a home-made sauna with wife and sons. Other poems, equally straight-from-the-sunburned shoulder, attack the bulldozer, the strip-miner, the nuclear reactor.

Is the ideal reader of this book conceived of as primarily an enjoyer of poems or as a conservationist? Presumably both, for at some point the preservation of poems depends on the preservation of people, standing, creeping, crawling, poetry-writing.

All interdepend, owl, lizard, whale, poet, if we are to have:

An owl winks in the shadow

A lizard lifts on tiptoe
        breathing hard
The whales turn and glisten
        plunge and
Sound, and rise again
Flowing like breathing planets

In the sparkling whorls

Of light.

Interview

Snyder was interviewed by James MacKenzie on 19 March 1974 during a writers' conference at the University of North Dakota. Also participating in the interview were John Little and Maggie Leventer of the University of North Dakota.

Moving the World a Millionth of an Inch
James MacKenzie
The Beat Diary, pp. 140–157

JM: I wanted to ask you if it's meaningful at all for you to think of the Beats as a cohesive group still, or if they have any continuing literary or cultural effects.

GS: Well, I never did know exactly what was meant by the term "The Beats," but let's say that that original meeting, association, comradeship of Allen, myself, Michael, Lawrence, Philip Whalen, who's not here, Lew Welch, who's dead, Gregory, for me, to a somewhat lesser extent (I never knew Gregory as well as the others) did embody a criticism and a vision which we shared in various ways, and then we went our own ways for many years. At least I did. I was out of the country for ten years.

JM: When it really became big, *Time* magazine and everybody making it "The Beats". . . .

GS: Yeah, I was gone all during that time, although I maintained constant correspondence with Allen and with Philip in particular, and less correspondence with Jack, less correspondence with Lawrence. Where we began to come really close together again, in the late 60's, and gradually working toward this point, it seems to me, was when Allen began to take a deep interest in Oriental thought and then in Buddhism which added another dimension to our levels of agreement; and later through Allen's influence, Lawrence began to draw toward that; and from another angle, Michael and I after a lapse of some years of contact, found our heads very much in the same place, and it's very curious and interesting now; and Lawrence went off in a very political direction for awhile, which none of us had any objection with, except that wasn't my main focus. It's very interesting that we find ourselves so much on the same ground again, after having explored divergent paths; and find ourselves united on this position of powerful environmental concern, critique of the future of the industrial state, and an essentially shared poetics, and only half-stated but in the background very powerfully there, a basic agreement on some Buddhist type psychological views of human nature and human possibilities. I was surprised today even by the way Lawrence was speaking, and Michael, to see how much unity we've arrived at without any effort really to arrive at it.

JM: You mean this wasn't planned? (laughing)

GS: No, it wasn't planned.

JM: Yeah, I know. I'm interested in a remark you dropped along the way there; you said that you still

Snyder in the doorway of the fire lookout tower on Sourdough Mountain in the state of Washington, summer 1953

Snyder in Berkeley, 1956 (Gary Snyder Collection)

have a shared poetics. One of the things that's interested me about your poetry is that although you were all lumped together when I first experienced you, reading you as the Beats, I find that with very few exceptions, you all seem to have quite different voices. And I suppose just in your own case, if I had to pick (of all the poets that I know) the person that you seem to be maybe closest to in some ways, I would say Rexroth, who you haven't mentioned. But I think of you as having in many ways quite different poetics. Ginsberg's being the very personal statements, whereas you retreat so much, avoiding the pronoun "I," leaving out those kinds of connections.

GS: It depends on what poems you read. (Pause) I should've mentioned Kenneth; Kenneth is such a catalytic figure for all of us–his presence in San Francisco; his house, literally, was the place that we met, and Kenneth provided for some of us a very valuable bridge between floundering in Stalinism/anti-Stalinism at a time when the *Partisan Review* was talking about the failure of intellectual America. I don't know if you know all this literary history–early 50's?

JM: I know some of it, yeah.

GS: At any rate San Francisco, as a place with a cultural background, with an ethnic background, and Rexroth as a person in that place at a certain time, was a very valuable aid and bridge and teacher in helping me, and I think some others, retain our radical vision and radical perspective without falling into the either/or of American capitalism or Stalinism.

JM: Would you say in political terms that that translates as his teaching you anarchism, perhaps, or getting out of those *Partisan Review* type fights?

GS: Yeah, anarchism as a credible and viable position was one of Rexroth's greatest contributions for us, intellectually. Also, linking that to Kenneth's sense of biology and nature, his belief in poetry as song which he states clearly in the introduction to *The Signature of All Things* in the original edition of it, his interest in American Indian song, his interest in Chinese and Japanese poetry, which I started studying before I met Kenneth. But it was beautifully reinforcing to meet Kenneth and get the sense that here was an American poet of an older generation who saw value in that. Because you know, like, when I started doing things I was doing, I didn't know Allen, I didn't know Kenneth, I didn't know anybody. It was simply my own blind courage in the dark, so to speak. And it gave me, it gave others a lot of reinforcement to begin to realize that we weren't, you know, entirely crazy;

that there were some other people who saw things the way we did.

JM: Yeah, there's that nice statement that Jack Kerouac quotes from you in *Dharma Bums* that you thought there were only three people, or something like that, who thought as you before the reading of *Howl* in Six Gallery.

GS: Yeah, it's very accurate. Now to go back to the poetics–I guess I meant that in the very broadest sense of the word, because I know what you mean: our poetics are different in other ways.

JM: Yeah, you really all have different voices, I think.

GS: Right. So when I said "shared poetics," I suppose I meant it in almost a Blakean sense of shared visionary poetics. You know, you can also say colloquial language, visionary, use of vernacular–all of that kind of thing. I don't know. I've never done analytics on my poetics.

ML: I've just been trying to think about what's happened since the late 50's till now because seeing you all on stage gave me a different sense of things than what I had previously thought. I mean most of us tend to think that so much of what we've wanted has gone down the drain, been smashed, that the things you were saying, like in the *Oracle* interview, have not come through. How do you see the kinds of things you wanted, let's say, in the early 60's right now? What do you feel has been accomplished? Because so much of what you were all talking about has become part of the counter-culture and has moved in.

GS: That's why we're not talking about it now. Those are battles you don't have to fight. And maybe some of the students that came to that talk today were expecting us to talk about those things.

ML: That's what I mean, and Corso seemed to stand for them, in a way, when he was saying get off your intellectual stuff, you know.

GS: You know what Allen whispered to me? "The last of the Beatniks."

JM: He kept referring to "daddies," which is a term you associate with the language of the 50's.

GS: Well, I mean, Gregory really probably *is* the last of the Beatniks in that sense in that he's manifesting the same style that he manifested in the 50's. It's a matter of style.

JM: Can I ask you a question that goes back to that original reading and to something that Kerouac says in *Dharma Bums?* Everyone always talks about "Howl" being read at that reading, and Kerouac talks about your reading some delightful coyote poems and I'm not sure what he refers to. There are a few in *Myths*

Snyder and Allen Ginsberg practicing calligraphy, 1963 (Gary Snyder Collection)

and Texts that fit that description, but I wonder if there are some others that he's referring to that have never been in print?

GS: You know what he's referring to specifically is "A Berry Feast" which was published in *The Back Country* finally. That was the poem I read there, the major poem I read there. I also read some things that later came out in *Myths and Texts,* but "A Berry Feast" was written before *Myths and Texts,* and I didn't have a place to publish it; I didn't have a cycle of poems that I thought it belonged with until I put together *The Back Country.*

JM: You were talking in class today earlier about your own development as a poet and your writing nature poems, you said, and poems about yourself when you were very young; and I think David Kherdian talks about your having been influenced by your mother reading poetry to you. And somewhere else, someone reports you as saying at the same time when you were at the University of Indiana taking anthropology for that one semester, something happened and you knew that you were going to abandon that at least professionally and that

Snyder in Japan, 1963 (Gary Snyder Collection)

you were a poet. And then you mentioned earlier burning all your poems at some point. Can you comment on what it was that happened?

GS: Let's see if I can remember what that was. I had set myself to the idea of becoming a linguistic anthropologist, and in graduate school with that intention, with the intention of doing it for the Ph.D. and so forth. It wasn't until I got into the graduate work that I began to really reflect on some of the things that I guess had happened to me the previous year. And what the reflections involved, as I recall, were first of all, I had come on my first Zen Buddhist literature which gave me reason to seriously question the usual occidental way of using the intellectual mind. I was really thinking about that. The second influence in that decision was the previous summer I had spent working in a logging camp with Indians, on the Warm Springs Indian Reservation and followed that by a long trip into the Olympic Mountains, back-packing. The Olympics had really soaked into me. And then something that Allen mentioned today at the talk which was something that he remembers (I'm surprised he remembered it)–I told him how I had this flash, you know, it happened to be during this summer, that everything was alive–you know, really had a gut level animistic perception which was shamanistic and animistic and maybe now when I look at it, ecological, but I didn't have those words for it then.

JM: This was on that back-packing trip in the Olympic Mountains?

GS: Well, actually it was in the spring before that even. So what I saw was that it was a matter of distributing one's energy properly. I realized that you can't do everything, and that if you want to do something well you have to limit your choices. And so I said there's some bridges you got to burn and there's some choices you have to make. And the work and the use of the mind and the energy, the nature of the energy required to get a Ph.D. would distract me too much, and so I'll go this other route. So that's what I did. But it was a very chancy feeling at the time, you know, like I had the kind of question that I was asking myself, the very prosaic question of like how am I going to make my living. So my answer to that was, I'll be a working man. So I worked for several years after that, logging, and I worked on the docks in San Francisco; I did just all kinds of things for a few years.

JM: But you were also a poet.

GS: Well yeah, sure. Yeah, that was part of it. That kind of choice, that was my own personal, and sort of scarey at that time; although looking back at it now it doesn't seem like it was a scarey choice at all, of course, but it seemed scarey then. And America was much poorer then than it is now and there wasn't any

Snyder in a diner booth, 1963 (photograph by Allen Ginsberg)

welfare. (Chuckling) That kind of choice really is what lies behind the Beat generation as a literary movement. We weren't high school dropouts. We were graduate school dropouts–all of us. And we all arrived at that choice which was at that time a real existential choice in that. . . . Like I remember talking with Allen when he was considering dropping out of graduate school at Berkeley, and Allen said, "Well, gee, I don't know if I should do it. How will I make my living?" And I said, "Allen, I used to worry about that but I don't worry about it anymore. Last summer I worked on a trail crew up in the Yosemite Park with a guy who was 60 years old and he could still handle a pick and shovel, and he could still handle dynamite. Now, if he can do it, we can. We can be working men till we're 60." I was serious at that time. We were serious at that time. We had in Eisenhower-McCarthy 1950's America . . . like there wasn't anything in our minds of any level of literary success. As far as we were concerned, it *was* a choice of remaining laborers for the rest of our lives to be able to be poets.

JM: Was there also something that happened in your poetry that changed, too–that made you know you should take that risk. The reason I ask that is what you said earlier today about burning the old stuff. Did something change, or was it related to that experience of knowing that everything was alive; or how did you know that the old stuff was no good, but now you were going to write this other stuff?

GS: Well, I burned the old stuff because I believed in the new criticism for awhile. (Laughter) Which I've never regretted actually because I had no desire to carry baggage around with me anyway. Leave no trace, ultimately. There's no reason to save things. I'm not a collector.

Now I'd like to go back to what Maggie's question was, which was how much do we think has been accomplished or changed in the meantime. You must remember that we never really articulated what we wanted except like what I recall articulating in several conversations with Allen and Jack and possibly with Phil was a critique of the national state as an unworkable entity, for one thing, and a critique of industrial civilization as being self-destructive because of its lack of understanding of the nature of biological systems. I remember working that out in the 50's. But there's another thing that has to be looked at in this, and since we're laying out a historical perspective, 56–57 is one point in time that started a chain of events. The next point in time (I've said this before), the next key point was Castro taking over Cuba. The apolitical quality of Beat thought changed with that. It sparked quite a discussion and quite a dialogue; many people had been basic pacifists with considerable disillusion with Marxian revolutionary rhetoric. At the time of Castro's victory, it had to be rethought again. Here was a revolution that had used violence and that was apparently a good thing. Many people abandoned the pacifist position at that time or at least began to give more thought to it. In any case, many people began to look to politics again as having possibilities. From that follows, at least on some levels, the beginnings of civil rights activism, which leads through one whole chain of events: the Movement. And all of us and the younger people whom we influenced in the 50's who are now not so young, I think, went through these processes. Like there are some interviews prior to Castro's takeover of Cuba in which the essential line was "drop out," except we didn't use the term. It was just detachment from the existing society.

JM: The cool 50's.

GS: Yeah. Our point of view at that time was you can't do anything about it, but you don't have to participate in it–sort of Thoreauvian, really. But we had little confidence of transforming; that's why I say when we said we were going to be working for the rest of our lives, we believed it. We had little confidence in our power to make any long range or significant changes. That *was* the 50's, you see. It seemed that bleak. So that our choices seemed entirely personal existential lifetime choices that there was no guarantee that we would have any audience, or anybody would listen to us; but it was a moral decision, a moral poetic decision. Then Castro changed things, then Martin Luther King changed things, and then the '65 on psychedelic scene brings us to the point where Allen, myself, Watts, and Leary find ourselves speaking in that *Oracle* interview. In some ways, daddies, you know, and accepted or actually called on as such by the editors of the San Francisco *Oracle* who called on us and said, "Come talk to us," because they were in that in-between generation that in high school had heard about the Beatniks.

JM: Yeah, that's us pretty much, I think.

GS: So that is the link; and so there's a double link there, the hippie generation, kids who feel like that in high school, are now *again* talking to us. In essence, that's what I think Corso meant when he said "Daddies."

JM: You seem to have gone, in some ways, to a less political stance again. I'm thinking of the poem, "Revolution within Revolution within Revolution," and "Spell Against Demons" in *The Fudo Trilogy* which talks about the revolution in terms of the back country of the mind. Have you turned to less political things? And the other thing I guess I'm interested in is the links between the political and the irrational or sacred such as you suggest in those poems and in some of those essays in *Earth House Hold.*

GS: Well, *Earth House Hold* is the summation for me of what I thought had happened between 1955 and 1969. And personally it was clearly that, and also it was an attempt to clarify and locate it up to '69.

Snyder with his mother, Lois Snyder Hennessy, to whom he dedicated Turtle Island

ML: I think I have my question a little clearer; I mean, what we've really been talking about is the relationship between let's say the private world, the political world and perhaps also the ecological world. Well, what I'm wondering is whether you feel that the sense of powerlessness and/or disillusionment which the Vietnam War seems to have left behind influenced you and the other poets in any way. Has it left you free in certain ways for other things?

GS: You see now, it's interesting that you say that because I don't think any of us feel a sense of powerlessness or disillusionment because of that. We've gone through that before. The difference between the people of the 60's and us is that perhaps they expected things to happen more easily and more quickly, whereas we were more seasoned, really. But our commitment to a vision of a different America is older and like it's deeply rooted, and we're willing to see that it won't happen tomorrow. The whole dope thing–like dope is, like it's "speed," you know. It speeds everything up and one of

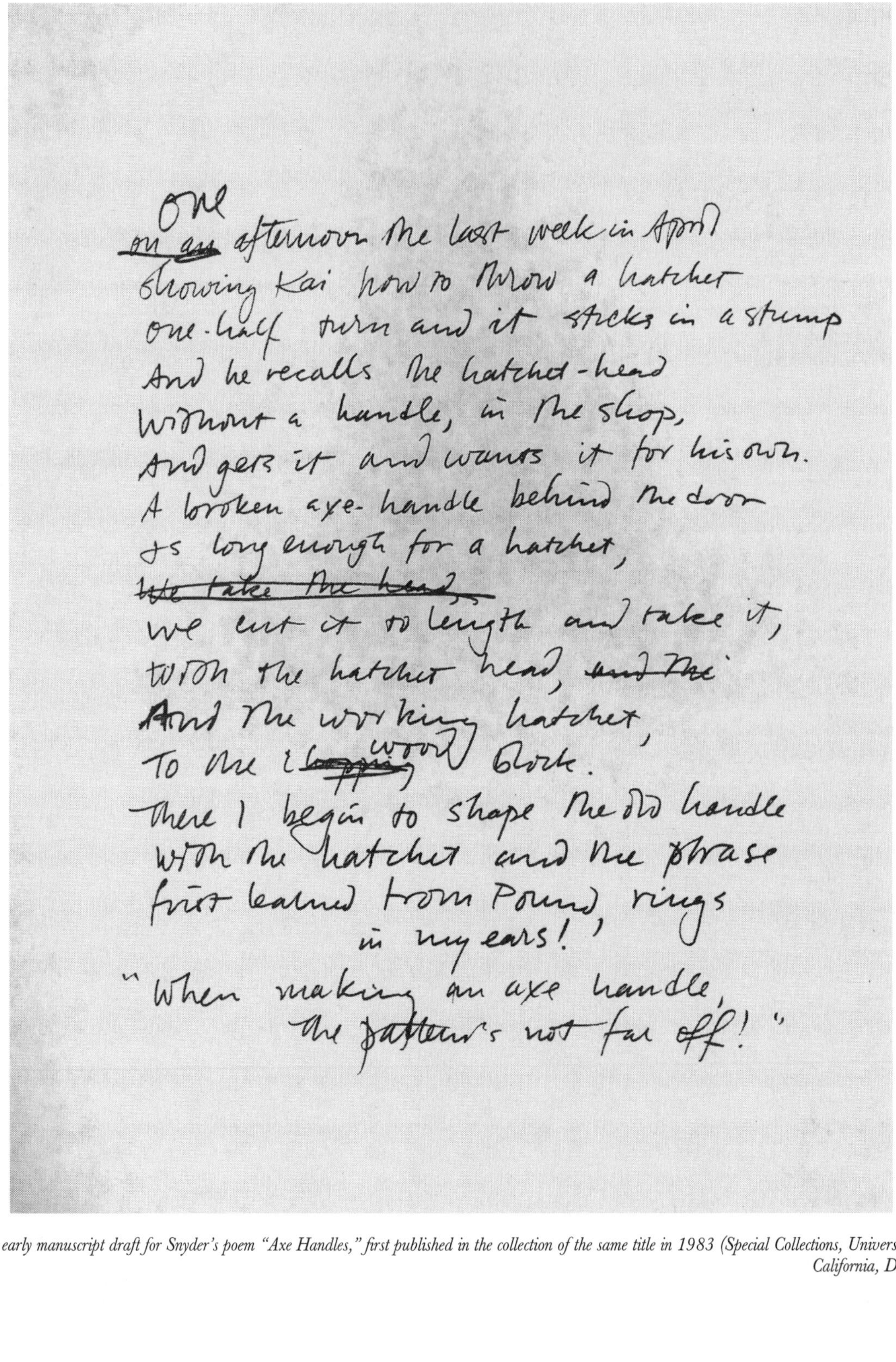

One ~~on an~~ afternoon the last week in April
Showing Kai how to throw a hatchet
One-half turn and it sticks in a stump
And he recalls the hatchet-head
Without a handle, in the shop,
And gets it and wants it for his own.
A broken axe-handle behind the door
Is long enough for a hatchet,
~~We take the head,~~
We cut it to length and take it,
With the hatchet head, ~~and the~~
And the working hatchet,
To the ~~chopping~~ wood block.
There I begin to shape the old handle
With the hatchet and the phrase
First learned from Pound, rings
in my ears!
"When making an axe handle,
the pattern's not far off!"

An early manuscript draft for Snyder's poem "Axe Handles," first published in the collection of the same title in 1983 (Special Collections, University of California, Davis)

-2-

And I say this to Kai,
"Look! We'll shape the
handle by checking the handle
of the axe we cut with!"
And he sees. And I get the
Right quote, from Lu Chi's Wen Fu
Preface, "In making the handle
of an axe
By cutting wood with an axe
The model is indeed ~~the han~~ as near at hand."
My teacher ~~E Hsch~~ Shih-hsiang Chen
Translated that ~~and taught~~ and
said it, years ago.
And I see—he was an axe,
And I am an axe
And my son is a handle, soon
To be shaping again, model
And tool, ~~living body human craft~~
craft ~~of human~~ of culture,
How we go on.

4.V.78

the drawbacks of LSD is perhaps that it's messianic and it makes you think that thinks are going to be accomplished right away. In some sense things are accomplished right away. But there was an overblown optimism quite clearly, like Timothy's messianism.

ML: Right. I'm thinking of your corrections of him in that interview. He seemed to think that the personal individual revolution or transforming one individual or a few will transform the country or the world.

GS: Well, I'd feel very happy if I could just make some changes in our local school board. (Laughter) On one level we talk in pretty vast terms, and in very visionary terms, but what Allen and I and the rest of us can say realistically, with absolute surety and with great pride, is we have moved the world a millionth of an inch. But it's a real millionth of an inch. That much happened. Not nearly as much as people think, perhaps, or would like to ascribe to it, but what it was, was real, and so, like, that much is possible, and the fact that that much was possible is what gives us a certain amount of confidence. If you can move it a millionth of an inch, you've got a chance. (chuckle)

ML: When you said you were seasoned you were then aware of the difference between yourselves and your readers or your audience or those people who have been caught up or influenced by you. Do you sense the difference between yourself and let's say your audience who reads your poetry; are you aware of that?

GS: I'm beginning to be aware of it. I had maybe kind of overlooked that for a long time, but I am actually becoming conscious of being older than my audience, of the fact that that does allow for certain differences. I am in a lot of contact with young people, not on the university teaching level, but like they're my neighbors. We do a lot of work together and so maybe I'm in more contact in some ways with them than maybe even with you. Because, you see, in the life I lead where I am, people don't think of me, people don't even *know* me as a poet, hardly. Or they don't know any of this history because they have no sense of history. We all just know each other for what we're doing, which is very nice. And consequently there's no shyness or hesitation on their part; like if I'm an old fuck, why then I'm an old fuck, you know; so they don't have any exaggerated respect. (Laughter) Which is charming. So like I live with a lot of people on a totally ahistorical non-intellectual level, that have only faintly heard about any of these things. So I have a good measure of where their heads are at.

JM: Are most of the people at Kitkitdizze totally nonacademic, and have never had much contact with the university?

GS: Oh, there's just every type coming out in the country nowadays. Some of them have just barely graduated from high school, and some of them are local to the ridge and were born there–not just at my place but like around the area as a whole. Some of them had incredible academic backgrounds–like one of my best friends, who's also one of my gurus in a way, stopped just short of his Ph.D. in biophysics, and now he fixes trucks. But whenever I have a really difficult question I go to him, on the scientific level. And he recommends books to me which I recommend to Michael sometimes, which you saw reflected in the talk at noon today.

ML: So if you're living with people who don't have that sense of the past, then do you turn to yourself and to books for most of the explorations that you're doing? You see, the way you're setting yourself up, you are apart from this community in certain ways.

GS: On some levels, I am, yeah; which is my choice: to continue in my own growth outside of the academic and the urban intellectual world and see what happens.

JM: This whole turn in the discussion brings up a question about how you perceive the university world, or the academic world, functioning in a society in process. You've purposely disassociated yourself from it for a long time. I suppose it goes all the way back to what you were talking about earlier when you left Indiana University.

GS: Well, I think actually it concerns me a lot. In the first place, it's my major source of income and you know I don't say that as a joke; in some ways I'm a good Maoist.

JM: In *Earth House Hold* too, you say that some of your friends might be in the academies.

GS: Sure, it's an existing structure in society which is certainly one of the most creative and potentially revolutionary structures in this society, perhaps *the* most, as we have seen.

JM: As structures go.

GS: As establishment structures go. And it is very clear that the kind of work that I and the rest of us have done, the kind of lives we're leading, has a relationship to what that structure is looking for. There is an ecological niche for us in that, so that all of us have an ongoing dialogue with the universities. Like they are one of the points of contact for me, the universities are, and I think that I would be less valuable in that dialogue if I did not choose to live in the back country. The very fact that I speak from such a completely different place. . . .

ML: But you've integrated some of the university too into yourself, the discipline.

GS: Oh, sure. That isn't necessarily university either. I have, but that makes an interesting play, you

Axe handles

re-type w/ 1 carbon

One afternoon the last week in April
Showing Kai how to throw a hatchet
One-half turn and it sticks in a stump
And he recalls the hatchet-head
Without a handle, in the shop,
And gets it, and wants it for his own.
A broken-off axe handle behind the door
Is long enough for a hatchet,
We cut it to length and take it,
With the hatchet head
And working hatchet, to the wood block.
There I begin to shape the old handle
With the hatchet, and the phrase
First learned from Pound, rings
          in my ears!
"When making an axe handle
     the pattern [redacted] is not far off!"
And I say this to Kai,
"Look! We'll shape the handle
By checking the handle
Of the axe[redacted] we cut with!"
And he sees. And I get the
Right quote, from Lu Chi's Wen Fu
Preface, "In making the handle
Of an axe
By cutting wood with an axe
The model is indeed near at hand."
My teacher [redacted] Shih-hsiang Chen
Translated that and said it years ago.
And I see--he was an axe,
And I am an axe
And my son a handle, soon
To be shaping again, model
And tool, craft of culture,
How we go on.

GS 4·V·78

Typescript of "Axe Handles" (Special Collections, University of California, Davis) know, and I have great respect for the possibilities of libraries, for the storing and transmission of lore. Actually for universities as a place of discipline and like nobody ever even talks about it properly to my mind and I'm thinking about it, maybe I'll try to write an essay about it myself if nobody else does. To try to put in a 40,000 year anthropological perspective what universities are. They're like giant kivas that people descend into for four years to receive the transmission of the lore.

JM: (Laughing) My experience of the university seems so far from transmission of lore, you know, and a kiva, that I just. . . .

GS: (Laughing) Well, it should be closer.

JM: That's what it *should* be, you're right.

GS: But that's what it *could* be. (Pause) Also, there are some things you don't have to learn in universities. But, like, universities are valuable as, like, shrines, like libraries are kind of shrines, and the librarians are priestesses in which an eternal flame is always burning. And you have to learn the rituals to approach the layers of knowledge. And the rituals of approach are how to use a card catalogue for example, and I suppose nine-tenths of your university education is finished when you learn how to use the bibliographies and the card catalogues. And you learn that there is a method of approach to any piece of information you wish to get–and you *can* get it. Like if you want some information you *can* get it, like that's *right there;* if people would just learn that, then they would have something. And then what goes with that of course is that in the right time, at the right place, a piece of information can move the world. The right piece of information at the right time is a key tool. The other things that universities do is they can provide learning situations that we cannot provide for ourselves, like we can read philosophy and literature of all sorts, but very few of us can maintain a botanical collection, or a working chemistry laboratory, or any other kind of scientific laboratory. So to have working laboratories available in which one could see how experiments proceed is valuable in the physical sciences–in other words, and in engineering and so forth. It's invaluable.

ML: You mentioned thinking of writing essays about something. Do you conceive of any dichotomy between what you would put in an essay and what you choose to put in your poetry?

GS: Well, yeah, there is a dichotomy in that I put things in essays that I can't put in poems.

JM: I know you keep journals a lot. What's published from them is really interesting, and you work in the Japanese journal poet tradition, but how do you know, or how do you decide when you're writing a poem, or when it's going to be just a journal jotting?

GS: I don't know at the time; sometimes. . . .

JM: Which may relate to another thing you were just talking about. You said in relationship to the university that you think that it's very vital for you to remain in the back country to make your connection with the university, the kind of connection you make, and one of the other things that you mean by "the back country" I think, is the subconscious. (G.S.: Yeah.) I'd like to get back to the *Earth House Hold* essays, especially "Poetry and the Primitive" and what you say about experiences of contact with the muse. Is that an experience that you sometimes have in writing some of your poetry, and other times don't?

GS: Well, the simplest way to answer that is to say that every poem that I write that I trust (and I know right away from the beginning whether it's that or not) comes from a place that I can't control, or call on, or make demands on. It comes from a place in myself which has its own life and requires it own kinds of respects. It demands absolute equality with my intellectual and analytical mind, and manifests itself according to its own whims, and that's one way of talking about the muse.

JM: So that means that a poem that you really trust and respect is one that you didn't have to choose to write.

GS: I never choose to write a poem.

JM: So the question of whether it's a journal or a poem is not really a question if it's a good poem, because you just know it's going to be a poem.

GS: Well, that's true of some poems. There are a few things that take place like in journal writings which I write almost automatically, where I don't see what's happening until later; for example a line here, a line there, six months later another three lines. I don't see it mixed in with other things. A couple of years later I look at it and say "Oh, that was one poem and here was the first line, here was the next line, and here are the last three lines," and I see it as one. So sometimes it spaces itself out and it's not quite as clear.

JM: But sometimes it's also the kind of experience that you talk about in "Poetry and the Primitive" in which the muse just takes over.

GS: Yes. Very definitely. And then, like, working with a lot of fragmentary and intractable material as I do when I'm working on poems that go into *Mountains and Rivers without End,* I work on that on every level I can, intellectually and so forth, until I push it to those limits, and then I just have to wait for the creative integrating force to come into it. And, like, I wait, that's all, you know, I just give myself the time.

JM: I wanted to ask you about *Mountains and Rivers without End.* You started on that a long time ago; Kerouac mentions it in *Dharma Bums,* I know. Is that something you still see as a viable ongoing poem?

GS: Well, I expect to finish that after I've finished a couple of other things. I'm working on a prose book right now which I have committed myself to and I have a deadline, so to speak, although the deadline is already two years in the past, and out of a sense of responsibility I'm giving all my energies to that, and then I'll return to *Mountains and Rivers,* and I have that pretty well blocked out now. I'm very glad that it's taken so much time to do it because it gets richer and riper by allowing more time to have taken place. But I have some other ideas about what I want to do when I finish that too, so I'd like to finish it.

JM: Would you care to comment on how you see it blocked out, or is it still too inchoate, because it implies that they have an end instead of like those scrolls that you talk about.

GS: Oh, it does have an end–absolutely. Like those scrolls all do come to an end. Yeah, it has an end. It has an end, and it serves a function–and it will have a use and a place. Then I have some other poems I want to write after that, like my head is leaping ahead of the structures of *Mountains and Rivers* to some extent. Or maybe I won't write anymore poems after that, I don't know. It depends. I'm going to be reading from a lot of new poems tomorrow night that are genuinely ecological-political, illustrating every point we've talked about with clarity. (Laughing) Poems of real clarity, Don Juan type clarity.

JM: Castaneda's Don Juan?

GS: Yeah.

JM: (Laughing) That's one of the enemies. Clarity is the second enemy on "the way," you know.

GS: Well, that's why you have to write a lot of them and, you know, get them out of the way. So then maybe *Mountains and Rivers* will be power. That only leaves old age.

JM: How much longer do you see *Mountains and Rivers without End* being?

GS: Well, after I finish the book I'm working on now which is about Japan, and wilderness, and the history of Asian thought then. . . . (Laughter)

JM: He said modestly. . . .

ML: You've only gone around the hemisphere a couple of times.

GS: That's why it's taking me a long time. (Laughter) I took on more than I realized when I took on that assignment, which originally was an assignment for the Friends of the Earth. They asked me if I would do a book on Hokkaido, which is the northern-most island of Japan, and the most wild, where the Ainu people used to live, a few still live there. They asked me if I would do a little book on that; not so little, you know, large format, with photographs, for their . . . what is it, *Wild Places of the Earth* series. So I said I would. And so it's become a fascinating project that is going to be like a circumpolar bear cult; questions about the nature of civilizations colonizing primitive people, and the questions that arise in one's mind whenever that happens; a look at Zen Buddhism in its rich temples in the capital from the position of greasy shamans on the margins; and a look at the actual place as it is today; a look at the background and the future of Japanese industrial civilization trying to address itself to the question of how come a traditional Asian country with a Buddhist background could end up being the most ecologically self-destructive in the world. But what I'm learning from the Hokkaido book is all going to be useful in *Mountains and Rivers.* I went to Hokkaido two summers ago and travelled in the wilderness there, and met some Ainu, and one thing and another, and a lot of research since. And it's taken me to Pleistocene studies, and geology, and botany to an extent that I hadn't gone before, but I really wanted to go. I mean, everything I'm learning, I wanted to study. But I think that by this intense focus on a place across the North Pacific, I'm going to really have the conceptual tools to come back and look at North America with a really fine eye. Like I'm really getting my geological understanding, and earth history understanding and organic evolution, and botanical taxonomy, and ethno-botany, and I'm really getting those tools down, and I see all of those now as tools.

JM: So that the garden that your Zen master mentioned is the world, you hope.

GS: Right. Well, it's not the whole world. I mean you've got to be realistic; it's western North America, the North Pacific, and the eastern coast of Asia. That's the territory that I have come to know. I pretty well know the plant life, the bird life, and the annual climactic changes of that whole space of territory: the north Pacific, what you call the North Pacific rim and Pacific basin. I'm completely at sea on this side of the Rockies; I don't know the trees or the plants very much.

JM: Well, it's good that you came to North Dakota.

GS: Well, I don't know what the use of that's going to be, really, except that it's part of what I want, what I have a feeling that I need to do–which is to try to talk about North America in a credible way. Which comes to this whole thing about how do we spend our winters in Grand Forks, North Dakota. Like, how do we find the magic where we are, and relate to that, and make that part of our lives instead of feeling that we're off in the sticks somewhere where nothing is interesting.

Axe Handles

One afternoon the last week in April
Showing Kai how to throw a hatchet
One-half turn and it sticks in a stump
And he recalls the hatchet-head
Without a handle, in the shop,
And go gets it, and wants it for his own.
A broken-off axe handle behind the door
Is long enough for a hatchet,
We cut it to length and take it,
With the hatchet head
And working hatchet, to the wood block.
There I begin to shape the old handle
With the hatchet, and the phrase
First learned from Ezra Pound, rings
in my ears!
"When making an axe handle
the pattern is not far off!"
And I say this to Kai,
"Look! We'll shape the handle
By checking the handle
Of the axe we cut with!"
And he sees. And I ~~got~~ remember that the original of Pound's
Quote, ~~right~~, it's from Lu Chi's Wen Fu, "Essay on Literature"—4th c. AD—
The Preface, "In making the handle
Of an axe
By cutting wood with an axe
The model is indeed near at hand."
My teacher Shih-hsiang Chen
Translated that and said it years ago.
And I see--he was an axe,
And I am an axe
And my son a handle, soon
To be shaping again, model
And tool, craft of culture,
How we go on.

Go back to original

GS 4.V.78

Revised typescript of "Axe Handles" (Special Collections, University of California, Davis)

JM: Does what you said about *Mountains and Rivers without End* mean that you don't see it as endless cantos?

GS: Oh, no. Not at all. No, I don't like that idea about endless things.

JM: But you say, "without end."

GS: That's the name; the name comes from Chinese scrolls. That's what they title them themselves, but only endless inasfar as they become cyclical finally. After that you can see where thy go so you don't have to keep on doing it; no need to, you know, state the thing ad infinitum. Let the universe be endless, works of art don't have to. In fact, you know, craft-wise, I have perhaps an excessive sense of structure.

JM: Yeah, I would certainly agree with that.

GS: And bringing things through to a close.

ML: You've been implying some of the ways in which your ecological interests might occupy you for the next few years, at least. I'm wondering especially because at least one generation was influenced by the way you chose to lead your lives, what kinds of personal growth you conceive of. I know that it's hard to separate that from your writing, and from the community you live in. Maybe I'm asking a question that includes all of these things.

GS: It really does. (Pause) My ongoing practice is Rinzai Zen Buddhism, with a big dose of Vajrayana Buddhism, and a big dose of native American shamanism. And I haven't by any means exhausted the need to do that practice, or what I want to learn from it, or how I hope to learn from it yet. And I share as much of that as I can with my neighbors. My wife and I work very much together on these things. One of the things I hope to do is be able to pursue that, to spend more time deeper in the mountains, farther away, you know, like from some people's standpoint where I am is at the end of the road. But from my standpoint where I am is at the beginning of the trail and . . . (chuckles)

JM: I can't help but think of Cold Mountain and what Kerouac said in *Dharma Bums,* that you're going to end up, you know, like Han-Shan.

GS: It's true. It's curiously true. But Han-Shan didn't live in a community. And another thing that is part of my personal world is erasing some parts of my ego increasingly into the cooperation of the group, and the decision-making of the group. And a third thing which I won't say too much about because it's too personal, is the ongoing erasure of sexual roles and sexual jealousies that all of us in our community are learning with each other, which is a difficult but very profound learning for all of us. And I don't know where that's going to lead. And that involves my wife, and others who. . . .

JL: Why is it too personal?

JM: Because the tape recorder is on.

GS: You know perfectly well why it's too personal, John Little. (scolding)

JL: Well, you see, I disagree with. . . .

JM: If it takes two years to tell somebody that he drives his car too much. . . .

JL: I'm disagreeing with the philosophy, is all. If it's valuable. . . .

GS: I mean it's too personal to talk onto this tape.

JM: That may be how his poetic voice is different from Ginsberg's. . . .

JL: But why? People can learn from what you have learned.

ML: It's violating the privacy of those people.

GS: She's quite right, it is violating the privacy of those people.

ML: They haven't agreed to this discussion; it's a community. . . .

GS: Like I would, if you turned off the tape, I would tell you everything and that's the difference. But the tapes go out into the university libraries and God knows where they all go.

JL: O.K. I accept that–there are other people involved. That's fine.

GS: And also that's a whole conversation in itself, but that is part of my personal growth. Very definitely. But you know, that's as much my wife Masa's territory as it is my territory. And we're very much together in that. It's very interesting.

JL: I want to reserve a few minutes of this interview to gossip about the Beats. I'm interested in Gregory Corso as the last of the Beats, and his life style. You know, watching Gregory is a good bit like reading *On The Road,* and I detect that he *is* the last of the Beats. And I detect, seeing you all together, that Gregory *has been* the last of the Beats. There has been a separation in life styles for some time.

GS: Yeah, that's true.

JL: How do you react to his life style? It seems to me like there's a great deal of distance between the collective group and Gregory Corso. Why? How?

GS: Well, this really is gossip, but Allen can probably answer that much better than I could because he's been much closer to Gregory and he's known everything that's happened to Gregory in a way that I haven't. Gregory has gone through a lot of stuff. He's gone through a heavy junk problem, which has been combined with a particular kind of ego sense, and his survival as a kind of hustler. Why that should not have happened to the rest of us in the same way, I'm not sure. Lew Welch died, and I'm going to read some of Lew's poems and speak about Lew when my turn comes to read poetry, because Lew was a very important person to us. He was a casualty.

JM: Kerouac was a casualty.

GS: Kerouac was a casualty too. And there were many other casualties that most people have never heard of, but were genuine casualties. Just as, in the 60's, when Allen and I for a period there were almost publicly recommending people to take acid. When I look back on that now I realize there were many casualties, responsibilities to bear.

ML: If you're talking about the change in time, though, I mean, what happened is everybody has seen freaked-out people on every single corner and it's no longer. . . .

GS: Oh, that's a good point Maggie, that's . . . well, excuse me. Let me go on with that. In the 50's we really did have to protect, defend, and nurture our freaks because they were valuable people. Something else has happened in the meantime. I mean, it's almost a matter of our sense of responsibility to project an image of a little bit more sanity. The Beats are responsible for plenty of freakouts.

JL: O.K. Does that bother you and does it bother the collective consciousness of the Beats?

GS: I don't know if it bothers anybody else but I take it into account. I mean, I see it as part of my karma. And I'll have to pay for it and I've had to pay for it. I've had people turn up at my door who are half insane, who told me that I had set them on their path. And I've had to deal with them, and it's not easy, because we're talking about real people, real situations.

JL: How have you dealt with it?

GS: As best I could. Which is to try to find out where the person is really at.

JL: You spent time with them then?

GS: Yeah. Sat down with them and talked and scared shit out of me and my wife one time, and my kids. And you know, like, not knowing really where these people are at, and trying to find out where they're at. You've got to realize that there's an underside to this, that at its bottom is Charlie Manson. But we have to live with that underside too, and in California we see that underside, and it's dangerous.

ML: You were identifying with Gregory in a curious way, John, but I think the difference is really that what I felt was a lot of anger too in him, and that's very scarey. It isn't always just a benevolent, crazy kind of thing. It really can strike out at other people.

GS: Gregory has certainly done that, and I haven't really tried to deal with where Gregory's at; but he's had a lot of self-created hard times, and he's had incredible opportunities because of his grace and his gift for gab and his charm; he's had many, many beautiful opportunities. And then he's hurt a lot of people, you know; he's really shit on a lot of scenes, egregious shit, as it were. I don't want to get into having to defend

Snyder looking over his correspondence during a visit to Kent State University

Gregory either. Like he's got a karma which I wouldn't want to have; it is not my karma, fortunately, and I'm not responsible for it either. But we're all responsible collectively in some sense for Gregory, so what I would like to do is all of us (Lawrence, myself, and Allen and so forth) sit down and have a collective meeting with Gregory. That's what I'm going to suggest, too. I've learned how to do that where I live. Collective meetings of mutual and personal self-criticism.

ML: What seems to be happening is he feels unloved.

GS: Oh, he always said that. That's just one of his arguments; "You don't love me." No, that's the bad little kid thing; you know, you do all the bad things and then you say, "You don't love me"–double bind. So I always tell Gregory, "Of course, I don't love you–you're not lovable." (Laughter)

JL: Which is an absolute lie, and something that parents learn to tell miscreant children. He is lovable.

GS: I know he is. But not when he fucks up *too* much, then you get mad at him. Well, now I'm going to be honest and personal with Gregory, too. When I get mad, I get mad. Why shouldn't I, you know, like that's my beat freedom, to get mad.

JL: How much of a sense of competition do you have when you have five egos up on stage? One of the things you want to erase is your ego. Does that come into play, is that more of a problem when you're on a stage with four other egos?

ML: You were running things, sort of. Allen sort of retreated into the background, and chose to.

JM: Yeah, he sure did.

GS: Allen is like the president of the board. He listens to all the arguments, then he makes the summation. And that's, you know, beautiful, how he does that.

JL: So answer my question. Is ego a problem with most of the panel?

GS: I really don't think it is, John.

JL: Does this turn in the questioning turn you off?

GS: No. We've worked these things out over the years. Like Allen and Michael worked it out in the middle 60's. Michael and I and Lawrence have worked it out in the last four or five years. Michael and I are really strong allies, really close allies, and I feel as much fondness for Michael as anyone I know in the world, although he is very different from me in many ways. And of course, Allen and I are very close. We're all really very close in different ways. So I don't think (maybe I'm fooling myself)–I don't think that there is any significant ego conflict play in our relationships.

JM: You said you were all very close in a lot of ways. If there was somebody else we should have invited here to this conference, would it have been Whalen? Or who?

GS: I don't think Whalen would have come at this point. Although if he had come, he would have been fine. And that would be to my mind the only lacking person, for the peculiar focus of this situation. Creeley, if it were slightly enlarged, would be appropriate. And you know you can think of a few augmentations.

JM: But you think that with seven people, these were the people that it should've been?

GS: Yeah. Creeley or Duncan would fit in perfectly well. I'm glad that Shig came, and I'm glad that Gregory and Peter came. And I think that fills it out. Peter provides the craziness, you know, which is a very right craziness.

JM: What about Burroughs?

GS: Burroughs would have been appropriate in every sense except San Francisco. He wasn't in San Francisco to my knowledge. Or if he was, it was just an overnight stop.

JL: Oh, a question I want to ask. I've had some friends in the past who tried to get me to think with Eastern thought, and I've struggled five or ten minutes, and sometimes as long as an hour reading this essay here and there and yonder, and really longer because I spent time with these friends who, one of whom is particularly brilliant and obtuse because he thinks in Eastern thoughts that are totally beyond my conception; I never know what the son of a bitch is talking about so I nod my head.

GS: I'd kick the fuck out of him, that's all.

JL: Well, hell, he loves me and I love him.

GS: But he don't make sense.

JL: Well, O.K., I never tried to kick the hell out of him but I'll keep that in mind.

GS: Say, "Make sense, you son of a bitch." That's what I do with people.

JL: I've tried, I've sincerely tried, to think Eastern and I have not made it. Have you made it?

GS: I don't know.

JL: Shit. You don't know. That's an Eastern answer, isn't it?

JM: (Laughing) John's got to categorize what he's thinking. He won't rest until you say Eastern or Western.

GS: I really don't know. Because I don't ask myself those questions anymore. In fact, I don't know if I ever did. (Laughing)

For Further Reading

This list of books related to Beat Generation writers is a selective one. Fuller bibliographies may be found in Lewis Leary and John Auchbard, eds., *Articles on American Literature, 1968–1975* (Durham, N.C.: Duke University Press, 1979); the annual MLA International Bibliographies; the annual bibliography in *The Journal of Modern Literature;* and David J. Nordloh and Gary Scharnhorst, eds., *American Literary Scholarship: An Annual Survey* (Durham, N.C.: Duke University Press, 1965–).

Allen, Donald M., ed. *The New American Poetry: 1945–1960.* New York: Grove, 1960.

Allen and George F. Butterick, eds. *The Postmoderns: The New American Poetry Revisited.* New York: Grove, 1982.

Allen and Robert Creeley, eds. *New American Story.* New York: Grove, 1965.

Allen and Warren Tallman, eds. *Poetics of the New American Poetry.* New York: Grove, 1974.

Ash, Mel. *Beat Spirit: The Way of the Beat Writers as a Living Experience.* New York: Jeremy P. Tarcher/Putnam, 1997.

Bartlett, Lee, ed. *The Beats: Essays in Criticism.* Jefferson, N.C.: McFarland, 1981.

Berthoff, Warner. *A Literature without Qualities: American Writing since 1945.* Berkeley: University of California Press, 1979.

Charters, Ann, ed. *The Portable Beat Reader.* New York: Viking, 1992.

Charters, ed. *Scenes along the Road: Photographs of the Desolation Angels, 1944–1960.* New York: Portents/Gotham Book Mart, 1970.

Charters, Samuel. *Some Poems/Poets: Studies in American Underground Poetry since 1945.* Berkeley: Oyez, 1971.

Cook, Bruce. *The Beat Generation.* New York: Scribners, 1971.

Cook, Ralph T. *The City Lights Pocket Poets Series: A Descriptive Bibliography.* La Jolla, Cal.: McGilvery/Atticus Books, 1982.

di Prima, Diane. *Memoirs of the Beatnik.* New York: Olympia, 1969.

Duberman, Martin. *Black Mountain: An Exploration in Community.* New York: Dutton, 1972.

Ehrlich, J. W., ed. *Howl of the Censor: The Four Letter Word on Trial.* San Carlos, Cal.: Nourse, 1961.

Faas, Ekbert. *Towards a New American Poetics: Essays and Interviews.* Santa Barbara, Cal.: Black Sparrow, 1979.

Feldman, Gene, and Max Gartenberg, eds. *The Beat Generation and the Angry Young Men.* New York: Citadel, 1958.

French, Warren. *The San Francisco Poetry Renaissance, 1955–1960.* Boston: Twayne, 1991.

Friebert, Stuart, and David Young, eds. *A Field Guide to Contemporary Poetry and Poetics.* New York: Longman, 1980.

Books for Further Reading

George-Warren, Holly, ed. *The Rolling Stone Book of the Beats.* New York: Hyperion Press, 1999.

Hassan, Ihab. *Contemporary American Literature 1945–1972.* New York: Ungar, 1973.

Hickey, Morgan. *Bohemian Register: An Annotated Bibliography of the Beat Literary Movement.* Metuchen, N.J.: Scarecrow Press, 1990.

Hoffman, Daniel, ed. *Harvard Guide to Contemporary Writing.* Cambridge, Mass.: Harvard University Press, 1979.

Hoffman, Frederick J. *Marginal Manners: The Variants of Bohemia.* Evanston, Ill.: Row, Peterson, 1962.

Hoffman. *The Modern Novel in America 1900–1950.* Chicago: Regnery, 1951.

Howard, Richard. *Alone with America: Essays on the Art of Poetry in the United States since 1950.* New York: Atheneum, 1980.

Johnson, Joyce. *Minor Characters.* Boston: Houghton Mifflin, 1983.

Jones, LeRoi, ed. *The Moderns: An Anthology of New Writing in America.* New York: Corinth Books, 1963.

Kaufman, Alan, ed. *The Outlaw Bible of American Poetry.* New York: Thunder's Mouth Press, 1999.

Kherdian, David. *Beat Voices: An Anthology of Beat Poetry.* New York: Holt, 1995.

Knight, Arthur, and Kit Knight, eds. *The Beat Diary,* the unspeakable visions of the individual, volume 5. California, Pa.: Knight, 1977.

Knight and Knight, eds. *The Beat Road,* the unspeakable visions of the individual, volume 14. California, Pa.: Knight, 1984.

Knight and Knight, eds. *The Beat Vision: A Primary Source Book.* New York: Paragon, 1987.

Knight, Brenda. *Women of the Beat Generation: The Writers, Artists, and Muses at the Heart of Revolution.* Berkeley, Cal.: Conari Press, 1996.

Kostelanetz, Richard. *Twenties in the Sixties.* Westport, Conn.: Greenwood Press, 1979.

Kramer, Jane. *Allen Ginsberg in America.* New York: Random House, 1969.

Lawlor, William. *The Beat Generation: A Bibliographical Teaching Guide.* Metuchen, N.J.: Scarecrow Press, 1998.

Lepper, Gary M. *A Bibliographical Introduction to Seventy-five Modern American Authors.* Berkeley, Cal.: Serendipity Books, 1976.

Lipton, Lawrence. *The Holy Barbarians.* New York: Messner, 1959.

Maynard, John Arthur. *Venice West: The Beat Generation in Southern California.* New Brunswick, N.J.: Rutgers University Press, 1991.

Meltzer, David, comp. *The San Francisco Poets.* New York: Ballantine, 1971.

Moore, Harry T., ed. *Contemporary American Novelists.* Carbondale: Southern Illinois University Press, 1964.

Ossman, David. *The Sullen Art: Interviews by David Ossman with Modern American Poets.* New York: Corinth Books, 1963.

Parkinson, Thomas, ed. *A Casebook on the Beat.* New York: Crowell, 1961.

Peabody, Richard, ed. *A Different Beat: Women of the Beat Generation.* New York: Serpent's Tail, 1997.

Perloff, Marjorie. *The Poetics of Indeterminacy: Rimbaud to Cage.* Princeton: Princeton University Press, 1981.

Perry, Paul. *On the Bus: The Complete Guide to the Legendary Trip of Ken Kesey and the Merry Pranksters and the Birth of the Counterculture.* New York: Thunder's Mouth Press, 1990.

Peters, Robert. *The Great American Poetry Bake-Off.* Metuchen, N.J.: Scarecrow Press, 1979.

Plimpton, George, ed. *Beat Writers at Work: The Paris Review.* New York: Modern Library, 1998.

Plimpton, ed. *Writers at Work: The Paris Review Interviews,* third series. New York: Viking, 1967.

Plimpton, ed. *Writers at Work: The Paris Review Interviews,* fourth series. New York: Viking, 1976.

Rexroth, Kenneth. *American Poetry in the Twentieth Century.* New York: Herder & Herder, 1971.

Rigney, Francis J., and L. Douglas Smith. *The Real Bohemia: A Sociological and Psychological Study of the Beats.* New York: Basic Books, 1961.

Sanders, Ed. *Tales of the Beatnik Glory.* New York: Stonehill, 1975.

Seaver, Richard, Terry Southern, and Alexander Trocchi, eds. *Writers in Revolt.* New York: Frederick Fell, 1963.

Shepard, Sam. *Rolling Thunder Logbook.* New York: Penguin, 1978.

Simpson, Louis. *A Revolution in Taste.* New York: Macmillan, 1978.

Stauffer, Donald Barlow. *A Short History of American Poetry.* New York: Dutton, 1974.

Sterritt, David. *Mad to Be Saved: The Beats, the '50s, and Film.* Carbondale: Southern Illinois University Press, 1998.

Tonkinson, Carol, ed. *Big Sky Mind: Buddhism and the Beat Generation.* New York: Riverhead, 1995.

Tytell, John. *Naked Angels: The Lives and Literature of the Beat Generation.* New York: McGraw-Hill, 1976.

Tytell. *Paradise Outlaws: Remembering the Beats.* New York: Morrow, 1999.

Vendler, Helen. *Part of Nature, Part of Us: Modern American Poets.* Cambridge, Mass.: Harvard University Press, 1980.

Waldman, Anne, ed. *The Beat Book: Writings from the Beat Generation.* Boulder, Colo.: Shambhala Publications, 1999.

Waldmeir, Joseph J., ed. *Recent American Fiction: Some Critical Views.* Boston: Houghton Mifflin, 1963.

Watson, Steve. *The Birth of the Beat Generation: Visionaries, Rebels, and Hipsters, 1944–1960.* New York: Pantheon, 1995.

Wolf, Daniel, and Edwin Fancher, eds. *The Village Voice Reader.* Garden City, N.Y.: Doubleday, 1962.

Note: page numbers in italics refer to illustrations or captions.